英和対照

税 金 ガ イ ド

30年度

GUIDE TO JAPANESE TAXES 2018

川 田 剛 著

財 経 詳 報 社

PREFACE

This book provides practical, extensive and up-to-date informa-tion on Japanese taxes based on laws, regulations, circulars etc., in effect as of the end of June 2018. Japanese tax laws are usually revised each spring, so new editions of this book appear in July every year, ensuring that it contains the most recent developments in the Japanese tax system.

This book has been written by my respected senior colleague Mr. Yuji Gomi. The writer and editor has changed to me. However, The basic style will not change.

Valuable information and detailed explanations have been refined and added based on the FY2018 Tax Reform. Accordingly, readers will be able to grasp, with greater ease, the main features of the Japanese tax system how it is enforced and find the key to resolving practical tax problems involving Japanese taxes. I believe this will make the book more accessible to a wider international audience.

Go Kawada
July 2018

本書は，平成30年6月末現在の法令及び通達を基に，わが国の税金に関する実務的，包括的かつ最新の情報を盛り込んだ書である。わが国の税法は毎年春に改正されるので，この改正事項を盛り込むために改訂版が店頭に置かれるのは，毎年7月頃になる。

ちなみに，本書は尊敬する先輩である五味雄治氏によって書かれてきたものを，川田が引き継いだものである。しかし，基本的なスタイルは変更していない。

本年も，平成30年度の税制改正に対応し，新たに必要な情報を追加するとともに説明についても見直し，追加した。これにより読者の皆さんは，わが国の税制及びその執行の全般を容易に把握でき，日本における実際の税務問題を解決するための手がかりをより容易に得ることができ，海外のより広い読者層にも一層親しみやすいものになったと信じている。

川 田 　 剛
2018年10月

CONTENTS

		Page
1	INTRODUCTION	8
2	MAIN FEATURES OF JAPANESE TAXES	36
3	NATIONAL TAXES ON INCOME	82
4	WITHHOLDING INCOME TAX	104
5	ASSESSMENT INCOME TAX	188
6	CORPORATION TAX	336
7	INHERITANCE TAX AND GIFT TAX	532
8	CONSUMPTION TAX	650
9	LOCAL TAX etc.	790
	INDEX	864

目　　次

1　はじめに……………………………………………………9
2　日本の租税の主な特色…………………………………37
3　所得に対する国税………………………………………83
4　源泉所得税…………………………………………… 105
5　申告所得税 ……………………………………………189
6　法人税 …………………………………………………337
7　相続税及び贈与税 ……………………………………533
8　消費税 …………………………………………………651
9　地方税等 ………………………………………………791
索　引 ……………………………………………………885

MAIN TABLES AND CHARTS

	Paragraph
National Tax Administration System	¶ 1-800
General View of Japanese Taxes	¶ 1-850
Tax Burden on Individual Income	¶ 2-050
Tax Burden on Corporate Income	¶ 2-060
Inheritance Tax Burden	¶ 2-320
Automobile Tax	¶ 2-350
Tax Burden on Real Estate	¶ 2-370
Liquor Tax	¶ 2-560
Stamp Tax	¶ 2-820
Registration and License Tax	¶ 2-830
Basic Structure of National Taxes on Income	¶ 3-010
General View of Withholding Income Tax	¶ 4-010
Withholding Tax Table for Monthly Salary Payment	¶ 4-250
Withholding Tax Table for Bonus Payments	¶ 4-270
Retirement Income Deduction for Withholding Tax	¶ 4-370
Withholding Tax Rates and Taxable Amounts	¶ 4-380
Computation of Assessment Income Tax	¶ 5-010
Ten Categories of Income	¶ 5-120
Rate of Income Tax	¶ 5-500
Corporation Tax Payable by Companies	¶ 6-002
Types of Corporations and the Object of Taxation	¶ 6-020
Selection of a Depreciation Method	¶ 6-275
Useful Life of Selected Depreciable Assets	¶ 6-295
Computation of Inheritance Tax	¶ 7-005
Tax Rates and Total Amount of Inheritance Tax	¶ 7-370
Rate of Gift Tax	¶ 7-890
Comparison of Income Tax and Income Levy	¶ 9-090
Table of Standard Remuneration and Monthly Premiums	¶ 9-860

主要計表及び図表

国税の執行機関の組織図	¶ 1-800
日本における各種租税の概要	¶ 1-850
給与所得の租税負担	¶ 2-050
法人の所得に対する租税負担	¶ 2-060
相続税負担	¶ 2-320
自動車税	¶ 2-350
不動産に係る租税	¶ 2-370
酒税	¶ 2-560
印紙税	¶ 2-820
登録免許税	¶ 2-830
所得に対する国税の基本的な仕組み	¶ 3-010
源泉所得税の概要	¶ 4-010
月額表	¶ 4 250
賞与に対する源泉徴収税額の算出率の表	¶ 4-270
源泉徴収のための退職所得控除額	¶ 4-370
源泉徴収の税率及び課税標準	¶ 4-380
申告所得税の計算	¶ 5-010
10種類の所得	¶ 5-120
所得税の税率	¶ 5-500
法人の納付すべき法人税	¶ 6-002
法人の種類と納税義務の範囲	¶ 6-020
償却の方法の選定	¶ 6-275
代表的な固定資産の耐用年数	¶ 6-295
相続税の計算	¶ 7-005
税率及び相続税の総額	¶ 7-370
贈与税の税率	¶ 7-890
各種の所得控除に係る所得税と所得割額の比較	¶ 9-090
健康保険 厚生年金保険 標準報酬月額・保険料額表	¶ 9-860

凡　　例

本書において引用している法令，通達の略語は次によるものです。

通則法	国税通則法
所法	所得税法
所令	所得税法施行令
所基通	所得税基本通達
法法	法人税法
法令	法人税法施行令
法基通	法人税基本通達
相法	相続税法
相令	相続税法施行令
相基通	相続税法基本通達
評基通	財産評価基本通達
消法	消費税法
消令	消費税法施行令
消規	消費税法施行規則
消基通	消費税法基本通達
措法	租税特別措置法
措令	租税特別措置法施行令
措通	租税特別措置法関係通達
地法	地方税法
地令	地方税法施行令
地法附	地方税法附則

※　英文と和文の対照は，同じパラグラフ・ナンバー（¶）をご覧下さい。

英和対照

税 金 ガ イ ド

30年版

CHAPTER 1

INTRODUCTION

	Paragraph
Key Tables and Charts	¶ 1-100
Summary of 2018 Tax Reform	¶ 1-200
Nondiscrimination on the Basis of Nationality	¶ 1-400
For Foreign Readers	¶ 1-420
A Person Who Needs Assistance	¶ 1-430
Administration System	¶ 1-450
Tax Disputes	¶ 1-500
Litigation	¶ 1-510
Competent Authority Assistance	¶ 1-520
Penalties	¶ 1-530
Certified Public Tax Accountant	¶ 1-540
Chart: National Tax Administration System	¶ 1-800
Table: General View of Japanese Taxes	¶ 1-850

第 1 章

は　じ　め　に

主要計表及び図表……………………………………………… ¶1-100
平成30年度税制改正の概要…………………………………… ¶1-200
国籍無差別……………………………………………………… ¶1-400
外国人読者のために…………………………………………… ¶1-420
納税相談をしたい者…………………………………………… ¶1-430
行政組織………………………………………………………… ¶1-450
不服申立て……………………………………………………… ¶1-500
訴訟……………………………………………………………… ¶1-510
権限のある当局による救済…………………………………… ¶1-520
罰則……………………………………………………………… ¶1-530
税理士…………………………………………………………… ¶1-540
国税の執行機関の組織図……………………………………… ¶1-800
日本における各種租税の概要………………………………… ¶1-850

10   INTRODUCTION

¶ 1-100 Key tables and charts

Readers are given a bird's-eye view of Japanese national and local taxes in the table "General View of Japanese Taxes" at ¶ 1-850. The main features of each kind of tax are described in detail at the paragraph numbers [¶] indicated there.

Similarly, the tables at ¶ 3-010, ¶ 4-010 and the charts at ¶ 5-010, ¶ 6-002, ¶ 7-005 show the basic structure of Japanese national taxes on income, withholding income tax, assessment income tax on individuals, corporation tax and inheritance tax respectively. The numbers in these tables and charts indicate the paragraphs in which the information is furnished in detail.

¶ 1-200 Summary of 2018 tax reform

As for the 2018 tax reform, individual income taxation is reviewed from the perspective of broadly supporting people regardless of their work-styles which is becoming diversified. Additionally, in order to overcome deflation and achieve economic revitalization, taxation measures were revised to spur wage hikes and productivity and promote business investment by local SMEs. Other measures include expanding the business succession tax system to facilitate business succession of SMEs, and creating International Tourist Tax (provisional) to promote tourism. Also, from the perspective of establishing financial bases for local taxes that support local communities, the, settlement standard for local consumption tax was fundamentally revised. The government also revised the international taxation system, promote electronic tax filing and revised the tobacco tax.

Outline of 2018 Tax Reform

The main revision points for 2018 are set out below with cross-references to the paragraphs.

1. Amendments to the individual income tax (national)
Effetive from January 1, 2018

   (1) The spouse deduction and special spouse deduction shall be amended (see ¶ 5-410).

   (2) The installment-type NISA shall be introduced (see ¶ 5-070(7)(c)).

¶ 1-100

はじめに　11

¶1-100　主要計表及び図表

　読者は¶1-850の「日本における各種租税の概要」により，わが国の国税及び地方税につき一覧することができよう。それぞれの租税の主な特色については，同頁に記した節番号〔¶〕の箇所で詳細に説明されている。

　また，¶3-010，¶4-010の各表及び¶5-010，¶6-002，¶7-005の各図表は，わが国における所得に対する課税，源泉所得税，個人の申告所得税，法人税，相続税のそれぞれについて示している。これらの各表又は図表に記した節の番号は，別に詳細な説明が行われている節の番号を示すものである。

¶1-200　平成30年度税制改正の概要

　平成30年度の税制改正においては，働き方の多様化等を踏まえ，個人所得課税の見直しが行われた。また，デフレ脱却と経済再生に向け，賃上げ・生産性向上のための税制上の措置が講じられた。さらに，中小企業の代替わりを促進する事業承継税制の拡充及び国際観光税の新設が行われた。あわせて，地方のコミュニティを支援するという観点から地方消費税の課税標準の見直しも行われた。また，国際課税制度の見直し，税務手続の電子化の推進やたばこ税の見直し等も行われている。

▶税制改正の主な内容◀

　主要な改正点は次のとおりである。参照項目は本文における改正部分を示す。

1．個人所得税の改正点
　（平成30年分以降適用）

　(1)　配偶者控除及び配偶者特別控除の見直しが行われる（¶5-410参照）。

　(2)　積立NISAが導入される（¶5-070(7)(c)参照）。

12   INTRODUCTION

Effetive from January 1, 2020

(1) The amount of employment income deduction and pension income deduction shall be transfered to the amount of basic deduction (see ¶ 5-470).

(2) Employment income deduction, pension income deduction and basic deduction shall be amended (see ¶ 5-130(5)(a), (8)(c), ¶ 5-470).

2. Amendments to the corporate income tax (national)

(1) The amounts of taxable revenue related to the sale of assets were clarified in the tax laws to be, in principle, the amounts equivalent to the value of the assets at the transfer, and to be included in the revenue in the accounting period during that the transfer was occurred (see ¶ 6-170).

(2) The rules for reserve for goods returned and the rules for income recognition for installment sales were eliminated (see ¶ 6-180, ¶ 6-385). Certain transitional measures were still given for certain corporations for accounting periods on and after April 1, 2018.

(3) Corporations whose amounts of capital are more than ¥100 million must file its tax returns with using e-Tax systems from the accounting periods beginning on and after April 1, 2020 (see ¶ 6-800, ¶ 6-805).

(4) Some of special depreciations and special tax credits were abolished, some of rates applicable to those were changed, some of their applicable periods were extended and some of those were newly introduced (see ¶ 6-310, ¶ 6-720 to ¶ 6-738).

(5) Certain revisions were made to the CFC rules (see ¶ 6-195). The revision applied to foreign subsidiaries' accounting periods beginning on and after April 1, 2018.

3. Amendments to inheritance/gift tax

(1) Tax exemption measurement for non-resident without Japanese nationality at the time of inheritance or donation who received foreign property from non-resident (see ¶ 7-100, ¶ 7-761).

(2) New inheritance taxation on general incorporated association (see ¶ 7-031).

(3) Tax deferral on inheritance/gift tax on unlisted shares (see ¶

¶ 1-200

（平成32年分以降適用）
 ⑴　給与所得控除及び公的年金等控除の控除額を基礎控除の控除額に振り
　　替える（¶5-470参照）。

 ⑵　給与所得控除，公的年金等控除及び基礎控除の見直しが行われる（¶
　　5-130⑸⒜，⑻⒞，¶5-470参照）。

２．法人税の改正点
 ⑴　資産の販売等に係る収益の額は，原則として，その資産の引渡しの
　　時における価額とし，当該引渡しの日の属する事業年度の益金の額に
　　算入することを法令上明確化する（¶6-170参照）。

 ⑵　返品調整引当金制度及び長期割賦販売等に係る延払基準の選択制度
　　は廃止する（¶6-180，¶6-385参照）。一定の法人については，平成30
　　年4月1日以後も経過措置がある。

 ⑶　大法人（資本金の額が1億円を超える法人）の法人税の申告書の提
　　出については，これらの申告書に記載すべきものとされる事項を電子
　　情報処理組織を使用する方法（e-Tax）により提出しなければならない
　　こととなった（¶6-800，¶6-805参照）。当該改正は，平成32年4月1
　　日以後に開始する事業年度について適用する。
 ⑷　特別償却，特別税額控除等について，所要の見直しが行われ，その
　　いくつかが廃止，縮減，延長又は創設された（¶6-310及び¶6-720～
　　¶6-738参照）。

 ⑸　外国子会社合算税制について，見直しが行われた（¶6-195参照）。
　　当該改正は，平成30年4月1日以後に開始する外国子会社の事業年度
　　から適用される。

３．相続税・贈与税の改正点
 ⑴　相続開始時又は贈与時において非居住者で日本国籍を有しない人が，
　　非居住者から相続等又は贈与があった国外財産は，相続税又は贈与税が
　　課税されなくなった（¶7-100，¶7-761参照）。
 ⑵　一般社団法人等に対する相続税が強化された（¶7-031参照）。

 ⑶　非上場株式等についての相続税・贈与税の納税猶予の特例が創設され

14   INTRODUCTION

7-312, ¶ 7-882).

(4) Inheritance tax deferral on certain art works (see ¶ 7-318).

4. Amendments to the consumption tax

(1) The consumption tax rate increase to 10% is rescheduled from April 1, 2017 to October 1, 2019 (see ¶ 8-010).

(2) After October 1, 2019, businesses of producing agricultural and fishery products of edible will be classified as the Secand-class businesses and 80% deemed purchase ratio (now 70%) will be applied (see ¶ 8-680).

(3) From October 1, 2023, the Invoice-based method will be introduced. Until then, simple methods could be applied (see ¶ 8-610).

5. Amendments to the Individual Inhabitant Taxes

After the year 2021, amount of Basic allowance will be reduced (see ¶ 9-090).

Amount of total income	Basic allowance
¥24,000,000 and under	¥430,000
¥24,500,000 and under	¥290,000
¥25,000,000 and under	¥150,000
more than ¥25,000,000	NIL

6. Tobacco tax

Tobacco tax rate shall be raised from October, 2018 (see ¶ 2-640).

7. International taxation revision of permanent Establishment

- From pro forma basis (based on the effective tax rates of foreign subsidiaries) to substance basis (based on the specifics of individual activities (e.g. types of income)). When making the revision, consideration will be given to the administrative burden on companies.

- So-called passive income, or income not generated with real economic substance, will be subject to the CFC taxation.

- Income generated through real economic activities will be exempted from the CFC taxation regardless of foreign subsidiaries' effective tax rates.

In order to prevent the international tax avoidance, expansion of permanent Establishment was made.

た（¶7-312，¶7-882）。
　⑷　特定の美術品についての相続税が見直された（¶7-318）。

4．消費税の改正点
　⑴　平成29年4月に予定されていた消費税率の10%への引上げ時期が平成
　　　31年10月1日に延長することとされた（¶8-010参照）。
　⑵　平成31年10月1日以降，食用の農林水産物を生産する事業を簡易課税
　　　制度の第二種事業とし，そのみなし仕入率が80%（現行70%）とされる
　　　こととなった（¶8-680参照）。
　⑶　平成35年10月1日から適格請求書等の保存が仕入税額控除の要件とさ
　　　れることとなった（¶8-610参照）。

5．個人住民税の改正点
　　所得割額の算定に関し，平成33年度分以降，基礎控除の額が減額されるこ
　ととなった（¶9-090参照）。
　　合計所得2,400万円以下　430,000円
　　　　　　　2,450万円以下　290,000円
　　　　　　　2,500万円以下　150,000円
　　　　　　　2,500万円以上　なし

6．たばこ税
　　たばこ税の税率が平成30年10月から引き上げられる（¶2-640参照）。

7．国際課税
　　恒久的施設関連規定の見直し
　　租税回避防止等のため，恒久的施設（PE）の範囲の見直しがなされた。

16 INTRODUCTION

¶ 1-400 Nondiscrimination on the basis of nationality

The Japanese tax system does not differentiate on the basis of the nationality or citizenship of a taxpayer. Therefore, foreign readers need to pay attention only to the differences of tax liabilities between residents and non-residents, except in cases where a particular tax treaty grants special concessions on account of nationality or citizenship.

¶ 1-420 For foreign readers

Foreign taxpayers should read the following paragraphs with attention:

Tax burden on individual income .... ¶ 2-040
Tax burden on corporate income .... ¶ 2-060
Inheritance tax (national) .... ¶ 2-310
Tax-free purchases by visitors to Japan .... ¶ 2-540
Resident and non-resident (individual) .... ¶ 3-210 to ¶ 3-250
Domestic corporation and foreign corporation.................. ¶ 3-340 to ¶ 3-360
Withholding from payments to non-residents and
    foreign corporations .... ¶ 4-620 to ¶ 4-680
Non-resident's income tax liability .... ¶ 5-850 to ¶ 5-920
Foreign corporations.. ¶ 6-870 to ¶ 6-910

Generally speaking, treatment of foreign taxpayers who fall into any of the following categories is as follows:

(1) **A person who receives investment income**

A person who receives investment income such as interest income, dividend income or royalties is liable to withholding income tax at source. Applicable tax rates differ depending upon the situation, e.g. residence or non-residence, or the existence of a tax treaty (see Chapter 4).

(2) **A person who carries on business**

(a) When such person establishes a Japanese corporation:

A Japanese (domestic) corporation is subject to corporation tax on its worldwide income at the rate of 30%. In addition to this national tax, it is also subject to local taxes such as inhabitant tax and enterprise tax (see ¶ 2-060, ¶ 2-090 to ¶ 2-240).

(b) When such person establishes a Japanese branch:

The Japanese branch of a foreign corporation is subject to corporation tax on income attributed to the Japanese branch. The tax rate is basically, the same as that of a domestic

¶ 1-400

はじめに　17

¶1-400　国籍無差別

わが国の税法は，納税者の国籍又は市民権を理由とする差別につき何ら規定していない。そこで，外国人の読者は，個々の租税条約で特典が与えられている場合を除けば，単に居住者と非居住者の区別に基づく租税負担の差異に注意すれば足りる。

¶1-420　外国人読者のために

外国人読者の場合には，とりわけ次の各節を参照されたい。

個人の所得の租税負担	¶2-040
法人の所得の租税負担	¶2-060
相続税	¶2-310
来日外国人の購入物品の免税	¶2-540
居住者及び非居住者（個人）	¶3-210～¶3-250
内国法人及び外国法人	¶3-340～¶3-360
非居住者及び外国法人への支払に対する源泉徴収	¶4-620～¶4-680
非居住者の所得税の納税義務	¶5-850～¶5-920
外国法人の所得に係る納税義務	¶6-870～¶6-910

おおまかにいって，次のいずれかに該当する外国の納税者は，それぞれ次のように取り扱われる。

(1)　投資所得を有する者

利子，配当及びロイヤルティなどの投資所得を有する者は，支払を受ける際，所得税の源泉徴収を受ける。適用される税率は，場合（居住・非居住の別，租税条約の適用の有無）により異なる（第4章参照）。

(2)　事業を営む者

(a)　日本法人を設立する場合

日本（内国）法人は，その全世界所得につき30％の税率による法人税を納付する義務がある。この国税である法人税の外に，住民税や事業税等の地方税を納付する義務もある（¶2-060，¶2-090～¶2-240参照）。

(b)　日本支店を設置する場合

外国法人の日本支店は，日本支店に帰属する所得について法人税の納税義務を負う。税率は，原則として内国法人と同様であり，支店利益に対する特別課税はない。地方税についても同様である。

18   INTRODUCTION

corporation and no special tax is levied on the profit of a branch in Japan. Local taxes are levied in the same way.

(c) When such person performs under a contract of partnership or as an individual (see ¶ 3-120 for partnership):
When an individual taxpayer carries on a business, he is liable to income tax. The scope of the tax base differs according to whether he is a resident or a non-resident (see ¶ 3-210 to ¶ 3-250).

(3) **A person who renders personal services**

(a) Employee (or director):
If a person renders personal services as an employee or director within Japan, he is liable to income tax. In this case, tax is withheld at source (see ¶ 3-210, ¶ 4-230 to ¶ 4-350, ¶ 4-620 to ¶ 4-650).

(b) Lawyer or certified public accountant:
Lawyers or certified public accountants can render their services either as employees or self-employed persons. Treatment of their income for tax purposes differs accordingly (see ¶ 3-210, ¶ 4-360, ¶ 4-620 to ¶ 4-650).

(c) Artist or athlete:
An artist or an athlete is subject to the same rules as a lawyer or a certified public accountant.

(4) **A person who transfers or rents real estate**
From the residential policy viewpoint, the tax treatment of a transfer or rental of real estate is very complicated (see ¶ 6-470 to ¶ 6-505 and ¶ 6-670 for corporations and ¶ 5-190 to ¶ 5-250 for individual taxpayers).

(5) **Filing, payment, refund**
As for the filing, determination of income, payment of tax amount and refund are assessed under the self-assessment system in Japan.

(a) Filing, payment, refund
Individual income tax, gifttax···until March 15, next year
Individual consumption tax···until March 31 next year
Corporate tax, corporate consumption tax···within 2 months after closing date (As for the filing due date of corporate tax maximum four months extension, when a company with an

¶ 1-420

はじめに　19

(c)　組合契約に基づき又は個人形態により事業を営む場合
　　　組合については¶3-120を参照されたい。
　　　個人形態により事業を営む場合には，所得税の納税義務を負う。課税
　　される所得の範囲は，居住者に該当するか非居住者に該当するかにより
　　異なる（¶3-210〜¶3-250参照）。

(3)　人的役務を提供する者
(a)　使用人（又は役員）
　　　日本国内で使用人又は役員として人的役務を提供する場合には，日本
　　の所得税の納税義務を負う。この場合には，所得税の源泉徴収が行われ
　　る（¶3-210，¶4-230〜¶4-350，¶4-620〜¶4-650参照）。

(b)　弁護士，公認会計士
　　　弁護士や公認会計士は，使用人として役務を提供することもあれば，
　　独立の事業者として役務を提供することもある。所得に対する課税の扱
　　いはいずれであるかにより異なる（¶3-210，¶4-360，¶4-620〜¶4-
　　650参照）。
(c)　芸能人，職業運動家
　　　芸能人，職業運動家等も，弁護士や公認会計士と同様に取り扱われ
　　る。

(4)　不動産の譲渡や賃貸をする者
　　　不動産の譲渡や賃貸の場合については，住宅政策の面もあり非常に複雑
　　である。法人の納税者の場合には¶6-470〜¶6-505まで及び¶6-670を，
　　また，個人の納税者の場合には¶5-190〜¶5-250までを参照されたい。

(5)　申告，納付，還付
　　　日本では，申告納税制度が採用されている。

(a)　申告，納付，還付
　　　個人所得税，贈与税…翌年3月15日まで
　　　個人消費税……………翌年3月31日まで
　　　法人税及び消費税……各事業年度終了の日の翌日から2月以内（ただ
　　　　　　　　　　　　　　し，法人税の申告にあっては，会計監査人設置
　　　　　　　　　　　　　　会社が事業年度終了後3か月を超えて株主総会

20   INTRODUCTION

accounting auditor sets the date of its general shareholders' meeting at a date more than three months after the end of its business year)

Inheritance tax···within 10 months after death

(b) Request for correction:

Miscalculation, miss use of legal provision etc···within 5 years after the filing due date.

¶ 1-430 A person who needs assistance

(1) At the regional and district tax office level, an information service is provided to person who visits the tax office and to telephone calls by taxpayers at any time during office hours. The offices are called Tax Counsellors' Offices.

(2) TAX ANSWER (Automatic answer Network System for Electrical Request) is also available. When taxpayers put a question by telephone, they receive the answer automatically in Japanese. This service is also provided through Internet (http://www.taxanswer.nta.go.jp).

Even if you do not speak English, English speaking tax counselors they are assigned at Tokyo, Nagoya and Osaka Regional Taxation Bureaus, and provide services in English.

(3) In addition, Tax office or Regional taxation Bureaus provides advance inquires (advance private ruling) how to apply tax law for specific questions.

¶ 1-450 Administration system

National taxes are levied and collected by the National Tax Administration, which is an external organization under the Ministry of Finance.

The National Tax Administration has one central office, 12 regional taxation bureaus (Okinawa Regional Taxation Office included), and 524 tax offices. Taxes on the income of foreign individuals, as well as foreign corporations, are examined by the officials of a regional taxation bureau.

The legislative work on the tax system is executed by the Tax Bureau of the Ministry of Finance.

The chart at ¶ 1-800 is a general outline of the national tax administration system.

Tax disputes are resolved at an administrative level by the National Tax Tribunal, which is an affiliated organization under the Commissioner

¶ 1-430

はじめに　21

期日を設定する場合に，最大4か月間の申告期
限の延長あり）

相続税……………………相続開始の日から10月以内
(b) 更正の請求
申告誤り，法令の適用誤り等があった場合には，法定申告期限の翌日
から5年以内に更正の請求をすることができるとされている。

¶1-430　納税相談をしたい者

(1) 国税局又は税務署では，執務時間中であればいつでも，直接面談し又
は電話により税務相談をすることができる。担当の機関は税務相談室と
呼ばれる。

(2) タックス・アンサーによる照会サービスも行われている。納税者は，
電話で税金に関する質問をすると，日本語による回答が得られる。この
サービスはインターネットを通じても提供されている（http://www.
taxanswer. nta. go. jp）。
なお，日本語のわからない方のため，東京，名古屋，大阪の各国税局
に英語を話す相談官も配置されている。

(3) さらに，特定の取引に係る税法の解釈適用の疑問に応えるため税務署
又は国税局では事前相談にも応じている。

¶1-450　行政組織

国税の賦課及び徴収は，財務省の外局である国税庁により行われる。
国税庁は，中央に1つの事務所，12の国税局（沖縄国税事務所を含む。），
及び524の税務署で構成されている。外国法人だけでなく外国人の所得税の
調査も，国税局の調査官により行われる。
税制の企画，立案は財務省主税局が行う。
¶1-800の表は，国に関する税務行政組織の概要である。
行政庁段階での租税に関する不服申立ては，国税庁の関係行政機関である
国税不服審判所がその処理に当たっている。国税不服審判所は，東京に本部
があるほか，12の地方支部を有している。
以上のほか，地方自治体は，地方税の賦課，徴収のために税務署とは別の
独自の事務所を設けている。

22   INTRODUCTION

of the National Tax Administration. The National Tax Tribunal has one central office in Tokyo, and 12 branches.

In addition, local organizations have their own offices, apart from national tax offices, to levy and collect local taxes.

¶ 1-500 Tax disputes

When a taxpayer objects to the determination or correction (¶ 5-740), he or she may request:

(i)   request for reinvestigation (review),

(ii) request for reconsideration,

(iii) litigation.

(1) **Request for reinvestigation (review) (to the Assessment Office)**

A taxpayer may request a tax office to reinvestigate again his or her tax liability as determined or corrected, within 3 months after receiving notice of such determination or correction. When the tax liability has been investigated by any staff member of Regional.

A taxpayer may request directly to the National Tax Tribunal to review the case within 3 months instead of request for reinvestigation by a tax office.

(2) **Request for reconsideration (to the National Tax Tribunal)**

A taxpayer may request to the National Tax Tribunal to review his or her tax liability within one month after receiving the decision of a tax office, a Regional Taxation Bureau, following a request for the reinvestigation, if he or she still has an objection to the said decision.

A taxpayer may also bring the case to the National Tax Tribunal, if no decision has been made within three months after the filing of a request for reinvestigation with the tax office or Regional Taxation Bureau.

In addition a taxpayer may request directly to the National Tax Tribunal without review process of reinvestigation request mentioned (1).

Decision made by the National Tax Tribunal (NTT) will bind the related administrative organization (Tax Authority). Tax Authority, therefore, will have to follow NTT decision even when that

¶ 1-500

はじめに　23

¶1-500　不服申立て

　納税義務者は，更正・決定に不服がある場合には，「再調査の請求」，「審査請求」及び「訴訟」を行うことができる。

(1)　再調査の請求（対原処分庁）

　納税義務者は，更正・決定された税額について，その通知を受けた日から3カ月以内に，税務署長に対して再調査の請求をすることができる。その税額が国税局の職員の調査によるものである場合には，当該国税局に直接再調査の請求をすることができる。

　なお，納税義務者は，再調査の請求に代えて更正・決定の通知を受けた日から3カ月以内に直接国税不服審判所に直接審査請求をすることもできる。

(2)　審査請求（国税不服審判所）

　納税義務者は，再調査の請求に対する決定についてなお不服がある場合には，決定の通知を受けた日から1月以内に国税不服審判所に対して審査請求することができる。

　また，再調査の請求をしてから3月以内に何らの決定がない場合にも，国税不服審判所に対して審査請求することができる（通則法75）。

※なお，(1)でもふれたように，納税義務者は，再調査の請求手続きを経ることなく，直接国税不服審判所に審査請求することもできる。

　審判所の裁決は，関係行政庁（税務当局）を拘束することとされている。

　したがって，税務当局は自己に不利な裁決が出されたとしても，それに従わなければならない。

24   INTRODUCTION

decision is against their position.

(National Tax Tribunal)

The role of The National Tax Tribunal is to reinvestigate and decide tax disputes brought by taxpayers, was established in 1970. It is more independent of the National Tax Administration Agency than the former Conference Group, which was abolished when the National Tax Tribunal was established.

The director of the National Tax Tribunal is appointed by the Commissioner of the National Tax Administration Agency with the consent of the Minister of Finance.

The director is authorized to decide cases on the basis of interpretations which differ from rulings issued by the National Tax Administration Agency, provided the consent of the Commissioner is obtained. In deciding whether to give consent or not, the Commissioner of the N.T.A.A. is required to pay due consideration to opinions reached by the National Tax Review Committee, which consists of members with academic know-ledge and practical experience.

¶ 1-510 Litigation

In principle, litigation cannot be brought in court unless a decision has been made by the administrative agency on an administrative appeal.

If a taxpayer wants to bring his case before the court, he must take legal action within six months after becoming aware of the decision made by the administrative agency (including the National Tax Tribunal).

In Japan, there is no special court such as the tax court; accordingly, litigation of a tax case is governed by the ordinary courts system.

Even if a tax case is under litigation, the validity and execution of the original action is not suspended.

Japanese litigation system consists of three steps, such as District Court, High Court and Supreme Court.

In case of litigation different from NTT decision, Tax Authorities as well as tax payers, are allow to compete against the decision by the Court.

¶ 1-510

はじめに 25

（国税不服審判所）

国税不服審判所は，国税に関する審査請求につき審査し，裁決する機関として，また，従来の協議団に比してより国税庁からの独立性の高い組織として，昭和45年に設置された。

国税不服審判所の所長は，財務大臣の承認を得て国税庁長官が任命する。

国税不服審判所長は，国税庁の通達と異なる解釈により裁決を行う権限を有するが，この場合には，国税庁長官の同意が必要である。国税庁長官が同意を与えるか否かを決定する場合には，学識経験者からなる国税審査会の議決に基づいてこれをしなければならないこととされている。

¶1-510　訴訟

訴訟の提起は，原則として行政庁に対する不服申立てに対する決定又は裁定があるまでは，することができない。訴訟の提起をしようとする場合には，税務当局（国税不服審判所を含む。）の決定（又は裁決）があったことを知った日から6カ月以内に行わなければならない。日本には，例えば租税裁判所のような特別裁判所はないため，税務に関する訴訟も通常の裁判所により審理される。訴訟が提起された場合においても，原処分の効力や処分の執行には影響を及ぼさない。

訴訟は，地方裁判所，高等裁判所及び最高裁判所の三審制となっている。

なお，審判所の裁決と異なり，判決に不服がある場合には，納税者だけでなく税務当局にも次のステップで争うことが認められている。

26   INTRODUCTION

¶ 1-520 Competent authority assistance

The interaction of Japanese and foreign tax systems generates many complex issues. The competent authority plays a key part in resolving such issues. Japan has concluded income tax conventions with 80 countries (as of 1 May, 2014), and under each treaty, the Japanese competent authority and the competent authority of the other country are empowered to negotiate agreements to provide relief to taxpayers in cases of double taxation and taxation contrary to the rules of the treaty. Generally, this negotiation is set in motion by a taxpayer's request for assistance. Such requests are properly directed to the competent authority of the country of which the taxpayer is a resident. In Japan, the competent authority is the Minister of Finance, the Commissioner of the National Tax Administration, or their authorized representatives.

Competent Authority assistance is provided separately from domestic dispute resolution process (including litigation process).

¶ 1-530 Penalties

(1) **Penalty taxes**

The following penalty taxes are collected as an administrative penalty:

(a) Penalty tax for under reporting

10% of the tax increment resulting from a correction or an amended return, when the original final return was filed on or before the due date (GL 65①).

If the tax amount due to pay is whichever higher over reported income amount or ¥500,000, this 15% on that penalties exceeding amount.

However, this penalty will not apply when the amendment return under the reasonable conditions (GL 65②).

(b) Penalty tax for non filing

15% (if the tax amount due to pay is over ¥500,000, 20% is applied to the excessive amount over ¥500,000) of the tax determined by a tax office or set out in a final or amended return when the original final return was not filed on or before the due date (GL 66①, ②).

However, when it was recognized by a tax office that a taxpayer had intension to file a final tax return before the due date such as a tax payer filed a tax return within 1 month

¶ 1-520

はじめに **27**

¶1-520　権限のある当局による救済

　日本の税制と外国の税制の相互作用は多くの困難な問題を惹起する。権限のある当局は，このような問題の解決に重要な役割を果す。日本は80カ国との間に租税条約を締結しているが（2014年5月1日時点），二重課税を受けたり，条約の規定に違反して課税を受けた納税者を救済するためのこれらの租税条約は，日本の権限ある当局と相手国の権限ある当局が協議する権限を与えている。通常の場合，この権限のある当局者間の協議は，納税者からの救済の申立てをまって行われる。この救済の申立ては，自己が居住者である国の権限のある当局に対して行わなければならない。日本の場合，この権限のある当局は，財務大臣，国税庁長官又は権限を与えられたその代理人である。

　この救済の申立ては，国内法に規定する救済手続（訴訟を含む。）とは別の制度として位置付けられている。

¶1-530　罰則

(1)　加算税

　次の加算税は，行政上の罰金として徴収される。

(a)　過少申告加算税

　期限内申告をした後，更正又は修正申告書の提出があったときには，修正申告又は更正により納付することになった税額の10％に相当する過少申告加算税が課される（通則法65①）。

　ただし，納付すべき金額から期限内申告納税相当額又は50万円のいずれか多い金額を超える場合には，超える部分に対してはその割合は15％となる（通則法65②）。

　なお，正当な理由がある場合には，過少申告加算税は課されない。

(b)　無申告加算税

　決定又は期限後申告書の提出及び期限後申告書の提出後に修正申告書の提出があったときには，その決定又は申告により納付することになった税額の15％に相当する無申告加算税が課される。ただし，納付すべき税額が50万円を超える場合には，超える部分に対しては20％に相当する無申告加算税が課される（通則法66①，②）。

　申告書が法定申告期限から1ヶ月以内に提出され，かつ，その申告書に係る納付すべき税額の全額が法定納期限までに納付されている等の期限内申告書を提出する意思があったと認められる場合には，無申告加算税は課

28   INTRODUCTION

from the due date and paid the tax amount due to pay in full
up to the legal due date to pay, penalty tax for no return will
not be assessed (GL 66⑥).

(c) Heavy penalty tax
In fraud tax cases, 35% of the additional tax instead of the
penalty tax is payable for a short return, and in case of no return filed 40% of the tax determined instead of the penalty tax
is payable for no return (GL 68①, ②).

(d) Heavy penalty tax addition
In order to prevent vicious fraud case, if taxpayers who were
changed heavy penalty tax within 5 previous years, 10% point
increase of penalty for non filing (no return) and heavy penalty tax.
Details of this systems are as follows

	Base rate	Increased rate
• non-filing case penalty tax		
for non-filing	15% (20%)	25% (30%)
• fraud case heavy penalty		
(review reporting		
on no payment)	35%	45%
heavy penalty		
(non filing)	40%	50%

(2) **Notification procedure**
If the District Director of a tax office believes a tax crime has
been committed, he is empowered to issue notification to the
taxpayer demanding payment of an amount equivalent to a fine.
When the taxpayer makes payment of this amount, he is released
from punishment on a criminal charge.
When taxpayer fails this payment, he will be prosecuted as a criminal charge.
This notification procedure is applicable only to indirect taxes
such as liquor tax and consumption tax.

(3) **Judicial penalty**
If a taxpayer fails to meet a tax obligation without reasonable
excuse, for instance by neglecting to file a tax return in accordance with the tax laws or making an incorrect tax return by omit-
ting any taxable income, a judicial penalty is imposed.

¶ 1-530

されない（通則法66⑥）。

(c) 重加算税

仮装・隠ぺいの場合には，過少申告加算税に代わって35％の重加算税が，無申告の場合にあっては，無申告加算税に代わって40％の重加算税が課される（通則法68①，②）。

(d) 加算税の加重措置

悪質な行為を防止する観点から過去5年以内に無申告加算税又は重加算税を賦課されたものが、再び「無申告又は仮装隠蔽」に基づく修正申告税の提出等を行っていた場合には、加算税が10％加重される。

	（原税）	（加重）
＜無申告の場合＞　無申告加算税	15％（20％）	25％（30％）
＜仮装隠蔽の場合＞		
重加算税（過少、不納付）	35％	45％
重加算税（無申告）	40％	50％

(2) **通告処分**

税務署長は，租税に関する犯則があると認めるときは，納税者に対し罰金に相当する金額の納付を求めることができる。納税者は，この金額を納付した場合には，刑事法廷において罰せられることはなくなる。

納税者が，通告を履行しなかった場合には刑事訴追を受ける。

この通告処分の手続は，酒税や消費税のような間接税についてのみ適用される。

(3) **刑事罰**

正当な理由なく納税義務を免れた場合，例えば税法の規定に基づく申告書を提出しなかった場合又は過少申告書を提出した場合には，刑事罰が科される。

典型的な犯罪及びこの犯罪に対する刑事罰は，次のとおりである。

30   INTRODUCTION

Typical offenses and their penalties are as follows:

(a) tax evasion:

• self assessment   (including fraudulent refund and its attempted one) (IT 239①, CT 159①) imprisonment for a term not exceeding 10 years and/or a fine not exceeding ¥10,000,000

• withholding agent   (IT 240)

tax evasion   imprisonment for a term not exceeding 10 years and/or a fine not exceeding ¥1,000,000

no payment   imprisonment for a term not exceeding 10 years and/or a fine not exceeding ¥2,000,000

(b) filing no return: imprisonment for a term not exceeding one year and/or a fine not exceeding ¥500,000 (IT 241, CT 160)

(c) willfull nonfiling: imprisonment for a term not exceeding 5 years or a fine not exceeding ¥5,000,000 (IT 239③, CT 159③)

(d) false or no reply   A fine not exceeding ¥300,000.
to a tax examiner:

(e) agitation   imprisonment for a term not exceeding 3
(anti-tax):   years and/or a fine not exceeding ¥200,000

¶ 1-540 Certified public tax accountant

No one can undertake the occupation of rendering the following services to a taxpayer without a license:

(a) acting as an agent for a taxpayer;

(b) preparing various documents for tax purposes;

(c) consulting with a taxpayer on tax issues.

A certified public tax accountant can render services with respect to all taxes except travel, stamp, registration and license tax and customs duty, etc.

A lawyer, a certified public accountant or a person who has passed a certified public tax accountant examination is entitled to become a certified public tax accountant. The subjects of this examination are income tax law, corporation tax law, inheritance tax law, either liquor tax law or consumption tax law, national tax collection law, local tax law and accounting.

¶ 1-540

はじめに　31

(a)　脱税
・申告納税
　　脱税　　10年以下の懲役又は1000万円以下の罰金（所得238①，法法159①）
・源泉徴収
　　不納付　10年以下の懲役又は200万円以下の罰金（所法240）

(b)　無申告　1年以下の懲役又は50万円以下の罰金（所法241，法法160）

(c)　故意の無申告　5年以下の懲役又は500万円以下の罰金（所法239③，法法159③）

(d)　調査官に対する不答弁又は虚偽の答弁　30万円以下の罰金

(e)　煽動　3年以下の懲役又は20万円以下の罰金

¶1-540　税理士

資格がない場合には，何人も次のサービス業務を業として行うことができない。
(a)　納税者の代理人として行動すること
(b)　税務上の種々の書類を作成すること
(c)　税務上の問題につき，納税者と相談すること

税理士は，通行税，印紙税，登録免許税，関税等を除くすべての租税につき，サービスを提供することができる。

弁護士，公認会計士又は税理士試験に合格した者は，税理士になることができる。

試験は，所得税法，法人税法，相続税法，酒税法又は消費税法のうちいずれかの法律，国税徴収法，地方税法及び会計学について行われる。

¶ 1-800 Chart: National Tax Administration System

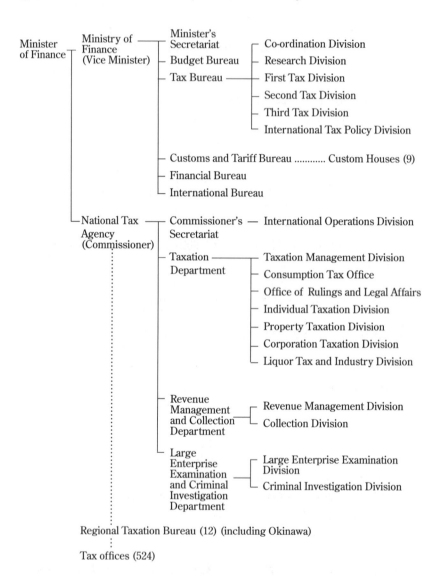

¶ 1-800

¶1-800　国税の執行機関の組織図

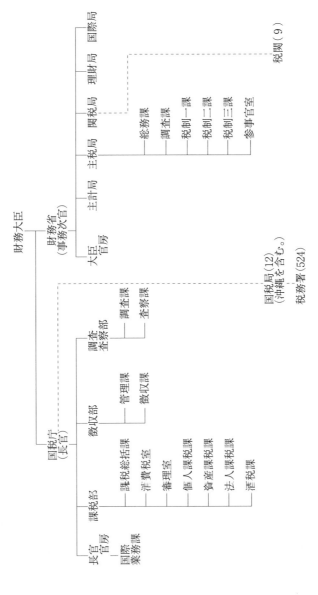

34 INTRODUCTION

¶ 1-850 Table: General View of Japanese Taxes

	National taxes	Local taxes (¶ 2-010)	
			Municipal taxes
Taxes on income and profits	Income tax (Withholding income tax and assessment income tax) (¶ 2-080) Corporation tax (¶ 2-090)	Prefectural inhabitant tax (¶ 2-110) Enterprise tax (¶ 2-240)	Municipal inhabitant tax (¶ 2-110)
Taxes on inheritances and gifts	Inheritance tax (¶ 2-310, ¶ 2-320) Gift tax (¶ 2-340)		
Taxes on property	Land value tax (¶ 2-345) Automobile tonnage tax (¶ 2-420)	Automobile tax (¶ 2-350)	Fixed assets tax (¶ 2-360) Special land holding tax (¶ 2-380) City planning tax (¶ 2-390) Light vehicle tax (¶ 2-410) Enterprise establishment tax (¶ 2-430)
Excise taxes (Taxes on consumption)	Consumption tax (¶ 2-510) Liquor tax (¶ 2-560) Gasoline tax and local road tax (¶ 2-580) Aircraft fuel tax (¶ 2-585) Petroleum coal tax (¶ 2-590) Petroleum gas tax (¶ 2-595) Tobacco tax, Special tobacco tax (¶ 2-640)	Prefectural tobacco tax (¶ 2-640) Golf course tax (¶ 2-650) Special local consumption tax (¶ 2-670) Diesel oil delivery tax (¶ 2-680)	Municipal tobacco tax (¶ 2-640) Bathing tax (¶ 2-710)
Taxes on transactions	Stamp tax (¶ 2-820) Registration and licence tax (¶ 2-830) Electric power resources development tax (¶ 2-890)	Real property acquisition tax (¶ 2-850) Automobile acquisition tax (¶ 2-870)	
Miscellaneous taxes		Mining allotment tax (¶ 2-950) Hunting tax (¶ 2-950) Other prefectural taxes (¶ 2-950)	Mineral product tax (¶ 2-950) Other municipal taxes (¶ 2-950)

¶ 1-850

はじめに　35

¶1-850　日本における各種租税の概要

	国　税	地方税　（¶2-010）	
		道府県税	市町村税
所得及び利潤に対する税	所得税（源泉所得税及び申告所得税）（¶2-080） 法人税（¶2-090）	道府県民税（¶2-110） 事業税（¶2-240）	市町村民税（¶2-110）
相続及び贈与に対する税	相続税（¶2-310, ¶2-320） 贈与税（¶2-340）		
財産に対する税	地価税（¶2-345） 自動車重量税（¶2-420）	自動車税（¶2-350）	固定資産税（¶2-360） 特別土地保有税（¶2-380） 都市計画税（¶2-390） 軽自動車税（¶2-410） 事業所税（¶2-430）
消費にかかる税	消費税（¶2-510） 酒税（¶2-560） 揮発油税及び地方道路税（¶2-580） 航空機燃料税（¶2-585） 石油石炭税（¶2-590） 石油ガス税（¶2-595） たばこ税，たばこ特別税（¶2-640）	道府県たばこ税（¶2-640） ゴルフ場利用税（¶2-650） 特別地方消費税（¶2-670） 軽油取引税（¶2-680）	市町村たばこ税（¶2-640） 入湯税（¶2-710）
取引に関する税	印紙税（¶2-820） 登録免許税（¶2-830） 電源開発促進税（¶2-890）	不動産取得税（¶2-850） 自動車取得税（¶2-870）	
その他の税		鉱区税（¶2-950） 狩猟税（¶2-950） その他の道府県税（¶2-950）	鉱区税（¶2-950） その他の市町村税（¶2-950）

CHAPTER 2

MAIN FEATURES OF JAPANESE TAXES

	Paragraph
Local Taxes	¶ 2-010
Taxes on Income and Profits	¶ 2-040
Taxes on Inheritances and Gifts	¶ 2-310
Taxes on Property	¶ 2-345
Taxes on Consumption	¶ 2-510
Taxes on Transactions	¶ 2-820
Miscellaneous Taxes	¶ 2-950

第　2　章

日本の租税の主な特色

地方税……………………………………………………… ¶2–010
所得及び利潤に対する租税……………………………… ¶2–040
相続及び贈与に対する租税……………………………… ¶2–310
財産に対する租税………………………………………… ¶2–345
消費に対する租税………………………………………… ¶2–510
取引に対する租税………………………………………… ¶2–820
その他の租税……………………………………………… ¶2–950

38   MAIN FEATURES OF JAPANESE TAXES

Local Taxes

¶ 2-010 Local taxes

Japan is divided into 47 prefectures which are the upper level local units, and about 1,720 municipalities which are the lower level local units. The prefectures are called *"ken"*, *"fu"*, *"do"* or *"to"* and the municipalities are called *"shi"*, *"cho"*, *"mura"* or *"ku"* (special ward of *"to"*).

Both the prefectures and the municipalities collect their own local taxes. As the main kinds of local taxes and their tax rates are regulated by national legislation, the tax burden in Japan is not substantially different from one district to another, although some local authorities collect more revenue than is envisioned under the standard local tax system.

Taxes on Income and Profits

¶ 2-040 Tax burden on individual income

Individuals are subject to income tax (national) (¶ 2-080) and prefectural inhabitant tax and municipal inhabitant tax (¶ 2-110, ¶ 2-240) on their income. The table at ¶ 2-050 shows some examples of the total burden of these taxes.

地　方　税

¶2-010　地方税

　日本の行政区画は，上位の区画として47の都道府県と，下位の約1,720の市町村に区分される。都道府県は，都・道・府・県と呼ばれ，また，市町村は市・町・村又は区（特別区）と呼ばれる。

　都道府県及び市町村は，それぞれ自らの地方税を賦課し徴収する。主要な地方税の税目及び税率は国の法律により規定されるので，日本では，各地方自治体の住民の税負担には大差がないが，地方自治体によっては標準税率以上の租税を課すことがある。

所得及び利潤に対する租税

¶2-040　個人の所得に対する租税負担

　個人の所得に対しては，所得税（国税）（¶2-080），都道府県民税及び市町村民税（地方税）（¶2-110，¶2-240）の各租税が課される。¶2-050の表は，これらの租税負担の総額の一例である。

40 MAIN FEATURES OF JAPANESE TAXES

¶ 2-050 Table: Tax Burden on Individual Income (2018)

(¥1,000)

Annual revenue (A)		Income tax (national)	Local inhabitant tax (prefectural and municipal)	Total (B)	$\dfrac{(B)}{(A)}$
3,000	(US$ 27,777)	20	64	84	2.8%
5,000	(46,296)	97	218	315	6.3
10,000	(92,592)	829	652	1,481	14.8
20,000	(185,185)	3,962	1,685	5,647	28.2
50,000	(462,962)	16,201	4,685	20,886	41.8
100,000	(925,925)	38,701	9,685	48,386	48.4

Note:

1. The above figures apply to an employee with a spouse and two children (16 and over, under 19 years old).
2. The kind of income is assumed to be employment income.
3. Exchange rate: ¥108 = US $1.

Income Deductions	Income tax (national)	Local inhabitant tax
Deduction for a spouse	¥380,000	¥330,000
Deduction for dependants	¥760,000	¥660,000
Basic deduction	¥380,000	¥330,000

In the case of doing business in Japan, enterprise tax (prefectural) is imposed on business income (¶ 2-240)

4. Earthquake restoration surtax (2.1% of the amount of income tax) is not included.

¶ 2-050

¶2-050　給与所得の租税負担（平成30年分）

年間収入 (A)	(米 $)	所得税 （国税）	住民税 （都道府県及び市町村）	計 (B)	(B) (A)
3,000千円	27,777	20千円	64千円	84千円	2.8%
5,000	46,296	97	218	315	6.3
10,000	92,592	829	652	1,481	14.8
20,000	185,185	3,962	1,685	5,647	28.2
50,000	462,962	16,201	4,685	20,886	41.8
100,000	925,925	38,701	9,685	48,386	48.4

(注)：
1．上記の数字は，配偶者と2人の子供（共に16歳以上19歳未満）を有する者に関するものである。
2．所得の種類は，給与所得とした。
3．換算レート：1ドル＝108円

《参考》

所得控除	所得税	住民税
配偶者控除	380,000円	330,000円
扶養控除	760,000	660,000
基礎控除	380,000	330,000

これらの租税のほか，日本の国内において事業を営む場合には，事業の所得を課税標準として事業税（都道府県民税）が課される（¶2-240）。
4．復興特別所得税（所得税額の2.1%）は含めていない。

42   MAIN FEATURES OF JAPANESE TAXES

¶ 2-060 Tax burden on corporate income

Corporations, both domestic and foreign, are subject to corporation tax (national) (¶ 2-090), prefectural inhabitant tax, municipal inhabitant tax (¶ 2-110, ¶ 9-010) and enterprise tax (prefectural) (¶ 9-760 to ¶ 9-840) on their income. The following table shows examples of the total tax burden on corporate income.

Tax Burden on Corporate Income
(Effective tax rate)

Part of income before tax	up to ¥4 million	¥4 million to ¥8 million	over ¥8 million
Corporation tax	13.96%	13.31%	19.95%
Inhabitant taxes			
(1) prefectural	0.48	0.48	0.75
(2) municipal	1.45	1.45	2.27
(3) local corporate tax	0.66	0.66	1.03
Enterprise tax	3.40	5.10	6.70
Local special corporate tax	1.47	2.20	2.89
	21.42	23.20	33.59

Note:

Enterprise tax and Local special corporate tax are deductible in computing the tax base for corporation tax and for enterprise tax itself. Indirectly it is also deductible in computing inhabitant tax as well.

The following assumptions have been made for the computation:

(1) Capital amount of the corporation is 100 million yen or less.

(2) Business year begins on and after April 1, 2018.

¶ 2-080 Income tax (national)

Income tax is composed of withholding income tax and assessment income tax.

Withholding income tax is withheld at source from payments to individuals as well as to corporations. The tax rate is usually a flat 20% or less. However, tax withheld from the salaries, wages, bonuses, retirement allowances, etc. paid to resident individuals is often higher than 20% because the amount of tax is computed by applying a progressive rate.

Assessment income tax is levied on individuals, only at progressive rates. Non-resident taxpayers are subject to assessment income tax only in certain cases (for example, if they possess a permanent establishment or real estate in Japan, etc.): (see ¶ 3-020 ff.)

¶ 2-060

¶2-060　法人の所得に対する租税負担

内国法人，外国法人を問わず，法人の所得に対して法人税（国税）（¶2-090），法人都道府県民税，法人市町村民税（¶2-110，¶9-010）及び事業税（都道府県税）（¶9-760～¶9-840）が課される。

次の表は法人の所得に対する租税負担の総額の一例である。

法人の所得に対する租税負担
（実効税率）

税引前所得部分	400万円以下	400万円超～800万円	800万円超
法人税	13.96%	13.31%	19.95%
住民税　(1) 都道府県	0.48	0.48	0.75
(2) 市町村	1.45	1.45	2.27
(3) 地方法人税	0.66	0.66	1.03
事業税	3.40	5.10	6.70
地方法人特別税	1.47	2.20	2.89
計	21.42	23.20	33.59

（注）：事業税及び地方法人特別税は，法人税及び事業税の課税標準を計算するに当たり控除される。同様に，住民税を計算するに当たっても，間接的に控除される。計算に当たっては，次の前提を置いている。
　(1) 法人の資本金は 1 億円以下である。
　(2) 事業年度は平成30年 4 月 1 日以降開始する事業年度である。

¶2-080　所得税（国税）

所得税は，源泉所得税と申告所得税とからなる。

源泉所得税は，個人・法人を問わず支払が行われる場合に，差し引かれる。税率は，通常20％又はそれ以下とされている。しかしながら，給料，賃金，賞与，退職手当等で居住者である個人に対して支払われるものについては，20％を超えることが多いが，これは累進税率により税額を計算するからである。

個人に対して課される申告所得税は，常に累進税率による。非居住者は，日本国内に恒久的施設あるいは不動産を持っている場合等，特定の場合にのみ申告所得税を課される（¶3-020以降を参照）。

44   MAIN FEATURES OF JAPANESE TAXES

¶ 2-090 Corporation tax (national)

Corporation tax is imposed on the income of domestic and foreign corporations.

Withholding income tax withheld at source is deducted from the amount of corporation tax, or is refunded when excess withholding has occurred (see ¶ 3-020 ff.).

¶ 2-100 Local special corporate tax (national)

Local special corporate tax was introduced as a temporary measure pending integrated tax reform including consumption tax. Local special corporate tax is separated off the specified portion of enterprise tax.

Local special corporate tax is levied on all corporation who is liable to pay corporation enterprise tax. The tax amount is computed on the basis of income or gross proceeds.

¶ 2-110 Inhabitant taxes (prefectural and municipal)

Inhabitant taxes are levied by the prefectures and the municipalities. However, prefectural inhabitant tax and municipal inhabitant tax may be regarded as two components of the one inhabitant tax, because the main features of both taxes are almost the same and especially because prefectural inhabitant tax on individuals is collected by the municipal tax offices.

Inhabitant taxes are composed of:

(1)   individual inhabitant taxes (see ¶ 9-010 to ¶ 9-160); and

(2)   corporate inhabitant taxes (see ¶ 9-180 to ¶ 9-320).

As part of the three-part-reform (integrated reform of subsidies, local allocation tax and transfer of tax revenue sources from national to local governments), the full-fledged transfer of tax revenue sources of ¥3 trillion from national income tax to local inhabitant tax will be carried out as a permanent measure.

This transfer of tax revenue sources will be applied to Income tax from 2007 Calendar year. In fiscal year 2006, transfer of tax revenue sources will be carried out through Income transfer tax as a temporary measure.

¶ 2-240 Enterprise tax (prefectural)

Enterprise tax is composed of enterprise tax on individuals and enterprise tax on corporations and levied by prefectures. With the exception of enterprise tax on corporations in businesses such as electric power

¶ 2-090

日本の租税の主な特色　45

¶2-090　法人税（国税）

　法人税は，内国法人，外国法人を問わず，法人に対して課される。支払の際に徴収された源泉所得税は，法人税から控除されるほか源泉所得税を納付し過ぎた場合には還付される（¶3-020以降を参照）。

¶2-100　地方法人特別税（国税）

　地方法人特別税は，消費税を含む税体系の抜本的改革が行われるまでの間の暫定措置として，法人事業税の一部を分離し，創設された。納税義務者は法人事業税の納税義務者とされ，標準税率により計算した所得割額又は収入割額に税率を乗じて計算される。

¶2-110　住民税（都道府県税及び市町村税）

　住民税は，都道府県及び市町村により課される。しかしながら，都道府県住民税も市町村住民税も一つの住民税の構成要因にすぎないと考えられている。その理由は，両税の主要点がほとんど同じであり，特に個人に課される都道府県住民税は市町村により徴収されるからである。

　住民税は，

　(1)　個人に対する住民税（個人住民税）と，
　(2)　法人に対する住民税（法人住民税）
に分けられる（¶9-010以降を参照）。

　また，三位一体改革の一環として，平成18年度税制改正において，所得税から個人住民税への恒久措置として，3兆円規模の本格的な税源移譲を実施する。

　この税源移譲は，平成19年分の所得税及び平成19年度分の個人住民税から適用し，平成18年度においては，暫定的措置として，税源移譲額の全額を所得譲与税によって措置する。

¶2-240　事業税（都道府県税）

　事業税は，個人事業税と法人事業税とからなっており，都道府県の課す税である。電気供給業等にかかる法人事業税を除いて，事業税の額は所得に基づいて計算される（¶9-340以降を参照）。

46   MAIN FEATURES OF JAPANESE TAXES

supply, etc, enterprise tax is computed on the basis of profits (see ¶ 9-340 to ¶ 9-560).

¶ 2-270 Taxation of Corporation by the size of their business

Taxation of corporation by the size of their business was incorporated into corporate enterprise tax.

Taxation of Corporation by the size of their business is newly introduced from the viewpoints of sharing the tax burden more broadly and thinly and clarifying the relationship between the burden and benefits in the local community.

Taxpayers are Corporations with capital of ¥100,000,000 and over and Tax base consists of profits, capital and other value added items such as wages, interest and rentals.

Taxation of Corporation by the size of their business is applicable for taxable year beginning after October 1, 2008.

Tax rates on per income, per capital and per value added are as follows.

(1) Per income

Over	Not over	
–	4,000,000	:0.395%
4,000,000	8,000,000	:0.635%
8,000,000	–	:0.88%

(2) Per capital   :0.525%

(3) Per value added   :1.26%

(see ¶ 9-480, ¶ 9-570)

Taxes on Inheritances and Gifts

¶ 2-310 Inheritance tax (national)

The inheritance tax system is constructed on the theory that an inheritance is supplementary income of a special character. Therefore, it is levied on heirs, legatees, etc, but not on the deceased's estate itself.

If a person who has Japanese nationality (except for certain cases) or is domiciled in Japan inherits property, inheritance tax is fully levied on the property inherited, whether or not the deceased resided in Japan at the time of death, and whether or not the properties were situated in Japan at the time of death. On the other hand, if an heir does not fall in above-mentioned category, inheritance tax is levied only on the inherited proper-

¶ 2-270

日本の租税の主な特色　47

¶2-270　外形標準課税

法人事業税に外形標準課税が適用されることとなった。

外形標準課税は税負担をより幅広くかつ薄く求め，応益課税を明確にする観点から導入されたものである。

外形標準課税の対象となる法人は，資本金の額又は出資金額が1億円を超える法人とされ，対象法人に対し，所得割，付加価値割及び資本割の合算額によって法人事業税を課するものであり，平成20年10月1日以後開始の事業年度から適用される。

所得割，付加価値割及び資本割に係る標準税率は，次のとおりである。

(1)　所得割
＊所得のうち年400万円以下の金額：0.395％
＊所得のうち年400万円を超え，年800万円以下の金額：0.635％
＊所得のうち年800万円を超える金額及び清算所得：0.88％

(2)　資本割　　　　　　　　　　　　　　　：0.525％
(3)　付加価値割　　　　　　　　　　　　　：1.26％
　　（¶9-480，¶9-570参照）

相続及び贈与に対する租税

¶2-310　相続税（国税）

相続税に関する制度は，相続は特殊の性格を有する補完的所得を得ることであるという考え方に基づいて構成されている。したがって，相続税は，相続人又は受遺者に対して課せられるものであり，被相続人の財団に課されるものではない。

日本国籍を有する一定の者又は日本に住所を有する者が財産を相続した場合は，被相続人が死亡の際日本に住所を有していたか否かを問わず，また，その死亡の際に財産が日本国内にあったか否かを問わず，相続した全財産につき相続税が課される。一方，上記以外の相続人の場合には，被相続人が死亡の際に日本国内に住所を有しているか否かを問わず，日本国内にある相続

48   MAIN FEATURES OF JAPANESE TAXES

ties which were situated in Japan, whether or not the deceased resided in Japan at the time of death.

The table at ¶ 2-320 shows the burden of Japanese inheritance tax (for further details, see ¶ 7-010 ff.).

¶ 2-320 Table: Inheritance Tax Burden

(unit : thousand yen)

Total of net taxable assets	Tax payable by wife	Tax payable by a child	Total tax payable	%
100,000	0	500	2,000	2.0
150,000	0	1,187	4,750	3.2
300,000	0	4,000	16,000	5.3
500,000	0	9,500	38,000	7.6

Note:
  (1) It is assumed that the deceased had a wife and four children who had reached full age at the time of death, and the estate was distributed among them in accordance with statutory shares.
  (2) Credit for the spouse is taken into consideration for tax payable by wife (see ¶ 7-400(2)).

¶ 2-340 Gift tax (national)

Gift tax is levied on an individual donee with regard to property donated by another individual (donation to an individual by a corporation is treated as occasional income and subject to income tax and inhabitant taxes). If a donee resides in Japan or has Japanese nationality (except for certain cases), all properties donated are taxable whether or not they are located in Japan, while a donee who does not fall in above-mentioned category is subject to gift tax only for properties located in Japan (For details, see ¶ 7-760 ff.).

Taxes on Property

¶ 2-345 Land Value Tax (national)

As a tentative measure, the implementation of Land Value Tax is suspended for the time being. This amendment is effective in 1998 tax period and after.

  (1) **Object of taxation**
       Land which includes land, leasehold, superficies and the like, located in Japan, owned by individuals or corporations.

¶ 2-320

財産についてのみ相続税が課される。

¶2-320の表は，日本の相続税の負担額を示すものである（詳細については，¶7-010以降を参照のこと）。

¶2-320　相続税負担

（単位：1,000円）

遺産の総額	妻 の 納 付すべき税額	子1人当たりの納付すべき税額	納 付 す べ き税額の合計額	％
100,000	0	500	2,000	2.0
150,000	0	1,187	4,750	3.2
300,000	0	4,000	16,000	5.3
500,000	0	9,500	38,000	7.6

（注）：1. 被相続人には，死亡の際，妻のほか4人の成年に達している子供があり，遺産はこれらの相続人が遺産分割により法定相続分に従って取得するものとする。
　　　　2. 妻の納付すべき税額は，配偶者の税額軽減額を控除した後のものである（¶7-400 (2) 参照）。

¶2-340　贈与税（国税）

贈与税は，他の個人からの贈与により財産を取得した個人に対して課される（個人への法人からの贈与は，一時所得として所得税及び住民税が課される。）。贈与を受けた者が日本に住所を有する場合又は日本国籍を有する場合（一定の場合を除く。）には，贈与の対象となった財産が日本国内にあったかどうかを問わず，贈与を受けた全財産が課税対象となるが，贈与を受けた者が上記に該当しない場合には，日本国内にあった財産のみに対して贈与税が課される（詳細については，¶7-760以降を参照のこと）。

財産に対する租税

¶2-345　地価税（国税）

臨時的措置として，当分の間地価税は課税しないこととされた。この改正は，平成10年の課税時期に係る地価税から適用される。

(1)　課税対象

個人又は法人が国内に有する土地等（土地，借地権及び地上権等）

50   MAIN FEATURES OF JAPANESE TAXES

(2) **Taxpayers**

Individuals or corporations who own land, etc, at the time of taxation (January 1 of each year).

(3) **Evaluation of land**

Land, etc. is evaluated under the Inheritance and Gift Tax Law and Evaluation Rulings.

(4) **Non-taxable land**

(a) Land owned by the national or local governments, etc.

(b) Land, owned by public interest corporations (except land not directly used for their proper activities).

(c) Land, etc. directly used for specified public welfare purposes.

(d) Site up to 1,000m^2 owned by an individual for residence (except second houses), and that owned by an individual or a corporation for rental purposes (except company houses for directors).

(e) Land with an assessment value of ¥30,000/m^2 or less.

(f) Agricultural land and forests.

(5) **Tax base**

The tax base is the total amount of the assessed value of land, etc. owned at the time of taxation.

(6) **Basic deduction**

The amount of basic deduction is (a) or (b), whichever is higher:

(a) Individuals or corporations with capital
of not more than 100 million yen   ¥1.5 billion
Corporations with capital of more than 100
million yen   ¥1 billion

(b) ¥30,000 × area of the land (m^2).

(7) **Tax rate:** 0.15%

(8) **Computation of tax amount**

(Tax base – Basic deduction) × Tax rate

(9) **Filing a return and tax payment**

Taxpayers must file returns, and pay half of the tax due, between October 1 and 31 every year. The other half of the tax due must be paid by March 31 of the next year.

¶ 2-350 Automobile tax (prefectural)

Automobile tax is paid each year by the owner of an automobile to the prefecture in which the usual parking place of the vehicle is situated. The

¶ 2-350

日本の租税の主な特色　51

(2)　納税義務者
　　課税時期（各年1月1日）において土地等を有する個人又は法人

(3)　土地等の評価
　　土地等の価額は，相続税評価額により算定する。

(4)　非課税とされる土地等
　　(a)　国及び地方公共団体等が有する土地等
　　(b)　公益法人等が有する土地等（本来の事業以外の事業の用に供されているもの等を除く。）
　　(c)　一定の公益的な用途に供されている土地等
　　(d)　個人が所有し居住している住宅（一つに限る。）敷地及び個人・法人所有の貸家（会社役員の住宅を除く。）敷地で1,000㎡以下の部分

　　(e)　1㎡当たりの評価額が30,000円以下である土地等
　　(f)　農地・森林
(5)　課税標準
　　課税時期において有する土地等の価額の合計額を課税標準とする。

(6)　基礎控除
　　次のいずれか多い金額が基礎控除額となる。
　　(a)　個人又は資本金1億円以下の法人　　　15億円
　　　　資本金1億円超の法人　　　　　　　　10億円

　　(b)　30,000円×土地等の面積（㎡）
(7)　税率：0.15%
(8)　税額計算
　　（課税標準－基礎控除額）×税率
(9)　申告と納税
　　納税義務者は毎年10月1日から10月31日までに申告書を提出し，税額の2分の1を納税しなければならない。残額の2分の1は翌年の3月31日までに納税しなければならない。

¶2-350　自動車税（都道府県税）
　自動車税は，自動車の所有者がその定置場の所在する都道府県に対して毎年納付するもので，4月1日現在の所有者に対して，納税通知書が送付され

52　MAIN FEATURES OF JAPANESE TAXES

tax notification is sent to the owner as of April 1, and the time limit for paying the tax is the end of May. If the tax liability occurs or terminates after April 1, the tax amount payable is determined on the prorated monthly basis (If there is eventual overpayment, the excess is refundable.).

The annual amount of automobile tax is as follow:

Classification		Commercial use	Others
	Displacement		
Ordinary car	1 litre or less	7,500 yen	29,500 yen
	over　1 litre　to　1.5　litres	8,500 yen	34,500 yen
	over　1.5　litres to　　2　litres	9,500 yen	39,500 yen
	over　　2　litres to　2.5　litres	13,800 yen	45,000 yen
	over　2.5　litres to　　3　litres	15,700 yen	51,000 yen
	over　　3　litres to　3.5　litres	17,900 yen	58,000 yen
	over　3.5　litres to　　4　litres	20,500 yen	66,500 yen
	over　　4　litres to　4.5　litres	23,600 yen	76,500 yen
	over　4.5　litres to　　6　litres	27,200 yen	88,000 yen
	over　　6　litres	40,700 yen	111,000 yen
Truck		6,500 yen~	8,000 yen~
Bus	Omnibus for regular travel (not for sightseeing)	12,000 yen ~ 29,000 yen	33,000 yen ~ 83,000 yen
	Others	26,500 yen ~ 64,000 yen	
Three wheel car		4,500 yen	6,000 yen

Note:
  (1) The tax rates mentioned above are standard rates. Actual rates adopted by a prefecture should not exceed 150% of the standard rates.
  (2) A new automobile, which promotes a good influence to environment, is applied to the tax rate reduced. And a new automobile, which promotes a harmful influence to environment, is applied to the tax rate increased. And this special measure will be extended up to March 31, 2019.

¶ 2-360　Fixed assets tax (municipal)

Fixed assets tax is paid to a municipality by the registered owner of land, buildings, ships or any other depreciable assets as at January 1 of each year. (Tax on assets designated by the governor as large-scale depreciable assets is paid to the municipality and prefecture). "Registered owner" means the person registered as the owner of such property in the registration book maintained by a national juridical office.

¶ 2-360

納期限は5月末日である。4月1日以降に納税義務が発生し,又は消滅した場合の税額は月数により按分される(過納となる場合は還付される。)。

自動車税の年額は次のとおりである。

区 分	排 気 量	営 業 用	自 家 用
乗 用 車	1リットル以下	7,500円	29,500円
	1リットル超1.5リットル以下	8,500円	34,500円
	1.5リットル超2リットル以下	9,500円	39,500円
	2リットル超2.5リットル以下	13,800円	45,000円
	2.5リットル超3リットル以下	15,700円	51,000円
	3リットル超3.5リットル以下	17,900円	58,000円
	3.5リットル超4リットル以下	20,500円	66,500円
	4リットル超4.5リットル以下	23,600円	76,500円
	4.5リットル超6リットル以下	27,200円	88,000円
	6リットル超	40,700円	111,000円
トラック		6,500円〜	8,000円〜
バ ス	(一般乗合用)	12,000円〜29,000円	33,000円〜83,000円
	(その他)	26,500円〜64,000円	
三 輪 車		4,500円	6,000円

(注):1. 上記の税率は標準税率であり,都道府県によって実際に採用される税率は,この標準税率の150%を超えることはできない。
2. 平成13年度より環境負荷の小さい新車登録自動車は税率が軽減され,大きい自動車は税率を重くする特例措置が講じられた。そして,この特例措置は,軽減対象の見直しを行った上,2019年3月31日まで延長された。

¶2–360　固定資産税（市町村税）

固定資産税は,毎年1月1日現在において,公簿上に土地・建物・船舶その他の償却資産の所有者として登記された者により,市町村(都道府県知事が指定する大規模償却資産については,都道府県及び市町村)に納付される租税である。登記された所有者とは,登記所の登記簿にこれらの財産の所有者として登記された者をいう。

自動車税,軽自動車税の対象となる自動車については,固定資産税は課さ

54   MAIN FEATURES OF JAPANESE TAXES

No fixed assets tax is levied on automobiles or other vehicles which are subject to automobile tax or light vehicle tax.

The annual tax rate is 1.4%. In some relatively poor municipalities, the tax rate is higher than 1.4%, but it may not be higher than 2.1% in any case.

Fixed assets tax is collected in four equal installments in April, July and December of the taxation year, and February of the following year (see ¶ 9-580 to ¶ 9-740).

¶ 2-370 Tax burden concerning land and buildings

The following table provides a bird's-eye view of the tax burden concerning land and buildings:

Tax Burden on Real Estate

Taxpayer	Name of tax	Tax base	Tax rate (standard)	To whom payable
Registered owner	Fixed assets tax	registered market value	1.4%	municipality
	City planning tax (in designated districts only)	registered market value	0.3%	
	Special tax on holding of land	acquisition price	1.4%	
Heir	Inheritance tax	market value	progressive (10 to 55%)	national government
Donee	Gift tax	market value	progressive (10 to 55%)	national government
Person acquiring real property	Real property acquisition tax	market value	3%	prefecture
	Special tax on holding of land	acquisition price	0%	municipality
Applicant for registration	Registration and license tax	market value	0.15%	national government (registration office)
* Seller (individual)	Income tax	long-term	15%	national government
		short-term	30%	national government
	Inhabitant tax	long-term	5%	municipality
		short-term	9%	and prefecture

¶ 2-370

日本の租税の主な特色　55

れない。

　年税額は1.4％である。財政が相対的に困窮状態にある市町村では，税率は1.4％よりも高くなることがあるが，2.1％を超えることはできない。

　固定資産税は，4回に分割して4月，7月，12月及び翌年の2月の各月に納付する（¶9-580～¶9-740参照）。

¶2-370　土地及び建物の租税負担

　次の表は土地及び建物の租税負担の概要である。

不動産に係る租税

納税義務者	租税の種類	課税標準	税率 （標準）	支払先
登記簿上の所有者	固定資産税	登記された時価	1.4％	市町村
	都市計画税 （特定の地区に限る。）	〃	0.3％	〃
	特別土地保有税	取得価額	1.4％	〃
相続人 受贈者	相続税 贈与税	時価 時価	累進（10～55％） 累進（10～55％）	国 国
不動産の取得者	不動産取得税	時価	3％	都道府県
	特別土地保有税	取得価額	0％	市町村
登記申請人	登録免許税	時価	0.15％	国（登記所）
＊譲渡人（個人）	所得税	長期 短期	15％ 30％	国 国
	住民税	長期 短期	5％ 9％	市町村及び 都道府県

56   MAIN FEATURES OF JAPANESE TAXES

Seller (corporation)	Corporation tax	net income	23.4% (basic rate)	national government
	Inhabitant tax	net income	12.9%	municipality and prefecture
	Enterprise tax	net income	(3.4 to 6.7%)	prefecture
Parties to purchase contract, etc.	Stamp tax	market value	up to ¥540,000	national government (by affixing stamps)
Renter (individual)	Income tax	net income from rent	progressive (5 to 45%)	national government
	Inhabitant tax	net income from rent	flat (10%)	municipality and prefecture
Renter (corporation)	Corporation tax	net income from rent	23.4% (basic rate)	national government
	Inhabitant tax	net income from rent	12.9%	municipality and prefecture
	Enterprise tax	net income from rent	(3.4 to 6.7%)	prefecture

Note: *Cf. ¶ 5-200, ¶ 5-555, ¶ 5-560.

¶ 2-380 Special land holding tax (municipal)

This tax is levied on both the holding and acquisition of land. It is levied by the municipality in which the land is located.

(1) **Object of taxation**

Acquisitions of land and holdings of land except the land, the holding period of which is more than ten years:

A holding of land the total area of which is less than the area listed below, or an acquisition of land (where the total area of land acquired within a year preceding July 1 or January 1 is less than the area listed below) is exempt from the tax:

(i) Land located in the ward district of designated cities or in the special ward district of Tokyo-to...................................... 2,000m²

(ii) Land located in municipalities which have the town planning area stipulated in Art. 5 of Town Planning and Zoning Act 5,000m²

(iii) Land located in municipalities other than above............. 10,000m²

(2) **Taxpayers**

Holders or acquirers of land which is the object of taxation.

(3) **Non-taxation**

(a) Land acquired or held by the government or local governments;

(b) Land of which ownership is transferred procedurally, for in-

¶ 2-380

譲渡人(法人)	法人税	所得	23.4% (基本税率)	国
	住民税	〃	12.9%	市町村及び 都道府県
	事業税	〃	3.4～6.7%	都道府県
売買契約の当事者等	印紙税	時価	最高 540,000円まで	国 (印紙をは り付ける。)
貸主(個人)	所得税	貸付による所得	累進 (5～45%)	国
	住民税	〃	一律 (10%)	市町村及び 都道府県
貸主(法人)	法人税	貸付による所得	23.4% (基本税率)	国
	住民税	〃	12.9%	市町村及び 都道府県
	事業税	〃	3.4～6.7%	都道府県

(注)：¶5–200，¶5–555，¶5–560参照。

¶2-380　特別土地保有税（市町村税）

この租税は土地の保有又は取得に対し，その土地の所在する市町村により課される。

(1)　課税対象

土地（ただし，その土地の保有期間が10年を超えるものを除く。）の保有及び土地の取得

（面積基準）

次の面積に満たない土地の保有又は1月1日もしくは7月1日前1年内に取得した土地の合計面積が次の面積に満たない場合には免税。

(i)　指定都市の区の区域及び都の特別区の区域……………………　2,000㎡

(ii)　都市計画法第5条に規定する都市計画区域を有する市町村の区域
………………………………………………………………………　5,000㎡

(iii)　その他の市町村の区域……………………………………………　10,000㎡

(2)　納税義務者

課税対象とされる土地の所有者又は取得者

(3)　非課税

(a)　国又は地方公共団体が取得し又は所有する土地

(b)　相続又は法人の合併等形式的な所有権の移転に係る土地

58   MAIN FEATURES OF JAPANESE TAXES

stance, by inheritance or merger of corporation, etc.;
  (c) Land for residence, etc.
(4) **Tax base**
    The acquisition cost of the land (in case of acquisition without consideration or with unreasonably low consideration — ordinary acquisition cost).
(5) **Tax rate**
  (a) Holdings of land 1.4%
  (b) Acquisitions of land 3%

(6) **Tax credit**
    The fixed assets tax amount and the real property acquisition tax amount are creditable against this tax.
(7) **Time limit for filing a return and tax payment**
  (a) Where a taxpayer holds taxable land on January 1: May 31 of that year.
  (b) Where a taxpayer acquired taxable land within a year preceding January 1 or July 1: end of February or August 31 of that year respectively.
(8) **From a current economical point of view, special and holding tax is not imposed in the future after 2003.**

¶ 2-390 City planning tax (municipal)

The city planning tax is, in substance, a tax in addition to the fixed assets tax. It is levied on land and buildings located in an area where a city planning scheme is in effect.

The tax rate is 0.3% of the value of the land and buildings, and is paid annually.

¶ 2-410 Light vehicle tax (municipal)

The light vehicle tax is levied on owners, as of April 1, of motor bicycles and small cars by the municipality in which the usual parking place of the vehicle is situated.

The annual tax rate is as follows:

(1) bicycle with a small engine

total displacement:	0.05 litre or less	¥2,000
	0.09 litre or less (two wheels)	¥2,000

¶ **2-390**

日本の租税の主な特色　59

　(c)　住宅の用に供する土地その他
(4)　課税標準
　　土地の取得価額（無償又は著しく低い価額による取得の場合その土地の取得に通常要する額）

(5)　税率
　(a)　土地の保有については$\dfrac{1.4}{100}$

　(b)　土地の取得については$\dfrac{3}{100}$
(6)　税額控除
　　固定資産税額及び不動産取得税額に相当する額は税額控除される。

(7)　申告及び納付期限
　(a)　1月1日に課税対象の土地を保有する場合…その年の5月31日

　(b)　1月1日又は7月1日前1年以内に課税対象の土地を取得した場合…それぞれの年の2月末日又は8月31日

(8)　現下の経済情勢等にかんがみ，平成15年以降，新たな課税は行わない。

¶2-390　都市計画税（市町村税）

　都市計画税は，固定資産税の附加税としての実質を有する。この租税は，都市計画区域内に所在する土地及び建物に対して課される。
　年税率は，土地及び建物の価額の0.3％である。

¶2-410　軽自動車税（市町村税）

　軽自動車税は，原動機付自転車その他の小型自動車を4月1日に所有する者に対し，その定置場の所在する市町村によって課税されるものである。
　税率年額は次のとおりである。

(1)　小型原動機付自転車
　　総排気量　0.05ℓ以下　　　　　　　　2,000円
　　　　　　　0.09ℓ〃（二輪）　　　　　　2,000円

60   MAIN FEATURES OF JAPANESE TAXES

	over 0.09 litre (two wheels)		¥2,400
	over 0.02 litre (three or more wheels)		¥3,900
(2) motor bicycle			¥6,000
(3) light car			
with two wheels			¥3,600
with three wheels			¥3,900
with four wheels			
for passengers	commercial use		¥6,900
	others		¥10,800
for cargo	commercial use		¥3,800
	others		¥5,000

¶ 2-420 Automobile tonnage tax (national)

The automobile tonnage tax is levied on automobile owners or users when they receive from a transportation office a periodical certificate of car inspection or a licensed number for a car which is not required to undergo inspection. The current 10 years provisional scheme on automobile tonnage tax is abolished, but the tax rate will be as below for the time being:

(Cars with inspection certificates valid for three years are subject to 150% higher tax rates than those with two-year certificates.)

(1) Passenger car used by a commercial enterprise (subject to car inspection once a year):

every 0.5 ton of car weight..¥2,600

(any fraction less than 0.5 ton counts as 0.5 ton for the computation)

(2) Passenger car used otherwise (subject to car inspection once every two years):

every 0.5 ton of car weight..¥8,200

(any fraction less than 0.5 ton counts as 0.5 ton for the computation)

(3) Truck and bus which does not fall into (1) (subject to car inspection once a year):

every 1 ton of total car weight..¥2,600

(any fraction less than 1 ton counts as 1 ton for the computation)

"total car weight" means (car weight + maximum loading capacity + 55kg × number of persons carried)

(4) Motor bicycle (subject to inspection once every two years):.....¥3,800

(5) Light car:

with three or four wheels (taxed only at the time of inspection) .¥6,600

with two wheels (taxed only at the time of receiving a licensed car number) ¥4,900

¶ 2-420

	0.09ℓ超（二輪）	2,400円
	0.02ℓ〃（三輪以上）	3,900円
(2)	二輪の小型自動車	6,000円
(3)	軽自動車	

二輪のもの			3,600円
三輪のもの			3,900円
四輪のもの			
乗用のもの		営業用	6,900円
		自家用	10,800円
貨物用のもの		営業用	3,800円
		自家用	5,000円

¶2-420　自動車重量税（国税）

　自動車重量税は，自動車の所有者又は使用者が，定期的に陸運局より自動車検査証の交付を受け，又は検査を受けることを要しないが車両番号の指定を受ける際に課される。税率は，現行の10年間の暫定税率を廃止し，本則税率を適用することとなるが，当分の間の措置として，次のとおりとする。

　しかしながら，自動車検査証の有効期間が3年とされる自動車については，2年とされる自動車の税率の1.5倍の税率が適用される。

(1)　営業用乗用車（毎年検査を受ける。）

　　車両重量0.5トンごとに　　　　　　　　　　　　　　　　　　2,600円

　　0.5トン未満の端数は，計算上0.5トンとみなす。

(2)　その他の乗用車（2年に一度検査を受ける。）

　　車両重量0.5トンごとに　　　　　　　　　　　　　　　　　　8,200円

　　0.5トン未満の端数は，計算上0.5トンとみなす。

(3)　トラック及び(1)に区分されないバス（毎年検査を受ける。）

　　車両総重量1トンごとに　　　　　　　　　　　　　　　　　　2,600円

　　（1トン未満の端数は，計算上1トンとみなす。）

　　「車両総重量」とは，（車両重量＋最大積載量＋55kg×定員）をいう。

(4)　小型二輪車（2年に一度検査を受ける。）　　　　　　　　　3,800円

(5)　軽自動車（検査の際にのみ課される。）

　　三輪又は四輪のもの　　　　　　　　　　　　　　　　　　　6,600円

　　二輪のもの（車両番号の指定を受ける際にのみ課される。）　4,900円

62   MAIN FEATURES OF JAPANESE TAXES

The automobile tonnage tax is temporarily exempted or reduced on owners or users when they receive a car inspection newly or continuously for the period from May 1, 2017 to March 31, 2019. This treatment is only applied to the cars with high environmental performance.

¶ 2-430 Enterprise establishment tax (municipal)

Enterprise establishment tax is levied on enterprises located in big cities such as Tokyo or Osaka. Tax bases and rates are as follows:

(1)   Enterprise establishment tax on establishment or extension was abolished after April 1, 2003.

(2)   Where buildings are already established, the tax amount consists of —

(a)   assets levy (600 yen per square meter of the floor space); and

(b)   number of employees levy (0.25% of the enterprise's gross wages bill).

The tax is collected on an annual basis.The taxpayer is the person who carries on business in the building.Filing a return and payment of tax are required within two months after the end of the business year (corporation) or until March 15 of the next year (individual).

Taxes on Consumption

¶ 2-510 Consumption tax (national, prefectural)

Under this law, transactions such as sale and leasing of goods, the provision of services carried out within Japan and imported goods delivered from bonded areas are subject to taxation. The tax rate is 6.3% (7.8% from October 1, 2019) for national tax and 1.7% (2.2%, ditto) for prefectural tax. Therefore the total effective tax rate is 8% (10.0%, ditto).

The consumption tax is to be levied on tobacco, liquor and petroleum along with tobacco tax, liquor tax and petroleum-related taxes.

A detailed explanation of the consumption tax is given in Chapter 8.

¶ 2-540 Tax-free purchases by visitors to Japan

A visitor to Japan who is a non-resident, as defined under the Japanese foreign exchange system (an "exchange non-resident"), may purchase some kinds of goods of which the total price is over ¥5,000 free of consumption tax. The definition of an exchange non-resident is different from that of a tax non-resident, that is, a non-resident for income tax purposes. A foreigner who visits Japan and stays for less than six months without engaging

¶ 2-430

平成29年5月1日から平成31年3月31日までの間に受ける新規・継続検査等の際に納付すべき自動車重量税については，特に環境性能に優れた自動車に対しては軽減・免除する。

¶2-430　事業所税（市町村税）

事業所税は，東京，大阪等の大都市に所在する事業に対し課される。課税標準及び税率は次のとおりである。

(1)　新増設に係る事務所税は平成15年3月31日をもって廃止された。

(2)　既設の建物の場合には，課税標準は，
　(a)　資産割（床面積1平方メートル当たり600円）及び
　(b)　従業者割（当該事業が従業者に支払う給与総額の0.25％）。

納税は毎年一度行う。納税義務者は，事業所において事業を行う者である。期末後2カ月以内（法人）又は翌年3月15日まで（個人）に申告・納付。

消費に対する租税

¶2-510　消費税（国税，都道府県税）

国内で行われる商品の販売及びサービスの提供並びに保税地域から引き取られる外国貨物に対しては国税6.3％（平成31年10月1日から7.8％），都道府県税1.7％（同2.2％）の消費税が課税される。したがって，合計8％（同10％）の消費税となる。

酒税，たばこ消費税及び石油関係諸税の対象物品については，消費税が併課される。

消費税の詳細については第8章を参照のこと。

¶2-540　来日外国人の購入物品の免税

来日した者で日本の"外国為替及び外国貿易法"に規定する非居住者（外為法上の非居住者）に該当する者は，対価の合計額が5千円を超える物品を消費税を課されることなく購入することができる。"外国為替及び外国貿易法"にいう非居住者の定義は，所得税課税上の非居住者の定義とは異なる。来日した外国人で6カ月以上日本国内に滞在しない者及び日本国内で事業に従事しない者は，"外国為替及び外国貿易法"上は非居住者として扱われる。

64   MAIN FEATURES OF JAPANESE TAXES

in any business in Japan, is usually treated as an exchange non-resident.

When an exchange non-resident desires to purchase tax-free goods, he must present, at the tax-free sales counter of a retail shop, a declaration that the purchases will be taken out of Japan on the purchaser's departure from Japan at the latest (Covenant of Purchaser of Consumption Tax-Exempt of Ultimate Export), and his passport or the like, to which will be attached a document recording the tax-free purchase (Record of Purchase of Consumption Tax Exemption for Export). This document should be presented to the Customs Office when the purchaser leaves Japan. If an exchange non-resident does not take the tax-free goods with him when he leaves Japan, he will be obliged to pay consumption tax on them.

A foreign visitor may make inquiries at any department store or other retail shop accustomed to dealing with foreigners for details concerning tax-free purchases (see ¶ 8-200).

¶ 2-560 Liquor tax (national)

Liquor tax is levied on a manufacturer of liquors (in the case of imported goods the taxpayer is the recipient from a bonded area).

The basic tax rate is as follows:

Kind of liquor	Tax amount per kilolitre
Refined "sake" (*seishu*)	¥120,000
Synthetic "sake" (*goseiseishu*)	100,000
Shochu	
Group A 25% (alcohol content)	250,000
Group B 25%	250,000
Mirin	20,000
Beer	220,000
Wine	80,000
Sweet Wine	120,000
Whiskey and Brandy	
40%	400,000
Other spirits	370,000
Liqueur	
12%	120,000
Miscellaneous liquors	
Sparkling liquors	
percentage of malt 50% or more	220,000
percentage of malt 25% or more ~ less than 50%	178,125
others	134,250
Powdered liquors	390,000
Others	140,000

¶ 2-560

外為法上の非居住者が免税物品を購入しようとする場合には，免税物品の販売場において，遅くとも自己が離日する日までに当該物品を輸出する旨を記載した誓約書（最終的に輸出となる物品の消費税免税購入についての購入者誓約書）及び旅券又はこれに類する書類に免税物品を購入した事実を記載した書類（輸出免税物品購入記録票）をはり付けて提出しなければならない。購入者が離日する場合には，税関においてこの書類を提示しなければならない。非居住者が，免税で購入した物品を帰国の際に携帯していなかった場合には，その購入物品に対する消費税を徴収される。

外国人旅行者は，どこの百貨店又は小売店でも，外国人の接遇に慣れている店員に対し免税物品の購入に関し照会することができる（¶8-200参照）。

¶2-560　酒税（国税）

酒税は，酒類の製造者（輸入酒類の場合には，保税地域から引き取る者）に対して課される。

基本税率は次のとおりである。

種類	1キロリットル当たりの税額
清　酒	120,000円
合成清酒	100,000
しょうちゅう	
甲類　25%	250,000
乙類　25%	250,000
みりん	20,000
ビール	220,000
果実酒	80,000
甘味果実酒	120,000
ウイスキー・ブランデー	
40%	400,000
その他のスピリッツ	370,000
リキュール	
12%	120,000
雑　酒	
発泡酒	
麦芽使用割合50%以上	220,000
麦芽使用割合25%以上～50%未満	178,125
その他のもの	134,250
粉末酒	390,000
その他	140,000

66   MAIN FEATURES OF JAPANESE TAXES

¶ 2-580 Gasoline tax and local gasoline tax (national)

Both gasoline tax and local gasoline tax are taxes levied on gasoline. The revenue from gasoline tax is appropriated for the expenditures of the national budget, while the revenue from local gasoline tax is distributed to local governments as their general source of revenue. However, from a consumer's or business point of view, both taxes may be considered as one aggregate tax. The taxpayer of these taxes is the refinery (in the case of imported gasoline the taxpayer is the recipient from a bonded area).

The tax rates are as follows (specific duty):

Gasoline tax	¥48,600/kl
Local gasoline tax	¥5,200/kl
Total	¥53,800/kl

Gasoline used as a solvent for rubber, export, aircraft fuel, chemical products, etc. is exempt from this tax under certain conditions.

Further, fuel for the registered automobile of a diplomatic establishment or an ambassador and the like is exempt from this tax.

¶ 2-585 Aircraft fuel tax (national)

Aircraft fuel tax is levied on fuel which an aircraft consumes. The tax is paid by the aircraft owners or users on or before the end of the month following the month of the loading. Fuel consumed for international flights is exempt from this tax. The tax rate is ¥18,000 per kilolitre.

¶ 2-590 Petroleum coal tax (national)

Petroleum coal tax is levied on crude oil, imported petroleum products, gaseous hydrocarbons and coal (hereinafter referred to as "crude oil, etc."). The taxpayer is the domestic extractor of crude oil etc., or those who withdraw crude oil, etc. from a bonded area. The tax is paid by the extractor on or before the end of the month following the month of delivery from the place of extraction and by those who withdraw from a bonded area at the time of withdrawal.

Special taxation of global warming countermeasure with the aim of controlling the emission of energy-originated CO_2 which accounts for about 90% of greenhouse gas causing global warming has been introduced. The following tax rates corresponding to the amount of CO_2 emission are added on the petroleum coal tax on fossil fuel.

¶ 2-580

¶2-580 揮発油税及び地方揮発油税 (国税)

揮発油税及び地方揮発油税は，いずれも揮発油に対して課せられる。揮発油税による歳入は国の予算に組み込まれ，地方揮発油税は地方自治体に配分されて一般財源となる。しかしながら，消費者又は企業の立場からは，両税は一個の租税とみることができる。両税の納税者は揮発油の製造者（輸入揮発油の場合には，保税地域からの引取者）である。

税率（従量税）は，次のとおりである。

揮発油税	48,600円／kℓ
地方揮発油税	5,200円／kℓ
合計	53,800円／kℓ

ゴムの溶剤，輸出用，航空機用，石油化学製品製造用等の各用途に消費される揮発油は，一定の条件の下で免税される。

また，外国公館及び大使等がその登録自動車の燃料用に使用する揮発油の揮発油税も免税される。

¶2-585 航空機燃料税 (国税)

航空機燃料税は，航空機燃料の消費に対して課される。この租税は，航空機に燃料が積み込まれた月の翌月末までに航空機の所有者又は使用者により支払われるものである。国際間を往来する航空機の燃料には課税されない。税率は，1キロリットル当たり18,000円である。

¶2-590 石油石炭税 (国税)

石油石炭税は，原油及び輸入石油製品，ガス状炭化水素並びに石炭（以下「原油等」という。）に課される。原油等の採取者は移出した月の翌月末までに，また原油等を保税地域から引き取る場合には引取りの際に，この租税を支払わなければならない。

地球温暖化の原因となる温室効果ガスの約9割を占めるエネルギー起源CO_2の排出を抑制する観点から，地球温暖化対策のための課税の特例が導入される。この特例により，原油及び石油製品については1キロリットル当たり760円（現行2,040円／kℓ），ガス状炭化水素は1トン当たり780円（現行1,080円／t），石炭は1トン当たり670円（現行700円／t）の税率が上乗せされる。これらは平成24年10月1日に施行され，平成28年3月31日までの間，所要の経過措置が講じられる。

68　MAIN FEATURES OF JAPANESE TAXES

Added tax rate : crude oil and petroleum products: ¥760/kl (current: ¥2,040/kl)

gaseous hydrocarbons: ¥780/t (current: ¥1,080/t)

coal : ¥670/t (current: ¥700/t)

These tax rates will be in force on October 1, 2012. Necessary interim measures will be taken until March 31, 2016.

Tax Rate

Classification	April 1, 2007~	October 1, 2012~	April 1, 2014~	April 1, 2016~
(1) crude oil and petroleum products	¥2,040/kl	2,290	2,540	2,800
(2) gaseous hydrocarbons (LPG · LNG)	¥1,080/t	1,340	1,600	1,860
(3) coal	¥700/t	920	1,140	1,370

¶ 2-595　Petroleum gas tax (national)

Petroleum gas tax is levied on liquefied petroleum gas for automobile fuel contained in a high pressure container. The tax rate is ¥17.5 per kilogram.

¶ 2-640　Tobacco tax (national and local)

Tobacco tax (national tax) and local tobacco tax are imposed on tobacco products.

(1)　**Tobacco tax (national)**

The taxpayer for tobacco tax is the manufacturer or the receiver of tobacco products from a bonded area. The tax rate is ¥5,302 (¥5,802 from October 1, 2018) per 1,000 pieces.

(2)　**Local tobacco tax**

The taxpayer for local tobacco tax (prefectural tobacco tax and municipal tobacco tax) is the manufacturer or the wholesale dealer of tobacco products.

Tax Rate

	October 1, 2010~	April 1, 2013~	October 1, 2018~
Prefectural tobacco tax	¥1,504 per 1,000 pieces	¥860	¥930
Municipal tobacco tax	¥4,618 per 1,000 pieces	¥5,262	¥5,692

¶ 2-595

日本の租税の主な特色　69

税　率

区　分		H19.4.1〜	H24.10.1〜	H26.4.1〜	H28.4.1〜
(1) 原油・石油製品	2,040円／kℓ	2,290	2,540	2,800
(2) ガス状炭化水素 （LPG・LNG）	1,080円／t	1,340	1,600	1,860
(3) 石炭（1t当たり）	700円／t	920	1,140	1,370

¶2–595　石油ガス税（国税）

　石油ガス税は，自動車燃料用として高圧の容器に充てんされている一定の品質の石油ガスに対して課される。税率は1キログラム当たり17円50銭である。

¶2–640　たばこ税

　たばこに対しては，たばこ税（国税）と，道府県たばこ税及び市町村たばこ税（地方税）が課される。
　(1)　たばこ税（国税）
　　　たばこ税の納税義務者は，製造たばこの製造者又は保税地域から製造たばこを引き取る者である。
　　　税率は，1,000本につき5,302円（平成30年10月1日以降5,802円）である。
　(2)　道府県たばこ税及び市町村たばこ税（地方税）
　　　道府県たばこ税及び市町村たばこ税の納税義務者は，製造たばこの製造者又は製造たばこの卸売販売を行う者である。

税　率

		H22.10.1〜	H25.4.1〜	H30.10.1〜
道府県たばこ税	1,000本につき	1,504円	860円	930円
市町村たばこ税		4,618円	5,262円	5,692円

70   MAIN FEATURES OF JAPANESE TAXES

¶ 2-650 Golf course tax (prefectural)

This tax is levied on visitors (including club members) to a golf course, or on the operators of a golf course. In the former case, however, the amount of tax is included in the charges paid at the counter of the golf course.

The tax rate is ¥800 per player per day.

The amount of this tax is excluded for the purpose of consumption tax.

¶ 2-680 Diesel oil delivery tax (prefectural)

This tax is levied on diesel oil delivered from a wholesaler to a retailer of diesel oil, and usually paid by the wholesaler to the prefecture monthly.

The tax rate is ¥32,100 per kilolitre.

¶ 2-710 Bathing tax (municipal)

The bathing tax is a municipal tax on persons taking mineral baths in spas. It is collected by the operators of mineral baths and transferred to the municipality.

The tax is ¥150 per person per day.

Taxes on Transactions

¶ 2-820 Stamp tax (national)

Stamp tax is paid by affixing and cancelling a stamp on the documents which are exhaustively listed in the Stamp Duty Act provisions.

The stamps are sold in post offices. It is possible for taxpayers to pay stamp tax in cash directly to a tax office and receive an imprint on the document from the tax office.

¶ 2-650

日本の租税の主な特色　71

¶2–650　ゴルフ場利用税（都道府県税）

このゴルフ場利用税は，ゴルフ場の利用者又は経営者に対して課される。利用者の負担する税額については，ゴルフ場を利用する際に支払う料金の中に含まれている。

標準税率は，1人1日につき800円である。

なお，この税は，消費税の計算上，除外される。

¶2–680　軽油引取税（都道府県税）

この税は元売業者から小売業者に引き取られる軽油に課され，通常は元売業者から毎月都道府県に支払われる。

税率は，1キロリットルにつき32,100円である。

¶2–710　入湯税（市町村税）

この税は，鉱泉浴場の経営者が鉱泉の入湯者から徴収して市町村に納付するものである。

税額は，1人1日当たり150円である。

取引に対する租税

¶2–820　印紙税（国税）

印紙税は，印紙税法に限定的に規定されている文書に印紙をはり付け，かつ，消印することにより納付される。

印紙は郵便局で販売されている。納税者は，税務署に直接現金で納付し，税務署から文書に税印の押なつを受けることにより納税することも可能である。

72   MAIN FEATURES OF JAPANESE TAXES

The tax rates are as follows:

Taxable Documents	Amount stated in Documents (Tax Base)	Tax Amount (Tax Rate)
(1) Agreements concerning transfers of title to real estate, rights to intangible property*, ships, aircraft and business. Agreements concerning creation and transfer of surface rights and land leasehold. Agreements concerning loans for consumption. Agreements concerning transportation.	(¥) less than 10,000	Exempt
	100,000 or less	¥200
	500,000 or less	400
	1,000,000 or less	1,000
	5,000,000 or less	2,000
	10,000,000 or less	10,000
	50,000,000 or less	20,000
	100,000,000 or less	60,000
	500,000,000 or less	100,000
	1,000,000,000 or less	200,000
	5,000,000,000 or less	400,000
	more than 5,000,000,000	600,000
	if no amounts is stated	200

    * Intangible property rights includes patents, utility model rights, trademark rights and trade names.

Taxable Documents	Amount stated in Documents (Tax Base)	Tax Amount (Tax Rate)
(2) Agreements concerning contracts for work.	less than 10,000	Exempt
	1,000,000 or less	¥200
	2,000,000 or less	400
	3,000,000 or less	1,000
	5,000,000 or less	2,000
	10,000,000 or less	10,000
	50,000,000 or less	20,000
	100,000,000 or less	60,000
	500,000,000 or less	100,000
	1,000,000,000 or less	200,000
	5,000,000,000 or less	400,000
	more than 5,000,000,000	600,000
	if no amounts is stated	200
(3) Promissory notes and bills of exchange.	less than 100,000	Exempt
	1,000,000 or less	¥200
	2,000,000 or less	400
	3,000,000 or less	600
	5,000,000 or less	1,000
	10,000,000 or less	2,000
	20,000,000 or less	4,000
	30,000,000 or less	6,000
	50,000,000 or less	10,000
	100,000,000 or less	20,000
	200,000,000 or less	40,000
	300,000,000 or less	60,000
	500,000,000 or less	100,000
	1,000,000,000 or less	150,000
	more than 1,000,000,000	200,000

¶ 2-820

日本の租税の主な特色　73

税率は次のとおりである。

課税文書	文書の記載金額(課税標準)		税額(税率)
(1) 不動産, 無体財産権*, 船舶, 航空機及び営業の譲渡に関する契約書 地上権又は土地の貸借権の設定又は譲渡に関する契約書 消費貸借契約書 運送に関する契約書	10,000円未満		非課税
	100,000	以下	200円
	500,000	〃	400
	1,000,000	〃	1,000
	5,000,000	〃	2,000
	10,000,000	〃	10,000
	50,000,000	〃	20,000
	100,000,000	〃	60,000
	500,000,000	〃	100,000
	1,000,000,000	〃	200,000
	5,000,000,000	〃	400,000
	5,000,000,000円超		600,000
	金額の記載のない場合		200

＊無体財産権には, 特許権, 実用新案権, 商標権及び商号を含む。

課税文書	文書の記載金額(課税標準)		税額(税率)
(2) 請負契約書	10,000円未満		非課税
	1,000,000	以下	200円
	2,000,000	〃	400
	3,000,000	〃	1,000
	5,000,000	〃	2,000
	10,000,000	〃	10,000
	50,000,000	〃	20,000
	100,000,000	〃	60,000
	500,000,000	〃	100,000
	1,000,000,000	〃	200,000
	5,000,000,000	〃	400,000
	5,000,000,000円超		600,000
	金額の記載のない場合		200

課税文書	文書の記載金額		税額
(3) 約束手形又は為替手形	100,000円未満		非課税
	1,000,000	以下	200円
	2,000,000	〃	400
	3,000,000	〃	600
	5,000,000	〃	1,000
	10,000,000	〃	2,000
	20,000,000	〃	4,000
	30,000,000	〃	6,000
	50,000,000	〃	10,000
	100,000,000	〃	20,000
	200,000,000	〃	40,000
	300,000,000	〃	60,000
	500,000,000	〃	100,000
	1,000,000,000	〃	150,000
	1,000,000,000円超		200,000

74   MAIN FEATURES OF JAPANESE TAXES

Note: A note or bill which (a) is payable at sight, (b) appoints a financial institution as the drawer or recipient, (c) which is indicated in foreign currency, (d) is to be settled through a non-resident's free yen account, or (e) is drawn in a yen amount for banker's acceptance, is taxed at the rate of ¥200.

(4) Articles of incorporation (limited to original articles prepared at the time of incorporation).. ¥40,000

(5) Basic agreements under which continuous transactions are carried on (such as agency contracts, third party contracts, agreements on banking transactions), but excluding agreements effective for not more than 3 months. ¥4,000

Note: There are 25 items which are listed as taxable documents in the Act. The remaining 20 items are not described above as their tax rates are almost uniformly ¥200.

¶ 2-830 Registration and license tax (national)

Registration and license tax is levied not only on the occasion of an entry in official books or documents with regard to property rights, companies, certain professions, etc., but also on the obtaining of business licenses.

However, it is also possible for a taxpayer to pay this tax directly to a tax office, and to submit an application for registration to a registration office together with a certificate of payment.

The important tax rates are as follows:

Items	Tax basis	Tax rate
(1) Registration of real estate		
(a) Acquisition by inheritance/legacy	value of real estate	0.4%
(b) Acquisition by merger	value of real estate	0.4
(c) Acquisition by purchase or gift	value of real estate	2.0[1]
(d) Preservation of ownership	value of real estate	0.4
(e) Additional entry or correction alteration or erasure of entry	per entry	¥1,000
(2) Registration of ships		
(a) Acquisition by inheritance	value of ship	0.4%
(b) Acquisition by merger	value of ship	0.4
(c) Acquisition by legacy or gift	value of ship	2.0
(d) Acquisition by purchase	value of ship	2.8
(e) Preservation of ownership	value of ship	0.4
(f) Provisional registration for acquisition	value of ship	0.4
(g) Acquisition by mortgage	amount of credit	0.4
(3) Registration of commercial companies (in case of a joint stock company)		
(a) Registration of incorporation	amount of capital	0.7%[2]
(b) Increase in capital	amount of capital increase	0.7
(c) Merger	amount of capital	0.15

¶ 2-830

日本の租税の主な特色　75

(注)：約束手形又は為替手形のうち(a) 一覧払のもの，(b) 金融機関を振出人及び受取人とする
もの，(c) 外国通貨で表示されているもの，(d) 非居住者自由円勘定を通じて決済されるも
の，(e) 円建銀行引受手形は，200円の税率で課税される。

(4)　会社の定款（会社設立のときに作成される定款の原本に限る）　　　40,000円

(5)　継続的取引の基本となる契約書（特約店契約書，代理店契約書，銀行取引約定書
等）。ただし，契約期間が3カ月以内のものを除く。　　　　　　　　4,000円
(注)：法律には課税文書として25のものが掲記されている。残りの20の項目は上には掲げな
かったが，税率はおおむね，統一的に200円である。

¶2-830　登録免許税（国税）

　登録免許税は，財産権，会社，特定の職業等に関し，公簿上に登録を受け
る際に課せられるだけでなく，営業の免許を受ける際にも課される。

　しかしながら，納税者はこの租税を直接税務署に納付し，納付証明書を添
付して登記所に対し登記を申請することもできる。

　主要な税率は次のとおりである。

事　　項	課税標準	税　　率
(1)　不動産の登記		％
(a)　相続（遺贈）による移転	不動産の価額	0.4
(b)　合併による移転	〃	0.4
(c)　売買又は贈与による移転	〃	2.0 (注) *(1)
(d)　所有権の保存	〃	0.4
(e)　附記登記，回復登記	不動産の個数	1,000円
登記の更正又は変更の登記		
(2)　船舶の登記		
(a)　相続による移転	船舶の価額	0.4％
(b)　合併による移転	〃	0.4
(c)　遺贈又は贈与による移転	〃	2.0
(d)　売買による移転	〃	2.8
(e)　所有権の保存	〃	0.4
(f)　所有権の移転の仮登記	〃	0.4
(g)　担保権の設定	債権金額	0.4
(3)　会社の登記（株式会社の場合）		
(a)　設立の登記	資本金額	0.7 *(2)
(b)　増資	増加した資本の額	0.7
(c)　合併	資本金額	0.15

76   MAIN FEATURES OF JAPANESE TAXES

(4) Registration of an advocate (new registration)		¥60,000
Registration of a certified public accountant (new registration)		¥60,000
Registration of a physician (new registration)		¥60,000

	copyright	patent
(5) Registration of copyright, patent, etc.		
(a) Transfer by sale	¥18,000	¥15,000
(b) Acquisition by inheritance or merger	¥18,000	¥3,000

(6) License for banking business	
(a) license for business	¥150,000
(b) approval of establishment of branch	¥150,000
(7) License for liquor business	
(a) license for manufacturing	¥150,000
(b) license for selling business	
(i) wholesale	¥90,000
(ii) retail	¥30,000

Note:

(1) The tax rate is reduced as follows in case of the registration of real estate by purchase acquisition for the period from April 1, 2009 through March 31, 2019.

April 1, 2009 to March 31, 2011	1.0%
April 1, 2011 to March 31, 2012	1.3%
April 1, 2012 to March 31, 2019	1.5%

(2) If the computed tax amount is less than ¥150,000, ¥150,000 must be paid for an application.

¶ 2-850 Real property acquisition tax (prefectural)

Real property acquisition tax is levied on the acquisition of land or buildings (inclusive of rebuilding). The tax is not levied on the acquisition of depreciable assets other than buildings. No tax is levied on the transfer of land or buildings on account of mergers of corporations or inheritance.

The tax base is the market value of the acquired land or buildings, usually substantially lower than the purchase price. The tax rate is 3%.

The tax is not levied if the tax base is less than:

(a)   ¥100,000 in the case of land;

(b)   ¥230,000 in the case of a new building constructed by the taxpayer himself; or

(c)   ¥120,000 in the case of other buildings.

There are some special exemptions and reductions. For example, a special deduction from the tax base amounting to ¥12,000,000 is allowed on or after April 1, 1989 for a new house with a floor area between 50 and 240 square meters, constructed for residential purposes.

¶ 2-850

(4)	弁護士の登録		
	（新規登録）		60,000円
	公認会計士の登録		
	（新規登録）		60,000円
	医師の登録		
	（新規登録）		60,000円
(5)	著作権，特許権の登録	著作権	特許権
	(a) 売買による移転	18,000円	15,000円
	(b) 相続又は合併による移転	18,000円	3,000円
(6)	銀行の営業の免許		
	(a) 営業の免許		150,000円
	(b) 支店の設置の認可		150,000円
(7)	酒類業の免許		
	(a) 製造の免許		150,000円
	(b) 販売業の免許		
	(ⅰ) 卸売		90,000円
	(ⅱ) 小売		30,000円

(注)：＊(1) 売買による所有権の移転登記については，平成21年4月1日から平成31年3月31日までの間は以下のとおり。

平成21年4月1日～平成23年3月31日	1.0%
平成23年4月1日～平成24年3月31日	1.3%
平成24年4月1日～平成31年3月31日	1.5%

(2) 計算した税額が15万円に満たないときは，申請件数1件につき15万円となる。

¶2-850　不動産取得税（都道府県税）

　不動産取得税は，土地又は建物の取得（改築を含む。）に対して課されるが，建物以外の償却資産の取得に対しては課されない。会社の合併又は相続による土地又は建物の移転についても課されない。

　課税標準は，取得した土地又は建物の時価であるが，これは通常の売買価額よりも相当低額に抑えられている。税率は3％である。

　課税標準が，土地の場合は10万円未満，新築家屋の場合は23万円未満，その他の家屋の場合は12万円未満の場合には，課されない。この税については，若干の免除又は軽減措置が講じられている。例えば，1989年4月1日以降については，床面積が50平方メートル以上240平方メートル以下の住宅用家屋の新築については1,200万円の控除が認められている。

　住宅用家屋を新築するために土地を取得した場合において，取得後一定期間内に住宅を建築したとき，又は既に新築していたときは，原則として次の金額が不動産取得税額から控除される。

　150万円×税率（4％）＝控除税額

　(注)：平成18年4月1日から平成32年3月31日まで，税率を3％とする。

78   MAIN FEATURES OF JAPANESE TAXES

Further special tax treatment is granted as follows:

The acquisition of land for constructing a new residential house within a certain period before or after the acquisition of that land—the following amount is generally deductible from the amount of real property acquisition tax:

¥1,500,000 × tax rate (4%) = deductible amount

Note:

Tax rate is reduced from 4% to 3% between April 1, 2006 and March 31, 2020.

¶ 2-870 Automobile acquisition tax (prefectural)

The automobile acquisition tax is levied on the acquisition of new or second-hand automobiles. The 10 years provisional scheme on automobile acquisition tax is abolished. However, as the current level of the tax rate is maintained for the time being, the tax rate is 3% of the purchase price of the automobile. If the price is not more than ¥500,000, the vehicle is exempt from the tax. The payment to the prefecture must normally be made at the same time as the registration of the automobile. A transport company which acquires an omnibus to operate in sparsely populated districts is exempt from the tax under certain conditions.

With the aim of promoting measures to control global warming etc., so-called "eco-car tax cut" on automobile acquisition tax has been extended for 2 years by April 2019, changing its environmental standard and focusing on vehicles with high environmental performance.

¶ 2-890 Electric power resources development tax (national)

This tax is levied on enterprises selling electric power (¥375 per 1,000 kw per hour).

Miscellaneous Taxes

¶ 2-950 Miscellaneous taxes

Miscellaneous taxes are not important to non-resident taxpayers.

- A mining allotment tax is levied on mining right holders. The standard tax rate is ¥200 to ¥400 per hectare of mining allotment area.
- A hunting tax is levied on hunters. The aggregate standard rate is ¥5,500, ¥8,200 or ¥16,500 per year according to the class of the license, etc.

¶ 2-870

日本の租税の主な特色　79

¶2-870　自動車取得税（都道府県税）

　自動車取得税は，新車であると中古車であるとを問わず，自動車の取得に対し課される。税率は，現行の10年間の暫定税率は廃止されるが，当分の間，現在の税率水準は維持されることから，自動車購入価格の3％となる。購入価格が50万円以下の場合には，課税されない。都道府県に対する納税は，通常の場合，自動車の登録と同時に行わなければならない。過疎地域において運行の用に供する乗合自動車を取得した運送会社は，一定の条件の下に，この租税を免除される。

　地球温暖化対策の推進等の観点を踏まえ，自動車取得税についても，いわゆる「エコカー減税」について，燃費基準の切り替えを行うとともに，環境性能に極めて優れた自動車に対する軽減措置を見直した上で，平成31年4月まで2年間延長された。

¶2-890　電源開発促進税（国税）

　この租税は，電気事業者の販売する電力量に対し課税するものである（1,000キロワット時につき，375円）。

その他の租税

¶2-950　その他の租税

　非居住者にとって，その他の租税はそれほど重要ではない。
- ・鉱区税は，鉱業権者に対し課税される。標準税率は，鉱区面積100アールにつき，200円から400円までである。
- ・狩猟税は，狩猟者に対して課せられる。標準税額は，免許の種類等に応じ，年額5,500円，8,200円又は16,500円とされる。

80   MAIN FEATURES OF JAPANESE TAXES

- A mineral product tax is levied on mine operators. The standard tax rate is usually 1.0% of the turnover of mineral products.

Prefectures and municipalities are entitled to levy other kinds of taxes, such as dog tax, etc., with the permission of the national government.

・鉱産税は，鉱業者に対して課税するものである。標準税率は，通常の場合，鉱物の価格の1.0%である。

なお，都道府県及び市町村は，政府の許可を得て犬税等のその他の種類の租税を課すことができる。

CHAPTER 3

NATIONAL TAXES ON INCOME

Paragraph

Table: Basic Structure of National Taxes on Income......¶ 3-010

Structure of Income Taxation ....¶ 3-020

Partnership and Non-juridical Organization ....¶ 3-120

Resident and Non-resident (Individual) ....¶ 3-210

Domestic Corporation and Foreign Corporation...........¶ 3-340

Exempt Corporation ....¶ 3-410

Tax Treaties ....¶ 3-510

Principle of Taxation Based on
    "Economic Substance"..¶ 3-710

第 3 章

所得に対する国税

所得に対する国税の基本的な仕組み…………………………………	¶3-010
所得に対する課税の仕組み……………………………………………	¶3-020
組合及び人格のない社団等……………………………………………	¶3-120
居住者又は非居住者（個人）…………………………………………	¶3-210
内国法人及び外国法人…………………………………………………	¶3-340
非課税法人………………………………………………………………	¶3-410
租税条約…………………………………………………………………	¶3-510
「経済的実質」に基づく課税の原則 …………………………………	¶3-710

84 NATIONAL TAXES ON INCOME

¶ 3-010 Table: Basic Structure of National Taxes on Income

Classification of taxpayers / Method of payment	Individual		Corporation* (¶ 3-140)	
	Resident	Non-resident	Domestic corporation	Foreign corporation
	(¶ 3-210 to ¶ 3-250)	(¶ 3-210 to ¶ 3-250)	(¶ 3-340 to ¶ 3-360)	(¶ 3-340 to ¶ 3-360)
Withholding at source** (¶ 3-050)	Withholding income tax	Withholding income tax	Withholding income tax	Withholding income tax
Return and payment (¶ 3-050)	Assessment income tax	Assessment income tax	Corporation tax	Corporation tax

Note: * A non-juridical organization is subject to withholding income tax and corporation tax in the same way as a corporation, but only to a limited extent.

** The payer of certain items of income which are subject to withholding income tax has the obligation, regardless of whether such payer is an individual, a corporation or a non-juridical organization, to withhold tax and transfer it to a tax office.

Structure of Income Taxation

¶ 3-020 Principle

The Japanese national tax system is based on the principle that "income" should be taxed, regardless of whether the person receiving the income is an individual, a corporation, or a non-juridical organization.

¶ 3-040 Capital gain, inheritance and gift

"Income" includes capital gains, but does not include any increase in an individual's net property value resulting from an inheritance or a gift from another individual.

¶ 3-050 Withholding income tax, assessment income tax and corporation tax

Japanese national taxes on income are divided into withholding tax and assessment tax according to the method of collection.

Withholding tax is always called income tax regardless of whether the recipient of the income is an individual, a corporation or a non-juridical organization.

Assessment tax is also called income tax when it is levied on an individual, but it is called corporation tax when it is levied on a corporation or

¶ 3-010

所得に対する国税　85

¶3-010　所得に対する国税の基本的な仕組み

納税者の分類／納税方法	個　人		法　人・(¶3-140)	
	居住者 (¶3-210～¶3-250)	非居住者 (¶3-210～¶3-250)	内国法人 (¶3-340～¶3-360)	外国法人 (¶3-340～¶3-360)
源泉徴収** (¶3-050)	源泉所得税	源泉所得税	源泉所得税	源泉所得税
申告納付 (¶3-050)	申告所得税	申告所得税	法人税	法人税

(注)：＊　　人格のない社団等は，一定範囲内で法人と同様に源泉所得税及び法人税を課される。
　　　＊＊　源泉所得税の対象となる特定の種類の所得の支払者は，個人，法人又は人格のない社団
　　　　　　等のいずれであるかを問わず，租税を源泉徴収して税務署に納付する義務を負う。

所得に対する課税の仕組み

¶3-020　原則

　日本の国税の仕組みは，所得を受領する者の人格，すなわち，個人，法人
又は人格のない社団等のいずれに該当するかを問わず，「所得」に対して課
税するという原則に基づいている。

¶3-040　譲渡による所得，相続及び贈与

　「所得」には譲渡による所得も含まれるが，他の個人からの相続又は贈与
を受けた結果に基づく個人の純資産価額の増加によるものは含まれない。

¶3-050　源泉所得税，申告所得税及び法人税

　所得に対する日本の国税は，納税の方法により，源泉所得税と申告所得税
とに分類される。
　源泉徴収される租税は，当該所得の受領者が個人，法人又は人格のない社
団等のいずれであるかを問わず，所得税と呼ばれる。
　申告所得税は，個人に課される場合には所得税と呼ばれるが，法人又は人
格のない社団等に課される場合には，法人税と呼ばれる。
　本書では混乱を避けるため，源泉徴収される租税は源泉所得税，個人の所
得に対する申告方式による租税は，申告所得税と呼ぶ。

86   NATIONAL TAXES ON INCOME

on a non-juridical organization.

In this book, withholding tax is referred to as withholding income tax and the assessment tax on an individual's income is referred to as assessment income tax in order to avoid confusion.

Partnership and Non-juridical Organization

¶ 3-120 Partnership

Partnerships in a wide sense are classified into two categories in Japan:

(1) a partnership to which a juridical personality pertains in accordance with the provisions of the Commercial Code ("gomeigaisha" or "goshigaisha"); and

(2) a partnership to which no juridical personality pertains and to which the provisions of the Civil Code should be applied (a partnership in a narrow sense).

The income of a partnership with juridical personality is subject to corporation tax, whether or not the income is distributed among its partners. If the income is subsequently distributed among the partners, the tax is levied again on each partner's income independently of the juridical person's tax liability, due consideration naturally being given to the avoidance of double taxation.

The income of a partnership with no juridical personality is, for tax purposes, deemed to be distributed among the partners at the end of its accounting period. Income tax is levied on the constructive distribution allocable to the individual partners, while corporation tax is levied on the constructive distribution allocable to corporate partners.

Silent partnership (Tokumei Kumiai) is provided under the Commercial Code, and is consisted of silent partners and a business party based on a Tokumei Kumiai contrast.

¶ 3-140 Non-juridical organization

The term "corporation" means an organization to which a juridical personality pertains under the Japanese Commercial Code, the Civil Code or other laws. Corporations created under any foreign law are treated as corporations, as well as corporations established under Japanese laws.

The term "non-juridical organization" means an organization which has its own existence independent of its members and has its own repre-

¶ 3-120

所得に対する国税　87

組合及び人格のない社団等

¶3-120　組合
　日本では，広義の組合は二種に分類される。
(1)　商法の規定により，法人格の認められる組合（合名会社又は合資会社と呼ばれる。）

(2)　法人格の認められないもので，民法の規定が適用される組合（狭義の組合）

　前者の所得に対しては，組合員に対して所得が分配されたか否かを問わず，法人そのものの所得として，法人税が課される。後日，組合の構成員に対して所得が分配される場合には，法人の納税義務とは独自に，各構成員の所得に対して再度課税されるが，二重課税を回避するための配慮がされている。
　一方，後者に対する所得については，課税上は事業年度の末日において組合の各構成員に対して分配されたものとみなして，個人又は法人の各構成員に対して分配されたものとみなされた所得に対して，所得税又は法人税が課される。
　この他に商法の規定に基づく匿名組合がある。匿名組合は営業者と匿名組合員から構成され，それぞれが納税義務者となる。

¶3-140　人格のない社団等
　「法人」とは，日本の商法，民法その他の法律により法人格の認められるものをいう。日本の法律だけではなく，外国の法律により設立された法人も，法人として扱われる。
　「人格のない社団等」とは，その構成員とは別個独自の存在を有するもので，代表者又は管理人を有するものをいうが，法人格はないものである（法法3）。狭義の組合は（¶3-120），通常その構成員とは別個独自の存在を有

88 NATIONAL TAXES ON INCOME

sentative or administrator, but which has no juridical personality (Corporation tax law 3). A partnership in the narrow sense (¶ 3-120) usually is not independent of its partners; therefore it is not treated as a non-juridical organization. A non-juridical organization is always subject to withholding income tax, but it is subject to corporation tax only for its profit-making activities (as set out in a Cabinet Order) (Corporation tax law 4①, Reg 5).

In this book, the term "corporation" includes "non-juridical organizations", when the context requires.

Resident and Non-resident (Individual)

¶ 3-210 Tax liability of individuals, significance of residence

Individual taxpayers are classified into resident taxpayers and non-resident taxpayers.

A resident taxpayer is subject to income tax on his worldwide income, from sources in any country (Income tax law 7①(1)). Withholding income tax is withheld at source from some kinds of income, then assessment income tax is levied on the income on a calendar year basis. The amount of withholding income tax is deducted from the amount of assessment income tax to arrive at the amount of tax payable for a calendar year.

A non-resident taxpayer is subject to Japanese income tax only on income derived from sources in Japan. The non-resident's tax liability is usually settled finally by the withholding of income tax, which covers a wider range of income for a non-resident than for a resident (Income tax law 7①(3)). Japanese assessment income tax is levied on a non-resident's income in only limited cases.

¶ 3-230 Non-permanent resident

A non-permanent resident belongs to the resident taxpayers group, but his tax liability on income from foreign sources is restricted. He is subject to assessment income tax on a so-called remittance basis with regard to income derived from sources abroad, i.e. the income derived from foreign sources is not subject to Japanese tax unless it is paid in Japan or it is remitted into Japan (Income tax law 7①(2)).

¶ 3-210

所得に対する国税　89

するものではない。それ故，人格のない社団等として扱われることはない。人格のない社団等は常に源泉所得税の納税義務を負うが，法人税については，政令で定める収益事業を行う場合に限られる（法法4①，法令5）。

　本書では，文脈により，「法人」には「人格のない社団等」を含む。

居住者又は非居住者（個人）

¶3-210　個人の制限納税義務又は無制限納税義務

　個人の納税者は，居住者と非居住者とに分類される。

　居住者は，所得の源泉地のいかんを問わず全世界所得に対して所得税が課される（所法7①一）。ある種の所得については，最初に源泉所得税が差し引かれ，次いでその所得について暦年基準により申告所得税が課される。その暦年の要納付税額を計算する際に，源泉所得税額は申告所得税額から控除される。

　非居住者は，日本の国内源泉所得についてのみ日本の所得税が課される。その納税義務は，通常，源泉所得税のみで最終のものとなる（所法7①三）。それは，居住者の場合に比して非居住者の場合には，源泉徴収義務が広範囲に規定されているからである。非居住者の所得に対して申告所得税が課されるのは特定の場合だけである。

¶3-230　非永住者

　非永住者は居住者の範ちゅうに属するが，国外源泉所得に対する納税義務は限定されている。国外源泉所得については，いわゆる送金基準により申告所得税の納税義務を負う。換言すれば，国外源泉所得については，日本国内で支払われるか，日本へ送金されない限り，日本の租税は課されない（所法7①二）。

90   NATIONAL TAXES ON INCOME

¶ 3-250 Definition of resident, non-resident, and non-permanent resident

(1) Resident

An individual who has his domicile in Japan is a resident. An individual who has had his residence in Japan for one year or more is also a resident (Income tax law 2①(3)).

"Domicile" means his centre of living. The concept of "domicile" is quite different for Japanese income tax purposes from the concept in the U.K., but rather similar to the American concept of domicile. An exact definition of "domicile" is difficult, but it is clear that if a foreigner enters Japan with his family with an intention to have his house anywhere in Japan and is actually in Japan for one year or more, he is domiciled in Japan.

"Residence" means the place where an individual stays continuously for a certain period but which cannot be said to be his centre of living.

When an individual who has his residence leaves Japan with the intention of returning to Japan after a short stay abroad, his period of residence in Japan is not considered to be broken.

(2) Non-permanent resident

A resident taxpayer who has no Japanese nationality and has lived in Japan for 5 years or less in the last 10 years is a non-permanent resident (Income tax law 2①(4)).

Non-permanent resident status is designed to absorb the financial strain from taxation which a foreigner might experience in the first few years he works in Japan.

For example, if a foreign citizen comes to Japan as an employee attached to the Tokyo branch of his firm for a three-year term, he will become a resident for Japanese tax purposes, and interest on any deposits with a bank in his home country, coupons of bonds or debentures issued in his home country, capital gains from the sale of real property situated in his home country, etc. would be subject to Japanese income tax. To avoid such tax liability, the non-permanent resident scheme makes it possible for him not to pay any Japanese income tax on such income from sources abroad, unless it is paid in Japan or remitted into Japan.

(3) Non-resident

All individuals other than residents are non-residents (Income tax law 2①(5)).

¶ 3-250

所得に対する国税　91

¶3-250　居住者，非居住者及び非永住者の定義

(1)　居住者

　日本の国内に住所を有する者が居住者である。日本に1年以上居所を有する者も居住者である（所法2①三）。

　「住所」とは生活の本拠地である。所得税の課税上における「住所」の概念は英国のそれとは全く異なり，むしろ米国のそれに類似している。「住所」の厳密な定義は困難であるが，外国人が家族を同伴して日本国内に家庭を1年以上構える意図の下に来日した場合には，同人が日本国内に住所を有していることは明らかである。

　「居所」とは，個人が相当期間継続して居住する場所であるが，生活の本拠という程度には至らないものをいう。

　居所を有する個人が短期間海外に滞在後再度日本へ帰国する意図で出国した場合には，同人の日本における居所を有する期間は中断されたものとはみなされない。

(2)　非永住者

　居住者のうち，日本国籍を有せず，かつ，過去10年間のうち5年以下の期間国内に住所又は居所を有する者が非永住者である（所法2①四）。

　この非永住者という居住形態は，外国人が日本において勤務する場合，最初の数年間に経験する課税という財政面の困難を回避するために考案されたものである。

　例えば，外国の一市民が自己の勤務する会社の日本支店に3年の任期で転勤になったとする。日本での課税上，同人が居住者となれば，本国の銀行にある預金の利子，本国で発行された公社債の利子，本国にある不動産の譲渡による所得などのすべてにつき，日本の所得税が課されることになる。これを回避するため，納税者は，このような所得が日本で支払われないか又は日本へ送金されない限り，この国外源泉所得を日本で課税されないで済むよう工夫することができるのである。

(3)　非居住者

　居住者以外のすべての者が非居住者である（所法2①五）。

92   NATIONAL TAXES ON INCOME

Domestic Corporation and Foreign Corporation

¶ 3-340 Tax liability of corporation, significance of nationality

Corporate taxpayers are classified into two categories, domestic and foreign.

A domestic corporation is subject to Japanese income tax on its worldwide income (Corporation tax law 5). Withholding income tax is withheld at source from some kinds of income paid to domestic corporations, thereafter corporation tax is levied on their income. The amount of withholding income tax is deducted from the amount of corporation tax.

A foreign corporation is subject to Japanese income tax only on income derived from sources in Japan (Corporation tax law 9). Its tax liability is usually settled finally by the withholding of tax, unless it has a branch office, agent (excluding independent agents), etc. in Japan, in which case corporation tax is levied on its income derived from sources in Japan in the regular manner.

¶ 3-360 Definition of domestic corporation and foreign corporation

A corporation which has its head office in Japan is a domestic corporation, and all corporations other than Japanese corporations are foreign corporations (Corporation tax law 2(3), (4)).

The place of management and control has no bearing on the nationality of corporations.

Exempt Corporation

¶ 3-410 Exempt corporation

Some corporations are fully or partially exempt from Japanese income tax, both withholding tax and assessment tax, because of their public character:

(a) Wholly exempt corporations: local governments, corporations wholly owned by the national government, etc.

(b) Partially exempt corporations: Japan Red Cross, Chamber of Commerce and Industry, religious corporations and other corporations related to the public interest as defined by law.

¶ 3-340

内国法人及び外国法人

¶3-340　法人の制限納税義務又は無制限納税義務

　法人の納税者は，内国法人と外国法人とに分類される。

　内国法人は，所得の源泉地のいかんを問わず全世界所得につき日本で課税される（法法5）。一定の種類の所得が同法人に支払われる場合には，源泉所得税が差し引かれる。次いで，法人税が課税される。源泉所得税額は法人税額から控除される。

　一方，外国法人は，日本の国内源泉所得についてのみ日本で課税される（法法9）。日本国内に支店，代理人（独立の地位を有する代理人等を除く。）を有しない限り，その納税義務は，通常，源泉所得税のみで最終的に清算されるが，支店等を有する場合には，日本の国内源泉所得については，通常の方法により課税される。

¶3-360　内国法人及び外国法人の定義

　日本国内に本店を有する法人が内国法人であり，内国法人以外の法人は，すべて外国法人である（法法2三，四）。

　管理，支配の場所は，両者の区分には関係がない。

非課税法人

¶3-410　非課税法人

　若干の法人は，その公共的性格の故に，全部又は一部の所得に対する日本での課税（源泉所得税及び申告納税による所得税）を免れる。

(a)　全額非課税となる法人……地方自治体，全額政府出資法人，その他の類似法人

(b)　一部非課税法人……日本赤十字社，商工会議所，宗教法人その他の公益法人で法律に規定するもの

94   NATIONAL TAXES ON INCOME

Partially exempt corporations are usually exempt from withholding income tax as well as corporation tax, but their income earned from profit-making activities (as set out in a Cabinet Order) is subject to corporation tax (Corporation tax law 4①, ③).

¶ 3-430 Tax liability of foreign corporations working for religious, charitable, scientific, educational and similar public purposes

Foreign corporations similar in character to the corporations mentioned in ¶ 3-410 are exempt from Japanese income taxation under the principle of reciprocity, in so far as the tax authorities of their home country extend tax exemptions to Japanese corporations of similar character (Corporation tax law 10).

Tax Treaties

¶ 3-510 Tax treaties

Japan has concluded treaties for the avoidance of double taxation on income with the U.S.A., the U.K., Canada, Sweden, Norway, Denmark, Austria, France, Germany, Belgium, Italy, Netherlands, Switzerland, Pakistan, India, Malaysia, Singapore, Thailand, Sri Lanka, Republic of Korea, New Zealand, Australia, United Arab Republic, Zambia, Brazil, Finland, Ireland, Spain, Romania, Czech, Slovakia, Hungary, Philippines, Poland, Indonesia, China, Bulgaria, Bangladesh, Luxemburg, Turkey, Israel, Vietnam, Mexico, South Africa, Kazakhstan, Brunei Darussalam, Kuwait, Fiji, Hong Kong, Saudi Arabia, Portugal, United Arab Emirates, Oman, Qatar, Taiwan, Latvia and Slovenia. Japan also concluded a tax treaty with the Union of Soviet Socialist Republics. This treaty is also applied to Russia, Kyrgyzstan, Georgia, Tajikistan, Uzbekistan, Turkmenistan, Ukraine, Armenia, Belarus, Azerbaijan and Moldova.

The special concessions granted under these treaties are described in ¶ 4-650, ¶ 5-900 and ¶ 6-900.

With respect to Taiwan, a framework equivalent to a tax treaty is established in combination of (1) a private-sector arrangement between the Interchange Association (Japan) and the Association of East Asian Relations (Taiwan) and (2) Japanese domestic legislation to implement the provisions of that private-sector arrangement in Japan.

¶ 3-430

所得に対する国税　95

　一部非課税法人は，通常，法人税のみならず源泉所得税も免除されるが，政令で規定する収益事業から生ずる所得については，法人税が課される（法法4①，③）。

¶3-430　外国法人で宗教，慈善，科学，教育その他類似の事業を行うものの納税義務

　¶3-410で述べた法人と同様の性質を有する外国法人は，本国の税務当局が，日本の法人で同様の性質を有するものに対し非課税の取扱いをする場合には，相互主義の原則に基づき日本でも課税されない（法法10）。

租　税　条　約

¶3-510　租税条約

　日本は，所得に対する二重課税の回避を目的として，米国，英国，カナダ，スウェーデン，ノルウェー，デンマーク，オーストリア，フランス，ドイツ，ベルギー，イタリア，オランダ，スイス，パキスタン，インド，マレーシア，シンガポール，タイ，スリランカ，韓国，ニュージーランド，オーストラリア，エジプト，ザンビア，ブラジル，フィンランド，アイルランド，スペイン，ルーマニア，チェコ，スロヴァキア，ハンガリー，フィリピン，ポーランド，インドネシア，中国，旧ソ連，ブルガリア，バングラデシュ，ルクセンブルク，トルコ，イスラエル，ヴェトナム，メキシコ，南アフリカ，カザフスタン，ブルネイ・ダルサラーム，クウェート，フィジー，香港，サウジアラビア王国，ポルトガル，アラブ首長国連邦，オマーン，カタール，台湾，ラトビア及びスロベニアの各国・地域と租税条約を締結している。なお，旧ソ連との間の租税条約については，ロシア，キルギスタン，ジョージア，タジキスタン，ウズベキスタン，トルクメニスタン，ウクライナ，アルメニア，ベラルーシ，アゼルバイジャン及びモルドヴァ各共和国との間で引き続き適用されることで合意されている。

　これらの租税条約において与えられている特典については，¶4-650，¶5-900及び¶6-900で述べられている。

　台湾については，公益財団法人交流協会（日本側）と亜東関係協会（台湾側）との間の民間取決め及びその内容を日本国内で実施するための法令によって，全体として租税条約に相当する枠組みが構築されている。

96   NATIONAL TAXES ON INCOME

¶ 3-540 Diplomatic privilege and exemption for foreign governments

Diplomatic privilege under international law is of course recognized by the Japanese tax authorities.

Diplomatic officials and their spouses are exempt from Japanese income tax.

Interest on Japanese bonds and deposits with a Japanese bank accrued to a foreign government are also exempt because of the government's immunity, even though they are derived from sources in Japan.

The following form is to be used by those who want to apply for this immunity:

The Commissioner   (Date)
National Tax Administration

Dear Sir,

We, the Central Bank of (*Name of Country*), hereby pledge that the deposit held with the (*Name of Bank*) in our name, amounting to $_____, substantially belongs to our assets and forms a part of our foreign reserves and is not held for commercial and/or industrial purposes.

In connection with the above, we request you consider granting an exemption of the income tax on the interest accruing from the above deposit through the (*Name of Bank*).

Yours faithfully,

(Authorized Signature)
(Status)
(Name of the Central Bank)

Principle of Taxation Based on "Economic Substance"

¶ 3-710 To whom income pertains

It is not always an easy question to determine to whom income pertains.

¶ 3-540

所得に対する国税　97

¶3-540　外交特権及び外国政府の非課税

　国際法に基づく外交特権は，当然，日本の税務当局によっても認められている。

　外交官及びその配偶者は日本の所得税を課されない。

　日本の公社債の利子や，日本の銀行に対する預金の利子で外国政府の保有に係るものは日本の国内源泉所得であるが，主権免税という見地から課税されない。

　この主権免税を申請しようとする者は，次の書式を用いて行わなければならない。

国税庁長官　　　　　　　　　　　　　　　　　　　年　月　日

拝啓
　当中央銀行（○○国）が，当行の名義で（○○銀行）に有する＿＿＿＿ドルの預金は，実質的にも当行の資産であり，当国の海外留保金であり，商業目的及び／又は事業目的のため保有するものではないことを誓約致します。
　ついては，上記預金の利子に対する所得税の非課税を御配慮願えれば幸甚です。
　この段，（○○銀行）を通じて申請致します。

　　　　　　　　　　　　　　　　　　　　　　　　　　敬　具

　　　　　　　　　　　　　　　　　　　（権限のある者の署名）
　　　　　　　　　　　　　　　　　　　（資　格）
　　　　　　　　　　　　　　　　　　　（中央銀行の名称）

「経済的実質」に基づく課税の原則

¶3-710　所得の帰属者

　所得の帰属者を決定することは，通常，容易ではない。

　A氏とB氏との間の契約により，A氏は第三者に対する関係では，一定の

98 NATIONAL TAXES ON INCOME

It sometimes happens that Mr. A presents himself to third parties as a person entitled to receive a certain item of income, while Mr. B enjoys fully the income which is channeled to him through Mr. A, according to an agreement concluded between them. This kind of agreement is often concluded with or without a clear intention to evade income tax. In such a case, Japanese income taxes are levied on the person to whom the income is finally allocable in an economic sense, namely, on Mr. B in the above-mentioned example, so as to fairly allocate the income tax burden.

For example, a company may happen to hold shares issued by itself, even though such holding is prohibited under the Commercial Code. In order to avoid the illegality of such holding, the company may conclude an agreement with one of its directors to the effect that he becomes a registered shareholder, even though the dividends paid nominally to the director are channeled to the said company and the director actually does not get any income at all. Applying the "economic substance principle of taxation", Japanese income taxes are levied on the company, but not on the director, for the said dividends.

This principle is a guide to taxation of trusts, as well as a denial of transactions and entries of a family corporation, although it does not deny the existence of a family corporation nor of a subsidiary corporation (Income tax law 12, Corporation tax law 11).

¶ 3-740 Taxation of trusts

The income derived from an entrusted property is deemed to be earned by the beneficiary of the trust. No income tax is levied on a trustee or the settlor of a trust, unless he is a beneficiary at the same time.

There is one exception to the above principle. Japanese trust companies often have funds which are invested in securities, loans to companies, etc. for many separate and independent beneficiaries. Under this kind of trust, the income attributable to such funds is not subject to corporation tax but only to withholding income tax. Tax is levied on the beneficiaries at the time of payment of benefits from trust companies (Income tax law 13, Corporation tax law 12).

Regarding tax treatments of trusts, taxation measures were improved corresponding to new types of trust under the revised Trust Law. In addition, with a view to preventing tax avoidance, necessary tax measures were introduced to ensure neutral and fair taxation such as application of corporate

¶ 3-740

所得に対する国税　99

所得を受領する権限を与えられた者として行動し，一方，B氏はA氏を通ずることにより得た所得を享受するということが，しばしば発生する。この者の契約は，所得税の税負担を免れようという明確な意図をもって行われることもあれば，そうでないこともある。このような場合，日本の所得税は，所得が経済的意味において最終的に配分された者に対し課税される。すなわち，上記の事案では，租税負担の適正な配分という見地からB氏に課税される。

　また，例えば，商法で禁止されているにもかかわらず自社発行の株式を保有する法人がある。このような法律違反を回避するために，法人は自社の役員と契約して，その者を株主名簿に株主として登録はするが，形式上役員に支払われた配当は法人に流れて行き，その役員は所得を全く得ていないということがある。日本での所得に対する課税に当たっては，「経済的実質に基づく課税の原則」が適用され，上記の配当については，役員ではなく，法人に対して課税が行われる。

　この原則は，同族会社やその子会社の存在までを否定するものではない。この原則が同族会社の行為・計算の否認だけではなく，信託財産に対する課税においても採り入れられている（所法12，法法11）。

¶3-740　信託財産に対する課税

　信託財産につき生じた所得は，信託の受益者が獲得したものとみなされる。信託の受託者又は信託契約者に対しては，その者が同時に信託の受益者に該当しない限り，所得に対する租税は課されない。

　上記の原則には一つの例外がある。日本の信託会社は，別個の分離・独立した多くの受益者のために，証券に投資したり貸付けを行うために基金を有する。この種の信託においては，基金に帰属する所得については法人税が課税されず，信託会社が受益者に対して信託利益を支払う際には源泉所得税が課される（所法13，法法12）。

　平成18年12月の信託法の改正に伴い，新たな類型の信託への税制が整備された。さらに，租税回避防止の観点から，受託者に対する法人課税を行う等課税の中立・公平を確保するための措置が講ぜられている（¶5-180，¶6-052，¶7-850，¶8-300参照）。

100 NATIONAL TAXES ON INCOME

income taxation to trustees (¶ 5-180, ¶ 6-052, ¶ 7-850, ¶ 8-300).

¶ 3-760 Denial of transactions or entries of family corporation

Transactions between a family corporation and its shareholders are not always carried on at arm's length. The same thing can be said of transactions between a subsidiary and a parent corporation or between two subsidiaries controlled by one parent corporation.

The book entries of such corporations are also often artificial.

In order to accomplish fair income taxation, the Japanese tax authorities are empowered to deny such transactions or book entries and compute the income by reconstructing the transactions or book entries on reasonable terms at their discretion (Corporation tax law 132).

¶ 3-780 Family corporation

The term "family corporation" is defined as a corporation, over 50% of whose capital is owned by one, two or three shareholders.

Therefore, the term "family corporation" includes a subsidiary.

In counting the number of shareholders, one shareholder and the persons specially connected with him are counted as one. The term "persons specially connected with a shareholder" means:

(i) his relatives,

(ii) any other individuals having special connection with the shareholder, e.g. de facto spouse, their servant or any individual economically supported by them,

(iii) relatives of these individuals living with the person described the above (ii), and

(iv) any corporation controlled by them.

A corporation is treated as "controlled" in this context when over 50% of its capital is directly or indirectly (extending as far as a great-grandfather corporation) owned by one shareholder and the persons specially connected with him.

If a shareholder controls two or more corporations, and these corporations together control a grandson corporation whose capital is not owned by the first-mentioned shareholder, then these two or more corporations are counted as one shareholder of the grandson corporation (Corporation tax law 2(10)).

¶ 3-760

所得に対する国税　101

¶3-760　同族会社の行為計算の否認

　同族会社とその株主との間の取引は，常に独立企業の原則に基づき行われるとは限らない。同様のことは，子会社と親会社又は同一の親会社によって支配されている二つの子会社の間においてもみられる。

　このような法人の帳簿の記入は，往々にして不自然である。

　公正な課税を行うために，日本の税務当局は，このような行為・計算を否認して，その裁量に基づき適正と認められる行為・計算に引直して所得を計算する権限を与えられている（法法132）。

¶3-780　同族会社

　同族会社とは，株式の50％超が，1人，2人又は3人の株主により所有されている会社をいう。

　したがって，同族会社には子会社が含まれる。株主の数を計算するに際し，1人の株主と特殊の関係のある者は1人と数えられる。「特殊の関係のある者」とは，

(i)　その親族，

(ii)　事実上婚姻関係と同様の事情にある者，その使用人その他の個人で株主により生計を維持されている者，

(iii)　上記(ii)に掲げる者の同居の親族，

(iv)　その株主により支配されている法人，

をいう。

　50％超株式が，直接又は間接に（曾祖父法人にまで遡る。）1人の株主により所有されており，その者と特殊の関係のある者は，この点については支配されているものとして取り扱われる。

　1人の株主が2以上の法人を支配しており，かつ，これらの法人が前者の株主により所有されていない孫会社を共同して支配している場合には，これらの2以上の法人は，孫会社の株主を計算する際には，1人として計算する（法法2十）。

102   NATIONAL TAXES ON INCOME

¶ 3-790 Nonpersonal family corporation

The family corporation is classified into two classes, namely, corporations controlled by a number of "individuals" and other corporations. The former is defined as a "personal family corporation" and the latter a "nonpersonal family corporation". A good example of a nonpersonal family corporation is a subsidiary of a corporation which is not itself a personal family corporation.

A nonpersonal family corporation is subject to the discretional adjustment of its transactions or book entries by the tax authorities, but is not subject to tax on undistributed profits (Corporation tax law 67) (¶ 6-640).

¶ 3-790

¶3-790　非同族の同族会社

　同族会社は，2種のものに分類される。すなわち，多くの個人により支配されている法人と，その他の法人である。前者は「同族会社」といわれ，後者は「非同族の同族会社」といわれる。非同族の同族会社の好例は，その法人自体は同族会社には該当しない法人の子会社である。

　非同族の同族会社は，税務当局の行う行為・計算の否認の対象になるが，留保金課税の対象にはならない（法法67）（¶6-640）。

CHAPTER 4

WITHHOLDING INCOME TAX

	Paragraph
Table: General View of Withholding Income Tax	¶ 4-010
Basic Structure of Withholding Income Tax	¶ 4-050
Withholding from Payments to Residents	¶ 4-130
Withholding from Payments to Domestic Corporations	¶ 4-510
Withholding from Payments to Non-residents and Foreign Corporations	¶ 4-620
Application Forms	¶ 4-830

第 4 章
源 泉 所 得 税

源泉所得税の概要………………………………………… ¶4-010
源泉所得税の基本的な仕組み……………………………… ¶4-050
居住者に対する支払に係る源泉徴収……………………… ¶4-130
内国法人に対する支払に係る源泉徴収…………………… ¶4-510
非居住者及び外国法人に対する支払に係る源泉徴収……… ¶4-620
租税条約に関する届出書…………………………………… ¶4-830

¶ 4-010 Table: General View of Withholding Income Tax

Kind of recipient / Items of income	Individual (¶ 3-210 ~ ¶ 3-250)		Corporations (¶ 3-340, ¶ 3-360)	
	Resident (¶ 4-130)	Non-resident (¶ 4-620)	Domestic corporation (¶ 4-510)	Foreign corporation (¶ 4-620)
Interest on bonds, debentures, deposits with a bank, etc.	¶ 4-150, ¶ 4-190	¶ 4-620 ~ ¶ 4-680	¶ 4-510, ¶ 4-540	¶ 4-620 ~ ¶ 4-680
Interest on loans	—	¶ 4-620, ¶ 4-650	—	¶ 4-620, ¶ 4-650
Dividends	¶ 4-210	¶ 4-620, ¶ 4-650	¶ 4-510, ¶ 4-540	¶ 4-620, ¶ 4-650
Rent on real property, etc.	—	¶ 4-620	—	¶ 4-620
Salaries, wages, bonuses	¶ 4-230 ~ ¶ 4-310	¶ 4-620, ¶ 4-650	—	—
Retirement allowances	¶ 4-340	¶ 4-620	—	—
Remuneration, etc. for independent personal services, etc.	¶ 4-360	¶ 4-620, ¶ 4-650	¶ 4-570	¶ 4-620, ¶ 4-650
Royalties	¶ 4-360	¶ 4-620, ¶ 4-650	—	¶ 4-620, ¶ 4-650
Rentals of equipment	—	¶ 4-620	—	¶ 4-620
Prizes	¶ 4-360	¶ 4-620	¶ 4-510, ¶ 4-570	¶ 4-620
Annuities	¶ 4-390	¶ 4-620	—	¶ 4-620

¶4-010 源泉所得税の概要

支払を受ける者 / 所得の種類	個人 (¶3-210~¶3-250)		法人 (¶3-340, 3-360)	
	居住者 (¶4-130)	非居住者 (¶4-620)	内国法人 (¶4-510)	外国法人 (¶4-620)
公社債, 預金等の利子	¶4-150, ¶4-190	¶4-620~¶4-680	¶4-510, ¶4-540	¶4-620~¶4-680
貸付金の利子	—	¶4-620, ¶4-650	—	¶4-620, ¶4-650
配当	¶4-210	¶4-620, ¶4-650	¶4-510, ¶4-540	¶4-620, ¶4-650
不動産等の賃貸料	—	¶4-620	—	¶4-620
給料, 賃金, 賞与	¶4-230~¶4-310	¶4-620, ¶4-650	—	—
退職手当	¶4-340	¶4-620	—	—
職業専門家に対する報酬	¶4-360	¶4-620, ¶4-650	¶4-570	¶4-620, ¶4-650
使用料	¶4-360	¶4-620, ¶4-650	—	¶4-620, ¶4-650
賃貸料	—	¶4-620	—	¶4-620
賞金	¶4-360	¶4-620	¶4-510, ¶4-570	¶4-620
年金	¶4-390	¶4-620	—	¶4-620

108   WITHHOLDING INCOME TAX

Basic Structure of Withholding Income Tax

¶ 4-050 Four kinds of withholding income tax

Japanese national taxes on income are divided into withholding tax and assessment tax according to the method of collection.

Withholding tax is always called income tax regardless of whether the recipient of the income is an individual, a corporation or a non-juridical organization.

Assessment tax is also called income tax when it is levied on an individual, but it is called corporation tax when it is levied on a corporation or on a non-juridical organization.

In this book, withholding tax is referred to as withholding income tax and assessment tax on an individual's income is referred to as assessment income tax in order to avoid confusion.

Withholding income tax is divided into four categories, according to the recipient of the payment from which the tax is withheld at source:

(1) an individual resident;

(2) a domestic corporation;

(3) an individual non-resident; and

(4) a foreign corporation.

The table at ¶ 4-010 gives a general view of the applicable range of these four categories of withholding income tax (see ¶ 5-070 for exempt income).

¶ 4-070 Withholding and payment

An income payer who withholds tax at source from the payment must transfer the tax so withheld to a tax office on or before the tenth day of the month following the month of payment.

Regarding the place for withholding income tax payment, if an office handling salary payments moves to a new place, the place for withholding income tax payment connected with salary payment made before moving to a new place is to be the place of a new office.

When the bonuses payable to a director of a corporation or the dividends payable to shareholders (except for distributed profits of securities investment trusts), have not yet been actually paid on a date one year

¶ 4-050

源　泉　所　得　税　109

源泉所得税の基本的な仕組み

¶4-050　源泉所得税の4分類

日本における所得に対して課される税は，納税の方法により，源泉所得税と申告所得税とに分類される。

源泉徴収される租税は，当該所得の受領者が，個人，法人又は人格のない社団等のいずれであるかを問わず所得税と呼ばれる。

申告所得税は，個人に課される場合には，所得税と呼ばれるが，法人又は人格のない社団等に課される場合には，法人税と呼ばれる。

本書では，混乱を避けるため，源泉徴収される租税は源泉所得税，個人の所得に対する申告方式による租税は，申告所得税と呼ぶ。

源泉所得税は，源泉徴収される支払の受領者別に，次の四つに分けることができる。すなわち，

(1)　居住者に係るもの
(2)　内国法人に係るもの
(3)　非居住者に係るもの
(4)　外国法人に係るもの

である。

¶4-010の表は，上記の四つの区分ごとに源泉所得税が課税される所得の種類を示している。

なお，非課税となる所得については，¶5-070で触れている。

¶4-070　源泉徴収と支払

源泉徴収すべき所得の支払を行う者は，源泉徴収した税額をその支払を行った月の翌月の10日までに税務署に納付しなければならない。

源泉所得税の納税地について，給与等の支払事務所等の移転があった場合には，当該移転前に支払った給与等に係る源泉所得税の納税地は，移転後の給与等の支払事務所等の所在地とする。

法人の役員に支払われるべき賞与あるいは株主に支払われるべき配当（証券投資信託の収益の分配を除く。）がその支払決定後1年以内に実際に支払われないときは，かかる賞与あるいは配当はその支払決定後1年を経過した日に支払が行われたものとみなされ，したがって，源泉所得税の納付義務が生ずる（所法181②，183②）。

110   WITHHOLDING INCOME TAX

after the amount payable was determined, such bonuses or dividends are deemed to be paid on that date, and withholding income tax must be transferred to a tax office accordingly (Law 181②, 183②).

When income is paid to a non-resident or a foreign corporation at a place outside Japan by a payer who has a residence or an office in Japan, the withheld tax is transferred at the end of the month following the month of payment (Law 212②).

Withholding from Payments to Residents

¶ 4-130 Withholding from payments to residents

The withholding tax scheme is applicable to the following income paid to resident individuals, unless they are paid abroad:

(a) interest (including profit from the redemption of certain discounted debentures);

(b) dividends;

(c) salaries, wages and similar types of remuneration as well as bonuses and other nonregular payments to employees;

(d) retirement allowances;

(e) remuneration and fees, etc. paid to non-employees.

¶ 4-150 Withholding from interest

Interest income (interest on bonds, debentures, deposits with a bank, etc.; see ¶ 5-120) and income which is not defined as interest income, but is similar to interest income in nature, is subject to separate withholding tax at the rate of 20.315% (15.315% for national tax and 5% for local tax) (Law 181, 182, 209-2, 209-3).

Interest on bonds, debentures issued outside Japan, and payments made through an agent in Japan are subject to withholding tax (SM 3-3①).

¶ 4-155 Withholding tax on income which is similar in nature to interest income

The following categories of income are similar in nature to interest income and, like interest income, are subject to withholding tax (Law 174, 209-2):

1. income derived from certain specific transactions involving gold and other valuable metals;

¶ 4-130

源 泉 所 得 税　111

　支払者がわが国に住所又は事務所を有する場合において，その支払が国外において非居住者又は外国法人に対して行われたときには，その源泉所得税は支払が行われた月の翌月末日までに納付すればよい（所法212②）。

居住者に対する支払に係る源泉徴収

¶4-130　居住者に対する支払に係る源泉徴収
　居住者に対して国内において行われる支払で源泉徴収の対象となるのは，主に以下の所得である。
　(a)　利子（特定の割引債の償還差益を含む。）

　(b)　配当
　(c)　給料，賃金及びその他類似の報酬並びに賞与及び被用者に支払われる臨時の支払
　(d)　退職手当
　(e)　被用者以外の者に支払われる報酬，料金等

¶4-150　利子に係る源泉徴収
　利子所得（公社債，預金等の利子をいう。¶5-120参照）及び利子所得と類似する性格を有する定期積金，相互掛金，抵当証券，金貯蓄口座等に係る収益について20.315％（国税15.315％，地方税5％）の税率の源泉分離課税による所得税が課される（所法181，182，209の2，209の3）。
　国外で発行した公社債等についても，その支払が国内の支払取扱者によって支払われる場合には，源泉所得税が課される（措法3の3①）。

¶4-155　金融類似商品等に対する源泉徴収
　次のものは，金融類似商品とされ，利子の場合と同様に源泉所得課税が行われる（所法174，209の2）。

1．金その他の貴金属等に関する一定の取引に該当するもの

112 WITHHOLDING INCOME TAX

2. income derived from certain specific contracts involving secured coupons; and

3. income derived from some foreign currency deposits.

¶ 4-160 Submission of payment slips for interest payments

Payers of interest paid in Japan on bonds, debentures and deposits must submit a payment slip to a district tax office by January 31 of the year following the year in which the interest accrued (Law 225①(1)).

Payment slips are not required for interest paid to residents or non-residents (SM 3③).

¶ 4-170 Exemption for interest on small deposits and government bonds

When the recipient is a qualified handicapped person or widow, interest income on bank deposits, joint operation trusts, public bonds, mortgaged debentures and stock investment trusts are exempt from income tax, as long as the sum total of the principal amount of deposits or face value of securities does not exceed ¥3,500,000 for each qualified handicapped person or widow who is domiciled in Japan. To obtain this exemption, taxpayers are required to file exemption certificates with a bank, trust company or securities dealer (Law 10, SM 3-4①).

An additional income tax exemption for a qualified handicapped person or widow is allowed for interest on national or local government bonds. This exemption is limited to government bonds with a face value not exceeding ¥3,500,000 for each qualified handicapped person or widow who is domiciled in Japan. An exemption certificate must be filed with the securities dealers from whom the bonds were purchased (SM 4②).

¶ 4-175 Non-taxable interest income from savings for formation of employees' property

A tax exemption is granted for interest on savings by an employee for the purpose of acquiring a residence based on the Employees' Property Formation Promotion Act, Law No. 92, 1971. Interest on deposits made, joint operation trusts, securities bought or insurance contracted by the employer with banks, securities dealers or insurance companies is exempt from the tax, if the necessary procedures are followed, as long as the amount of principal does not exceed ¥5,500,000 for each taxpayer (SM 4-2).

¶ 4-160

2．抵当証券に関する一定の契約に基づく取引に該当するもの

3．外貨建預貯金によるものの差益のうち特定のもの

¶4-160　利子に関する支払調書の提出
　国内において公社債及び預貯金の支払をする者は，その支払に関する調書をその利子の支払の確定した日の属する年の翌年1月31日までに税務署長に提出しなければならない（所法225①一）。
　居住者又は非居住者が支払を受ける利子については支払調書の提出は必要とされない（措法3③）。

¶4-170　一定の障害者，寡婦に対する少額貯蓄及び国債の利子の非課税
　日本国内に住所を有する一定の障害者等は，銀行預金，合同運用信託，公債，政府保証債及び証券投資信託の利子について，元本又は額面金額の合計額が納税者1人につき350万円を超えない限り，非課税とされる。この非課税措置を受けるためには，銀行，信託会社又は証券会社に非課税申告書を提出しなければならない（所法10，措法3の4①）。
　国債及び地方債の利子についても，国内に住所を有する障害者等は，額面350万円までは非課税とされる。この場合は，債券を購入した証券会社に非課税申告書を提出する必要がある（措法4②）。

¶4-175　勤労者財産形成住宅貯蓄の利子の非課税
　勤労者財産形成促進法（昭和46年法律第92号）に基づいて勤労者が住宅の取得のために貯蓄等を行う場合には，その利子は非課税とされている。すなわち，勤労者は，住宅の取得のために，銀行，証券会社，保険会社と締結された契約に従って払い込まれる貯蓄，合同運用信託，購入された証券又は生命保険に係る利子については，所定の手続の下に納税者1人につき元本550万円まで非課税とされる（措法4の2）。
　なお，勤労者財産形成年金貯蓄の利子についても住宅の取得のための貯蓄等の場合と同様にその利子が非課税とされている（措法4の3）。

114   WITHHOLDING INCOME TAX

Further, a similar tax exemption for interest on savings for the purpose of a pension based on the Employees' Property Formation Promotion Act is applicable. For these tax exemptions to apply to interest earned, the total principal both for the acquisition of housing and the pension must not exceed ¥5,500,000 (SM 4-3).

¶ 4-190 Withholding from debentures issued at discount

(1)   Discounted debentures are subject to tax at the rate of 18.378% (income tax 18%, earthquake restoration surtax 0.378%) (16.336% rate applies to some specific discount bond) on the excess of the amount redeemed over the amount paid in at the time of issuance. The tax is imposed on the purchaser of the debenture and collected from its issuer, and is deemed to be withholding income tax. When the purchaser is an individual, the excess amount redeemed is not subject to assessment income tax.

This special treatment of discounted debentures is limited to national bond, debenture on telephone and telegram, and debentures issued by certain banks and financial institutions (SM 41-12).

(2)   In 2013 tax reform, the excess of the amount redeemed over the amount paid in at the issuance after January 1, 2016 is not subject to withholding tax at the rate of 18.378%, and the excess amount is subject to withholding tax at the rate of 15.315% (besides 5% local tax) when the discounted debentures are redeemed by its issuer.

¶ 4-210 Withholding from dividends

Dividend income (dividends other than dividends of listed stocks, distributions by securities investment trusts, etc. — see ¶ 5-120), is subject to withholding income tax at a rate of 20.42% (in the case of the distributed income of a securities investment trust 15.315% for national tax and 5% for local tax no assessment income tax is levied). The tax so withheld is deducted from the amount of assessment income tax to arrive at the amount of tax payable for a calendar year, with credits for dividends taken into account.

And 10% (or 5% where his taxable income is more than ¥10 million) of the dividend income (dividends minus the interest paid on borrowings for the acquisition of the shares) is credited against the amount of assessment income tax (see credit for dividends, ¶ 5-580).

¶ 4-190

源 泉 所 得 税　115

　非課税の限度額は，上記の住宅の取得のための貯蓄等と年金のための貯蓄等の合計額550万円までとされている。

¶4-190　割引債に係る源泉徴収

(1)　国内で発行される割引債は，その償還差益に対して18.378％（所得税18％，復興特別所得税0.378％）（特定のものについて16.336％）の税率で課税される。これは割引債の購入者に対して課されるもので割引債の発行の際に源泉徴収により課税が行われる。購入者が個人の場合は，その償還差益には申告所得税は課されない。上記の償還差益に関する特別の規定は，国債，電信電話債券，特定の銀行その他のものに限定される（措法41の12）。

(2)　平成25年度税制改正により，平成28年1月1日以降に発行される割引債の償還差益については，発行時の源泉徴収（18.378％）を適用しないこととされ，償還時に15.315％（他に地方税5％）の税率による源泉徴収をしなければならないこととされた。

¶4-210　配当に係る源泉徴収

　配当所得（上場株式以外の配当，証券投資信託の収益の分配等をいう。¶5-120参照）に対しては，20.42％（証券投資信託の収益の分配については，国税15.315％，地方税5％の計20.315％の分離課税となっている。）の税率の源泉所得税が課され，この源泉所得税額はその年の所得に課される申告所得税額から控除されることになっている。また，配当控除制度の適用がある。

　そして配当所得（配当額から負債利子を控除したもの）の10％（課税所得が1,000万円以上の場合は5％）相当額の税額控除が認められる（¶5-580参照）。

　次に，居住者又は国内に恒久的施設を有している非居住者は，一法人から支払を受ける配当の額が5万円（支払法人の事業年度が1年以上の場合は10万円）以下である場合には，申告所得税の申告に当たりこれを課税所得に含める必要はない。

116   WITHHOLDING INCOME TAX

Further, if the dividends paid by one company to an individual resident, or a non-resident having a permanent establishment in Japan, do not exceed ¥50,000 (¥100,000 where the accounting period of the paying company is 12 months or more), he is not required to include it in his taxable income when he files a return for assessment income tax.

The distributed profit of public bonds and debenture investment trusts is subject to the same tax treatment as interest income (Law 181, 182 and SM 8-2, 8-3) (¶ 4-150).

¶ 4-211 Withholding from dividends of listed stocks

Dividends of listed stocks are taxed as follows:

January 1, 2013 to December 31, 2013	10.147% (income tax and earthquake restoration surtax 7.147%, local inhabitant tax 3%)
January 1, 2014 to December 31, 2037	20.315% (income tax and earthquake restoration surtax 15.315%, local inhabitant tax 5%)

With regard to dividends of certain listed stocks paid to stockholders after April 1, 2003, the upper limitation of the amount of one-time payment not required to be reported to tax authority by filing a tax return is lifted. Accordingly, tax is paid by withholding and no filing of returns is required.

If a taxpayer receives dividends of listed stocks from the company he owns 3% or more of whose issued stocks, the withholding tax rate is 20.42% (income tax 20%, earthquake restoration surtax 0.42%) on January 1, 2013 and after.

¶ 4-212 Withholding from distribution from publicly traded stock investment funds

Distribution from publicly traded stock investment funds is taxed at the reduced rate of 10.147%(7.147% for income tax and earthquake restoration surtax, 3% for local inhabitant tax) for the period from January 1,2013 to December 31, 2013. And from January 1, 2014, the tax rate is 20.315% (income tax and earthquake restoration surtax 15.315%, local inhabitant tax 5%).

Tax is paid by withholding and no filing of returns is required.

¶ 4-211

源 泉 所 得 税　117

　公社債投資信託の収益の分配についても，利子所得（¶4-150参照）に対するものと同様の取扱いが認められている（所法181，182，措法8の2，8の3）。

¶4-211　上場株式等の配当等に係る源泉徴収

　上場株式等の配当等に係る源泉徴収税率については，次のとおりである。

| 平成25年1月1日～平成25年12月31日 | 10.147%（所得税及び復興特別所得税7.147%，住民税3%） |
| 平成26年1月1日～平成49年12月31日 | 20.315%（所得税及び復興特別所得税15.315%，住民税5%） |

　平成15年4月1日以後に支払を受ける一定の上場株式等の配当等につき，申告不要とされる，いわゆる少額配当の1回の支払金額の上限額が撤廃された。したがって，源泉納付で終了し，申告納付する必要はない。
　上記取扱いについて，配当等の支払を受ける者が株式等の発行済株式等の総数の3%以上を保有する場合は，平成25年以降20.42%（所得税20%，復興特別所得税0.42%）である。

¶4-212　投資信託の収益の分配に係る源泉徴収

　公募株式投資信託の収益の分配に係る源泉徴収税率については，平成25年1月1日から平成25年12月31日までは10.147%（所得税及び復興特別所得税7.147%，住民税3%）の優遇税率を適用する。平成26年以降は20.315%（所得税及び復興特別所得税15.315%，住民税5%）である。
　源泉納付で終了し，申告納付する必要はない。

118   WITHHOLDING INCOME TAX

¶ 4-230 Withholding from employment income

Salaries, wages or similar remuneration paid periodically to employees as well as bonuses or similar remuneration paid to employees are subject to withholding income tax. However, no withholding of tax is required when a person employs no more than one or two domestic servants for his household (Law 183, 184).

The amount to be withheld is determined by the "withholding tax table for salaries, wages, etc." and the "withholding tax table for bonuses".

Entertainment expenses which are not related to business activities are classified as "salary" to a director or employee who has paid entertainment expenses.

An allowance for commuting, of up to 150,000 yen per month, is not included in taxable salary (Reg 20-2).

A reasonable amount paid by an employer for an employee's night meal when the employee works overtime is not included in taxable salary (R 36-24).

¶ 4-250 Withholding from salaries, wages, etc.

The withholding tax table for salaries, wages, etc. is composed of a "monthly table" with two columns, A and B, and a "daily table" with three columns, A, B and C.

The monthly table is applicable to monthly payments and to payments for periods which are a multiple or a fraction of a month.

The daily table is applicable to daily payments or other payments to which the monthly table is not applicable.

"Column A" in both the monthly table and the daily table applies to the payment of an employee who does not earn any remuneration from other employers or who earns no higher remuneration from any other employer.

"Column B" in both the monthly table and the daily table is applicable to payments to which neither column A nor column C applies.

"Column C" in the daily table is applicable to a casual day laborer.

¶ 4-230

源 泉 所 得 税　119

¶4-230　給与所得に係る源泉徴収

　給料，賃金その他被用者に定期的に支払われる類似の報酬並びに賞与その他賞与の性質を有するものには，源泉所得税が課される。ただし，2人以下の家事使用人を雇用しているだけの場合は，源泉所得税は課されない（所法183，184）。

　源泉徴収税額は，"給与所得の源泉徴収税額表"及び"賞与に対する源泉徴収税額の算出率の表"により計算される。

　役員又は使用人の交際費で事業のために使用したことが明らかでないものは報酬又は給与とされる。

　通勤手当で月額150,000円以下のものは課税の対象から除かれる（所令20の2）。残業のための夜食で通常必要とされる金額以下のものは課税の対象から除かれる（所基通36-24）。

¶4-250　給料，賃金等に係る源泉徴収

　給与所得の源泉徴収税額表は，甲欄と乙欄とからなる"月額表"と甲欄，乙欄及び丙欄からなる"日額表"の2種類がある。

　月額表は，毎月又は月の整数倍若しくは月の2分の1若しくは3分の1の期間ごとに支払われることになっている給料等に適用される。

　日額表は，毎日支払われることになっている給料等及び月額表が適用されない給料等に適用される。

　月額表及び日額表の甲欄は，他の者から給料等の支払を受けていない雇用者又は受けていてもその額が少ない者に対して支払われる給料等に係るものである。

　月額表及び日額表の乙欄は，甲欄又は丙欄のいずれについても適用対象にならない給料等に係るものである。

　日額表の丙欄は，日雇労働者に対して支払われる賃金に係るものである。

120 WITHHOLDING INCOME TAX

Withholding tax table for monthly salary payment

(Applicable for 2018)

Amount of salary after deduction of social insurance premiums		{A}								{B}
		Number of dependants								Amount of tax
		0	1	2	3	4	5	6	7	
from	less	Amount of tax								
yen	yen	yen	yen	yen	yen	yen	yen	yen	yen	yen
less than 88,000		0	0	0	0	0	0	0	0	3.063 percent of salary after deduction of social insurance premiums
88,000	89,000	130	0	0	0	0	0	0	0	3,200
89,000	90,000	180	0	0	0	0	0	0	0	3,200
90,000	91,000	230	0	0	0	0	0	0	0	3,200
91,000	92,000	290	0	0	0	0	0	0	0	3,200
92,000	93,000	340	0	0	0	0	0	0	0	3,300
93,000	94,000	390	0	0	0	0	0	0	0	3,300
94,000	95,000	440	0	0	0	0	0	0	0	3,300
95,000	96,000	490	0	0	0	0	0	0	0	3,400
96,000	97,000	540	0	0	0	0	0	0	0	3,400
97,000	98,000	590	0	0	0	0	0	0	0	3,500
98,000	99,000	640	0	0	0	0	0	0	0	3,500
99,000	101,000	720	0	0	0	0	0	0	0	3,600
101,000	103,000	830	0	0	0	0	0	0	0	3,600
103,000	105,000	930	0	0	0	0	0	0	0	3,700
105,000	107,000	1,030	0	0	0	0	0	0	0	3,800
107,000	109,000	1,130	0	0	0	0	0	0	0	3,800
109,000	111,000	1,240	0	0	0	0	0	0	0	3,900
111,000	113,000	1,340	0	0	0	0	0	0	0	4,000
113,000	115,000	1,440	0	0	0	0	0	0	0	4,100
115,000	117,000	1,540	0	0	0	0	0	0	0	4,100
117,000	119,000	1,640	0	0	0	0	0	0	0	4,200
119,000	121,000	1,750	120	0	0	0	0	0	0	4,300
121,000	123,000	1,850	220	0	0	0	0	0	0	4,500
123,000	125,000	1,950	330	0	0	0	0	0	0	4,800
125,000	127,000	2,050	430	0	0	0	0	0	0	5,100
127,000	129,000	2,150	530	0	0	0	0	0	0	5,400
129,000	131,000	2,260	630	0	0	0	0	0	0	5,700
131,000	133,000	2,360	740	0	0	0	0	0	0	6,000
133,000	135,000	2,460	840	0	0	0	0	0	0	6,300
135,000	137,000	2,550	930	0	0	0	0	0	0	6,600
137,000	139,000	2,610	990	0	0	0	0	0	0	6,800
139,000	141,000	2,680	1,050	0	0	0	0	0	0	7,100
141,000	143,000	2,740	1,110	0	0	0	0	0	0	7,500
143,000	145,000	2,800	1,170	0	0	0	0	0	0	7,800
145,000	147,000	2,860	1,240	0	0	0	0	0	0	8,100
147,000	149,000	2,920	1,300	0	0	0	0	0	0	8,400
149,000	151,000	2,980	1,360	0	0	0	0	0	0	8,700
151,000	153,000	3,050	1,430	0	0	0	0	0	0	9,000
153,000	155,000	3,120	1,500	0	0	0	0	0	0	9,300
155,000	157,000	3,200	1,570	0	0	0	0	0	0	9,600
157,000	159,000	3,270	1,640	0	0	0	0	0	0	9,900
159,000	161,000	3,340	1,720	100	0	0	0	0	0	10,200
161,000	163,000	3,410	1,790	170	0	0	0	0	0	10,500
163,000	165,000	3,480	1,860	250	0	0	0	0	0	10,800
165,000	167,000	3,550	1,930	320	0	0	0	0	0	11,100

¶ 4-250

源 泉 所 得 税　121

月　額　表（平成30年分）

その月の社会保険料等控除後の給与等の金額		甲								乙
		扶養親族等の数								
		0人	1人	2人	3人	4人	5人	6人	7人	
以上	未満	税額								税額
円	円	円	円	円	円	円	円	円	円	円
88,000円未満		0	0	0	0	0	0	0	0	その月の社会保険料等控除後の給与等の金額の3.063％に相当する金額
88,000	89,000	130	0	0	0	0	0	0	0	3,200
89,000	90,000	180	0	0	0	0	0	0	0	3,200
90,000	91,000	230	0	0	0	0	0	0	0	3,200
91,000	92,000	290	0	0	0	0	0	0	0	3,200
92,000	93,000	340	0	0	0	0	0	0	0	3,300
93,000	94,000	390	0	0	0	0	0	0	0	3,300
94,000	95,000	440	0	0	0	0	0	0	0	3,300
95,000	96,000	490	0	0	0	0	0	0	0	3,400
96,000	97,000	540	0	0	0	0	0	0	0	3,400
97,000	98,000	590	0	0	0	0	0	0	0	3,500
98,000	99,000	640	0	0	0	0	0	0	0	3,500
99,000	101,000	720	0	0	0	0	0	0	0	3,600
101,000	103,000	830	0	0	0	0	0	0	0	3,600
103,000	105,000	930	0	0	0	0	0	0	0	3,700
105,000	107,000	1,030	0	0	0	0	0	0	0	3,800
107,000	109,000	1,130	0	0	0	0	0	0	0	3,800
109,000	111,000	1,240	0	0	0	0	0	0	0	3,900
111,000	113,000	1,340	0	0	0	0	0	0	0	4,000
113,000	115,000	1,440	0	0	0	0	0	0	0	4,100
115,000	117,000	1,540	0	0	0	0	0	0	0	4,100
117,000	119,000	1,640	0	0	0	0	0	0	0	4,200
119,000	121,000	1,750	120	0	0	0	0	0	0	4,300
121,000	123,000	1,850	220	0	0	0	0	0	0	4,500
123,000	125,000	1,950	330	0	0	0	0	0	0	4,800
125,000	127,000	2,050	430	0	0	0	0	0	0	5,100
127,000	129,000	2,150	530	0	0	0	0	0	0	5,400
129,000	131,000	2,260	630	0	0	0	0	0	0	5,700
131,000	133,000	2,360	740	0	0	0	0	0	0	6,000
133,000	135,000	2,460	840	0	0	0	0	0	0	6,300
135,000	137,000	2,550	930	0	0	0	0	0	0	6,600
137,000	139,000	2,610	990	0	0	0	0	0	0	6,800
139,000	141,000	2,680	1,050	0	0	0	0	0	0	7,100
141,000	143,000	2,740	1,110	0	0	0	0	0	0	7,500
143,000	145,000	2,800	1,170	0	0	0	0	0	0	7,800
145,000	147,000	2,860	1,240	0	0	0	0	0	0	8,100
147,000	149,000	2,920	1,300	0	0	0	0	0	0	8,400
149,000	151,000	2,980	1,360	0	0	0	0	0	0	8,700
151,000	153,000	3,050	1,430	0	0	0	0	0	0	9,000
153,000	155,000	3,120	1,500	0	0	0	0	0	0	9,300
155,000	157,000	3,200	1,570	0	0	0	0	0	0	9,600
157,000	159,000	3,270	1,640	0	0	0	0	0	0	9,900
159,000	161,000	3,340	1,720	100	0	0	0	0	0	10,200
161,000	163,000	3,410	1,790	170	0	0	0	0	0	10,500
163,000	165,000	3,480	1,860	250	0	0	0	0	0	10,800
165,000	167,000	3,550	1,930	320	0	0	0	0	0	11,100

122 WITHHOLDING INCOME TAX

Amount of salary after deduction of social insurance premiums		{A} Number of dependants								{B}
		0	1	2	3	4	5	6	7	
from	less					Amount of tax					Amount of tax
yen	yen	yen	yen	yen	yen	yen	yen	yen	yen	yen
167,000	169,000	3,620	2,000	390	0	0	0	0	0	11,400
169,000	171,000	3,700	2,070	460	0	0	0	0	0	11,700
171,000	173,000	3,770	2,140	530	0	0	0	0	0	12,000
173,000	175,000	3,840	2,220	600	0	0	0	0	0	12,400
175,000	177,000	3,910	2,290	670	0	0	0	0	0	12,700
177,000	179,000	3,980	2,360	750	0	0	0	0	0	13,200
179,000	181,000	4,050	2,430	820	0	0	0	0	0	13,900
181,000	183,000	4,120	2,500	890	0	0	0	0	0	14,600
183,000	185,000	4,200	2,570	960	0	0	0	0	0	15,300
185,000	187,000	4,270	2,640	1,030	0	0	0	0	0	16,000
187,000	189,000	4,340	2,720	1,100	0	0	0	0	0	16,700
189,000	191,000	4,410	2,790	1,170	0	0	0	0	0	17,500
191,000	193,000	4,480	2,860	1,250	0	0	0	0	0	18,100
193,000	195,000	4,550	2,930	1,320	0	0	0	0	0	18,800
195,000	197,000	4,630	3,000	1,390	0	0	0	0	0	19,500
197,000	199,000	4,700	3,070	1,460	0	0	0	0	0	20,200
199,000	201,000	4,770	3,140	1,530	0	0	0	0	0	20,900
201,000	203,000	4,840	3,220	1,600	0	0	0	0	0	21,500
203,000	205,000	4,910	3,290	1,670	0	0	0	0	0	22,200
205,000	207,000	4,980	3,360	1,750	130	0	0	0	0	22,700
207,000	209,000	5,050	3,430	1,820	200	0	0	0	0	23,300
209,000	211,000	5,130	3,500	1,890	280	0	0	0	0	23,900
211,000	213,000	5,200	3,570	1,960	350	0	0	0	0	24,400
213,000	215,000	5,270	3,640	2,030	420	0	0	0	0	25,000
215,000	217,000	5,340	3,720	2,100	490	0	0	0	0	25,500
217,000	219,000	5,410	3,790	2,170	560	0	0	0	0	26,100
219,000	221,000	5,480	3,860	2,250	630	0	0	0	0	26,800
221,000	224,000	5,560	3,950	2,340	710	0	0	0	0	27,400
224,000	227,000	5,680	4,060	2,440	830	0	0	0	0	28,400
227,000	230,000	5,780	4,170	2,550	930	0	0	0	0	29,300
230,000	233,000	5,890	4,280	2,650	1,040	0	0	0	0	30,300
233,000	236,000	5,990	4,380	2,770	1,140	0	0	0	0	31,300
236,000	239,000	6,110	4,490	2,870	1,260	0	0	0	0	32,400
239,000	242,000	6,210	4,590	2,980	1,360	0	0	0	0	33,400
242,000	245,000	6,320	4,710	3,080	1,470	0	0	0	0	34,400
245,000	248,000	6,420	4,810	3,200	1,570	0	0	0	0	35,400
248,000	251,000	6,530	4,920	3,300	1,680	0	0	0	0	36,400
251,000	254,000	6,640	5,020	3,410	1,790	170	0	0	0	37,500
254,000	257,000	6,750	5,140	3,510	1,900	290	0	0	0	38,500
257,000	260,000	6,850	5,240	3,620	2,000	390	0	0	0	39,400
260,000	263,000	6,960	5,350	3,730	2,110	500	0	0	0	40,400
263,000	266,000	7,070	5,450	3,840	2,220	600	0	0	0	41,500
266,000	269,000	7,180	5,560	3,940	2,330	710	0	0	0	42,500
269,000	272,000	7,280	5,670	4,050	2,430	820	0	0	0	43,500
272,000	275,000	7,390	5,780	4,160	2,540	930	0	0	0	44,500
275,000	278,000	7,490	5,880	4,270	2,640	1,030	0	0	0	45,500
278,000	281,000	7,610	5,990	4,370	2,760	1,140	0	0	0	46,600
281,000	284,000	7,710	6,100	4,480	2,860	1,250	0	0	0	47,600
284,000	287,000	7,820	6,210	4,580	2,970	1,360	0	0	0	48,600
287,000	290,000	7,920	6,310	4,700	3,070	1,460	0	0	0	49,500

¶ 4-250

源 泉 所 得 税 123

その月の社会保険料等控除後の給与等の金額		甲								乙
		扶養親族等の数								
		0人	1人	2人	3人	4人	5人	6人	7人	
以上	未満	税額								税額
円	円	円	円	円	円	円	円	円	円	円
167,000	169,000	3,620	2,000	390	0	0	0	0	0	11,400
169,000	171,000	3,700	2,070	460	0	0	0	0	0	11,700
171,000	173,000	3,770	2,140	530	0	0	0	0	0	12,000
173,000	175,000	3,840	2,220	600	0	0	0	0	0	12,400
175,000	177,000	3,910	2,290	670	0	0	0	0	0	12,700
177,000	179,000	3,980	2,360	750	0	0	0	0	0	13,200
179,000	181,000	4,050	2,430	820	0	0	0	0	0	13,900
181,000	183,000	4,120	2,500	890	0	0	0	0	0	14,600
183,000	185,000	4,200	2,570	960	0	0	0	0	0	15,300
185,000	187,000	4,270	2,640	1,030	0	0	0	0	0	16,000
187,000	189,000	4,340	2,720	1,100	0	0	0	0	0	16,700
189,000	191,000	4,410	2,790	1,170	0	0	0	0	0	17,500
191,000	193,000	4,480	2,860	1,250	0	0	0	0	0	18,100
193,000	195,000	4,550	2,930	1,320	0	0	0	0	0	18,800
195,000	197,000	4,630	3,000	1,390	0	0	0	0	0	19,500
197,000	199,000	4,700	3,070	1,460	0	0	0	0	0	20,200
199,000	201,000	4,770	3,140	1,530	0	0	0	0	0	20,900
201,000	203,000	4,840	3,220	1,600	0	0	0	0	0	21,500
203,000	205,000	4,910	3,290	1,670	0	0	0	0	0	22,200
205,000	207,000	4,980	3,360	1,750	130	0	0	0	0	22,700
207,000	209,000	5,050	3,430	1,820	200	0	0	0	0	23,300
209,000	211,000	5,130	3,500	1,890	280	0	0	0	0	23,900
211,000	213,000	5,200	3,570	1,960	350	0	0	0	0	24,400
213,000	215,000	5,270	3,640	2,030	420	0	0	0	0	25,000
215,000	217,000	5,340	3,720	2,100	490	0	0	0	0	25,500
217,000	219,000	5,410	3,790	2,170	560	0	0	0	0	26,100
219,000	221,000	5,480	3,860	2,250	630	0	0	0	0	26,800
221,000	224,000	5,560	3,950	2,340	710	0	0	0	0	27,400
224,000	227,000	5,680	4,060	2,440	830	0	0	0	0	28,400
227,000	230,000	5,780	4,170	2,550	930	0	0	0	0	29,300
230,000	233,000	5,890	4,280	2,650	1,040	0	0	0	0	30,300
233,000	236,000	5,990	4,380	2,770	1,140	0	0	0	0	31,300
236,000	239,000	6,110	4,490	2,870	1,260	0	0	0	0	32,400
239,000	242,000	6,210	4,590	2,980	1,360	0	0	0	0	33,400
242,000	245,000	6,320	4,710	3,080	1,470	0	0	0	0	34,400
245,000	248,000	6,420	4,810	3,200	1,570	0	0	0	0	35,400
248,000	251,000	0,530	4,920	3,300	1,680	0	0	0	0	36,400
251,000	254,000	6,640	5,020	3,410	1,790	170	0	0	0	37,500
254,000	257,000	6,750	5,140	3,510	1,900	290	0	0	0	38,500
257,000	260,000	6,850	5,240	3,620	2,000	390	0	0	0	39,400
260,000	263,000	6,960	5,350	3,730	2,110	500	0	0	0	40,400
263,000	266,000	7,070	5,450	3,840	2,220	600	0	0	0	41,500
266,000	269,000	7,180	5,560	3,940	2,330	710	0	0	0	42,500
269,000	272,000	7,280	5,670	4,050	2,430	820	0	0	0	43,500
272,000	275,000	7,390	5,780	4,160	2,540	930	0	0	0	44,500
275,000	278,000	7,490	5,880	4,270	2,640	1,030	0	0	0	45,500
278,000	281,000	7,610	5,990	4,370	2,760	1,140	0	0	0	46,600
281,000	284,000	7,710	6,100	4,480	2,860	1,250	0	0	0	47,600
284,000	287,000	7,820	6,210	4,580	2,970	1,360	0	0	0	48,600
287,000	290,000	7,920	6,310	4,700	3,070	1,460	0	0	0	49,500

124 WITHHOLDING INCOME TAX

| Amount of salary after deduction of social insurance premiums | | {A} Number of dependants | | | | | | | | {B} |
from	less	0	1	2	3	4	5	6	7	Amount of tax
					Amount of tax					
yen	yen	yen	yen	yen	yen	yen	yen	yen	yen	yen
290,000	293,000	8,040	6,420	4,800	3,190	1,570	0	0	0	50,500
293,000	296,000	8,140	6,520	4,910	3,290	1,670	0	0	0	51,600
296,000	299,000	8,250	6,640	5,010	3,400	1,790	160	0	0	52,300
299,000	302,000	8,420	6,740	5,130	3,510	1,890	280	0	0	52,900
302,000	305,000	8,670	6,860	5,250	3,630	2,010	400	0	0	53,500
305,000	308,000	8,910	6,980	5,370	3,760	2,130	520	0	0	54,200
308,000	311,000	9,160	7,110	5,490	3,880	2,260	640	0	0	54,800
311,000	314,000	9,400	7,230	5,620	4,000	2,380	770	0	0	55,400
314,000	317,000	9,650	7,350	5,740	4,120	2,500	890	0	0	56,100
317,000	320,000	9,890	7,470	5,860	4,250	2,620	1,010	0	0	56,800
320,000	323,000	10,140	7,600	5,980	4,370	2,750	1,130	0	0	57,700
323,000	326,000	10,380	7,720	6,110	4,490	2,870	1,260	0	0	58,500
326,000	329,000	10,630	7,840	6,230	4,610	2,990	1,380	0	0	59,300
329,000	332,000	10,870	7,960	6,350	4,740	3,110	1,500	0	0	60,200
332,000	335,000	11,120	8,090	6,470	4,860	3,240	1,620	0	0	61,100
335,000	338,000	11,360	8,210	6,600	4,980	3,360	1,750	130	0	62,000
338,000	341,000	11,610	8,370	6,720	5,110	3,480	1,870	260	0	63,000
341,000	344,000	11,850	8,620	6,840	5,230	3,600	1,990	380	0	64,000
344,000	347,000	12,100	8,860	6,960	5,350	3,730	2,110	500	0	65,000
347,000	350,000	12,340	9,110	7,090	5,470	3,850	2,240	620	0	66,200
350,000	353,000	12,590	9,350	7,210	5,600	3,970	2,360	750	0	67,200
353,000	356,000	12,830	9,600	7,330	5,720	4,090	2,480	870	0	68,200
356,000	359,000	13,080	9,840	7,450	5,840	4,220	2,600	990	0	69,200
359,000	362,000	13,320	10,090	7,580	5,960	4,340	2,730	1,110	0	70,200
362,000	365,000	13,570	10,330	7,700	6,090	4,460	2,850	1,240	0	71,300
365,000	368,000	13,810	10,580	7,820	6,210	4,580	2,970	1,360	0	72,300
368,000	371,000	14,060	10,820	7,940	6,330	4,710	3,090	1,480	0	73,200
371,000	374,000	14,300	11,070	8,070	6,450	4,830	3,220	1,600	0	74,200
374,000	377,000	14,550	11,310	8,190	6,580	4,950	3,340	1,730	100	75,100
377,000	380,000	14,790	11,560	8,320	6,700	5,070	3,460	1,850	220	76,100
380,000	383,000	15,040	11,800	8,570	6,820	5,200	3,580	1,970	350	77,000
383,000	386,000	15,280	12,050	8,810	6,940	5,320	3,710	2,090	470	77,900
386,000	389,000	15,530	12,290	9,060	7,070	5,440	3,830	2,220	590	78,800
389,000	392,000	15,770	12,540	9,300	7,190	5,560	3,950	2,340	710	80,600
392,000	395,000	16,020	12,780	9,550	7,310	5,690	4,070	2,460	840	82,300
395,000	398,000	16,260	13,030	9,790	7,430	5,810	4,200	2,580	960	83,900
398,000	401,000	16,510	13,270	10,040	7,560	5,930	4,320	2,710	1,080	85,700
401,000	404,000	16,750	13,520	10,280	7,680	6,050	4,440	2,830	1,200	87,400
404,000	407,000	17,000	13,760	10,530	7,800	6,180	4,560	2,950	1,330	89,000
407,000	410,000	17,240	14,010	10,770	7,920	6,300	4,690	3,070	1,450	90,800
410,000	413,000	17,490	14,250	11,020	8,050	6,420	4,810	3,200	1,570	92,500
413,000	416,000	17,730	14,500	11,260	8,170	6,540	4,930	3,320	1,690	94,100
416,000	419,000	17,980	14,740	11,510	8,290	6,670	5,050	3,440	1,820	95,900
419,000	422,000	18,220	14,990	11,750	8,530	6,790	5,180	3,560	1,940	97,600
422,000	425,000	18,470	15,230	12,000	8,770	6,910	5,300	3,690	2,060	99,200
425,000	428,000	18,710	15,480	12,240	9,020	7,030	5,420	3,810	2,180	101,000
428,000	431,000	18,960	15,720	12,490	9,260	7,160	5,540	3,930	2,310	102,600
431,000	434,000	19,210	15,970	12,730	9,510	7,280	5,670	4,050	2,430	104,300
434,000	437,000	19,450	16,210	12,980	9,750	7,400	5,790	4,180	2,550	106,100
437,000	440,000	19,700	16,460	13,220	10,000	7,520	5,910	4,300	2,680	107,700

¶ 4-250

源 泉 所 得 税 125

その月の社会保険料等控除後の給与等の金額		甲								乙
		扶養親族等の数								
		0人	1人	2人	3人	4人	5人	6人	7人	
以上	未満	税額								税額
円	円	円	円	円	円	円	円	円	円	円
290,000	293,000	8,040	6,420	4,800	3,190	1,570	0	0	0	50,500
293,000	296,000	8,140	6,520	4,910	3,290	1,670	0	0	0	51,600
296,000	299,000	8,250	6,640	5,010	3,400	1,790	160	0	0	52,300
299,000	302,000	8,420	6,740	5,130	3,510	1,890	280	0	0	52,900
302,000	305,000	8,670	6,860	5,250	3,630	2,010	400	0	0	53,500
305,000	308,000	8,910	6,980	5,370	3,760	2,130	520	0	0	54,200
308,000	311,000	9,160	7,110	5,490	3,880	2,260	640	0	0	54,800
311,000	314,000	9,400	7,230	5,620	4,000	2,380	770	0	0	55,400
314,000	317,000	9,650	7,350	5,740	4,120	2,500	890	0	0	56,100
317,000	320,000	9,890	7,470	5,860	4,250	2,620	1,010	0	0	56,800
320,000	323,000	10,140	7,600	5,980	4,370	2,750	1,130	0	0	57,700
323,000	326,000	10,380	7,720	6,110	4,490	2,870	1,260	0	0	58,500
326,000	329,000	10,630	7,840	6,230	4,610	2,990	1,380	0	0	59,300
329,000	332,000	10,870	7,960	6,350	4,740	3,110	1,500	0	0	60,200
332,000	335,000	11,120	8,090	6,470	4,860	3,240	1,620	0	0	61,100
335,000	338,000	11,360	8,210	6,600	4,980	3,360	1,750	130	0	62,000
338,000	341,000	11,610	8,370	6,720	5,110	3,480	1,870	260	0	63,000
341,000	344,000	11,850	8,620	6,840	5,230	3,600	1,990	380	0	64,000
344,000	347,000	12,100	8,860	6,960	5,350	3,730	2,110	500	0	65,000
347,000	350,000	12,340	9,110	7,090	5,470	3,850	2,240	620	0	66,200
350,000	353,000	12,590	9,350	7,210	5,600	3,970	2,360	750	0	67,200
353,000	356,000	12,830	9,600	7,330	5,720	4,090	2,480	870	0	68,200
356,000	359,000	13,080	9,840	7,450	5,840	4,220	2,600	990	0	69,200
359,000	362,000	13,320	10,090	7,580	5,960	4,340	2,730	1,110	0	70,200
362,000	365,000	13,570	10,330	7,700	6,090	4,460	2,850	1,240	0	71,300
365,000	368,000	13,810	10,580	7,820	6,210	4,580	2,970	1,360	0	72,300
368,000	371,000	14,060	10,820	7,940	6,330	4,710	3,090	1,480	0	73,200
371,000	374,000	14,300	11,070	8,070	6,450	4,830	3,220	1,600	0	74,200
374,000	377,000	14,550	11,310	8,190	6,580	4,950	3,340	1,730	100	75,100
377,000	380,000	14,790	11,560	8,320	6,700	5,070	3,460	1,850	220	76,100
380,000	383,000	15,040	11,800	8,570	6,820	5,200	3,580	1,970	350	77,000
383,000	386,000	15,280	12,050	8,810	6,940	5,320	3,710	2,090	470	77,900
386,000	389,000	15,530	12,290	9,060	7,070	5,440	3,830	2,220	590	78,800
389,000	392,000	15,770	12,540	9,300	7,190	5,560	3,950	2,340	710	80,600
392,000	395,000	16,020	12,780	9,550	7,310	5,690	4,070	2,460	840	82,300
395,000	398,000	16,260	13,030	9,790	7,430	5,810	4,200	2,580	960	83,900
398,000	401,000	16,510	13,270	10,040	7,560	5,930	4,320	2,710	1,080	85,700
401,000	404,000	16,750	13,520	10,280	7,680	6,050	4,440	2,830	1,200	87,400
404,000	407,000	17,000	13,760	10,530	7,800	6,180	4,560	2,950	1,330	89,000
407,000	410,000	17,240	14,010	10,770	7,920	6,300	4,690	3,070	1,450	90,800
410,000	413,000	17,490	14,250	11,020	8,050	6,420	4,810	3,200	1,570	92,500
413,000	416,000	17,730	14,500	11,260	8,170	6,540	4,930	3,320	1,690	94,100
416,000	419,000	17,980	14,740	11,510	8,290	6,670	5,050	3,440	1,820	95,900
419,000	422,000	18,220	14,990	11,750	8,530	6,790	5,180	3,560	1,940	97,600
422,000	425,000	18,470	15,230	12,000	8,770	6,910	5,300	3,690	2,060	99,200
425,000	428,000	18,710	15,480	12,240	9,020	7,030	5,420	3,810	2,180	101,000
428,000	431,000	18,960	15,720	12,490	9,260	7,160	5,540	3,930	2,310	102,600
431,000	434,000	19,210	15,970	12,730	9,510	7,280	5,670	4,050	2,430	104,300
434,000	437,000	19,450	16,210	12,980	9,750	7,400	5,790	4,180	2,550	106,100
437,000	440,000	19,700	16,460	13,220	10,000	7,520	5,910	4,300	2,680	107,700

126   WITHHOLDING INCOME TAX

Amount of salary after deduction of social insurance premiums		{A} Number of dependants								{B}
from	less	0	1	2	3	4	5	6	7	Amount of tax
yen	yen	yen	yen	yen	yen	yen	yen	yen	yen	yen
440,000	443,000	20,090	16,700	13,470	10,240	7,650	6,030	4,420	2,800	109,500
443,000	446,000	20,580	16,950	13,710	10,490	7,770	6,160	4,540	2,920	111,200
446,000	449,000	21,070	17,190	13,960	10,730	7,890	6,280	4,670	3,040	112,800
449,000	452,000	21,560	17,440	14,200	10,980	8,010	6,400	4,790	3,170	114,600
452,000	455,000	22,050	17,680	14,450	11,220	8,140	6,520	4,910	3,290	116,300
455,000	458,000	22,540	17,930	14,690	11,470	8,260	6,650	5,030	3,410	117,900
458,000	461,000	23,030	18,170	14,940	11,710	8,470	6,770	5,160	3,530	119,700
461,000	464,000	23,520	18,420	15,180	11,960	8,720	6,890	5,280	3,660	121,400
464,000	467,000	24,010	18,660	15,430	12,200	8,960	7,010	5,400	3,780	123,000
467,000	470,000	24,500	18,910	15,670	12,450	9,210	7,140	5,520	3,900	124,800
470,000	473,000	24,990	19,150	15,920	12,690	9,450	7,260	5,650	4,020	126,500
473,000	476,000	25,480	19,400	16,160	12,940	9,700	7,380	5,770	4,150	128,100
476,000	479,000	25,970	19,640	16,410	13,180	9,940	7,500	5,890	4,270	129,900
479,000	482,000	26,460	20,000	16,650	13,430	10,190	7,630	6,010	4,390	131,600
482,000	485,000	26,950	20,490	16,900	13,670	10,430	7,750	6,140	4,510	133,200
485,000	488,000	27,440	20,980	17,140	13,920	10,680	7,870	6,260	4,640	135,000
488,000	491,000	27,930	21,470	17,390	14,160	10,920	7,990	6,380	4,760	136,600
491,000	494,000	28,420	21,960	17,630	14,410	11,170	8,120	6,500	4,880	138,300
494,000	497,000	28,910	22,450	17,880	14,650	11,410	8,240	6,630	5,000	140,100
497,000	500,000	29,400	22,940	18,120	14,900	11,660	8,420	6,750	5,130	141,700
500,000	503,000	29,890	23,430	18,370	15,140	11,900	8,670	6,870	5,250	143,500
503,000	506,000	30,380	23,920	18,610	15,390	12,150	8,910	6,990	5,370	145,200
506,000	509,000	30,880	24,410	18,860	15,630	12,390	9,160	7,120	5,490	146,800
509,000	512,000	31,370	24,900	19,100	15,880	12,640	9,400	7,240	5,620	148,600
512,000	515,000	31,860	25,390	19,350	16,120	12,890	9,650	7,360	5,740	150,300
515,000	518,000	32,350	25,880	19,590	16,370	13,130	9,890	7,480	5,860	151,900
518,000	521,000	32,840	26,370	19,900	16,610	13,380	10,140	7,610	5,980	153,700
521,000	524,000	33,330	26,860	20,390	16,860	13,620	10,380	7,730	6,110	155,400
524,000	527,000	33,820	27,350	20,880	17,100	13,870	10,630	7,850	6,230	157,000
527,000	530,000	34,310	27,840	21,370	17,350	14,110	10,870	7,970	6,350	158,800
530,000	533,000	34,800	28,330	21,860	17,590	14,360	11,120	8,100	6,470	160,300
533,000	536,000	35,290	28,820	22,350	17,840	14,600	11,360	8,220	6,600	161,900
536,000	539,000	35,780	29,310	22,840	18,080	14,850	11,610	8,380	6,720	163,500
539,000	542,000	36,270	29,800	23,330	18,330	15,090	11,850	8,630	6,840	165,000
542,000	545,000	36,760	30,290	23,820	18,570	15,340	12,100	8,870	6,960	166,600
545,000	548,000	37,250	30,780	24,310	18,820	15,580	12,340	9,120	7,090	168,200
548,000	551,000	37,740	31,270	24,800	19,060	15,830	12,590	9,360	7,210	169,800
551,000	554,000	38,280	31,810	25,340	19,330	16,100	12,860	9,630	7,350	171,300
554,000	557,000	38,830	32,370	25,890	19,600	16,380	13,140	9,900	7,480	173,000
557,000	560,000	39,380	32,920	26,440	19,980	16,650	13,420	10,180	7,630	174,500
560,000	563,000	39,930	33,470	27,000	20,530	16,930	13,690	10,460	7,760	175,900
563,000	566,000	40,480	34,020	27,550	21,080	17,200	13,970	10,730	7,900	177,300
566,000	569,000	41,030	34,570	28,100	21,630	17,480	14,240	11,010	8,040	178,900
569,000	572,000	41,590	35,120	28,650	22,190	17,760	14,520	11,280	8,180	180,300
572,000	575,000	42,140	35,670	29,200	22,740	18,030	14,790	11,560	8,330	181,800
575,000	578,000	42,690	36,230	29,750	23,290	18,310	15,070	11,830	8,610	183,300
578,000	581,000	43,240	36,780	30,300	23,840	18,580	15,350	12,110	8,880	184,700
581,000	584,000	43,790	37,330	30,850	24,390	18,860	15,620	12,380	9,160	186,200
584,000	587,000	44,340	37,880	31,410	24,940	19,130	15,900	12,660	9,430	187,700
587,000	590,000	44,890	38,430	31,960	25,490	19,410	16,170	12,940	9,710	189,200

¶ 4-250

その月の社会保険料等控除後の給与等の金額		甲								乙
		扶養親族等の数								
以上	未満	0人	1人	2人	3人	4人	5人	6人	7人	
		税額								税額
円	円	円	円	円	円	円	円	円	円	円
440,000	443,000	20,090	16,700	13,470	10,240	7,650	6,030	4,420	2,800	109,500
443,000	446,000	20,580	16,950	13,710	10,490	7,770	6,160	4,540	2,920	111,200
446,000	449,000	21,070	17,190	13,960	10,730	7,890	6,280	4,670	3,040	112,800
449,000	452,000	21,560	17,440	14,200	10,980	8,010	6,400	4,790	3,170	114,600
452,000	455,000	22,050	17,680	14,450	11,220	8,140	6,520	4,910	3,290	116,300
455,000	458,000	22,540	17,930	14,690	11,470	8,260	6,650	5,030	3,410	117,900
458,000	461,000	23,030	18,170	14,940	11,710	8,470	6,770	5,160	3,530	119,700
461,000	464,000	23,520	18,420	15,180	11,960	8,720	6,890	5,280	3,660	121,400
464,000	467,000	24,010	18,660	15,430	12,200	8,960	7,010	5,400	3,780	123,000
467,000	470,000	24,500	18,910	15,670	12,450	9,210	7,140	5,520	3,900	124,800
470,000	473,000	24,990	19,150	15,920	12,690	9,450	7,260	5,650	4,020	126,500
473,000	476,000	25,480	19,400	16,160	12,940	9,700	7,380	5,770	4,150	128,100
476,000	479,000	25,970	19,640	16,410	13,180	9,940	7,500	5,890	4,270	129,900
479,000	482,000	26,460	20,000	16,650	13,430	10,190	7,630	6,010	4,390	131,600
482,000	485,000	26,950	20,490	16,900	13,670	10,430	7,750	6,140	4,510	133,200
485,000	488,000	27,440	20,980	17,140	13,920	10,680	7,870	6,260	4,640	135,000
488,000	491,000	27,930	21,470	17,390	14,160	10,920	7,990	6,380	4,760	136,600
491,000	494,000	28,420	21,960	17,630	14,410	11,170	8,120	6,500	4,880	138,300
494,000	497,000	28,910	22,450	17,880	14,650	11,410	8,240	6,630	5,000	140,100
497,000	500,000	29,400	22,940	18,120	14,900	11,660	8,420	6,750	5,130	141,700
500,000	503,000	29,890	23,430	18,370	15,140	11,900	8,670	6,870	5,250	143,500
503,000	506,000	30,380	23,920	18,610	15,390	12,150	8,910	6,990	5,370	145,200
506,000	509,000	30,880	24,410	18,860	15,630	12,390	9,160	7,120	5,490	146,800
509,000	512,000	31,370	24,900	19,100	15,880	12,640	9,400	7,240	5,620	148,600
512,000	515,000	31,860	25,390	19,350	16,120	12,890	9,650	7,360	5,740	150,300
515,000	518,000	32,350	25,880	19,590	16,370	13,130	9,890	7,480	5,860	151,900
518,000	521,000	32,840	26,370	19,900	16,610	13,380	10,140	7,610	5,980	153,700
521,000	524,000	33,330	26,860	20,390	16,860	13,620	10,380	7,730	6,110	155,400
524,000	527,000	33,820	27,350	20,880	17,100	13,870	10,630	7,850	6,230	157,000
527,000	530,000	34,310	27,840	21,370	17,350	14,110	10,870	7,970	6,350	158,800
530,000	533,000	34,800	28,330	21,860	17,590	14,360	11,120	8,100	6,470	160,300
533,000	536,000	35,290	28,820	22,350	17,840	14,600	11,360	8,220	6,600	161,900
536,000	539,000	35,780	29,310	22,840	18,080	14,850	11,610	8,380	6,720	163,500
539,000	542,000	36,270	29,800	23,330	18,330	15,090	11,850	8,630	6,840	165,000
542,000	545,000	36,760	30,290	23,820	18,570	15,340	12,100	8,870	6,960	166,600
545,000	548,000	37,250	30,780	24,310	18,820	15,580	12,340	9,120	7,090	168,200
548,000	551,000	37,740	31,270	24,000	19,060	15,830	12,590	9,360	7,210	169,000
551,000	554,000	38,280	31,810	25,340	19,330	16,100	12,860	9,630	7,350	171,300
554,000	557,000	38,830	32,370	25,890	19,600	16,380	13,140	9,900	7,480	173,000
557,000	560,000	39,380	32,920	26,440	19,980	16,650	13,420	10,180	7,630	174,500
560,000	563,000	39,930	33,470	27,000	20,530	16,930	13,690	10,460	7,760	175,900
563,000	566,000	40,480	34,020	27,550	21,080	17,200	13,970	10,730	7,900	177,300
566,000	569,000	41,030	34,570	28,100	21,630	17,480	14,240	11,010	8,040	178,900
569,000	572,000	41,590	35,120	28,650	22,190	17,760	14,520	11,280	8,180	180,300
572,000	575,000	42,140	35,670	29,200	22,740	18,030	14,790	11,560	8,330	181,800
575,000	578,000	42,690	36,230	29,750	23,290	18,310	15,070	11,830	8,610	183,300
578,000	581,000	43,240	36,780	30,300	23,840	18,580	15,350	12,110	8,880	184,700
581,000	584,000	43,790	37,330	30,850	24,390	18,860	15,620	12,380	9,160	186,200
584,000	587,000	44,340	37,880	31,410	24,940	19,130	15,900	12,660	9,430	187,700
587,000	590,000	44,890	38,430	31,960	25,490	19,410	16,170	12,940	9,710	189,200

128 WITHHOLDING INCOME TAX

Amount of salary after deduction of social insurance premiums		{A} Number of dependants								{B}
		0	1	2	3	4	5	6	7	
from	less				Amount of tax					Amount of tax
yen	yen	yen	yen	yen	yen	yen	yen	yen	yen	yen
590,000	593,000	45,440	38,980	32,510	26,050	19,680	16,450	13,210	9,990	190,600
593,000	596,000	46,000	39,530	33,060	26,600	20,130	16,720	13,490	10,260	192,100
596,000	599,000	46,550	40,080	33,610	27,150	20,690	17,000	13,760	10,540	193,600
599,000	602,000	47,100	40,640	34,160	27,700	21,240	17,280	14,040	10,810	195,000
602,000	605,000	47,650	41,190	34,710	28,250	21,790	17,550	14,310	11,090	196,500
605,000	608,000	48,200	41,740	35,270	28,800	22,340	17,830	14,590	11,360	198,000
608,000	611,000	48,750	42,290	35,820	29,350	22,890	18,100	14,870	11,640	199,400
611,000	614,000	49,300	42,840	36,370	29,910	23,440	18,380	15,140	11,920	200,900
614,000	617,000	49,860	43,390	36,920	30,460	23,990	18,650	15,420	12,190	202,400
617,000	620,000	50,410	43,940	37,470	31,010	24,540	18,930	15,690	12,470	203,900
620,000	623,000	50,960	44,500	38,020	31,560	25,100	19,210	15,970	12,740	205,300
623,000	626,000	51,510	45,050	38,570	32,110	25,650	19,480	16,240	13,020	206,800
626,000	629,000	52,060	45,600	39,120	32,660	26,200	19,760	16,520	13,290	208,300
629,000	632,000	52,610	46,150	39,680	33,210	26,750	20,280	16,800	13,570	209,700
632,000	635,000	53,160	46,700	40,230	33,760	27,300	20,830	17,070	13,840	211,200
635,000	638,000	53,710	47,250	40,780	34,320	27,850	21,380	17,350	14,120	212,700
638,000	641,000	54,270	47,800	41,330	34,870	28,400	21,930	17,620	14,400	214,100
641,000	644,000	54,820	48,350	41,880	35,420	28,960	22,480	17,900	14,670	215,600
644,000	647,000	55,370	48,910	42,430	35,970	29,510	23,030	18,170	14,950	217,000
647,000	650,000	55,920	49,460	42,980	36,520	30,060	23,590	18,450	15,220	218,000
650,000	653,000	56,470	50,010	43,540	37,070	30,610	24,140	18,730	15,500	219,000
653,000	656,000	57,020	50,560	44,090	37,620	31,160	24,690	19,000	15,770	220,000
656,000	659,000	57,570	51,110	44,640	38,180	31,710	25,240	19,280	16,050	221,000
659,000	662,000	58,130	51,660	45,190	38,730	32,260	25,790	19,550	16,330	222,100
662,000	665,000	58,680	52,210	45,740	39,280	32,810	26,340	19,880	16,600	223,100
665,000	668,000	59,230	52,770	46,290	39,830	33,370	26,890	20,430	16,880	224,100
668,000	671,000	59,780	53,320	46,840	40,380	33,920	27,440	20,980	17,150	225,000
671,000	674,000	60,330	53,870	47,390	40,930	34,470	28,000	21,530	17,430	226,000
674,000	677,000	60,880	54,420	47,950	41,480	35,020	28,550	22,080	17,700	227,100
677,000	680,000	61,430	54,970	48,500	42,030	35,570	29,100	22,640	17,980	228,100
680,000	683,000	61,980	55,520	49,050	42,590	36,120	29,650	23,190	18,260	229,100
683,000	686,000	62,540	56,070	49,600	43,140	36,670	30,200	23,740	18,530	230,100
686,000	689,000	63,090	56,620	50,150	43,690	37,230	30,750	24,290	18,810	231,200
689,000	692,000	63,640	57,180	50,700	44,240	37,780	31,300	24,840	19,080	232,700
692,000	695,000	64,190	57,730	51,250	44,790	38,330	31,860	25,390	19,360	234,200
695,000	698,000	64,740	58,280	51,810	45,340	38,880	32,410	25,940	19,630	235,700
698,000	701,000	65,290	58,830	52,360	45,890	39,430	32,960	26,490	20,030	237,300
701,000	704,000	65,840	59,380	52,910	46,450	39,980	33,510	27,050	20,580	238,900
704,000	707,000	66,400	59,930	53,460	47,000	40,530	34,060	27,600	21,130	240,400
707,000	710,000	66,950	60,480	54,010	47,550	41,090	34,610	28,150	21,690	242,000
710,000	713,000	67,500	61,040	54,560	48,100	41,640	35,160	28,700	22,240	243,500
713,000	716,000	68,050	61,590	55,110	48,650	42,190	35,710	29,250	22,790	245,000
716,000	719,000	68,600	62,140	55,660	49,200	42,740	36,270	29,800	23,340	246,600
719,000	722,000	69,150	62,690	56,220	49,750	43,290	36,820	30,350	23,890	248,100
722,000	725,000	69,700	63,240	56,770	50,300	43,840	37,370	30,910	24,440	249,700
725,000	728,000	70,260	63,790	57,320	50,860	44,390	37,920	31,460	24,990	251,300
728,000	731,000	70,810	64,340	57,870	51,410	44,940	38,470	32,010	25,550	252,800
731,000	734,000	71,360	64,890	58,420	51,960	45,500	39,020	32,560	26,100	254,300
734,000	737,000	71,910	65,450	58,970	52,510	46,050	39,570	33,110	26,650	255,900
737,000	740,000	72,460	66,000	59,520	53,060	46,600	40,130	33,660	27,200	257,400

¶ 4-250

源　泉　所　得　税　129

その月の社会保険料等控除後の給与等の金額		甲								乙
		扶養親族等の数								
		0人	1人	2人	3人	4人	5人	6人	7人	
以上	未満	税額								税額
円	円	円	円	円	円	円	円	円	円	円
590,000	593,000	45,440	38,980	32,510	26,050	19,680	16,450	13,210	9,990	190,600
593,000	596,000	46,000	39,530	33,060	26,600	20,130	16,720	13,490	10,260	192,100
596,000	599,000	46,550	40,080	33,610	27,150	20,690	17,000	13,760	10,540	193,600
599,000	602,000	47,100	40,640	34,160	27,700	21,240	17,280	14,040	10,810	195,000
602,000	605,000	47,650	41,190	34,710	28,250	21,790	17,550	14,310	11,090	196,500
605,000	608,000	48,200	41,740	35,270	28,800	22,340	17,830	14,590	11,360	198,000
608,000	611,000	48,750	42,290	35,820	29,350	22,890	18,100	14,870	11,640	199,400
611,000	614,000	49,300	42,840	36,370	29,910	23,440	18,380	15,140	11,920	200,900
614,000	617,000	49,860	43,390	36,920	30,460	23,990	18,650	15,420	12,190	202,400
617,000	620,000	50,410	43,940	37,470	31,010	24,540	18,930	15,690	12,470	203,900
620,000	623,000	50,960	44,500	38,020	31,560	25,100	19,210	15,970	12,740	205,300
623,000	626,000	51,510	45,050	38,570	32,110	25,650	19,480	16,240	13,020	206,800
626,000	629,000	52,060	45,600	39,120	32,660	26,200	19,760	16,520	13,290	208,300
629,000	632,000	52,610	46,150	39,680	33,210	26,750	20,280	16,800	13,570	209,700
632,000	635,000	53,160	46,700	40,230	33,760	27,300	20,830	17,070	13,840	211,200
635,000	638,000	53,710	47,250	40,780	34,320	27,850	21,380	17,350	14,120	212,700
638,000	641,000	54,270	47,800	41,330	34,870	28,400	21,930	17,620	14,400	214,100
641,000	644,000	54,820	48,350	41,880	35,420	28,960	22,480	17,900	14,670	215,600
644,000	647,000	55,370	48,910	42,430	35,970	29,510	23,030	18,170	14,950	217,000
647,000	650,000	55,920	49,460	42,980	36,520	30,060	23,590	18,450	15,220	218,000
650,000	653,000	56,470	50,010	43,540	37,070	30,610	24,140	18,730	15,500	219,000
653,000	656,000	57,020	50,560	44,090	37,620	31,160	24,690	19,000	15,770	220,000
656,000	659,000	57,570	51,110	44,640	38,180	31,710	25,240	19,280	16,050	221,000
659,000	662,000	58,130	51,660	45,190	38,730	32,260	25,790	19,550	16,330	222,100
662,000	665,000	58,680	52,210	45,740	39,280	32,810	26,340	19,880	16,600	223,100
665,000	668,000	59,230	52,770	46,290	39,830	33,370	26,890	20,430	16,880	224,100
668,000	671,000	59,780	53,320	46,840	40,380	33,920	27,440	20,980	17,150	225,000
671,000	674,000	60,330	53,870	47,390	40,930	34,470	28,000	21,530	17,430	226,000
674,000	677,000	60,880	54,420	47,950	41,480	35,020	28,550	22,080	17,700	227,100
677,000	680,000	61,430	54,970	48,500	42,030	35,570	29,100	22,640	17,980	228,100
680,000	683,000	61,980	55,520	49,050	42,590	36,120	29,650	23,190	18,260	229,100
683,000	686,000	62,540	56,070	49,600	43,140	36,670	30,200	23,740	18,530	230,100
686,000	689,000	63,090	56,620	50,150	43,690	37,230	30,750	24,290	18,810	231,200
689,000	692,000	63,640	57,180	50,700	44,240	37,780	31,300	24,840	19,080	232,700
692,000	695,000	64,190	57,730	51,250	44,790	38,330	31,860	25,390	19,360	234,200
695,000	698,000	64,740	58,280	51,810	45,340	38,880	32,410	25,940	19,630	235,700
698,000	701,000	65,290	58,830	52,360	45,890	39,430	32,900	26,490	20,030	237,300
701,000	704,000	65,840	59,380	52,910	46,450	39,980	33,510	27,050	20,580	238,900
704,000	707,000	66,400	59,930	53,460	47,000	40,530	34,060	27,600	21,130	240,400
707,000	710,000	66,950	60,480	54,010	47,550	41,090	34,610	28,150	21,690	242,000
710,000	713,000	67,500	61,040	54,560	48,100	41,640	35,160	28,700	22,240	243,500
713,000	716,000	68,050	61,590	55,110	48,650	42,190	35,710	29,250	22,790	245,000
716,000	719,000	68,600	62,140	55,660	49,200	42,740	36,270	29,800	23,340	246,600
719,000	722,000	69,150	62,690	56,220	49,750	43,290	36,820	30,350	23,890	248,100
722,000	725,000	69,700	63,240	56,770	50,300	43,840	37,370	30,910	24,440	249,700
725,000	728,000	70,260	63,790	57,320	50,860	44,390	37,920	31,460	24,990	251,300
728,000	731,000	70,810	64,340	57,870	51,410	44,940	38,470	32,010	25,550	252,800
731,000	734,000	71,360	64,890	58,420	51,960	45,500	39,020	32,560	26,100	254,300
734,000	737,000	71,910	65,450	58,970	52,510	46,050	39,570	33,110	26,650	255,900
737,000	740,000	72,460	66,000	59,520	53,060	46,600	40,130	33,660	27,200	257,400

130   WITHHOLDING INCOME TAX

Amount of salary after deduction of social insurance premiums		{A} Number of dependants								{B}
		0	1	2	3	4	5	6	7	
from	less					Amount of tax				Amount of tax
yen	yen	yen	yen	yen	yen	yen	yen	yen	yen	yen
740,000	743,000	73,010	66,550	60,080	53,610	47,150	40,680	34,210	27,750	259,000
743,000	746,000	73,560	67,100	60,630	54,160	47,700	41,230	34,770	28,300	260,600
746,000	749,000	74,110	67,650	61,180	54,720	48,250	41,780	35,320	28,850	262,100
749,000	752,000	74,670	68,200	61,730	55,270	48,800	42,330	35,870	29,400	263,600
752,000	755,000	75,220	68,750	62,280	55,820	49,360	42,880	36,420	29,960	265,200
755,000	758,000	75,770	69,310	62,830	56,370	49,910	43,430	36,970	30,510	266,700
758,000	761,000	76,320	69,860	63,380	56,920	50,460	43,980	37,520	31,060	268,200
761,000	764,000	76,870	70,410	63,940	57,470	51,010	44,540	38,070	31,610	269,900
764,000	767,000	77,420	70,960	64,490	58,020	51,560	45,090	38,620	32,160	271,400
767,000	770,000	77,970	71,510	65,040	58,570	52,110	45,640	39,180	32,710	272,900
770,000	773,000	78,530	72,060	65,590	59,130	52,660	46,190	39,730	33,260	274,400
773,000	776,000	79,080	72,610	66,140	59,680	53,210	46,740	40,280	33,820	276,000
776,000	779,000	79,630	73,160	66,690	60,230	53,770	47,290	40,830	34,370	277,500
779,000	782,000	80,180	73,720	67,240	60,780	54,320	47,840	41,380	34,920	279,000
782,000	785,000	80,730	74,270	67,790	61,330	54,870	48,400	41,930	35,470	280,700
785,000	788,000	81,280	74,820	68,350	61,880	55,420	48,950	42,480	36,020	282,200
788,000	791,000	81,830	75,370	68,900	62,430	55,970	49,500	43,040	36,570	283,700
791,000	794,000	82,460	75,920	69,450	62,990	56,520	50,050	43,590	37,120	285,300
794,000	797,000	83,100	76,470	70,000	63,540	57,070	50,600	44,140	37,670	286,800
797,000	800,000	83,730	77,020	70,550	64,090	57,630	51,150	44,690	38,230	288,300
800,000	803,000	84,370	77,580	71,100	64,640	58,180	51,700	45,240	38,780	290,000
803,000	806,000	85,000	78,130	71,650	65,190	58,730	52,250	45,790	39,330	291,500
806,000	809,000	85,630	78,680	72,210	65,740	59,280	52,810	46,340	39,880	293,000
809,000	812,000	86,260	79,230	72,760	66,290	59,830	53,360	46,890	40,430	294,600
812,000	815,000	86,900	79,780	73,310	66,840	60,380	53,910	47,450	40,980	296,100
815,000	818,000	87,530	80,330	73,860	67,400	60,930	54,460	48,000	41,530	297,600
818,000	821,000	88,160	80,880	74,410	67,950	61,480	55,010	48,550	42,090	299,200
821,000	824,000	88,800	81,430	74,960	68,500	62,040	55,560	49,100	42,640	300,800
824,000	827,000	89,440	82,000	75,510	69,050	62,590	56,110	49,650	43,190	302,300
827,000	830,000	90,070	82,630	76,060	69,600	63,140	56,670	50,200	43,740	303,800
830,000	833,000	90,710	83,260	76,620	70,150	63,690	57,220	50,750	44,290	305,400
833,000	836,000	91,360	83,930	77,200	70,720	64,260	57,800	51,330	44,860	306,900
836,000	839,000	92,060	84,630	77,810	71,340	64,870	58,410	51,940	45,480	308,400
839,000	842,000	92,770	85,340	78,420	71,950	65,490	59,020	52,550	46,090	310,000
842,000	845,000	93,470	86,040	79,040	72,560	66,100	59,640	53,160	46,700	311,600
845,000	848,000	94,180	86,740	79,650	73,180	66,710	60,250	53,780	47,310	313,100
848,000	851,000	94,880	87,450	80,260	73,790	67,320	60,860	54,390	47,930	314,700
851,000	854,000	95,590	88,150	80,870	74,400	67,940	61,470	55,000	48,540	316,200
854,000	857,000	96,290	88,860	81,490	75,010	68,550	62,090	55,610	49,150	317,700
857,000	860,000	97,000	89,560	82,130	75,630	69,160	62,700	56,230	49,760	319,300
860,000		97,350	89,920	82,480	75,930	69,470	63,010	56,530	50,070	320,900
860,001~ 969,999		the amount of tax when the salary, after deduction of social insurance premiums, is 860,000 yen plus 23.483% of the amount which exceeds 860,000 yen								320,900 yen plus 40.84% of the amount which exceeds 860,000 yen, after deduction of social insurance premiums

¶ 4-250

源　泉　所　得　税　131

その月の社会保険料等控除後の給与等の金額		甲								乙
		扶養親族等の数								
以上	未満	0人	1人	2人	3人	4人	5人	6人	7人	
		税額								税額
円	円	円	円	円	円	円	円	円	円	円
740,000	743,000	73,010	66,550	60,080	53,610	47,150	40,680	34,210	27,750	259,000
743,000	746,000	73,560	67,100	60,630	54,160	47,700	41,230	34,770	28,300	260,600
746,000	749,000	74,110	67,650	61,180	54,720	48,250	41,780	35,320	28,850	262,100
749,000	752,000	74,670	68,200	61,730	55,270	48,800	42,330	35,870	29,400	263,600
752,000	755,000	75,220	68,750	62,280	55,820	49,360	42,880	36,420	29,960	265,200
755,000	758,000	75,770	69,310	62,830	56,370	49,910	43,430	36,970	30,510	266,700
758,000	761,000	76,320	69,860	63,380	56,920	50,460	43,980	37,520	31,060	268,200
761,000	764,000	76,870	70,410	63,940	57,470	51,010	44,540	38,070	31,610	269,900
764,000	767,000	77,420	70,960	64,490	58,020	51,560	45,090	38,620	32,160	271,400
767,000	770,000	77,970	71,510	65,040	58,570	52,110	45,640	39,180	32,710	272,900
770,000	773,000	78,530	72,060	65,590	59,130	52,660	46,190	39,730	33,260	274,400
773,000	776,000	79,080	72,610	66,140	59,680	53,210	46,740	40,280	33,820	276,000
776,000	779,000	79,630	73,160	66,690	60,230	53,770	47,290	40,830	34,370	277,500
779,000	782,000	80,180	73,720	67,240	60,780	54,320	47,840	41,380	34,920	279,000
782,000	785,000	80,730	74,270	67,790	61,330	54,870	48,400	41,930	35,470	280,700
785,000	788,000	81,280	74,820	68,350	61,880	55,420	48,950	42,480	36,020	282,200
788,000	791,000	81,830	75,370	68,900	62,430	55,970	49,500	43,040	36,570	283,700
791,000	794,000	82,460	75,920	69,450	62,990	56,520	50,050	43,590	37,120	285,300
794,000	797,000	83,100	76,470	70,000	63,540	57,070	50,600	44,140	37,670	286,800
797,000	800,000	83,730	77,020	70,550	64,090	57,630	51,150	44,690	38,230	288,300
800,000	803,000	84,370	77,580	71,100	64,640	58,180	51,700	45,240	38,780	290,000
803,000	806,000	85,000	78,130	71,650	65,190	58,730	52,250	45,790	39,330	291,500
806,000	809,000	85,630	78,680	72,210	65,740	59,280	52,810	46,340	39,880	293,000
809,000	812,000	86,260	79,230	72,760	66,290	59,830	53,360	46,890	40,430	294,600
812,000	815,000	86,900	79,780	73,310	66,840	60,380	53,910	47,450	40,980	296,100
815,000	818,000	87,530	80,330	73,860	67,400	60,930	54,460	48,000	41,530	297,600
818,000	821,000	88,160	80,880	74,410	67,950	61,480	55,010	48,550	42,090	299,200
821,000	824,000	88,800	81,430	74,960	68,500	62,040	55,560	49,100	42,640	300,800
824,000	827,000	89,440	82,000	75,510	69,050	62,590	56,110	49,650	43,190	302,300
827,000	830,000	90,070	82,630	76,060	69,600	63,140	56,670	50,200	43,740	303,800
830,000	833,000	90,710	83,260	76,620	70,150	63,690	57,220	50,750	44,290	305,400
833,000	836,000	91,360	83,930	77,200	70,720	64,260	57,800	51,330	44,860	306,900
836,000	839,000	92,060	84,630	77,810	71,340	64,870	58,410	51,940	45,480	308,400
839,000	842,000	92,770	85,340	78,420	71,950	65,490	59,020	52,550	46,090	310,000
842,000	845,000	93,470	86,040	79,040	72,560	66,100	59,640	53,160	46,700	311,600
845,000	848,000	94,180	86,740	79,650	73,180	66,710	60,250	53,780	47,310	313,100
848,000	851,000	94,880	87,450	80,200	73,790	07,320	00,800	54,390	47,930	314,700
851,000	854,000	95,590	88,150	80,870	74,400	67,940	61,470	55,000	48,540	316,200
854,000	857,000	96,290	88,860	81,490	75,010	68,550	62,090	55,610	49,150	317,700
857,000	860,000	97,000	89,560	82,130	75,630	69,160	62,700	56,230	49,760	319,300
860,000円		97,350	89,920	82,480	75,930	69,470	63,010	56,530	50,070	320,900
860,000円を超え970,000円に満たない金額		860,000円の場合の税額に，その月の社会保険料等控除後の給与等の金額のうち860,000円を超える金額の23.483％に相当する金額を加算した金額								320,900円に，その月の社会保険料等控除後の給与等の金額のうち860,000円を超える金額の40.84％に相当する金額を加算した金額

132 WITHHOLDING INCOME TAX

Amount of salary after deduction of social insurance premiums	{A} Number of dependants								{B}
	0	1	2	3	4	5	6	7	
970,000 yen	yen 123,190	yen 115,760	yen 108,320	yen 101,770	yen 95,310	yen 88,850	yen 82,370	yen 75,910	320,900 yen plus 40.84% of the amount which exceeds 860,000 yen, after deduction of social insurance premiums
970,001~ 1,719,999 yen	the amount of tax when the salary, after deduction of social insurance premiums, is 970,000 yen plus 33.693% of the amount which exceeds 970,000 yen								
1,720,000 yen	yen 375,890	yen 368,460	yen 361,020	yen 354,470	yen 348,010	yen 341,550	yen 335,070	yen 328,610	yen 672,200
1,720,001~ 3,549,999 yen	the amount of tax when the salary, after deduction of social insurance premiums, is 1,720,000 yen plus 40.84% of the amount which exceeds 1,720,000 yen								672,200 yen plus 45.945% of the amount which exceeds 1,720,000 yen, after deduction of social insurance premiums
3,550,000 yen	yen 1,123,270	yen 1,115,840	yen 1,108,400	yen 1,101,850	yen 1,095,390	yen 1,088,930	yen 1,082,450	yen 1,075,990	
More than 3,550,000 yen	the amount of tax when the salary, after deduction of social insurance premiums, is 3,550,000 yen plus 45.945% of the amount which exceeds 3,550,000 yen								
When the number of dependants exceeds 7, the amount of tax is that for 7 dependants minus 1,610 yen for each additional dependant.									If sub application form for dependants is submitted, the amount of tax is reduced 1,610 yen for each dependant from the amount of tax listed above.

¶ 4-250

源 泉 所 得 税　133

その月の社会保険等控除後の給与等の金額	甲（扶養親族等の数）								乙
	0人	1人	2人	3人	4人	5人	6人	7人	
970,000円	円 123,190	円 115,760	円 108,320	円 101,770	円 95,310	円 88,850	円 82,370	円 75,910	320,900円に，その月の社会保険料等控除後の給与等の金額のうち860,000円を超える金額の40.84％に相当する金額を加算した金額
970,000円を超え1,720,000円に満たない金額	970,000円の場合の税額に，その月の社会保険料等控除後の給与等の金額のうち970,000円を超える金額の33.693％に相当する金額を加算した金額								
1,720,000円	円 375,890	円 368,460	円 361,020	円 354,470	円 348,010	円 341,550	円 335,070	円 328,610	672,200
1,720,000円を超え3,550,000円に満たない金額	1,720,000円の場合の税額に，その月の社会保険料等控除後の給与等の金額のうち1,720,000円を超える金額の40.84％に相当する金額を加算した金額								672,200円に，その月の社会保険料等控除後の給与等の金額のうち1,720,000円を超える金額の45.945％に相当する金額を加算した金額
3,550,000円	円 1,123,270	円 1,115,840	円 1,108,400	円 1,101,850	円 1,095,390	円 1,088,930	円 1,082,450	円 1,075,990	
3,550,000円を超える金額	3,550,000円の場合の税額に，その月の社会保険料等控除後の給与等の金額のうち3,550,000円を超える金額の45.945％に相当する金額を加算した金額								
扶養親族等の数が7人を超える場合には，扶養親族等の数が7人の場合の税額から，その7人を超える1人ごとに1,610円を控除した金額									従たる給与についての扶養控除等申告書が提出されている場合には，当該申告書に記載された扶養親族等の数に応じ，扶養親族等1人ごとに1,610円を，上の各欄によって求めた税額から控除した金額

134   WITHHOLDING INCOME TAX

¶ 4-260 Basic elements taken into account in table

The monthly table assumes that each monthly payment amounts to one twelfth of the annual payment. The daily table assumes that each daily payment amounts to one three-hundred-and-sixtieth of the annual payment, except that column C assumes that a day laborer works 22 days each month.

The following table shows which elements are taken into account in the withholding tax tables:

Elements	Column A	Column B	Column C
Employment income deduction	o	o	o
Deduction for accidental loss (¶ 5-320)	×	×	×
Deduction for medical expenses (¶ 5-330)	×	×	×
Deduction for social insurance premiums (¶ 5-340)	o •,*	o	o
Deduction for life insurance premiums (¶ 5-370)	•,*	×	×
Deduction for earthquake insurance premiums (¶ 5-380)	•,*	×	×
Deduction for contributions (¶ 5-390)	×	×	×
Allowance for a physically handicapped person (¶ 5-430)	o*	×	×
Allowance for a widow or widower (¶ 5-450)	o*	×	×
Allowance for a working student (¶ 5-460)	o*	×	×
Allowance for spouse (¶ 5-410)	o*	#*	@
Allowance for dependant (¶ 5-420)	o*	#*	@
Basic allowance (¶ 5-470)	o	#	o
Tax rate (¶ 5-500)	o	#	o
Credit for dividends (¶ 5-580)	×	×	×
Special credit for acquisition of house (¶ 5-600)	•,*	×	×
Credit for experimental and research expenses (¶ 5-610)	×	×	×
Credit for foreign taxes (¶ 5-630)	×	×	×

Note:

"o"   means that the element is taken into account.

"×"   means that the element is not taken into account.

"•,"   means that the element is not taken into account in the withholding tax table for salaries, wages, etc., but is taken into account in the year-end adjustment. In the case of the deduction for social insurance premiums, it means that social insurance premiums withheld from salaries, etc. are always taken into account, but other social insurance premiums are taken into account only in the year-end adjustment.

"#"   means that the element is taken into account only to a certain extent because the benefits of the allowances or the low rates are enjoyed in the payments from other employers to which Column A is applicable.

"@"   means that the element is taken into account on the assumption that the employee has a spouse and two children.

"*"   means that an employee cannot enjoy the benefit unless he submits an application to his employer in due time.

¶ 4-260

源　泉　所　得　税　135

¶4-260　税額表の仕組み

　月額表は，各月ごとに支払われる給料等が年間支払額の12分の１であるものとして作成されている。日額表については，甲欄及び乙欄は毎日支払われる給料等が年間支払額の360分の１であるものとして，丙欄は日雇労働者が月に22日働くものとして，それぞれ作成されている。

　次の表は，源泉徴収のための税額表の中で考慮されている要素を示すものである。

要　素	甲　欄	乙　欄	丙　欄
給与所得控除	○	○	○
雑損控除（¶5-320参照）	×	×	×
医療費控除（¶5-330参照）	×	×	×
社会保険料控除（¶5-340参照）	○◎*	○	○
生命保険料控除（¶5-370参照）	◎*	×	×
地震保険料控除（¶5-380参照）	◎*	×	×
寄付金控除（¶5-390参照）	×	×	×
障害者控除（¶5-430参照）	○*	×	×
寡婦（寡夫）控除（¶5-450参照）	○*	×	×
勤労学生控除（¶5-460参照）	○*	×	×
配偶者控除（¶5-410参照）	○*	△*	□
扶養控除（¶5-420参照）	○*	△*	□
基礎控除（¶5-470参照）	○	△	○
税率（¶5-500参照）	○	△	○
配当控除（¶5-580参照）	×	×	×
住宅取得控除（¶5-600参照）	◎*	×	×
試験研究費税額控除（¶5-610参照）	×	×	×
外国税額控除（¶5-630参照）	×	×	×

（注）：
○印──当該要素が考慮されていることを示す。
×印──当該要素が考慮されていないことを示す。
◎印──当該要素は，「給与所得の源泉徴収税額表」においては考慮されていないが，年末調整の際に考慮されることを示す。
　　　社会保険料控除については，給料から差し引かれた社会保険料はすべて考慮されているが，その他の社会保険料は年末調整の際にのみ考慮される。
△印──当該要素は，一定期限まで考慮されていることを示す。これは，甲欄が適用される他の雇用者からの支払について控除が行われ又は低税率が適用されていることを反映している。
□印──当該要素は，夫婦２人という前提で，考慮されていることを示す。
＊印──雇用者に対して所定の期日までに適用を受けるための申告書を提出している場合に限り，当該要素が考慮されることを示す。

136   WITHHOLDING INCOME TAX

¶ 4-270   Withholding tax table for bonus payments

Withholding tax rate for bonus payments	0 person		1 person		2 persons		3 persons	
	the amount of salary, after deduction of social							
	from	less	from	less	from	less	from	less
% 0.000	less than 68		less than 94		less than 133		less than 171	
2.042	68	79	94	243	133	269	171	295
4.084	**79**	**252**	**243**	**282**	**269**	**312**	**295**	**345**
6.126	252	300	282	338	312	369	345	398
8.168	300	334	338	365	369	393	398	417
10.210	**334**	**363**	**365**	**394**	**393**	**420**	**417**	**445**
12.252	363	395	394	422	420	450	445	477
14.294	395	426	422	455	450	484	477	513
16.336	**426**	**550**	**455**	**550**	**484**	**550**	**513**	**557**
18.378	550	647	550	663	550	678	557	693
20.420	647	699	663	720	678	741	693	762
22.462	**699**	**730**	**720**	**752**	**741**	**774**	**762**	**796**
24.504	730	764	752	787	774	810	796	833
26.546	764	804	787	826	810	852	833	879
28.588	**804**	**857**	**826**	**885**	**852**	**914**	**879**	**942**
30.630	857	926	885	956	914	987	942	1,017
32.672	926	1,321	956	1,346	987	1,370	1,017	1,394
35.735	1,321	1,532	1,346	1,560	1,370	1,589	1,394	1,617
38.798	1,532	2,661	1,560	2,685	1,589	2,708	1,617	2,732
41.861	2,661	3,548	2,685	3,580	2,708	3,611	2,732	3,643
45.945	**3,548 or over**		**3,580 or over**		**3,611 or over**		**3,643 or over**	

源 泉 所 得 税 137

(Applicable for 2018)

Unit: 1,000 yen

dependants								{B}		Withholding tax rate for bonus payments
4 persons		5 persons		6 persons		7 persons or more				
insurance premiums, which are paid in previous month										
from	less	from	less	from	less	from	less	from	less	
less than 210		less than 243		less than 275		less than 308				0.000 %
210	300	243	300	275	333	308	372			2.042
300	**378**	**300**	**406**	**333**	**431**	**372**	**456**			**4.084**
378	424	406	450	431	476	456	502			6.126
424	444	450	472	476	499	502	527			8.168
444	**470**	**472**	**496**	**499**	**525**	**527**	**553**	less than 239		**10.210**
470	504	496	531	525	559	553	588			12.252
504	543	531	574	559	602	588	627			14.294
543	**591**	**574**	**618**	**602**	**645**	**627**	**671**			**16.336**
591	708	618	723	645	739	671	754			18.378
708	783	723	804	739	825	754	848	239	296	20.420
783	**818**	**804**	**841**	**825**	**865**	**848**	**890**			**22.462**
818	859	841	885	865	911	890	937			24.504
859	906	885	934	911	961	937	988			26.546
906	**970**	**934**	**998**	**961**	**1,026**	**988**	**1,054**			**28.588**
970	1,048	998	1,078	1,026	1,108	1,054	1,139	296	528	30.630
1,048	1,419	1,078	1,443	1,108	1,468	1,139	1,492			32.672
1,419	1,645	1,443	1,674	1,468	1,702	1,492	1,730			35.735
1,645	2,756	1,674	2,780	1,702	2,803	1,730	2,827	528	1,135	38.798
2,756	3,675	2,780	3,706	2,803	3,738	2,827	3,770			41.861
3,675 or over		**3,706 or over**		**3,738 or over**		**3,770 or over**		**1,135 or over**		**45.945**

138 WITHHOLDING INCOME TAX

¶4-270 賞与に対する源泉徴収税額の

賞与の金額に乗ずべき率	甲							
	扶　養　親　族							
	0　人		1　人		2　人		3　人	
	前　月　の　社　会　保　険　料　等　控　除　後							
	以上	未満	以上	未満	以上	未満	以上	未満
%	千円	千円	千円	千円	千円	千円	千円	千円
0.000	68 千円未満		94 千円未満		133 千円未満		171 千円未満	
2.042	68	79	94	243	133	269	171	295
4.084	79	252	243	282	269	312	295	345
6.126	252	300	282	338	312	369	345	398
8.168	300	334	338	365	369	393	398	417
10.210	334	363	365	394	393	420	417	445
12.252	363	395	394	422	420	450	445	477
14.294	395	426	422	455	450	484	477	513
16.336	426	550	455	550	484	550	513	557
18.378	550	647	550	663	550	678	557	693
20.420	647	699	663	720	678	741	693	762
22.462	699	730	720	752	741	774	762	796
24.504	730	764	752	787	774	810	796	833
26.546	764	804	787	826	810	852	833	879
28.588	804	857	826	885	852	914	879	942
30.630	857	926	885	956	914	987	942	1,017
32.672	926	1,321	956	1,346	987	1,370	1,017	1,394
35.735	1,321	1,532	1,346	1,560	1,370	1,589	1,394	1,617
38.798	1,532	2,661	1,560	2,685	1,589	2,708	1,617	2,732
41.861	2,661	3,548	2,685	3,580	2,708	3,611	2,732	3,643
45.945	3,548 千円以上		3,580 千円以上		3,611 千円以上		3,643 千円以上	

¶ 4-270

算出率の表（平成30年分）

扶養親族等の数 4人		5人		6人		7人以上		乙 前月の社会保険料控除後の給与等の金額		賞与の金額に乗ずべき率
以上（千円）	未満（千円）	以上（千円）	未満（千円）	以上（千円）	未満（千円）	以上（千円）	未満（千円）	以上（千円）	未満（千円）	％
210千円未満		243千円未満		275千円未満		308千円未満				0.000
210	300	243	300	275	333	308	372			2.042
300	378	300	406	333	431	372	456			4.084
378	424	406	450	431	476	456	502			6.126
424	444	450	472	476	499	502	527			8.168
444	470	472	496	499	525	527	553	239千円未満		10.210
470	504	496	531	525	559	553	588			12.252
504	543	531	574	559	602	588	627			14.294
543	591	574	618	602	645	627	671			16.336
591	708	618	723	645	739	671	754			18.378
708	783	723	804	739	825	754	848	239	296	20.420
783	818	804	841	825	865	848	890			22.462
818	859	841	885	865	911	890	937			24.504
859	906	885	934	911	961	937	988			26.546
906	970	934	998	961	1,026	988	1,054			28.588
970	1,048	998	1,078	1,026	1,108	1,054	1,139	296	528	30.630
1,048	1,419	1,078	1,443	1,108	1,468	1,139	1,492			32.672
1,419	1,645	1,443	1,674	1,468	1,702	1,492	1,730			35.735
1,645	2,756	1,674	2,780	1,702	2,803	1,730	2,827	528	1,135	38.798
2,756	3,675	2,780	3,706	2,803	3,738	2,827	3,770			41.861
3,675千円以上		3,706千円以上		3,738千円以上		3,770千円以上		1,135千円以上		45.945

140 WITHHOLDING INCOME TAX

¶ 4-290 Withholding from bonuses (resident)

The withholding tax table for bonuses (see ¶ 4-270) indicates the rate by which the gross amount of the bonuses should be multiplied for computing the amount of the tax to be withheld.

The rates are calculated on the assumption that an employee receives bonuses amounting to 4.5 times the salary received in the immediately preceding month in addition to regular annual payments.

¶ 4-310 Year-end adjustment

The year-end adjustment is a device to equalize:

    (i)   the total amount of withholding income tax actually withheld in a year from payments to an employee; and

    (ii) his annual tax liability to be retained from the total of those payments.

The year-end adjustment should be reflected in the last salary payment to a Column A employee in a year. It proceeds through the following three steps:

    (1) Aggregate the tax amounts actually withheld at source from the payments to an employee in a calendar year.

    (2) Find the correct annual tax amount to be withheld from the annual total of the employment income (¶ 5-120(5)) paid to him in a year.

    (3) If the aggregate tax amount computed in (1) is less than the correct amount in (2), the difference should be withheld from the last payment.

If the tax amount in (1) is more than the correct tax amount in (2), the difference should be refunded to the employee.

The year-end adjustment, however, does not apply to an employee whose gross amount of employment income receivable during a year exceeds ¥20 million (Law 190).

> **Note:**
> As the amounts withheld from salaries and bonuses etc. are total amounts of income tax and earthquake restoration surtax, the year-end adjustment is also applied to the total amounts of them.

¶ 4-340 Withholding from retirement allowances (resident)

Retirement allowances are subject to withholding income tax. The tax amount can be found in the "withholding tax table for retirement income".

As payment of retirement allowances does not often take place and

¶ 4-290

源 泉 所 得 税　141

¶4-290　賞与に対する源泉徴収（居住者）

「賞与に対する源泉徴収税額の算出率の表」（¶4-270参照）が示す率を賞与の額に乗じて得られる額が，源泉徴収すべき税額となる。

この率は，賞与の額が前月の給料の4.5倍であるという前提で作られている。

¶4-310　年末調整

年末調整は，

(i)　1年の間に支払われた給料から実際に源泉徴収された税額の総額と，

(ii)　その給料の総額から源泉徴収すべき税額とを一致させるために行われる。

年末調整は，1年間甲欄適用を受けた給与所得者に支払われる最終の給料について行われる。その手続は，次の三段階による。

(1)　暦年中の当該被用者に対する給与支払額から実際に源泉徴収した金額を合計する。
(2)　当該被用者に支払ったその年の給与所得の額（¶5-120(5)参照）から源泉徴収すべき金額を計算する。
(3)　上記(1)の合計額が上記(2)の税額より少ないときは，その差額を最後の支払給与額から源泉徴収する。逆の場合は還付する。

ただし，この年末調整は，年間の給与収入額が2,000万円を超える給与所得者には適用されない（所法190）。

（注）：給与等から源泉徴収する税額は，所得税と復興特別所得税の合計額となっているので，年末調整も所得税と復興特別所得税の合計額で行う。

¶4-340　退職手当に対する源泉徴収（居住者）

退職手当には，源泉所得税が課される。その税額は，「退職所得の源泉徴収税額表」による。

退職手当の支払はそう頻繁に行われるものではなく，また，退職所得に係

142   WITHHOLDING INCOME TAX

income tax on retirement income is computed separately from the tax on other kinds of income, the tax liability on a retirement allowance must be finally settled by withholding at source as far as possible.

Following the procedure provided for in the law, first, the amount of the special deduction for retirement income (see ¶ 4-370 and ¶ 5-130(10)) should be deducted from the gross amount of the payment on the basis of an application submitted to the payer by the recipient. Then, the tax amount due corresponding to the amount of payment after this deduction can be found in the withholding tax table for retirement income.

If a person receives a retirement allowance two or more times in a year, the second payment of retirement allowance is subject to withholding at source on a cumulative basis. The payer of the second retirement allowance is to be provided with the information about the first retirement allowance, which should be submitted by the recipient, so that the cumulative basis can be applied. The tax amount to be withheld is the tax on the aggregate retirement allowances paid in a year minus the tax withheld earlier in the year.

If such information is not given, tax amounting to 20% of the gross amount of retirement allowance should be withheld at source (Law 201).

¶ 4-350 Calculation of withholding tax on retirement allowances

Withholding tax on retirement allowances is calculated in accordance with the following formula (Law 30).

(amount of retirement allowance − amount of deduction) × 1/2 (Note) × tax rate = amount of tax

The amount of the deduction is based on the number of years the employee worked for the employer. If the period of service does not exceed 20 years, 400,000 yen per year is deducted. If the number of years exceeds 20 years, the deduction is 8,000,000 yen plus 700,000 yen for each year exceeding 20 years (see ¶ 4-370).

In calculating the number of years worked for the employer, a period of less than twelve months is counted as one year.

(concerning the above tax rate, see ¶5-522)

> **Note:**
> In the case of short-term executives whose term is 5 years or below, so called "50% taxation" is not applied to the computation of retirement income received by them from 2013 (see ¶5-130(10)).

¶ 4-350

源 泉 所 得 税 143

る所得税額は他の所得に係る所得税額と分離して計算されるので，退職手当に係る租税負担は，できるだけ，源泉徴収だけで完結することとされている。

手続は次のとおりである。まず，退職所得控除額（¶4-370及び¶5-130⑩参照）を退職手当から控除する。この場合，適用申告書を退職手当の支払者に提出しておく必要がある。次に，この退職所得控除後の退職手当の額に応じて計算された源泉徴収税額を「退職所得の源泉徴収税額表」により求める。

仮に，1年間に2回以上退職手当が支払われる場合には，2回目以降の退職手当の支払について，累積計算により源泉徴収を行うことができる。この場合，2回目の退職手当の支払者に対して累積計算ができるよう最初の退職手当についての情報が示される必要がある。このようにして，その年に支払われた退職手当の合計額に係る税額からこれまでに徴収された税額を差し引いた差額が源泉徴収されることになる。

支払済みの他の退職手当についての情報が与えられなかった場合には，退職手当の20％相当額が源泉徴収される（所法201）。

¶4-350 退職所得に対する源泉徴収税額の算定

退職所得に対する源泉徴収税額は，次の方式で算定される（所法30）。

（退職手当等の収入金額−退職所得控除額）$\times \frac{1}{2}$（注）×税率＝退職所得に対する税額

退職所得控除額は，その者の勤務年数によって計算されるが，勤務年数が20年以下の場合は，勤続1年につき400,000円，勤務年数が20年を超える場合には，800万円に20年を超える勤続1年につき700,000円を加算した金額とされる（¶4-370参照）。

この勤続年数の算定上1年に満たない端数の月は1年として計算される。
（税率については，¶5-522参照）

（注）：平成25年分以後，勤続年数が5年以下の役員等が支払を受ける退職手当等については，いわゆる，2分の1課税は適用されない（¶5-130⑩参照）。

144   WITHHOLDING INCOME TAX

¶ 4-360 Withholding from remuneration, fees, etc. (resident)

The following payments (excluding payments to employees) are subject to withholding income tax under the following conditions (unless the payer is an individual who does not have any obligation to withhold income tax from the employment income): (Law 204).

(a) Remuneration for manuscripts, illustrations, music compositions, recordings, broadcasting, lectures, dramatization, designs, translations, proofreading, stenography, block copy art work or bookbinding, or royalties on copyright, patents, know-how, remuneration for instruction of sports or arts, etc.

(b) Remuneration paid to:

(i)   lawyers, licensed tax accountants, certified public accountants, patent attorneys, accountants, assistant accountants, architects, real estate appraisers, assistant real estate appraisers, land surveyors, assistant land surveyors, building agents, business consultants, registered technicians, assistant technicians, fire or automobile damage appraisers;

(ii) judicial scriveners, land and house inspectors, marine agents.

(c) Remuneration paid to doctors or dentists from "Social Insurance Treatment Remuneration Payment Funds".

(d) Remuneration paid to:

(i)   baseball players, jockeys, motorcar racers, motorboat racers, cycle racers, golfers, wrestlers, bowlers, soccer players, tennis players;

(ii) models;

(iii) boxers;

(iv) salesmen, bill collectors or electric meter men.

(e) Remuneration paid to:

(i)   actors, movie or stage directors, producers, conductors of music, band players;

(ii) persons who perform as public entertainers.

(f) Remuneration paid to hostesses includes companion and banquet hostesses who serve as partners for such amusements as dancing and drinking at cabarets, nightclubs and bars.

(g) Lump sum payments for furnishing personal services (e.g. base-

¶ 4-360

源 泉 所 得 税　145

¶4-360　報酬，料金等に係る源泉徴収（居住者）

　下記の支払（被用者に対する支払を除く。）については，以下に述べる条件の下で，源泉所得税が課される（所法204）。ただし，給与所得につき源泉徴収する義務を有しない個人については，ここでも源泉徴収義務はない。

⒜　原稿，さし絵，作曲，レコード吹込み，放送，講演，脚本，脚色，デザイン，翻訳，校正，速記，版下，又は書籍の装ていに係る報酬又は著作権，特許権，ノウ・ハウ等の使用料，技法・スポーツ等の教授，指導等の報酬

⒝⒤　弁護士，税理士，公認会計士，弁理士，計理士，会計士補，建築士，不動産鑑定士，不動産鑑定士補，測量士，測量士補，建築代理士，企業診断員，技術士，技術士補又は火災若しくは自動車等の損害鑑定人

　⒤　司法書士，土地家屋調査士，海事代理士
　　　に対して支払われる報酬
⒞　社会保険診療報酬支払基金から医師又は歯科医師に支払われる診療報酬
⒟⒤　野球選手，競馬の騎手，自動車競争の選手，モーターボート競争の選手，自転車競争の選手，ゴルファー，レスラー，ボウラー，プロサッカーの選手，プロテニスの選手，自動車のレーサー

　⒤　モデル
　⒤　拳闘家
　⒤　外交員，集金人又は電力量計の検針人
　　　に対して支払われる報酬
⒠⒤　俳優，映画又は演劇の演出家，製作者，音楽の指揮者，演奏者

　⒤　芸能人として出演する者に対して支払われる報酬
⒡　キャバレー，ナイトクラブ及びバーにおけるダンス又は飲食といった遊興のため客に侍して接待するホステスに対して支払われる報酬，ホテル・旅館等における接客・配膳をする者の報酬
⒢　役務の提供につき支払われる一時金（例えば野球選手に対して）

146 WITHHOLDING INCOME TAX

ball players).

(h) Prizes, etc.:

(i) prizes or other benefits paid in advertising promotions;

(ii) prizes for horse-racing paid to horse owners.

(i) Annuity payments (Law 207).

(j) Distributions of profit to "silent" partners in a partnership (Tokumei Kumiai) (Law 210).

The withholding tax rates applicable to these categories of payment are set out in ¶ 4-380.

¶ 4-360

源　泉　所　得　税　147

(h)(i)　広告宣伝のための賞金

　(ii)　馬主が受ける競馬の賞金
(i)　生命保険年金等（所法207）
(j)　匿名組合（所法210）から受ける利益の配当
これらの源泉徴収に係る適用税率については¶4-380を参照。

148   WITHHOLDING INCOME TAX

¶ 4-370 Retirement income deduction for withholding tax

Unit: 1,000 yen

Years of employment	Retirement income deduction		Years of employment	Retirement income deduction	
	Ordinary deduction	Special deduction		Ordinary deduction	Special deduction
2 years	800	1,800	24 years	10,800	11,800
			25 years	11,500	12,500
			26 years	12,200	13,200
3 years	1,200	2,200	27 years	12,900	13,900
4 years	1,600	2,600	28 years	13,600	14,600
5 years	2,000	3,000	29 years	14,300	15,300
6 years	2,400	3,400	30 years	15,000	16,000
7 years	2,800	3,800	31 years	15,700	16,700
8 years	3,200	4,200	32 years	16,400	17,400
9 years	3,600	4,600	33 years	17,100	18,100
10 years	4,000	5,000	34 years	17,800	18,800
11 years	4,400	5,400	35 years	18,500	19,500
12 years	4,800	5,800	36 years	19,200	20,200
13 years	5,200	6,200	37 years	19,900	20,900
14 years	5,600	6,600	38 years	20,600	21,600
15 years	6,000	7,000	39 years	21,300	22,300
16 years	6,400	7,400	40 years	22,000	23,000
17 years	6,800	7,800			
18 years	7,200	8,200	41 years or over	22,000,000 yen plus 700,000 yen for each year which exceeds 40 years	23,000,000 yen plus 700,000 yen for each year which exceeds 40 years
19 years	7,600	8,600			
20 years	8,000	9,000			
21 years	8,700	9,700			
22 years	9,400	10,400			
23 years	10,100	11,100			

Note:
The special deduction applies in cases where an injury causes the retirement.

¶ 4-370

源　泉　所　得　税　149

¶4-370　源泉徴収のための退職所得控除額

勤続年数	退職所得控除額		勤続年数	退職所得控除額	
	一般退職の場合	障害退職の場合		一般退職の場合	障害退職の場合
	千円	千円		千円	千円
2 年以下	800	1,800	24　年	10,800	11,800
			25　年	11,500	12,500
			26　年	12,200	13,200
3　年	1,200	2,200	27　年	12,900	13,900
4　年	1,600	2,600	28　年	13,600	14,600
5　年	2,000	3,000	29　年	14,300	15,300
6　年	2,400	3,400	30　年	15,000	16,000
7　年	2,800	3,800	31　年	15,700	16,700
8　年	3,200	4,200	32　年	16,400	17,400
9　年	3,600	4,600	33　年	17,100	18,100
10　年	4,000	5,000	34　年	17,800	18,800
11　年	4,400	5,400	35　年	18,500	19,500
12　年	4,800	5,800	36　年	19,200	20,200
13　年	5,200	6,200	37　年	19,900	20,900
14　年	5,600	6,600	38　年	20,600	21,600
15　年	6,000	7,000	39　年	21,300	22,300
16　年	6,400	7,400	40　年	22,000	23,000
17　年	6,800	7,800			
18　年	7,200	8,200	41年以上	22,000千円に，勤続年数が40年を超える1年ごとに700千円を加算した金額	23,000千円に，勤続年数が40年を超える1年ごとに700千円を加算した金額
19　年	7,600	8,600			
20　年	8,000	9,000			
21　年	8,700	9,700			
22　年	9,400	10,400			
23　年	10,100	11,100			

(注)：障害退職とは，障害を基因とする退職をいう。

150   WITHHOLDING INCOME TAX

¶ 4-380 Withholding tax rates and taxable amounts

The conditions (the withholding tax rate and the taxable amount) which apply to the categories of payment set out in ¶ 4-360 are as follows:

Payments	Taxable Amount	Tax Rate***
(a), (b)(i), (d)(i), (d)(ii), (e) & (g)	gross amount of payment	10.21%, provided 20.42% is applied to the excess over ¥1,000,000 of each payment to a person
(b)(ii)	amount after deduction of ¥10,000 from each payment to a person	10.21%
(c)	amount after deduction of ¥200,000 from monthly payment to a person	10.21%
(d)(iii)	amount after deduction of ¥50,000 from each payment to a person	10.21%
(d)(iv)	amount after deduction of ¥120,000 from monthly payment to a person*	10.21%
(f)	amount after deduction from each payment of ¥5,000 multiplied by the number of days for which such payment is made*	10.21%
(h)(i)	amount after deduction of ¥500,000 from each payment to a person	10.21%
(h)(ii)	amount after deduction of ¥600,000 plus 20% of the prize from each payment to a person	10.21%
(i)	amount after deduction of that portion of payment attributable to the paid-in premiums**	10.21%
(j)	amount of profit distributed (Law 204, 205 and Reg 320 to 322)	20.42%

---

*   When the payee receives a salary, the amount of salary is deducted from the above-mentioned figures.

**   When the amount after such deduction is less than ¥250,000, it is free from withholding income tax.

***For the period from January 1, 2013 to December 31, 2037, earthquake restoration surtax (2.1% of withholding income tax amount) shall be added. The above tax rates are total tax rates of withholding income tax and earthquake restoration surtax.

¶ 4-380

源　泉　所　得　税　151

¶4-380　源泉徴収の税率及び課税標準

¶4-360 の源泉徴収についての税率及び課税標準は次のとおりである。

支　払	課　税　標　準	税　　率***
(a),(b)(i), (d)(i)(ii),(e),(g)	支払われる金額	10.21％，ただし，同一人に対し1回に支払われる金額のうち100万円を超える部分については20.42％
(b)(ii)	同一人に対し1回支払われる金額から1万円を控除した金額	10.21％
(c)	同一人に対しその月分として支払われる金額から20万円を控除した金額	10.21％
(d)(iii)	同一人に対し1回に支払われる金額から5万円を控除した金額	10.21％
(d)(iv)	同一人に対しその月中に支払われる金額から12万円を控除した金額*	10.21％
(f)	同一人に対し1回に支払われる金額から5,000円に当該支払金額の計算期間の日数を乗じて計算して金額を控除した金額*	10.21％
(h)(i)	同一人に対し1回に支払われる金額から50万円を控除した金額	10.21％
(h)(ii)	同一人に対し1回に支払われる金額から60万円に当該賞金の20％相当額を加えた金額を控除した金額	10.21％
(i)	支払われる金額から払込保険料に対応する額を控除した金額**	10.21％
(j)	利益の配当の額 （所法204，205，所令320～322）	20.42％

*　受取人が給料の支払も受ける場合には，12万円又は5,000円から当該給料を控除した後の金額となる。

**　控除後の金額が25万円未満の場合には，源泉徴収不適用となる。

***　平成25年1月1日から平成49年12月31日までの間，復興特別所得税（源泉徴収されるべき所得税額の2.1％）が加算される。上記の税率は，源泉所得税と復興特別所得税の合計税率である。

152   WITHHOLDING INCOME TAX

¶ 4-390 Withholding from public pensions

With respect to public pension the payments are subject to withholding income tax at the rate of 5.105% (income tax 5%, earthquake restoration surtax 0.105%) of the amount remaining after deducting the amounts specified by law (Law 203-2, 203-3).

There are various types of public pensions, and the precise amounts which should be deducted to calculate the tax base is provided by law.

¶ 4-400 Withholding tax on capital gains derived from transactions involving stock in listed companies

Capital gain of listed stocks in the designated account applied to withholding by election is subject to withholding income tax at source.

Withholding tax rates as follows.

January 1, 2013 to December 31, 2013	10.147% (income tax and earthquake restoration surtax 7.147%, local inhabitant tax 3%)
January 1, 2014 to December 31, 2037	20.315% (income tax and earthquake restoration surtax 15.315%, local inhabitant tax 5%)

¶ 4-410 Personal taxation for expatriates who work in Japan

1. A person who has no Japanese nationality and has lived in Japan for 5 years or less in the last 10 years is categorized as a non-permanent resident.

An expatriate who is a non-permanent resident is subject to tax on Japanese-source income and foreign-source income which is paid in Japan or remitted to Japan.

Japanese-source income is calculated by the following formula. (Income other than Japanese-source income is treated as foreign-source income.) (R 161-28)

$$\text{the amount of salary for the year} \times \frac{365 \text{ days} - \left(\substack{\text{days spent as home leave} \\ \text{and business trips abroad}}\right)}{365 \text{ days} - \text{days spent as home leave}}$$

¶ 4-390

源 泉 所 得 税　153

¶4-390　公的年金等についての源泉徴収

公的年金については，その支払の際，一定の金額を控除した残額について
5.105％（所得税 5 ％，復興特別所得税0.105％）の税率で源泉徴収される
（所法203の 2，203の 3 ）。

公的年金は，広範囲にわたる種類があるが，課税額算定のための一定の控
除額については，それぞれ細かく規定されている。

¶4-400　上場株式等に係る譲渡所得についての源泉徴収

源泉徴収を選択した特定口座内上場株式等の譲渡をした場合，源泉徴収さ
れる税率は以下のとおりである。

平成25年 1 月 1 日〜平成25年12月31日	10.147％（所得税及び復興特別所得税7.147％，住民税 3 ％）
平成26年 1 月 1 日〜平成49年12月31日	20.315％（所得税及び復興特別所得税15.315％，住民税 5 ％）

¶4-410　外国から日本に所在する子会社等に出向する者に対する給与についての所得税の課税関係

1 ．日本国籍を有せず，かつ，日本に滞在する期間が過去10年間のうち 5 年
以下の者は非永住者とされる。

非永住者については，その給与のうち国内源泉所得及び国外源泉所得のう
ち日本国内で支払われたもの又は国外から送金されたものが課税の対象とさ
れる。その給与の国内源泉所得と国外源泉所得は，次のとおり計算される。

$$国内源泉所得＝その年分の給与\times\frac{365日－（ホーム・リーブの日数＋国外勤務の日数）}{365日－ホーム・リーブの日数}$$

国外源泉所得＝国内源泉所得以外のもの（所基通161-28）

154   WITHHOLDING INCOME TAX

2. The following are the main items of non-taxable benefits.

① Rent.

The difference between the rent paid by the employer to the housing owner and the rent paid by the director or the employee to the employer is non-taxable, if the director or the employee pays at least the amount of the rent which is calculated by the following formula.

(a) In the case of rent paid for a director, 50% of the actual payment made by the employer to the owner of the housing or the amount calculated by the following formula, whichever is greater, is non-taxable (R 36-40).

$$\left\{ \begin{array}{l} \text{tax base for fixed} \\ \text{asset tax on the} \\ \text{housing for the year} \end{array} \times 12\% + \begin{array}{l} \text{tax base for fixed asset} \\ \text{tax on the land used for} \\ \text{the housing for the year} \end{array} \times 6\% \right\} \times \frac{1}{12}$$

Where the housing is of non-timber construction, the above 12% is changed to 10%.

Where the space of the housing is 132m² or less the following formula is applied (R 36-41):

$$\begin{array}{l} \text{tax base for} \\ \text{fixed asset} \\ \text{tax on the} \\ \text{housing} \\ \text{for the year} \end{array} \times 0.2\% + 12 \text{ yen} \times \frac{\begin{array}{c} \text{total space} \\ \text{of the housing} \\ (m^2) \end{array}}{3.3 \text{ m}^2} + \begin{array}{l} \text{tax base for} \\ \text{fixed asset tax} \\ \text{on the land used} \\ \text{for the housing} \\ \text{for the year} \end{array} \times 0.22\%$$

Where the housing is of non-timber construction, the above 132m² is changed to 99m².

(b) In the case of rent paid for an employee the amount calculated by the following formula is non-taxable.

$$\begin{array}{l} \text{tax base for} \\ \text{fixed asset} \\ \text{tax on the} \\ \text{housing} \\ \text{for the year} \end{array} \times 0.2\% + 12 \text{ yen} \times \frac{\begin{array}{c} \text{total space} \\ \text{of the housing} \\ (m^2) \end{array}}{3.3 \text{ m}^2} + \begin{array}{l} \text{tax base for} \\ \text{fixed asset tax} \\ \text{on the land used} \\ \text{for the housing} \\ \text{for the year} \end{array} \times 0.22\%$$

In practical administration, the amount of 5% to 10% of the actual rent is deemed to be the amount which is calculated by the above formula.

② Home leave expenses.

③ Business trip expenses.

④ Japanese language lessons.

⑤ Economic benefits for school tuition fees, where the employer con-

¶ 4-410

源 泉 所 得 税 155

2．非課税とされるもの

次のものは課税の対象から除外される。

① 次の算式で計算された家賃以上を会社がその役員又は従業員から徴収している場合の会社が負担する家賃と役員又は従業員が会社に支払う家賃との差額

(a) 役員については実際の支払家賃の50％相当額又は次の算式で計算された額のいずれか多い金額（所基通36-40）

$$\left\{\text{その年度の家屋の固定資産税の課税標準額}\times12\%\left(\begin{matrix}\text{木造家屋以}\\\text{外の家屋に}\\\text{ついて10\%}\end{matrix}\right)+\text{その年度の敷地の固定資産税の課税標準額}\times6\%\right\}\times\frac{1}{12}$$

その家屋の床面積が132㎡（木造家屋以外の場合は99㎡）以下であるときには，次の算式による（所基通36-41）。

$$\text{その年度の家屋の固定資産税の課税標準額}\times0.2\%+12\text{円}\times\frac{\text{その家屋の床面積(㎡)}}{3.3\text{㎡}}+\text{その年度の敷地の固定資産税の課税標準額}\times0.22\%$$

(b) 従業員については次の算式で計算された額

$$\text{その年度の家屋の固定資産税の課税標準額}\times0.2\%+12\text{円}\times\frac{\text{その家屋の床面積(㎡)}}{3.3\text{㎡}}+\text{その年度の敷地の固定資産税の課税標準額}\times0.22\%$$

実務的には，実際の家賃の5％から10％を徴収している場合には，その計算が認められている。

② ホーム・リーブ費用
③ 出張手当
④ 日本語を習得するための授業料
⑤ 会社が一定の学校に対する寄付を行っている場合に，その学校に在学

156   WITHHOLDING INCOME TAX

tributes to qualified schools such as the American School.

⑥ Expenses for commuting, up to 150,000 yen per month, paid by the employer.

⑦ Moving expenses for a new assignment.

3. The following are the main items of taxable economic benefits:

① Expenses for utilities.

② Expenses for furniture.

③ Expenses for maid service.

④ Fees for private clubs.

Withholding from Payments to Domestic Corporations

¶ 4-510 Withholding from payments to domestic corporations

The following items of income paid to a domestic corporation are subject to withholding income tax unless they are paid abroad (Law 174, 212③):

(1) interest income (including profit from redemption of certain discounted debentures (¶ 4-190);

(2) dividends;

(3) prizes for horse racing paid to horse owners.

(4) distribution of profit paid to silent partners in a silent partnership (Tokumei Kumiai).

¶ 4-540 Withholding from interest and dividends (domestic corporations)

The withholding tax system explained in ¶ 4-150, ¶ 4-190 and ¶ 4-210 is also applicable to interest income and dividend income paid to domestic corporations.

In case of interest, 15.315% for income tax and earthquake restoration surtax and 5% for local tax (total 20.315%) are applicable.

In case of dividend, 20.42% for income tax is applicable (local tax is not applicable). However, in case of dividends on listed shares, the reduced tax rate (7.147%) is applicable up to December 31, 2012.

However, the description in those paragraphs with regard to assessment income tax is not applicable, because corporation tax is always fully assessed on those classes of income received by domestic corporations, unless they are exempt under the law (Law 175).

¶ 4-510

する子女の授業料が免除されるときの経済的利益

⑥　通勤手当　150,000円（月額）

⑦　転勤手当

3．課税されるもの

次のものは給与として，その経済的利益が課税の対象とされる。

①　会社が従業員のために負担する水道・光熱費
②　会社が支給する家具等
③　メイドの費用
④　個人の所属するクラブの会費

内国法人に対する支払に係る源泉徴収

¶4-510　内国法人に対する支払に係る源泉徴収

内国法人に対して支払われる次の所得項目は，国外で支払われる場合を除き，源泉所得税が課される（所法174，212③）。

(1)　利子所得（特定の割引債の償還差益を含む。¶4-190参照）

(2)　配当所得
(3)　馬主が受ける競馬の賞金
(4)　匿名組合契約に基づく利益の分配

¶4-540　利子又は配当に係る源泉徴収

内国法人に対して支払われる利子又は配当に係る源泉徴収については，¶4-150，¶4-190及び¶4-210で説明したところと同様である。

利子については，所得税及び復興特別所得税15.315％並びに地方税5％の税率で源泉所得税が課される。

配当については，所得税20.42％の税率で源泉所得税が課される。ただし，上場株式等に係る配当に対しては，平成25年12月31日までは7.147％が適用される。

もっとも，申告所得税に関する説明部分は関係がない。法人税の場合は，法律上免税とされない限り，内国法人のすべての所得が課税所得にとり込まれることになっている（所法175）。

158   WITHHOLDING INCOME TAX

¶ 4-550 Withholding tax for income which is similar to interest

Income which is not defined as interest income, but is similar to interest income in nature, is subject to withholding tax at the rate of 20.315% (15.315% for income tax and earthquake restoration surtax and 5% for local tax).

¶ 4-570 Withholding from payments to public entertainers for performances and payments to horse owners as prizes (domestic corporations)

The remuneration paid to a domestic corporation for furnishing public entertainers' performances after April 1, 2003 is not subject to withholding income tax.

A prize paid to a corporation which owns a horse for a horse race is subject to withholding income tax. The tax rate of 10.21% is applied to the amount after deducting ¥600,000 plus 20% of the gross amount of the prize.

¶ 4-580 Distribution of profit based on the silent partnership (Tokumei Kumiai) agreement

Distribution of profit based on the silent partnership (Tokumei Kumiai) agreement is subject to withholding tax at the rate of 20.42%.

Withholding from Payments to Non-residents and Foreign Corporations

¶ 4-620 Withholding from payments to non-residents and foreign corporations

The following items of income paid to a non-resident individual or a foreign corporation are subject to Japanese withholding income tax at a rate of 20.42% (15.315% for the following (1) and (14), 18.378% for profits from redemption of discounted debentures issued in Japan). The tax applies if they are paid in Japan or if they are paid abroad and the payer also has an office, domicile, residence, etc. within Japan at the same time. The due date for the transfer of the withheld tax to a tax office is the end of the calendar month following the month of payment, when they are paid abroad; if the payment is made in Japan, it is the tenth day of the month following the month of the payment (Law 212, 213).

The items of income to which the withholding income tax applies are:

¶ 4-550

¶4-550　利子所得に類似する所得の源泉徴収

　その収益が利子とされているが利子所得と類似する性格を有する定期積金，相互掛金，抵当証券，金貯蓄口座等に係る収益について20.315％（所得税及び復興特別所得税15.315％，地方税5％）の源泉徴収が行われる。

¶4-570　芸能人の役務提供事業に係る報酬又は競馬の賞金

　平成15年4月1日以降に内国法人に支払われる芸能人の役務提供事業に係る報酬に対する源泉徴収は不要となった。

　法人たる馬主に対して支払われる競馬の賞金には源泉所得税が課される。税率は10.21％で，課税標準は，賞金総額から60万円に賞金総額の20％相当額を加えた額を控除した金額である。

¶4-580　匿名組合契約に基づく利益の分配

　内国法人に対して支払われる匿名組合契約に基づく利益の分配についてはその支払額につき20.42％の税率の源泉所得税が課される。

非居住者及び外国法人に対する支払に係る源泉徴収

¶4-620　非居住者及び外国法人に対する支払に係る源泉徴収

　非居住者又は外国法人に対し支払われる次の所得項目については，それが国内で支払われる場合には，又は，それが国外で支払われる場合でも支払者が国内に事務所，住所，居所等を有している場合には，20.42％（下記(1)及び(14)については15.315％，(13)については18.378％）の税率で源泉所得税が課される。源泉徴収した税額の納付期限は，その支払が国外で行われた場合には支払が行われた月の翌月末日，その支払が国内で行われた場合には支払が行われた月の翌月10日となっている（所法212，213）。

160   WITHHOLDING INCOME TAX

(1)   Interest on:
   (a)   bonds or debentures issued by the Japanese Government, local governments in Japan, or a Japanese domestic corporation;
   (b)   deposits with a bank office situated in Japan, or similar credit.
(2)* Interest on loans extended for business carried on in Japan.
(3)   Dividends on shares or securities investment trust certificates issued by a Japanese domestic corporation.
(4)* Rent for the use of real property and similar property located in Japan. Payments for the use of a ship or aircraft rented to a Japanese resident.
(5)   Salaries, wages, bonuses or similar remuneration paid to an employee for personal services performed in Japan.
(6)   "Retirement allowances paid which are attributable to personal services rendered as a resident of Japan, or pensions paid based upon Japanese domestic laws and regulations".
(7)* Remuneration paid to an individual for independent personal services performed in Japan.
(8)* Remuneration paid to a person for furnishing the performances of public entertainers or professional or technical services.
(9)* Royalties (whether in the form of a lump sum or periodical payments) or capital gains derived from patents, know-how, copyright, motion picture films, etc. used for business carried on in Japan.
(10)* Rental received for the use of industrial or commercial equipment by an enterprise in Japan.
(11)* Prizes or other benefits paid for advertising in Japan (after the deduction of ¥500,000 from each payment).
(12)* Annuities paid on contracts concluded with offices or agents in Japan (after the deduction of that portion of payment attributable to the paid-in premiums).
(13)   Profit from redemption of discounted debentures issued in Japan (¶ 4-190).
(14)   Income which is not defined as interest income, but is similar to interest income in nature (¶ 4-550).
(15)* The purchaser of real estate from a non-resident or foreign corporation must withhold an amount equal to 10.21% of the consideration for that real estate. This does not apply, however, when the

¶ 4-620

源泉所得税　161

(1)(a)　日本国の国債若しくは地方債又は内国法人が発行する社債の利子

　(b)　国内にある営業所に預け入れられた預貯金の利子
(2)*　国内において行われる業務に係る貸付金の利子
(3)　内国法人が発行する株式又は証券投資信託証券に係る配当

(4)*　国内にある不動産その他類似の財産の使用の対価，居住者又は内国法人に対する船舶又は航空機の賃貸料

(5)　給料，賃金，賞与又はこれらに類する報酬のうち，国内において行う役務提供に基因するもの
(6)　居住者としての役務提供に基因する退職手当又は年金（日本の法令に基づいて支給されるもの）

(7)*　国内において行われた自由職業の役務提供に対する報酬

(8)*　芸能人，自由職業者又は技術者の役務提供事業を行う者に対するこれらの事業に係る報酬
(9)*　特許権，ノウ・ハウ，著作権，映画フィルム等の使用料（一時払か定期払かを問わない。）又は譲渡の対価のうち国内において行われる業務に係るもの

(10)*　機械，装置等の使用の対価で国内において行われる業務に係るもの

(11)*　国内において行う広告宣伝のための賞金（一回の支払につき50万円の控除がある。）
(12)*　国内にある営業所又は代理人を通じて締結した契約に基づき支払われる年金（払込保険料に対応する年金額の控除がある。）

(13)　国内で発行される割引債の償還差益（¶4-190参照）

(14)　利子所得に類似するもの（¶4-550参照）

(15)*　非居住者又は外国法人が土地等又は建物等を譲渡する場合には，その譲受者は譲渡価額の10.21％相当額を源泉徴収し，国に納付しなければならない。ただし，その譲受者の取得した土地等又は建物等の対価

162   WITHHOLDING INCOME TAX

value of the real estate is 100 million yen or less, and the property is solely for the purchaser's residence or the purchaser's family's residence.

(16) Distribution of profit based on the silent partnership (Tokumei Kumiai) agreement.

(17)* Allocable income to a non-resident partner which is earned through partnership activities in Japan conducted based on the partnership contract stipulated by Civil Law (Nin-i Kumiai).

Note:

(1) If the recipient of income is a non-resident or a foreign corporation having a permanent establishment in Japan, the asterisked (*) items of income mentioned above are exempt from withholding income tax, on condition that the recipient obtains from the taxation office and presents to the payer of income a certificate showing that such income is taxable together with his income from business in Japan. However, where the recipient has a special type of permanent establishment (agent, construction site for more than one year, etc. other than branch, office, etc.) this exemption does not apply to income which is not attributable to the special type of permanent establishment.

(2) Alternative withholding tax treatment (35%, but no assessment income tax) and release from filing a final return applicable to dividend income by an individual resident (¶ 4-210), also apply to an individual non-resident, provided that he has an ordinary type of permanent establishment (branch, office, factory, etc.) or a special type of permanent establishment to which this income is attributable.

(3) Interest paid to a foreign corporation by a financial institution on deposits or loans belonging to a special account for offshore banking is exempt from income tax as a special concession from April 1, 1998 (SM 7).

¶ 4-650 Concessions under tax treaties (withholding income tax)

Some special concessions are granted under tax treaties. Such concessions are usually granted to a resident individual or a resident corporation in a foreign country which has concluded a treaty with Japan, if they are not at the same time a resident in Japan or a Japanese domestic corporation according to Japanese tax laws.

Some tax treaties provide that a person with dual residence may be determined to be a person with single residence by mutual agreement between the competent authorities.

Japan has concluded tax treaties with 68 countries and regions. These are listed   below in order of the date of signature of the original treaty.

¶ 4-650

が１億円以下で，かつ，その土地等又は建物等を自己又は親族の居住の用に供する場合には，この源泉徴収の規定の適用はない。

⒃　匿名組合契約に基づいて支払を受ける利益の分配

⒄*　国内において民法に規定する組合契約に基づいて行う事業から生ずる利益で当該組合契約に基づいて配分を受けるもの

（注）： 1 ．支払を受ける非居住者又は外国法人が国内に恒久的施設を有している場合には，上記＊印の所得項目は，これが事業所得に合算して課税されることを明らかにする所轄税務署の証明書を支払者に提出することを条件に，源泉所得税が免除される。ただし，支払を受ける者が有している恒久的施設が支店，事務所等ではなく，代理人又は 1 年を超える建設工事現場等の特定の恒久的施設である場合には，当該特定の恒久的施設に帰属しない所得については，源泉徴収免除の適用はない。
 2 ．居住者に適用される利子，配当所得に係る源泉分離課税選択制度及び申告不要制度は，通常の恒久的施設（支店，事務所，工場等）又は当該利子，配当所得が帰属する特定の恒久的施設を有する非居住者にも同様に適用される。
 3 ．外国法人が金融機関に預入等した預金等で特別国際金融取引勘定に経理されたものに係る利子について，平成10年 4 月 1 日から非課税とされる（措法 7 ）。

¶4-650　租税条約による特例

　租税条約によりいくつかの特例措置が認められる。これらの特例措置は，通常，わが国が条約を締結した相手国の居住者たる個人又は法人（わが国の税法においてわが国の居住者又は内国法人とされない者である必要がある。）に対して認められる。なお，租税条約の中には，双方居住者を権限ある当局間の協議によりいずれの一方の居住者にする規定を有するものもある。

　わが国は，次の68カ国・地域との間で租税条約を締結している。

164   WITHHOLDING INCOME TAX

1. U.S.A.
2. Sweden
3. Pakistan
4. Norway
5. Denmark
6. India
7. Singapore
8. Austria
9. United Kingdom
10. New Zealand
11. Thailand
12. Malaysia
13. Canada
14. France
15. The Federal Republic of Germany
16. Brazil
17. Sri Lanka
18. Belgium
19. Egypt
20. Italy
21. Australia
22. Zambia
23. The Netherlands
24. The Republic of Korea
25. Switzerland
26. Finland
27. Spain
28. Ireland
29. Romania
30. Czech
31. Slovakia
32. Philippines
33. Hungary
34. Poland
35. Indonesia
36. The People's Republic of China

¶ 4-650

（原条約の署名順）

① アメリカ合衆国
② スウェーデン
③ パキスタン
④ ノルウェー
⑤ デンマーク
⑥ インド
⑦ シンガポール
⑧ オーストリア
⑨ 英国
⑩ ニュージーランド
⑪ タイ
⑫ マレーシア
⑬ カナダ
⑭ フランス
⑮ ドイツ連邦共和国
⑯ ブラジル
⑰ スリ・ランカ
⑱ ベルギー
⑲ エジプト
⑳ イタリア
㉑ オーストラリア
㉒ ザンビア
㉓ オランダ
㉔ 韓国
㉕ スイス
㉖ フィンランド
㉗ スペイン
㉘ アイルランド
㉙ ルーマニア
㉚ チェコ
㉛ スロヴァキア
㉜ フィリピン
㉝ ハンガリー
㉞ ポーランド
㉟ インドネシア
㊱ 中華人民共和国

166   WITHHOLDING INCOME TAX

37. Russia (the Union of Soviet Socialist Republics)
38. Kyrgyzstan
39. Georgia
40. Tajikistan
41. Uzbekistan
42. Turkmenistan
43. Ukraine
44. Armenia
45. Belarus
46. Azerbaijan
47. Moldova
48. Bangladesh
49. Bulgaria
50. Luxemburg
51. Turkey
52. Israel
53. Vietnam
54. Mexico
55. South Africa
56. Fiji
57. Kazakhstan
58. Brunei Darussalam
59. Kuwait
60. Hong Kong
61. Saudi Arabia
62. Portugal
63. United Arab Emirates
64. Oman
65. Qatar
66. Taiwan
67. Latvia
68. Slovenia

Japan also concluded a tax treaty with the Union of Soviet Socialist Republics. This treaty is also applied to Russia, Kyrgyzstan, Georgia, Tajikistan, Uzbekistan, Turkmenistan, Ukraine, Armenia, Belarus, Azerbaijan and Moldova.

The following description is concerned only with the important con-

¶ 4-650

㊲ ロシア（旧ソ連）
㊳ キルギスタン
㊴ ジョージア
㊵ タジキスタン
㊶ ウズベキスタン
㊷ トルクメニスタン
㊸ ウクライナ
㊹ アルメニア
㊺ ベラルーシ
㊻ アゼルバイジャン
㊼ モルドヴァ
㊽ バングラデシュ人民共和国
㊾ ブルガリア共和国
㊿ ルクセンブルク
(51) トルコ
(52) イスラエル
(53) ヴェトナム
(54) メキシコ
(55) 南アフリカ
(56) フィジー
(57) カザフスタン
(58) ブルネイ・ダルサラーム
(59) クウェート
(60) 香港
(61) サウジアラビア王国
(62) ポルトガル
(63) アラブ首長国連邦
(64) オマーン
(65) カタール
(66) 台湾
(67) ラトビア
(68) スロベニア

日本は旧ソ連との間で租税条約の締結があるが，この条約については，ロシア，キルギスタン，ジョージア，タジキスタン，ウズベキスタン，トルクメニスタン，ウクライナ，アルメニア，ベラルーシ，アゼルバイジャン及びモルドヴァ各共和国との間で引き続き適用されることが合意されている。

以下の説明は，日本が締結した租税条約のうち大多数の読者が関心を有し

168   WITHHOLDING INCOME TAX

cessions granted to non-residents and foreign corporations under the treaties which Japan has concluded with the U.S.A., Canada, the United Kingdom, France, Germany, Sweden, Australia, New Zealand, the People's Republic of China, Malaysia, Singapore, Korea and Thailand, as the majority of readers are assumed to be interested in those treaties. The provisions of the treaties themselves should be referred to for details.

(1) **Interest (including interest on loans)**

Japanese withholding income tax on interest from sources within Japan is reduced, unless the interest is attributable to a permanent establishment in Japan, from 20% to 10% when the interest is paid to individual or corporate residents in Canada, France, Australia, the People's Republic of China, Singapore, Korea and Malaysia. And also, in the U.S.A, the reduced tax rate of 10% is applicable and, in addition, interests paid to specified financial institutions are exempted. The reduced tax rate of 10% is only applicable when the recipient is a financial institution, according to the Japan-Thailand tax treaty. There is no provision in the Japan-New Zealand tax treaty for reducing rates of withholding tax on interest.

(2) **Dividends**

Japanese withholding income tax on dividends paid by a Japanese domestic corporation to a shareholder who is a resident (individual or corporate) in the People's Republic of China, the United Kingdom, France, Australia and Sweden is reduced from 20% to 10% and in Canada, Germany, New Zealand, Malaysia, Singapore or Korea is reduced from 20% to 15%, unless the dividends are attributable to a permanent establishment in Japan.

In addition, dividends paid by a Japanese domestic corporation (subsidiary) to a corporate shareholder (parent company) can be subject to the more reduced tax rate.

In the case of France, Australia and Sweden, the 10% or 15% rate is reduced to zero or 5% in accordance to the ownership ratio of the voting shares of the subsidiary by the parent company.

In the case of Singapore, Malaysia, Canada or Korea, the 15% rate is reduced to 5% on dividends paid by a Japanese domestic corporation to a corporate shareholder who owns at least 25% of the voting shares of the subsidiary by the parent company.

In the case of Germany, the 15% rate is reduced to 10% on dividends

¶ 4-650

源 泉 所 得 税　169

ていると思われるアメリカ，カナダ，英国，フランス，ドイツ，スウェーデ
ン，オーストラリア，ニュージーランド，中華人民共和国，マレーシア，シ
ンガポール，韓国及びタイとの間の租税条約において非居住者及び外国法人
に対して認められている主要な特例についてである。詳しくは条約本文の規
定を参照されたい。

(1)　利子（貸付金の利子を含む。）

　わが国源泉の利子については，それが国内にある恒久的施設に帰せられな
い限り，20％の源泉徴収税率が，カナダ，フランス，オーストラリア，中華
人民共和国，シンガポール，韓国及びマレーシアの居住者たる個人又は法人
に支払われるものにあっては10％に，それぞれ軽減される。アメリカの居住
者たる個人又は法人に支払われるものにあっては，10％の軽減税率を定める
とともに，一定の金融機関に対する利子に対しては免税としている。日・タ
イ租税条約においては，利子の受領者が金融機関に限って，10％の税率に軽
減される。日・ニュージーランド租税条約においては，利子についての軽減
税率を定めた条項はない。

(2)　配当

　日本の内国法人が支払う配当については，それが国内にある恒久的施設に
帰せられない限り，20％の源泉徴収税率が，中華人民共和国，英国，フラン
ス，オーストラリア及びスウェーデンの居住者たる個人又は法人株主に支払
われるものは10％に軽減され，カナダ，ドイツ，ニュージーランド，マレー
シア，シンガポール及び韓国の居住者たる個人又は法人の株主に支払われる
ものにあっては15％に軽減される。
　この10％又は15％の税率は，親子会社間配当の場合，フランス，オースト
ラリア及びスウェーデンについては，持株割合に応じて免税又は５％，シン
ガポール，マレーシア，カナダ，韓国については５％，その他の国について
は10％まで軽減される。親子会社の要件は，株主がスウェーデン，カナダ，
ドイツ，マレーシア又はシンガポールの会社の場合には，日本の子会社の議
決権ある株式の25％以上を有していること，株主がフランスの会社の場合に
は，日本の子会社の議決権ある株式の15％以上を有していること，オースト
ラリアの会社の場合には，10％若しくは80％以上を有していることである。
中国及びニュージーランドとの租税条約においては，このような親子会社配
当についての軽減税率の規定はない。
　日・仏租税条約においては，適格居住者である親会社が子会社から受ける
配当は免税とされている。

170 WITHHOLDING INCOME TAX

paid by a Japanese domestic corporation to a corporate shareholder who own at least 25% of the voting shares of the subsidiary by the parent company.

In the case of the People's Republic of China and New Zealand, there is no provision to reduce the dividends paid to a parent corporation.

In case of Japan France tax treaty, the above ownership of 25% is reduced to 15%.

In the case of Thailand, the dividends paid by a Japanese corporation to a corporate who owns at least 25% of the voting share of that corporation are taxed at 20%.

Dividends paid by a Japanese domestic corporation to a shareholder (individual or corporate) who is a resident of the U.S.A., and not a resident or a domestic corporation of Japan, are subject to withholding income tax at the rate of 10%, unless the dividends are attributable to a permanent establishment in Japan. The 10% rate is reduced to 5% or dividends are exempted from withholding tax if dividends are paid to any U.S.A. corporation fulfilling certain conditions.

*The 5% tax rate will apply if: The beneficial owner is a company that owns directly or indirectly, on the date on which entitlement to the dividends is determined, at least 10% of the voting stock of the company paying the dividends.

The withholding tax exemption will apply if:

*The beneficial owner of the dividends is:

(a) 1) a company that is a resident of U.S.A., that has owned, directly or indirectly through one or more residents of U.S.A. or Japan, more than 50% of the voting stock of the company paying the dividends for the period of 12 months ending on the date on which entitlement to the dividends is determined, and

2) a company that satisfies the conditions described in the article 22.

(b) A pension fund that is a resident of U.S.A. provided that such dividends are not derived from the carrying on of a business, directly or indirectly, by such pension fund.

In the case of the United Kingdom, the dividends are subject to withholding income tax at the rate of 10%. In addition, the 10% rate is reduced to 5% or dividends are exempted from withholding tax under the certain requirements.

¶ 4-650

タイの場合には，持株比率25％以上の会社の支払配当については20％の税率で課税される。

日本の内国法人がアメリカの居住者であり，かつ，日本の居住者又は内国法人でない株主（個人又は法人を問わない。）に支払う配当については，日本に所在する恒久的施設に帰せられない限り，10％の税率の源泉所得税が課される。一定の要件を満たすアメリカ法人に支払われる配当については，この10％の税率が5％に軽減若しくは免税となる。その要件は次のとおりである。

＊軽減税率（5％）が適用される場合：
　配当の受益者が，その配当の支払を受ける者が特定される日に，その配当を支払う法人の議決権のある株式の10％以上を直接又は間接に所有する法人であること。

＊免税が適用される場合：
　(a)　アメリカの居住者であり，かつ，その配当の支払を受ける者が特定される日をその末日とする12カ月の期間を通じ，その配当を支払う日本法人の議決権のある株式の50％を超える株式を直接に又はアメリカ，日本のいずれかの国の一若しくは二以上の居住者を通じて間接に所有する法人であって，一定の要件を満たす法人であること。

　(b)　アメリカの居住者である年金基金。ただし，その配当が，年金基金が直接又は間接に事業を遂行することにより取得されたものでない場合に限る。
　英国の場合には，10％の税率の源泉所得税が課されるが，親子会社間配当の場合，一定の要件の下で，この10％の税率が5％に軽減若しくは免税となる。

172   WITHHOLDING INCOME TAX

(3) **Salaries, wages, bonuses, etc.**

Salaries, wages, bonuses, etc. are exempt from Japanese income tax if a resident of the U.S.A, Canada, the United Kingdom, France, Germany, Sweden, Australia, New Zealand, the People's Republic of China, Malaysia, Singapore, Korea or Thailand visits Japan and stays temporarily (183 days or less in a calendar year or in 12 months) and receives such remuneration from an employer in one of those countries. In the case of Thailand, the above 183 days is changed to 180 days.

A similar exemption is also applicable to compensation from the practice of professional services, under treaties with New Zealand, and Thailand. Under treaties with the United Kingdom, Canada, France, Germany, Sweden and Australia, income from professional services or other independent activities is not subject to Japanese tax, unless a fixed place is established in Japan for the performance of such activities.

In the case of Singapore, Korea, Malaysia and the People's Republic of China income from the professional who stays in Japan more than 183 days in 12 months or has a fixed place of business in Japan is subject to tax.

In the case of U.S., income from the professional is not subject to tax unless a fixed place is established in Japan and the professional stays in Japan more than 183 days. U.S. entertainers' profits is not subject to tax except to the profits of a public entertainer who provides an independent service when the profits exceed 10,000 US dollars or the equivalent of 10,000 US dollars in yen.

A special exemption is granted to professors and students visiting Japan.

(4) **Royalties, capital gains from the transfer of ownership of patents etc.**

Japanese withholding income tax levied on royalties on any patents, know-how, copyright, design, etc. with a Japanese source is reduced from 20% to 10% when such royalties are paid to a resident of Canada, Oman, the People's Republic of China, Malaysia, Singapore, Korea or United Arab Emirates unless they are attributable to a permanent establishment in Japan. In case of the United Kingdom, France, Sweden and Germany royalties are exempted from withholding tax. And in the case of Australia, the tax rate is reduced from 20% to 5%.

According to the new Japan-U.S.A. tax treaty, royalties are exempted

¶ 4-650

源 泉 所 得 税 173

⑶ 給料，賃金，賞与等

給料，賃金，賞与等については，アメリカ，カナダ，英国，フランス，ドイツ，スウェーデン，オーストラリア，ニュージーランド，中華人民共和国，マレーシア，シンガポール又は韓国の居住者が日本に一時的に（年間又は12カ月のうち183日以下）滞在し，かつ，本国の雇用者から報酬の支払を受ける場合に，一定条件の下で所得税が免除される。

タイの場合には，上記の183日の条件は180日とされて同様の免税措置がある。

このような免税措置は，自由職業活動の対価についても，ニュージーランド及びタイとの条約において認められている。英国，カナダ，フランス，ドイツ，スウェーデン及びオーストラリアとの間の条約では，自由職業ないし独立の活動から取得する所得については，日本国内にその活動のための固定的施設を有していない限り，免税とされる。日・シンガポール条約においては，自由職業者については，固定的施設を有する場合に課税が行われ，固定的施設を有しない場合には12カ月のうち183日超滞在するときに課税が行われる。

アメリカの場合には，自由職業者については，固定的施設を有する場合に課税が行われ，固定的施設がない場合には課税年度のうち183日超滞在するときに課税が行われる。アメリカの芸能人が10,000ドルを超える所得を得た場合には課税されることとなる。

なお，日本を訪問する教授又は学生についても，一定の条件で，免税措置が認められている。

⑷ 使用料，特許権等の譲渡益

特許権，ノウハウ，著作権，デザイン等に関する国内源泉所得に該当する使用料につき，カナダ，オマーン，中華人民共和国，マレーシア，シンガポール，韓国又はアラブ首長国連邦の居住者に支払われる使用料に課される源泉所得税の税率は，当該使用料が日本国内に所在する恒久的施設に帰せられない限り，20％が10％に軽減される。英国，フランス，スウェーデン及びドイツの場合は，免税となり，オーストラリアの場合は5％となる。

新日米租税条約によると，使用料は免除となる。ただし，使用料の支払者と支払を受ける者との間の特別の関係により，使用料の額が，その関係がないとしたならば合意したとみられる額を超えるときは，その合意したとみられる額についてのみ免税となる。この場合，支払われた額のうち超過分に対

174   WITHHOLDING INCOME TAX

from withholding tax unless they are attributable to a permanent establishment in Japan. However, by reason of a special relationship between the payer and the beneficial owner, when the amount of the royalties exceeds the amount which would have been agreed upon such relationship, the tax exemption applies only to the amount seemed to be agreed. In this case, the excess part of the payment is subject to withholding tax at the rate of 5%.

A similar tax reduction, but to 15% instead of 10%, is granted to Thai residents.

In the case of New Zealand, tax rate on royalties is reduced to 5%. Capital gains accruing from a genuine alienation of a patent or similar property to a Japanese resident (individual or corporate), without leaving the alienable any right to such property, are exempt from Japanese tax when they are derived by a German or a British resident and such property does not form part of the business property of a permanent establishment in Japan. Such capital gains derived by a U.S.A. resident are also exempt from Japanese tax, provided that the amounts realized on such alienation for consideration are not contingent on the productivity, use, or disposition of such property or rights. Such capital gains derived by a resident of Singapore, Malaysia or Korea are taxable, with the tax rate reduced from 20% to 10% (12%).

In the case of Thailand, the tax rate is reduced from 20% to 15%.

The resident of Sweden, New Zealand, Canada or the People's Republic of China is subject to Japanese income tax based on the provisions of Japanese domestic law, and is taxed at the rate of 20%, as there is no applicable reduced tax rate in tax treaties.

¶ 4-680 Unilateral concessions

For the purpose of taxation for non-resident and foreign corporation, interest on debenture issued outside Japan by a domestic corporation is exempt from Japanese income tax when the taxpayer submits the application for exemption to the district tax office through the payer of the interest.

However, this tax-exemption is not applicable if the interest is attributable to the permanent establishment located in Japan (SM 6).

For the purpose of taxation for non-resident, discounts on debenture

¶ 4-680

源 泉 所 得 税 175

しては，5％を超えない。

タイの場合には，10％ではなく15％ではあるが，同様に軽減税率の適用が認められる。ニュージーランドとの租税条約においては，5％の軽減税率で課税される。

日本の居住者又は内国法人に対する特許権又は類似の資産の真正な譲渡（譲渡者にいかなる権利も残さないこと）から生ずる所得については，ドイツ又はイギリスの居住者が所得を得る場合には，当該所得が日本に所在する恒久的施設に帰せられない限り，免除とされる。アメリカの居住者の場合には，対価を得て行う処分によって実現する収益が，その財産又は権利の生産性，使用又は処分に対応しないものであれば，免税となる。シンガポール，マレーシア及び韓国の場合は，課税対象とされるが，20％の税率が10％（12％）に軽減される。

タイの場合には，その税率は20％が15％に軽減される。

スウェーデン，カナダ，ニュージーランド及び中華人民共和国との租税条約においては，譲渡の場合の軽減税率の規定がないので，国内法どおり20％の税率で課税される。

¶4-680　国内法による特例措置

(1) 非居住者又は外国法人が民間国外債につき支払を受ける利子について，これらの者が非課税申告書をその利子の支払者を経由して税務署長に提出する場合にはその利子についての所得税は課されない。ただし，利子がこれらの者の日本に所在する恒久的施設に帰せられる場合には，課税の対象とされる（措法6）。

(2) 非居住者が民間国外債につき支払を受ける発行差金については所得税を課さない。ただし，発行差金が非居住者の日本に所在する恒久的施設に帰せられる場合には，課税の対象とされる（措法41の13）。

176   WITHHOLDING INCOME TAX

issued outside Japan by a domestic corporation is exempt from Japanese income tax.

However, this tax exemption is not applicable if the discounts are attributable to the permanent establishment located in Japan (SM 41-13).

For the purpose of taxation for foreign corporation, discounts on debenture issued outside Japan by a domestic corporation are exempt from Japanese corporate tax.

However, this tax exemption is not applicable if the discounts are attributable to the permanent establishment located in Japan (SM 67-17).

¶ 4-830 Application forms

Exemption from, or reduction of, Japanese withholding income tax under the tax treaties usually means no further collection of Japanese assessment income tax or Japanese corporation tax.

Following are titles of application forms for exemption or deduction granted under tax treaties. Of these forms, forms with respect to dividends and interest are shown at ¶ 4-830 ff.

Form 1: Relief from Japanese Income Tax on Dividends

Form 2: Relief from Japanese Income Tax on Interest

Form 3: Relief from Japanese Income Tax on Royalties

Form 4: Extension of Time for Withholding of Tax on Dividends with respect to Foreign Depositary Receipt

Form 5: Relief from Japanese Income Tax on Dividends with respect to Foreign Depositary Receipt

Form 6: Relief from japanese tax on Remuneration Derived from Rendering Personal Services

Form 7: Relief from Japanese Income Tax on Income Earned by Professionals, Entertainers, Sportsmen and Temporary Visitors

Form 8: Relief from Japanese Income Tax on Remunerations, Grants, etc., Received by Professors, Students or Business Apprentices

Form 9: Relief from Japanese Income Tax on Pensions, Annuities, etc.

Form 10: Relief from Japanese Income Tax on Income Not Expressly Mentioned in the Income Tax Convention

Form 11: Application Form for Refund of the Overpaid Withholding

¶ 4-830

源　泉　所　得　税　177

(3)　外国法人が民間国外債につき支払を受ける発行差金については法人税を課さない。ただし，発行差金が外国法人の日本に所在する恒久的施設に帰せられる場合には課税の対象とされる（措法67の17）。

¶4-830　租税条約に関する届出書

　租税条約においてわが国の源泉所得税を免除し又は軽減することは，通常，申告所得税又は法人税がもはや課されないということである。

　なお，租税条約に基づく減免措置を受けるための申請様式には次のものがあるが，参考のためこのうち利子と配当に関する様式を以下に掲げてある。

様式 1　配当に対する所得税の軽減・免除
様式 2　利子に対する所得税の軽減・免除
様式 3　使用料に対する所得税の軽減・免除
様式 4　外国預託証券に係る配当に対する所得税の源泉徴収の猶予

様式 5　外国預託証券に係る配当に対する所得税の軽減

様式 6　人的役務提供事業の対価に対する所得税の免除

様式 7　自由職業者・芸能人・運動家・短期滞在者の報酬・給与に対する所得税の免除

様式 8　教授等・留学生・事業等の修習者・交付金等の受領者の報酬・交付金等に対する所得税の免除

様式 9　退職年金・保険年金等に対する所得税の免除

様式10　所得税法第161条第 3 号から第 7 号まで，第 9 号，第11号又は第12号に掲げる所得・割引債の償還差益に対する所得税の免除
様式11　租税条約に関する源泉徴収税額の還付請求書

178 WITHHOLDING INCOME TAX

Tax other than Redemption of Securities and Remuneration Derived from Rendering Personal Services Exercised by an Entertainer or a Sportsman in accordance with the Income Tax Convention

Form 12: Application Form for Refund of the Withholding Tax on Remuneration Derived from Rendering Personal Services Exercised by an Entertainer or a Sportsman in accordance with the Income Tax Convention

Form 13: Application Form for Refund of the Withholding Tax on Profit from Redemption of Securities in accordance with the Income Tax Convention (Discount government bonds only)

Form 14: Application Form for Refund of the Withholding Tax on Profit from Redemption of Securities in accordance with the Income Tax Convention (for Discount debentures other than Discount government bonds)

Form 15: Application Form for Income Tax Convention

Form 16: List of the Members of Foreign Company or List of the Partners of Entity

Form 17: Attachment Form for Limitation on Benefits Article

¶ 4-830

様式12　租税条約に関する芸能人等の役務提供事業の対価に係る源泉徴収税額の還付請求書

様式13　租税条約に関する割引債の償還差益に係る源泉徴収税額の還付請求書（割引国債用）

様式14　租税条約に関する割引債の償還差益に係る源泉徴収税額の還付請求書（割引国債以外の割引債用）

様式15　租税条約に関する届出書
様式16　外国法人の株主等の名簿兼相手国団体の構成員の名簿

様式17　特典条項に関する付表

180   WITHHOLDING INCOME TAX

Form 1

様式 1
FORM

支払者受付印　税務署受付印

租税条約に関する届出書

APPLICATION FORM FOR INCOME TAX CONVENTION

(配当に対する所得税の軽減・免除)
(Relief from Japanese Income Tax on Dividends)

この届出書の記載に当たっては、別紙の注意事項を参照してください。
See separate instructions.

税務署整理欄
For official use only

適用；有、無

To the District Director of ＿＿＿＿＿ 税務署長殿 Tax Office

1　適用を受ける租税条約に関する事項；
　　Applicable Income Tax Convention
　　日本国と＿＿＿＿＿＿との間の租税条約第＿＿条第＿＿項
　　The Income Tax Convention between Japan and ＿＿＿＿＿＿ ,Article ＿＿ ,para. ＿＿

□ 限度税率　　　％
　 Applicable Tax Rate
□ 免　税
　 Exemption

2　配当の支払を受ける者に関する事項；
　　Details of Recipient of Dividends

氏　名　又　は　名　称 Full name		
個人の場合 Individual	住　所　又　は　居　所 Domicile or residence	（電話番号 Telephone Number）
	国　　　　籍 Nationality	
法人その他の団体の場合 Corporation or other entity	本店又は主たる事務所の所在地 Place of head office or main office	（電話番号 Telephone Number）
	設立又は組織された場所 Place where the Corporation was established or organized	
	事業が管理・支配されている場所 Place where the business is managed or controlled	（電話番号 Telephone Number）
下記「4」の配当につき居住者として課税される国、納税地（注8） Country where the recipient is taxable as resident on Dividends mentioned in 4 below and the place where he is to pay tax (Note8)		（納税者番号　Taxpayer Identification Number）
日本国内の恒久的施設の状況 Permanent establishment in Japan □有(Yes) , □無(No) If "Yes",explain:	名　　　称 Name	
	所　在　地 Address	（電話番号 Telephone Number）
	事　業　の　内　容 Details of Business	

3　配当の支払者に関する事項；
　　Details of Payer of Dividends

(1)　名　　　　　　　称 Full name	
(2)　本　店　の　所　在　地 Place of head office	（電話番号 Telephone Number）
(3)　発行済株式のうち議決権のある株式の数(注9) Number of voting shares issued (Note 9)	

4　上記「3」の支払者から支払を受ける配当で「1」の租税条約の規定の適用を受けるものに関する事項（注10）；
　　Details of Dividends received from the Payer to which the Convention mentioned in 1 above is applicable (Note 10)

元　本　の　種　類 Kind of Principal	銘柄又は名称 Description	名義人の氏名又は名称（注11） Name of Nominee of Principal(Note 11)	証券の記号・番号 Registered Number	元　本　の　取　得　年　月　日 Date of Acquisition of Principal
□出資・株式・基金 Shares (Stocks) □株式投資信託 Stock investment trust				

元　本　の　数　量 Quantity of Principal	左のうち議決権のある株式数 Of which Quantity of Voting Shares	配　当　の　支　払　期　日 Due Date for Payment	配　当　の　金　額 Amount of Dividends

5　その他参考となるべき事項（注12）；
　　Others (Note 12)

¶ 4-830

源 泉 所 得 税 181

6 日本の税法上、届出書の「2」の外国法人が納税義務者とされるが、「1」の租税条約の相手国では、その外国法人の株主等が納税義務者とされており、かつ、租税条約の規定によりその株主等である者（相手国居住者に限ります。）の所得として取り扱われる部分に対して租税条約の適用を受けることとされている場合の租税条約の適用に関する割合に関する事項等(注4)；
Details of proportion of income to which the convention mentioned in 1 above is applicable, if the foreign company mentioned in 2 above is taxable as a company under Japanese tax law, and the member of the company is treated as taxable person in the other contracting country of the convention; and if the convention is applicable to income that is treated as income of the member (limited to a resident of the other contracting country) of the foreign company in accordance with the provisions of the convention (Note 4)

届出書の「2」の欄に記載した外国法人は、「4」の配当につき、「1」の租税条約の相手国において次の法令に基づいて、次の日以後、その株主等である者が課されることとされています。
The member of the foreign company mentioned in 2 above is taxable in the other contracting country mentioned in 1 above regarding the dividends mentioned in 4 above since the following date under the following law of the other contracting country

根拠法令 _____ 効力を生じる日 ___ 年 ___ 月 ___ 日
Applicable law   Effective date

届出書の「2」の外国法人の株主等で租税条約の適用を受ける者の名称 Name of member of the foreign company mentioned in 2 above, to whom the Convention is applicable	間接保有 Indirect Ownership	持分の割合 Ratio of Ownership	受益の割合＝ 租税条約の適用を受ける割合 Proportion of benefit = Proportion for Application of Convention
	☐	___ %	___ %
	☐	___ %	___ %
	☐	___ %	___ %
	☐	___ %	___ %
	☐	___ %	___ %
合計 Total		___ %	___ %

7 日本の税法上、届出書の「2」の団体の構成員が納税義務者とされるが、「1」の租税条約の相手国ではその団体が納税義務者とされており、かつ、租税条約の規定によりその団体の所得として取り扱われる部分に対して租税条約の適用を受けることとされている場合の記載事項等(注5)；
Details if, while the partner of the entity mentioned in 2 above is taxable under Japanese tax law, the entity is taxable person in the other contracting country of the convention mentioned in 1 above, and if the convention is applicable to income that is treated as income of the entity in accordance with the provisions of the convention (Note 5)

届出書の「2」の欄に記載した団体は、「4」の配当につき、「1」の欄に掲げる租税条約の相手国において次の法令に基づいて、次の日以後、法人として課税されることとされています。
The entity mentioned in 2 above is taxable as a corporation regarding the dividends mentioned in 4 above since the following date under the following law in the other contracting country of the convention mentioned in 1 above

根拠法令 _____ 効力を生じる日 ___ 年 ___ 月 ___ 日
Applicable law   Effective date

他のすべての構成員から通知を受けこの届出書を提出する構成員の氏名又は名称 _____
Full name of the partner of the entity who has been notified by all other partners and is to submit this form

私は、この届出書の「4」に記載した配当が「1」に掲げる租税条約の規定の適用を受けるものであることを、「租税条約の実施に伴う所得税法、法人税法及び地方税法の特例等に関する法律の施行に関する省令」の規定により届け出るとともに、この届出書(及び付表)の記載事項が正確かつ完全であることを宣言します。

In accordance with the provisions of the Ministerial Ordinance for the Implementation of the Law concerning the Special Measures of the Income Tax Law, the Corporation Tax Law and the Local Tax Law for the Enforcement of Income Tax Conventions, I hereby submit this application form under the belief that the provisions of the Income Tax Convention mentioned in 1 above is applicable to Dividends mentioned in 4 above and also hereby declare that the statement on this form (and attachment form) is correct and complete to the best of my knowledge and belief.

Date___ 年 ___ 月 ___ 日
      配当の支払を受ける者又はその代理人の署名
      Signature of the Recipient of Dividends or his Agent _____

8 権限ある当局の証明 （注13）
Certification of competent authority (Note 13)

私は、届出者が、日本国と_____との間の租税条約第___条第___項___に規定する居住者であることを証明します。
I hereby certify that the applicant is a resident under the provisions of the Income Tax Convention between Japan and _____, Article_____, para._____.

Date___ 年 ___ 月 ___ 日   Signature_____

○ 代理人に関する事項 ； この届出書を代理人によって提出する場合には、次の欄に記載してください。
Details of the Agent ； If this form is prepared and submitted by the Agent, fill out the following Columns.

代理人の資格 Capacity of Agent in Japan	氏名 （名称） Full name	納税管理人の届出をした税務署名 Name of the Tax Office where the Tax Agent is registered
☐ 納税管理人 ※ Tax Agent ☐ その他の代理人 Other Agent	住所 （居所・所在地） Domicile (Residence or location)　（電話番号 Telephone Number）	税務署 Tax Office

※ 「納税管理人」とは、日本国の国税に関する申告、申請、請求、届出、納付等の事項を処理させるため、国税通則法の規定により選任し、かつ、日本国における納税地の所轄税務署長に届出をした代理人をいいます。

※ "Tax Agent" means a person who is appointed by the taxpayer and is registered at the District Director of Tax Office for the place where the taxpayer is to pay his tax, in order to have such agent take necessary procedures concerning the Japanese national taxes, such as filing a return, applications, claims, payment of taxes, etc., under the provisions of the General Law for National Taxes.

○ 適用を受ける租税条約が特典条項を有する租税条約である場合
If the applicable convention has article of limitation on benefits

特典条項に関する付表の添付 ☐有Yes
"Attachment Form for Limitation on Benefits Article attached" ☐添付省略 Attachment not required
（特典条項に関する付表を添付して提出した租税条約に関する届出書の提出日
Date of previous submission of the application for income tax convention with the "Attachment Form for Limitation on Benefits Article ___ 年 ___ 月 ___ 日）

182   WITHHOLDING INCOME TAX

様 式　1
FORM

「租税条約に関する届出書(配当に対する所得税の軽減・免除)」に関する注意事項

INSTRUCTIONS FOR "APPLICATION FORM FOR RELIEF FROM JAPANESE INCOME TAX ON DIVIDENDS"

─注　意　事　項─

届出書の提出について

1　この届出書は、配当に係る日本国の所得税の源泉徴収税額について租税条約の規定に基づく軽減又は免除を受けようとする場合に使用します。

2　この届出書は、配当の支払者ごとに作成してください。

3　この届出書は、正副2通を作成して配当の支払者に提出し、配当の支払者は、正本を、最初にその配当の支払をする日の前日までにその支払者の所轄税務署長に提出してください。この届出書の提出後その記載事項に異動が生じた場合も同様です。
　　なお、記載事項に異動が生じた場合において、異動が生じた記載事項が届出書の「4」の「元本の数量」や「配当の金額」の増加又は減少によるものである場合には、異動に係る届出書の提出を省略することができます。
　　無記名の受益証券等に係る配当については、その支払を受ける都度、この届出書を正副2通作成して配当の支払者に提出し、配当の支払者は、正本をその支払の所轄税務署長に提出してください。

4　外国法人であって、米国ではその株主等が納税義務者とされるものが支払を受ける所得については、米国居住者である株主等（その株主等の受益する部分に限ります。）についての日米租税条約の規定の適用を受けることができます。上記に該当する外国法人は、次の書類を添付して提出してください。
　① 届出書の「2」の欄に記載した外国法人が米国においてその株主等が課税を受けていることを明らかにする書類
　② 「外国法人の株主等の名簿(様式16)」
　③ 日米租税条約の適用を受けることができる株主等がその外国法人の株主等であることを明らかにする書類
　　なお、この場合には、「特典条項に関する付表(様式17)」(その添付書類を含みます。)については、③の各株主等のものを添付してください。

5　日米租税条約の米国の居住者に該当する団体であって、日本ではその構成員が納税義務者とされる団体の構成員(その団体の居住地国の居住者だけでなく、それ以外の国の居住者や日本の居住者も含みます。以下同じです。)は、この届出書に次の書類を添付して提出してください。
　　なお、その団体の構成員のうち特定の構成員が他のすべての構成員から「相手国団体の構成員の名簿(様式16)」に記載すべき事項について通知を受けかつその事項を記載した「相手国団体の構成員の名簿(様式16)」を提出した場合には、すべての構成員が届出書を提出しているものとみなされます。
　① 届出書の「2」の欄に記載した団体が居住地国において法人として課税を受けていることを明らかにする書類
　② 「相手国団体の構成員の名簿(様式16)」
　③ 「相手国団体の構成員の名簿」に記載された構成員が届出書の「2」の団体の構成員であることを明らかにする書類
　　なお、この場合には、「特典条項に関する付表(様式17)」(その添付書類も含みます。)は、届出書の「2」の欄に記載した団体のものを添付してください。

6　この届出書を納税管理人以外の代理人によって提出する場合には、その委任関係を証する委任状をその翻訳文とともに添付してください。

届出書の記載について

7　届出書の□欄には、該当する項目について✓印を付してください。

8　納税者番号とは、租税の申告、納付その他の手続を行うために用いる番号、記号その他の符号でその手続をすべき者を特定することができるものをいいます。支払を受ける者が納税者番号を有しない場合や支払を受ける者の居住地である国に納税者番号に関する制度が存在しない場合には納税者番号を記載する必要はありません。

9　届出書の「3」の「③」の欄には、配当の支払を受ける者が配当の支払者の議決権のある発行済株式の10%以上を所有している場合に記載してください。

10　届出書の「4」の各欄には、配当の支払を受ける者が日本国内に支店等の恒久的施設を有する場合は、その恒久的施設に帰せられない配当について記載してください。

【裏面に続きます】

─INSTRUCTIONS─

Submission of the FORM

1　This form is to be used by the Recipient of Dividends in claiming the relief from Japanese Income Tax under the provisions of the Income Tax Convention.

2　This form must be prepared separately for each Payer of Dividends.

3　This form must be submitted in duplicate to the Payer of Dividends , who has to file the original with the District Director of Tax Office for the place where the Payer resides, by the day before the payment of the Dividends is made. The same procedures must be followed when there is any change in the statements on this form except if the change results in an increase or decrease in the "Quantity of Principal", or "Amount of Dividends" mentioned in column 4.
　　However, in case of Dividends from bearer securities, this form must be submitted in duplicate at the time of each payment of such Dividends .

4　In case of income that is received by a foreign company whose member is treated as taxable person in the United States, the Japan-US Income Tax Convention is applicable only to US resident members (to the extent that the income is a benefit of the members). Such foreign companys should attach the following documents to this form:
　① Documents showing that the member of the foreign company mentioned in 2 is treated as taxable person in the United States.
　② "List of the Members of Foreign Company (Form 16)"
　③ Documents showing that the member to whom the Japan-US Income Tax Convention is applicable is a member of the foreign company.
　　Also attach "Attachment Form for Limitation on Benefits Article (Form 17)"(including attachment) completed for each of the members described in ③.

5　A Partner of an entity that is a US resident under the Japan-US Income Tax Convention (including a partner that is resident of Japan or any other country, in addition to the country of which the entity is a resident; the same applies below) and whose partners are taxable persons in Japan must submit this form attached with the following documents.
　　If a specific partner of the entity is notified of required information to enter in "List of the Partners of Entity (Form 16)" by all of the other partners and "List of the Partners of Entity (Form 16)" filled with the notified information, all of the partners are deemed to submit the application form.
　① Documents showing that the entity mentioned in 2 is taxable as a corporation in its residence country.
　② "List of the Partners of Entity (Form 16)"
　③ Documents showing that the partners mentioned in "List of the Partners of Entity (Form 16)" are partners of the entity mentioned in 2.
　　In this case, attach "Attachment Form for Limitation on Benefits Article (Form17)" (including attachment) for the entity mentioned in 2.

6　An Agent other than the Tax Agent must attach a power of attorney together with its Japanese translation.

Completion of the FORM

7　Applicable blocks must be checked.

8　The Taxpayer Identification Number is a number, code or symbol which is used for filing of return and payment of due amount and other procedures regarding tax, and which identifies a person who must take such procedures. If a system of Taxpayer Identification Number does not exist in the country where the recipient resides, or if the recipient of the payment does not have a Taxpayer Identification Number, it is not necessary to enter the Taxpayer Identification Number.

9　Column (3) of 3 must be filled in if the Recipient of Dividends owns not less than 10% of the total voting shares issued by the Payer of such Dividends.

10　Enter into Column 4 Dividends which are not attributed to a permanent establishment in Japan of the Recipient (such Dividends as are not accounted for in the books of the permanent establishment).

【Continue on the reverse】

¶ 4-830

源泉所得税　183

11　届出書の「4」の「名義人の氏名又は名称」欄には、元本がその真実の所有者以外の者―配当の支払を受ける者以外の者―の名義によって所有されている場合に、その名義人の氏名又は名称を記載してください。この場合、届出書「2　配当の支払を受ける者に関する事項」欄に記載された者が元本の真実の所有者であること及びその元本が真実の所有者以外の者の名義によって所有されている理由を証するその名義人の発行した証明書を、その翻訳文とともに添付してください。

12　届出書の「5」の欄には、「2」から「4」までの各欄に記載した事項のほか、租税の軽減又は免除を定める「1」の租税条約の適用を受けるための要件を満たす事情の詳細を記載してください。
　なお、配当の支払を受ける者が、日仏租税条約議定書3 (b) (i) の規定に規定する組合又はその他の団体である場合には、その旨（組合その他の団体の種類、設立根拠法を記載してください。）、支払を受ける総額、フランスの居住者たる組合員は構成員の持ち分の割合を記載し（組合員又は構成員全体の持ち分の明細を添付してください。）、また、フランスにおいて法人課税を選択している場合には、その選択している旨を記載してください。

13　支払を受ける配当が、租税条約の規定により免税となる場合には、支払者に提出する前に、届出書の「8」の欄に権限ある当局の証明を受けてください（注意事項14の場合を除きます。）。

14　注意事項13の場合において権限ある当局が証明を行わないこととしているため、その証明を受けることができない場合には、届出書の「5」の欄に記載した「要件を満たす事情の詳細」を明らかにする書類（その書類が外国語で作成されている場合には、その翻訳文を含みます。）及び権限ある当局の発行した居住者証明書を添付してください（平成16年4月1日以後適用開始となる租税条約の適用を受ける場合に限ります。）。

この届出書に記載された事項その他租税条約の規定の適用の有無を判定するために必要な事項については、別に説明資料を求めることがあります。

11　Enter into item "Name of Nominee of Principal" in 4 the registered name of the owner of shares in question.
　If the registered name is different from the name of Recipient of Dividends, attach the certificate issued by the nominee to clarify that the beneficial owner of such shares is the Recipient stated in Column 2, together with its Japanese translation and why the shares are registered in a name other than that of the beneficial owners.

12　Enter into line 5 details of circumstance that the conditions for the application of the convention mentioned in 1 are satisfied, in addition to information entered in 2 thought 4.
　If the Recipient of Dividends is the partnership or other group of persons in the sense of the Article 3 (b)(i) of Protocol of the Convention between Japan and the French Republic, enter details into this Column to that effect (kind of partnership or other group of persons, and the basis law for the establishment), total amount of Dividends, and the ratio of an interest of the French resident partners to that of all partners, together with the full details of interests of all partners. If said partnership or other group of persons elects to be liable to the corporation tax in France, enter information into this Column to that effect.

13　If the Dividends are subject to the tax exemption under the provisions of the Income Tax Convention, the Column 8 must be filled with the certification by the competent authority before submitting this form to the payer(except for cases described in Note 14).

14　If the competent authority does not make such a certification as mentioned in Note 13, documents showing "the details of circumstance that the conditions are satisfied" entered in line 5 (including Japanese translation if the documents are written in foreign language.) and the certification of residency issued by the competent authority must be attached (only for the application of the convention that went into entered into effect on and after April 1, 2004).

If necessary, the applicant may be requested to furnish further information in order to decide whether relief under the Convention should be granted or not.

184 WITHHOLDING INCOME TAX

Form 2

様 式 2
FORM

租 税 条 約 に 関 す る 届 出 書
APPLICATION FORM FOR INCOME TAX CONVENTION

(利子に対する所得税の軽減・免除
Relief from Japanese Income Tax on Interest)

支払者受付印　　税務署受付印

この届出書の記載に当たっては、別紙の注意事項を参照してください。
See separate instructions.

税務署整理欄
For official use only

適用；有、無

　　　　　　税務署長殿
To the District Director of_____Tax Office

1　適用を受ける租税条約に関する事項；
　Applicable Income Tax Convention
　日本国と_____との間の租税条約第___条第___項___
　The Income Tax Convention between Japan and_____, Article____, para.____

☐ 限度税率_____ %
　Applicable Tax Rate
☐ 免　税
　Exemption

2　利子の支払を受ける者に関する事項；Details of Recipient of Interest

	氏　名　又　は　名　称 Full name	
個人の場合 Individual	住　所　又　は　居　所 Domicile or residence	（電話番号 Telephone Number）
	国　　　籍 Nationality	
法人その他の団体の場合	本店又は主たる事務所の所在地 Place of head office or main office	（電話番号 Telephone Number）
	設立又は組織された場所 Place where the Corporation was established or organized	
Corporation or other entity	事業が管理・支配されている場所 Place where the business is managed or controlled	（電話番号 Telephone Number）
	下記「4」の利子につき居住者として課税される国及び納税地(注8) Country where the recipient is taxable as resident on Interest mentioned in 4 below and the place where he is to pay tax (Note 8)	（納税者番号 Taxpayer Identification Number）
日本国内の恒久的施設の状況 Permanent establishment in Japan	名　　　称 Name	
	所　在　地 Address	（電話番号 Telephone Number）
☐有(Yes)，☐無(No) If "Yes", explain:	事　業　の　内　容 Details of business	

3　利子の支払者に関する事項；Details of Payer of Interest

	氏　名　又　は　名　称 Full name	
	住所（居所）又は本店（主たる事務所）の所在地 Domicile (residence) or Place of head office (main office)	（電話番号 Telephone Number）
日本国内の恒久的施設の状況 Permanent establishment in Japan	名　　　称 Name	（事業の内容 Details of Business）
☐有(Yes)，☐無(No) If "Yes", explain:	所　在　地 Address	（電話番号 Telephone Numb.）

4　上記「3」の支払者から支払を受ける利子で「1」の租税条約の規定の適用を受けるものに関する事項（注9）；
　Details of Interest received from the Payer to which the Convention mentioned in 1 above is applicable (Note 9)
　〇 元本の種類：　☐ 公社債　　　　　☐ 公社債投資信託　　☐ 預貯金、合同運用信託　　　☐ 貸付金 ☐ その他
　　Kind of principal:　Bonds and debentures　Bond investment trust　Deposits or Joint operation trust　　Loans　Others

(1)　債券に係る利子の場合；In case of Interest derived from securities

債　券　の　銘　柄 Description of Securities	名義人の氏名又は名称（注10） Name of Nominee of Securities (Note 10)	債券の記号・番号（登録番号） Registered Number	債券の取得年月 Date of Acquisition of Securities
額　面　金　額 Face Value of Securities	債　券　の　数　量 Quantity of Securities	利子の支払期日 Due Date for Payment	利　子　の　金　額 Amount of Interest

(2)　債券以外のものに係る利子の場合；In case of other Interest

支払の基因となった契約の内容 Content of Contract under Which Interest is paid	契約の締結年月日 Date of Contract	契　約　期　間 Period of Contract	元　本　の　金　額 Amount of Principal	利子の支払期日 Due Date for Payment	利　子　の　金　額 Amount of Interest

¶ 4-830

源 泉 所 得 税　185

5　その他参考となるべき事項（注11）；
　　Others (Note 11)

6　日本の税法上、届出書の「2」の外国法人が納税義務者とされるが、「1」の租税条約の相手国では、その外国法人の株主等が納税義務者とされており、かつ、租税条約の規定によりその株主である者（相手国居住者に限ります。）の所得として取り扱われる部分に対して租税条約の適用を受けることとされている場合の課税の割合に関する事項（注4）；
　　Details of proportion of income to which the convention mentioned in 1 above is applicable, if the foreign company mentioned in 2 above is taxable as a company under Japanese tax law, and the member of the company is treated as taxable person in the other contracting country of the convention; and if the convention is applicable to income that is treated as income of the member (limited to a resident of the other contracting country) of the foreign company in accordance with the provisions of the convention (Note 4)
　　届出書の「2」の欄に記載された外国法人は、「4」の利子につき、「1」の租税条約の相手国において次の法令に基づいて、次の日以後、その株主等が課税されることとされています。
　　The member of the foreign company mentioned in 2 above is taxable in the other contracting country mentioned in 1 above regarding the interest mentioned in 4 above since the following date under the following law of the other contracting country.

根拠法令＿＿＿＿＿＿＿＿＿＿＿＿＿＿＿＿＿＿＿＿＿　効力を生じる日＿＿＿＿＿年＿＿＿月＿＿＿日
Applicable law　　　　　　　　　　　　　　　　　　　　Effective date

届出書の「2」の外国法人の株主等で租税条約の適用を受ける者の名称 Name of member of the foreign company mentioned in 2 above, to whom the Convention is applicable	間接保有 Indirect Ownership	持分の割合 Ratio of Ownership	受益の割合＝ 租税条約の適用を受ける割合 Proportion of benefit = Proportion for Application of Convention
	☐	％	％
	☐	％	％
	☐	％	％
	☐	％	％
	☐	％	％
合計 Total		％	％

7　日本の税法上、届出書の「2」の団体の構成員が納税義務者とされるが、「1」の租税条約の相手国ではその団体が納税義務者とされており、かつ、租税条約の規定により団体の所得として取り扱われる部分に対して租税条約の適用を受けることとされている場合の記載事項等（注5）；
　　Details if, while the partner of the entity mentioned in 2 above is taxable under Japanese tax law, the entity is treated as taxable person in the other contracting country of the convention mentioned in 1 above, and if the convention is applicable to income that is treated as income of the entity in accordance with the provisions of the convention (Note 5)
　　届出書の「2」に記載した団体は、「4」の利子につき、「1」の租税条約の相手国において次の法令に基づいて、次の日以後、法人として課税されることとされています。
　　The entity mentioned in 2 above is taxable as a corporation regarding the interest mentioned in 4 above since the following date under the following law in the other contracting country of the convention mentioned in 1 above.

根拠法令＿＿＿＿＿＿＿＿＿＿＿＿＿＿＿＿＿＿＿＿＿　効力を生じる日＿＿＿＿＿年＿＿＿月＿＿＿日
Applicable law　　　　　　　　　　　　　　　　　　　　Effective date
他のすべての構成員から通知を受けたこの届出書を提出する構成員の氏名又は名称＿＿＿＿＿＿＿＿＿＿
　　Full name of the partner of the entity who has been notified by all other partners and is to submit this form

私は、この届出書の「4」に記載した利子が「1」に掲げる租税条約の規定の適用を受けるものであることを、「租税条約の実施に伴う所得税法、法人税法及び地方税法の特例等に関する法律の施行に関する省令」の規定により届け出るとともに、この届出書（及び付表）の記載事項が正確かつ完全であることを宣言します。
In accordance with the provisions of the Ministerial Ordinance for the Implementation of the Law concerning the Special Measures of the Income Tax Law, the Corporation Tax Law and the Local Tax Law for the Enforcement of Income Tax Conventions, I hereby submit this application form under the belief that the provisions of the Income Tax Convention mentioned in 1 above is applicable to Interest mentioned in 4 above and also hereby declare that the statement on this form (and attachment form) is correct and complete to the best of my knowledge and belief.

Date＿＿＿＿＿年＿＿＿月＿＿＿日

利子の支払を受ける者又はその代理人の署名
Signature of the Recipient of Interest or his Agent ＿＿＿＿＿＿＿＿＿＿＿＿＿

8　権限ある当局の証明（注12）
　　Certification of competent authority (Note 12)

私は、届出者が、日本国と＿＿＿＿＿＿＿＿＿＿＿＿＿＿＿＿との間の租税条約第＿＿＿条第＿＿＿項＿＿＿に規定する居住者であることを証明します。
I hereby certify that the applicant is a resident under the provisions of the Income Tax Convention between Japan and ＿＿＿＿＿＿＿＿＿＿＿, Article＿＿＿＿＿, para.＿＿＿＿＿.

Date＿＿＿＿＿年＿＿＿月＿＿＿日　　　Signature＿＿＿＿＿＿＿＿＿＿＿

○　代理人に関する事項　；　この届出書を代理人によって提出する場合には、次の欄に記載してください。
　　Details of the Agent　；　If this form is prepared and submitted by the Agent, fill out the following columns.

代理人の資格 Capacity of Agent in Japan	氏名（名称） Full name		納税管理人の届出をした税務署名 Name of the Tax Office where the Tax Agent is registered
☐　納税管理人　※ Tax Agent ☐　その他の代理人 Other Agent	住所（居所・所在） Domicile (Residence or location)	（電話番号 Telephone Number）	税務署 Tax Office

※　「納税管理人」とは、日本国の国税に関する申告、申請、請求、届出、納付等の事項を処理させるため、国税通則法の規定により選任し、かつ、日本国における納税地の所轄税務署長に届出をした代理人をいいます。

※　"Tax Agent" means a person who is appointed by the taxpayer and is registered at the District Director of Tax Office for the place where the taxpayer is to pay his tax, in order to have such agent take necessary procedures concerning the Japanese national taxes, such as filing a return, applications, claims, payment of taxes, etc., under the provisions of the General Law for National Taxes.

○　適用を受ける租税条約が特典条項を有する租税条約である場合；
　　If the applicable convention has article of limitation on benefits
特典条項に関する付表の添付　☐有Yes
"Attachment Form for Limitation on Benefits Article attached　☐添付省略 Attachment not required
特典条項に関する付表を添付して提出した租税条約に関する届出書の提出日
Date of previous submission of the application for income tax convention with the "Attachment Form for Limitation on Benefit Article　＿＿＿＿＿年＿＿＿月＿＿＿日

186 WITHHOLDING INCOME TAX

様 式 2
FORM

「租税条約に関する届出書(利子に対する所得税の軽減・免除)」に関する注意事項

INSTRUCTIONS FOR "APPLICATION FORM FOR RELIEF FROM JAPANESE INCOME TAX ON INTEREST"

――――注 意 事 項――――

届出書の提出について

1 この届出書は、利子に係る日本国の所得税の源泉徴収額について租税条約の規定に基づき軽減又は免除を受けようとする場合に使用します。

2 この届出書は、利子の支払者ごとに作成してください。

3 この届出書は、正副2通を作成して利子の支払者に提出し、利子の支払者は、正本を、最初にその利子の支払をする日の前日までにその支払者の所轄税務署長に提出してください。この届出書の提出後その記載事項に異動が生じた場合も同様です。
　なお、記載事項に異動が生じた場合において、異動が生じた記載事項が届出書の「4」の「額面金額」、「数量」又は「利子の金額」の増加又は減少によるものである場合には、異動に係る届出書の提出を省略することができます。
　無記名の債券に係る利子については、その支払を受ける都度、この届出書を正副2通作成して利子の支払者に提出し、利子の支払者は、正本をその支払者の所轄税務署長に提出してください。

4 外国法人であって、米国ではその株主等が納税義務者とされるものが支払を受ける所得については、米国居住者である株主等（その株主等の受益する部分に限ります。）についてのみ日米租税条約の規定の適用を受けることができます。上記に該当する外国法人は、次の書類を添付して提出してください。
　① 届出書の「2」の欄に記載した外国法人が米国においてその株主等が課税を受けていることを明らかにする書類
　② 「外国法人の株主等の名簿（様式16）」
　③ 日米租税条約の適用を受けることができる株主等がその外国法人の株主等であることを明らかにする書類
　なお、この場合には、「特典条項に関する付表（様式17）」（その添付書類を含みます。）については、③の各株主等のものを添付してください。

5 日米租税条約の米国の居住者に該当する団体であって、日本ではその構成員が納税義務者とされる団体の構成員（その団体の居住地国の居住者だけでなく、それ以外の国の居住者も日本の居住者も含みます。以下同じです。）は、この届出書に次の書類を添付して提出してください。
　なお、その団体の構成員のうち特定の構成員が他のすべての構成員から支払を受けるべき事項の名簿（様式16）」に記載すべき事項について通知を受けその事項を記載した「相手国団体の構成員の名簿（様式16）」を提出した場合には、すべての構成員が届出書を提出しているものとみなします。
　① 届出書の「2」の欄に記載した団体が居住地国において法人として課税を受けていることを明らかにする書類
　② 「相手国団体の構成員の名簿（様式16）」
　③ 「相手国団体の構成員の名簿」に記載された構成員が届出書の「2」の団体の構成員であることを明らかにする書類
　なお、この場合には、「特典条項に関する付表（様式17）」（その添付書類を含みます。）は、届出書の「2」の欄に記載した団体のものを添付してください。

6 この届出書を納税管理人以外の代理人によって提出する場合には、その委任関係を証する委任状をその翻訳文とともに添付してください。

届出書の記載について

7 届出書の□欄には、該当する項目について✓印を付してください。

8 納税者番号とは、納税の申告、納付その他の手続を行うために用いる番号、記号その他の符号でその手続を特定することができるものをいいます。支払を受ける者が納税者番号を有しない場合や支払を受ける者の居住地国である国に納税者番号に関する制度が存在しない場合には納税者番号を記載する必要はありません。

9 届出書の「4」の各欄には、利子の支払を受ける者が日本国内に支店等の恒久的施設を有する場合は、その恒久的施設に帰せられない利子について記載してください。

10 届出書の「4」の「名義人の氏名又は名称」欄には、元本がその真実の所有者以外の者―利子の支払を受ける者以外の者―の名義によって所有されている場合に、その名義人の氏名又は名称を記載してください。この場合には、届出書の「2　利子の支払を受ける者に関する事項」欄に記載された者が元本の真実の所有者であること及びその元本が真実の所有者以外の者の名義によって所有されている理由を証するその名義人の発行した証明書を、その翻訳文とともに添付してください。

【裏面に続きます】

――――INSTRUCTIONS――――

Submission of the FORM

1 This form is to be used by the Recipient of Interest in claiming the relief from Japanese Income Tax under the provisions of the Income Tax Convention.

2 This form must be prepared separately for each Payer of Interest.

3 This form must be submitted in duplicate to the Payer of Interest, who has to file the original with the District Director of Tax Office for the place where the Payer resides, by the day before the payment of the Interest is made. The same procedures must be followed when there is any change in the statements on this form except if the change results in an increase or decrease in the "Face Value of Securities", Quantity of Securities", or "Amount of Interest" mentioned in column 4.
　However, in case of Interest from bearer securities, this form must be submitted in duplicate at the time of each payment of such Interest.

4 In case of income that is received by a foreign company whose member is treated as taxable person in the United States, the Japan-US Income Tax Convention is applicable only to US resident members (to the extent that the income is a benefit of the members). Such foreign companys should attach the following documents to this form:
　① Documents showing that the member of the foreign company mentioned in 2 is treated as taxable person in the United States.
　② List of the Members of Foreign Company (Form 16)"
　③ Documents showing that the member to whom the Japan-US Income Tax Convention is applicable is a member of the foreign company.
　Also attach "Attachment Form for Limitation on Benefits Article (Form 17)"(including attachment) completed for each of the members described in ③.

5 A Partner of an entity that is a US resident under the Japan-US Income Tax Convention (including a partner that is resident of Japan or any other country, in addition to the country of which the entity is a resident; the same applies below) and whose partners are taxable persons in Japan must submit this form attached with the following documents.
　If a specific partner of the entity is notified of required information to enter in "List of the Partners of Entity (Form 16)"by all of the other partners and submits "List of the Partners of Entity (Form 16)"filled with the notified information, all of the partners are deemed submit the application form.
　① Documents showing that the entity mentioned in 2 is taxable as a corporation in its residence country.
　② List of the Partners of Entity (Form 16)"
　③ Documents showing that the partners mentioned in "List of the Partners of Entity (Form 16)"are partners of the entity mentioned in 2.
　In this case, attach "Attachment Form for Limitation on Benefits Article (Form 17)" (including attachment) for the entity mentioned in 2.

6 An Agent other than the Tax Agent must attach a power of attorney together with its Japanese translation.

Completion of the FORM

7 Applicable blocks must be checked.

8 The Taxpayer Identification Number is a number, code or symbol which is used for filing of return and payment of due amount and other procedures regarding tax, and which identifies a person who must take such procedures. If a system of Taxpayer Identification Number does not exist in the country where the recipient resides, or if the recipient of the payment does not have a Taxpayer Identification Number, it is not necessary to enter the Taxpayer Identification Number .

9 Enter into column 4 the Interest which is not attributed to a permanent establishment in Japan of Recipient (such Interest as are not accounted for in the books of the permanent establishment).

10 Enter into item "Name of Nominee of Securities" of column 4 the registered name of the owner of securities in question. If the registered name is different from the name of Recipient of Interest, attach the certificate issued by the nominee to clarify that the beneficial owner of such security is the Recipient stated in column 2, together with its Japanese translation and why the securities are registered in a name other than that of the beneficial owners.

【Continue on the reverse】

¶ 4-830

源 泉 所 得 税 187

11　届出書の「5」の欄には、「2」から「4」までの各欄に記載した事項のほか、租税の軽減又は免除を定める「1」の租税条約の適用を受けるための要件を満たす事情の詳細を記載してください。
　なお、利子の支払を受ける者が、日仏租税条約議定書3（b）（i）の規定に規定する組合又はその他の団体である場合には、その旨（組合その他の団体の種類、設立根拠法を記載してください。）、支払を受ける総額、フランスの居住者たる組合員又は構成員の持ち分の割合を記載し（組合員又は構成員全体の持ち分の明細を添付してください。）、また、フランスにおいて法人課税を選択している場合には、その選択している旨を記載してください。

12　支払を受ける利子が、租税条約の規定により免税となる場合には、支払者に提出する前に、届出書の「8」の欄に権限ある当局の証明を受けてください（注意事項13の場合を除きます。）。

13　注意事項12の場合において権限ある当局が証明を行わないこととしているため、その証明を受けることができない場合には、届出書の「5」の欄に記載した「要件を満たす事情の詳細」を明らかにする書類（その書類が外国語で作成されている場合には、その翻訳文を含みます。）及び権限ある当局の発行した居住者証明書を添付してください（平成16年4月1日以後適用開始となる租税条約の適用を受ける場合に限ります。）。

この届出書に記載された事項その他租税条約の規定の適用の有無を判定するために必要な事項については、別に説明資料を求めることがあります。

11　Enter into line 5 details of circumstance that the conditions for the application of the convention mentioned in 1 are satisfied, in addition to information entered in 2 thought 4.
　If the Recipient of Dividends is the partnership or other group of persons in the sense of the Article 3 (b) (i) of Protocol of the Convention between Japan and the French Republic, enter details into this Column to that effect (kind of partnership or other group of persons, and the basis law for the establishment), total amount of Dividends, and the ratio of an interest of the French resident partners to that of all partners, together with the full details of interests of all partners. If said partnership or other group of persons elects to be liable to the corporation tax in France, enter information into this Column to that effect.

12　If the Interest is subject to tax exemption under the provisions of the Income Tax Convention, Column 8 must be entered with the certification by the competent authority before this form is submitted to the payer. (except for cases described in Note 13).

13　If the competent authority does not make such a certification as mentioned in Note 12, documents showing "the details of circumstance that the conditions are satisfied" entered in line 5 (including Japanese translation if the documents are written in foreign language.) and the certification of residency issued by the competent authority must be attached (only for the application of the convention that went into entered into effect on and after April 1, 2004).

If necessary, the applicant may be requested to furnish further information in order to decide whether relief under the Convention should be granted or not.

CHAPTER 5

ASSESSMENT INCOME TAX

	Paragraph
Chart: Computation of Assessment Income Tax	¶ 5-010
General Information	¶ 5-020
Exempt Income	¶ 5-070
Method of Computation of Assessment Income Tax (Resident)	¶ 5-090
Ten Categories of Income (Step 1)	¶ 5-120
Aggregation for Ordinary Income Amount (Step 2)	¶ 5-230
Net Loss	¶ 5-270
Deductions and Allowances (Step 3)	¶ 5-310
Application of Tax Rate (Step 4)	¶ 5-500
Tax Credits (Step 5)	¶ 5-570
Examples of Computation of Income Tax	¶ 5-650
Return, Payment, Assessment and Tax Disputes	¶ 5-710
Information Return	¶ 5-810
Non-resident's Income Tax Liability	¶ 5-850
How to Fill Out Your Final Return (for Type B)	¶ 5-950

第 5 章
申 告 所 得 税

申告所得税の計算……………………………………………	¶5-010
概要………………………………………………………………	¶5-020
非課税所得………………………………………………………	¶5-070
居住者に係る申告所得税の計算方法………………………	¶5-090
10種類の所得（第1段階）……………………………………	¶5-120
総所得金額の合計（第2段階）………………………………	¶5-230
純損失……………………………………………………………	¶5-270
所得控除（第3段階）…………………………………………	¶5-310
税率の適用（第4段階）………………………………………	¶5-500
税額控除（第5段階）…………………………………………	¶5-570
計算例……………………………………………………………	¶5-650
申告，納付，賦課及び不服審査……………………………	¶5-710
資料の提出………………………………………………………	¶5-810
非居住者の納税義務…………………………………………	¶5-850
所得税の確定申告書…………………………………………	¶5-950

¶ 5-010 Chart: Computation of Assessment Income Tax

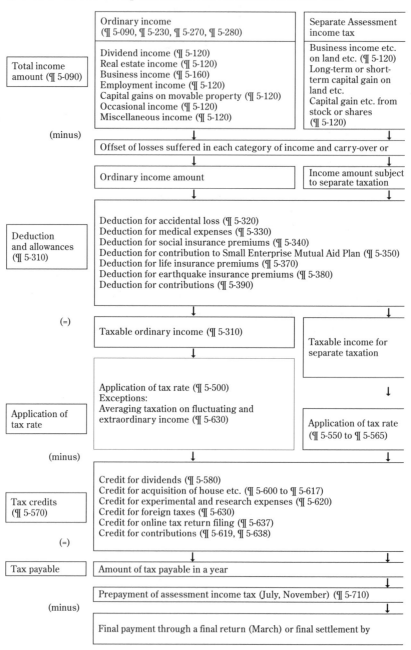

¶ 5-010

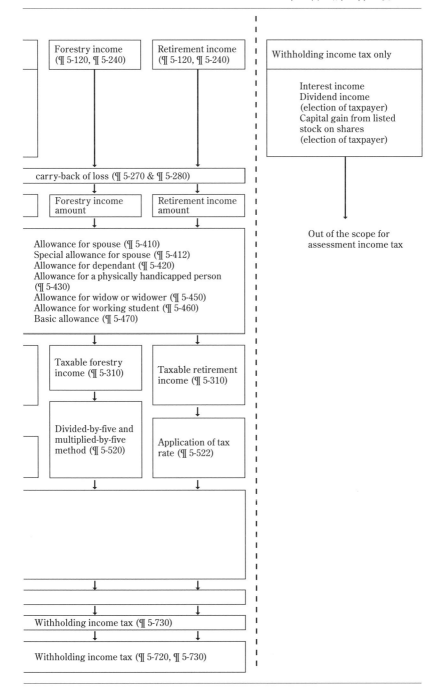

¶5-010　申告所得税の計算

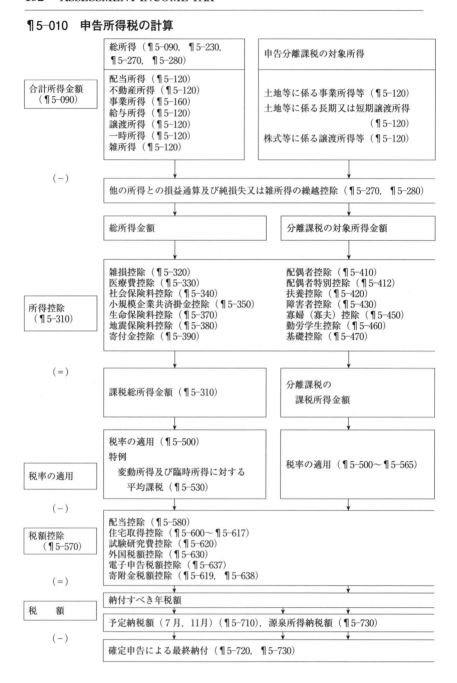

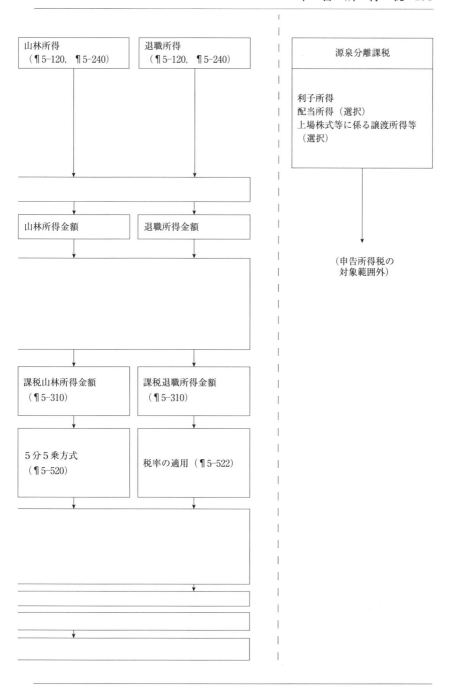

194   ASSESSMENT INCOME TAX

General Information

¶ 5-020 Basic structure of assessment income tax (and earthquake restoration surtax)

Assessment income tax is levied on the income of an individual in a calendar year.

The annual amount of income tax is computed first on the basis of the annual income of an individual in a calendar year, then, after deducting the total amount of withholding income tax withheld at source and the total amount of prepayments from the said annual amount of income tax, the balance should be paid by the individual to a tax office as final payment of assessment income tax.

The prepayments usually become payable twice in the year in which the said annual income accrues (in July and November), and the final payment becomes due on March 15 of the following year in accordance with the taxpayers own final return. The amount of the final payment is the annual amount of income tax less the amounts of withholding and prepayments.

If the tax amount payable as the final payment shows a negative amount due to prepayment or withholding of more than the annual amount of income tax, then the minus figure is refunded in accordance with the final return.

The special measures to secure the financial resources to implement the restoration from the Tohoku Earthquake were promulgated on December 2, 2012 and the earthquake restoration surtax was introduced. An individual who is required to pay income tax is also required to pay the earthquake restoration surtax for the period from 2013 to 2037. The amount of the earthquake restoration surtax would be computed on the basis of the standard income tax at the fixed rate of 2.1%.

The basic structure of the earthquake restoration surtax is almost same as the one of assessment income tax described the above.

¶ 5-030 Blue return

An individual taxpayer who has business income (¶ 5-120(4)), real estate income (¶ 5-120(3)) or forestry income (¶ 5-120(9)) may file a blue return in the same manner as a corporate taxpayer, with the approval of the tax office. A blue return taxpayer must keep a journal, a general ledger and other

¶ 5-020

申 告 所 得 税 195

概　　要

¶5-020　申告所得税の仕組み

　申告所得税は，一暦年中における個人の所得に対して課される。

　所得税額は，年間の所得を基に計算されるが，この所得税額から既に当該所得につき源泉徴収された税額及び予定納税した税額を差し引いた差額が申告所得税として最終的に納付されることになる。

　予定納税は，通常，所得が生ずる年に2回（7月及び11月）行われ，最終納付は，翌年の3月15日までに確定申告をした上で行う。最終納付額は年税額から源泉所得税額と予定納税額とを差し引いた額である。もしも，年税額が源泉所得税額と予定納税額との合計額に満たなければ，その差額は，還付申告することにより還付される。

　平成23年12月2日に東日本大震災からの復興のための施策を実施するために必要な財源に関する特別措置法が公布され，「復興特別所得税」が創設された。所得税を納める義務のある個人は，平成25年分から平成49年分まで，復興特別所得税も併せて納める義務があり，復興特別所得税の課税標準はその年分の基準所得税額とされ，税率は一律2.1％となる。

　復興特別所得税の仕組みは，既述の申告所得税の仕組みとほぼ同様である。

¶5-030　青色申告

　事業所得（¶5-120(4)），不動産所得（¶5-120(3)）又は山林所得（¶5-120(9)）を有する個人納税者は，法人納税者と同様，税務署の承認を受けて青色申告書を提出することができる。青色申告納税者は仕訳帳，総勘定元帳，その他の必要な帳簿を備え，課税所得を正確に計算し得るようにするため，そ

196 ASSESSMENT INCOME TAX

necessary books, and record all transactions affecting assets, liabilities and capital in the books clearly and in good order according to the principles of double entry so that taxable income can be calculated correctly (Law 143, 148).

The taxpayer must also settle accounts on the basis of the records, prepare balance sheets, profit and loss statements and other statements, and keep the books and documents for seven years.

(1) **Privileges of blue returns**

Privileges granted to blue return taxpayers in the calculation of income include:

(a) Blue return special deduction is allowed (see ¶ 5-160).

(b) A net loss (see ¶ 5-280) may be carried back to the preceding calendar year and the taxpayer can qualify for a refund of income tax, if he has a net loss in the year (Law 140).

(c) The greater part of the special depreciation allowances provided in the Special Taxation Measures Act apply to blue return taxpayers only.

(d) The various tax-free reserves provided in the Special Taxation Measures Act are permitted to be deducted as expenses on the condition that a blue return is filed.

(2) **Procedural privileges of blue returns**

Privileges granted to blue return taxpayers in respect of taxation procedures include:

(a) The tax office cannot make corrections unless any mistakes made by the taxpayer in the calculation of income and other matters are ascertained from an audit of books and documents (Law 155).

(b) The tax office must give the reasons for correction in a correction notice (Law 1552).

(c) A blue return taxpayer can request immediate reconsideration by the National Tax Tribunal without asking the tax office for a reinvestigation (GL 75④). Unless he is a blue return taxpayer, he is called a "white return taxpayer".

¶ 5-040 Book-keeping

A white return taxpayer whose business income, real estate income or forestry income for the year before the preceding year amounted to more than ¥3,000,000, is required to keep brief accounts for seven years from January 1 of the following year (Law 231-2). In addition, every white return

¶ 5-040

申 告 所 得 税　197

の資産，負債及び資本に影響を及ぼす一切の取引につき，複式簿記の原則に従い，整然と，かつ，明りょうに記録しなければならない（所法143, 148）。

さらに，当該納税者は，その記録，貸借対照表，損益計算書その他の資料に基づき決算を行い，それらの帳簿書類を7年間保存しなければならない。

(1)　青色申告者の特典

青色申告納税者に対して所得の計算に関して与えられている特典は次のとおりである。

(a)　青色申告特別控除が適用される（¶5-160参照）。

(b)　その年において生じた純損失の金額がある場合には，その年の前年分の所得に繰り戻して，所得税の還付が受けられる（所法140）（¶5-280参照）。

(c)　租税特別措置法に規定される特別償却のほとんどは，青色申告納税者についてのみ認められる。

(d)　租税特別措置法に規定される種々の準備金は，青色申告書の提出を条件として必要経費の額に算入することが認められる。

(2)　青色申告の手続上の特典

青色申告納税者に対しては，課税手続上次の特典が認められている。

(a)　税務署は納税者の帳簿書類を調査し，所得その他の計算に誤りがあると認められる場合に限り，更正することができる（所法155）。

(b)　税務署は更正通知書に更正の理由を附記しなければならない（所法155②）。

(c)　青色申告納税者は税務署へ異議申立てをすることなく，直ちに，国税不服審判所へ審査請求をすることができる（通則法75④）。

青色申告納税者以外の納税者は，白色申告納税者とよばれる。

¶5-040　記帳

前々年分の事業所得，不動産所得及び山林所得の合計額が300万円を超える個人は白色申告納税者の場合も取引に関し，簡易な記帳をしなければならない（所法231の2）。300万円以下の白色申告納税義務者についても，平成26年1月から記帳しなければならない。

198   ASSESSMENT INCOME TAX

taxpayer who has business income, real estate income or forestry income is
required to keep brief accounts for seven years from January 1, 2014.

Exempt Income

¶ 5-070 Exempt income

The following items of income are exempt from assessment income
tax as well as withholding income tax. (Expenses necessary for deriving
such items of income are not deductible in computing the net amount of
income assessable.)

(1) Interest received by a certain handicapped person, etc. on small savings, postal savings and government bonds, if the invested amount
does not exceed ¥3,500,000 for each item (Law 10, SM 4).

(2) Interest on specified savings for housing, etc. by a salary-income
earner, if the invested amount does not exceed ¥5,500,000 (SM 4-2).

(3) The following payments from a present or former employer (Law 9
①(3) to (7)):

(a) travel expenses, including daily travel allowances paid to an employee for business trips;

(b) allowance for commuting expenses between an employee's
home and place of employment;

(c) allowances in kind to employees which are used exclusively in
the performance of their duties;

(d) allowance for an employee's service performed abroad;

(e) pension paid to a former employee who retired on account of
an injury sustained or disease contracted while performing his
duty, or paid to the surviving family of a former employee;

(f) The economic benefits derived from the exercise of specified
stock option which was granted by an employer.

Note:
Special tax treatment for Stock Options.
Together with the generalization of stock option under the amendment
of Commercial Law, non-taxable treatment on economic benefits derived
from stock or shares specified directors etc. acquire under the stock option plan are amended as follows.
① The stock option is to be granted as an underwriting right for issuance of new stocks granted at the shareholders' meeting or a right to
purchase the stocks granted at the shareholders' meeting to directors
or employees of "kabushiki-kaisha" (K.K.) (including directors or

¶ 5-070

申　告　所　得　税　199

非課税所得

¶5-070　非課税所得

　次に掲げる所得には，申告所得税並びに源泉所得税が課されない。なお，これらの所得を稼得するために要した費用は，課税所得の計算に当たり控除されない。

(1)　一定の障害者等が受領する少額預金及び少額公債の利子（いずれも元本350万円を限度とする。）（所法10，措法4）

(2)　勤労者財産形成住宅貯蓄に係る利子（元本550万円を限度とする。）（措法4の2）

(3)　雇用主からの次の支払（所法9①三～七）

　(a)　出張旅費

　(b)　通勤手当

　(c)　業務を遂行するためにもっぱら使用される現物支給

　(d)　在外勤務手当

　(e)　業務上の事由による負傷又は疾病に基因して退職した者に支払われる年金，死亡した従業員の遺族に支払われる年金

　(f)　従業員及び役員に付与された特定のストック・オプションの行使に伴う株式の取得に係る経済的利益

　(注)：ストック・オプションに係る税制上の措置

　　　商法改正によるストック・オプションの一般化に伴い，特定の取締役等が受ける新株の発行に係る株式の取得に係る経済的利益の非課税等の特例措置は以下のとおり。

　　　①　株式会社の取締役又は使用人等（保有割合50％超の子会社の取締役又は使用人を含む。）が，

　　　イ　その株式会社の定時総会の決議に基づきその株式会社と締結した契約により与えられた権利で，あらかじめ定めた価額でその株式会社からその株式をその者に譲渡すべき旨を請求するもの，又は

　　　ロ　その株式会社の株主総会の特別決議に基づきその株式会社と締結した契約により

200   ASSESSMENT INCOME TAX

employees of 50% subsidiaries and sub-subsidiaries.).

And when directors or employees acquired stocks or shares by exercising the stock option meeting with the following requirement, economic benefits in connection with the acquisition of stocks or shares are treated non-taxable under the certain conditions.

A: Exercise of the stock option is prohibited within 2 years from the date of the shareholders' meeting at which the option is granted.

B: The annual amount of the stock option exercised does not exceed ¥12,000,000.

C: The stocks or shares acquired by the exercise of the stock option are deposited by the employer with securities company or bank under the certain measure.

② When directors and employees sold the stocks or shares after acquisition of stocks or shares by the exercise of the stock option under the above ①, the capital gains is taxed at 15% for income tax and 5% for local tax. In this case, the acquisition cost of stocks or shares sold comes to the exercise price of the stock option and withholding tax system which is alternatively applied to the capital gains of listed stocks in the designated account can't be applied.

(g) Employer's contribution under corporation type defined contribution pension plan will be treated non-taxable benefit to employee.

Note:

Special tax treatment for defined contribution pension plan.

Accompanying with introduction of defined contribution pension plan, tax measure was established at the stage of contribution, fund earnings and distribution on this plan.

(1) Contribution
① Employer contribution (Company type)
Employer's contribution is considered as expenses and is non-taxable benefits to employee.
② Participant contribution (Individual type)
Participant contribution is deductible from income amount.
③ Employee contribution (Company type)
Employee's contribution is deductible from income amount (see ¶ 5-350).

(2) Fund earnings
① The income derived from an entrusted property related to the defined contribution pension plan (company type) does not apply to the taxation of trusts set forth at ¶ 3-740.
② The Special Corporation Tax
The Special corporation tax on pension funds should be imposed on the premium paid by employers and its investment returns.
The Special corporation tax on pension funds should be imposed on the premium paid by individual beneficiaries and its investment returns.

(3) Distribution
① A public pension's deduction can be applicable to a distribution for Old Age, if a distribution for Old Age is paid by installment.

¶ 5-070

申　告　所　得　税　201

　　　　与えられた新株の引受権
　　で，次に掲げる要件等を満たすものを行使して株式を取得した場合の経済的利益については，一定の要件の下で，所得税を課さない。
　　A　その権利の行使が株主総会の決議の日から2年以内はできないこと
　　B　その権利の行使に係る譲受価額等の年間の合計額が1,200万円を超えないこと
　　C　その権利の行使により取得をする株式はその株式会社により，その者に代わって，一定の方法によって証券会社，銀行等に保管の委託等がされているものであること
　②　上記①の非課税措置の適用を受けて取得した株式をその取得の日以後に譲渡した場合には，その特定株式の譲渡による所得については，行使価額を取得価額とした上で，株式等に係る譲渡所得等の申告分離課税を行うこととし，上場株式等に係る譲渡所得等の源泉分離課税選択は適用しない。

(g)　企業年金型の事業主掛金については，従業員に対しては課税しない。

(注)：確定拠出型年金制度に係る税制上の措置
　　確定拠出型年金制度の創設に伴い，同制度における拠出，運用及び給付の各段階について，次の措置を講ずる。

　(1)　拠出段階
　　①　企業年金型の事業主掛金
　　　事業主は損金（必要経費）に算入するとともに，従業員に対しては課税しない。
　　②　個人型年金の加入者掛金
　　　所得控除の対象とする。
　　③　企業年金型の従業員掛金（¶5-350参照）
　　　所得控除の対象とする。

　(2)　運用段階
　　①　企業型年金に係る信託については，信託財産に帰せられる収入及び支出等の帰属の原則（¶3-740参照）を適用しない。
　　②　特別法人税
　　　事業主掛金及びその運用益を対象として特別法人税を課税する。
　　　個人型加入者掛金及びその運用益を対象として特別法人税を課税する。

　(3)　給付段階
　　①　年金としての老齢給付金については，公的年金等控除を適用する。
　　②　一時払いの老齢給付金については，退職手当等とみなす。

202　ASSESSMENT INCOME TAX

    ② A lump-sum distribution for Old Age is deemed retirement allowance.

    ③ A distribution for Injury and Diseases is non-taxable benefits.

    ④ A lump-sum distribution for Death is subject to inheritance tax.

    ⑤ A lump-sum distribution for withdrawal from plan is subject to income tax

  (4) Rollover - Switch

    ① Rollover from defined contribution pension plan to another one. Necessary measures should continue to be taken.

    ② Switch from defined distribution pension plan to defined contribution pension plan. Necessary measures should continue to be taken.

(4) Foreigners' staff (Law 9①(8)):

  (a) all income belonging to an ambassador or diplomat;

  (b) salary income for staff of foreign governments or local entities or specific staff of specific international organizations.

(5) Capital gains accruing from the sale of furniture, clothes, etc. which are necessary for the normal daily life of a taxpayer or his family (Law 9①(9)).

(6) Other kinds of exempt income (Law 9①(14) to (16)):

  (a) the acquisition of assets on account of inheritance, donation, bequest or demise (inheritance tax or gift tax is imposed thereon);

  (b) insurance money, compensation or consolation money paid on account of any physical or mental injury or accidental damage to property (excluding inventory);

  (c) money granted for the education or support of dependants.

  (d) Child allowances

  (e) High School education at no charge

  (f) Child support allowance paid to a father and child family

  (g) Support allowance for a job-hunting person

(7) Dividends and capital gains from small investments in listed stocks in non-taxable account

  (a) A Japanese version of Individual Saving Account (NISA) shall be introduced from January 1, 2014 to December 31, 2023. NISA shall allow individuals to invest up to 1 million yen (1.2 million from 2016) of listed stocks to each account. They shall be allowed to open one NISA account per year and up to 5 NISA accounts in total. Dividends and capital gains from listed stocks up to 5 million yen or 6 million yen in the accounts shall not be

¶ 5-070

③ 傷害給付金については，課税しない。
④ 死亡一時金については，相続税の課税対象とする。
⑤ 脱退一時金については，所得税を課税する。

(4) 移管・移行
① 確定拠出型年金間の移管
一定の手続を前提として税制上の措置を継続する。
② 確定給付型年金等からの移行
所要の措置を講ずる。

(4) 外国人職員 （所法9①八）
　(a) 外国の大公使及び外交官のすべての所得
　(b) 外国の政府，地方公共団体又は特定の国際機関の特定の職員の給与

(5) 日常生活に必要な家具，衣類等の譲渡から生ずる譲渡所得 （所法9①九）

(6) その他の非課税所得 （所法9①十四～十六）
　(a) 相続，贈与，遺贈による資産の取得 （相続税又は贈与税が課される。）

　(b) 保険金，損害賠償金又は慰謝料で，心身に加えられた傷害又は突発的な事故により資産 （たな卸資産を除く。） に加えられた損害に基因するもの
　(c) 学資に充てるため給付される金品及び扶養義務者から給付される金品
　(d) 子ども手当
　(e) 高校の実質無償化
　(f) 父子家庭に支給されることとなる児童扶養手当
　(g) 求職者支援給付
(7) 非課税口座内の少額上場株式等に係る配当所得及び譲渡所得

　(a) 少額上場株式等に係る配当所得及び譲渡所得を非課税とする口座，日本版ISA（NISA）が，平成26年1月1日から平成35年12月31日まで開設される。個人はこのNISA口座に1年ごとに1勘定100万円（平成28年から120万円）まで，合計5勘定に500万円又は600万円までの上場株式等を投資することができ，その口座から得られる5年内の配当及び譲渡所得が，非課税とされる（下図参照）。
　　平成27年1月からは，1年単位でNISA口座を開設する金融機関の変

taxed for up to 5 years (see the chart below).

From January 1, 2017, users of NISA accounts shall be allowed to switch their NISA accounts to a different financial institution every year, as well as reopen their NISA accounts after the accounts are closed.

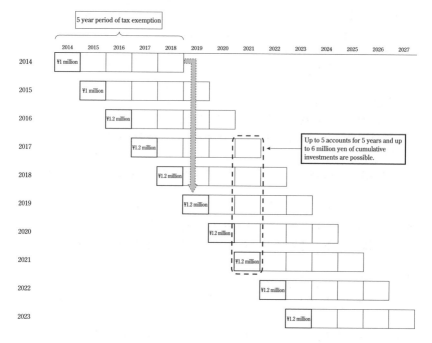

(b) People less than 20 years old shall open a Junior NISA account with the maximum amount of the annual investments set at 800,000 yen. Dividends and capital gains from listed stocks up to 4 million yen in the account will not be taxed for up to 5 years.

(c) Effective from January 1, 2018

Introduction of the installment-type NISA

The installment-type NISA, whereby investment is made in investment trusts suitable for installment and diversified investment through a periodic and continuous method, shall be introduced (the upper limit on the annual investment amount : 400,000yen, non-taxability period : 20years, users can select either the installment-type NISA or the existing NISA).

¶ 5-070

更が認められるとともに，NISA口座を廃止した場合にNISA口座の再開設も認められる。

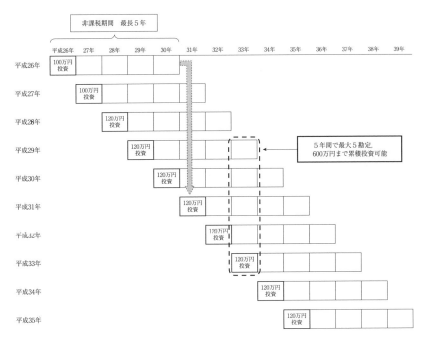

(b) 20歳未満の人が開設するジュニアNISA口座内の少額上場株式等の配当，譲渡益が非課税とされる。年間投資上限額は80万円，5年間で400万円までである。

(c) 平成30年分以降の取扱い
　　積立NISAの創設
　　積立・分散投資に適した一定の投資信託に対して定期的かつ継続的な方法で投資を行う積立NISAが創設され，その配当及び譲渡益が非課税とされる（年間投資上限額は40万円，非課税期間は20年，現行のNISAとは選択適用となる）。

206   ASSESSMENT INCOME TAX

Method of Computation of Assessment Income Tax (Resident)

¶ 5-090   Outline of computation

The annual amount of assessment income tax payable by a taxpayer is computed using the following six steps (see ¶ 5-010):

(1)   Compute, according to the statutory formulae, the amount of each of the ten categories of income into which assessable income is divided (see ¶ 5-120 and following).

Note:

The ten categories of income mentioned above can be divided into "withholding income tax only", "separate assessment income tax" and "comprehensive assessment income tax" according to taxation method.

1.   Interest income

Interest income is taxable by withholding income tax only, and is not subject to assessment income tax in general. But interest on public bonds and debentures will be subject to separate assessment income tax at the rate of 15% from January 1, 2016 (SM 3).

2.   Dividend income

Dividend income is subject to withholding income tax and taxable by comprehensive assessment income tax, in general. In addition, dividend income of listed stock can be taxed at the separate assessment income taxation with a resident taxpayer's choice (see ¶ 5-540).

But, dividend income from the distribution of profits of securities investment trusts is subject to withholding income tax only at the rate of 15% (SM 8-2, 8-3).

3.   Real estate income

Real estate income is taxable by comprehensive assessment income tax.

4.   Business income

Business income is taxable by comprehensive assessment income tax.

But business income from stock or shares (hereinafter "capital gains etc. from shares") is taxable by separate assessment income tax in the same manner as capital gains (SM 37-10).

5.   Employment income

Employment income is taxable by comprehensive assessment income tax. But the great number of salary income earners do not need to file an income tax return because of year end adjustment (Law 121) (see ¶ 4-310).

6.   Capital gains

Capital gains is taxable by comprehensive assessment income tax.

But, long-term capital gains on land and buildings and rights thereon (hereinafter "long-term capital gains on land etc.") and short-term capital gains on land and buildings and rights thereon (hereinafter "short-term capital gains on land etc.") is taxable by separate assessment income tax (SM 31 to 37-9).

Capital gains from shares etc. are taxable by separate assessment income tax. But, on the other hand, capital gains from listed stock or shares are taxable by withholding income tax only according to election of taxpayer

¶ 5-090

申 告 所 得 税　207

居住者に係る申告所得税の計算方法

¶5-090　概要

　納付すべき申告所得税の額は，次の 6 段階で計算される（¶5-010参照）。

⑴　課税されるべき所得を，法律の定めるところに従って，10の種類に分
　け，それぞれの金額を計算する（¶5-120以降参照）。

　　（注）：10種類の所得は課税の方法として，「源泉分離課税」，「申告分離課税」及び「申告総合
　　　　課税」に分けられるが，10種類の所得ごとにみると，次のとおりである。

　　　1.　利子所得──利子所得は源泉分離課税であり，原則として，申告所得税の対象とな
　　　　　　らない。ただし，公社債の利子は，平成28年 1 月 1 日以降15％の税率
　　　　　　による申告分離課税の対象となる（措法 3 ）。

　　　2.　配当所得──配当所得は原則として，源泉徴収の対象となり，申告総合課税の対象
　　　　　　となるが，上場株式等に係る配当所得については，15％の税率で申告
　　　　　　分離課税の選択適用ができる（¶5-540参照）。
　　　　　　　しかし，証券投資信託の収益の分配に係る配当所得については15％
　　　　　　の源泉分離課税とされる（措法 8 の 2 , 8 の 3 ）。

　　　3.　不動産所得─不動産所得は申告総合課税の対象となる。

　　　4.　事業所得──事業所得は申告総合課税の対象となる。
　　　　　　　しかし，株式等に係る事業所得（以下「株式等に係る譲渡所得等」
　　　　　　という。）は譲渡所得と同様に分離課税の対象とされる（措法37の10）。

　　　5.　給与所得──給与所得は申告総合課税の対象となる。しかし，大半の給与所得者は年
　　　　　　末調整により，確定申告の提出を要しない（所法121）（¶4-310参照）。

　　　6.　譲渡所得　　譲渡所得は申告総合課税の対象となる。
　　　　　　　ただし，土地及び建物並びにこれらの上に存する権利に係る長期譲
　　　　　　渡所得（以下「土地等に係る長期譲渡所得」という。）及び，土地及び
　　　　　　建物並びにこれらの上に存する権利の短期譲渡所得（以下「土地等に
　　　　　　係る短期譲渡所得」という。）は申告分離課税される（措法31～37
　　　　　　の 9 ）。
　　　　　　　また，株式等に係る譲渡所得は申告分離課税される。しかし，上場
　　　　　　株式に係る譲渡所得は納税者の選択により源泉分離課税の対象となる
　　　　　　（措法37の10, 37の11）。

208 ASSESSMENT INCOME TAX

(SM 37-10, 37-11).
7. Occasional income
   Occasional income is taxable by comprehensive assessment income tax.
8. Miscellaneous income
   Miscellaneous income is taxable by comprehensive assessment income tax.
   But, miscellaneous income from shares (hereinafter "capital gains etc. from shares") is taxable by separate assessment income tax (SM 37-10).
9. Forestry income
   Forestry income is taxable by comprehensive assessment income tax, the income is not included in ordinary income (Law 22).
10. Retirement income
    Retirement income is taxable by comprehensive assessment income tax, the income is not included in ordinary income (Law 22).
    But the great number of retirement income earners do not need to file an income tax return because of withholding income tax settlement.

(2) Aggregate the amounts of interest income (rare case), dividend income, real estate income, business income, employment income, capital gains, occasional income and miscellaneous income which are not subject to the tax method of "withholding income tax only" or "separate assessment income tax". The total of these 8 categories of income is known as "ordinary income amounts" (see ¶ 5-230 and following).

These "ordinary income amounts", added to the total of forestry income, retirement income, and the 8 categories of income mentioned above which are subject to "separate assessment income tax", are called the "total income amounts".

Note:
Three categories of income which are subject to separate assessment income tax are as follows:
(1) Long-term or short-term capital gains on land etc.
(2) Capital gains etc. from shares etc.
(3) Dividend income from listed shares (with a taxpayer's choice)

(3) Deduct the fourteen kinds of deductions or allowances from the amount of ordinary income, forestry income, retirement income, and income which is subject to separate assessment income tax, in the prescribed order. The balances are called the "taxable ordinary income amount", "taxable forestry income amount", "taxable retirement income amount" and the "taxable amount of income which is subject to separate assessment income tax" (see ¶ 5-310 and following).

(4) Apply the progressive tax rate to the taxable amounts of ordinary

¶ 5-090

申 告 所 得 税　209

7.　一時所得————一時所得は申告総合課税の対象となる。

8.　雑所得————雑所得は申告総合課税の対象となる。
　　　　　　しかし，株式に係る雑所得（以下「株式等に係る譲渡所得等」とい
　　　　　　う。）は申告分離課税される（措法37の10）。

9.　山林所得————山林所得は申告総合課税の対象となるが，総所得金額には含められな
　　　　　　い（所法22）。

10.　退職所得————退職所得は申告総合課税の対象となるが，総所得金額には含められな
　　　　　　い（所法22）。
　　　　　　しかし，大半の退職所得者は源泉徴収の調整により所得税の確定申
　　　　　　告書の提出を必要とされていない。

(2)　「源泉分離課税」又は「申告分離課税」の対象とならない利子所得（稀
　　な事例），配当所得，不動産所得，事業所得，給与所得，譲渡所得，一時
　　所得及び雑所得を合計する。この8種類の合計した金額を「総所得金額」
　　という（¶5-230以降参照）。
　　　この総所得金額に，山林所得，退職所得及び上記8種類の所得のうち申
　　告分離課税の対象となる所得を加えた金額を「合計所得金額」という。

(注)：8種類の所得のうち申告分離課税の対象となるものは，次のものである。
　　　⑴　土地等に係る長期又は短期譲渡所得
　　　⑵　株式等に係る譲渡所得等
　　　⑶　上場株式等に係る配当所得（選択）

(3)　総所得金額，山林所得金額，退職所得金額及び申告分離課税の対象所得
　　金額から，一定の順序で，14種類の所得控除を行う。控除後の額は，「課
　　税総所得金額」，「課税山林所得金額」，「課税退職所得金額」，及び「分離
　　課税の対象とされる課税所得金額」という（¶5-310以降参照）。

(4)　課税総所得金額，課税山林所得金額，課税退職所得金額に対して，法律

210   ASSESSMENT INCOME TAX

income, forestry income, retirement income, and apply the proportionate tax rate to the taxable amounts of income which is subject to separate assessment income tax, according to the statutory formula (see ¶ 5-500 and following).

(5) Deduct the tax credits from the total of the tax amounts resulting from (4): the tax amount after deducting tax credits is the annual amount of income tax (see ¶ 5-570 and following).

(6) Deduct from the annual tax amount in (5) the amount of withholding income tax withheld at source from annual income and the amount of prepayment. The balance is the annual amount of assessment income tax, which is payable or refundable by means of the final payment.

Ten Categories of Income (Step 1)

¶ 5-120 Ten categories of income

The following table shows ten categories of income and the method by which the amount of each category of income should be computed. Care is needed concerning the deductibility of expenses.

Category of income	What belongs to the category	Method of computation
(1)　Interest　income	Interest on public bonds and debentures, deposits with a bank, distribution of profits of joint operation trusts, and public bonds and debentures investment trusts.	Withholding income tax only
(comprehensive taxation)		
(2)　Dividend　income	Dividends, distribution of profits of securities investment trust, etc.	Gross receipts minus interest paid on borrowings for the acquisition of shares, etc.
Note: Dividend income is required to be included in the ordinary income amount unless a taxpayer elects final settlement by withholding income tax (¶ 4-210).		
(3)　Real estate　income	Rent from real estate (houses, land, etc.) and any initial lump sum payment received for rented houses or land, except when such a lump sum payment on rented land exceeds half of the value of the land (see (6a) below).	Gross receipts minus deductible necessary expenses
Note: The rental loss on account of interest paid on loans for the acquisition of land will not be allowed to be offset against other income and also to be carried forward.		

¶ 5-120

申　告　所　得　税　211

で定めるところにより，累進税率を適用し，「分離課税の対象とされる課税所得金額」に対して法律の定めるところにより比例税率を適用する（¶5-500以降参照）。

(5)　上記(4)により計算した税額の合計額から税額控除を行う。この税額控除後の金額が，その年の所得税額となる（¶5-570以降参照）。

(6)　上記(5)の所得税額からその年の所得に対して課された源泉所得税額と予定納税額とを差し引いた残額が，その年の申告所得税額で，最終的に納付又は還付しなければならないものである。

10種類の所得（第1段階）

¶5-120　10種類の所得

　次の表は，10種類の所得とそれぞれの種類の所得の金額の計算方法を示すものであるが，控除できる経費について留意する必要がある。

所得の種類	範　　　　囲	計　算　方　法
(1)　利子所得	公社債及び預貯金の利子並びに合同運用信託及び公社債投資信託の収益の分配	収入金額

（総合課税）

所得の種類	範　　　　囲	計　算　方　法
(2)　配当所得	配当，証券投資信託の利益の分配等	収入金額－株式等を取得するための借入金の利子

(注)：配当所得は，納税者が源泉課税で課税関係を終了させる方法を選択しない場合に，総所得金額に含まれる（¶4-210参照）。

所得の種類	範　　　　囲	計　算　方　法
(3)　不動産所得	不動産（家屋，土地等）の賃貸料，賃貸家屋・土地に係る敷金（土地の価額の2分の1を超える場合を除く。）	総収入金額－必要経費

(注)：各年分の不動産所得の損失の金額のうち，土地等を取得するために要した負債の利子の額に相当する部分の金額については，損益通算の対象とはならない。また，繰越控除の対象とされる純損失の金額とはならない。

212 ASSESSMENT INCOME TAX

Category of income	What belongs to the category	Method of computation
(4) Business income	Profits from business activities or professions such as wholesaling, retailing, manufacturing, agriculture, fishing, hotels, restaurants, attorneys, certified public accountants, actors, musicians, etc.	Gross receipts minus deductible necessary expenses
(5) Employment income	Salaries, wages, allowances, bonuses.	Gross receipts minus standard employment income deduction or specified payment deductions and standard employment income deduction
(6) Capital gains (as rule)	Income derived from the transfer of assets	Gross receipts minus costs incurred for the acquisition, installation, or improvement of the assets and expenses incurred in connection with the transfer minus "special deductions for capital gains"
(7) Occasional income	Gifts received from a corporation, prizes, and other income of an occasional nature	Gross receipts minus expenses paid in order to acquire the income concerned minus "special deduction for occasional income"
(8) Miscellaneous income	Royalties on books, compensation for manuscripts or lectures and other miscellaneous income not classified in the other categories (professional writers fees are classed as business income). The same proportion of the reserved income of a specified foreign subsidiary corporation as the ratio of a taxpayer's share to the total shares of the corporation, where the taxpayer's share is not less than 5% Public pensions	Gross receipts minus deductible necessary expenses Gross receipts minus public pension deduction

¶ 5-120

所得の種類	範　　囲	計　算　方　法
(4) 事業所得	卸売業，小売業，製造業，農業，漁業，旅館業，飲食店業，弁護士，公認会計士，俳優，音楽家など事業活動又は専門職業から生ずる所得	総収入金額－必要経費
(5) 給与所得	給料，賃金，歳費，賞与	収入金額－給与所得控除額又は 収入金額－給与所得控除額－特定支出控除額
(6) 譲渡所得 　　（原則）	土地及び建物並びにこれらの上に存する権利以外の資産の譲渡から生ずる所得	総収入金額－取得費，据付費又は改良費及び譲渡経費－譲渡所得の特別控除額
(7) 一時所得	法人からの贈与，賞金その他一時の所得	総収入金額－その収入を得るために支出した金額－一時所得の特別控除額
(8) 雑所得	著作権の使用料，原稿料など他の所得のいずれにも該当しない所得（作家等著述業に係る報酬は事業所得に該当する。） 　特定外国子会社の留保所得のうち，当該会社の株式を5％以上有している者の持分に対応する金額	総収入金額－必要経費
	公的年金	収入金額－公的年金控除額

214   ASSESSMENT INCOME TAX

Category of income	What belongs to the category	Method of computation
(9) Forestry income	Income derived from the sale of timber whether cut or uncut, but excluding the sale of timber which was acquired within five years before the sale	Total receipts minus costs for acquisition, afforestation, management and lumbering of the forest and other necessary expenses (a taxpayer may (i) elect to apply the "standard deduction method" and (ii) deduct "special deduction for afforestation plan" as well) minus "special deduction for forestry income".
(10) Retirement income	A lump sum payment received by a retiring employee, such as retirement allowance and the like, including payments from the social insurance scheme	First deduct "retirement income deduction" then take one half of the remainder.
(separate taxation)		
(11) Dividend income	Dividends of listed stocks etc.	Gross receipts minus interest paid on borrowings for the acquisition of shares, etc
(12) Business income etc. on land etc.	Business income or miscellaneous income with respect to transfers of land and buildings and the rights thereon (Note 1, 2)	Gross receipts minus acquisition costs etc. minus deductible necessary expenses
(13) Long-term or short-term capital gains on land etc. (Note 3)	Capital gains derived from the transfer of land and buildings and the rights thereon (Note 1)	Gross receipts minus acquisition costs etc. minus expenses incurred in connection with the transfer minus special deduction
(14) Capital gains etc. from stocks or shares	Business income, capital gain miscellaneous income from the sales of stock or shares, or convertible bonds	According to each category of comprehensive income, the method of computation is different.

Note:

1. "Long-term or short-term" refers to the periods during which land is owned. The taxation method, tax rate and the amount of special deduction is different for each.

¶ 5-120

申 告 所 得 税 215

所得の種類	範　　　　囲	計 算 方 法
(9)　山林所得	山林の伐採又は譲渡による所得。ただし，山林をその取得の日以後5年以内に伐採し又は譲渡することによる所得は含まない。	総収入金額－山林の取得費，植林費，伐採費その他の必要経費（(i)概算経費控除の選択適用あり(ii)森林計画特別控除の追加控除あり）－山林所得の特別控除額
(10)　退職所得	退職手当その他退職により一時に受ける所得。社会保障制度に基づく支払金を含む。	「退職所得控除額」を控除した額の2分の1に相当する金額

(分離課税)

所得の種類	範　　　　囲	計 算 方 法
(11)　配当所得	上場株式等の配当	収入金額－株式等を取得するための借入金の利子
(12)　土地等に係る事業所得等	土地及び建物並びにこれらの上に存する権利の譲渡に係る事業所得又は雑所得(注1, 2)	総収入金額－取得費等－必要経費
(13)　土地等に係る長期又は短期譲渡所得(注3)	土地及び建物並びにこれらの上に存する権利に係る譲渡所得(注1)	総収入金額－取得費等－譲渡経費－特別控除
(14)　株式等に係る譲渡所得等	株式，持分及び転換社債の譲渡による事業所得，譲渡所得及び雑所得	それぞれの総合課税上の所得の種類ごとにその計算方法による

(注)：1．土地の価額の2分の1を超えて支払われる貸地賃貸料の一括払いは土地の譲渡があったものと取り扱われる。

216 ASSESSMENT INCOME TAX

2. With respect to business income or miscellaneous income taxation on the sale of lands etc., short-term capital gain for the period from January 1, 1998 to March 31, 2017 is suspended.
3. If an initial lump sum payment received for rented land exceeds half the value of the land, the rental is treated as a transfer of land.

¶ 5-130 Computation of each category of income

In computing the amount of each category of income, the following supplementary explanation may be useful:

(1) **Interest income:**

Withholding income tax only (Law 23, SM 3). But interest on public bonds and debentures are subject to separate assessment income tax from January 1, 2016.

(2) **Dividend income (Law 24, 25):**

(a) In computing the amount of dividend income, only interest paid on borrowings incurred for the acquisition of the shares etc. is deductible. Other kinds of expenses are not deductible (Law 24).

(b) "Constructive dividends" should be included in dividend income. Constructive dividends include, for example, a portion of the money paid by a company to shareholders as compensation for its capital reduction, when such payment is, in its nature, a distribution of earnings retained in the past within the company (Law 25).

(3) **Real estate income (Law 26):**

Depreciation costs of buildings, fixed assets tax, city planning tax, fire insurance premiums, etc. are deductible (Law 26). Taxpayers having real estate income can be blue return taxpayers.

If a taxpayer who is a partner of a Nin-i Kumiai or a partnership similar to a Nin-i Kumiai involving in rental real property activity incurs losses from the rental activity, such losses will be considered nothing. That is, such losses can't be offset against other income and can't be carried over to the following years.

(4) **Business income:**

See ¶ 5-160 and ¶ 5-170 (Law 27).

(5) **Employment income:**

As a rule a standard employment income deduction is deductible when computing the amount of employment income for normal payments by an employer. As an exceptional case, when the

¶ 5-130

申 告 所 得 税 217

　2．土地の譲渡等に係る事業所得及び雑所得の課税の特例については，平成10年1月1日
　　から平成29年3月31日までの間の短期所有土地の譲渡等については適用しない。

　3．長期又は短期とは保有期間を示し，課税方法，税率，特別控除の金額がそれぞれ
　　に異なる。

¶5-130　各所得の計算

　各所得の計算について補足すれば次のとおりである。

(1)　利子所得

　　源泉分離課税（所法23，措法3）。ただし，公社債の利子は，平成28年
　1月1日以降申告分離課税の対象である。

(2)　配当所得（所法24，25）
　(a)　配当所得の計算に当たっては，株式等を取得するためにした借入金の
　　　利子だけが控除でき，他の経費は控除されない。

　(b)　みなし配当は配当所得に含まれる。みなし配当には，例えば，減資に
　　　より株主に交付される金銭で過去の留保利益の分配としての性格を有す
　　　るものなどが含まれる。

(3)　不動産所得（所法26）
　　建物の減価償却費，固定資産税，都市計画税，火災保険料等が控除され
　る。不動産所得を有する納税者は青色申告納税者となり得る。
　　不動産所得を生ずべき事業を行う民法組合等の当該民法組合等に係る不
　動産所得の金額の計算上生じた損失については，なかったものとみなす。

(4)　事業所得
　　¶5-160及び¶5-170参照（所法27）。
(5)　給与所得
　　給与所得者の通常の支払負担を考慮して(a)給与所得控除が認められる。
　特定の支出が(a)給与所得控除金額の50％（給与等の収入金額が1,500万円
　超の場合，125万円。）を超えるときは，(a)給与所得控除額に加えて(b)その

218   ASSESSMENT INCOME TAX

amount of the specified payment mentioned below is greater than the amount of one-half of the standard income deduction (upper limit is ¥1,250,000), a taxpayer can deduct the excess amount of the specified payment in addition to the amount of the standard employment income deduction.

(a)   Standard employment income deduction (Law 28):

The standard employment income deduction amounts to:

when gross receipt is not over ¥1,800,000
40% × gross receipt (minimum amount ¥650,000)
when gross receipt is over ¥1,800,000 but not over ¥3,600,000
30% × gross receipt + ¥180,000
when gross receipt is over ¥3,600,000 but not over ¥6,600,000
20% × gross receipt + ¥540,000
when gross receipt is over ¥6,600,000 but not over ¥10,000,000
10% × gross receipt + ¥1,200,000
when gross receipt is over ¥10,000,000
¥2,200,000

Effective from January 1, 2020

when gross receipt is not over ¥1,625,000
¥550,000
when gross receipt is over ¥1,625,000 but not over ¥1,800,000
gross receipt × 40% – ¥100,000
when gross receipt is over ¥1,800,000 but not over ¥3,600,000
gross receipt × 30% + ¥80,000
when gross receipt is over ¥3,600,000 but not over ¥6,600,000
gross receipt × 20% + ¥440,000
when gross receipt is over ¥6,600,000 but not over ¥8,500,000
gross receipt × 10% + ¥1,1000,000
when gross receipt is over ¥10,000,000
¥1,950,000

(b)   Specified payment deduction (Law 57-2):

When an employment income earner has been paid a specified payment under specific conditions, and the amount of the specified payment paid in the year is greater than the amount of the one-half of the standard employment income deduction (upper limit is ¥1,250,000), the excess amount is deductible in computing the amount of employment income.

¶ 5-130

超える部分の金額についても，特定支出控除が認められる。

(a) 給与所得控除（所法28）

給与所得控除額は収入金額に比例しており，次のとおりである。

収入金額が180万円以下の場合

収入金額×40%（最低限度額65万円）

収入金額が180万円を超え360万円以下の場合

収入金額×30%＋18万円

収入金額が360万円を超え660万円以下の場合

収入金額×20%＋54万円

収入金額が660万円を超え1,000万円以下の場合

収入金額×10%＋120万円

収入金額が1,000万円を超える場合

220万円

（平成32年分以降適用）

収入金額が162万5,000円以下の場合

55万円

収入金額が162万5,000円超180万円以下の場合

収入金額×40%－10万円

収入金額が180万円超360万円以下の場合

収入金額×30%＋8万円

収入金額が360万円超660万円以下の場合

収入金額×20%＋44万円

収入金額が660万円超850万円以下の場合

収入金額×10%＋110万円

収入金額が850万円超の場合

195万円

(b) 特定支出控除（所法57の2）

給与所得者が一定の要件に当てはまる特定支出をした場合において，その年中の特定支出の合計額が(a)の給与所得控除額の50%（給与等の収入金額が1,500万円超の場合，125万円。）を超えるときは，その超える部分の金額についても，給与所得の計算上，控除が認められる。

この「特定支出」とは，次のものをいい，雇用者から補てんされる部分を除いた金額である。この特例は確定申告書の提出により適用を受け

220 ASSESSMENT INCOME TAX

The amount of the specified payment is calculated on the amount excluding amounts reimbursed by the employer for expenses paid on its behalf for business purposes. This deduction is allowed when a final return is filed by a taxpayer, and the final return must be accompanied by a receipt for the specified payment, or a certificate approved by the employer.

A "specified payment" means the following:

(i) a transport or car allowance paid for using means of transportation or automobiles while away from home in the performance of services as an employee;

(ii) a payment for such moving expenses as would usually be necessary on transfer from one place of work to another;

(iii) a payment for acquiring a qualification (excluding lawyer, tax accountant, etc. except certification or permission required for the particular business) which is directly necessary for performing the employee's services;

(iv) a specific payment for travel from a temporary residence to the taxpayer's home where the taxpayer's spouse and family live, as reasonably necessary, when a taxpayer moves his or her residence as a result of a transfer of his or her place of work.

(v) a payment for obtaining certain qualifications such as attorneys, CPAs, tax accountants and etc which is directly necessary for performing the employee's services.

(vi) business expenses, for instance, expenses for books and clothing, social expenses, business–related membership fees. The deductible amount is limited up to ¥650,000.

(6) **Capital gains (Law 33):**

  (a) The cost incurred for the acquisition, installation or improvement of buildings and other depreciable assets is computed on the cost incurred for the acquisition, installation or improvement in the past, minus the total of depreciation cost.

  (b) The special deduction for capital gains which should be deducted in computing taxable capital gains is ¥500,000, or the amount of capital gains, whichever is smaller.

(7) **Occasional income (Law 34):**

The principle that expenses necessary for acquiring income are deductible is interpreted very strictly in this category. For example,

¶ 5-130

られ，その際には，特定支出に関する明細書，雇用者の証明書等が必要とされている。

  (i)　通勤のために必要な交通機関の利用又は交通用具の使用のための支出

  (ii)　転任に伴い，通常必要とされる転居のための支出

  (iii)　人の資格（弁護士，税理士などその資格を有する者に限り特定の業務を営むことができるものを除く。）を取得するための支出で，その者の職務の遂行に直接必要なもの

  (iv)　転任に伴い，配偶者と別居を常況とすることとなった場合，その者の居所と配偶者等が居住する場所との間の旅行に通常要する支出のうち，特定のもの

  (v)　職務の遂行に直接必要な弁護士，公認会計士，税理士，弁理士などの資格取得費

  (vi)　職務と関連のある図書の購入日，職場で着用する衣服の衣服費，職務に通常必要な交際費及び職業上の団体の経費（勤務必要経費）
    合計額が65万円を超える場合には，65万円を限度とする。
(6)　譲渡所得（通則）（所法33）
 (a)　建物及びその他の減価償却資産の取得費，据付費及び改良費は，過去に支出された取得費，据付費及び改良費から減価償却累計額を控除して算出する。

 (b)　譲渡所得特別控除額は，50万円又は譲渡益のいずれか小さい金額である。

(7)　一時所得（所法34）
  控除できる必要経費の解釈は厳格である。例えば，競馬の場合，馬券代と払戻金とはレースごとで計算され，純益を合計するが，損失とは相殺し

222   ASSESSMENT INCOME TAX

in horse racing the price of betting-tickets and the amount of gains are usually compared for each race, and net profits are totalled, but net losses are not set off against profits.

The special deduction for occasional income is ¥500,000 or the amount of occasional income, whichever is smaller.

(8) **Miscellaneous income (Law 35):**

  (a) Miscellaneous income includes:

    (i)   interest on a loan when a taxpayer does not carry on any professional financial business;

    (ii) fee for manuscripts, when the taxpayer is not engaged in a literary profession;

    (iii) the same proportion of the reserved income of a specified foreign subsidiary corporation as an individual taxpayer's share bears to the total shares of the corporation, when the individual taxpayer owns shares of not less than 5% of the total shares of the corporation (Note);

    (iv) profits from other kinds of activities when they are not classified as business income;

    (v) annuities; public pensions;

    (vi) other kinds of income not belonging to other categories.

Note:

A specified foreign subsidiary corporation means a foreign corporation which has a head office in one of the so-called tax haven countries, which impose no tax or very light tax on the income of the corporation, and is controlled by Japanese corporations and individual residents owning 50% or more of the shares. This measure was introduced in the 1978 Tax Reform. Forty-one countries was designated as tax haven countries by the Minister of Finance (SM 40-4) (see ¶ 6-195).

In the 1992 Tax Reform, the designation system was eliminated in accordance with the abolishment of the existing designation system for tax haven countries and areas. It must now be determined on a subsidiary by subsidiary basis whether an overseas subsidiary of a Japanese company is subject to the legislation.

  (b) In computing the income accruing from annuities, premiums paid for the purchase of the annuity can be deducted, applying a specific method of calculation.

  (c) Public pensions (Law 35③)

    A public pensions deduction can be deducted in computing the

¶ 5-130

申　告　所　得　税　223

ない。

一時所得の特別控除額は，50万円又は一時所得金額のいずれか小さい額
である。

(8)　雑所得（所法35）

　(a)　次のようなものは雑所得とされる。

　　(i)　事業に関係しない貸付金の利子

　　(ii)　著述業を営む者以外の者が取得する原稿料

　　(iii)　特定外国子会社の留保所得のうち，当該会社の株式を5％以上有し
　　　ている者のその持分に対応する金額[注]

　　(iv)　事業所得に該当しない諸活動からの所得

　　(v)　保険年金，公的年金

　　(vi)　そのほか他の所得に属さない所得

　[注]：特定外国子会社とは，法人の所得に対する課税がないか又は軽課しているいわゆるタッ
　　　クス・ヘイブン国に本店を有し，かつ，日本の国内法人及び居住者がその株式の50％以上
　　　を所有して支配している外国法人をいう。この制度は昭和53年の税制改正で導入されたも
　　　のである。タックス・ヘイブン国は財務大臣により41カ国が指定されていたが，平成4年
　　　の税制改正により，タックス・ヘイブン国の指定制度は廃止され，タックス・ヘイブン国
　　　に該当するか否かは各外国法人ごとに判定される（措法40の4）（¶6-195参照）。

　(b)　保険年金に係る所得の計算に当たっては，支払った保険料が所定の計
　　算方式に従い控除される。

　(c)　公的年金（所法35③）

　　　公的年金については，収入金額から公的年金控除額を控除した残額が

224 ASSESSMENT INCOME TAX

amount of miscellaneous income from the gross receipts from public pensions. Public pensions means public servant pensions, approved fund pensions, national pensions or the other pensions paid under social insurance schemes. The public pensions deduction is as follows.

(less than 65 years old)   unit: ¥1,000

gross receipts (A)	deductions
1,300 or less	700
over 1,300 less than 4,100	(A) ×25% + 375
over 4,100 less than 7,700	(A) ×15% + 785
over 7,700	(A) × 5 % + 1,555

(over 65 years old)   unit: ¥1,000

gross receipts (A)	deductions
3,300 or less	1,200
over 3,300 less than 4,100	(A) ×25% + 375
over 4,100 less than 7,700	(A) ×15% + 785
over 7,700	(A) × 5 % + 1,555

Effective from January 1, 2020

(less than 65 years old)   unit: ¥1,000

gross receipts of public pensions (A)	total income other than public pensions		
	10,000 or less	over 10,000 and 20,000 or less	over 20,000
1,300 or less	600	500	400
over 1,300 and 4,100 or less	(A) ×25% + 275	(A) ×25% + 175	(A) ×25% + 75
over 4,100 and 7,700 or less	(A) ×15% + 685	(A) ×15% + 585	(A) ×15% + 485
over 7,700 and 10,000 or less	(A) × 5 % + 1,455	(A) × 5 % + 1,355	(A) × 5 % + 1,255
over 10,000	1,955	1,855	1,755

(over 65 years old)   unit: ¥1,000

gross receipts of public pensions (A)	total income other than public pensions		
	10,000 or less	over 10,000 and 20,000 or less	over 20,000
3,300 or less	1,100	1,000	900
over 3,300 and 4,100 or less	(A) ×25% + 275	(A) ×25% + 175	(A) ×25% + 75
over 4,100 and 7,700 or less	(A) ×15% + 685	(A) ×15% + 585	(A) ×15% + 485
over 7,700 and 10,000 or less	(A) × 5 % + 1,455	(A) × 5 % + 1,355	(A) × 5 % + 1,255
over 10,000	1,955	1,855	1,755

¶ 5-130

雑所得金額とされる。

　公的年金とは，恩給，厚生年金又は国民年金等の社会保険制度に基づき支給される年金をいい，公的年金控除額は，以下のようになる。

65歳未満の者

その年中の公的年金等の収入金額の合計額（A）	公的年金等控除額
130万円未満	70万円
130万円以上410万円未満	（A）×25％＋ 37万5千円
410万円以上770万円未満	（A）×15％＋ 78万5千円
770万円以上	（A）× 5％＋155万5千円

65歳以上の者

その年中の公的年金等の収入金額の合計額（A）	公的年金等控除額
330万円未満	120万円
330万円以上410万円未満	（A）×25％＋ 37万5千円
410万円以上770万円未満	（A）×15％＋ 78万5千円
770万円以上	（A）× 5％＋155万5千円

（平成32年分以降適用）

65歳未満の者

公的年金等の収入金額（A）	公的年金等に係る雑所得以外の所得に係る合計所得金額		
	1,000万円以下	1,000万円超 2,000万円以下	2,000万円超
130万円以下	60万円	50万円	40万円
130万円超 410万円以下	（A）×25％＋ 27.5万円	（A）×25％＋ 17.5万円	（A）×25％＋ 7.5万円
410万円超 770万円以下	（A）×15％＋ 68.5万円	（A）×15％＋ 58.5万円	（A）×15％＋ 48.5万円
770万円超 1,000万円以下	（A）× 5％＋145.5万円	（A）× 5％＋135.5万円	（A）× 5％＋125.5万円
1,000万円超	195.5万円	185.5万円	175.5万円

65歳以上の者

公的年金等の収入金額（A）	公的年金等に係る雑所得以外の所得に係る合計所得金額		
	1,000万円以下	1,000万円超 2,000万円以下	2,000万円超
330万円以下	110万円	100万円	90万円
330万円超 410万円以下	（A）×25％＋ 27.5万円	（A）×25％＋ 17.5万円	（A）×25％＋ 7.5万円
410万円超 770万円以下	（A）×15％＋ 68.5万円	（A）×15％＋ 58.5万円	（A）×15％＋ 48.5万円
770万円超 1,000万円以下	（A）× 5％＋145.5万円	（A）× 5％＋135.5万円	（A）× 5％＋125.5万円
1,000万円超	195.5万円	185.5万円	175.5万円

226   ASSESSMENT INCOME TAX

(9) **Forestry income (Law 32):**

(a) The computation method applicable to capital gains as described in ¶ 5-190 (1) and (2) below is applicable also to forestry income.

(b) If the "standard deduction method" is chosen, deductible expenses amount to the total of (SM 30):

(i) a certain percentage (50%) of the gross receipts less expenses for cutting, transportation and selling; and

(ii) expenses for cutting, transportation and selling.

(c) The "special deduction for an afforestation plan" amounts to the lesser of either 20% of receipts or 50% of receipts minus deductible expenses with respect to the cutting or selling of timber under an afforestation plan designated by the Minister of Agriculture, Forestry and Fisheries or an authorized prefectural governor (SM 30-2).

(d) The "special deduction for forestry income (¥500,000)" is same amount as the special deduction for capital gains on movable property.

(e) The amount remaining after the special deduction in (d) is called the "forestry income amount".

(10) **Retirement income (Law 30, 31):**

(a) Nothing but the "special deduction for retirement income" is deductible in computing the amount of retirement income.

The special deduction for retirement income amounts to:

(i) When the number of years of service is 20 years or less — ¥400,000 multiplied by the number of years of service or ¥800,000, whichever is greater.

(ii) When the number of years of service is longer than 20 years —¥8,000,000 plus ¥700,000 multiplied by the number of years of service in excess of 20 years.

An additional special deduction of ¥1,000,000 will be allowed for a taxpayer who has retired as a result of being handicapped.

(b) A half of the remainder after deducting the special deduction for retirement income represents the "retirement income amount". However, regarding retirement income received by short-term executives (whose term is 5 years or below), the "retirement income amount" is to be the amount after deducting the special deduction for retirement income.

¶ 5-130

申 告 所 得 税　227

(9)　山林所得（所法32）
　(a)　後述する譲渡所得の計算方法（¶5-190(1), (2)参照）が，山林所得に
　　　も適用される。
　(b)　概算控除を選択した場合の控除し得る経費の額は次の(i)と(ii)との合計
　　　額である（措法30）。
　　(i)　伐採費，運搬費及び売却費を控除した収入金額の一定割合（50％）
　　　　に相当する金額
　　(ii)　伐採費，運搬費及び売却費
　(c)　森林計画特別控除額は，農林水産大臣又は権限ある都道府県知事が認
　　　定した森林施業計画に基づく山林の伐採又は譲渡に係る収入金額の20％
　　　相当額又は収入金額の50％相当額から必要経費を控除した残額のいずれ
　　　か低い金額（措法30の２）。

　(d)　山林所得の特別控除額は，譲渡所得（原則）の場合と同じである。

　(e)　上記(d)の特別控除後の金額が山林所得の金額である。

(10)　退職所得（所法30, 31）
　(a)　退職所得控除額以外の控除はない。
　　　退職所得控除額は次のとおりである。

　　(i)　勤続年数が20年以下の場合
　　　　勤続年数に40万円を乗じて計算した金額と80万円とのいずれか大き
　　　　い金額
　　(ii)　勤続年数が20年を超える場合
　　　　800万円と勤続年数から20年を控除した年数に70万円を乗じて計算
　　　　した金額との合計額
　　　　なお，障害を受けたことにより退職した場合には，100万円が加算
　　　される。
　(b)　退職手当等の収入金額から退職所得控除額を控除した残額の２分
　　　の１に相当する金額が退職所得金額である。但し，役員等（役員等とし
　　　ての勤続年数が５年以下の者（「短期在任役員」）に限る。）が当該退職
　　　手当等の支払者から役員等の勤続年数に対応するものとして支払を受け
　　　るものについては，退職所得控除額を控除した残額に対して所得税が課
　　　され，いわゆる，２分の１課税は適用されない。

228   ASSESSMENT INCOME TAX

That is, 50% taxation is not applied to the computation of retirement income received by short-term executives.

(c) Lump sum payments paid according to the "Welfare pensions insurance law" are deemed to be retirement income.

¶ 5-140 Accrual basis

The tax law requires a taxpayer to use the accrual basis in the calculation of his income, regardless of the category of income, with a few exceptions. Dividends are considered to accrue when a dividend payment is declared at a shareholders' general meeting.

An exception is dividend income on bearer stocks or shares, which is recognized on a cash basis (Law 36).

Further, a cash basis is allowed for a taxpayer filing a blue return whose total business income and real estate income in two years before was not more than ¥3,000,000 (Law 67-2).

¶ 5-150 Receipts and expenses in kind (usual taxation)

Receipts and expenses in kind should be included in gross receipts or expenses respectively at a fair market value (Law 36②).

¶ 5-160 Computation of business income (usual taxation)

Generally accepted accounting principles are applicable to the computation of business income, with a few exceptions. The following description indicates important rules applicable to individuals, some of which are different from the rules applicable to corporations:

(1) Expenses necessary for carrying on a business are deductible, but expenses disbursed for private purposes are not deductible (Law 45).

(2) Income tax, inhabitant taxes and fines are not deductible (Law 45).

(3) Payments to a taxpayer's family members are deductible only within certain limits, whatever their nature might be (salaries, rent, interest, etc.), namely:

(a) in the case of a taxpayer filing a blue return, only salaries or wages paid to family members engaged exclusively in the taxpayer's business (during more than 6 months as a rule) are deductible, provided that the salaries or wages do not exceed the amount reported in advance to the tax office by March 15 of the year, and must be reasonable in view of their service

¶ 5-140

申　告　所　得　税　229

(c)　厚生年金保険法による一時金は退職手当とみなされる。

¶5-140　発生主義

若干の例外を除き，所得は発生主義により計算される。配当は，株主総会において配当の支払が決議された時に生じたものとされる（所法36）。

例外としては，無記名株式に係る配当は現金主義による。

また，前々年の事業所得及び不動産所得の合計額が300万円以下の青色申告者は，現金主義によることが認められる（所法67の2）。

¶5-150　金銭以外の収入及び支出（原則）

現物による受取り又は支払は，その市場価格で収入又は支出されたものとして扱われる（所法36②）。

¶5-160　事業所得の計算

事業所得の計算に当たっては，若干の例外を除き，一般に認められた会計基準によることとなる。以下に述べることは，個人の事業についての重要な原則であり，法人の場合と異なるものもある。

(1)　事業を行うための必要経費は控除できるが，家事関連費は控除できない（所法45）。
(2)　所得税，住民税及び罰金は控除できない（所法45）。
(3)　家族に対する支払については，それが給与，賃料，利子等であっても，控除額には一定の限度がある。

(a)　青色申告者である場合には，もっぱらその事業に（原則として6カ月を超える期間）従事する家族に支払われる給与等だけが控除できる。この場合，その給与等の額はあらかじめその年の3月15日までに税務署に届け出た額を超えず，かつ，納税者の他の従業員あるいは他の同業者の勤務時間，職務内容，給与水準に照らし妥当なものである必要がある（所法57）。

230   ASSESSMENT INCOME TAX

time, job description, salary level of other employees of the taxpayer or other taxpayers engaged in a similar business of similar size (Law 57).

(b) in the case of other taxpayers, the smaller of the following amounts (i) or (ii) shall be deemed to be the necessary expenses, and that amount is taxable as salary income of the family employees (Law 57):

(i)   ¥500,000 (in the case of a spouse, ¥860,000)

(ii)   (amount of business income accrued from that business) ÷ (the number of family employees + 1)

Note:
When a taxpayer elects to deduct payments for his family members, he is unable to deduct an allowance for a spouse (¶ 5-410) or allowances for dependents (¶ 5-420).

(4) Entertainment expenses for carrying on business and those directly related to the business are deductible, and not subject to restrictions as in the case of the corporation tax (Law 22).

(5) The cost of goods sold is computed by adding the opening inventory at the beginning of the year to the cost of goods purchased or produced during the year and deducting from this total the closing inventory at the end of the year. The taxpayer may elect one of the methods for evaluating inventories. In the absence of notification of the election, the "most recent purchased" method (see ¶ 6-255) is deemed to have been adopted by the taxpayer (Law 47).

(6) (a) Depreciation is always automatically deducted from the assessable income of individual taxpayers, while in the case of corporations, depreciation is deducted only if the corporation has included depreciation in its profit and loss statement for business purposes.

(b) The acquisition cost of an asset costing less than ¥100,000 is deductible as an expense in the year when such an asset is put into operation (Reg 138).

Depreciable assets which acquisition cost are less than ¥200,000 can be amortized in the three succeeding years.

For depreciable assets acquired for the period from April 1, 2006 to March 31, 2018, the acquisition cost of the asset costing less than ¥300,000 is deductible as an expense in

¶ 5-160

申　告　所　得　税　231

　(b)　その他の納税者については，次のいずれか低い金額を必要経費とみな
　　し，かつ，その金額は事業専従者の給与所得の収入金額とみなされる
　　（所法57）。

　　(i)　50万円（配偶者については86万円）
　　(ii)　その年分の当該事業に係る事業所得の金額÷（事業専従者の数＋1）

　(注)：専従者給与を選択した場合には，配偶者控除（¶5-410）又は扶養控除（¶5-420）を受
　　けられない。

(4)　交際費は，事業を営むためにその事業と直接的に関連するものにつき控
　除され，法人税法上のような制限の対象とならない。

(5)　たな卸資産の売上原価は，年の始めの期首たな卸資産に期中の仕入高又
　は製造原価を加え，この合計額から年の終わりの期末たな卸資産を差し引
　くことにより計算される。
　　納税者はたな卸資産の評価方法のいずれか一つを選択できるが，届出が
　ないときは最終仕入原価法（¶6-255参照）を採用したものとみなされる
　（所法47）。

(6)(a)　減価償却費は，課税所得計算上必ず控除される。なお，法人の場合に
　　は損金経理した場合にだけ控除が認められることになっているものであ
　　る。

　(b)　取得価額が10万円未満のものは，事業の用に供した年に全額経費とし
　　て控除する（所令138）。
　　　取得価額が20万円未満の減価償却資産については，業務の用に供した
　　年ごとに一括して，その取得価額の合計額を3年間で均等に必要経費に
　　算入することができる。
　　　平成18年4月1日から平成30年3月31日までの間に青色申告者が取得
　　した30万円未満の減価償却資産については，事業の用に供した年に全額
　　経費として控除する。ただし，資産の価額の合計額が各年300万円を超

232   ASSESSMENT INCOME TAX

the year when the assets are put into operation. However, if the total acquisition costs of such assets being acquired are over ¥3,000,000 each year, the acquisition cost exceeding ¥3,000,000 is not applicable.

(c)   For depreciable assets acquired on or after April 1, 2007, the final depreciable limit (currently 95% of their acquisition costs) will be abolished and such assets can be depreciated to ¥1 (memorandum price) at the end of their useful life with the introduction of 250% declining balance method.

For depreciable assets acquired before March 31, 2007, will be allowed to be depreciated to ¥1 in five years using the straight line method after having depreciated to the final depreciable limit (95% of their acquisition costs).

(d)   For the depreciation rate of the declining balance method on the depreciable assets acquired on or after April 1, 2012, 200% declining balance method is applied.

(e)   Reducing balance method is no longer applicable to newly acquired buildings only the straight line method is applicable to building acquired on or after April 1, 1998.

(f)   Goodwill acquired after April 1, 1998 must be amortized by the straight line method over five years.

(g)   Leased assets used by a non-resident or a foreign corporation operating outside Japan must be depreciated by the straight line method for the lease period.

(h)   The taxpayer may select one of the depreciation methods. In the absence of notification of the election, the "straight line" method (see ¶ 6-270) is deemed to have been adopted by the taxpayer (Law 49).

(i)   The amortization of deferred assets is computed in the same way as intangible assets by applying the "straight line" method (Law 50).

(7)   A lease transaction with conditions of non-cancelable and full pay-out contracted on April 1, 2008 or later is deemed as sale (see ¶ 6-309).

(8)   When an individual taxpayer files a blue return, as an example, the following special additional depreciation is deductible, the same as for a corporate taxpayer:

¶ 5-160

申　告　所　得　税　233

える場合には，その超える取得価額は該当しない。

(c)　平成19年4月1日以降に取得した減価償却資産については，償却可能
限度額（現行では取得価額の5％）は廃止され，耐用年数経過時点
に1円まで償却することでができるとともに，250％定率法が導入された。
　　平成19年3月31日以前に取得をした減価償却資産については，償却可
能限度額まで償却した後，5年間で1円まで均等償却することができる。

(d)　平成24年4月1日以後に取得する減価償却資産の定率法の償却率につ
いて，定額法の償却率を2.0倍した割合とされる。いわゆる，200％定率
法が導入された。
(e)　平成10年4月1日以後に取得する建物の償却方法は定額法のみとす
る。
(f)　平成10年4月1日以後に取得する営業権の償却方法は定額法のみとす
る。
(g)　リース取引の目的とされている減価償却資産で，非居住者又は外国法
人の国外において行う事業の用に供されるものの償却方法は，リース期
間定額法とする。
(h)　納税者は減価償却の方法のいずれか一つを選択できるが，届出がない
場合には，定額法（¶6-270参照）を採用したものとみなされる（所法
49）。

(i)　繰延資産の償却費については有形固定資産と同じく定額法により計算
される（所法50）。

(7)　平成20年4月1日以後に締結する契約に係る所有権移転外ファイナン
ス・リース取引については，資産の売買取引として取り扱う（¶6-309参
照）。
(8)　個人事業所得者も法人と同様に，特別償却が青色申告書を提出している
ことを条件として認められる。例えば，次のものがある。

234   ASSESSMENT INCOME TAX

    (a) A special additional depreciation for specified equipment (SM 11).

    (b) A special additional depreciation for qualifying assets contributing to the use of sun energy, wind energy etc (SM 10-2-2).

    (c) A special additional depreciation for specified machines used by medium or small enterprises (SM 10-3).

    (d) Additional depreciation for machines used by an enterprise which employs a handicapped person (SM 13).

(9) (a) An allowance for bad debts is deductible to a limit of 5.5% (3.3% for financial enterprises) of receivables outstanding at the year-end (Law 52).

      The allowable limit for the allowance for bad debts consists of the allowable limits of Doubtful receivables and Other receivables.

    (b) Bonus payment reserve, Reserve for special repair, Reserve for aftercare of construction work or products are abolished.

    (c) Reserves for goods returned unsold (Law 53) and other taxfree reserves are allowed.

(10) In calculating the amount of business income earned by an independent worker in a taxpayer's residence, the taxpayer in whose residence he works can deduct ¥650,000, with a proportionate deduction for a part-time worker (eligible for the standard employment income deduction), if the amount of his necessary expenses is under ¥650,000 (SM 27).

(11) If the taxpayer is a blue return taxpayer (see ¶ 5-030) and keeps an accounting book in compliance with Principle of orderly bookkeeping, the blue return special deduction of ¥650,000 is allowed.

     If the taxpayer is a blue return taxpayer (see ¶ 5-030) other than the above, the blue return special deduction of ¥100,000 is allowed.

¶ 5-170   Capital gain's taxation on commodity futures trading

Capital gains arise from commodity futures trading is subject to separate taxation at the rate of 20% (national tax 15% & local tax 5%).

(1) Capital gains, which are treated as business income or miscellaneous income, arise from commodity futures trading made by a resident taxpayer and settled by the balance are subject to income

¶ 5-170

申　告　所　得　税　235

　(a)　特定設備等の特別償却（措法11）

　(b)　太陽光，風力エネルギー等の利用設備の特別償却（措法10の2の2）

　(c)　中小企業者の機械等の特別償却（措法10の3）

　(d)　障害者を雇用する場合の機械等の割増償却（措法13）

(9)(a)　貸倒引当金については，年末の貸金額の5.5％（金融業の場合は3.3％）まで引き当てることができる（所法52）。
　　　貸倒引当金の繰入限度額の計算を，期末貸金を個別に評価する債権と一括して評価するその他の債権とに区分して計算する方法とする。

　(b)　賞与引当金，特別修繕引当金，製品保証等引当金を廃止する。

　(c)　返品調整引当金（所法53）及びその他の非課税準備金が認められる。

(10)　家内労働者等の事業所得の計算については，パート所得者（給与所得控除が受けられる。）との課税の均衡を考慮して，その必要経費の金額が65万円に満たないときでも，最低65万円の控除が認められる（措法27）。

(11)　青色申告納税者（¶5-030参照）で，取引を正規の簿記の原則に従って記録している者については，650,000円の青色申告特別控除額が認められる。
　　　上記以外の青色申告納税者（¶5-030参照）については，100,000円の青色申告特別控除が認められる。

¶5-170　商品先物取引による所得課税
　商品先物取引による所得に対して，20％（所得税15％，地方税5％）の税率により申告分離課税が適用される。
(1)　商品先物取引を行い，かつ，当該商品先物取引の差金決済をした場合には，当該商品先物取引による事業所得及び雑所得については，他の所得と分離して確定申告を通じて課税する。

236   ASSESSMENT INCOME TAX

tax through the process of filing a final tax return, separate from other income.

(2) Capital losses generated from commodity or stock futures trading are not allowed to offset against income other than income from commodity or stock future trading.

(3) To the extent that there are capital losses generated from commodity or stock futures trading, the amount of capital losses can be carried forward for the succeeding 3 years and allowed to deduct from capital gains generated from commodity or stock futures trading under the specified conditions.

¶ 5-180 Taxation of trusts

1. Regarding trusts issuing securities representing beneficiary rights, an income distribution from trust dividend income, and capital gains from the sale of securities representing beneficiary rights are treated as capital gains from the sale of stocks.

2. Regarding such a trust as beneficiaries don't exist,

    (1) When such a trust is created, the transfer of the asset to the trust is treated as the transfer of the asset from a settlor to a trustee and a settlor is subject to income tax on the capital gains. On the other hand, a trustee is subject to gift tax on the fair market value of the entrusted property.

    (2) Only if a trust which beneficiaries don't exist turned to a trust which beneficiaries do exist, income tax will not be imposed on the benefits from the acquisition of the beneficiary rights by the beneficiary.

3. When rental losses from the trust are incurred by an individual beneficiary of the trust and such losses are classified as rental income from real property, such losses are disregarded and can't be offset against other income.

¶ 5-190 Computation of capital gains (general rule)

The following shows the important points to be kept in mind in computing the amount of capital gains:

(1) A property is deemed to have been sold at a fair market value (Law 59):

    (i)   if the property is donated or bequeathed to a corporation, in-

¶ 5-180

申 告 所 得 税　237

⑵　商品先物取引等による所得の金額の計算上生じた損失の金額は，商品先物取引による所得以外の所得との通算は認めない。

⑶　商品先物取引又は有価証券等先物取引に係る差金等決済をしたことにより生じた損失の金額のうちに，一定の要件の下で，その控除しきれない金額についてその年の翌年以後３年内の各年分の商品先物取引又は有価証券等先物取引に係る雑所得等の金額から繰越控除を認める。

¶5-180　信託財産に対する課税

１．受益証券発行信託において，個人受益者が受ける収益の分配は配当所得として，その受益証券の譲渡による所得は株式等に係る譲渡所得等として課税される。

２．受益者等の存在しない信託において，
　⑴　受益者等の存在しない信託を設定した場合には，委託者においてはみなし譲渡課税を，受託者においてはその信託財産の価額に相当する金額について受贈益課税を行う。

　⑵　受益者等の存在しない信託に受益者等が存在することとなった場合に限り，当該受益者等の受益権の取得による受贈益については，所得税を課税しない。

３．受益者段階課税される信託の個人受益者等の当該信託に係る不動産所得の損失は，生じなかったものとみなし，損益通算等が制限されている。

¶5-190　譲渡所得の計算（通則）

次の事項は，譲渡所得計算上重要な点である。

⑴　次の場合には，譲渡資産は適正な市場価格で売買されたものとされる（所法59）。
　⒤　法人に対する寄付又は遺贈，限定承認に係る相続又は包括遺贈のうち

238   ASSESSMENT INCOME TAX

herited with qualified acceptance of heritage, or bequeathed to an individual in the form of a universal legacy with qualified acceptance, without receiving any compensation for it; and

(ii) if the property is sold to a corporation at an unreasonably low price (less than one half of the fair market value).

(2) Movable property acquired by a taxpayer before January 1, 1953, is deemed to have been acquired at the price valued for inheritance tax purposes as of January 1, 1953 (Law 61).

(3) The acquisition cost of a property used for non-business purposes may not be fully deducted in computing the amount of capital gains. In this case the acquisition cost minus depreciation costs may be deducted. In computing depreciation costs, the useful life of non-business assets is treated as 150% of the useful life applicable to business assets (Reg 85).

(4) When an inherited property is transferred within three years after the date when the inheritance tax return regarding such inherited property is due, the inheritance tax on such inherited property is deductible in computing the capital gains derived from the transfer (SM 39).

(5) Capital gains from the exchange of a fixed asset for another fixed asset are deemed not to have accrued, provided the following requirements are met (Law 58):

(i) both the old and new fixed assets belong to the same classification and are used for the same purposes,

(ii) both the old and new fixed assets are owned for one year or more,

(iii) the fair market price of the old fixed assets is not different from 20% or less of the price of new fixed assets.

(6) No capital gain is deemed to accrue, if (SM 40, 40-2, 40-3):

(i) a person contributes his or her property to the government, local government, etc.,

(ii) a person transfers his or her property as a payment in kind for inheritance tax.

(7) Capital gains are divided into two categories for tax purposes based on the length of ownership before the transfer. Capital gains derived from a transfer of movable properties after five years' ownership are defined as long-term capital gains (Law 33③) (see ¶ 5-230 (6) and Note).

¶ 5-190

申　告　所　得　税　239

限定承認に係るもの

(ii)　法人に対する著しく低い価格（適正市場価格の2分の1未満）による譲渡

(2)　昭和28年1月1日前に取得した動産は，同日における相続税評価額で取得したものとみなされる（所法61）。

(3)　非事業用資産の取得費は，使用されて減価している場合には，譲渡所得の計算上，その取得費全額の控除は認められない。この場合は，取得費から減価償却費を差し引いた額が控除される。減価償却費の計算に当たっては，非事業用資産の耐用年数は事業用資産の1.5倍とされる（所令85）。

(4)　相続により取得した資産を当該資産に係る相続税の申告期限後3年以内に譲渡した場合には，その譲渡所得計算上当該資産に係る相続税額を控除できる（措法39）。

(5)　固定資産と他の固定資産の交換により生じる譲渡所得は，次のことを要件として生じなかったものとみなされる（所法58）。

(i)　譲渡資産と取得資産とが同一の種類に属し，同一の用途に供されること

(ii)　譲渡資産と取得資産とも1年以上所有されていたこと

(iii)　譲渡資産の価額と取得資産の価額との差額が20%を超えないこと

(6)　次の場合も譲渡所得がないものとみなされる（措法40，40の2，40の3）。
(i)　政府，地方自治体等に寄付した場合

(ii)　相続税を物納した場合

(7)　譲渡所得は，譲渡資産の所有期間により2種に分けられる（所法33③）。すなわち，5年を超えて所有していた資産に係る長期譲渡所得と5年以内の期間所有していた資産に係る短期譲渡所得とである。なお，¶5-230(6)及び（注）を参照のこと。

240   ASSESSMENT INCOME TAX

(8)   A special deduction of ¥500,000 is deductible in computing the income amount of capital gain (Law 33④).

¶ 5-195 Computation of business income etc. on land etc.

1.   If a taxpayer, for example a real estate agent, acquired capital gains from its land etc. which is situated in Japan and has been owned for 5 years, and the capital gains belong to Business income, or Miscellaneous income, "business income etc. on land etc." is computed using the following formula (SM 28-4);

The amount of Business income on land etc.

= gross receipts from alienation of land etc.

– acquisition cost of lands sold

– interest paid in that year in connection with the transaction

– selling and general administrative expenses in connection with the transaction.

2.   However, the above-mentioned treatment on short-term capital gain from the sale of lands etc. for the period from January 1, 1998 to March 31, 2017 is suspended.

3.   If a taxpayer alienates land etc. to any of the following, the business income or miscellaneous income is not given special tax treatment.

(1)   The national and local government.

(2)   Urban Renaissance Agency or the designated organizations.

(3)   The other person for the expropriation.

¶ 5-200 Computation of long-term or short-term capital gains on land etc.

(1)   Capital gains derived from land (including directly related rights) and buildings are taxable separately from other income.

These gains are broken into two categories as follows:

(a)   Long-term capital gains on land etc. (SM 31).

Capital gains derived from the transfer of land and buildings owned by an individual for more than 5 years as of January 1 of the year when the transfer was made.

(b)   Short-term capital gains on land etc. (SM 32).

Capital gains derived from the transfer of land and buildings other than long-term capital gains on land etc.

(2)   The following shows the important points to be kept in mind in

¶ 5-195

申　告　所　得　税　241

⑻　譲渡所得の金額の計算上，50万円の特別控除が認められる（所法33④）。

¶5-195　土地等に係る事業所得等の計算

1．不動産業者等がその年の1月1日において所有期間が5年以下の土地等で事業所得又は雑所得の基因となる土地等の譲渡をした場合には，「土地等に係る事業所得等の金額」として，次により所得金額を計算する（措法28の4）。

$$
\begin{pmatrix} 土地等に係る事 \\ 業所得等の金額 \end{pmatrix} = \begin{bmatrix} 土地の譲渡等に \\ よる収入金額 \end{bmatrix} - \left\{ \begin{bmatrix} 土地の譲渡等に \\ 係る原価の額 \end{bmatrix} \right.
$$
$$
\left. + \begin{bmatrix} 土地の譲渡等に \\ 係る負債の利子 \end{bmatrix} + \begin{bmatrix} 土地の譲渡等に要した \\ 販売費・一般管理費 \end{bmatrix} \right\}
$$

2．ただし，平成10年1月1日から平成29年3月31日までの間の短期所有土地の譲渡等については，土地の譲渡等に係る事業所得及び雑所得の課税の特例は適用しない。

3．次に掲げる者に土地等を譲渡した場合には，その事業所得及び雑所得は特例課税の対象とならない。
　⑴　国又は地方公共団体
　⑵　独立行政法人都市再生機構又はその他の指定法人
　⑶　収用による第三者

¶5-200　土地等の長期又は短期譲渡所得

⑴　土地（土地の上に存する権利を含む。）及び建物の譲渡による所得は他の所得と分離して課税される。
　　その譲渡所得は課税上次のように二区分に分類される。
　⒜　土地等の長期譲渡所得（措法31）
　　　納税者が土地及び建物を譲渡した日の属する年の1月1日において5年を超えて所有していたものに係る譲渡所得

　⒝　土地等の短期譲渡所得（措法32）
　　　長期譲渡所得以外の土地等の譲渡所得

⑵　土地等の譲渡所得の計算上特に留意すべき点を挙げれば次のとおりであ

242   ASSESSMENT INCOME TAX

computing the amount of capital gains on land or buildings:

(a) If a person permits another person to construct a building on his land and receives a lump sum payment in excess of one half of its fair market value, the usufruct of the land is deemed to have been sold and capital gains are deemed to have accrued accordingly.

(b) The acquisition cost of land or buildings acquired by a taxpayer before January 1, 1953 is deemed, as a rule, to be 5% of the amount of gross receipts from the transfer of the land or buildings.

(c) Any losses in other categories of income, or the nondeductible amount of deductions and allowances, may be offset against this category of income, and in this case, the offset against the capital gains amount is made as follows:

- first.........short-term capital gains from land etc.
- second....short-term capital gains from property other than land etc.
- third.......long-term capital gains from land etc.
- fourth.....long-term capital gains from property other than land etc.

(3) Special deduction for capital gains.

Instead of the special deduction of ¥500,000 determined in capital gains (general rule) (see ¶ 5-190), the following special deduction regulated by the Tax Special Measures Law is deductible.

Special treatment of the special deduction:

The following special treatment of the special deduction is permitted, in which the special deduction is deducted from long-term capital gains or short-term capital gains according to a specified order:

(i) A special deduction of ¥50,000,000 is allowed for compensation money paid upon expropriation (SM 33-4).

(ii) A special deduction of ¥30,000,000 is allowed for capital gains derived from land and buildings used for residence (SM 35).

(iii) A special deduction for capital gains from sale of inherited vacant houses (SM 35).

A special deduction of ¥30,000,000 is applied to capital gains for the cases where an inherited vacant house only meets the old earthquake proof standards and the successor sells the house or property after conducting necessary anti-seismic renovation or demolition of the house for the period from

¶ 5-200

る。
(a) 建物の所有を目的とする借地権の設定の場合，その対価が土地の市場価額の2分の1相当額を超えるときは，借地権が譲渡されたものとされ，したがって，譲渡所得が生じたものとされる。

(b) 昭和28年1月1日前に取得した土地等の取得費は，原則として，土地等の譲渡の対価の5％相当額とみなされる。

(c) 他の所得の種類における損失又は所得控除の控除不足額は，この譲渡所得から控除できるが，譲渡所得からの控除の順序は次のとおりである。

　・第1……土地等の短期譲渡所得
　・第2……土地等以外の資産の短期譲渡所得
　・第3……土地等の長期譲渡所得
　・第4……土地等以外の資産の長期譲渡所得

(3) 譲渡所得に係る特別控除
　　譲渡所得（通則）（¶5-190参照）に述べた500,000円の特別控除に代えて，租税特別措置法に定められている次に掲げる特別控除が適用される。
　・特別控除の特例：譲渡所得には，次のような特別控除の特例があり，これらの特別控除額は，長期譲渡所得，短期譲渡所得のいずれからも一定の順序で差し引くことができる。

　　(i) 収用などにより資産を譲渡した場合の5,000万円控除の特例（措法33の4）
　　(ii) 居住用財産を譲渡した場合の3,000万円控除の特例（措法35）

　　(iii) 被相続人の空き家に係る譲渡所得の特別控除の特例（措法35条）
　　　　相続により生じた空き家で旧耐震基準のみ満たしているものに関し，平成28年4月1日から平成31年12月31日の間に，相続人が必要な耐震改修又は除却を行った上で家屋又は土地を売却した場合の譲渡所得について，3,000万円の特別控除が適用できることとされた。

244   ASSESSMENT INCOME TAX

April 1, 2016 to December 31, 2019.

(iv) A special deduction of ¥20,000,000 is allowed for capital gains derived from land for a specified land development project (SM 34).

(v) A special deduction of ¥15,000,000 is allowed for capital gains derived from land for a specified housing area creation project (SM 34-2).

(vi) A special deduction of ¥8,000,000 is allowed for capital gains derived from farm land for a farm land development project (SM 34-3).

(vii) With regard to the sale of the land purchased in 2009 or 2010 after ownership of the land for at least 5 years, a taxpayer can apply the special tax deduction up to 10 million yen to the profit gains from the sale of the land.

The ceiling of these special deductions is ¥50,000,000 in any case.

Note:
In the computation of capital gains on land and buildings, the provisions mentioned in items (1), (3) to (7) of ¶ 5-190 likewise apply.

¶ 5-210 Exchange, replacement, donation of land and buildings

(1) If a taxpayer receives compensation for old expropriated property and acquires property which replaces the former property, that part of the compensation which is allocated for certain expenses is deemed not to have accrued (SM 33).

(2) Replacement of business property.
80% of the capital gains are deemed not to have accrued, where the proceeds of a sale of land or buildings used for business purposes are used by the taxpayer to acquire land or buildings replacing the former in accordance with the established rule of land policy, provided that the tax office is informed of the taxpayer's intention to have the acquisition cost of the former replaced by the latter and that certain other requirements are met (SM 37).

(3) Tax roll-over treatment for sale of residential property. If a taxpayer sells his house and land owned for more than 10 years and used for his residential purposes for 10 years or more at the price of ¥200,000,000 or less, and purchases his residential house during April 1, 1993 to December 31, 2017, he can enjoy tax roll-over treat-

¶ 5-210

(ⅳ) 特定土地区画整理事業等のために土地等を譲渡した場合の2,000万円控除の特例（措法34）

(ⅴ) 特定住宅地造成事業等のために土地等を譲渡した場合の1,500万円控除の特例（措法34の2）

(ⅵ) 農地保有の合理化等のために農地等を譲渡した場合の800万円の控除の特例（措法34の3）

(ⅶ) 個人が，平成21年1月1日から平成22年12月31日までの間に取得をした国内にある土地等で，その1月1日において所有期間が5年を超えるものの譲渡をした場合には，その年中の当該譲渡に係る長期譲渡所得の金額から1,000万円（当該長期譲渡所得の金額が，1,000万円に満たない場合には，当該長期譲渡所得の金額）を控除する。

これらの特別控除の額は合計で5,000万円が限度とされている。

(注)：土地等の譲渡所得の計算については，¶5-190の(1)及び(3)から(7)までの記述が同様にあてはまる。

¶5-210　土地及び建物の交換，買換え，贈与

(1) 収用資産

個人の資産が収用された場合において他の資産を取得しないときは，取得資産の取得原価を超える収用補償金の額は譲渡益として取り扱われる（措法33）。

(2) 事業用資産の買換え

土地政策に資する特定の事業用資産の買換え，すなわち，土地又は建物の買換資産を取得するため，土地又は建物の譲渡資産を譲渡した場合の収入金額は買換資産の取得に充てることを税務署へ届け出，かつ，一定の要件を満たすことを条件としてその譲渡所得の80％相当額が生じなかったものとされる（措法37）。

(3) 特定の居住用財産の買換え

平成5年4月1日から平成29年12月31日までの間に所有期間が10年を超え，かつ，居住期間が10年以上である家屋及びその敷地を譲渡した場合，取得価額の引継ぎによる課税の繰延べを認めることとされた（措法36の2）。

246   ASSESSMENT INCOME TAX

ment by booking the acquisition cost of sold assets as the acquisition cost of the purchased assets (SM 36-2).

This special treatment will be applied to an old house which a taxpayer purchased as a replacement of residential property without the limitation on the number of years from construction if an old houses is satisfied with anti-earthquake safety standards.

(4) Capital gains are deemed not to have accrued when they have been derived from the transfer of land suitable for supplying multi-storey fire-proof apartment houses in a specified urban area or large scale housing lots, subject to certain conditions (SM 37-5).

¶ 5-220 Capital gains etc. from stock or shares

(1) The taxation methods for capital gains, business income or miscellaneous income are as follows (SM 37-10).

Since 1953, an individual taxpayer has not as a rule been taxed on capital gains derived from stocks or shares; but from 1989, with a view to fair taxation of property under the 1988 tax reform, such capital gains are taxable under the following circumstances. When an individual taxpayer sells stocks or shares from April 1, 1989, then business income, capital gain, or miscellaneous income derived from stocks or shares (¶ 5-120) is taxable on the income amount in each separate category.

In this case, "stocks or shares" means stocks or shares of a limited corporation or bonds convertible to stocks.

(2) In calculating the income amount, the taxpayer can deduct necessary costs and various expenses from the proceeds, but not including the stock or shares represented by securities futures transactions or interests in golf-clubs.

Necessary costs are computed as the amount of stock or shares at the end of the year valued by the weighted-average method.

Aggregation for Ordinary Income Amount (Step 2)

¶ 5-230 Aggregation of seven categories of income

The total of the following amounts is called the ordinary income amount (as described in ¶ 5-090 (2)) (Law 22②):

(1) the amount of interest income;

¶ 5-220

申　告　所　得　税　247

　　年数に関係なく，地震に対する安全基準を満たしている既存住宅を買い換えた場合もこの特例が受けられる。ただし，平成17年4月1日以後に取得した場合に適用する。

⑷　その他
　　市街地における中高層耐火共同住宅あるいは大規模な住宅地の供給に資する土地の譲渡については，一定条件の下で，譲渡所得は生じなかったものとされる（措法37の5）。

¶5-220　株式等に係る譲渡所得等

⑴　株式等に係る譲渡所得等の課税方法は次のとおりである（措法37の10）。
　　個人の有価証券の譲渡による所得については，昭和28年以来，原則として非課税とされてきたところだが，昭和63年の税制改正により，平成元年から資産に対する課税の適正化の見地から次のように課税されることとなった。
　　すなわち，個人が平成元年4月1日以後に株式等を譲渡した場合には，その株式等の譲渡による事業所得，譲渡所得及び雑所得（¶5-120）については，他の所得と分離して，それぞれの所得金額に対し，課税される。
　　この場合，株式等とは，株式，有限会社の社員の持分及び転換社債をいい，有価証券先物取引によるもの及びゴルフ場経営に係るものを除外する。

⑵　所得金額の算定に当たっては，収入金額から取得原価及び諸費用を控除するものとされている。
　　取得原価は，年末における株式等の価額を総平均法により評価して算定する。

総所得金額の合計（第2段階）

¶5-230　7項目の所得の種類の合計

　　次の所得の合計が，¶5-090⑵に述べた総所得金額である（所法22②）。

⑴　利子所得

248   ASSESSMENT INCOME TAX

(2)   the amount of dividend income;

(3)   the amount of real estate income;

(4)   the amount of business income;

(5)   the amount of employment income;

(6)   the full amount of "short-term capital gains" and one half of the amount of "long-term capital gains";

(7)   one half of the amount of occasional income;

(8)   the amount of miscellaneous income.

However, the income which is subject to separate assessment income tax is excluded in the ordinary income amount.

Note:

When a property is sold within five years after its acquisition, capital gains derived from that sale are short-term capital gains, but if a property is sold after longer ownership, capital gains derived from that sale are long-term capital gains.

¶ 5-240 Forestry income amount and retirement income amount

The amount of forestry income and the amount of retirement income as computed in ¶ 5-120(9),(10) and ¶ 5-130(9),(10) are called the forestry income amount and the retirement income amount respectively (Law 22③).

¶ 5-250 Business income etc. on land etc.

The amount of business income etc. (business income or miscellaneous income (¶ 5-120(12))) on land etc. (land and buildings) is called the business   income etc. on land (SM 28-4①) (see ¶ 5-550).

¶ 5-252 Long-term capital gains on land etc.

The amount of long-term capital gains on land etc., as computed in ¶ 5-120(13) and ¶ 5-200, is called the long-term capital gains amount on land etc.

¶ 5-254 Short-term capital gains on land etc.

The amount of short-term capital gains on land etc., as computed in ¶ 5-200, is called the short-term capital gains amount on land etc.

¶ 5-256 Capital gain etc. from stock or shares

The amount of capital gain etc. from stock or shares, as computed in ¶ 5-220, is called the capital gain etc. from stock or shares.

¶ 5-240

申　告　所　得　税　249

(2)　配当所得の金額

(3)　不動産所得の金額

(4)　事業所得の金額

(5)　給与所得の金額

(6)　動産の短期譲渡所得の金額及び動産の長期譲渡所得の2分の1の金額

(7)　一時所得の2分の1の金額

(8)　雑所得の金額

　しかしながら，分離課税の対象となる所得は，総所得金額には含まれない。

(注)：取得後5年以内に譲渡した資産の譲渡所得が短期譲渡所得で，それ以上の期間所有していた資産の譲渡所得が長期譲渡所得である。

¶5-240　山林所得金額及び退職所得金額

　山林所得の金額及び退職所得の金額は¶5-120(9)，(10)及び¶5-130(9)，(10)で計算方法を示しているが，それぞれ，山林所得金額又は退職所得金額という（所法22③）。

¶5-250　土地等に係る事業所得等の金額

　¶5-120(12)で言及した土地等（土地及び建物）の譲渡から生ずる事業所得等（事業所得又は雑所得）の金額を，土地等に係る事業所得等の金額という（措法28の4①）（¶5-550参照）。

¶5-252　土地等の長期譲渡所得金額

　¶5-120(13)及び¶5-200で示すように計算される土地等の長期譲渡所得の金額を，土地等の長期譲渡所得金額という。

¶5-254　土地等の短期譲渡所得金額

　¶5-200で示すように計算された土地等の短期譲渡所得の金額を，土地等の短期譲渡所得金額という。

¶5-256　株式等に係る譲渡所得等

　¶5-220で示すように計算された株式等に係る譲渡所得等の金額を株式等に係る譲渡所得等の金額という。

250   ASSESSMENT INCOME TAX

In calculating the taxable income amount of each income category mentioned above, the following exceptions apply:

(1) Interest paid on borrowings for the acquisition of stocks or shares is deductible when those stocks or shares are sold and is deductible from dividends when those stocks or shares are not sold and are held if that income derived from the transfer of those stocks or shares is categorized as capital gain. However, if that income is categorized as business or miscellaneous income, the interest can't be deducted from dividend. The interest is treated necessary expenses in computing business or miscellaneous income.

(2) Capital loss derived from the sale of stocks or shares is deemed not to arise. But capital loss may be deducted from net capital gain categorized as other income with respect to stocks or shares.

(3) In determining the amount of capital gain, business income or miscellaneous income with respect to stocks or shares, the amount of loss in computing the other income categories may not be deducted (see ¶ 5-270).

(4) The special deduction of ¥500,000 in computing the income amount of capital gains (see ¶ 5-190(8)) is not deductible.

(5) The provision for taxing only one-half of the amount of long-term capital gains on movable property (see ¶ 5-230(5)) does not apply.

(6) Net loss incurred by the transfer of specified stocks issued by specified small or medium corporation may be fully carried forward to the following three years under specified conditions if a taxpayer files a tax return for the year the net loss is incurred. The net loss is deducted from only capital gain by the transfer of stocks of the following three calendar years.

(7) If an individual who acquired stocks set forth at ¶ 5-256 (6) by investing capital in cash for the period from April 1, 2000 to April 29, 2008 disposed such stocks, capital gains arising from the disposal of such stocks are applied to one-half taxation under the certain conditions.

(8) If there are capital losses incurred by the sale of listed stocks on January 1, 2003 or later which can't be deducted from other capital gains of stocks, such net capital loss is deducted from capital gains of stocks of the following 3 years.

(9) Cost of listed stocks sold between January 1, 2003 and December

¶ 5-256

申　告　所　得　税　251

　なお，それぞれの課税所得金額の算定に当たっては，次の特例が設けられている。

(1)　株式等の取得に要した負債利子については，譲渡所得に分類される場合には，譲渡したときに控除され，譲渡しないで所有しているときは，事業所得又は雑所得に分類される場合を除き，配当を受領したときに控除される。

(2)　損失の金額は生じなかったものとみなされる。ただし，株式等に係る三つの所得分類の間では，その譲渡損失を譲渡利益から控除することができる。

(3)　他の所得金額の計算上生じた損失は株式等の譲渡による所得から控除できない（¶5-270参照）。

(4)　譲渡所得の計算上認められている50万円の特別控除は認められない（¶5-190(8)参照）。

(5)　所有期間5年以上のものに係る長期譲渡所得の2分の1課税は適用されない（¶5-230(5)参照）。

(6)　特定中小会社が発行する株式に係る譲渡損失の金額を有するときは，一定の要件の下で，その年の翌年以後3年間各年分の株式等に係る譲渡所得等の金額からの繰越控除を認めることとした。

(7)　特定中小会社が発行した株式に係る譲渡損失の繰越控除等の特例の対象となる特定中小会社の特定株式を平成12年4月1日から平成20年4月29日までの間に払込みにより取得した一定の個人が，その特定株式を譲渡をした場合には，一定の要件の下で，その譲渡による株式等に係る譲渡所得等の金額をその2分の1に相当する金額とする。

(8)　平成15年1月1日以後に上場株式等を譲渡したことにより生じた損失の金額のうち，その年に控除しきれない金額については，翌年以後3年間にわたり，株式等に係る譲渡所得等の金額からの繰越控除を認めることとした。

(9)　平成15年1月1日から平成22年12月31日までの間に譲渡した上場株式等

252   ASSESSMENT INCOME TAX

31, 2010 and purchased before October 1, 2001 may deem to be 80% of the price of such stocks on October 1, 2001 by election. This is not applied to the stocks sold on or after January 1, 2011.

¶ 5-257   **Special measures for capital gains of listed stocks in a designated account**

(1)   When a taxpayer holds the same listed stocks in a designated account and in other account, capital gain of listed stocks held in a designated account will be calculated independently from those in other account.

(2)   There are two kinds of designated accounts, which are subject to withholding income tax and not subject to withholding income tax by a taxpayer's election.

(3)   Capital gain of listed stocks in the designated account subject to withholding income tax may be through withholding tax at source at the rate of 10.147% (income tax and earthquake restoration surtax 7.147%, local inhabitant tax 3%) from January 1, 2013 and 20.315% (income tax and earthquake restoration surtax 15.315%, local inhabitant tax 5%) for the period from January 1, 2014 to December 31, 2037. And a taxpayer is not required to report these capital gains by a tax return.

(4)   Capital gain of listed stocks in the designated account not subject to withholding income tax is to be reported by a tax return based on the annual transaction reports issued by security companies.

(5)   Open stock investment funds are added to the scope of assets that may be held in a designated account under which tax will be paid by withholding and the filing of returns will not be required.

(6)   Bank is allowed to operate a designated account.

(7)   The amount of loss derived from the case, where the corporation issuing stocks deposited in a designated control account have ended to the liquidation and the economic value of the stock issued by the corporation becomes worthless, is deemed to be capital loss from the disposition of the stock and can be applied to the special treatment described in ¶ 5-256(8).

(8)   Japan Post Co., Ltd. is permitted to handle a designated account.

¶ 5-257

申　告　所　得　税　253

で平成13年 9 月30日以前に取得したものの取得費については，選択により，平成13年10月 1 日における価額の80％相当額とすることができる。
　　平成23年 1 月 1 日以後に譲渡したものについては，適用されない。

¶5-257　特定口座内の上場株式等の譲渡所得金額等の特例

(1)　特定口座を通じて取得した上場株式等を譲渡した場合，特定口座外に特定口座内上場株式と同一銘柄の上場株式等を有しているとき，これらの同一銘柄の上場株式等は，それぞれその銘柄の異なるものとして，これらの同一銘柄の上場株式等の譲渡に係る譲渡所得金額の計算を行う。
(2)　特定口座には，源泉徴収の対象となるものと，源泉徴収の対象とならないものがある。納税者はそのいずれかを選択することができる。

(3)　源泉徴収の対象となる特定口座内上場株式等の譲渡をした場合，一定の方法により計算した差益について，平成25年 1 月 1 日からは10.147％（所得税及び復興特別所得税7.147％，住民税 3 ％），平成26年 1 月 1 日から平成49年12月31日までの期間については，20.315％（所得税及び復興特別所得税15.315％，住民税 5 ％）の税率が適用され，申告は不要とされる。

(4)　源泉徴収の対象とならない特定口座内上場株式等の譲渡をした場合，特定口座年間取引報告書等により譲渡所得の金額の計算を行い，確定申告を行うこととなる。
(5)　特定口座内保管上場株式等の範囲に，公募株式投資信託の受益証券を加える。

(6)　銀行が特定口座の取扱者となった。
(7)　特定管理株式を発行した株式会社に清算結了等の事実が生じ，当該特定管理株式の価値を失ったことによる損失の金額については，譲渡損失とみなして，譲渡所得等の課税の特例を適用することができる。

(8)　特定口座の取扱者の範囲に日本郵便株式会社が加えられた。

254   ASSESSMENT INCOME TAX

¶ 5-258 Special measures for capital losses of open stock investment funds

Capital losses of open stock investment funds are carried forward for 3 years.

¶ 5-260 Taxation of income from public and corporate bonds and stocks

(1) Interest income from public and corporate bonds is not subject to withholding separate taxation at the rate of 15%, and is subject to assessment separate taxation from January 1, 2016.

(2) Capital gains from public and corporate bonds become taxable and be subject to assessment separate taxation at the rate of 15% from January 1, 2016.

(3) Capital losses from public and corporate bonds, similar to capital losses from listed stocks, also become deductible against interest income from public and corporate bonds, dividend income and capital gains from listed stocks. Besides, capital losses from public and corporate bonds are carried forward up to 3 years.

¶ 5-262 Special measure for taxation on unrealized capital gains of financial assets at the time of move from Japan

A resident who has lived in Japan for more than 5 years in the last 10 years before moving out of Japan and has financial assets like securities with a value of 100 million yen or more at the time of moving out of Japan is imposed income tax with special restoration tax on the unrealized capital gains of the assets from July 1, 2015.

A person subject to this taxation is required to file a tax return until time of departure from Japan if a tax agent is not designated. Under certain conditions, a person subject to this taxation may be granted a tax payment grace period for 5 years or the tax will be reduced by submitting a request for correction.

Net Loss

¶ 5-270 Offset of losses suffered in each category of income

In determining the amount of real estate income, business income (including business income on land etc. and excluding business income from

申 告 所 得 税　255

¶5-258　公募株式投資信託の受益証券の譲渡所得金額等の特例
　公募株式投資信託の受益証券の譲渡による損失について，上場株式等に係る譲渡損失の繰越控除の対象とする。

¶5-260　公社債及び株式に係る所得の課税

(1)　特定公社債等の利子等については，15％源泉分離課税の対象から除外した上，平成28年1月1日以降15％の税率による申告分離課税の対象とされた。
(2)　特定公社債等の譲渡所得等については，非課税の対象から除外した上で，平成28年1月1日以降15％の税率による申告分離課税の対象とされた。
(3)　特定公社債等の譲渡損失も，上場株式等の譲渡損失と同様に，特定公社債等の利子所得，上場株式の配当所得及び上場株式の譲渡所得との損益通算が可能とされた。さらに，特定公社債等の譲渡損失のうち損益通算しても控除しきれない金額は，翌年以降3年間の繰越控除が可能とされた。

¶5-262　国外転出をする場合の譲渡所得の特例
　平成27年7月1日以降に国外転出をする一定の居住者が，1億円以上の有価証券等を所有している場合には，その対象資産の含み益に所得税（復興特別所得税を含む。）が課税される。
　該当者は，所得税の確定申告の手続を行う必要がある。また，一定の場合は，5年間の納税猶予制度や税額を減額するなどの措置を受けることができる。

純　損　失

¶5-270　各種所得間での損失の通算
　不動産所得，事業所得（土地等に係る事業所得を含み，株式等に係る事業所得を除く。），山林所得又は譲渡所得（土地等の譲渡所得，株式等に係る譲

256   ASSESSMENT INCOME TAX

stock or shares), forestry income or capital gains (excluding capital gains on land etc. and stock or shares) respectively, if one or more of these categories of income result in loss, the amount of loss may be deducted in computing ordinary income, business income with respect to land, forestry income and retirement income in accordance with the statutory order for deductions (Law 69① and SM 31⑤, 32①) (¶ 5-090 (3)).

If a loss still remains after applying it as a deduction against other categories of income, it is called a "net loss".

Loss arising from publicly traded stock investment funds can be aggregated with capital gain, if any, of stocks.

If there are capital losses incurred by the sale of listed stocks in the current year or capital losses incurred by the sale of listed stocks in the past 3 years, such net capital losses are deducted from the dividend income only which is subject to the separate assessment income taxation (see ¶ 5-540) in the current year.

Note:
> Capital losses from the sale of land etc. can be allowed to deduct from other capital gains from the sale of land etc., but can't be allowed to deduct from income amounts other than capital gains from the sale of land etc.

¶ 5-280   Carry-over or carry-back of loss

The net loss of a certain year may be fully carried forward to the following three calendar years if a taxpayer files a blue return for the year the net loss is incurred (Law 70①).

If the taxpayer does not file a blue return, a certain component of net loss representing losses sustained in relation to fluctuating income (¶ 5-530) or damaged business assets may be carried forward in a similar way. An accidental loss may also be carried forward (Law 69②, 71) (see ¶ 5-320).

Further, a net loss may be fully carried back to the preceding calendar year if a taxpayer files a blue return. In such a case his tax liability for the preceding calendar year is recalculated by deducting the net loss of the present year from the income of the preceding year according to a statutory formula, and he will be entitled to a refund of the tax overpaid for the preceding year (Law 70②).

Note:
> As a general, long-term and short-term capital losses from the sale of land etc. can't be allowed to carry forward for the succeeding calendar year.

¶ 5-280

渡所得を除く。）についてそれぞれの金額を計算するに際して，これらの所得の種類の一部に損失が生じた場合には，その損失の金額は，法の定める順序（¶5-090(3)参照）に従って，総所得，土地等に係る事業所得，山林所得及び退職所得の計算に当たり控除することができる。それでもなお控除しきれない損失がある場合に，これを「純損失」という（所法69①，措法31⑤，32①）。

公募株式投資信託の償還・中途解約による損失については，株式等に係る譲渡所得等の金額と通算することができる。

その年分の上場株式等の譲渡所得等の金額の計算上生じた損失の金額があるとき又はその年の前年以前3年以内の各年に生じた上場株式等の譲渡損失の金額があるときは，これらの損失の金額を上場株式等の配当所得の金額（申告分離課税を選択したものに限る。）から控除する（¶5-540参照）。

　　（注）：土地，建物等の譲渡損失は同一年において発生した土地，建物等の譲渡利益との相殺
　　　　は認められるが，その他の所得との相殺は認められない。

¶5-280　損失の繰越し及び繰戻し

ある年の純損失は，納税者がその年分について青色申告書を提出している場合には，次の3年間にわたり繰り越して控除が認められる（所法70①）。

青色申告書を提出していない場合には，変動所得（¶5-530参照）の金額の計算上生じた損失及び被災事業用資産の損失については，同様の繰越控除が認められる。なお，雑損失も，¶5-320で述べるように繰越しすることができる（所法69②，71）。

さらに，純損失は，青色申告書を提出している場合には，前年に繰り戻すこともできる。この場合，前年の所得税額は再計算され，税額の還付を受けることができる（所法70②）。

　　（注）：土地，建物等の長期譲渡所得の金額又は短期譲渡所得の金額の計算上生じた損失の金
　　　　額については，原則として，翌年以降の繰越しを認めない。

258   ASSESSMENT INCOME TAX

¶ 5-290 Carry-forward of long-term capital loss on replacement of residential property

(1) If a taxpayer sells his house or land owned for more than 5 years and used for his residential purpose for the period from January 1, 1998 to December 31, 2019 and,

(2) If a taxpayer purchases his residential house or lands for the period from January 1 of the year in which the sale was made to December 31 of the year following the sale, and use or will use this replacement house or lands for his residential purpose for the period from the purchase date to December 31 of the year following the purchase,

(3) To the extent that there are capital losses generated from the sale of a residential house of lands, the amount of capital losses can be carried forward for the succeeding 3 years and allowed to deduct from income amount if the following conditions (the conditions are mitigated after January 1, 2004) are satisfied:

However, when a taxpayer sells residential house including land and the land is more than 500 m^2 in area, the capital loss related to the area in excess is not allowed to carry forward.

Note:

The amount of capital losses means the amount of capital losses still remained after applying it as a deduction against other categories of income.

① (a) There must exist a certain balance of the housing loan related to the acquisition of residential property at the certain date of the year the sale was made and (b) A certain balance of the housing loan related to replacement residential property exists at the end of the year to apply the carry-forward capital loss as a deduction against other categories of income.

② When the taxpayer has disposed a specified residential property before December 31, 1998, the taxpayer has the alternative of carry-forward of long-term capital losses or tax credit for acquisition of residential house.

¶ 5-300 Carry-forward of capital loss on the sale of residential property

If a taxpayer sells his house or land owned for more than 5 years and used for his residential purpose for the period from January 1, 2004 to December 31, 2019, to the extent that there are capital losses generated from the sale of residential property, the amount of capital losses can be carried forward for the succeeding 3 years and allowed to deduct from income amount if the certain conditions are satisfied.

¶ 5-290

申 告 所 得 税　259

¶5-290　居住用財産の買換えの場合の譲渡損失の繰越控除制度

個人が,

(1)　平成10年１月１日から平成31年12月31日までの間にその有する家屋又は土地等でその年１月１日において所有期間が５年を超えるもののうち当該個人の居住の用に供しているものの譲渡をし, かつ,

(2)　当該譲渡の日の属する年の１月１日から翌年12月31日までの間に当該個人の居住の用に供する家屋又はその敷地等で一定のものの取得をして, 当該取得の日から翌年12月31日までの間に当該買換資産を当該個人の居住の用に供した場合, 又は供する見込みである場合において,

(3)　当該譲渡の日の属する年に当該譲渡資産に係る譲渡損失の金額があるときは, 一定の要件（平成16年以降については, 要件が緩和された。）の下で, その譲渡損失の金額についてその年の翌年以後３年以内の各年分の総所得金額等からの繰越控除を認める。ただし, 当該譲渡資産のうちに家屋の敷地等が含まれている場合には, 当該敷地等に係る譲渡損失の金額のうち面積500㎡を超える部分に相当する金額を除く。

(注)：譲渡資産に係る譲渡損失の金額とは, 譲渡資産に係る譲渡所得の金額の計算上生じた損失の金額のうち損益通算をしてもなお控除しきれない部分の金額をいう。
①　この繰越控除は, 当該個人が,(イ)その譲渡資産の譲渡をした年の一定の日において当該譲渡資産の取得に係る一定の住宅借入金等の残高を有し, かつ(ロ)繰越控除の適用を受けようとする年の年末においてその買換資産の取得に係る一定の住宅借入金等の残高を有する場合に限り適用する。
②　平成10年12月31日以前に特定譲渡を行った場合には, この繰越控除とその買換資産の取得に係る住宅借入金等に係る住宅取得促進税制とは, 選択適用とする。

¶5-300　特定の居住用財産の譲渡損失の繰越控除等

個人が, 平成16年１月１日から平成31年12月31日までの間にその有する家屋又は土地等でその年１月１日において所有期間が５年を超えるものの当該個人の居住の用に供しているものの譲渡をした場合において, 当該譲渡の日の属する年に当該譲渡資産に係る譲渡損失の金額があるときは, 一定の要件の下で, その譲渡損失の金額についてその年の翌年以後３年内の各年分の総所得金額等からの繰越控除を認める。

260   ASSESSMENT INCOME TAX

Deductions and Allowances (Step 3)

¶ 5-310 Kinds of deductions and allowances

Fourteen deductions or allowances may be made (in a certain order) from the amounts of ordinary income, business income etc. on land etc, long-term capital gains on land etc., short-term capital gains on land etc. and capital gains etc. from stock or shares, forestry income, retirement income.

The 14 deductions and allowances are:

(1) deduction for accidental loss,

(2) deduction for medical expenses,

(3) deduction for social insurance premiums,

(4) deduction for contributions to the Small Enterprise Mutual Aid Plan,

(5) deduction for life insurance premiums,

(6) deduction for earthquake insurance premiums,

(7) deduction for contributions,

(8) allowance for a spouse,

(9) special allowance for a spouse,

(10) allowance for dependants,

(11) allowance for a physically handicapped person,

(12) allowance for a widow or widower,

(13) allowance for a working student, and

(14) basic allowance.

What remains after the deduction of these deductions and allowances are respectively called the taxable ordinary income amount; taxable forestry income amount; taxable retirement income; taxable business income etc. on land etc; taxable long-term capital gains on land etc.; taxable short-term capital gains on land etc. taxable capital gains etc. from stock or shares etc.

¶ 5-320 Deduction for accidental loss

A deduction for accidental loss is allowed to a taxpayer who sustains a loss (including unusual expenditures) on properties (excluding inventories and other business assets as well as properties used for luxury purposes) owned by him or his dependant relatives due to earthquake, storm, flood, fire, theft, usurpation, etc. (Law 72).

The deductible amount is the amount of the loss calculated at the present price level, less the insurance money or compensation if any, and

¶ 5-310

申 告 所 得 税　261

所得控除（第 3 段階）

¶5-310　所得控除の種類

　総所得金額，山林所得金額，退職所得金額，土地等に係る事業所得等の金額，土地等の長期譲渡所得金額，土地等の短期譲渡所得金額及び株式等に係る事業所得等の金額から，一定の順序で，14種類の所得控除を行うことができる。

　14種類の所得控除は次のとおりである。

(1)　雑損控除

(2)　医療費控除

(3)　社会保険料控除

(4)　小規模企業共済等掛金控除

(5)　生命保険料控除

(6)　地震保険料控除

(7)　寄付金控除

(8)　配偶者控除

(9)　配偶者特別控除

(10)　扶養控除

(11)　障害者控除

(12)　寡婦（寡夫）控除

(13)　勤労学生控除

(14)　基礎控除

　これらの所得控除を行った後の金額が，それぞれ，課税総所得金額，課税山林所得金額，課税退職所得金額，土地等に係る課税事業所得等の金額，土地等の課税長期譲渡所得金額，土地等の課税短期譲渡所得金額及び株式等に係る課税事業所得等の金額となる。

¶5 320　雑損控除

　雑損控除は，地震，嵐，洪水，火災，盗難，横領等により本人又はその扶養親族の資産（たな卸資産その他事業用資産及び生活に通常必要でない資産を除く。）について生じた損害（異常の支出を含む。）について認められる。

　控除額は，当該損失の金額から当該損失に係る補償金等の額及び合計所得金額（¶5-090参照）の10％＊相当額を控除した金額である（所法72）。

　　＊　災害に直接関連する損失については，合計所得金額の10％相当額と 5 万円のいずれか小さい金額とされている。

262   ASSESSMENT INCOME TAX

10%* of the "total income amount" (¶ 5-090).

> * with respect to a loss caused directly by a disaster, 10% of the "total income amount" or ¥50,000, whichever is less.

Instead of this allowance, a special tax exemption or reduction may be allowed to the taxpayer at his or her option, if his or her annual income amounts to ¥10,000,000 or less.

When a deductible accidental loss cannot be fully deducted from the ordinary income amount of a certain year, nor from the forestry income amount, nor from the retirement income amount, nor from the income subject to separate taxation, because these income amounts are smaller sums, the balance may be carried forward to the following three years, and is deductible in computing the ordinary income amount (not the taxable ordinary income amount), the forestry income amount, the retirement income amount or the income subject to separate taxation (¶ 5-280).

¶ 5-330 Deduction for medical expenses

This deduction is allowed to a taxpayer who pays medical or dental expenses (excluding any portion recovered as insurance proceeds) for himself or herself or for dependent relatives (Law 73).

The deductible amount is the actual amount paid for medical or dental expenses, less 5% of his total income or ¥100,000 whichever is less, with a ceiling of ¥2,000,000.

¶ 5-332 Deduction for switch OTC drugs (a special measure for medical expenses deduction)

An income deduction system for promoting self-medication (a special measure concerning the calculation of medical expenses deduction) shall be applied to the purchase costs of switch OTC drugs (the amount exceeding ¥12,000 and with limit of ¥88,000) for individuals or their dependent relatives who receive health checks, vaccinations, etc. for the period from January 1, 2017 to December 31, 2021.

¶ 5-340 Deduction for social insurance premiums

The amount of premiums for social insurance paid (including deductions from a withholding agent) for a taxpayer or for his or her dependant relatives may be deducted from the taxpayer's total income amount without any ceiling (Law 74).

¶ 5-330

年間所得が1,000万円以下の場合には，この雑損控除に代えて，税額の減免を選択することができる。

その年の総所得金額，山林所得金額，退職所得金額又は分離課税の対象所得金額からその全額を控除しきれない雑損控除額は，3年間の繰越控除が認められ，爾後の総所得金額，山林所得金額，退職所得金額又は分離課税の対象所得金額から控除することができる（¶5-280参照）。

¶5-330　医療費控除

医療費控除は，本人又はその扶養親族に係る医療費（保険金等により補てんされる部分の金額を除く。）を支払った場合に適用される。

控除額は，支払った医療費の金額から合計所得金額の5％又は10万円のいずれか小さい額を差し引いた額で，200万円を限度とする（所法73）。

¶5-332　スイッチOTC薬控除（特定一般用医薬品等購入費を支払った場合の医療費控除の特例）

健診，予防接種等を受けている個人又は自己と生計を一にする扶養親族を対象として，セルフメディケーション推進のため，平成29年1月1日から平成33年12月31日までの間，いわゆるスイッチOTC医薬品の購入費用（年間12,000円を超える部分の金額で88,000円が限度）を所得控除額とすることができることとされた。

¶5-340　社会保険料控除

社会保険料控除は，本人又はその扶養親族の負担すべき社会保険料を支払った場合（源泉徴収義務者が差し引く場合を含む。）に認められるもので，控除限度額はない（所法74）。

国民年金の保険料等に係る社会保険料控除の適用について，その保険料等

264   ASSESSMENT INCOME TAX

For the purpose of applying deductions for social insurance premiums, it will be made obligatory to attach copy (certificate) of national pension premium receipts when filing tax returns.

When a resident has paid a specified social insurance premium to his home country in accordance with the social insurance system in his home country concluding tax treaty with Japan, such premiums within the limit are treated as deductible social insurance premiums for Japanese tax purposes. And a resident taxpayer can deduct such premiums from total income amount.

¶ 5-350 Deduction for contributions to a Small Enterprise Mutual Aid Plan

A deduction is allowed when a taxpayer who is a proprietor or director of a small-size business pays contributions to the Small Enterprise Mutual Aid Plan which will provide the taxpayer with a lump sum payment at the time of his or her retirement from business.

A deduction is allowed when a taxpayer pays premiums for mentally or physically handicapped dependants to a Mentally or Physically Handicapped Persons Mutual Aid Plan which will provide them with a lump sum payment or annuity at the time of the taxpayer's death, at a maturity date, etc. (Law 75).

With regard to Defined Contribution Pension Plan, individual contributions which will be introduced into corporate defined contribution pension plans are deductible in full.

Individual contributions are, so called, matching contributions. And matching contributions must be satisfied with the following items.

The amount of matching contributions must not exceed the amount contributed by the employer.

The total amount contributed by an employee and an employer must not exceed the contribution limit.

The contribution limit per month is as follows.

Corporate type

Without other corporate pension plans	¥51,000
With other corporate pension plans	¥25,500

Individual type

Without corporate pension plans	¥23,000

¶ 5-350

の支払をした旨を証する書類を，確定申告書に添付等しなければならない。

居住者が租税条約の相手国の社会保障制度の下で支払った一定の保険料については，一定の金額を限度として社会保険料とみなし，その年の所得税に係る総所得金額等から控除される。

¶5-350　小規模企業共済等掛金控除

小規模企業共済等掛金控除は，中小企業の事業主又は役員本人が，事業廃止の際に一時金を支払うという小規模企業共済制度に加入し，その掛金を支払った場合に認められる。

心身障害者を扶養する者が，本人の死亡，廃疾等を原因として当該心身障害者に一時給付金又は年金を支払うという心身障害者扶養共済制度に加入し，心身障害者扶養共済掛金を支払った場合にも認められる（所法75）。

企業型確定拠出年金について，事業主拠出額を限度とし，かつ，事業主拠出と合計して拠出限度額の範囲内で行う個人拠出（いわゆるマッチング拠出）が導入されることに伴い，その掛金の全額を所得控除の対象とする。

確定拠出年金の拠出限度額については，以下のとおり。

企業型
　　他の企業年金がない場合　　　月額5.1万円
　　他の企業年金がある場合　　　月額2.55万円
個人型
　　企業年金がない場合　　　　　月額2.3万円

266   ASSESSMENT INCOME TAX

¶ 5-370 Deduction for life insurance premiums

The amount of life insurance premiums or similar payments, employee contributions to approved pension funds paid by a taxpayer and the long term care and medical insurance premium for the benefit of relatives or for himself or herself may be deducted from the tax payer's total income each category as follows.

(1)   Deduction for General life insurance premiums

(2)   Deduction for Individual annuity premiums

(3)   Deduction for Long-term care and medical insurance premiums

Deductible amounts are limited ¥40,000 as follows each the above category.

The annual amount of the premiums paid	Deductible amount
Not over ¥20,000	The premium
Over ¥20,000 Not over ¥40,000	¥10,000 plus 50% of the premium
Over ¥40,000 Not over ¥80,000	¥20,000 plus 25% of the premium
Over ¥80,000	¥40,000

With regard to life insurance premiums paid on the basis of the insurance contract concluded with a life insurance company or a general insurance company before December 31, 2011, those premiums apply to the former method such as the deduction for life insurance premiums and individual annuity premiums respectively.

The annual amount of the premiums paid	Deductible amount
Not over ¥25,000	The premium
Over ¥25,000 Not over ¥50,000	¥12,500 plus 50% of the premium
Over ¥50,000 Not over ¥100,000	¥25,000 plus 25% of the premium
Over ¥100,000	¥50,000

When the taxpayer claims the deduction for life insurance premiums based on both of the contracts of life insurance concluded before and after December 31, 2011, the deductible amount is limited to ¥40,000 respectively.

¶ 5-380 Deduction for earthquake insurance premiums

Earthquake insurance premiums paid by a taxpayer covering the taxpayer's house or furniture or a dependent relative's house or furniture may be deducted from the taxpayer's total income. Deductible amount is limited up to ¥50,000. And when the taxpayer claims both the deduction for long-term fire and other accident insurance premiums and the deduction for earthquake insurance premiums, deductible amount is limited up to ¥50,000. This deduction will be available from 2007 for income tax.

申　告　所　得　税　267

¶5-370　生命保険料控除

　本人及びその親族を受取人とする生命保険の支払保険料（類似の支払を含む．），適格退職年金の掛け金，介護保障又は医療保障を内容とする保険契約に係る支払保険料を支払った場合には，その額を合計所得金額から控除することができる。つまり，一般生命保険料控除，個人年金生命保険料控除及び介護保障又は医療保障保険料控除それぞれ別枠で控除することができる。

　控除額は以下の通りである。それぞれ４万円を限度として，合計12万円が適用限度額となる。

年間の支払保険料等	控除額
20,000円以下	支払保険料等の全額
20,000円超40,000円以下	支払保険料等×1/2＋10,000円
40,000円超80,000円以下	支払保険料等×1/4＋20,000円
80,000円超	一律40,000円

　平成23年12月31日以前に生命保険会社又は損害保険会社等と締結した保険契約等については，従前の一般生命保険料控除及び個人年金保険料控除を適用する。

年間の支払保険料等	控除額
25,000円以下	支払保険料等の全額
25,000円超 50,000円以下	支払保険料等×1/2＋12,500円
50,000円超100,000円以下	支払保険料等×1/4＋25,000円
100,000円超	一律50,000円

　新契約と旧契約の双方について、保険料控除の適用を受ける場合，それぞれの控除額の合計額（上限40,000円）とされる。

¶5-380　地震保険料控除

　地震保険料控除は，居住者等の有する居住用家屋・生活用動産を保険又は共済の目的とし，かつ，地震等を原因とする火災等による損害に基因して保険金又は共済金が支払われる地震保険契約に係る地震等相当部分の保険料又は掛金の全額をその年分の総所得金額等から控除する（最高５万円）。

　長期損害保険契約等に係る保険料を併せて適用する場合には合わせて最高５万円とする。平成19年分以後の所得税について適用する。

268   ASSESSMENT INCOME TAX

¶ 5-390   Deduction for contributions

When a taxpayer has made approved contributions, so much of the contributions as exceeds ¥2,000 in a year may be deducted from the amount of total income. There is a further restriction, that the allowable amount for contributions may not exceed 40% of the taxpayer's "total income amount" (Law 78).

The term "approved contributions" means:

(a)   contributions to government or municipalities for public purposes,

(b)   contributions to organizations or foundations for educational, scientific, social welfare or other public interest purposes, which are individually designated by the Minister of Finance, and

(c)   contributions to the Japan Red Cross, or schools or corporations for scientific or educational purposes as defined in the Cabinet Order on income tax.

(d)   contributions to the specified NPO Corporations.

When a resident or a non-resident setting up the permanent establishment in Japan have bought shares of designated small sized enterprises within 3 years since their establishment, he or she is allowed to apply the deduction for contributions up to ¥10,000,000.

¶ 5-410   Allowance for spouse/special allowance for spouse

(1)   Allowance for spouse

The income limit shall be set with respect to taxpayers who are eligible for the spouse allowance of 380,000 yen. The amount of the spouse allowance shall be reduced starting at the taxpayers' annual salary of 11.20 million yen (total income of 9 million yen) and eliminated at the annual salary of 12.20 million yen (total income of 10 million yen).

(2)   Special allowance for spouse

The upper limit on the annual salary of spouses eligible for the special spouse allowance of 380,000 yen shall be raised from 1.03 million yen (total income of 380,000 yen) to 1.50 million yen (total income of 850,000 yen). The amount of special spouse allowance shall be gradually reduced in proportion to the amount of spouse's annual salary and eliminated at the annual salary of 2.01 million yen (total income of 1.23 million yen).

¶ 5-390

申 告 所 得 税　269

¶5-390　寄附金控除

　特定の寄附金を支出したときは，その年中に支出した特定の寄附金のうち，2,000円を超える部分を総所得金額から控除することができる。ただし，支出額は総所得金額の40%相当額までを限度とする（所法78）。

　特定の寄附金とは次のものをいう。
(a)　政府，地方自治体に対してする寄附金
(b)　教育，科学，社会福祉その他の公益を目的とする団体又は基金に対してする寄附金で財務大臣が個別に指定するもの

(c)　日本赤十字社，学校法人又は科学若しくは教育を目的とする団体で所得税法施行令で列挙するものに対する寄附金

(d)　認定NPO法人に対する寄附金
　居住者又は国内に恒久的施設を有する非居住者が，その年中に特定中小会社であって一定の要件を満たす株式会社に出資した金額について，1,000万円を限度として，寄附金控除を適用することができる。

¶5-410　配偶者控除・配偶者特別控除

(1)　配偶者控除
　配偶者控除38万円が適用される納税者本人に所得制限が導入される。給与収入金額1,120万円（合計所得金額900万円）で配偶者控除額が低減を開始し，1,220万円（合計所得金額1,000万円）で消失する。

(2)　配偶者特別控除
　配偶者特別控除額38万円の対象となる配偶者の給与収入金額の上限を103万円（合計所得金額38万円）から150万円（合計所得金額85万円）に引き上げる。配偶者特別控除額は逓減し，配偶者の給与収入金額201万円（合計所得金額123万円）で消失する。

(3) The amounts of spouse allowance and special spouse allowance

spouse's annual salary (total income)   (unit : 10 thousand yen)

taxpayer's annual salary (total income)	spouse allowance	special spouse allowance									
		~103 (~38)	~150 (~85)	~155 (~90)	~160 (~95)	~167 (~100)	~175 (~105)	~183 (~110)	~190 (~115)	~197 (~120)	~201 (~123)	201~ (123~)
~1,120 (~900)	38	38	36	31	26	21	16	11	6	3	—
~1,170 (~950)	26	26	24	21	18	14	11	8	4	2	—
~1,220 (~1,000)	13	13	12	11	9	7	6	4	2	1	—
1,220~ (1,000~)	—	—	—	—	—	—	—	—	—	—	—

¶ 5-420 Allowance for dependent

If a taxpayer has children and other relatives (up to 15 years old) who meet the same requirements as described in ¶ 5-410, ¥380,000 for each one is deductible as an allowance for dependents. The amount of ¥630,000 is deducted, if the dependent is 19 years or more but less 23 years, taking into account consideration educational expenses.

If the dependent is 70 years old or more, the amount of the allowance is ¥480,000. In addition, if the dependent is a parent, a grandparent of a great-grandparent of the taxpayer or the taxpayer's spouse and lives with them, the amount of the allowance is ¥580,000.

The term "relatives" means, for the purposes of this allowance:
  (a) any relative by blood to the sixth degree,
  (b) any relative by marriage to the third degree, or
  (c) any foster child or aged person approved by a governor.

¶ 5-430 Allowance for a physically handicapped person

When a taxpayer, a taxpayer's spouse (¶ 5-410) or a taxpayer's dependent (¶ 5-420) is a physically handicapped person, an allowance of ¥270,000 may be deducted from the amount of the taxpayer's total income.

The allowance for a severely disabled person is increased to ¥400,000.

When a taxpayer's dependent or a taxpayer's spouse is a severely handicapped person and lives with the taxpayer, ¥350,000 is added to the amount of the allowance for a severely disabled person (¥400,000).

¶ 5-450 Allowance for a widow or widower

When a taxpayer is a widow or widower but not an aged person (¶ 5-440), and satisfies the following requirements, an allowance of

申　告　所　得　税　271

(3)　控除額

配偶者の給与収入（合計所得金額）　　　　　　　　　　（単位：万円）

納税者本人の給与収入（合計所得金額）	配偶者控除	配偶者特別控除									
	～103 （～38）	～150 （～85）	～155 （～90）	～160 （～95）	～167 （～100）	～175 （～105）	～183 （～110）	～190 （～115）	～197 （～120）	～201 （～123）	201～ （123～）
～1,120（～900）	38	38	36	31	26	21	16	11	6	3	－
～1,170（～950）	26	26	24	21	18	14	11	8	4	2	－
～1,220（～1,000）	13	13	12	11	9	7	6	4	2	1	－
1,220～（1,000～）	－	－	－	－	－	－	－	－	－	－	－

¶5-420　扶養控除

　上記¶5-410で述べたと同一の要件を満たす子供その他の親族（扶養親族のうち，年齢16歳未満の者を除く。）を有するものは，その１人につき38万円ずつの扶養控除が認められる。扶養親族が年齢19歳以上23歳未満である場合には，教育費の支出を考慮して控除額は63万円となる。

　扶養親族が70歳以上の老人扶養親族である場合には，控除額は48万円となる。さらに，この老人扶養親族が納税者又はその配偶者の直系尊属で，かつ，納税者又はその配偶者と同居している場合には，控除額は58万円とされる。

　親族とは，この場合，(a)六親等までの血族，(b)三親等までの姻続及び(c)里子又は都道府県知事が認める養護委託老人をいう。

¶5-430　障害者控除

　納税者，控除対象配偶者又は扶養親族が障害者の場合は，１人につき27万円の障害者控除が認められる。

　また，障害の程度が特別である場合は，控除額は40万円となる。

　扶養親族又は控除対象配偶者が同居の特別障害者である場合において，特別障害者控除の額に35万円を加算する。

¶5-450　寡婦（寡夫）控除

　納税者本人が老年者（¶5-440）に該当せず，かつ，次の要件を満たす場合には27万円の所得控除を受けられる（所法81）。

272   ASSESSMENT INCOME TAX

¥270,000 may be deducted from the total income (Law 81):

Widow: (a) she has a dependant who is not married

(b) she has not married after her husband's death and her total income does not exceed ¥5,000,000.

If she satisfies all the requirements of (a) and (b), a deduction of ¥350,000 applies.

Widower: (a) he has not married after his wife's death or their divorce,

(b) he has a dependant and,

(c) his total income does not exceed ¥5,000,000.

¶ 5-460 Allowance for a working student

When a taxpayer is a working student, an allowance of ¥270,000 may be deducted from his or her total income amount. However, none is allowed where total income exceeds ¥650,000 nor if income other than earned income (as listed in ¶ 5-120 above) exceeds ¥100,000 (Law 2①(32), 82).

¶ 5-470 Basic allowance

A taxpayer may deduct ¥380,000 as a basic allowance from the amount of total income (Law 86).

(Effective from January 1, 2020)

The amount of Basic allowance will be raised to 480,000 yen, but for the people with total income exceeding 24,000,000 yen, the amount of basic allowance will be further reduced gradually to zero when total income exceeds 25,000,000 yen.

unit: ¥1,000

total income	basic allowance
24,000 or less	480
over 24,000 and 24,500 or less	320
over 24,500 and 25,000 or less	160
over 25,000	0

¶ 5-460

申 告 所 得 税　273

(1)　寡婦の要件

　(a)　死別・離婚後婚姻しておらず扶養親族がいること

　(b)　死別後婚姻しておらず合計所得が500万円以下であること

　　ただし，(a)と(b)の双方の要件を満たす場合には，35万円の控除が受けられる。

(2)　寡夫の要件

　(a)　死別・離婚後婚姻しておらず

　(b)　扶養親族がいて，かつ，

　(c)　合計所得が500万円以下であること

¶5-460　勤労学生控除

　勤労学生は，合計所得金額から27万円を控除することができる。ただし，合計所得が65万円を超える場合及び給与所得等（¶5-120に列挙した所得）以外の所得が10万円を超える場合には，控除が認められない（所法2①三十二，82）。

¶5-470　基礎控除

　基礎控除として，合計所得金額から38万円を控除する（所法86）。

（平成32年分以降適用）

　基礎控除について，一律10万円引き上げるとともに，合計所得金額が2,400万円を超える個人はその合計所得金額に応じて控除額が逓減し，合計所得金額が2,500万円を超えると基礎控除の適用はできないこととされた。

合計所得金額	控除額
2,400万円以下	48万円
2,400万円超2,450万円以下	32万円
2,450万円超2,500万円以下	16万円
2,500万円超	0円

274   ASSESSMENT INCOME TAX

Application of Tax Rate (Step 4)

¶ 5-500 Progressive tax rates

The following tax rates apply to the taxable ordinary income amount and the taxable retirement income amount separately (Law 89):

Rate of income tax
(Applicable from 2007 to 2014)

Brackets of taxable income   Unit : 1,000 yen

Over	Not over	Tax rate %
—	1,950	5
1,950	3,300	10
3,300	6,950	20
6,950	9,000	23
9,000	18,000	33
18,000		40

Rate of income tax
(Applicable from 2015)

Brackets of taxable income   Unit : 1,000 yen

Over	Not over	Tax rate %
—	1,950	5
1,950	3,300	10
3,300	6,950	20
6,950	9,000	23
9,000	18,000	33
18,000	40,000	40
40,000		45

¶ 5-505 Tax table

The tax table given below is not the simplified tax table, but is convenient in calculating the amount of tax.

Tax table
(Applicable from 2007 to 2014)

Unit : 1,000 yen

Over	Not over	Tax rate %	Amount of deduction
—	1,950	5	—
1,950	3,300	10	97.5
3,300	6,950	20	427.5
6,950	9,000	23	636
9,000	18,000	33	1,536
18,000		40	2,796

¶ 5-500

申　告　所　得　税　275

税率の適用（第4段階）

¶5-500　累進税率

次の税率は，課税総所得金額及び課税退職所得金額に対してそれぞれ適用される（所法89）。

所　得　税　の　税　率（平成19年分から平成26年分）

課税所得の区分		税　　率
千円超	千円以下	%
－	1,950	5
1,950	3,300	10
3,300	6,950	20
6,950	9,000	23
9,000	18,000	33
18,000		40

所　得　税　の　税　率（平成27年分以降）

課税所得の区分		税　　率
千円超	千円以下	%
－	1,950	5
1,950	3,300	10
3,300	6,950	20
6,950	9,000	23
9,000	18,000	33
18,000	40,000	40
40,000		45

¶5-505　税額表

下記の表は，所得税の簡易税額表ではないが，税額計算上，便宜的なものである。

税　額　表（平成19年分から平成26年分）　単位：千円

所　得　区　分		税　率	控除額
超	以下	%	円
－	1,950	5	－
1,950	3,300	10	97.5
3,300	6,950	20	427.5
6,950	9,000	23	636
9,000	18,000	33	1,536
18,000		40	2,796

276   ASSESSMENT INCOME TAX

Tax table

(Applicable from 2015)

Unit : 1,000 yen

Over	Not over	Tax rate %	Amount of deduction
—	1,950	5	—
1,950	3,300	10	97.5
3,300	6,950	20	427.5
6,950	9,000	23	636
9,000	18,000	33	1,536
18,000	40,000	40	2,796
40,000		45	4,796

¶ 5-520 Tax rate on forestry income

The tax on forestry income is computed in the following way (Law 89):

(1)   divide the taxable forestry income by five;

(2)   apply the progressive tax rate stated in ¶ 5-500 to the taxable forestry income amount so divided; and

(3)   multiply the tax amount resulting from (2) by five.

This formula has the effect of mitigating the steepness of the progressive tax rate, taking into account the fact that timber is usually cut at long intervals.

¶ 5-522 Tax rate for retirement income

The same rate as in ¶ 5-500 is applied (Law 89).

¶ 5-530 Fluctuating and extraordinary income

A special taxation averaging device may be applied to "fluctuating income" and "extraordinary income", taking into consideration the fact that these kinds of income fluctuate from year to year (Law 90①).

The term "fluctuating income" means profits from fisheries, gathering of laver (edible seaweed) or cultivation of oysters, eels, scallops, pearls, etc., compensation for manuscripts or musical compositions, and royalties for copyrights.

The term "extraordinary income" means a lump sum payment to a baseball player, or a lump sum payment received by a lessor for granting a lease for three years or longer when it amounts to twice the annual rent or more, etc.

Under the averaging taxation scheme which may be applied at a taxpayer's option, the tax amount is computed by applying a progressive

¶ 5-520

申　告　所　得　税　277

税　額　表 (平成27年分以降)

所　得　区　分		税　率	控除額 単位：千円
超	以下	%	円
－	1,950	5	－
1,950	3,300	10	97.5
3,300	6,950	20	427.5
6,950	9,000	23	636
9,000	18,000	33	1,536
18,000	40,000	40	2,796
40,000		45	4,796

¶5-520　山林所得に係る税率

山林所得に係る税額は次により計算する。

(1)　まず，課税山林所得金額の5分の1相当額を算出する。

(2)　次に，上記の計算で算出された額に，¶5-500で示した累進税率を適用する。

(3)　上記(2)で算出された額を5倍する。

この方式は，山林が通常長期的な間隔で伐採されるという事実を考慮し，税率の累進度を緩和するものである (所法89)。

¶5-522　退職所得に係る税率

¶5-500の一般税率に同じ (所法89)。

¶5-530　変動所得及び臨時所得

「変動所得」及び「臨時所得」については，これらの所得がその年々で変動することを考慮し，特別に平均課税の途がある (所法90①)。

「変動所得」とは，漁獲，のりの採取，かき，うなぎ，ほたて貝，真珠等の養殖から生ずる所得，原稿若しくは作曲の報酬に係る所得，著作権の使用料に係る所得をいう。

「臨時所得」とは，職業野球の選手等に対して支払われる一時金又は資産の賃貸に係る一時金で3年以上の使用を認め，かつ，年額の2倍以上であるもの等をいう。

平均課税は納税者の選択により適用されるものであるが，変動所得及び臨時所得が総所得金額の20％相当額以上である場合，次の算式により累進税率を適用して税額が計算される。

278   ASSESSMENT INCOME TAX

tax rate according to the following formula, if the amount of fluctuating income and extraordinary income is 20% or more of the ordinary income amount:

$$\bullet \left[\begin{array}{l} \text{taxable ordinary} \\ \text{income amount (A)} \end{array} - \left\{ \begin{array}{l} \text{(fluctuating income of this year} - \text{half the} \\ \text{total fluctuating income of the two preced-} \\ \text{ing years)} + \text{extraordinary income of this} \\ \text{year (B)} \end{array} \right\} \times 4/5 \right.$$

$$\times \text{ tax rate} = \text{(C)}$$

$$\bullet \text{ (C)} + \text{(B)} \times 4/5 \times \frac{\text{(C)}}{\text{(A)} - \text{(B)} \times 4/5} = \text{the amount of tax}$$

¶ 5-540 Separate assessment income taxation on dividend

With regard to the dividend of listed stock paid to a resident taxpayer after January 1, 2009, the dividend can be taxed at the separate assessment income taxation at the rate of 20% (income tax 15%, local inhabitant tax 5%) by a resident taxpayer's choice. But, if a taxpayer receives dividends from the company he owns 3% or more of whose issued stocks, the dividends which he received from the company don't apply the above treatment.

The reduced tax rate (7%) is applied to the dividend income from the listed shares from January 1, 2009 to December 31, 2013.

In addition to the above income tax, earthquake restoration surtax of 2.1% to income tax amount shall be added for the period from January 1, 2013 to December 31, 2037.

¶ 5-550 Tax rate on business income etc. on land etc.

The amount of tax on business income etc. on land etc. is (a) or (b), whichever is the greater (SM 28-4):

(a)
$$\left\{ \left[\begin{array}{l} \text{taxable ordinary} \\ \text{income amount} \end{array} + \begin{array}{l} \text{taxable amount of business} \\ \text{income etc. o land, etc.} \end{array} \right] \right.$$
$$\left. \times \begin{array}{l} \text{the progressive} \\ \text{tax rate} \end{array} - \begin{array}{l} \text{taxable ordinary} \\ \text{income amount} \end{array} \times \begin{array}{l} \text{the progressive} \\ \text{tax} \end{array} \right\} \times 110\%$$

(b) 40% tax rate on the taxable amount of business income etc. on land etc.

¶ 5-555 Tax Rates for long-term capital gains on land etc.

(1) **Usual case (SM 31)**

15% for capital gains.

¶ 5-540

申 告 所 得 税　279

$$\left[課税総所得金額(A)-\left\{(当年の変動所得-前2年の変動所得の2分の1の額)+当年の臨時所得(B)\right\}\times\tfrac{1}{5}\right]\times税率=(C)$$

$$(C)+(B)\times\tfrac{1}{5}\times\frac{(C)}{(A)-(B)\times\tfrac{1}{5}}=税額$$

¶5-540　配当所得に係る申告分離課税

　平成21年1月1日以後に居住者等が支払を受ける上場株式等の配当所得については，当該居住者等は20％（所得税15％，住民税5％）の税率による申告分離課税を選択できる。但し，配当等の支払を受ける者が株式等の発行済株式等の総数の3％以上を保有する場合は，この取扱いの適用を受けることはできない。

　平成21年1月1日から平成25年12月31日までの間の上場株式等の配当所得及び譲渡所得等に対する税率を7％（住民税とあわせて10％）軽減税率とする。

　また，平成25年1月1日から平成49年12月31日までの間，所得税額に対して2.1％の復興特別所得税が課税される。

¶5-550　土地等に係る事業所得

　土地等に係る課税事業所得等の金額については，次の(a)と(b)とのいずれか大きい額が税額とされる（措法28の4）。

　(a)

$$\left\{\left(\begin{array}{c}課税総所得\\金\qquad額\end{array}+\begin{array}{c}土地等に係る\\事業所得等金額\end{array}\right)\times\begin{array}{c}累進\\税率\end{array}-\begin{array}{c}課税総所得\\金\qquad額\end{array}\times\begin{array}{c}累進\\税率\end{array}\right\}\times110\%$$

　(b)　土地等に係る課税事業所得等の金額の40％相当額

¶5-555　土地等の長期譲渡所得に対する税率

(1)　通例（措法31）

　譲渡益に対して一律15％

280   ASSESSMENT INCOME TAX

The special deductions (¥1,000,000) for long term capital gains of land and housing are abolished on or after January 1, 2004.

(2) **Special tax rate**

(a) Capital gains from sales of land etc. which will contribute to the promotion of the supply of good quality housing (SM 31-2)

(i) Where the taxable amounts after special deduction is not more than ¥20,000,000......10% of the taxable amounts.

(ii) Where the taxable amounts after special deduction is over ¥20,000,000......15% of the taxable amounts in excess of ¥20,000,000.

Note:

Capital gains include;

(i) land transferred to the national or local governments.

(ii) land transferred to a housing and urban development special corporation, an airport special corporation, or a land development corporation; and

(iii) land transferred in accordance with cities' planning law.

When a taxpayer enjoys other special treatments (see ¶ 5-200, ¶ 5-210, ¶ 5-290, ¶ 5-300), a taxpayer is not permitted to apply this special treatment.

(b) Capital gains for residential house and land—

Long-term capital gains derived from the transfer of a house and its land which has been owned by an individual for 10 years are taxable at the following tax rates for capital gains after deducting the special deduction of ¥30,000,000 (see ¶ 5-200(3)).

(i) where the taxable amount of long-term capital gains is not more than ¥60,000,000......10% of the taxable amount

(ii) where the taxable amount of long-term capital gains is over ¥60,000,000......15% of the taxable amount over ¥60,000,000 — ¥6,000,000

¶ 5-560 Tax rate for short-term capital gains on land etc.

Tax rate on short-term capital gains derived from the sale of land and housing on or after January 1, 2004.

¶ 5-560

申　告　所　得　税　281

　平成16年１月１日以後の譲渡において，長期譲渡所得の100万円の特別控除は廃止された。
(2)　特例
　(a)　優良住宅地の供給促進に係る土地等の譲渡益（措法31の２）

　　(i)　課税所得金額が2,000万円以下であるときは……課税所得金額に対して10％
　　(ii)　課税所得金額が2,000万円超であるときは……2,000万円を超える課税所得金額に対して15％

　(注)：この軽減税率は次に掲げる譲渡益に限られる。
　　　(i)　国又は地方公共団体へ譲渡した土地
　　　(ii)　都市基盤整備公団，空港公団，土地開発公社へ譲渡した土地
　　　(iii)　都市計画法に従って譲渡された土地

　　　収用交換等により代替資産等を取得した場合の課税の特例，換地処分等に伴い資産を取得した場合の課税の特例その他の課税の繰延措置並びに収用交換等の5,000万円特別控除，特定土地区画整理事業等のための2,000万円特別控除，特定住宅地造成事業等のための1,500万円特別控除，農地保有合理化のための800万円特別控除及び居住用財産の3,000万円特別控除を適用した場合には，この軽減税率の特例は適用しない（¶5-200,¶5-210,¶5-290,¶5-300参照）。
　(b)　居住用財産の譲渡益
　　　所有期間10年を超える居住用家屋及びその敷地を譲渡した場合の長期譲渡所得については，3,000万円の特別控除（¶5-200(3)）を差し引いた譲渡益に対して，次の税率により課税される。

　　(i)　6,000万円以下の課税所得金額に対して……10％

　　(ii)　6,000万円超の課税所得金額に対して………15％

¶5-560　土地等の短期譲渡所得
　土地等の短期譲渡所得に係る税額は，次の税額による。
　譲渡益の30％相当額

282   ASSESSMENT INCOME TAX

30% (tax rate) of the taxable amount of short-term capital gains on Land etc.

However, 15% (tax rate) of the taxable amount of short-term capital gains derived from land etc. transfered to the National or Local Governments.

¶ 5-565 Tax rate on capital gains etc. from stock or shares

(1) Capital gains etc. (that is, capital gains, business income or miscellaneous income) derived from the sale of stock or shares are, in general, taxed

Tax rate: 20% (income tax 15%, local inhabitant tax 5%).

(2) Capital gains of listed stocks from the sale are taxed as follows:

January 1, 2013 to December 31, 2013	10.147% (income tax and earthquake restoration surtax 7.147%, local inhabitant tax 3%)
January 1, 2014 to December 31, 2037	20.315% (income tax and earthquake restoration surtax 15.315%, local inhabitant tax 5%)

¶ 5-566 Tax rate on capital gains on open stock investment funds (stock-type investment trusts)

Capital gains on open stock investment fund (stock-type investment trusts) are also taxed at the same rate as capital gains of listed stocks.

Tax Credits (Step 5)

¶ 5-570 Tax credits

The following tax credits may be deducted from the tax amounts computed above:

(1) credit for dividends (Note);

(2) special credit for housing loan (Note);

(3) special credit for contributions to political parties (Note);

(4) credit for experimental and research expenses (Note);

(5) credit for foreign taxes

(6) credit for contributions to certified nonprofit corporations (see ¶ 5-638)

¶ 5-565

申 告 所 得 税　283

ただし，国等に対する譲渡については，次の税額による。
譲渡益の15％相当額

¶5-565　株式等に係る譲渡所得等に対する税率

(1)　株式等の譲渡による譲渡所得等（すなわち，譲渡所得，事業所得又は雑所得）については，次の税率により課税される。
　　　株式等の課税所得金額に対して20％（所得税15％，住民税５％）

(2)　上場株式等の譲渡所得等については，株式等の課税所得金額に対して，次の税率により課税される。

平成25年１月１日〜平成25年12月31日	10.147％（所得税及び復興特別所得税7.147％，住民税３％）
平成26年１月１日〜平成49年12月31日	20.315％（所得税及び復興特別所得税15.315％，住民税５％）

¶5-566　公募株式投資信託の受益証券に係る譲渡所得等に対する税率

公募株式投資信託の受益証券を譲渡した場合における譲渡所得等の金額についても，上記(2)の上場株式等を譲渡した場合と同様の税率により課税される。

税額控除（第５段階）

¶5-570　税額控除

前述のように算出された税額から次のような税額控除が認められる。

(1)　配当控除 (注)
(2)　住宅借入金等特別控除 (注)
(3)　政党等寄附金特別控除
(4)　試験研究費控除 (注)
(5)　外国税額控除
(6)　認定NPO法人等への寄附金税額控除（¶5-638参照）

284   ASSESSMENT INCOME TAX

Note:
No tax refund will be allowed when the amount of tax credits is greater than the tax amount before the tax credits.

¶ 5-580 Credit for dividends

To eliminate double taxation, credit for dividends may be deducted from the tax resulting from the application of the tax rate (¶ 6-010). Credit for dividends is allowed for dividend income received by a taxpayer (Law 92).

The amount of credit for dividends is the amount of dividends (less interest on money borrowed for the acquisition of shares) multiplied by the following percentages:

When dividend income belongs to the bracket*	Not more than ¥10 million	More than ¥10 million
Dividends paid to shareholders	10%	5%
Distribution of securities investment trust paid to beneficiaries	5%	2.5%

* Dividends paid to shareholders are treated as the top layer of income, and distribution of securities investment trusts paid to beneficiaries is treated as the next lower layer of income.

¶ 5-600 Special credit for housing loan

(1) A tax credit is available under certain conditions when a taxpayer acquires a new house or an existing house, or starts construction of a house for residential purpose or starts additional construction of a existing house for residential purpose, or makes certain reforms of an existing house for residential purpose from January 1, 1999 to June 30, 2019, and borrows the necessary funds from a public financial institution based on a loan contract in which repayments are made by installments over 10 years or longer (SM 41) .

Certain conditions are as follows;

(a) The floor space of the house is more than 50 square meters.

(b) In the acquisition of the existing house, the existing house with fireproof must be built within 25 years and the existing house with non-fireproof must be built within 20 years. In the acquisition of the existing house after 2005, if the existing house is satisfied with anti-earthquake safety standards, it is irrespective of the limitation on the number of years from construction.

¶ 5-580

申　告　所　得　税　285

(注)：税額控除額が税額控除前の額より大きくても還付はない。

¶5-580　配当控除

　配当控除は，二重課税（¶6-010参照）を除去するために配当所得について認められるものである（所法92）。

　配当控除の額は，配当収入（株式等の取得のためにした借入金に係る利子を控除する）に次の率を乗じて得られる額である。

配当所得に係る所得区分*	1,000万円以下	1,000万円超
株主に対して支払われる配当	10%	5%
証券投資信託の受益者に支払われる収益の分配	5%	2.5%

　＊株主に対して支払われる配当は，所得の最上積みとして，証券投資信託の受益者に支払われる収益の分配はその次の上積みとして扱われる。

¶5-600　住宅借入金等特別控除

(1)　納税者が平成11年1月1日から平成31年6月30日までの間に，自己の居住用に供するために新築住宅又は既存住宅を取得し又は家屋の建設を開始し，あるいは既存住宅を増改築した場合又はマンション等に一定のリフォームした場合，かつ，その必要資金に充てるため公的金融機関又は私的金融機関から賦払期間10年以上の融資を受けた場合には，一定の条件のもとで住宅借入金等特別控除が認められる（措法41）。

　一定の条件とは，
(a)　取得した住宅の床面積は50㎡以上であること
(b)　既存住宅を取得した場合，更に耐火建築物は25年以内，耐火建築物以外の建築物は20年以内に建築されたものであること及び年数に関係なく地震に対する安全基準を満たした住宅については平成17年以後に取得したものであること

286 ASSESSMENT INCOME TAX

(c) The additional floor space of additional construction for the existing house is more than 50 square meters.

(d) The taxpayer's annual income for the said year is not more than ¥30,000,000.

(e) The taxpayer did not enjoy a tax incentive on the replacement of his or her residential property (see ¶ 5-210).

(2) The following table is applied to an individual tax payer who has started residing a house meeting with the above conditions.

Year of inhabitation	Deductible period	Balance of Housing loans as the year-end (maximum)	Tax credit rate (maximum amount)
1999	15 years	¥50,000,000	Year1-year6:1% (¥500,000) Year7-year11:0.75% (¥375,000) Year12-year15:0.5% (¥250,000)
2000	15 years	¥50,000,000	Year1-year6:1% (¥500,000) Year7-year11:0.75% (¥375,000) Year12-year15:0.5% (¥250,000)
2001/1/1-2001/6/30	15 years	¥50,000,000	Year1-year6:1% (¥500,000) Year7-year11:0.75% (¥375,000) Year12-year15:0.5% (¥250,000)
2001/7/1-2001/12/31	10 years	¥50,000,000	Year 1-year10:1% (¥500,000)
2002	10 years	¥50,000,000	Year 1-year10:1% (¥500,000)
2003	10 years	¥50,000,000	Year 1-year10:1% (¥500,000)
2004	10 years	¥50,000,000	Year 1-year10:1% (¥500,000)
2005	10 years	¥40,000,000	Year 1-year8:1% (¥400,000) Year9-year10:0.5% (¥200,000)
2006	10 years	¥30,000,000	Year 1-year7:1% (¥300,000) Year 8-year10:0.5% (¥150,000)
2007 (Note1)	10 years	¥25,000,000	Year 1-year6:1% (¥250,000) Year 7-year10:0.5% (¥125,000)
2007 (Note1)	15 years	¥25,000,000	Year1-year10:0.6% (¥150,000) Year11-year15:0.4% (¥100,000)
2008 (Note2)	10 years	¥20,000,000	Year1-year6:1% (¥200,000) Year7-year10:0.5% (¥100,000)
2008 (Note2)	15 years	¥20,000,000	Year1-year10:0.6% (¥120,000) Year11-year15:0.4% (¥80,000)
2009	10 years	¥50,000,000	Year1-year10:1% (¥500,000)
2010	10 years	¥50,000,000	Year1-year10:1% (¥500,000)
2011	10 years	¥40,000,000	Year1-year10:1% (¥400,000)
2012	10 years	¥30,000,000	Year1-year10:1% (¥300,000)
2013	10 years	¥20,000,000	Year1-year10:1% (¥200,000)
2014/1/1-2014/3/31	10 years	¥20,000,000	Year1-year10:1% (¥200,000)
2014/4/1-2019/6/30	10 years	¥40,000,000	Year1-year10:1% (¥400,000)

¶ 5-600

申 告 所 得 税　287

(c)　既存住宅の増改築の場合には，当該家屋の増改築の床面積が50㎡以上であること

(d)　年間所得が3,000万円以下であること

(e)　居住用財産の買換制度の特例を受けていないこと（¶5-210参照）

(2)　居住の用に供した場合の控除期間，住宅借入金等の年末残高の限度額及び控除率は次のとおりである。

居住年	控除期間	住宅借入金等の 年末残高の限度額	適用年・控除率
平成11年	15年	50,000,000円	1年目から6年目：1％（最高50万円） 7年目から11年目：0.75％（最高37万5千円） 12年目から15年目：0.5％（最高25万円）
平成12年	15年	50,000,000円	1年目から6年目：1％（最高50万円） 7年目から11年目：0.75％（最高37万5千円） 12年目から15年目：0.5％（最高25万円）
平成13年6月 30日まで	15年	50,000,000円	1年目から6年目：1％（最高50万円） 7年目から11年目：0.75％（最高37万5千円） 12年目から15年目：0.5％（最高25万円）
平成13年12月 31日まで	10年	50,000,000円	1年目から10年目：1％（最高50万円）
平成14年	10年	50,000,000円	1年目から10年目：1％（最高50万円）
平成15年	10年	50,000,000円	1年目から10年目：1％（最高50万円）
平成16年	10年	50,000,000円	1年目から10年目：1％（最高50万円）
平成17年	10年	40,000,000円	1年目から8年目：1％（最高40万円） 9年目から10年目：0.5％（最高20万円）
平成18年	10年	30,000,000円	1年目から7年目：1％（最高30万円） 8年目から10年目：0.5％（最高15万円）
平　成　19　年 （※）	10年	25,000,000円	1年目から6年目：1％（最高25万円） 7年目から10年目：0.5％（最高12万5千円）
平　成　19　年 （※）	15年	25,000,000円	1年目から10年目：0.6％（最高15万円） 11年目から15年目：0.4％（最高10万円）
平　成　20　年 （※）	10年	20,000,000円	1年目から6年目：1％（最高20万円） 7年目から10年目：0.5％（最高10万円）
平　成　20　年 （※）	15年	20,000,000円	1年目から10年目：0.6％（最高12万円） 11年目から15年目：0.4％（最高8万円）
平成21年	10年	50,000,000円	1年目から10年目：1％（最高50万円）
平成22年	10年	50,000,000円	1年目から10年目：1％（最高50万円）
平成23年	10年	40,000,000円	1年目から10年目：1％（最高40万円）

288 ASSESSMENT INCOME TAX

Note:
  1 When the year of inhabitation is 2007, a taxpayer can choose whichever it is advantageous for you.
  2 When the year of inhabitation is 2008, a taxpayer can choose whichever it is advantageous for you.

(3) When the taxpayer files a return to take the above tax credit in Year1, from the following year he can choose a year-end adjustment by the employer (who will act as the withholding agent).

(4) When a taxpayer enjoying the above tax credit stopped using his own house for living, he couldn't have enjoyed the above tax credit since then. However, only if there are unavoidable reasons of the stop using his own house for living after April 1, 2003, a taxpayer is allowed to enjoy the above tax credit for housing loan after starting the use of his own house for living again.

(5) In addition, a taxpayer is allowed to enjoy a tax credit for housing loan after starting the use of his own house for living again when there is a fact that he bought his own house and used it for living at the same year, but he stopped using his own house for living by the end of the same year.

This treatment is applied only if there are unavoidable reasons of the stop of using his own house for living after January 1, 2009.

¶ 5-610 Special tax credit for housing loan for the acquisition of a qualified long-term high quality house

A tax credit is available under certain conditions when a taxpayer acquired a qualified long-term high quality house which is newly built or has been not used for any purpose since it was built with a qualified housing loan and used it for his residential purpose from January 1, 2009 to June 30, 2019, you can choose this tax credit instead of the tax credit for housing

¶ 5-610

申 告 所 得 税 289

平成24年	10年	30,000,000円	1年目から10年目：1％（最高30万円）
平成25年	10年	20,000,000円	1年目から10年目：1％（最高20万円）
平成26年1月から平成26年3月まで	10年	20,000,000円	1年目から10年目：1％（最高20万円）
平成26年4月から平成31年6月まで	10年	40,000,000円	1年目から10年目：1％（最高40万円）

（注）：居住年が平成19年もしくは平成20年の場合，いずれかを選択。

⑶　納税者が適用を受ける最初の年に確定申告書を提出している場合には，適用2年目以降の年においては給与所得に対する年末調整に際し住宅借入金等特別控除の適用を受けることができる。

⑷　住宅の取得等をして住宅借入金等特別控除の適用を受けていた居住者が，勤務先から転勤の命令その他これに準ずるやむを得ない事由によりその住宅を居住の用に供しなくなった後，当該事由が解消し再び当該住宅に入居した場合には，一定の要件の下で当該住宅の取得等に係る住宅借入金等特別控除の適用年のうちその者が再び入居した日の属する年以後の各適用年（当該再入居年）について住宅借入金等特別控除の再適用を受けることができる。平成15年4月1日以後に居住の用に供しなくなった場合について適用する。

⑸　また，住宅の取得等をして居住の用に供した居住者が，住宅を取得した年の12月31日までの間に勤務先から転任の命令その他これに準ずるやむを得ない事由によりその住宅をその者の居住の用に供しなくなった後，当該事由が解消し，再び当該住宅を居住の用に供した場合には，当初居住年において居住の用に供していたことを証する書類の提出等の一定の要件の下で，当該住宅の取得等に係る住宅借入金等を有する場合の所得税額の特別控除の適用年のうちその者が再び居住の用に供した日の属する年以後の各適用年について住宅借入金等を有する場合の所得税額の特別控除の適用を受けることができる。平成21年1月1日以後に自己の居住の用に供しなくなった場合について適用する。

¶5-610　認定長期優良住宅の新築等を行った場合の住宅借入金等特別控除

　長期優良住宅の普及の促進に関する法律に規定する認定長期優良住宅に該当する家屋で一定のもの（以下「認定長期優良住宅」という。）の新築又は建築後使用されたことのない認定長期優良住宅を取得し，平成21年から平成31年6月までの間に居住の用に供した場合においてその認定長期優良住宅の新築又は取得のための住宅借入金等を有するときは，一般の「住宅借入金等特別控除」との選択により，各年分の所得税額から控除することができる。

290   ASSESSMENT INCOME TAX

loan (see ¶ 5-600) alternatively.

The following table is applied to an individual tax payer who has started residing a house meeting with the above conditions.

Year of inhabitation	Deductible period	Balance of Housing loans as the year-end (maximum)	Tax credit rate (maximum amount)
2009	10years	¥50,000,000	1.2% (¥600,000)
2010	10years	¥50,000,000	1.2% (¥600,000)
2011	10years	¥50,000,000	1.2% (¥600,000)
2012	10years	¥40,000,000	1% (¥400,000)
2013	10years	¥30,000,000	1% (¥300,000)
2014/1/1-2014/3/31	10years	¥30,000,000	1% (¥300,000)
2014/4/1-2019/6/30	10years	¥50,000,000	1% (¥500,000)

¶ 5-611   Special tax credit for housing loan for the acquisition of a qualified low-carbonic house

A tax credit is available under certain conditions when a taxpayer acquired a qualified low-carbonic house which is newly built or has been not used for any purpose since it was built with a qualified housing loan and used it for his residential purpose from January 1, 2012 to June 30, 2019, you can choose this tax credit instead of the tax credit for housing loan (see ¶ 5-600) alternatively.

The following table is applied to an individual tax payer who has started residing a house meeting with the above conditions.

Year of inhabitation	Deductible period	Balance of Housing loans as the year-end (maximum)	Tax credit rate (maximum amount)
2012	10years	¥40,000,000	1% (¥400,000)
2013	10years	¥30,000,000	1% (¥300,000)
2014/1/1-2014/3/31	10years	¥30,000,000	1% (¥300,000)
2014/4/1-2019/6/30	10years	¥50,000,000	1% (¥500,000)

¶ 5-611

申　告　所　得　税　291

その控除期間，住宅借入金等の年末残高の限度額及び控除率は次のとおりである（¶5-600参照）。

居住年	控除期間	住宅借入金等の年末残高の限度額	控除率
平成21年	10年	50,000,000円	1.2％（最高60万円）
平成22年	10年	50,000,000円	1.2％（最高60万円）
平成23年	10年	50,000,000円	1.2％（最高60万円）
平成24年	10年	40,000,000円	1 ％（最高40万円）
平成25年	10年	30,000,000円	1 ％（最高30万円）
平成26年 1 月〜平成26年 3 月	10年	30,000,000円	1 ％（最高30万円）
平成26年 4 月〜平成31年 6 月	10年	50,000,000円	1 ％（最高50万円）

¶5-611　認定低炭素住宅の新築等を行った場合の住宅借入金等特別控除

　都市の低炭素化の促進に関する法律の制定に伴い，認定低炭素住宅の新築又は建築後使用されたことのない認定低炭素住宅の取得をして，平成24年から平成31年 6 月30日までの間に居住の用に供した場合において，その認定低炭素住宅の新築又は取得のための住宅借入金等を有するときは，一般の「住宅借入金等特別控除」との選択により，各年分の所得税額から控除することができる。住宅借入金等の年末残高の限度額及び控除率は次のとおりである（¶5-600参照）。

居住年	控除期間	住宅借入金等の年末残高の限度額	控除率
平成24年	10年	40,000,000円	1 ％（最高40万円）
平成25年	10年	30,000,000円	1 ％（最高30万円）
平成26年 1 月〜平成26年 3 月	10年	30,000,000円	1 ％（最高30万円）
平成26年 4 月〜平成31年 6 月	10年	50,000,000円	1 ％（最高50万円）

292   ASSESSMENT INCOME TAX

¶ 5-614 Special tax credit for additional construction or home improvement of a house

(1) In case of home barrier-free improvement

When a qualified resident makes additional construction on his or her own existing house including home improvements to make houses free of barriers and such house is actually used for residential purposes for the period from April 1, 2007 to June 30, 2019, he or she is allowed to take a tax credit in accordance with the qualified amount of outstanding loan as follows. A taxpayer has the option to take the tax credit as described in ¶ 5-610 or this tax credit.

Year of inhabitation	Deductible period	Qualified amount of outstanding loan	Amount of tax credit
April 1, 2007 to March 31, 2014	5 years	¥10million or less	2% : home improvement loan connected with the cost making houses free of barriers (limit is ¥2million) and 1% : home improvement loan connected with the cost other than the cost making houses free of barriers.
April 1, 2014 to June 30, 2019	5 years	¥10million or less	2% : home improvement loan connected with the cost making houses free of barriers (limit is ¥2,500,000) and 1% : home improvement loan connected with the cost other than the cost making houses free of barriers.

(2) In case of home improvement for better energy saving performances

When a resident makes additional construction on his or her own existing house including home improvements to make the house better energy saving performances and such house is actually used for residential purposes for the period from April 1, 2008 to June 30, 2019, he or she is allowed to take a tax credit in accordance with the qualified amount of outstanding loan as follows under a certain conditions. A taxpayer has the option to take the tax

¶ 5-614

申 告 所 得 税　293

¶5-614　特定増改築等住宅借入金等特別控除

⑴　住宅バリアフリー改修工事の場合

　一定の居住者が，その者の居住の用に供する家屋について一定のバリアフリー改修工事を含む増改築等を行った場合において，当該家屋を平成19年４月１日から平成31年６月30日までの間にその者の居住の用に供したときは，そのバリアフリー改修工事等に充てるために借り入れた住宅借入金等の年末残高の一定割合を所得税の額から控除する。住宅の増改築等に係る住宅借入金等を有する場合の所得税額の特別控除との選択適用をし，控除期間，住宅借入金等の年末残高の限度額及び控除率は次のとおりである。

居住の用に供する時期	控除期間	住宅借入金等の年末残高	控除率
平成19年４月１日から平成26年３月31日まで	５年間	1,000万円以下の部分	イ　一定のバリアフリー改修工事に係る工事費用相当部分（200万円を限度）：２％ ロ　イの「一定のバリアフリー改修工事に係る工事費用相当部分」以外の工事費用相当部分：１％
平成26年４月１日から平成31年６月30日まで	５年間	1,000万円以下の部分	イ　一定のバリアフリー改修工事に係る工事費用相当部分（250万円を限度）：２％ ロ　イの「一定のバリアフリー改修工事に係る工事費用相当部分」以外の工事費用相当部分：１％

⑵　住宅省エネ改修工事の場合

　居住者が，その者の居住の用に供する家屋について一定の省エネ改修工事を含む増改築等を行った場合において，当該家屋を平成20年４月１日から平成31年６月30日までの間にその者の居住の用に供したときは，一定の要件の下で，その省エネ改修工事等に充てるために借り入れた住宅借入金等の年末残高の1,000万円以下の部分の一定割合を所得税の額から控除する。住宅の増改築等に係る住宅借入金等を有する場合の所得税額の特別控除との選択適用をし，控除期間，住宅借入金等の年末残高の限度額及び控除率は次のとお

294   ASSESSMENT INCOME TAX

credit as described in ¶5-610 or this tax credit.

Year of inhabitation	Deductible period	Qualified amount of outstanding loan	Amount of tax credit
April 1, 2008 to March 31, 2014	5 years	¥10million or less	2% : home improvement loan connected with the cost making houses better energy saving performances (limit is ¥2million) and 1% : home improvement loan connected with the cost other than the cost making houses better energy saving performances
April 1, 2014 to June 30, 2019	5 years	¥10million or less	2% : home improvement loan connected with the cost making houses better energy saving performances (limit is ¥2,500,000) and 1% : home improvement loan connected with the cost other than the cost making houses better energy saving performances

¶ 5-616 Special credit for the acquisition of newly built long-term quality houses

A resident taxpayer who purchases the newly built long-term quality house and uses it for living up to December 31, 2017, under certain requirements, can credit 10% of the standard cost (limit: 5 million yen from January 2012 to March 2014 and 6.5 million yen from April 2014 to June 2019) for the acquisition of the above long-term quality house against the income tax liability. And if the amount of tax credit for the year exceeds the income tax liability for the year, the excess amount will be credited against the income tax liability for the following year.

¶ 5-617 Special credit for promotion of home improvement for better energy saving performances and the promotion of home barrier-free improvement

(1) A resident taxpayer who makes additional construction to make his own existing houses better energy saving performance and uses for living it from January 1, 2013 to June 30, 2019, under certain requirements, can credit 10% of the specified amount against the income tax liability for the year. The upper limitation of the

¶ 5-616

申　告　所　得　税　295

りである。

居住の用に供する時期	控除期間	住宅借入金等の年末残高	控除率
平成20年4月1日から平成26年3月31日まで	5年間	1,000万円以下の部分	イ　特定の省エネ改修工事に係る工事費用相当部分（200万円を限度）：2％ ロ　イの「省エネ改修工事に係る工事費用相当部分」以外の工事費用相当部分：1％
平成26年4月1日から平成31年6月30日まで	5年間	1,000万円以下の部分	イ　特定の省エネ改修工事に係る工事費用相当部分（250万円を限度）：2％ ロ　イの「省エネ改修工事に係る工事費用相当部分」以外の工事費用相当部分：1％

¶5-616　認定長期優良住宅新築等特別税額控除

　居住者が，国内において，住宅の用に供する認定長期優良住宅の新築又は建築後使用されたことのない認定長期優良住宅の取得をして，平成29年12月31日までの間に居住の用に供した場合には，一定の要件の下で，当該認定長期優良住宅の新築等に係る標準的な性能強化費用相当額（限度額：平成24年1月～平成26年3月の間は500万円，平成26年4月～平成31年6月の間は650万円）の10％に相当する金額をその年分の所得税額から控除（当該控除をしてもなお控除しきれない金額がある場合には，翌年分の所得税額から控除）する。

¶5-617　住宅特定改修特別税額控除

⑴　居住者が，その者の居住の用に供する家屋について一定の省エネ改修工事を行った場合において，当該家屋を平成25年1月1日から平成31年6月30日までの間にその者の居住の用に供したときは，一定の要件の下で，当該省エネ改修工事の費用の額と当該省エネ改修工事に係る標準的な工事費用相当額のいずれか少ない金額（200万円（平成26年4月1日から平成31

296　ASSESSMENT INCOME TAX

tax credit amount is ¥200,000 until March 31, 2014 and ¥250,000 for the period from April 1, 2014 to June 30, 2019.

(2) A qualified resident taxpayer who make additional construction to make house free of barriers and uses it for living from January 1, 2013 to June 30, 2019, under certain requirements, can credit 10% of the specified amount (the upper limit: ¥2,000,000) against the income liability for the year.

Regarding the specified amount as the basis of the tax credit calculation, if a resident taxpayer would receive the subsidy from local government the specified amount must be net of subsidy.

This treatment is not applied to the taxpayer who has the total amount of income exceeding ¥30 million.

¶ 5-618　Special credit for renovation for houses to accommodate three generations

A special tax credit is applied concerning the renovation of houses that accommodate three generations using a loan or self-financing (loan: 1 or 2% of the outstanding mortgage as of the end of year / self-financing: 10% of the value equivalent to the standard construction costs) for the period from April 1, 2016 to June 30, 2019.

¶ 5-619　Special credit for contributions to political parties

When a taxpayer paid contributions to political parties in accordance with Political Funds Control Act, he could apply the special credit for contributions to political parties with his choice in replacement of the deduction for contributions to political parties.

The creditable tax amount is the lesser of ① or ②.

① = (total amount of contribution–¥2,000) × 30%

② = income tax amount × 25%

Documents for tax credit for donations stamped by the Election Administration Commission must be attached to a final income tax return.

¶ 5-620　Credit for experimental and research expenses

When a taxpayer who files a blue tax return spends experimental and research expenses considered necessary expenses in computing his

¶ 5-618

年 6 月30日までの間は250万円）を限度）の10％に相当する金額をその年分の所得税額から控除する。

(2)　一定の居住者が，その者の居住の用に供する家屋について一定のバリアフリー改修工事を行った場合において，当該家屋を平成25年 1 月 1 日から平成31年 6 月30日までの間にその者の居住の用に供したときは，一定の要件の下で，当該バリアフリー改修工事の費用の額と当該バリアフリー改修工事に係る標準的な工事費用相当額のいずれか少ない金額（200万円を限度）の10％に相当する金額をその年分の所得税額から控除する。税額控除額の計算の基礎となる省エネ改修費用の額について，補助金等の交付がある場合は，当該補助金等の額を控除した後の金額とする。

その年分の合計所得金額が3,000万円を超える場合には適用しない。

¶5-618　三世代同居に対応した住宅リフォームに係る税額控除の特例

三世代同居に対応した住宅リフォームについて，平成28年 4 月 1 日から平成31年 6 月30日までの間に，借入金を利用してリフォームを行った場合や自己資金でリフォームを行った場合に，所定の額（借入金：住宅借入金等の年末残高の 1 又は 2 ％，自己資金：標準的な工事費用相当額の10％）を所得税から控除することができることとされた。

¶5-619　政党等寄附金特別控除

政治団体に対する政治活動に関する寄附に係る支出で，政治資金規正法に基づいてその政治団体の収入及び支出の報告者により総務大臣又は都道府県の選挙管理委員会に報告されたものについては，選択により，寄附金控除に代えて，政党等寄附金特別控除額を所得税額から控除することができる。

控除額は次の①又は②のいずれか低い金額である。
①　（寄附金の額の合計額－2,000円）×30％
②　所得税の額の25％に相当する金額

なお，政党又は政治資金団体を経由して交付される総務大臣又は都道府県の選挙管理委員会の確認印のある「寄附金（税額）控除のための書類」を確定申告書に添付しなければならない。

¶5-620　試験研究費控除

青色申告者のその年分において，その事業所得の金額の計算上必要経費に算入される試験研究費の額がある場合には，その年分の総所得金額に係る所

298   ASSESSMENT INCOME TAX

business income, a taxpayer is allowed to enjoy a tax credit equal to the amount which is computed as follows.

A tax credit amount =the experimental and research expenses × tax credit ratio

In this case, maximum amounts of the tax credit are 30% of the income tax corresponding to business income for the year.

Tax credit ratio is as follows in accordance to the ratio of the experimental and research expenses ("the ratio of the expenses").

| The ration of the expenses $\geqq 0.1$ | 0.1 |
| The ration of the expenses < 0.1 | The ratio of the expenses × 0.2 + 8/100 |

If the amount of the experimental and research expenses incurred during the year exceeds the amount of comparative experiment and research expenses, and also exceeds the amount of standard experimental and research expenses, a taxpayer is allowed to enjoy a tax credit equal to 5% of the portion exceeding the amount of comparative experimental and research expenses among the experimental and research expenses additionally for the period from 2009 to 2015.

¶ 5-630 Credit for foreign taxes

A taxpayer who pays foreign taxes, national or local, which are similar to Japanese income tax may choose to have the amount of those foreign taxes credited against his or her Japanese income tax (Law 95).

The principle is the same as for corporation tax (see ¶ 6-745), except that an indirect foreign tax credit is not allowed for an individual taxpayer.

When the amount of foreign income taxes to be credited against Japanese income taxes were reduced by foreign tax authorities in the following year, the reduced tax amounts was deducted from the amount of foreign taxes paid in the year the foreign taxes were reduced.

Foreign income taxes which are imposed by foreign governments and are not available to foreign tax credit in accordance with tax treaty are excluded from the scope of foreign income tax subject to foreign tax credit.

¶ 5-636 Special credit for earthquake-proof improvement of an existing house

When a resident improves the own existing house located in the

¶ 5-630

得税額から，その年分の試験研究費の額に税額控除割合を乗じて計算した金額を控除することができる。

この場合の税額控除限度額は，その適用を受ける年分の事業所得に係る所得税額の30％相当額を限度とする。

税額控除割合は，試験研究費割合に応じ，次のとおりとされる。

試験研究費割合≧0.1	0.1
試験研究費割合＜0.1	試験研究費割合×0.2＋8/100

なお，平成21年から平成27年までの各年の年分の事業所得の金額の計算上，必要経費に算入される試験研究費の額が，比較試験研究費の額を超え，かつ，基準試験研究費の額を超える場合には，比較試験研究費の額を超える部分の税額控除割合につき，5％が加算される。

¶5-630　外国税額控除

日本の所得税に相当する外国の租税（国税，地方税を問わない。）を納付した場合には，日本の所得税からその外国税額を控除することを選択できる。

外国税額控除は，個人の場合には間接税額控除が認められないことを除き，基本的には法人税における説明と同じである（所法95）（¶6-745参照）。

外国税額控除の適用を受けた外国所得税の額がその後の年分において外国で減額された場合には，その減額された年分において納付した外国所得税の額から控除する。

控除対象となる外国所得税の範囲から，租税条約の相手国において課された外国所得税のうち租税条約の規定により外国税額控除の対象とされないこととされたものを除外する。

¶5-636　既存住宅の耐震改修をした場合の所得税額の特別控除

居住者が，平成23年6月30日から平成31年6月30日までの間に，一定の区域内において，その者の居住の用に供する家屋の耐震改修をした場合には，

300   ASSESSMENT INCOME TAX

specified area for the purpose of earthquake-proof for the period between June 30, 2011 and June 30, 2019, the resident can credit 10% of the cost of earthquake-proof improvement with limit of ¥200,000 (¥250,000 from April 2014 to December 2017) from the tax-payer's total tax amount for the year of the earthquake-proof improvement.

¶ 5-637 Credit for online tax return filing

For an online tax return for 2011 or 2012 filed by individuals who obtained electronic certificate, income tax credit for online tax return is permitted under the certain conditions. The amount of tax credit is ¥4,000 for 2011 tax return or ¥3,000 for 2012 tax return.

¶ 5-638 Credit for contributions to certified nonprofit corporations

When a taxpayer paid contributions (upper limitation is 40% of his or her total income amount) to certified nonprofit corporations and the amount of donations is over ¥2,000, he or she could apply the tax credit with his choice in replacement of the deduction for contributions to certified nonprofit corporations.

The creditable tax amount is the lesser of 1 or 2

1=(total amount of contributions − ¥2,000) × 40%
2=income tax amount × 25%

When a taxpayer paid contributions (upper limitation is 40% of his or her total income amount) to public interest incorporated association and foundation, educational institution, social-welfare service corporation, and relief- and rehabilitation-service corporation and the amount of contributions is over ¥2,000, he or she could apply the tax credit with his choice in replacement of the deduction for contributions to the above corporations.

The creditable tax amount is the lesser of 1 or 2

1=(total amount of contributions − ¥2,000) × 40%
2=income tax amount × 25%

¶ 5-637

申　告　所　得　税　301

その者のその年分の所得税の額から，当該住宅耐震改修に要した費用の額の10％相当額を20万円（平成26年4月から平成29年12月の間は25万円）を限度として控除する。

¶5-637　電子申告税額控除

電子証明書を取得した個人が，平成23年分又は平成24年分の所得税の納税申告書の提出を，その者の電子署名及びその電子署名に係る電子証明書を付して各年の翌年3月15日までに電子情報処理組織を使用して行う場合には，一定の要件の下で，その者のその年分の所得税の額から4,000円（平成24年分については，3,000円）を控除する。

¶5-638　認定NPO法人等への寄附金税額控除

個人が，各年において支出した認定NPO法人に対する寄附金（総所得金額等の40％相当額を限度）で，その寄附金の額が2,000円を超える場合には，所得控除との選択により，その超える金額の40％相当額（所得税額の25％相当額を限度）をその者のその年分の所得税額から控除する。

個人が，各年において支出した公益社団法人，公益財団法人，学校法人，社会福祉法人又は更生保護法人に対する寄附金（総所得金額等の40％相当額を限度）で，その寄附金の額が2,000円を超える場合には，所得控除との選択により，その超える金額の40％相当額（所得税額の25％相当額を限度）をその者のその年分の所得税額から控除する。なお，平成28年分から上記公益社団法人等について，個人寄附に係る税額控除の対象となるために必要な寄附者数の要件が，事業規模に応じて緩和された。

また，平成28年分から，国立大学法人等が行う学生の修学支援事業のために充てられる個人寄附についても，この税額控除制度に加えられた。

302   ASSESSMENT INCOME TAX

And regarding public interest corporations, the requirements concerning the number of donors for tax deductions on private donations are eased according to the size of the project from 2016.

Besides, this tax deduction system is introduced concerning private donations used for student support programs by national university corporations, etc. from 2016.

Examples of Computation of Income Tax

¶ 5-650 Case I

Salary: ¥9,000,000
   Tax withheld at source: ¥800,000
Dividend income: ¥600,000
   Tax withheld at source: ¥120,000
Family composition: a couple with three children (none receiving income and all of three children are less than 16.)
Payment of social insurance premiums: ¥1,260,000

1. Computation of ordinary income amount

Employment income	¥9,000,000
less employment income deduction	¥2,100,000
	¥6,900,000
Dividend income	¥600,000
Ordinary income amount	¥7,500,000

2. Deductions and allowances

Deduction for social insurance premiums	¥1,260,000
Allowance for spouse	¥380,000
Basic allowance	¥380,000
Total	¥2,020,000

3. Taxable ordinary income amount

(¥7,500,000 – ¥2,020,000)	¥5,480,000
Tax computed (¥5,480,000 × 20% – ¥427,500)	¥668,500
less credit for dividends ¥600,000 × 10%	– ¥60,000
Net tax computed	¥608,500
Special income tax for reconstruction (¥608,500 × 2.1%)	¥12,778
less tax withheld at source (¥800,000 + ¥120,000)	¥920,000
Tax refund	– ¥298,722

¶ 5-650

申 告 所 得 税　303

計　算　例

¶5-650　所得税の計算例〈第1例〉

給与収入　9,000,000円：　源泉徴収税額　800,000円

配当所得　600,000円：　　　〃　　　　120,000円

家族構成　夫婦及び子3人（妻収入なし及び子3人とも16歳未満）

社会保険料　1,260,000円

1．総所得金額の計算

給与所得

（給与収入9,000,000円－給与所得控除2,100,000円）　6,900,000円

配当所得　600,000円

総所得金額　7,500,000円

2．諸控除

社会保険料控除　1,260,000円

配偶者控除　380,000円

基礎控除　380,000円

計　2,020,000円

3．課税総所得金額

（7,500,000円－2,020,000円）（千円未満切捨て）　5,480,000円

算出税額　（5,480,000円×20％－427,500円）　668,500円

配当控除　　（600,000円×10％）　－60,000円

差引税額　608,500円

復興特別所得税額（608,500円×2.1％）　12,778円

源泉徴収税額　（800,000円＋120,000円）　920,000円

確定申告税額　　　　　　　　　　　　（還付）△298,722円

304   ASSESSMENT INCOME TAX

¶ 5-660 Case II

Salary: ¥7,000,000

Tax withheld at source	¥430,000

Family composition: a couple with three children (none receiving income and the age of three children are less than 16 for one, 16 or more but less than 19 for two.)

Payment of social insurance premiums	¥980,000
Actual payment of medical expenses	¥300,000

1. Computation of ordinary income amount

Employment income	¥7,000,000
less employment income deduction	¥1,900,000
Ordinary income amount	¥5,100,000

2. Deductions and allowances

Deduction for social insurance premiums	¥980,000
Allowance for spouse	¥380,000
Allowance for dependants (¥380,000 × 2)	¥760,000
Basic allowance	¥380,000
Deduction for medical expenses	
actual payment (¥300,000) – (¥255,000, that is 5% of	
total income or ¥100,000, whichever is the lesser)	¥200,000
Total	¥2,700,000

3. Computation of taxable income amount

Taxable ordinary income amount (¥5,100,000 – ¥2,700,000)	¥2,400,000

4. Computation of tax

Tax computed on taxable ordinary income amount	¥142,500
(¥2,400,000 × 10% – ¥97,500)	
Special income tax for reconstruction (¥142,500 × 2.1%)	¥2,992
less tax withheld at source	¥430,000
Tax refund	– ¥284,508

¶ 5-670 Case III

Business income: ¥6,900,000	
Real estate income: ¥1,550,000	
Taxable amount of long-term capital gains on land	¥150,000,000
(a) contributing to the supply of good housing lots	¥50,000,000
(b) others	¥100,000,000

Family composition: a couple with three children (none receiving income and each of three children is all less than 16.)

¶ 5-660

申 告 所 得 税　305

¶5-660 〈第 2 例〉

給与収入　　7,000,000円：　　源泉徴収税額　430,000円

家族構成　　夫婦及び子 3 人（妻収入なし及び子16歳未満 1 人，16歳以
上19歳未満 2 人）

社会保険料　　980,000円

支払った医療費　　300,000円

1．総所得金額の計算

給与所得

（給与収入7,000,000円 − 給与所得控除1,900,000円）　　5,100,000円

総所得金額 <u>5,100,000円</u>

2．諸控除

社会保険料控除 980,000円

配偶者控除 380,000円

扶養控除（380,000円 × 2 ） 760,000円

基礎控除 380,000円

医療費控除 <u>200,000円</u>

（300,000円 − 合計所得の 5 ％相当額すなわち255,000円

又は10万円のいずれか小さい額）

計 <u>2,700,000円</u>

3．課税所得金額の計算

（5,100,000円 − 2,700,000円）（千円未満切捨て） 2,400,000円

4．算出税額（2,400,000円 × 10％ − 97,500円） 142,500円

復興特別所得税額（142,500円 × 2.1％） 2,992円

源泉徴収税額 <u>430,000円</u>

確定申告税額 （還付）<u>△284,508円</u>

¶5-670 〈第 3 例〉

事業所得 6,900,000円

不動産所得 1,550,000円

土地等の課税長期譲渡所得金額 150,000,000円

内(a)　優良住宅地供給に寄与するもの 50,000,000円

(b)　その他のもの 100,000,000円

家族構成　　夫婦及び子 3 人（妻収入なし及び子いずれも16歳未満）

306   ASSESSMENT INCOME TAX

1. Computation of ordinary income amount

Business income	¥6,900,000
Real estate income	¥1,550,000
Ordinary income amount	¥8,450,000

2. Allowances

Allowance for spouse	¥0
Basic allowance	¥380,000
Total	¥380,000

3. Computation of tax

Tax on taxable ordinary income amount

(¥8,450,000 – ¥380,000 = ¥8,070,000)

(¥8,070,000 × 23% – ¥636,000)	¥1,220,100
Tax on long-term capital gains on land (see Note)	¥21,500,000
	¥22,720,100
Special income tax for reconstruction (¥22,720,100 × 2.1%)	¥477,122
Total tax amount	¥23,197,200

Note:

Tax amount is calculated on the tax rate for the period from January 1, 2013 to December 31, 2019 in which the land is sold by the following process (see ¶ 5-555).

(a) contributing to the supply of good housing lots

20,000,000	×	10%	=	2,000,000	
30,000,000	×	15%	=	4,500,000	
		Total	=	6,500,000	

(b) others

100,000,000 × 15% = 15,000,000

¶ 5-680 Case IV

Business income	¥5,000,000

¥2,000,000 (income arising from sources outside Japan and remitted to Japan — ¥400,000 of foreign tax has been paid for this income)

¥3,000,000 (income from sources within Japan)

Real estate income	¥500,000
Forestry income	¥2,500,000
Interest on debentures issued by U.S. companies	¥300,000

(interest is neither paid in Japan nor remitted to Japan)

Taxpayer's status: non-permanent resident

Family composition: a couple with three children (none receiving in-

¶ 5-680

申　告　所　得　税　307

1．総所得金額の計算
　　事業所得 6,900,000円
　　不動産所得 1,550,000円
　　総所得金額 8,450,000円
2．諸控除
　　配偶者控除 0円
　　基礎控除 380,000円
　　計 380,000円
3．税額の計算
　　総所得金額に係る税額
　　　（8,450,000円－380,000円＝8,070,000円）
　　　（8,070,000円×23％－636,000円） 1,220,100円
　　課税長期譲渡所得に係る税額（（注）参照） 21,500,000円
　　　 22,720,100円
　　復興特別所得税額（22,720,100円×2.1％） 477,122円
　　確定申告税額 23,197,200円

　　（注）：平成25年1月1日から平成31年12月31日までの間に譲渡するものに係る税率に
　　　　　より次の算式により算出している（¶5-555参照）。
　　　　　⒜　優良住宅地
　　　　　　　20,000,000×10％＝2,000,000
　　　　　　　30,000,000×15％＝4,500,000
　　　　　　　　　　計　　6,500,000
　　　　　⒝　その他のもの
　　　　　　　100,000,000×15％＝15,000,000

¶5-680〈第4例〉
　　事業所得 5,000,000円
　　　内　国外源泉所得　2,000,000円（日本に送金。外国税額400,000円）
　　　　　国内源泉所得　3,000,000円
　　不動産所得 500,000円
　　山林所得 2,500,000円
　　米国法人の発行する社債に係る利子所得 300,000円
　　　（国外支払で日本に送金されていない。）
　　非永住者
　　家族構成　夫婦及び子3人（妻収入なし及び子いずれも16歳未満）
　　社会保険料 920,000円

308   ASSESSMENT INCOME TAX

come and the age of three children are all less than 16.)

Payment of social insurance premiums	¥920,000

1. Computation of total income amount

Business income	¥5,000,000
Real estate income	¥500,000
(interest income (¥300,000) is excluded from taxable income because it is neither paid in Japan nor remitted to Japan)	¥0
Ordinary income amount	¥5,500,000
Forestry income amount (¥2,500,000 – special deduction for forestry income ¥500,000)	¥2,000,000

2. Deductions and allowances

Deduction for social insurance premiums	¥920,000
Allowance for spouse	¥380,000
Basic allowance	¥380,000
Total	¥1,680,000

3. Computation of tax

Taxable ordinary income amount (¥5,500,000 – ¥1,680,000)	¥3,820,000
Tax thereon (¥3,820,000 × 20% – ¥427,500)	¥336,500
Taxable forestry income amount	¥2,000,000
Tax thereon	
(¥2,000,000 × 1/5) = ¥400,000 (tax rate: 5%)	
¥20,000 × 5 =	¥100,000
Total tax (¥336,500 + ¥100,000)	¥436,500
Special income tax for reconstruction (¥436,500 × 2.1%)	¥9,166
less foreign tax credit	¥118,844
Total tax amount	¥326,800

$$\left(\text{Japanese tax} \atop (¥445,666) \times \frac{\text{total income from sources outside Japan } (¥2,000,000)}{\text{total income from sources outside and in Japan } (¥5,500,000 \ + \ ¥2,000,000)} \right) = ¥118,844*$$

Total tax to be paid upon filing return (¥445,666 – ¥118,844)   ¥326,800

* The amount of foreign tax (¥400,000) exceeds the maximum amount of foreign tax credit (¥118,844). The excess amount may be carried forward or carried back on certain conditions.

¶ 5-680

申　告　所　得　税　309

1．課税所得の計算
　　事業所得　　　　　　　　　　　　　　　　　　　　5,000,000円
　　不動産所得　　　　　　　　　　　　　　　　　　　　500,000円
　　利子所得（300,000円は課税所得から除外される。）　　　　──
　　総所得金額　　　　　　　　　　　　　　　　　　　5,500,000円
　　山林所得（2,500,000円－特別控除500,000円）　　　　2,000,000円

2．諸控除
　　社会保険料控除　　　　　　　　　　　　　　　　　　920,000円
　　配偶者控除　　　　　　　　　　　　　　　　　　　　380,000円
　　基礎控除　　　　　　　　　　　　　　　　　　　　　380,000円
　　計　　　　　　　　　　　　　　　　　　　　　　　1,680,000円
3．税額の計算
　　課税総所得金額（5,500,000円－1,680,000円）　　　　3,820,000円
　　算出税額（3,820,000円×20％－427,500円）　　　　　　336,500円
　　課税山林所得金額　　　　　　　　　　　　　　　　2,000,000円
　　算出税額
　　　（2,000,000円×⅕）＝400,000（税率5％）
　　　20,000円×5＝　　　　　　　　　　　　　　　　　100,000円
　　合計金額（336,500円＋100,000円）　　　　　　　　　436,500円
　　復興特別所得税額（436,500円×2.1％）　　　　　　　　9,166円
　　外国税額控除　　　　　　　　　　　　　　　　　　　118,844円
　　確定申告税額　　　　　　　　　　　　　　　　　　　326,800円

$$\left(\begin{array}{l}\text{所得税額と復興特別}\\\text{所得税額との合計額}\\\text{（436,500円＋9,166円）}\end{array}\times\dfrac{\text{国外源泉所得（2,000,000円）}}{\begin{array}{l}\text{国外源泉所得と国内源泉所得との}\\\text{合計額（5,500,000円＋2,000,000円）}\end{array}}\right)=118,844円^{*}$$

　　確定申告税額　（445,666円－118,844円）（百円未満切捨て）326,800円
　　＊　外国税額400,000円は外国税額控除限度額118,844円を超えているので，その超過額は
　　　　一定の要件の下で繰戻し又は繰越しが認められる。

310   ASSESSMENT INCOME TAX

Return, Payment, Assessment and Tax Disputes

¶ 5-710 Prepayment

A taxpayer who submits before March 15 in a given year a final return for income of the preceding year should pay the prepayment of assessment income tax on the income of the given year in July and November of that year. The amount of each prepayment is calculated as one-third of the adjusted annual amount of assessment income tax on the income of the preceding year, due consideration being paid to the tax reduction in the given year. Prepayment is required only if the adjusted annual amount of assessment income tax on the income of the preceding year exceeds ¥150,000 (Law 105, 106).

The tax office must notify the amount of prepayment to a taxpayer on or before June 15. A taxpayer must pay the amount of the first prepayment between July 1 and July 31, and the second prepayment between November 1 and November 30 (Law 104).

If a taxpayer has a reasonable expectation that the income of the present year will be substantially less than in the preceding year, he or she may request the tax office to reduce the amount of the prepayment (Law 111).

¶ 5-720 Final return

A resident taxpayer should submit a final return for the income of a given year between February 16 and March 15 of the following year, unless:

- his or her income is very small, as stated in (1) below; or
- his or her tax liability is fully or almost fully settled by withholding at source in such a way as started in (2) below (Law 120, 121).

However, if a taxpayer who is required to submit a final return files a final return not for the tax payment but for the tax refund, he or she is allowed to submit a final return from January 1 of the following year.

Separate final return forms have been prepared (i) for Global Taxation, (ii) for refund returns by salaried income earners, and (iii) for Separate Taxation. The final return form for Global Taxation is shown at ¶ 5-950.

(1) A taxpayer is not required to file a final return if:

(a) his or her total income amount does not exceed the total of the

¶ 5-710

申　告　所　得　税　311

申告，納付，賦課及び不服審査

¶5-710　予定納税

その年の3月15日までに前年の所得について確定申告をした者は，その年の所得に係る税額を7月及び11月に予定納税しなければならない。各予定納税額は，前年の所得に係る申告所得税額から当該所得に係る源泉徴収税額を控除した額（予定納税基準額）の3分の1相当額である。ただし，予定納税基準額が15万円未満であるときは，予定納税を要しない（所法105，106）。

税務署長は，6月15日までに納税者に対して予定納税額を通知しなければならない。納税者は第1期分について7月1日から7月31日まで，第2期分について11月1日から11月30日までに納付しなければならない（所法104）。

当年の所得が前年の所得に満たないと見込まれるときは，税務署長に対し予定納税額の減額申請をすることができる（所法111）。

¶5-720　確定申告

居住者は，下記に述べるような(1)所得金額が小さい場合又は(2)源泉徴収により納税が完了している場合を除き，その年の所得について，翌年の2月16日から3月15日の間に確定申告書を提出しなければならない（所法120，121）。ただし，所得税の確定申告書の提出期間（その年の翌年2月16日から3月15日まで）について，申告義務のある者の還付申告書は，その年の翌年1月1日から提出することができる。

確定申告書の様式は，(イ)一般用，(ロ)給与所得者の還付申告用，及び(ハ)分離課税用がある。確定申告書（一般用）の様式は¶5-950に掲げた。

(1)　確定申告書の提出を要しない者

　(a)　合計所得金額が諸控除（¶5-310〜¶5-470）の合計額を超えない者

312   ASSESSMENT INCOME TAX

14 deductions or allowances described in ¶ 5-310 to ¶ 5-470, if any, or

(b) his or her tax, as computed by applying the tax rate on the total income amount less the total of deductions or allowances described in (a) above, does not exceed the amount of credit for dividends.

(c) he or she receives ¥4,000,000 or less of public pension and his or her other income amount is ¥200,000 or less in the year.

(2) A taxpayer whose gross receipt of employment income is not more than ¥20,000,000 is usually not required to file a final return:

(a) if:

(i) he or she was employed by only one person during a year and his or her other income amounts is ¥200,000 or less in that year, or

(ii) he or she was employed by two or more persons and his or her total employment income (excluding main employment income) and other income amounts is ¥200,000 or less in a year;

(b) with regard to retirement income, if withholding income tax withheld at source is considered to be enough for settling the taxpayer's annual tax liability.

Note:
For example, Japanese staff members employed by foreign diplomats are required to file final returns, because salaries paid to employees are not subject to withholding income tax.

A taxpayer may file a final return, even though he or she is not required to do so. It is possible to obtain a tax refund by filing a final return (Law 122, 123).

Note:
A salaried income earner may file a final return if that income earner is entitled to a deduction for accidental loss (¶ 5-320), a deduction for medical expenses (¶ 5-330), a deduction for an approved contribution (¶ 5-390) or is entitled to a special credit for housing loan (¶ 5-600 to ¶ 5-614), or if that income earner did not apply for a years-end adjustment because of retirement during the year.

¶ 5-721 Submission of statement of assets and liabilities to tax authority

A resident whose total income for a year exceeds ¥20,000,000, and whose total value of assets is ¥300,000,000 or more or total value of finan-

¶ 5-721

申 告 所 得 税　313

(b)　合計所得金額から諸控除を差し引いた残額に係る税額が配当控除額を超えない者

(c)　公的年金等の収入金額が400万円以下で，かつ，当該年金以外の他の所得の金額が20万円以下の者
(2)　給与収入が2,000万円を超えない者は，通常，確定申告書の提出を要しない。
(a)　次の場合には，確定申告を要しない。
(i)　1カ所から給与の支払を受ける場合であって他の所得が20万円以下である場合

(ii)　2カ所以上から給与の支払を受ける場合であって，従たる給与収入金額と他の所得の合計額が20万円以下である場合

(b)　源泉徴収により納税が完結したと認められる場合には，退職所得について確定申告を要しない。

(注)：外国の在日公館に勤務する人などで，給与の支払を受ける際に所得税を源泉徴収されない人は確定申告書を提出しなければならない。

確定申告を要しない者が確定申告をすることは差し支えない。また，確定申告により還付を受けることもできる（所法122，123）。

(注)：給与所得者で雑損控除（¶5-320），医療費控除（¶5-330），寄附金控除（¶5-390）又は住宅借入金等特別控除（¶5-600～¶5-614）が受けられる人及び年の中途で退職し，その後年末調整（¶4-310）を受けなかった人は確定申告書を提出することができる。

¶5-721　財産債務調書の提出
所得税の確定申告書を提出しなければならない居住者で，その年分の総所得金額等の合計額が2,000万円を超え，かつ，その年の12月31日において，価額の合計額が3億円以上の財産又は1億円以上の有価証券等を有する居住

314   ASSESSMENT INCOME TAX

cial assets such as securities is ¥100,000,000 or more at the end of a year is required to submit the statement of assets and liabilities with tax office by March 15th of the following year. Kind, volume and values of the assets and amounts of the liabilities are described into the statement.

¶ 5-722 Submission of offshore asset statement to Tax authority
A resident who has assets equivalent to ¥50,000,000 or more located outside Japan as of December 31 of the year is required to submit the statement of the assets located outside Japan with a tax office by March 15 of the following year.

Kind, volume and Value of each asset are described into the statement of the assets outside Japan.

¶ 5-730 Final payment and refund
If a taxpayer is required to file a final return (¶ 5-720), the excess of the annual tax liability over the total of prepayments of assessment income tax and withholding income tax should be paid on or before March 15 in the year following the tax year (Law 128). In the reverse case, the excess of the total of prepayments of assessment income tax and withholding income tax over the annual tax liability will, in due course, be refunded (Law 138 to 140). If the tax is not paid or refunded until after the due date, delinquency tax at the interest rate of 2.7% (the official discount rate plus 1.0%) per annum or interest on the refund at the interest rate of 1.7% accrues. The rate of delinquency tax is raised to 9.1% per annum, after two months has elapsed from the due date (GL 56, 58, 60).

The due date for the final payment may be postponed by a tax office on the application of a taxpayer if necessary requirements are met (Law 131).

¶ 5-740 Correction or determination of tax liability
If a taxpayer is required to file a final return according to the provisions of the law and fails to do so, a tax office will assess his or her tax liability by "determination" and inform the taxpayer of the tax liability so determined (GL 25).

Generally speaking, in the usual case, a taxpayer may file an amended return, if it is found that the tax amount shown in the original final return is short.

If the tax office suggests the taxpayer file an amended return as a re-

¶ 5-722

申 告 所 得 税　315

者は，その財産の種類，数量及び価額並びに債務の金額その他必要な事項を
記載した財産債務調書を提出しなければならない。

¶5-722　国外財産調書の提出

　その年の12月31日において価額の合計額が5,000万円を超える国外に所在
する国外財産を有する居住者は，当該財産の種類，数量及び価額その他必要
な事項を記載した調書を，翌年 3 月15日までに，税務署に提出しなければ
ならない。

¶5-730　確定申告による納付及び還付

　確定申告を要する者は，その年の所得税額から予定納税した額及び源泉徴収
された額の合計額を控除した額を翌年の 3 月15日までに納付しなければならな
い（所法128）。逆に，その年の所得税額が予定納税した額及び源泉徴収された額
の合計額より少ないときは，その差額の還付を受けることができる（所法138～
140）。所定の期限までに納付又は還付されないときは年2.7％（特例基準割合＋
1.0％）の延滞税が課され，又は還付加算金（1.7％）が付される（通則法56，58，
60）。なお，納期限から 2 月を過ぎると延滞税は年利9.1％に引き上げられる。

　なお，納税者の申請に基づき税務署の承認により一定の要件を満たせば延
納が認められる（所法131）。

¶5-740　更正，決定

　確定申告を要する納税義務者がこれを怠った場合には，税務署長は税額を
決定して当該納税義務者に通知する（通則法25）。

　納税義務者が，確定申告した税額が過少であることを知った場合には，修
正申告書を提出するのが通例である。

　税務当局は調査に基づき修正申告書を提出するよう納税義務者に対してし
ょうようし，修正申告書を提出した納税義務者はその税額について異議申立
てをすることができない。

　しかしながら，確定申告した税額が過少であり，かつ，納税義務者がその

316   ASSESSMENT INCOME TAX

sult of an audit, and if the taxpayer files an amended return, he or she may not request the tax office to reinvestigate his or her tax liability.

However, if the amount of tax liability shown in the taxpayer's final return is short and no amended return is filed in order to correct it, a tax office may, within 5 years of the filing of the return, correct it by "correction" and inform the taxpayer of the tax liability so corrected (7 years in the case of fraud or tax evasion) (GL 24).

A taxpayer is required to pay the tax so determined or increased by the correction within one month after notification thereof, in order to be fully released from the tax liability (GL 35).

When a tax liability is overstated in a final return, the taxpayer is entitled to request a tax office within 5 years of the filing of the return to refund the amount of overpayment (GL 23).

Information Return

¶ 5-810 **Information to the tax authority**

Taxpayers or other persons engaging in transactions with taxpayers are required to supply information to the Tax Authority in the following way in order to ensure fair taxation of income tax and corporation tax.

(1)   A person who withholds withholding income tax at source from the payment to a taxpayer must report the details of the income paid to the taxpayer (Law 226).

(2)   Insurance companies, buyers of real estate, trustees, lessees, etc. are required to report certain transactions to a tax office (Law 225).

(3)   Taxpayers or other persons engaging in transactions with taxpayers should supply all information which may have bearing on the tax liability of any given taxpayer, if requested by a tax official to do so (Law 234).

(4)   Foreign property owners more than 50 million yen, are required to report their foreign properties to a tax office (Foreign Account Reporting law 5).

(5)   Financial institutions are required to report to a tax office, the list those who send or receive more than 1 million yen at one time (Foreign Account Reporting law 4).

A person whose gross receipts of business income, real estate income and forestry income in a given year amount to more than ¥30,000,000 must

¶ 5-810

申　告　所　得　税　317

不足税額について修正申告書を提出しない場合には，税務当局は確定申告期限から 5 年間（偽りその他不正によるものについては 7 年間）までに不足税額を更正し，これを納税義務者に通知する（通則法24）。

　納税義務者は，更正又は決定に係る税額を，更正又は決定の通知後 1 月以内に納付することを要す（通則法35）。

　確定申告した税額が過大であるときは，申告期限から 5 年以内に，税務署長に対して更正の請求をすることができる（通則法23）。

資料の提出

¶5-810　税務当局に対する資料の提出

　所得税及び法人税の公平な課税を確保するために，納税義務者又は納税義務者と取引のある者は，次のように情報を税務当局に提出しなければならない。

(1)　源泉徴収義務者は，支払った所得の明細を報告しなければならない（所法226）。

(2)　保険会社，不動産の購入者，受託者，賃貸人等はその取引について税務署に報告しなければならない（所法225）。

(3)　納税義務者又は納税義務者と取引のある者は，税務職員から求められた場合には，納税義務者の納税義務に関するすべての情報を提供しなければならない（所法234）。

(4)　その年の12月31日において5,000万円超の国外財産を有するものは，国外財産調書を提出しなければならない（国外送金等調書法 5 ）。

(5)　金融機関は，1国当たり100万円超の国外送金等に関する調書を税務署に報告しなければならない（同法 4 ）。

　なお，その年の事業所得，不動産所得及び山林所得に係る総収入金額の合計が3,000万円を超える者は，確定申告書を提出する場合を除き，所得の種類ごとの収入金額を税務署に報告しなければならない（所法231の 3 ）。

318   ASSESSMENT INCOME TAX

inform the tax office of the amount of such gross receipts by categories of income if he or she is not required to file a final return in that year (Law 231-3).

¶ 5-820 Information to persons concerned

An employer should provide employees with the details of withholding income tax deducted from their salaries necessary for them to file their tax returns.

Non-resident's Income Tax Liability

¶ 5-850 Taxable income of non-resident taxpayer

An individual who is domiciled in Japan or who has had residence in Japan one year or more is defined a resident.

Non-residents are defined as individuals who are not residents (Law 2①(3), (5)) (see ¶ 3-250).

Residents are subject to income tax on their world-wide income from sources in any country, while non-residents are subject to income tax on income from sources in Japan (Law 5①, ②) (see ¶ 3-210).

¶ 5-860 Income from sources in Japan

Income from sources in Japan includes the following (Law 161):

(1)   Income attributable to a PE in Japan of non-residents or income derived from the use, the ownership or the sale of property situated in Japan (excluding income falling into the categories below) or income of miscellaneous items from sources in Japan enumerated in any Cabinet Order.

Note:
Capital gains derived from the sale of stocks or other comparable rights in a company which derives at least 50% of its value directly or indirectly from real property in Japan is considered Japan Source Income which is subject to filing a tax return.

(1A) Allocable income to a non-resident partner which earned through partnership activities by a PE in Japan conducted based on the partnership contract stipulated by Civil Law (Nin-i Kumiai).

(1B) Capital gains accruing from the alienation of lands or the rights thereon, or buildings or their annex equipment, or structures.

(2)   Remuneration paid to a person for furnishing the performances of professional services etc. and from the profits from performing

¶ 5-820

申 告 所 得 税　319

¶5-820　関係者に対する情報

雇用主は，確定申告を提出するために必要な給与に係る源泉徴収税額の明細を被用者に提供しなければならない。

非居住者の納税義務

¶5-850　非居住者の課税所得

日本の国内に住所を有する者及び日本に1年以上居所を有する者が居住者と定義され，居住者以外の者が非居住者と定義されている（所法2①三，五）（¶3-250参照）。

居住者は所得の源泉地のいかんを問わず，全世界所得について所得税が課され，一方，非居住者は日本の国内源泉所得についてのみ所得税が課される（所法5①，②）（¶3-210参照）。

¶5-860　国内源泉所得

国内源泉所得とは，次に掲げるものをいう（所法161）。

(1)　非居住者の日本に有する恒久的施設に帰せられる所得又は国内にある資産の運用，保有若しくは譲渡により生ずる所得（(2)から(12)までに該当するものを除く。）その他その源泉が国内にある所得

> （注）：国内にある不動産が総資産の50％以上である法人が発行する一定の株式等又は国内にある不動産か信託財産の価額の総額の50％以上である特定信託の一定の受益権の譲渡による対価が，申告対象となる国内源泉所得として取り扱われる。

(1A)　国内において民法に規定する組合契約に基づいて恒久的施設を通じて行う事業から生ずる利益で当該組合契約に基づいて配分を受けるもの

(1B)　国内にある土地若しくは土地の上に存する権利又は建物及びその附属設備若しくは構築物の譲渡による対価

(2)　国内において人的役務の提供を主たる内容とする事業で政令で定めるものを行う者が受ける当該人的役務の提供に係る対価

320 ASSESSMENT INCOME TAX

personal services in Japan.

(3) Rent for the use of real property and similar property located in Japan and royalties for the leasing of ships or aircraft to resident or domestic corporations.

(4) In the scope of interest income (see ¶ 5-120), the following income:

  (a) interest on bonds or debentures issued by Japanese central or local governments or Japanese domestic corporations, interest on bonds or debentures issued by foreign corporations and related to businesses carried through PE in Japan;

  (b) interest on deposits with a bank office situated in Japan or similar credits;

  (c) distribution of profits of joint operation trusts, and public bond and debentures investment trusts with offices situated in Japan.

(5) Dividends on shares or securities investment trust certificates issued by a Japanese domestic corporation.

(6) Interest on loans extended for business carried on in Japan.

(7) The following royalties or rental received from the business carried on in Japan:

  (a) royalties or capital gains derived from patent, know-how and similar rights;

  (b) royalties or capital gains derived from copyrights, motion picture films;

  (c) rental for the use of machines, or industrial or commercial equipment.

(8) The following salaries, remuneration or pensions:

  (a) salaries, wages, bonuses or similar remuneration paid to an employee for personal services performed in Japan;

  (b) public pensions etc.;

  (c) retirement allowances or pensions paid for past performance of personal services.

(9) Prizes or other benefits paid for advertising in Japan (after the deduction of ¥500,000 from each payment).

(10) Annuities paid on contracts concluded with offices or agents in Japan (after the deduction of that portion of payment attributable to the paid-in premiums).

(11) Profit from redemption of discounted debentures issued in Japan (¶ 4-190).

¶ 5-860

申 告 所 得 税　321

(3)　国内にある不動産，国内にある不動産の上に存する権利の貸付け又は居住者若しくは内国法人に対する船舶若しくは航空機の貸付けによる対価

(4)　利子所得のうち次に掲げるもの（¶5–120参照）
　(a)　公社債のうち日本国の国債若しくは地方債又は内国法人の発行する債券の利子，外国法人が発行する債権の利子のうち恒久的施設を通じて行う事業に係るもの

　(b)　国内にある営業所に預け入れられた預貯金の利子

　(c)　国内にある営業所に信託された合同運用信託又は公社債投資信託の収益の分配
(5)　内国法人が発行する株式又は証券投資信託証券に係る配当

(6)　国内において行われる業務に係る貸付金の利子
(7)　国内において業務を行う者から受ける次に掲げる使用料又は対価で当該業務に係るもの
　(a)　工業所有権又はノウハウ及びこれらに準ずるものの使用料又はその譲渡による対価
　(b)　著作権，映画フィルムの使用料又はその譲渡による対価

　(c)　機械，装置の使用料

(8)　次に掲げる給与，報酬又は年金
　(a)　国内において行われた役務提供に基因する退職手当又は年金

　(b)　公的年金等
　(c)　給料，賃金，賞与又はこれらに類する報酬のうち，国内において行う役務提供に基因するもの
(9)　国内において行う広告宣伝のための賞金（1回の支払につき50万円の控除がある。）
(10)　国内にある営業所又は代理人を通じて締結した契約に基づき支払われる年金（払込保険料に対応する年金額の控除がある。）

(11)　国内で発行される割引債の償還差益（¶4–190参照）

322   ASSESSMENT INCOME TAX

(12) Distribution of profits of non-named partnership for the shares of a business carried on in Japan.

¶ 5-870 Classification of non-resident taxpayers

Non-resident taxpayers are taxed on income derived in Japan. They are classified into the following four classes (Law 164) (see ¶ 6-870):

(1) non-residents carrying on business in Japan through a branch, office, factory or other fixed place of business situated in Japan;

(2) non-residents carrying on business in Japan only through:

  (a) building construction, assembly or similar activities continuing for a period longer than one year, or

  (b) certain kinds of agents (excluding independent agents) in Japan;

(3) non-residents not carrying on business in Japan as stated above, but deriving:

  (a) profits from furnishing professional services or public entertainer's activities in Japan;

  (b) rents on fixed assets situated in Japan;

  (c) income or capital gains accruing from assets situated in Japan and other miscellaneous items of minor importance as enumerated in ¶ 6-870 (3) (c) to (e);

  (d) employment income paid for personal services performed in Japan, if it is not subject to Japanese withholding income tax; and

  (e) retirement income subject to Japanese withholding income tax, if a taxpayer elects to make such income subject to Japanese assessment income tax;

(4) non-residents not falling into the categories (1), (2) or (3) above.

Note:

A foreign individual partner of investment fund will be considered not to have a permanent establishment in Japan if the following requirements are satisfied.

1. to be a limited partner of the investment fund.
2. not to be in charge of management of the investment fund.
3. to hold an interest of less than 25% for the asset of the investment fund.
4. not to have a specified relationship with the general partners of the investment fund.
5. not to have any permanent establishment in Japan other than a permanent establishment connected with the investment fund.

¶ 5-870

申　告　所　得　税　323

⑿　国内において事業を行う者に対する出資につき，匿名組合契約に基づい
て受ける利益の分配

¶5-870　非居住者の区分

非居住者は，国内源泉所得について課税され，次の四つに区分される（所
法164）（¶6-870参照）。
(1)　日本に支店，事務所，工場その他事業を行う一定の場所を有して事業を
行っている非居住者
(2)　日本において
　(a)　建設，組立てその他これに類する活動を1年を超えて継続して有し，

　(b)　国内の特定の代理人（独立の地位を有する代理人等を除く。）を通じ
て，事業を行っている非居住者
(3)　上記のような形で日本において事業は行っていないが，

　(a)　専門職業家としてあるいは芸能人として日本で役務を提供することに
より報酬を得ている非居住者，
　(b)　日本に所在する固定資産の貸付により所得を得ている非居住者，
　(c)　日本に所在する資産から生ずる所得又は譲渡所得及び¶6-870(3)の(c)
～(e)までに掲げられている所得を得ている非居住者，

　(d)　日本で提供した役務に対して支払われる給与所得でわが国の源泉所得
税の対象とならないものを得ている非居住者及び

　(e)　わが国の申告所得税の課税を受けることを選択している場合におい
て，わが国の源泉所得税の対象とされる退職所得を得ている非居住者

(4)　上記(1)，(2)又は(3)のいずれにも該当しない非居住者
　　（注）：次の要件を満たす外国組合員は，国内に恒久的施設を有しない非居住者に該当する者
　　　とみなすこととする。
　　　1．投資組合の有限責任組合員であること
　　　2．投資組合の業務を執行しないこと
　　　3．投資組合の組合財産に対する持分の割合が25％未満であること
　　　4．投資組合の無限責任組合員と特殊の関係にある者でないこと
　　　5．国内に投資組合の事業以外の事業に係る恒久的施設を有しないこと
　　　平成21年4月1日以後の外国組合員の恒久的施設の有無の判定について適用する。

324   ASSESSMENT INCOME TAX

The above treatment will be available from April 1, 2009.

¶ 5-880 Assessable income of non-residents

In the case of a class (1) non-resident, described in ¶ 5-870 above, the whole income derived from sources in Japan is subject to Japanese assessment income tax, namely:

- all income subject to Japanese withholding income tax;
- other income assessable in the case of class (2) or (3) non-residents; and
- other income derived from a business situated in Japan (¶ 6-880).

In the case of a class (2) non-resident, described in ¶ 5-870 above, his or her assessable income is:

- the income derived from his or her business as enumerated in ¶ 5-870 (2),
- the income enumerated in ¶ 5-870 (3), and
- the income subject to Japanese withholding income tax in so far as such income is attributable to the taxpayer's business as enumerated in ¶ 5-870 (2).

In the case of a class (3) non-resident, described in ¶ 5-870 above, the assessable income is limited to the income enumerated in (3) of ¶ 5-870. When profits or income enumerated in (3) (a), (b), or (d) are subject to Japanese withholding income tax, such Japanese withholding income tax may be credited against assessment income tax. The amount of assessment income tax on employment income enumerated in (3) (d) is always 20% of the gross amount of salaries, wages, etc.

The tax liability of the class (4) non-resident described in ¶ 5-870 above is finally settled by withholding at source, with the exception of capital gains on land and buildings or real estate income; therefore no assessment income tax is levied on him or her (Law 164).

In other words, a non-resident who merely invests in Japanese securities without holding any other business or assets in Japan is not required to pay any Japanese assessment income tax (Law 165).

A non-resident taxpayer has the option of having his or her retirement income assessed like a resident taxpayer (Law 171).

¶ 5-880

申　告　所　得　税　325

¶5-880　非居住者の課税所得

(1)　上記¶5-870に掲げた(1)に属する非居住者については，国内源泉所得の
　すべてに申告所得税を課される。すなわち，
　　源泉所得税の適用対象となるすべての所得，
　　(2)及び(3)に属する非居住者の場合におけるその他の課税所得，
　　国内にある事業から生ずる所得（¶6-880参照）である。

(2)　上記¶5-870に掲げた(2)に属する非居住者の課税所得は，
　　¶5-870(2)に掲げる事業から生ずる所得，
　　¶5-870(3)に掲げる所得，
　　¶5-870(2)に掲げる事業に帰属する所得である限り，源泉所得税の適用
　対象となる所得である。

(3)　上記¶5-870に掲げた(3)に属する非居住者の場合は，課税所得は¶5-870
　(3)に掲げた所得に限られる。(3)の(a)，(b)又は(d)に掲げる所得が源泉所得税
　の適用対象となるものであるときは，その源泉所得税額は申告所得税額か
　ら控除される。(3)の(d)に掲げる給与所得に係る税額は，給与等の総額の
　20％相当額である。

(4)　上記¶5-870に掲げた(4)に属する非居住者は，不動産の譲渡，貸付によ
　る所得などを除き源泉徴収だけで納税義務が完結し，したがって，申告所
　得税は課されない（所法164）。

　　換言すれば，日本に事業や資産を有せず単なる証券投資をするにとどま
　る非居住者には，申告所得税の納税義務はない（所法165）。

　　非居住者は，退職所得について，居住者と同様の課税を受けることを選
　択することができる（所法171）。

326   ASSESSMENT INCOME TAX

¶ 5-890 Computation of tax amount

The annual amount of assessment income tax levied on non-resident taxpayers is computed in a similar way to resident taxpayers. It is also computed in six steps (Law 165):

(1)   The amount of each category of income is computed in the same way as described in ¶ 5-120 to ¶ 5-200, except that only expenses necessary for acquiring the assessable income are deductible from the gross amount of each category of income. Expenses not necessary for acquiring income assessable to Japanese assessment income tax are not deductible.

(2)   The amounts of the ten categories of income should be aggregated to make "ordinary income amount", "forestry income amount" and "retirement income amount" and the income subject to separate taxation (see ¶ 5-120) as described in ¶ 5-230, ¶ 5-240 and ¶ 5-250 excluding interest income.

(3)   In the case of a non-resident, only three of the fifteen deductions and allowances (see ¶ 5-310), namely "deduction for accidental loss," "deduction for contributions" and "basic allowance" may be deducted in reaching the "taxable ordinary income amount".

Note:
A deduction for accidental loss is allowed only for losses of assets situated in Japan.

(4)   The tax rate is applied to the five taxable income amounts in the same way as for resident taxpayers.

(5)   Out of the tax credits deductible for resident taxpayers (see ¶ 5-570), only the credits for dividends and for experimental and research expenses may be deducted.

(6)   In order to reach the amount of assessment income tax to be paid to a tax office, only withholding income tax withheld from income subject to assessment income tax may be deducted from the tax amount resulting after Step 5.

¶ 5-900 Concessions under tax treaties (assessment income tax)

Refer to ¶ 4-650 and ¶ 6-900 for concessions granted under tax treaties. The information concerning withholding income tax and corporation tax in those paragraphs also applies to assessment income tax.

¶ 5-890

申 告 所 得 税　327

¶5-890　税額の計算

非居住者に課される申告所得税額は，居住者の場合と同様の方法で計算される。計算過程は 6 段階である（所法165）。

(1)　各種所得の金額を¶5-120～¶5-200に述べたと同じ方法で計算する。ただし，各種所得の合計金額から控除できるのは，課税所得を得るために要した必要経費だけであり，それ以外の経費は課税所得計算上控除されない。

(2)　10種の所得の金額は利子所得を除き，「総所得金額」，「山林所得金額」，「退職所得金額」及び分離課税の対象所得金額（¶5-120参照）とに区分して合計する（¶5-230，¶5-240及び¶5-250参照）。

(3)　非居住者にあっては，15種の所得控除のうち「雑損控除」，「寄附金控除」及び「基礎控除」の 3 控除だけが認められる。これらの所得控除を行って，「課税総所得金額」を算出する（¶5-310参照）。

　(注)：なお，雑損控除は，日本国内に所在する資産に係る損失についてのみ適用がある。

(4)　税率は，居住者の場合と同じように，適用される。

(5)　税額控除のうち，非居住者に対しては，配当控除と試験研究費控除だけが認められる（¶5-570参照）。

(6)　申告所得税の対象となる所得に係る源泉所得税が上記の(5)により算出される税額から控除され，その差額が納付すべき税額となる。

¶5-900　租税条約上の特例

租税条約上の特例については¶4-650及び¶6-900を参照のこと。源泉所得税及び法人税の説明における記述は，申告所得税にも当てはまる。

328   ASSESSMENT INCOME TAX

¶ 5-910 Return

A final return should be filed by a non-resident taxpayer in the same way as by a resident taxpayer (¶ 5-720), except that where a non-resident taxpayer leaves Japan without appointing a tax representative in Japan and notifying the appointment to a tax office, he or she is required to file a final return before departure from Japan (Law 166).

A typical form for the final return with respect to income accruing in 2013 is shown at ¶ 5-950.

¶ 5-920 Payment

Prepayment by a non-resident taxpayer takes place in the same way as in the case of a resident taxpayer (¶ 5-710).

The final payment by a non-resident taxpayer should be made in the same way as by a resident taxpayer (¶ 5-730), provided that a non-resident who is required to file a final return before departure from Japan should also make his or her final payment before departure from Japan (Law 166).

申　告　所　得　税　329

¶5-910　申告

　非居住者は，居住者と同じように，確定申告書を提出しなければならない（¶5-720参照）。ただし，納税管理人を指定しこれを税務署長に報告することなく出国する非居住者は，出国前に確定申告書を提出する必要がある。

　　＊平成25年分所得に係る確定申告書の典型的な様式を，¶5-950に掲げてある（所法166）。

¶5-920　納付

　非居住者による予定納税は，居住者の場合と同じように行われる（¶5-710）。

　非居住者の確定申告による納付も居住者の場合と同じであるが，ただ，出国前に確定申告をする必要がある非居住者は出国前に確定申告による納付をしなければならない（所法166）（¶5-730）。

330   ASSESSMENT INCOME TAX

¶ 5-950 How to Fill Out Your Final Return (for Type B)

税務署長　平成□年分の　所得税及び復興特別所得税の　申告書B　FA0123

第一表（平成二十九年分以降用）

住所 又は 事業所 事務所 居所など

個人番号

フリガナ

氏名　㊞

性別　職業　屋号・雅号　世帯主の氏名　世帯主との続柄
男 女

生年月日

電話番号　自宅・勤務先・携帯

翌年以降送付不要

（単位は円）　種類

収入金額等	事業	営業等	㋐	
		農業	㋑	
	不動産		㋒	
	利子		㋓	
	配当		㋔	
	給与		㋕	
	雑	公的年金等	㋖	
		その他	㋗	
	総合譲渡	短期	㋘	
		長期	㋙	
	一時		㋚	

所得金額	事業	営業等	①	
		農業	②	
	不動産		③	
	利子		④	
	配当		⑤	
	給与	区分	⑥	
	雑		⑦	
	総合譲渡・一時 ⑦+{(㋘+㋙)×½}		⑧	
	合計		⑨	

所得から差し引かれる金額	雑損控除	⑩	
	医療費控除 区分	⑪	
	社会保険料控除	⑫	
	小規模企業共済等掛金控除	⑬	
	生命保険料控除	⑭	
	地震保険料控除	⑮	
	寄附金控除	⑯	
	寡婦、寡夫控除	⑱	0000
	勤労学生、障害者控除	⑲〜⑳	0000
	配偶者（特別）控除 区分	㉑〜㉒	0000
	扶養控除	㉓	0000
	基礎控除	㉔	0000
	合計	㉕	

特例適用条文等　整理番号

税金の計算	課税される所得金額 (⑨−㉕)又は第三表	㉖	000
	上の㉖に対する税額 又は第三表の⑧	㉗	
	配当控除	㉘	
		㉙	
	（特定増改築等）住宅借入金等特別控除 区分	㉚	
	政党等寄附金等特別控除	㉛〜㉝	
	住宅耐震改修特別控除 住宅特定改修・認定住宅 新築等特別税額控除 区分	㉞〜㊱	
	差引所得税額 (㉗−㉘−㉙−㉚−㉛−㉝−㉞)	㊳	
	災害減免額	㊴	
	再差引所得税額 (基準所得税額) (㊳−㊴)	㊵	
	復興特別所得税額 (㊵×2.1%)	㊶	
	所得税及び復興特別所得税の額 (㊵+㊶)	㊷	
	外国税額控除 区分	㊸	
	所得税及び復興特別所得税の源泉徴収税額	㊹	
	所得税及び復興特別所得税の申告納税額 (㊷−㊸−㊹)	㊺	
	所得税及び復興特別所得税の予定納税額 (第1期分・第2期分)	㊻	
	所得税及び復興特別所得税の第3期分の税額 (㊺−㊻)	納める税金 ㊼	00
		還付される税金 ㊽	

その他	配偶者の合計所得金額	㊾	
	専従者給与（控除）額の合計額	㊿	
	青色申告特別控除額	51	
	雑所得・一時所得等の源泉徴収税額 所得税及び復興特別所得税の源泉徴収税額の合計額	52	
	未納付の所得税及び復興特別所得税の源泉徴収税額	53	
	本年分で差し引く繰越損失額	54	
	平均課税対象金額	55	
	変動・臨時所得金額	56	

| 延納の届出 | 申告期限までに納付する金額 | 57 | 00 |
| | 延納届出額 | 58 | 000 |

還付される税金の受取場所

銀行・金庫・組合・農協・漁協　本店・支店　出張所　本所・支所

郵便局 名等

預金種類　普通 当座 納税準備 貯蓄

口座番号 記号番号

整理欄	区分	A	B	C	D	E	F	G	H	I	J	K	
	異動											
	管理補完					L			名簿			確認

税理士署名押印 電話番号　㊞

税理士法第30条の書面提出有　税理士法第33条の2の書面提出有

¶ 5-950

申 告 所 得 税 331

¶5-950　所得税の確定申告書

FA0077

整理番号

平成　　年分の所得税及び復興特別所得税の確定申告書B

第二表（平成二十九年分以降用）

○ 所得から差し引かれる金額に関する事項

住所
屋号
フリガナ
氏名

⑩ 雑損控除　損害の原因　損害年月日　損害を受けた資産の種類など
損害金額　保険金などで補填される金額　差引損失額のうち災害関連支出の金額

⑪ 医療費控除　支払医療費等　保険金などで補填される金額

⑫ 社会保険料控除　社会保険の種類　支払保険料
⑬ 小規模企業共済等掛金控除　掛金の種類　支払掛金
合計　合計

○ 所得の内訳（所得税及び復興特別所得税の源泉徴収税額）

所得の種類	種目・所得の生ずる場所又は給与などの支払者の氏名・名称	収入金額	所得税及び復興特別所得税の源泉徴収税額
		円	円

⑭ 生命保険料控除　新生命保険料の計　旧生命保険料の計
新個人年金保険料の計　旧個人年金保険料の計
介護医療保険料の計

⑮ 地震保険料控除　地震保険料の計　旧長期損害保険料の計

⑯ 寄附金控除　寄附先の所在地・名称　寄附金

⑰〜⑲ 寡婦（寡夫）控除　□死別　□生死不明　□離婚　□未帰還　□勤労学生控除　学校名

㊹ 所得税及び復興特別所得税の源泉徴収税額の合計

○ 雑所得（公的年金等以外）、総合課税の配当所得・譲渡所得、一時所得に関する事項

所得の種類	種目・所得の生ずる場所	収入金額	必要経費等	差引金額
		円	円	円

⑳ 氏名
㉑・㉒ 配偶者の氏名　生年月日　明・大　昭・平　□配偶者控除　□配偶者特別控除
個人番号　国外居住

○ 特例適用条文等

㉓ 扶養控除　控除対象扶養親族の氏名　続柄　生年月日　控除額
個人番号　明・大　昭・平　万円　国外居住
㉓ 扶養控除額の合計

○ 事業専従者に関する事項

事業専従者の氏名	個人番号	続柄	生年月日	従事月数・程度・仕事の内容	専従者給与（控除）額
			明・大　昭・平		
			明・大　昭・平		

㊿ 専従者給与（控除）額の合計額

○ 住民税・事業税に関する事項

16歳未満の扶養親族	扶養親族の氏名	個人番号	続柄	生年月日	別居の場合の住所	寄附金税額控除
				平		都道府県、市区町村分
				平		住所地の共同募金会、日赤など
				平		条例指定　都道府県　市区町村

配当に関する住民税の特例　非居住者の特例
配当割額控除額　株式等譲渡所得割額控除額
給与・公的年金等に係る所得以外（平成30年4月1日において65歳未満の方は給与所得以外）の所得に係る住民税の徴収方法の選択　□給与から差引き　□自分で納付

非課税所得など　所得金額　損益通算の特例適用前の不動産所得　前年中の開（廃）業　開始・廃止　月　日
不動産所得から差し引いた青色申告特別控除額　事業用資産の譲渡損失など　他都道府県の事務所等

別居の控除対象配偶者・控除対象扶養親族・事業専従者の氏名・住所　氏名　住所　所得税で控除対象配偶者などとした専従者　氏名　給与　一連番号

332   ASSESSMENT INCOME TAX

Page 1   Note: Enter the following items into your return that corresponds to the circled letter:

Ⓐ	Tax year
Ⓑ	A kind of tax return
Ⓒ	Name of the tax office where your return should be filed.
Ⓓ	Date of filing your return.
Ⓔ	Present address
Ⓕ	Address as of January 1, 2017.
Ⓖ	Individual number

Ⓗ	Name (last, first, middle initial)
Ⓘ	Occupation
Ⓙ	Pen name, if applicable
Ⓚ	Name of house-holder
Ⓛ	Relationship between you and the above.
Ⓜ	Date of Birth
Ⓝ	Telephone number

Please enclose with a circle, if applicable.

Ⓞ	When you are allowed to file a blue tax return.
Ⓟ	When you have some income subject to separate taxation.
Ⓠ	When you have income subject to Exit tax system.
Ⓡ	When your income was in deficit etc.
Ⓢ	When you will amend your original tax return.
Ⓣ	If you are a special agricultural income earner.
Ⓤ	If you have received your return form by post from the Tax Office and will not required a form next year and beyond

Amount of earnings

Business income	⑦	Amount of earnings (sales etc)
	⑦	Amount of earnings (agriculture)
Real estate income	⑦	Amount of earnings (real estate)
Interest income	⑦	Amount of earnings (interest)
Dividends income	⑦	Amount of earnings (dividends)
Employment income	⑦	Amount of earnings (employment income)
Miscellaneous income	⑦	Amount of earnings (government pension etc)
	⑦	Amount of earnings (other than the above)
Capital gains subject to aggregate taxation		Amount of income (short-term capital gains)
	⑦	Amount of income (long-term capital gains)
Occasional income	⑦	Amount of income (occasional)

Amount of income

Business income	①	Amount of income (sales etc)
	②	Amount of income (agriculture)
Real estate income	③	Amount of income (real estate)
Interest income	④	Amount of income (interest)
Dividends income	⑤	Amount of income (dividends)
Employment income	⑥	Amount of income (employment income)
Miscellaneous income	⑦	Amount of income (government pension etc)
Capital gains & Occasional income + ((ⓙ + ⑪) × 1/2)	⑧	Amount of income (capital gains & occasional)
Total	⑨	Total amount of income

Deduction from income

⑩	Deduction for casualty losses
⑪	Deduction for medical expenses
⑫	Deduction for social insurance premiums
⑬	Deduction for small business mutual aid premiums
⑭	Deduction for life insurance premiums
⑮	Deduction for earthquake insurance premiums
⑯	Deduction for donations
⑱	Exemption for widow and widower
⑲~⑳	Exemption for working students, the disables
㉑	Exemption for spouse
㉒	Special exemption for spouse
㉓	Exemption for dependents
㉔	Basic exemption
㉕	Total amount of deductions and exemption from income

¶ 5-950

税金の計算	課税される所得金額 (⑨－㉕)又は第三表	㉖	000
	上の㉖に対する税額 又は第三表の㊱	㉗	
	配当控除	㉘	
	区分	㉙	
	(特定増改築等) 住宅借入金等特別控除 区分	㉚	
	政党等寄附金等特別控除	㉛～㉝	
	住宅耐震改修特別控除 住宅特定改修・認定住宅新築等特別税額控除 区分	㉟～㊲	
	差引所得税額 (㉗－㉘－㉙－㉚－㉛－㉜－㉝－㉟－㊱－㊲)	㊳	
	災害減免額	㊴	
	再差引所得税額 (基準所得税額) (㊳－㊴)	㊵	
	復興特別所得税額 (㊵×2.1%)	㊶	
	所得税及び復興特別所得税の額 (㊵＋㊶)	㊷	
	外国税額控除 区分	㊸	
	所得税及び復興特別所得税の源泉徴収税額	㊹	
	所得税及び復興特別所得税の申告納税額 (㊷－㊸－㊹)	㊺	
	所得税及び復興特別所得税の予定納税額 (第1期分・第2期分)	㊻	
	所得税及び復興特別所得税の第3期分の税額 (㊺－㊻) 納める税金	㊼	00
	還付される税金	㊽	△
その他	配偶者の合計所得金額	㊾	
	専従者給与(控除)額の合計額	㊿	
	青色申告特別控除額	51	
	雑所得・一時所得等の所得税及び復興特別所得税の源泉徴収税額の合計額	52	
	未納付の所得税及び復興特別所得税の源泉徴収税額	53	
	本年分で差し引く繰越損失額	54	
	平均課税対象金額	55	
	変動・臨時所得金額 区分	56	
延納の届出	申告期限までに納付する金額	57	00
	延納届出額	58	000

Calculation of your tax

㉖	Amount of taxable income (⑨ - ㉕)
㉗	Amount of tax imposed on the above taxable income
㉘	Credit for dividends
㉙	When you are running a business and filing a blue return and you are allowed to apply the special measure, it is necessity to fill out.
㉚	Special credit for loans relating to (acquisition of) a dwelling
㉛~㉞	Special credit for contributions to political parties.
㉟~㊲	Special deduction for anti-earthquake improvement made to an exisiting house, specified housing improvements and new building, etc. of a certified long-life quality house.
㊳	Balance of tax amount (㉗-㉘-㉙-㉚-㉛-㉜-㉝-㉞-㉟-㊱-㊲)
㊴	Credit for officially proclaimed natural disasters.
㊵	Balance of tax amount (㊳-㊴)
㊶	Special income tax for reconstruction (㊵×2.1%)
㊷	Total tax amount (㊵+㊶)
㊸	Foreign tax credit
㊹	Deduction for withholding tax
㊺	Balance of tax amount (㊷-㊸-㊹)
㊻	Amount of estimated tax (total amount of first and second installment tax)
㊼	Amount of third installment tax (㊺-㊻)
㊽	When the amount of ㊺ is in deficit, fill in this column (㊺-㊻)

Other items

㊾	Total amount of spouse's income
㊿	Total amount of deduction for salaries of family employees
51	Special reduction for blue returns
52	Total amount of withholding tax for miscellaneous and occasional income
53	Amount of unpaid withholding tax
54	Amount of carried-over losses subtracted from amount of income in 2007
55	Amount of income subject to averaging taxation
56	Amount of income to be considered fluctuating income and temporary income
57	Amount of tax to be paid by due date of filing return
58	Amount of deferred payment

Where to receive your tax refund

Ⓐ	The name of the bank
Ⓑ	The name of the branch
Ⓒ	The name of the post office (when you receive refund from post office)
Ⓓ	A type of account
Ⓔ	Account number

還付される税金の受取場所	Ⓐ	銀行 金庫・組合 農協・漁協	Ⓑ	本店・支店 出張所 本所・支所					
	郵便局名等 Ⓒ	Ⓓ 預金種類	普通	当座	納税準備	貯蓄			
	口座番号 記号番号	Ⓔ							

334   ASSESSMENT INCOME TAX

平成 ☐☐ 年分の所得税及び復興特別所得税の確定申告書B

Page 2

Ⓐ	Tax year
Ⓑ	Present address
Ⓒ	Name (last, first, middle initial)

Ⓐ

住　所
屋　号
フリガナ
氏　名　Ⓒ

Ⓑ

○ 所得の内訳（所得税及び復興特別所得税の源泉徴収税額）

所得の種類	種目・所得の生ずる場所又は給与などの支払者の氏名・名称	収 入 金 額	所得税及び復興特別所得税の源泉徴収税額
Ⓓ	Ⓔ	Ⓕ 円	Ⓖ 円
	㊹ 所得税及び復興特別所得税の源泉徴収税額の合計額	Ⓗ 円	

Withholding tax of income tax and special income tax of reconstruction

Ⓓ	Type of income
Ⓔ	Place where the income was generated
Ⓕ	Amount of earnings
Ⓖ	Amount of withholding tax
Ⓗ	Total amount of withholding tax

○ 雑所得（公的年金等以外）、総合課税の配当所得・譲渡所得、一時所得に関する事項

所得の種類	種目・所得の生ずる場所	収 入 金 額	必 要 経 費 等	差 引 金 額
Ⓘ	Ⓙ	Ⓚ 円	Ⓛ 円	Ⓜ 円

Items regarding miscellaneous income, dividends income, capital gains and occasional income

Ⓘ	Type of income
Ⓙ	Place where the income was generated
Ⓚ	Amount of earnings
Ⓛ	Amount of necessary expenses
Ⓜ	Amount of net income

○ 事業専従者に関する事項

事業専従者の氏名	個 人 番 号	続柄	生 年 月 日	従事月数・程度・仕事の内容	専従者給与(控除)額
Ⓝ	Ⓞ	Ⓟ	明·大昭·平 　Ⓠ　.	Ⓡ	Ⓢ
			明·大昭·平 　.　.		
				㊿ 専従者給与(控除)額の合計額	Ⓣ 円

Items regarding family employees

Ⓝ	Name of family employee
Ⓞ	Individual number
Ⓟ	Relationship to you
Ⓠ	Date of birth
Ⓡ	Period of participation in the family business Particulars of work and extent of participation

Ⓢ	Amount of family employee salary (deduction)
Ⓣ	Total amount of family employee salary (deduction)

¶ 5-950

申 告 所 得 税 335

| 番号 | | 一連番号 | |

○ 所得から差し引かれる金額に関する事項

| | | | |

Items regarding deduction from income

⑩	ⓐ	Cause of damage
	ⓑ	Date of damage
	ⓒ	Type of asset subjected to damage
	ⓓ	Amount of Loss
	ⓔ	Amount reimbursed by insurance, etc.
	ⓕ	Amount of unusual expenditures due to disaster
⑪	ⓐ	Amount of medical expenses paid
	ⓑ	Amount reimbursed by insurance, etc.
⑫	ⓐ	Type of social insurance
	ⓑ	Insurance premiums paid
	ⓒ	Amount of deduction
⑬	ⓐ	Type of contribution
	ⓑ	Amount of contribution
	ⓒ	Amount of deduction
⑭	ⓐ	New life insurance premiums
	ⓑ	New personal pension insurance premiums
	ⓒ	Medical care insurance premiums
	ⓓ	Old life insurance premiums
	ⓔ	Old personal pension insurance premiums
⑮	ⓐ	Amount of earthquake insurance premiums
	ⓑ	Amount of former long-term casualty insurance premiums
⑯	ⓐ	Title and address of the entity to which the contribution was made
	ⓑ	Amount of earthquake-related contribution to be made to Prefectures, municipal government etc.
	ⓒ	Amount of contribution other than (b)
⑳	ⓐ	If you are considered a disabled person, please write your name.
㉑~㉒	ⓐ	Name of your spouse
	ⓑ	Date of Birth
	ⓒ	Individual number
㉓	ⓐ	Name of your dependents
	ⓑ	Relationship to you
	ⓒ	Date of Birth
	ⓓ	Amount of deduction
	ⓔ	Individual number
	ⓕ	Total amount of deduction

○ 住民税・事業税に関する事項

	扶養親族の氏名	個 人 番 号	続柄	生 年 月 日	別居の場合の住所	寄附金額控除

336

CHAPTER 6

CORPORATION TAX

	Paragraph
Chart: Corporation Tax Payable by Companies	¶ 6-002

Outline of Corporation Tax
Basic Structure of Corporation Tax	¶ 6-005
Tax on Ordinary Income	¶ 6-060
Tax on Liquidation Income	¶ 6-070
Tax on Specific Funds	¶ 6-090

Ordinary Income
Basic Concepts in Computing Ordinary Income	¶ 6-100
Gross Income	¶ 6-150
Total Cost	¶ 6-205
Valuation of Inventory	¶ 6-250
Depreciation	¶ 6-265
Deferred Assets	¶ 6-320
Loss Due to Changes in Book Value	¶ 6-340
Tax-free Reserves	¶ 6-350
Exchange, Replacement or Donation of Properties	¶ 6-470
Other Deductions	¶ 6-520
Net Loss	¶ 6-570
Corporate Reorganization	¶ 6-600
Consolidated Taxation System	¶ 6-630
Undistributed Profits (for a family corporation)	¶ 6-640
Special Taxation on Capital Gains from Land	¶ 6-670
Special Taxation of Beneficiary-concealed-disbursement	¶ 6-675
Tax on Ordinary Income and Tax Credits	¶ 6-680
Examples of Computation	¶ 6-770
Return and Payment of Tax on Ordinary Income	¶ 6-800
Tax on Liquidation Income	¶ 6-820
Tax on Specific Funds	¶ 6-855
Other Procedural Matters	¶ 6-860
Foreign Corporations	¶ 6-870

第 6 章
法　人　税

法人の納付すべき法人税………………………………	¶6-002

一般的説明

法人税の基本的な仕組み…………………………………	¶6-005
各事業年度の所得に対する法人税………………………	¶6-060
清算所得に対する法人税…………………………………	¶6-070
退職年金等積立金に対する法人税………………………	¶6-090

各事業年度の所得に対する法人税

所得の計算の通則…………………………………………	¶6-100
益金…………………………………………………………	¶6-150
損金…………………………………………………………	¶6-205
たな卸資産の評価…………………………………………	¶6-250
減価償却……………………………………………………	¶6-265
繰延資産……………………………………………………	¶6-320
資産の評価損………………………………………………	¶6-340
引当金・準備金……………………………………………	¶6-350
資産の交換，買換え，贈与………………………………	¶6-470
その他の控除………………………………………………	¶6-520
欠損金………………………………………………………	¶6-570
企業組織再編成……………………………………………	¶6-600
連結納税制度………………………………………………	¶6-630
同族会社の留保金課税……………………………………	¶6-640
土地譲渡益に対する特別課税……………………………	¶6-670
使途秘匿金に対する特別課税……………………………	¶6-675
各事業年度の所得に対する法人税額及び税額控除………	¶6-680
計算例………………………………………………………	¶6-770
各事業年度の所得に対する法人税の申告及び納付………	¶6-800

清算所得に対する法人税…………………………………	¶6-820
退職年金等積立金に対する法人税………………………	¶6-855
その他の手続………………………………………………	¶6-860
外国法人……………………………………………………	¶6-870

¶ 6-002 Chart: Corporation Tax Payable by Companies

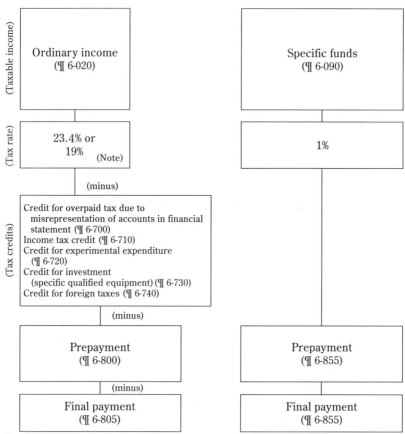

Note:
1. Additional tax on undistributed profits of a family corporation (¶ 6-640 to ¶ 6-660)
2. Additional tax (5 or 10%) on capital gains from land (¶ 6-670)
3. Additional tax (40%) on "beneficiary-concealed-disbursement" (¶ 6-675)

法　人　税　339

¶6-002　法人の納付すべき法人税

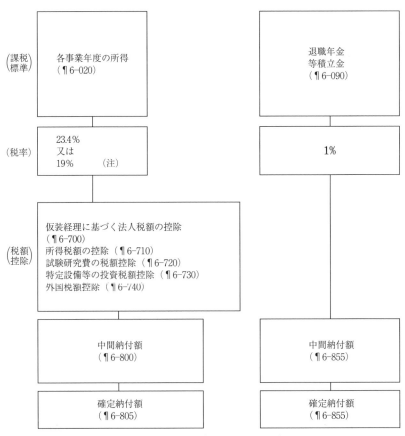

(注)：1．同族会社の留保金に対する追加課税（¶6-640～¶6-660）
　　　2．土地譲渡に対する5％又は10％の税率による追加課税（¶6-670）
　　　3．使途秘匿金に対する40％の税率による特別課税（¶6-675）

340   CORPORATION TAX

OUTLINE OF CORPORATION TAX

Basic Structure of Corporation Tax

¶ 6-005 Types of corporation tax

Japanese corporation tax is composed of:

(1) tax on ordinary income;

(2) tax on liquidation income (abolished from October 1, 2010); and

(3) tax on specific funds (The taxation is suspended from April 1, 1999 until March 31, 2017.).

The tax on ordinary income is the tax levied on net income accruing to a corporation in a business year. As this type of tax is internationally very well-known, it should be unnecessary to explain its nature to foreign readers.

However, it should be noted that ordinary income tax includes special taxation on undistributed profits of a family corporation (except a non-personal family corporation, see ¶ 3-790), and on capital gains from land and on "beneficiary-concealed-disbursement".

The tax on undistributed profits is levied only on the undistributed profits of a domestic personal family corporation. (For definitions of a family corporation and a personal family corporation, see ¶ 3-780 and ¶ 3-790.) A personal family corporation is apt to avoid the distribution of profits to its individual shareholders, because they are reluctant to pay income tax on dividends received. When a family corporation retains profits derived in a business year which exceed the prescribed limit, tax on the undistributed profits is levied automatically, without any specific action by the Tax Authority, in order to overcome this kind of tax avoidance (see ¶ 6-640).

The special taxes on land and on "beneficiary-concealed-disbursement" are both temporary measures (see ¶ 6-670 and ¶ 6-675).

The tax on liquidation income is levied on the liquidation income of a corporation when it is liquidated or merged. This tax is intended to catch the income which was actually gained before or during a liquidation or merger but not yet taxed.

The tax on specific funds is intended to collect interest on deferred income tax liability assessable against such funds as approved pension funds, employees' welfare pension funds and employees' assets formation

¶ 6-005

法　人　税　341

一般的説明

法人税の基本的な仕組み

¶6-005　法人税の種類

日本の法人税は,
(1)　各事業年度の所得に対する法人税,
(2)　清算所得に対する法人税（平成22年10月1日より廃止）及び,
(3)　退職年金等積立金に対する法人税（平成11年4月1日より平成29年3月31日まで課税なし。）
から構成される。

各事業年度の所得に対する法人税は, 法人の各事業年度の所得に対して課される租税である。この種の租税は国際的にもよく知られているので, その性格についての説明は省くことにする。

ただし, これに加え, 同族会社の留保金に対する特別の課税並びに土地の譲渡益に対する特別の課税及び使途秘匿金に対する特別課税があることに留意する必要がある。

留保金に対する課税は, 内国法人である同族会社（非同族の同族会社を除く。）の留保所得金額についてのみ課される。同族会社及び非同族の同族会社の定義については¶3-780及び¶3-790を参照されたい。個人的な同族会社は, その個人株主に対する利益の分配を回避する傾向があるが, これは個人株主が受取配当に対する所得税の支払に消極的であることによる。このような租税回避に対処するために, 同族会社が各事業年度において所得を一定限度を超えて留保した場合には, 留保金額に対する租税が課される（¶6-640参照）。

土地に対する特別課税及び使途秘匿金に対する特別課税は, いずれも臨時的措置である（¶6-670及び¶6-675参照）。

清算所得に対する租税は, 法人が解散又は合併したときに法人の清算所得について課される。この租税は, 法人の解散又は合併の際にそれ以前に事実上稼得しながらこれまで課税されなかった所得を捕捉するためのものである。

退職年金等積立金に対する法人税は, 適格退職年金契約, 厚生年金基金契約及び勤労者財産形成給付契約に係る積立金について課税し得る所得税の繰延べに対する利子相当分を徴収しようとするものである。すなわち, 使用者からこの種の年金基金への支払額は法人の課税所得の計算上損金に算入されるが, 使用人に帰属する期待給付は基金への支払時点では課税所得を構成せず, 使用人が実際に受領する時点で課税されることになる。このような租税

342   CORPORATION TAX

funds. Payments from an employer into this kind of fund are deductible in computing his or her taxable income. The expected benefits attributable to employees do not become taxable at this point, but later at the time of actual payment to employees. Since the time of the tax collection is deferred, specific funds must pay the interest. This tax is deductible in computing the tax base for ordinary income tax.

(The tax qualified pension fund regime was abolished from April 1, 2002 and a new pension fund agreement is not treated as a tax qualified agreement. Existing agreements are, however, treated as tax qualified pension fund agreements until March 31, 2012.)

¶ 6-010 Avoidance of double taxation

When dividends received by individual or corporate shareholders are taxable, even though the income of the paying corporation was subject to corporation tax, it causes so-called double taxation of dividends. The corporation tax system in Japan, like the income tax system, attempts to avoid double taxation to some extent.

An individual shareholder enjoys the benefit of a tax credit for dividends received (¶ 5-580), while dividends received by a corporate shareholder are exempt to a certain extent from corporation tax (¶ 6-150).

¶ 6-020 Types of corporations and the object of taxation

(1) Corporations including non-juridical organizations (associations or foundations without juridical personality) are subject to corporation tax (Law 3, 4). For the purposes of the tax, there are various types of corporations, each of which is subject to corporation tax in its own way.

(2) Corporations are classified as either domestic corporations (resident corporations) or foreign corporations. Domestic corporations are those that have a head or main office located in Japan. Domestic corporations include public corporations, public interest corporations, cooperatives, ordinary corporations and non juridical organizations. Foreign corporations include ordinary corporations and non juridical corporations.

(3) The following shows the effect of corporation tax on each type of corporation (Law 5 to 10-3).

¶ 6-010

法　人　税　343

の徴収の繰延べについて，特定の年金基金は利子を負担しなければならないというものである。この退職年金等積立金に対する法人税は各事業年度の所得に対する法人税の課税標準の計算上損金に算入される。

　（なお，適格退職年金制度は，平成14年3月31日において廃止され，平成14年4月1日以後は，原則として新たな契約の締結は適格退職年金契約として認められないこととなった。ただし，現に締結されている適格退職年金制度については，平成24年3月31日までに限り経過的に存続することとされている。）

¶6-010　二重課税の回避

　配当が個人又は法人株主へ支払われたときに，配当支払法人の所得が既に法人税の課税対象となっているにもかかわらず，その受取配当が課税されることになれば配当について二重課税を生ずる。日本における法人税制度は所得税制度と同様このような二重課税を部分的に回避しようとしている。すなわち，所得税課税上個人株主は受取配当について税額控除の利益を享受し（¶5-580参照），一方，法人株主が受領する配当についてはその一定割合を益金の額に算入しない（¶6-150参照）。

¶6-020　法人の種類と納税義務の範囲

⑴　法人は法人税の納税義務を負う（法法4）。人格のない社団等は法人税法上，法人とみなされることになっている（法法3）。法人税は，法人の種類によって課税の範囲が異なる。

⑵　法人税法上，法人は内国法人と外国法人とに分けられる。内国法人は国内に本店又は主たる事務所を有する法人である。
　　内国法人は，公共法人，公益法人等，協同組合等，普通法人及び人格のない社団等に分類される。外国法人は，普通法人及び人格のない社団等に分類される。

⑶　法人の種類別に法人税の課税範囲を示せば次のとおりである（法法5〜10の3）。

344   CORPORATION TAX

		Tax on ordinary income	Tax on liquidation income	Tax on specific funds
DOMESTIC CORPORATION	ordinary corporations	taxable	taxable	taxable
	cooperatives			
	public interest corporations	taxable (only on income from profit-making businesses)	non-taxable	
	non-juridical organizations			
	public corporations	non-taxable		
FOREIGN CORPORATION	ordinary corporations	taxable (only on income from sources in Japan)	non-taxable	
	non-juridical organizations	taxable (only on income from profit-making businesses in Japan)	non-taxable	

¶ 6-025 Public corporations

Public corporations are non-taxable corporations, and include agencies of the national government, the local authorities and corporations (other than companies) whose capital is fully paid by the government (and which are listed in Schedule I of the Corporation Tax Law).

¶ 6-030 Cooperatives

The term "cooperative" means any kind of mutual aid organization listed in Schedule III of the Corporation Tax Law, and established by persons engaged in specified occupations or by consumers. For example, agricultural cooperatives and small enterprise cooperatives.

The tax rate applicable to cooperatives is lower than that for ordinary corporations (Law 66③) (¶ 6-060).

If a cooperative pays refunds to its members according to the degree of utilization of the facility provided by the cooperative, such refunds are deductible in computing the income of the cooperative (Law 60-2).

¶ 6-040 Public interest corporations (1)

Public interest corporations are incorporated associations, foundations and other juridical persons which are engaged in education, charitable work and other activities for public interest, and which are listed in

¶ 6-025

		各事業年度の所得に対する法人税	清算所得に対する法人税	退職年金等積立金に対する法人税
内国法人	普通法人	課　税	課　税	課　税
内国法人	協同組合等	課　税	課　税	課　税
内国法人	公益法人等	収益事業所得についてのみ課税	非　課　税	
内国法人	人格のない社団等	収益事業所得についてのみ課税	非　課　税	
内国法人	公共法人	非　課　税		
外国法人	普通法人	国内源泉所得についてのみ課税	非　課　税	
外国法人	人格のない社団等	国内源泉収益事業所得についてのみ課税	非　課　税	

¶6-025　公共法人

　公共法人とは，地方公共団体，国又は地方公共団体がその全額を出資する法人などのうち，法人税法別表第一に掲名された法人をいう。

　公共法人は，法人税が課されない。

¶6-030　協同組合等

　協同組合等とは，農業協同組合，中小企業協同組合などのような相互扶助組織であり，具体的には法人税法別表第三に掲名されている。

　協同組合等に適用される税率は普通法人に適用される税率よりも低い（法法66③）（¶6-060参照）。

　協同組合等がその組合員に対し協同組合等の事業を利用した分量に応じて分配する場合における当該事業分量配当は，協同組合等の所得の金額の計算上損金の額に算入される（法法60の2）。

¶6-040　公益法人等(1)

　公益法人等には，教育，福祉，その他の公益活動を行う法人でその拠出者に利益を分配しない法人が該当するが，具体的には法人税法別表第二に掲名されている法人をいう。

346   CORPORATION TAX

Schedule II of the Corporation Tax Law.

Corporations designated as public interest corporations by the Corporation Tax Law are exempt from corporation tax, but profits accruing to them from profit-making businesses* are subject to corporation tax at a reduced rate (Law 7, 66③) (¶ 6-060).

A public interest corporation whose annual revenue exceeds 80 million yen has to report his balance sheet, whether he carries on any profit-making business or not (SM 68-6).

Public interest corporations should keep account books showing clearly the income from their profit-making business (Reg 6). In computing the taxable income accruing from the profit-making business, contributions of up to 20% of ordinary income (in the case of a social welfare corporation or a qualified private educational institution, 50% of ordinary income or ¥2 million, whichever is larger) by a profit-making branch to another branch of that corporation or to any other corporation are deductible.

Taxes on undistributed profits (¶ 6-640) are not levied on a public interest corporation, because it is not a family company.

As the tax on liquidation income is not levied on a public interest corporation, the tax on ordinary income is levied on its income accruing after the opening of liquidation proceedings just as it is levied before the opening of the proceedings.

> * The following activities carried on continuously are considered profit-making businesses, with reasonable exceptions (Reg 5):
> ① retail activities
> ② sales of real estate
> ③ granting loans
> ④ renting goods
> ⑤ renting real estate
> ⑥ manufacturing activities
> ⑦ communication services
> ⑧ transport services
> ⑨ undertaking services
> ⑩ printing services
> ⑪ publishing businesses
> ⑫ photo studios
> ⑬ renting rooms, halls etc.
> ⑭ hotels
> ⑮ restaurants
> ⑯ acting as a broker
> ⑰ acting as an agent
> ⑱ acting as an intermediary
> ⑲ wholesale activities

¶ 6-040

法　人　税　347

　法人税法上公益法人等と指定された法人（法法別表二）は，収益事業*から生じた所得については軽減税率により法人税が課されるが，これら以外の所得は非課税とされる（法法7，66③）（¶6-060参照）。

　公益法人等は，年間収入が8,000万円を超える場合には，収益事業を営むか否かにかかわらず，収支計算書を税務当局に提出しなければならない（措法68の6）。

　公益法人等は，収益事業から生ずる所得を他の所得と区分して記帳しなければならない（法令6）。収益事業から生ずる所得の計算上，収益部門から他の部門又は他の法人へ支出した寄附金は各事業年度の所得の金額の20％（社会福祉法人及び特定の私立学校については，所得の50％又は200万円のうちいずれか多い金額）までの範囲内で損金の額に算入される。

　公益法人等は同族会社ではないので留保金額に対する法人税は課されない。また，清算所得は非課税とされるが，清算手続開始後に生じた所得については清算手続開始前に課税されると同様に各事業年度の所得に対する法人税が課される。

＊収益事業には原則として次のものが該当する（法令5）。

① 物品販売業
② 不動産販売業
③ 金銭貸付業
④ 物品貸付業
⑤ 不動産貸付業
⑥ 製造業
⑦ 通信業
⑧ 運送業
⑨ 請負業
⑩ 印刷業
⑪ 出版業
⑫ 写真業
⑬ 席貸業
⑭ 旅館業
⑮ 料理店業その他の飲食店業
⑯ 周旋業
⑰ 代理業
⑱ 仲立業
⑲ 問屋業

348   CORPORATION TAX

㉑ mining
㉑ quarrying
㉒ carrying on a public bath
㉓ barber
㉔ carrying on a beauty parlor
㉕ show business
㉖ carrying on an amusement park business or the like
㉗ medical services
㉘ providing instruction in flower arrangement, Lettering, etc.
㉙ renting parking lots
㉚ providing credit guarantees
㉛ selling or granting the right to use a patent or the like

¶ 6-042 Public interest corporations (2)

Following the introduction of new corporations under the reform of law with regard to public interests corporations, from April 1, 2008, a corporate juridical person and a foundation are treated as follows:

1. Public interests corporate juridical persons or foundations
   (1) Its business income is subject to tax at tax rates applicable to ordinary corporations.

   Public interests businesses are exempted from the business.
   (2) If assets used for its business are disbursed for its public interests business, it is treated as donation for the public interests business (Law 37⑤).
   (3) Limitation of deductible amounts for the donation is larger of two below;
      ① 50% of its business income
      ② The amount of (2) above provided that it is clearly used or to be used for public interests business

2. Corporate juridical persons or foundations described below (Non-business oriented corporation) (Law 2(9)-(2))
      ① Its article of association stipulates that retained surplus will not be distributed, or
      ② its main purposes are to attain its members' common interested.
   (1) Its business income is subject to tax at tax rates applicable to ordinary corporations.

3. Corporate juridical persons or foundations other than 1. and 2. above
   (1) It is treated as an ordinary corporation for tax purposes (Law 66①).

¶ 6-042

法　人　税　349

 ⑳ 鉱業
 ㉑ 土石採取業
 ㉒ 浴場業
 ㉓ 理容業
 ㉔ 美容業
 ㉕ 興行業
 ㉖ 遊覧所業
 ㉗ 医療保険業
 ㉘ 技芸教授業
 ㉙ 駐車場業
 ㉚ 信用保証業
 ㉛ 無体財産権提供業

¶6-042　公益法人等(2)

　公益法人制度改革による新たな法人制度の創設に伴い，平成20年4月1日より，公益法人のうち，次の法人は，次のように取り扱う。

1．公益社団法人及び公益財団法人
 (1)　収益事業から生じた所得について普通法人に適用される税率で法人税を課税する。
  なお，収益事業の範囲から公益目的事業に該当するものを除外する。
 (2)　収益事業に属する資産のうちから自らの公益目的事業のために支出した金額は，その収益事業に係る寄附金の額とみなす（法法37⑤)。

 (3)　寄附金の損金算入限度額は，次のいずれか多い金額とする。

  ①　所得の金額の50%相当額
  ②　上記(2)の金額のうち，公益目的事業のために充当し，又は充当することが確実であると認められるもの

2．次の要件等に該当する一般社団法人及び一般財団法人（非営利型法人）
 （法法2九の二）
  ①　剰余金の分配を行わない旨が定款において定められていること

  ②　会員に共通する利益を図る活動を行うことを主たる目的としていること
 (1)　収益事業から生じた所得について普通法人に適用される税率で法人税を課税する。
3．上記1．及び2．のいずれにも該当しない一般社団法人及び一般財団法人
 (1)　法人税法上，普通法人とする（法法66①)。

350   CORPORATION TAX

¶ 6-045   Medical care corporations

Medical care corporations are included in ordinary corporations. However, medical care corporations which contribute to the promotion of medical care and are operated publicly, with the approval of the Minister of Finance, are subject to tax at a reduced rate (SM 67-2) (¶ 6-060).

¶ 6-050   Non-juridical organizations

Non-juridical organizations are non-juridical associations or foundations which carry on business independently with designated representatives or managers (Law 2(8), 3).

For tax purposes, non-juridical organizations are treated as corporations (Law 3).

However, non-juridical organizations are subject to ordinary income tax on profits accruing from profit-making business in the same way as public interest corporations, except that the tax rate and the limit of deductible contributions are the same as those applicable to ordinary corporations (Law 7, 37, 66 and Reg 73).

¶ 6-052   Trust

(1) Certain types of Beneficial Interest Certificate Issuing Trusts ("BICIT") under the Trust Law are classified as Specified BICITs if they meet certain requirements such that 97.5% or more of profits in the trusts are distributed to beneficiaries when earned by the trusts and so on. The Specified BICIT, the Joint Management Trust and the Investment Trust, except certain types of Investment Trust, are classified as the Collective Investment Trusts (Law 2).

(2) Certain types of BICIT, Trust with no beneficiary and Trust with a corporate trustee are, together with certain types of the Investment Trust and the Special Purpose Trust, classified as the Corporate Taxation Trusts. The Collective Investment Trusts, the Pension Fund Trusts and the Specified Public Interest Trusts are excluded from the Corporate Taxation Trusts (Law 2).

(3) If it is the Corporate Taxation Trust, the trust is subject to corporate tax on income attributable to the trust assets. Its trustee must file final returns with regard to the income by each trusted assets (Law 4-6).

¶ 6-045

法 人 税 351

¶6-045　医療法人

医療法人は普通法人に該当する。ただし医療の普及，向上に寄与し，かつ，公的に運営されているものとして財務大臣の承認を受けた特定の医療法人は，軽減税率が適用される（措法67の2）（¶6-060参照）。

¶6-050　人格のない社団等

人格のない社団等は，法人でない社団又は財団で定款等に代表者又は管理人の定めがあるものなど独立の活動を行う組織体をいい，法人税の課税上は法人とみなされる（法法2八，3）。

人格のない社団等は，公益法人等と同じように収益事業から生ずる所得に各事業年度の所得に対する法人税が課される（法法7，37，66，法令73）。

¶6-052　信託

(1) 信託法上の受益証券発行信託のうち一定の要件（信託に係る未分配利益の額が信託の元本総額の1,000分の25相当額以下であること等）を満たすものを特定受益証券発行信託という。これを合同運用信託及び投資信託（一定のものを除く。）と併せて集団投資信託という（法法2）。

(2) 受益証券発行信託，受益者が存しない信託，法人が委託者となる信託のうち一定の要件に該当する信託を一定の投資信託及び特定目的信託と併せて法人課税信託という。ただし，集団投資信託並びに退職年金等信託及び特定公益信託等を除く（法法2）。

(3) 法人課税信託の受託者について，信託資産等及び固有資産等ごとに，受託者をそれぞれ別の者とみなして法人税法の規定を適用する（法法4の6）。

352   CORPORATION TAX

(4) Entrustment of assets by a trustee into the Corporate Taxation Trust is deemed as a capital investment into a trustee provided that it is not a Trust with no beneficiary (Law 4-7).

(5) Trusted assets in trusts other than the Collective Investment Trust, the Corporate Taxation Trust, the Pension Fund Trusts and the Specified Public Interest Trusts are deemed to be owned by beneficiaries of the trusts and income and expenses attributable to the trusted assets are treated as those of beneficiaries' for the corporate tax purposes (Law 12).

¶ 6-055 Place for tax payment

A corporation is required to file returns, pay tax and supply details of the computation of taxable income to the tax office having jurisdiction over the place where the corporation is required to pay tax.

The place of tax payment of a domestic corporation is the place where its head or main office is located (Law 16). However, if that place is inconvenient because of the corporation's business or estate, the tax authority may designate another place as its place of tax payment (Law 18).

In the case of a foreign corporation, the place of tax payment is where the corporation's main permanent establishment or estate in Japan is located, or at the Kojimachi tax office (Law 17, Reg 16).

¶ 6-056 Blue returns

A corporation may file a blue return in the same manner as an individual taxpayer, with the approval of the tax office (Law 121). A blue return corporation must keep a journal, a general ledger and other necessary books, and record all transactions affecting assets, liabilities and capital in the books clearly and in good order according to the principles of double entry so that its taxable income can be calculated correctly.

The corporation must also settle accounts on the basis of the records, prepare balance sheets, profit and loss statements and other statements, and keep almost all books and documents for seven years (Law 126).

A corporation is required to apply for approval to file a blue return by the day before the first day of commencement of the business year (Law 122). With respect to the first business year of a new corporation, the application for approval must be made by the day within three months from the date of incorporation or by the last day of the first business year, which-

¶ 6-055

法　人　税　353

(4)　委託者がその有する資産を法人課税信託（受益者が存しない信託を除く。）に信託した場合にはその受託者に対する出資があったものとみなす（法法4の7）。

(5)　集団投資信託，法人課税信託，退職年金等信託等以外の信託については，信託財産に属する資産，負債，収益及び費用はその受益者に属するものとみなして法人税法を適用する（法法12）。

¶6-055　納税地

　法人はその納税地を所轄する税務署に法人税の申告，その他の手続を行う。内国法人の納税地は，その法人の本店又は主たる事務所の所在地である（法法16）。ただし，その法人の本店又は主たる事務所の所在地がその法人の事業又は資産の状況からみて法人税の納税地として不適当である場合には，税務当局が納税地を指定する（法法18）。

　外国法人の納税地は，原則として，国内にある主たる恒久的施設の所在地又は主たる資産の所在地である（法法17，法令16）。

¶6-056　青色申告書

　法人は，個人納税者と同様，税務署の承認を受けて青色申告書を提出することができる（法法121）。青色申告法人は仕訳帳，総勘定元帳，その他の必要な帳簿を備え，課税所得を正確に計算し得るようにするため，その資産，負債及び資本に影響を及ぼす一切の取引につき，複式簿記の原則に従い，整然と，かつ，明りょうに記録しなければならない。

　当該法人は，更に，その記録，貸借対照表，損益計算書その他の資料に基づき決算を行い，それらの帳簿書類を原則として7年間保存しなければならない（法法126）。

　青色申告書を提出することについての税務署に対する承認申請は，事業年度開始の日の前日（新設法人の場合は，設立後3ヶ月を経過した日と設立後最初の事業年度終了の日とのいずれか早い日の前日）までに行わなければならない（法法122）。

354   CORPORATION TAX

ever is earlier.

Privileges of blue returns

Privileges granted to blue return corporations in the calculation of income include:

(1) Carried-over net losses for nine years (ten years in case the losses are incurred in accounting periods beginning on and after April 1, 2017), which are incurred from business years for which blue returns have been filed can be deducted as expenses in the accounting period (Law 57) (¶ 6-570).

(2) Carried-back losses incurred within one year before an accounting period qualify for a refund of corporation tax provided the tax office accepts the calculation (Law 80) (¶ 6-570).

(3) Most of the special depreciation allowances and the special tax credits provided for in the Special Taxation Measures Law apply to blue return corporations only.

(4) The various tax-free reserves provided for in the Special Taxation Measures Law are permitted to be deducted as expenses on condition that a blue return is filed.

Procedures privileges of blue returns

Privileges granted to blue return corporations in respect of taxation procedures include:

(1) The tax office cannot make corrections unless any mistakes made by the corporation in the calculation of income and other matters are ascertained from an audit of books and documents (Law 130①).

(2) The tax office must give the reasons for correction in a correction notice (Law 130②).

(3) A blue return corporation can request immediate reconsideration by the National Tax Tribunal without requesting the tax office for a reinvestigation (GL 75④(1)).

¶ 6-057 White returns

A corporation (unless it is a blue return corporation, as mentioned in ¶ 6-056 above) is required to keep accounting books and record all transactions in the specified simple manner (Law 150-2①). These books include invoices, receipts and records of all transactions.

The tax office will audit these books in the case of a tax investigation (Law 150-2②).

¶ 6-057

法　人　税　355

（青色申告の特典）

青色申告法人に対して所得の計算に関して与えられている特典は次のとおりである。

(1)　当該事業年度開始の日前9年（平成29年4月1日以後に開始した事業年度において生じた欠損金については10年）以内に開始した事業年度で，青色申告書を提出した事業年度において生じた欠損金の繰越額は，当該事業年度の損金の額に算入される（法法57）（¶6-570参照）。

(2)　当該事業年度において欠損金が生じた場合は，欠損事業年度開始の日前1年以内に開始した事業年度に繰り戻して，税務署の調査したところにより，法人税の還付を受けられる（法法80）（¶6-570参照）。

(3)　租税特別措置法に規定される特別償却や税額控除のほとんどは，青色申告法人についてのみ認められる。

(4)　租税特別措置法に規定される種々の準備金は，青色申告書の提出を条件として損金の額に算入することが認められる。

（青色申告の手続上の特典）

青色申告法人に対しては，課税手続上次の特典が認められている。

(1)　税務署は法人の帳簿書類を調査し，所得その他の計算に誤りがあると認められる場合に限り，更正することができる（法法130①）。

(2)　税務署は更正通知書に更正の理由を附記しなければならない（法法130②）。

(3)　青色申告法人は税務署へ異議申立てをすることなく，直ちに，国税不服審判所へ審査請求をすることができる（通則法75④一）。

¶6-057　白色申告書

法人（上記の青色申告法人を除く。）は，帳簿を備え付けてこれに全取引を一定の簡易な方法により記録しなければならない（法法150の2①）。当該帳簿には，送り状，領収書及び取引の記録書類を含む。

税務職員は，調査に際しては，当該帳簿を検査するものとする（法法150の2②）。

356   CORPORATION TAX

Tax on Ordinary Income

¶ 6-060 Tax basis and tax rate

Tax on ordinary income is computed by applying the following formula:

Ordinary income (a) × tax rate (b)

+ [(undistributed profits of a family corporation (c) − allowance for undistributed profits (d)) × tax rate (e)]

+ (Capital gains from lands (f) × tax rate (g))

+ (Beneficiary-concealed-disbursement (h) × 40%)

− tax credits (i)

= tax on ordinary income

= prepayment (j) and final payment (k)

(a)   Ordinary income should be computed as described in ¶ 6-130.

(b)   The tax rate on ordinary income (Law 66) is as follows:

Ordinary corporations*, corporate juridical persons, non-juridical organizations

(i) not more than ¥8 million of income per annum of a small enter-prise (a corporation** whose capital amounts to ¥100 million or less)   19%

(ii) others	23.2%
Cooperatives (¶ 6-030)	19%***
Public interest corporations (¶ 6-040)	
(other than corporate juridical persons.)	19%
Specified medical care corporations (¶ 6-045)	19%****

Note:

1. Tax rate applicable to taxable income corresponding to the amounts up to ¥8 million or less of ordinary corporations whose capital are ¥100 million or less, public interest corporations, cooperatives and non-juridical organizations is 15% as a tentative measure for accounting periods ending during April 1, 2012 through March 31, 2017 (SM 42-3-2).
2. Corporate tax rates applied to an accounting period of ordinary corpora-tions beginning on and after April 1, 2016 during March 31, 2018 are 23.4%.
*   Ordinary corporation means a corporation other than a cooperative or public interest corporation. Limited Corporation (Kabushiki Kaisha), Limited Liability Corporation (Godo Kaisha) and mutual insurance com-panies are typical examples of ordinary corporations.
** This is not applicable to a corporation in 100 percent group if capital of

¶ 6-060

法　人　税　357

各事業年度の所得に対する法人税

¶6-060　課税標準及び税率

各事業年度の所得に対する法人税の額は次の算式によって計算した金額である。

各事業年度の所得(a)×税率(b)

+〔(同族会社の留保金額(c)−留保控除額(d))×特別税率(e)〕

+(土地の譲渡益(f)×特別税率(g))

+(使途秘匿金(h)×40%)

−税額控除額(i)

=各事業年度の所得に対する法人税の額

=中間納付額(j)及び最終納付額(k)

(a)　各事業年度の所得の金額の計算については，¶6-130以下のとおり。

(b)　各事業年度の所得に対する税率は次のとおりである（法法66）。

普通法人*，一般社団法人，人格のない社団等

(ⅰ)　資本の金額が1億円以下の法人**の
　　　年800万円以下の金額　　　　　　　　　　　　　　　19%

(ⅱ)　その他　　　　　　　　　　　　　　　　　　　　　23.2%

協同組合等（¶6-030参照）　　　　　　　　　　　　　　　19%***

一般社団法人以外の公益法人等（¶6-040参照）　　　　　19%
特定医療法人（¶6-045参照）　　　　　　　　　　　　　19%****

　(注)：1.　以上において，普通法人のうち資本等の金額が1億円以下の法人，公益法人等，協同組合等及び人格のない社団等の所得金額のうち年800万円以下の部分の税率は，平成24年4月1日から平成29年3月31日の間に終了する各事業年度については，暫定的に15%である（措法42の3の2）。
　　　　2.　なお，平成28年4月1日から平成30年3月31日の間に開始した各事業年度の普通法人の法人税率は原則23.4%である。

　　*　　　普通法人とは協同組合等及び公益法人等以外の法人をいう。株式会社，合同会社，相互保険会社などの会社は普通法人の典型である。

　　**　　資本の金額が5億円以上の法人の100%子法人には適用しない（¶6-590（完全支配

358   CORPORATION TAX

whose parent is ¥500 million or more (see ¶ 6-590 (Transactions within 100 percent group)).

*** If a cooperative has over 5 hundred thousand members and mainly supplies goods to consumers, the rate of 22% applies to the income over one billion yen for business years in which retail sales exceed one hundred billion yen (SM 68).

**** Medical care corporations are included in ordinary corporations. The reduced tax rate 19% applies to the income of specified medical care corporations which are similar to public interest corporations (SM 67-2).

(c)   The amount of undistributed profits is computed, as stated in ¶ 6-640 to ¶ 6-660, by the following method:

   (i)   by adjusting the amount of ordinary income so as to reflect the actual distributable profits without taking into account any deviation from common accounting practice, then

   (ii)   deducting the actual distribution from distributable profits.

(d)   The allowance for undistributed profits of a family corporation is equivalent to the largest of the following three amounts:

   (i)   40% of the amount of ordinary income of that business year, or

   (ii)   ¥20 million per annum, or

   (iii)   the amount necessary for the accumulated retained earnings outstanding at the end of the business year to reach a target amounting to 25% of the paid in capital.

(e)   The tax rate on undistributed profits of a family corporation is as follows:

Not more than ¥30 million per annum 10%
Over ¥30 million but not more than
¥100 million per annum 15%
Over ¥100 million per annum 20%

(f)   Additional taxation on capital gains from land is set out in ¶ 6-670.

(g)   The tax rate on capital gains from land is 5 or 10% (This taxation has been suspended from 1998 to December 31, 2013) (¶ 6-670).

(h)   Special taxation on "Beneficiary-concealed-disbursement" is set out in (¶ 6-675).

(i)   The following tax credits (see ¶ 6-690) are deductible from tax:

   (i)   a credit for overpaid tax due to misrepresentation of the accounts in the financial statement,

   (ii)   an income tax credit amounting to the income tax withheld at

¶ 6-060

法 人 税 359

関係がある法人間の取引）参照）。

＊＊＊　特定の地域において1,000億円以上の売上の物品供給事業を行う組合員50万人以上の協同組合等の年所得10億円を超える部分については22%の税率が適用される（措法68）。

＊＊＊＊医療法人は普通法人に該当するが，特定医療法人として認められたものに限り税率が19%に軽減される（措法67の2）。

(c)　留保金額は¶6-640から¶6-660に述べるように，

　(ｉ)　実際の配当可能利益を反映するように各事業年度の所得金額を調整し，

　(ⅱ)　配当可能利益から実際の支払配当額を控除して計算する。

(d)　留保控除額とは次に掲げる三つの金額のうち最も多い金額をいう。

　(ｉ)　各事業年度の所得等の金額の100分の40に相当する金額

　(ⅱ)　年2,000万円

　(ⅲ)　当該事業年度終了のときにおける利益積立金額がそのときにおける資本の金額の100分の25に相当する金額に満たない場合におけるこの満たない部分の金額に相当する金額

(e)　同族会社の特別税率は次のとおりである。

年3,000万円以下の金額　　　　　　　　　　　100分の10

年3,000万円を超え，年１億円以下の金額　　　100分の15

年１億円を超える金額　　　　　　　　　　　　100分の20

(f)　土地の譲渡益に対する課税については，¶6-670で説明。

(g)　土地の譲渡益に対する特別税率は５％又は10%である（ただし，平成10年から平成25年12月31日までの間は，不適用）（¶6-670参照）。

(h)　使途秘匿金に対する特別課税については，¶6-675で説明。

(i)　税額控除とは算出税額から控除するものであり，次のものがある（¶6-690参照）。

　(ｉ)　仮装経理に基づく過大申告により納付された法人税額のうち，その過大部分の法人税額の控除

　(ⅱ)　源泉徴収される所得税額の控除

360 CORPORATION TAX

source,

    (iii) a tax credit for experimental expenditure, an investment tax credit for specified equipment, etc. and

    (iv) a credit for foreign taxes to eliminate international double taxation.

(j) When the accounting period of an ordinary corporation exceeds six months, the prepayment should be made for the first six months of the accounting period (see ¶ 6-800).

(k) Where the total of income tax credits and prepayments exceeds the amount of tax on ordinary income, the excess is refunded to the corporation (see ¶ 6-805).

¶ 6-065 Annual basis

The provisions of the tax legislation are often expressed in terms of a 12-month business year. If a corporation has a business year (see ¶ 6-100) shorter than a calendar year, then each figure regarding its income should be converted into a figure in annual terms. For example, the rate of tax on ordinary income of a small corporation in the range up to ¥8 million per annum is reduced. In this case, if a corporation has a business year of six months, this reduced rate should be applied in the range up to ¥4 million (six-twelfths of ¥8 million) accruing in its six-month business year (Law 66④).

Tax on Liquidation Income
(Special taxation rule for liquidation income was abolished from October 1, 2010.)

¶ 6-070 Tax basis and rates

The tax on liquidation income is computed in the following way:

Liquidation income (a) × tax rate (b) + additional tax on capital gains from lands (¶ 6-670) and on beneficiary-concealed-disbursement (¶ 6-675) – tax credits (c)

= tax on liquidation income (d), which should be paid through

(i) periodic prepayment, (ii) non-periodic prepayment, or (iii) final payment.

(a) Liquidation income is the value of the residual assets of a corporation which is being wound up or dissolved, which are to be distributed to shareholders, less the total of its capital, capital

¶ 6-065

法　人　税　361

(iii)　試験研究支出に係る法人税額の特別控除，特定設備を取得した場合の法人税額の特別控除（投資税額控除）等及び

(iv)　国際的二重課税を排除するための外国税額の控除

(j)　中間納付税額とは普通法人の事業年度が6ヶ月を超える場合に，当該事業年度の最初の6ヶ月に対応するものとして，予納しなければならないものである（¶6-800参照）。

(k)　所得税額控除の額及び外国税額控除並びに中間納付額の合計額が各事業年度の所得に対する法人税の額を超える場合には，その超過額は法人に還付される（¶6-805参照）。

¶6-065　1年間の基準

　税法では12ヶ月の事業年度を基準とする規定がしばしば用いられている。法人の事業年度（¶6-100参照）が1暦年に満たない場合には，所得に係る各種の金額は当該事業年度の月数に応じて調整した金額とされる。例えば，中小法人の年800万円以下の所得金額については，その法人税率は軽減される。この場合，事業年度が6ヶ月である法人については，この軽減税率は当該6ヶ月の事業年度に対応して400万円（800万円×6／12）以下の金額に適用される（法法66④）。

清算所得に対する法人税
（平成22年10月1日から，清算所得課税は廃止され，通常の所得課税に移行した。）

¶6-070　課税標準及び税率

　清算所得に対する法人税は次の方式により計算される。

　　清算所得(a)×税率(b)＋土地重課（¶6-670）及び使途秘匿金課税（¶6-675）－税額控除(c)＝清算所得に対する法人税額(d)

　この税額は，(i)清算中の予納，(ii)残余財産の一部分配に係る予納，及び(iii)確定納付により納付しなければならない。

(a)　清算所得とは，解散した法人が株主へ分配する残余財産の価額から資本金額，資本積立金額及び利益積立金額（¶6-080参照）の合計額を控除した金額である（法法93）。

362 CORPORATION TAX

surplus and retained earnings (¶ 6-080) (Law 93).

(b) The tax rate on liquidation income (Law 99) is:

Ordinary corporations.. 27.1%

Cooperatives.. 20.5%

(c) Income tax credit (¶ 6-840) may be deducted from the tax amount reached by applying the tax rate (Law 100).

(d) The tax on liquidation income can be paid in any of the following three ways, if a corporation is liquidated.

(i) **Periodic prepayment:** A corporation must pay tax periodically on income accruing in every business year even after the opening of liquidation proceedings (Law 102 and 105). The amount of tax payable is equivalent to tax on ordinary income, but the tax represents a tax on liquidation income prepaid, because the corporation is exempt from tax on ordinary income after the opening of liquidation proceedings (¶ 6-825).

(ii) **Non-periodic prepayment:** If a corporation makes any interim distribution of its residual assets during the liquidation proceedings, it must make a non-periodic prepayment before making such an interim distribution (Law 103, 106) (¶ 6-830).

(iii) **Final payment:** The residue of the tax on liquidation income should be paid immediately before the last distribution of the residual assets by the liquidating corporation itself (Law 104, 107) (¶ 6-835).

If the tax credits or prepayments exceed the amount of tax on liquidation income, the excess is to be refunded (Law 109, 110).

¶ 6-080 Capital etc, retained earnings

Amounts of capital etc. mean contributed amounts from shareholders into a corporation, that is, amounts of capital and reserves (Law 2).

Amounts of retained earnings mean retained income in a corporation (Law 2).

¶ 6-080

法　人　税　363

(b) 清算所得に対する法人税率は次のとおりである（法法99）。
普通法人　　　　　　　　　　　　　　27.1%
協同組合等　　　　　　　　　　　　　20.5%
(c) 税率を適用して算出した税額から所得税額控除（¶6-840参照）が行われる（法法100）。
(d) 清算所得に対する法人税は次の三つの方法により納付される。

(i) **清算中の予納：**　法人は清算手続開始後においても各事業年度に生じた所得に対する税を納付するものとされる（法法102，105）。納付すべき税額は，法人は清算中の事業年度においては各事業年度の所得に対する法人税は非課税とされるため，予納すべき清算所得に対する税額で示されるが，各事業年度の所得に対する法人税に相当するものである（¶6-825参照）。

(ii) **残余財産の一部分配に係る予納：**　法人が清算中に残余財産の一部を分配する場合には，当該一部分配を行う前に予納額を納付しなければならない（法法103，106）（¶6-830参照）。

(iii) **確定納付：**　清算所得に対する法人税の残りの金額は，残余財産の最後の分配が行われる直前に法人自身が納付しなければならない（法法104，107）（¶6-835参照）。

税額控除額及び予納額が清算所得に対する法人税額を超える場合には，その超過額は還付される（法法109，110）。

¶6-080　資本金等の額，利益積立金額

資本金等の額とは，法人が株主等から出資を受けた金額で，法人の資本金の額及び準備金の額等をいう（法法2）。

利益積立金額とは，法人の所得の金額のうち留保している金額をいう（法法2）。

364   CORPORATION TAX

Tax on Specific Funds

¶ 6-090 Tax on specific funds (The taxation is suspended from April 1, 1999 until March 31, 2017.)

Tax on specific funds is levied on insurance companies, trust companies, banking companies, stock companies and cooperatives carrying on either an approved pension business, an employees' welfare pension business or an employees' assets formation business (Law 8). These businesses may be carried on by domestic corporations (Foreign corporations are included in taxable corporations from April 1, 2000). The tax amounts are 1% per annum of the specific funds at the beginning of the business year (Law 87).

(The tax qualified pension fund regime was abolished from April 1, 2002 and a new pension fund agreement is not treated as a tax qualified agreement. Existing agreements are, however, treated as tax qualified pension fund agreements until March 31, 2012.)

ORDINARY INCOME

Basic Concepts in Computing Ordinary Income

¶ 6-100 Business year

The business year for tax purposes usually means the accounting period provided for in the statute of a corporation (Law 13). If a corporation's accounting period is a calendar year, corporation tax is usually levied on the income accruing in a calendar year. If a corporation's accounting periods are, for example, April 1 to September 30 and October 1 to March 31, the corporation tax is levied on the income accruing in each accounting period.

If a corporation's accounting period is longer than one year, each year and fraction of a year in such an accounting period are treated as separate business years.

¶ 6-110 Adjustment of net profit for tax purposes

The computation of taxable net income follows generally accepted accounting principles as far as possible (Law 22).

The 1967 Amendment added a provision stating that revenues, costs and expenses must be calculated in accordance with generally accepted

¶ 6-090

法　人　税　365

退職年金等積立金に対する法人税

¶6-090　退職年金等積立金に対する法人税（平成11年4月1日から平成29年3月31日まで課税なし。）

退職年金等積立金に対する法人税は，適格退職年金契約，厚生年金基金契約又は勤労者財産形成給付契約の業務を行う法人（平成12年4月1日より外国法人を含む。）である保険会社，信託会社，銀行及び証券会社並びに協同組合等に対して課される（法法8）。その税額は各事業年度の期首における退職年金等積立金額について，毎年100分の1の税率により算出される（法法87）。

（なお，適格退職年金制度は，平成14年3月31日において廃止され，平成14年4月1日以後は，原則として新たな契約の締結は適格退職年金契約として認められないこととなった。ただし，現に締結されている適格退職年金制度については，平成24年3月31日までに限り経過的に存続することとされている。）

各事業年度の所得に対する法人税

所得の計算の通則

¶6-100　事業年度

課税上，事業年度は，通常，法人の定款に定められた会計期間をいう（法法13）。法人の会計期間が暦年である場合には，法人税は原則として暦年中に生じた所得について課される。例えば，法人の会計期間が4月1日から9月30日までの期間と10月1日から3月31日までの期間である場合には，法人税は各会計期間中に生じた所得について課される。

法人の会計期間が1年を超える場合には，当該会計期間中の1年間とその端数の期間はそれぞれ独立した別個の事業年度として取り扱われる。

¶6-110　企業利益の課税目的上の調整

課税所得は一般に公正妥当と認められる会計処理の基準に従って計算されるのが原則である（法法22）。

昭和42年の税制改正において，収益，原価及び費用は一般に公正妥当と認められる会計処理の基準に従って計算される旨の規定が追加された（法法22④）。

366   CORPORATION TAX

accounting principles (Law 22④).

However, the method of computing taxable net income deviates from generally accepted accounting principles at several points, and it is important to understand the interrelation between the two methods.

The revenues, costs and expenses of the profit and loss statement may be divided into several categories:

(1) Some items will be identical in the business accounts and the computation of taxable net income. Therefore an amount treated as expenses in the business accounts can be deducted from revenue in computation of taxable income. However, if the amount is over the limit prescribed for the purpose of corporation tax, the excess amount should be adjusted in the tax return.

(2) Some items in the business accounts must be adjusted in the tax return so as to conform with the requirements of the Corporation Tax Law and the Special Taxation Measures Law, if the figures in the business accounts are over the limits prescribed by these tax laws.

(3) Some items in the business accounts may, at the discretion of the corporation, be adjusted in computing the taxable net income and such adjustments may not be ignored or readjusted by the Tax Authority, in so far as they are legal.

Examples of these categories are given below.

(1) Identical items are:
  (a) depreciation of fixed assets,
  (b) amortization of some deferred assets, and
  (c) credits to various reserve accounts.

(2) Items which must be adjusted are:
  (a) contributions paid out,
  (b) entertainment expenses,
  (c) taxes and fines not deductible for tax purposes, and
  (d) bonuses paid to directors (not deductible for tax purposes).

(3) Items which may be adjusted at the discretion of a corporation are:
  (a) dividends received (exempt), and
  (b) withholding income tax and foreign taxes (which may be credited or deducted).
  (c) special income deductions.

¶ 6-110

法　人　税　367

　しかしながら，課税所得の計算方法は一般に公正妥当と認められる会計処理の基準とはいくつかの点で異なるので，この二つの計算方法の関連を理解することが重要である。

　損益計算書上の収益，原価及び費用は，いくつかの項目に分けられる。

(1)　第一は，企業経理上費用として経理されない限り，課税所得計算上控除されない項目である。ただし，企業経理上費用として経理されていても，課税所得計算上の限度額を超える部分は確定申告書において調整される必要がある。

(2)　第二は，企業経理上の処理が課税所得計算上の要件と合わない場合に，企業経理上計算された所得を税法上の要件に合致させるために確定申告書において調整しなければならない項目である。

(3)　第三は，法人の任意により課税所得の計算上調整できる項目であり，当該調整はそれらが適法である限り課税当局により無視されたり，再調整されることはない。

例示
(1)　企業経理が必要な項目
　(a)　固定資産の減価償却
　(b)　繰延資産の償却
　(c)　種々の引当金又は準備金勘定への繰入れ
(2)　税務調整が必要な項目
　(a)　支払寄附金
　(b)　交際費
　(c)　損金不算入の租税及び罰金
　(d)　役員への支払賞与（課税上控除されない）
(3)　法人が任意に調整できる項目
　(a)　受取配当（非課税）
　(b)　源泉所得税及び外国法人税（損金算入又は税額控除）

　(c)　種々の所得控除の特例

368   CORPORATION TAX

¶ 6-120 Accrual basis

The amount of ordinary income for each business year is computed on an accrual basis, unless the contrary is clearly provided.

¶ 6-125 Capital gains

No tax concession is granted on capital gains derived by a corporation, with the exceptions regarding exchange, replacement and expropriation described in ¶ 6-495 and ¶ 6-505.

¶ 6-130 Ordinary income

The tax base for ordinary income tax is the corporation's net income for each business year. Net income is the excess of "gross income" over "total costs" for each business year (Law 21, 22).

"Gross income" is the increase in the value of assets from all transactions including the sale or manufacture of goods, the provision of services, gifts of goods, other than gain from capital transactions (see ¶ 6-135 and ¶ 6-150 to ¶ 6-200).

"Total costs" is the decrease in value of assets from all causes including the cost of acquisitions, business expenses and losses other than from certain capital transactions such as reimbursement of capital or distribution of profits (see ¶ 6-140 and ¶ 6-205 to ¶ 6-580).

In short, gross income minus total cost represents ordinary income for tax purposes. Though the tax laws require or allow some adjustments of corporate profit calculated in accordance with generally accepted accounting principles in reaching the ordinary income, the calculation of corporate net income generally follows normal accounting principles and practice.

¶ 6-135 Gross income

Transactions giving rise to gross income (Law 22②) are as follows:

(1) Sales of assets (sales of goods, products, etc).

(2) Transfer of assets (transfer of assets such as securities and fixed assets, etc).

(3) Provision of service (contracts and the provision of other services).

(4) Free transfer of assets or provision of services.

(5) Free reception of assets.

(6) Other transactions (interest on deposits, interest on loans and others).

¶ 6-120

法 人 税　369

¶6-120　発生主義
各事業年度の収益の金額は，明らかに反対の規定がない限り発生主義により計算される。

¶6-125　キャピタル・ゲイン
法人の取得するキャピタル・ゲインは¶6-495及び¶6-505に記述する交換，買換及び収用に関する例外を除き，課税上の特別措置がない。

¶6-130　各事業年度の所得
各事業年度の所得に対する法人税の課税標準となる各事業年度の所得の金額は，各事業年度の益金の額から損金の額を控除した金額である（法法21，22）。

収益（益金）とは，資本取引以外のすべての取引（商品又は製品の販売，役務の提供，資産の無償譲受けを含む。）による資産の増加額である。

費用（損金）とは，資本等取引以外の資産の減少額（原価，費用，損失）である（¶6-140，¶6-205～¶6-580参照）。

要するに，益金の額から損金の額を控除した差額が課税上の各事業年度の所得である。税法上，各事業年度の所得を計算するために，一般に公正妥当と認められる会計処理の基準に従って計算された法人の利益から若干の調整が要求され又は認められているが，法人の課税所得の計算は，原則として一般の会計原則及び慣行に従って行われる。

¶6-135　益金
益金を生じる取引は次のとおりである（法法22②）。
(1)　資産の販売（商品，製品等の販売）
(2)　有償による資産の譲渡（有価証券，固定資産等の資産の譲渡）
(3)　有償による役務の提供（請負及びその他の役務の提供）
(4)　無償による資産の譲渡又は役務の提供
(5)　無償による資産の譲受け
(6)　その他の取引（預金の利子，貸付金等の利子）

370 CORPORATION TAX

Note:

Corporations, as economic entities, should not behave unreasonably from an economic point of view. So even when they transfer their assets free of charge, the amount equivalent to the current price of the assets is included in gross income. Similarly, when a corporation receipts assets free of charge or at an extraordinarily low price compared with the current price of the assets, the amount equivalent to the current price or the amount equivalent to the difference between the current price and the extraordinarily low price is also included in gross income.

If a corporation receives contributions in money or in kind, the amount of the money received or the fair market value of property received is usually included in the gross income of the corporation.

If a corporation is released from its debts by the action of any other person, the corporation is usually deemed to have received a contribution from that person.

Special stipulations

Those items of gross income which accrue from transactions by corporations and which are stipulated to be excluded from gross revenue by special provisions and regulations are not included in gross income.

Examples of exclusions from gross income include dividends received, increases in the book value of assets, tax refunds.

There are also regulations which specifically stipulate items to be included in gross income. Examples of inclusions in gross income include amounts added back in full into gross income in the following accounting period out of a reserve for bad debts or reserves for loss on the return of unsold goods. The tax haven countermeasure (¶ 6-195) and the taxation measure for transfer pricing (¶ 6-200) are also included in special stipulations.

¶ 6-140 Total costs (business expenses)

A corporation's "total costs" (or business expenses) for a business year is used to determine net income. Total costs are categorized as follows (Law 22③):

(1) Costs of acquisitions, costs of completed construction work, and other costs corresponding to the gross income derived in the business year under review.

(2) Besides those mentioned above, sales expenses, general administrative expenses and other expenses accrued in the business year under review.

(3) Losses incurred in the business year under review accruing from

¶ 6-140

法　人　税　371

(注)：経済人である法人は経済的に合理性のない活動を行うはずがない。したがって，たとえ法人が対価を受領することなく資産を譲渡した場合であっても，法人はその資産の譲渡により通常受領する時価相当額の収入があったものとみなされる。すなわち，資産の時価に相当する金額は益金の額に算入される。また，法人が資産を無償又は時価と比べて著しく低い価額により譲り受けた場合には，時価に相当する金額又は時価と著しく低い価額との差額に相当する金額は益金の額に算入される。

　　　法人が金銭その他の寄付金を受領する場合には，受領した金銭の額及び受領した資産の価額は，原則として法人の益金の額に算入する。

　　　法人が第三者の行為により債務免除を受けた場合には，法人は当該第三者から寄付金を受領したものとみなされるのが原則である。

(別段の規定)

　法人の取引から生じる収益であっても，法令上益金の額に算入しないとして別段の定めがあるものは，収益の額に含まれない。

　例えば，受取配当，資産の評価益，還付税額につき，益金不算入の規定がある。

　また，法令上，特別に益金の額に算入するものとする別段の定めもある。例えば，貸倒引当金や返品調整引当金については計上の翌事業年度において全額洗い直して益金の額に算入することとなる。さらに，タックスヘイブン対策税制（¶6-195参照）及び移転価格税制（¶6-200参照）も別段の定めである。

¶6-140　損金
　損金は次のように分類される（法法22③）。

(1)　当該事業年度の収益に係る売上原価，完成工事原価その他これらに準ずる原価の額

(2)　上記のほか，当該事業年度に発生した販売費，一般管理費その他の費用

(3)　当該事業年度の損失の額で資本等取引以外の取引に係るもの

372 CORPORATION TAX

transactions other than capital transactions, etc.

Costs

"Costs" include the outlays needed to derive gross income, such as the cost of buying commodities sold, the cost of manufacturing products sold, fixed assets acquired, transfer costs of securities, etc, the costs of construction work, contract costs, etc.

Expenses

"Expenses" include various expenditures incurred in the business year including selling expenses, etc. Expenses which have not become payable in that accounting period are not recognized as expenses except for the depreciation. Usually a corporation sets aside money to cover expenses if the cause of a liability has come into being, even if the liability itself has not been established. Under the tax law, amounts set aside as security for such expenses are not recognized except in the case of special stipulations, such as reserves, special depreciation, etc.

Special stipulations

The above-mentioned costs, sales expenses and other expenses, as well as those which are not normally regarded as expenses such as losses, or which have been specifically stipulated by laws and regulations as deductible expenses, are included in expenses under the Corporation Tax Law.

For instance, the following items are included in expenses: the amount credited to various kinds of reserves such as reserves for bad debts, etc. (¶ 6-350); the reduced amount of the book value of assets acquired by government subsidies, insurance compensation, etc. (¶ 6-495, ¶ 6-500); seven-year carried-over losses (¶ 6-570); and special deductions for profit from transfer of assets expropriated (¶ 6-505).

Some expenses that correspond to expenditures and losses for accounting purposes are not included as expenses for the purposes of the Corporation Tax Law. For instance, the following items are excluded from expenses: corporation tax and fines, etc.; amounts exceeding a reasonable amount of contributions (¶ 6-235); amounts exceeding a reasonable amount for entertainment expenses; amounts exceeding a reasonable amount for depreciation of depreciable assets or for deferred expenses; loss of assets by unreasonable reevaluations; officers' bonuses; and excessive officers' salaries. A special stipulation includes the taxation measure for transfer pricing (¶ 6-200).

¶ 6-140

（原価の額）

　原価の額とは，商品の売上原価，販売した製品の製造原価，譲渡資産の取得原価，証券等の取得原価，完成工事原価，請負契約の請負原価などの収益を稼得するのに必要とされる原価である。

（費用の額）

　費用の額とは，商品及び製品の販売費，一般管理費等を含む当該事業年度に属する種々の支出の額である。これらの費用は減価償却費を除き，当該事業年度において債務として確定していなければならない。一般に，法人は債務が確定していなくとも，債務の原因が発生している場合には経費として計上する。しかし，税法上は，別段の定め（例えば引当金制度）があるものを除き，当該経費は認められない。

（別段の定め）

　上記の原価，販売経費及びその他の費用（損失とされない経費を含む。）のほか，法令上損金の額に算入されるものとして別段の定めのあるものは，損金の額に算入される。

　例えば，貸倒引当金などのような種々の引当金計上額，国庫補助金，保険差益，工事負担金により取得した資産の帳簿価額の圧縮額（¶6-495，6-500），7年以内の繰越欠損金（¶6-570），収用資産の譲渡益に係る特別控除額（¶6-505）は損金の額に算入される。

　各事業年度における費用又は損失に相当する金額であっても，法人税法上別段の定めがあるものは，損金の額に算入されない。例えば，法人税及び罰科金，寄附金の限度超過額，交際費の限度超過額，減価償却資産及び繰延資産の償却費の限度超過額，資産の不適切な再評価による評価損，役員の過大退職給与，過大役員報酬などは損金の額に算入されない。また，移転価格税制（¶6-200参照）も別段の定めである。

374   CORPORATION TAX

¶ 6-145 Capital transactions

Gross income from capital transactions is not included in the amount of taxable gross income, and loss from capital transactions is not included in the amount of deductible losses either. Capital transactions are transactions which bring about increases or decreases in the amount of the capital of a corporation, and include distribution of profits and surpluses (Law 22⑤).

Amounts of capital etc. mean contributed amounts from shareholders into a corporation, that is, amounts of capital and reserves (Law 2).

Items excluded from gross income

The following are not included in the amount of gross income according to what is mentioned above:

(1) The amount of capital paid.

(2) The amount of the prices of issued stock exceeding the amount capitalized.

(3) Profits from capital reduction when capital is reduced free of charge or when capital is reduced by buying back shares below their face value.

Items excluded from expenses

(1) Reductions in value of assets from reductions in face value of shares.

(2) The amount of dividends or bonuses expended as distribution of profit or surpluses.

Gross Income

¶ 6-150 Dividends received (exclusion from gross income)

Dividends* received by domestic corporations from other domestic corporations, less the interest chargeable to the shares on which those dividends were paid, are excluded from gross income in computing the amount of ordinary income (Law 23).

The exclusion ratios from the dividends are as follows;

(1) 100%, if it owns shares more than 1/3 of those issued by the corporation

(2) 50%, in case other than (1) and (3)

(3) 20%, if it owns shares less than 5% of those issued by the corporation

If dividends are received on shares which were acquired within one

¶ 6-145

法　人　税　375

¶6-145　資本等取引

資本等取引からの収益は益金の額に算入されず，また，資本等取引からの損失は損金の額に算入されない。これらの資本等取引とは，法人の資本等の金額の増加，利益又は剰余金の分配など資産の増加又は減少をもたらす取引をいう（法法22⑤）。

資本金等の額とは，法人が株主等から出資を受けた金額で，法人の資本金の額及び準備金の額等をいう（法法2）。

（益金の額に算入されないもの）

次に掲げる項目は，上に述べた理由により益金の額に算入されない。

(1)　出資払込金額
(2)　株式の発行価額のうち資本に組み入れられなかった金額

(3)　有償又は無償減資による減資差益

（損金の額に算入されないもの）

(1)　減資による資産の減少額

(2)　利益又は剰余金の分配として支出される配当

益　　金

¶6-150　受取配当（益金不算入）

内国法人が他の内国法人から支払を受ける配当の額（負債利子を控除した金額）については，所得の金額の計算上，その一定割合を益金の額に算入しない（法法23）。

益金不算入割合は以下のとおりである。
(1)　法人が他の法人の発行済株式等の3分の1を超える株式等を有する場合，100％
(2)　(1)及び(3)以外の場合，50％
(3)　法人が他の法人の発行済株式等の5％以下に相当する株式等を有する場合，20％
法人が支払を受ける配当の元本である株式を当該配当の計算期間の末日以

376   CORPORATION TAX

month prior to the end of the business year of the issuing corporation and sold within two months after the end of the same business year, those dividends are not excluded from gross income.

> * "Dividends" includes interim dividends as provided in the Commercial Code and constructive dividends (¶ 6-155).

¶ 6-152   Exemption of dividends received from foreign subsidiary

Dividends received from a foreign subsidiary are exempted from taxable income of its Japanese parent company. The foreign subsidiary is defined as a foreign company whose 25% or more capital has been owned by a Japanese corporation for more than 6 months before the determination date of payment of the dividends. If a tax treaty applicable to the foreign subsidiary has a different percentage from the 25%, the percentage stipulated in the tax treaty shall be applied (Law 23-2).

If, however, the dividends are deducted as expenses for tax purposes in the country where the head office of the foreign subsidiary is located, the dividends are excluded from the dividends income exemption rule.

Exempted amounts are 95% of that of the dividends. Foreign withholding taxes assessed on the dividends are neither deducted as expenses (Law 39-2) nor credited against Japanese corporate taxes of the parent company. The indirect foreign tax credit system was abolished (see ¶ 6-750).

¶ 6-155   Constructive dividends received

Cash distributions exceeded reduced capital amounts due to a capital reduction, or the dissolution of a corporation, etc. are treated as dividends (Law 24).

¶ 6-158   Revaluation profits (exclusion from gross income)

Profit from the revaluation of an asset is excluded from gross income, regardless of whether or not the new book value of the asset is its fair market value.

However, the following types of reevaluations are exceptions for tax purposes and the revaluation profits are included in gross income (Law 25):

(1) Revaluations of assets in accordance with the Corporation Reorganization Law or the Civil Rehabilitation Law; and

(2) Revaluations of stock by an insurance company, based on the Insurance Business Law.

¶ 6-152

法　人　税　377

前 1 ヶ月以内に取得し，かつ，同日後 2 ヶ月以内に譲渡した場合には，その
受取配当については益金不算入は適用されない。

　　（注）：配当には，商法で定める中間配当及びみなし配当（¶6-155）を含む。

¶6-152　外国子会社から受ける配当等の益金不算入

　内国法人が外国法人から受ける配当等のうち，その内国法人が発行済株式
等の25％以上の株式等を配当等の支払義務が確定する日以前 6 ヶ月以上引き
続き直接に有している外国法人（外国子会社）から受ける配当等の額は，所
得の金額の計算上益金の額に算入されない。なお，当該25％の基準について
は，租税条約で異なる割合が定められている場合には，その割合による（法
法23の 2 ）。
　ただし，その配当等の額の全部又は一部が当該外国子会社の本店所在地国
等の法令において当該外国子会社の所得の金額の計算上損金の額に算入する
こととされている場合には，その配当等の額は，外国子会社配当益金不算入
制度の適用対象から除外される。
　益金不算入とされる額は，当該配当等の額の95％相当額である。その配当
等の額に対して課される外国源泉税等の額は，所得の金額の計算上損金の額
に算入されず（法法39の 2 ），また，外国税額控除の対象にならない。なお，間
接外国税額控除制度は，経過措置等を講じた上，廃止された（¶6-750参照）。

¶6-155　みなし受取配当

　法人の減資，解散等により出資額を超えて支払を受けた場合における当該
超えて支払を受けた金額は配当の支払とみなされる（法法24）。益金不算入の
規定（¶6-150参照）は当該みなし配当を受領する法人に適用される。

¶6-158　資産の評価益

　課税所得の計算上，法人の有する資産の評価換えによる帳簿価額の変更に
よる損益は，当該評価換えが時価を反映していると否とを問わず，原則とし
てこれを考慮しない。
　資産の評価益は，次の場合等を除き，益金の額に算入されない（法法25）。

　(1)　会社更生法及び民事再生法の規定に従い行う資産の評価換え

　(2)　保険会社が保険業法の規定に基づき行う株式の評価換え

378   CORPORATION TAX

*See ¶ 6-340 (for loss due to changes in book value).

¶ 6-160 Tax refunded (exclusion from gross income)

Refunds of taxes, payments of which are not deductible in computing ordinary income, such as corporation tax, withholding income tax and inhabitant tax, are not included in gross income (Law 26).

¶ 6-170 Ordinary sales

The amounts of taxable revenue related to the sale of assets and provision of services are, in principle, the amounts equivalent to the value of the assets at the transfer or value of services at provision. The amounts shall be included in the revenue in the accounting period during that the transfer is occurred (Law 22-2).

¶ 6-175 Sales reduction, discount, rebate and return of goods

Sales reduction is the reduction of a reasonable amount from sales because the commodities or products sold had material defects such as short weight, poor quality or damage. The amount of sales reduction is deducted from the sales of the current accounting period, irrespective of when the item concerned was sold.

A sales discount means a discount due for payment before the agreed time, and is treated as an expense or deducted from the sales amount in the accounting period in which the sales discount was made.

A sales rebate means a rebate paid to a customer who purchases large quantities in a certain period. The time when a sales rebate should be accounted for is normally decided as follows (R 2-5-1):

(1) if the method of calculating the sales rebate is fixed beforehand, for instance by proportioning it to the amount or quantity of sales, and the other party is informed of it—when the commodities or products are sold;

(2) in other cases—when actual payment is made or the buyer is informed of the amount of the sales rebate.

If commodities or products are returned by the customer after they are sold, their value is deducted from the value of sales in the accounting period in which information of return is received from the customer or the accounting period in which the seller accepted the request for return of the goods, irrespective of when the returned commodities or products

¶ 6-160

法　人　税　379

(注)：評価損については¶6-340参照。

¶6-160　還付金（益金不算入）

法人税，源泉所得税，住民税などのようにその支払について所得金額の計算上損金に算入されない租税の還付金は，益金の額に算入されない（法法26）。

¶6-170　通常の販売

資産の販売，譲渡又は役務の提供に係る収益の額として所得の金額の計算上益金の額に算入する金額は，原則として，その販売をした資産の引渡しの時における価額又はその提供した役務につき通常収受すべき対価に相当する額とし，当該引渡しの日の属する事業年度の益金の額に算入する（法法22の2）。

¶6-175　商品の売上値引，売上割引，売上割戻及び返品

売上値引とは，量目不足，品質不良及び損傷などの品質上の欠陥のために商品又は製品の販売に際して，通常の売価から合理的な金額が減額されるものである。売上値引の金額は，値引の対象となった商品が販売された年度とは関係なく，当該値引の行われた事業年度の売上高から差し引くこととされる。

売上割引は，約定支払期限前に支払を受けたことに対する売価の減額であり，その売上割引が行われた事業年度の損金の額に算入されるか，売上高から差し引くこととされる。

売上割戻は，一定期間内に多額又は多量の取引をした得意先に対する売上代金の返戻金であるが，売上割戻の計上時期は次により決められる（法基通2-5-1）。

(1)　例えば売上の金額又は数量に比例して，というように売上割戻の算定基準があらかじめ定められており，かつ，相手方に通知されている場合──商品又は製品の販売の時

(2)　その他の場合──売上割戻の支払を実際に行った時又は買手が売上割戻額の通知を受けた時

商品又は製品が販売後に販売先から返品された場合には，返品の金額は，当該商品又は製品が実際にいつ販売されたかを問わず，返品の通知を販売先から受けた日又は販売先から返品の要求を受けた日の属する事業年度の売上高から控除する。

380   CORPORATION TAX

were sold.

¶ 6-178 Consignment sales

Revenue from consignment sales is treated as gross income arising in the business year in which the consignee despatched the goods or the business year in which the consignor received the consignment note for the goods from the consignee (R 2-1-3).

¶ 6-180 Installment sales, etc.

The special income recognition rule for installment sale was eliminated on April 1, 2020. The current treatment described below is, however, applicable until the accounting period beginning on or before March 31, 2023 for the corporations which have elected the rules before April 1, 2018. Furthermore, transitional measures were given where the corporation could amortize one tenth of the deferred income for 10 years after it ceases to adopt the income recognition rule.

A taxpayer has the option of keeping his or her accounts on an installment basis, provided that it is consistently applied to certain deferred payment transactions with deferred payment clauses (Law 63).

When accounting on an installment basis is applied, the net profit accruing in a business year is computed as follows:

$$\left(\text{considera-}\atop\text{tion (A)} - {\text{costs of goods, etc.,}\atop\text{mentioned in (A),}\atop\text{including commissions}\atop\text{paid to sales agents}}\right) \times \frac{\text{installment payments which became receivable in a business year or which were received before maturity in a business year}}{\text{(A)}}$$

Deferred payment transactions with deferred payment clauses are sales of properties, contracts for construction work or provision of services, but nevertheless meet the following conditions:

(i)   payment must be made in three or more installments, either monthly, annually or otherwise periodically;

(ii) the period from the date of delivery of the object of the sale or contract to the due date for the last installment must be at least two years; and

法 人 税　381

¶6-178　商品の委託販売

委託販売による収益の額は，その委託品について受託者が販売をした日（受託者からの売上計算書の到着日とすることが認められる場合もある。）を含む事業年度の益金に計上される（法基通2-1-3）。

¶6-180　長期割賦販売等

長期割賦販売等に該当する資産の販売等について延払基準により収益の額及び費用の額を計算する下記の選択制度は，平成30年3月31日をもって廃止された。なお，平成30年4月1日前に長期割賦販売等に該当する資産の販売等を行った法人について，平成35年3月31日までに開始する各事業年度について現行の延払基準により収益の額及び費用の額を計算することができることとするとともに，平成30年4月1日以後に終了する事業年度において延払基準の適用をやめた場合の繰延割賦利益額を10年均等等で収益計上する等の経過措置がある。

納税者は，長期割賦販売等について，継続的に適用することを条件として，延払基準の方法により経理することを選択できる（法法63）。

延払基準の方法が適用される場合には，各事業年度の純損益の額は次により算出される。

$$\left[\text{当該取引の対価の額}☒ - \text{☒に係る原価の額（販売手数料を含む。）}\right] \times \frac{\text{賦払金のうち当期に支払期日が到来するもの又は当期に支払期日未到来のものの受領額}}{☒}$$

長期割賦販売等は，資産の譲渡，工事の請負又は役務の提供で次に掲げる要件に適合するものが該当する。

(i) 月賦，年賦その他の賦払いの方法により3回以上に分割して対価が支払われること
(ii) その販売又は請負の目的物の引渡しの期日の翌日から最後の賦払金の支払の期日までの期間が2年以上であること

382 CORPORATION TAX

(iii) the amount payable by the date of delivery must not exceed two-thirds of the total liability for the sale or contract.

¶ 6-185 Long-term contracts

Net profit accruing from a contract is, in principle, reported in the business year in which the contract is fulfilled, despite the fact that it may cover more than one business year. This rule may be referred to as the completed contract rule.

Under certain circumstances a partial completion rule is applicable.

The partial completion rule may be applied when:

(1) many units of buildings, etc. of the same or similar type are constructed under one contract, but they are accepted unit by unit as they are completed and the proceeds of the contract are received as the units are accepted; or

(2) in accordance with a contract or commercial custom the proceeds of the contract are divided into several parts, each of which is paid as the construction is accepted in parts.

Under the partial completion rule, gross income and expenditures attributable to completed and accepted parts are taken into account in the business year in which such parts were accepted (R 2-1-9).

However, a percentage of completion method has to be applied to long-term and large-scale contracts.

A percentage of the completion method may be applied only when the work lasts one year or more, the contract price of the work is 1 billion yen or over, and that more than half of construction fees are determined to be paid within one year after delivery of the asset (Law 64). Under this rule, net profits of a business year is usually computed as follows:

$$\text{estimated total profits from the work} \times \frac{\text{total costs of the work which became payable in the business year}}{\text{estimated total expenses for the work}} - \text{total profits of the previous business years with respect to the work}$$

¶ 6-188 Remuneration and fees, etc., for technical services

Remuneration and fees, etc., for technical services such as the supervision of a plan or of construction work and the like and technical consultation, etc., are included in the gross income of the business year in which those technical services were completed (R 2-1-12).

¶ 6-185

法　人　税　383

(iii)　引渡しの期日までの支払金額が譲渡又は請負のすべての対価の3分の2以下となっていること

¶6-185　長期大規模工事の請負

　工事請負契約に基づく損益は，その工事が2事業年度以上にわたる場合においても，原則としてその工事が完成した事業年度に帰属する。この原則は工事完成基準といわれる。

　また，一定の条件のもとに部分完成基準が適用される。
　部分完成基準とは，
(1)　一つの契約により同一又は同様の建築工事の多くの単位が施工され，完了した工事の単位ごとに承認され，かつ，承認された単位ごとに工事代金が支払われるものであるとき，又は，

(2)　契約又は商慣習によって工事代金がいくつかに区分され，その区分ごとに工事が承認されてその区分ごとに支払われるときに適用される。

　部分完成基準では，当該区分工事が承認された事業年度において，完了又は承認された区分工事に係る収益の額及び費用の額が帰属する（法基通2-1-9）。
　しかしながら，長期大規模工事については，課税上，工事進行基準が適用されなければならない。
　工事進行基準は，その工事が1年以上継続するもので，その工事の対価が10億円以上で，かつ，その請負の対価の額の2分の1以上がその工事の目的物の引渡しの期日から1年を経過する日後に支払われることが定められていないものについて適用される（法法64）。この基準では，各事業年度の利益金額は，通常次のように計算される。

$$\text{工事により見積もられる利益の合計額} \times \frac{\text{各事業年度において支出した工事原価の合計額}}{\text{工事により見積もられる工事原価の合計額}} - \text{前事業年度までの工事利益の合計額}$$

¶6-188　技術役務の提供対価等

　設計，作業の指揮監督，技術指導その他の技術役務の提供を行ったことにより受ける報酬の額は，役務の全部の提供を完了した日又はその報酬の額が確定した日の属する事業年度の益金の額に算入するのが原則である（法基通2-1-12）。

384   CORPORATION TAX

¶ 6-189 Sales of securities

Capital gains from the sales of securities are included in the income of the business year in which an agreement is concluded (Law 61-2).
(Short term sale commodity)

If a corporation transfers a Short Term Sale Commodity, the capital gain shall be recorded in the accounting period where it enters into the sale agreement (Law 61).

¶ 6-190 Capital gains

Capital gains are also accounted for under the delivery rule. Revenue from the transfer of a fixed asset is included in the gross income of the business year in which delivery was made.

However, with respect to land, buildings and the like, capital gains are derived on the date when the contract for the transfer of the asset was made (R 2-1-14).

¶ 6-193 Leasehold

Premiums paid by a lessee should be included in gross income.

Note:
> If the value of land decreases by more than 50% due to the grant of a lease, that part of the book value corresponding to depreciation of the land may be included in total costs (Reg 138).

Even if a landlord grants a lease without receiving a premium, he or she is deemed to receive the amount which the lessee has to pay as premium and, therefore, that amount should be included in the gross income of the landlord. In this case, the premium amount is deemed to be a contribution to the lessee by the landlord for the purpose of calculating the net income of the landlord (Reg 137). This treatment is not applied if the agreement provides that the lease can be terminated without compensation (R 13-1-7).

¶ 6-195 Undistributed profits of foreign subsidiaries (tax haven countermeasure)

When a domestic corporation (including its directors, corporations controlled by the directors and a family corporation group) owns 10% or more of the issued stocks of a foreign subsidiary in a tax haven, such portion of undistributed profits as is appropriate to the share is included in the gross

¶ 6-189

法　人　税　385

¶6-189　有価証券の譲渡収益

　法人が有価証券の譲渡をした場合の譲渡損益は契約をした日に発生したものとする（法法61の2）。

（短期売買商品）

　法人が短期売買商品の譲渡をした場合の譲渡損益はその譲渡に係る契約をした日の属する事業年度の損益の額に算入する（法法61）。

¶6-190　固定資産の譲渡収益

　固定資産の譲渡による収益は，その引渡しの日の属する事業年度の益金の額に算入する。ただし，その固定資産が土地，建物その他これに類する資産である場合には，譲渡契約の効力発生の日の属する事業年度の益金の額に算入することが認められる（法基通2-1-14）。

¶6-193　借地権の設定に伴う権利金

　土地に借地権を設定し，又はこれを更新するときに取得する権利金は，益金の額に算入される。

　　（注）：借地権の設定により土地の価額が2分の1以下に下った場合には，その土地の帳簿価額のうち地価の下落に対応する部分の金額は損金の額に算入される（法令138）。

　権利金を支払う慣行がある土地に借地権を設定させた場合において，権利金を取得しないときは，その権利金の取得があったものとみなされ，賃貸人の所得計算上，当該金額の益金算入が行われるとともに，その権利金相当額を相手方に贈与したものとして扱われる（法令137）。ただし，借地契約書にその土地を無償で返還することが定められており，その旨を土地所有者と借地人とが連名で税務署長に届け出たときは，権利金の取得があったものとみなされない（法基通13-1-7）。

¶6-195　外国会社の留保金額（タックスヘイブン対策税制）

　内国法人（同族株主グループ及び当該内国法人の役員及び当該役員等が支配する法人を含む。）がタックスヘイブン所在外国子会社の株式の10％以上を所有している場合には，その外国子会社の留保所得のうち当該持分に対応する部分の金額は内国法人の益金の額に算入する（措法66の6）。

　タックスヘイブン所在外国子会社とは，その発行済株式又は議決権ある株

income of that domestic corporation. A foreign subsidiary in a tax haven includes a foreign corporation more than 50% of whose issued stocks or voting-right stocks or preferred stocks is directly or indirectly owned by residents (including non-residents specially connected with them and directors of domestic corporations) or domestic corporations (including corporations controlled by the directors), and whose head office is located in a country or territory whose income tax burden is (a) under 30% or less in case that the corporation is classified as a Paper Company or a Cash Box, or (b) under 20% or less in case that the corporation is classified as other than those (SM 66-6).

If a foreign subsidiary issues several classes of voting shares and/or several classes of preferred shares, 50% test and 5% test shall be judged by the largest percentage of those calculated based on all of the shares, the voting shares and the preferred shares (SM 66-6).

Example: (% represents shareholding ratio)

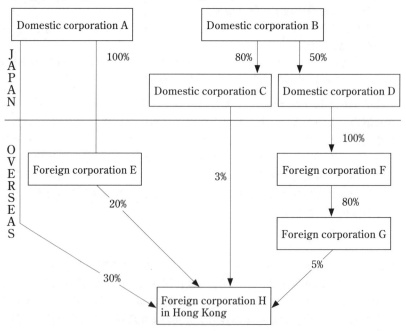

式等の50％超が居住者（内国法人の役員，居住者と特殊関連のある非居住者を含む。）及び内国法人（当該内国法人の役員が支配する法人を含む。）により直接又は間接に所有されている外国法人で，(1)その法人がペーパーカンパニー及びキャッシュフローボックスに該当する場合，その法人の所得に対する税が所得の30％未満，(2)その他のものの場合，20％未満であるものをいう（措法66の6）。

なお，50％超の株式保有割合の判定については，議決権（剰余金の配当等に関するものに限る。）の異なる株式又は請求権の異なる株式を発行している場合には，株式の数の割合，議決権の数の割合又は請求権に基づき分配される剰余金の配当等の金額の割合のいずれか多い割合で行う（措法66の6）。

〔例示〕

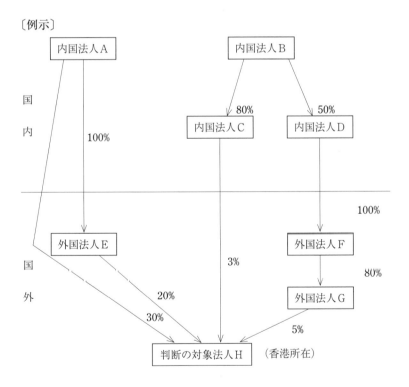

388   CORPORATION TAX

Foreign corporation H qualifies as a foreign subsidiary in a tax haven. Ratio of shares owned by domestic corporations

$$= A \ (30\% + 100\% \times 20\%) + C \ (3\%) + D \ (100\% \times 80\% \times 5\%)$$
$$= 57\% > 50\%$$

The countermeasure regarding tax havens is applicable to domestic corporations A, C and D.

Shareholding ratio:

A: $30\% + 100\% \times 20\% = 50\%$

C: 3% ⎫ Family corporation group
D: $100\% \times 80\% \times 5\% = 4\%$ ⎭ $3\% + 4\% = 7\% > 5\%$

Undistributed profits principally mean net income, excluding losses incurred within previous 7 years and corporation tax imposed on the undistributed profits of a foreign subsidiary.

However, even the ratio of tax burden of the foreign subsidiary in the country where its head office is located is less than 20%, only its passive income is subject to CFC rule, if the foreign subsidiary could satisfy all of the condition below:

(1)   Main business of the foreign subsidiary is not those such as holding stocks, offering intangible asset, or leasing ships or aircrafts (business criterion). A certain foreign subsidiary which is supervising other related corporations or running airplane-leasing business for itself could satisfy the business criterion.

(2)   The foreign subsidiary has a fixed facility necessary to conduct its business in the country where its main office is located (substance criterion).

(3)   The foreign subsidiary manages and controls its own business in the country where its main office is located (management and control criterion).

(4)   In case where the main business of the foreign subsidiary is a wholesale business, banking, trust business, financial instruments business, insurance, shipping or air transport, and the foreign subsidiary conducts its business mainly with non-related persons (non-related person criterion), or if the main business of the foreign subsidiary is other than those stated above, and the foreign subsidiary conducts its business mainly in the country where its main office is located (location criterion).

¶ 6-195

例示の法人Hはタックスヘイブン所在外国子会社となる。

内国法人による出資割合＝A（30％＋100％×20％）＋C（3％）＋D（100％
　　　　　　　　　　　　×80％×5％）＝57％＞50％

また，タックスヘイブン対策税制の対象となる内国法人はA，C，Dである。

株式の保有割合

A　30％＋100％×20％＝50％

C　3％　　　　　　　　　　　┐同族株主グループ

D　100％×80％×5％＝4％ ┘　3％＋4％＝7％＞5％

　留保所得とは，当該事業年度前7年以内に生じた欠損金を控除する等調整された留保所得をいい，一定の例外を除き純所得から留保所得に対して課せられた法人税額を控除したものをいう。

　しかしながら，その外国子会社の税負担率が20％未満でも，次の要件のすべてを満たす場合には，その子会社の受動的所得のみが合算課税の対象になる。

⑴　主たる事業が株式の保有，無形資産の提供，船舶・航空機リース等でないこと（事業基準）。一定の要件を満たす統括会社及び航空機リース会社は事業基準を満たしている。

⑵　本店所在地国に主たる事業に必要な事業所等を有すること（実体基準）。

⑶　本店所在地国において事業の管理，支配及び運営を自ら行っていること（管理支配基準）。

⑷　主たる事業が卸売業，銀行業，信託業，金融商品取引業，保険業，水運業又は航空運送業で，その取引を主として関連者以外の者と行っていること（非関連者基準），又は主たる事業が上記の卸売業等以外の法人で，その事業を主として本店所在地国で行っていること（所在地国基準）。

390   CORPORATION TAX

The exemption of anti-tax haven rule shall, however, not be allowed in principle if a company dose not keep or attach evidence that the activities of the related foreign subsidiary in a tax haven country meet the requirements in the rule.

¶ 6-197 Taxation of retained earnings in a foreign specified trust of Japanese corporations

As for a foreign specified trust similar to a Japanese specified trust related to Japanese corporations, retained earnings of the trust are aggregated to the Japanese corporations' taxable income alike to the anti-tax haven provision (SM 66-6⑦).

¶ 6-198 Taxation of retained income in a specified foreign subsidiary owned by a specially related Japanese corporations

If shareholders of a Japanese company own 80% or more shares of the Japanese company through a foreign subsidiary with no substance and located in a tax haven country after a company restructure, retained income in the foreign subsidiary is subject to Japanese taxation at the shareholders of the subsidiary provided that the Japanese company is owned 80% or more by a group of a few shareholders before the company restructure. If the foreign subsidiary further owns a sub-subsidiary with no substance, in a tax haven country, its retained income is also subject to Japanese taxation at the shareholders of the subsidiary (SM 66-9-2).

¶ 6-200 Taxation of transactions between corporations and foreign related persons for transfer pricing

When a corporation sells to, purchases from, provides services for or carries on other transactions with a foreign related person which has a special relationship with the corporation, and if its taxable income is less than the amount calculated upon arm's length principles, these transactions (the foreign related transactions) will be deemed to have been conducted at arm's length prices and the differential amount either will be included in or will not be deductible from the taxable income of the corporation (Law 66-4).

The differential amount which arises during the liquidation of a corporation will be added to the residual assets for the purposes of computing

¶ 6-197

法　人　税　391

ただし，当該適用除外は，原則として，必要な書類等の添付又は保存がない限り認められない。

¶6-197　内国法人に係る特定外国信託の留保金額の益金算入

内国法人に係る外国において設定された特定信託に類する一定の信託について，特定外国子会社等に係る所得の課税の特例と同様，当該信託に留保された所得を，当該内国法人等の所得金額の計算上益金の額に算入することとする。なお，当該信託については，適用除外基準を設けない（措法66の6⑦）。

¶6-198　特殊関係株主等である内国法人に係る特定外国法人の留保金額の益金算入

内国法人の株主が，組織再編成等により，軽課税国に所在する実体のない外国法人を通じてその内国法人の持分の80％以上を保有することとなった場合には，その外国法人に留保した所得を，その持分割合に応じて，その外国法人の株主である内国法人の所得に合算して課税する（合算対象となる所得には，その外国法人に係る外国子会社のうち，軽課税国に所在する実体のないものに留保した所得も含める。）。対象となる内国法人は，組織再編成等の前に少数の株主グループによってその持分の80％以上を保有されていたものに限る（措法66の9の2）。

¶6-200　国外関連者との取引に係る課税の特例（多国籍企業の同一関連グループ内の移転価格に対する課税）

法人が国外関連者（法人と特殊の関係を有する外国法人をいう。）との間で商品の販売あるいは購入，役務の提供又はその他の取引を行い，その対価が独立企業原則により算出された金額と異なることにより課税所得が少なくなる場合には，当該国外関連取引は独立企業間価格で行われたものとみなされ，その差額は法人の所得の金額の計算上損金の額に算入されない（措法66の4）。

法人の清算中に生じた差額は，当該法人の解散による清算所得の金額の計算上，残余財産の価額に算入する。

この特例の適用対象取引には単なる金銭の贈与や債務の免除等は原則として含まれない（なお，国外関連者に対する寄附金は¶6-235(ⅲ)にかかわらず

392 CORPORATION TAX

the liquidation income due to the dissolution of the corporation.

In principle, contributions and forgiveness of liabilities are not included in the above-mentioned transactions (Notwithstanding ¶ 6-235 (iii), if a corporation makes a contribution to its foreign related person, the full amount of the contribution is not deductible when calculating the income of the corporation.).

A corporation which conducts transactions with a foreign affiliated person during a business year must attach to its final tax return for that year a document (schedule 17 (4)) which contains, among other details, the name and location of the head or main office of the foreign related person.

   (1) "A special relationship" means:

      (a) A relationship in which either of two corporations owns directly or indirectly at least 50% of either the shares or the investment capital of the other corporation.

      (b) A relationship in which at least 50% of either the shares or the investment capital of two corporations are owned, directly or indirectly, by the same person.

In the following cases, A and B have a special relationship with each other (% represents shareholding ratio).

This method of computing the shareholding ratio is different from that of the tax haven counter measure (see ¶ 6-195 for an example).

Case (a) — 1

A —50%→ B

Case (a) — 2

A —50%→ ⓐ —50%→ B

Case (a) — 3

A —50%→ ⓐ —40%→ B ; A —50%→ ⓑ —10%→ B

Case (a) — 4

A —50%→ ⓐ —50%→ ⓒ —40%→ B ; A —50%→ ⓑ —10%→ B

Case (a) — 5

A —50%→ ⓐ —40%→ ⓒ —50%→ B ; A —50%→ ⓑ —10%→ ⓒ

Case (a) — 6

A —50%→ ⓐ —40%→ B ; A —10%→ B

Case (b) — 1

C —50%→ A ; C —50%→ B (A ↕ B)

Case (b) — 2

C —50%→ ⓐ —50%→ A ; C —50%→ B (A ↕ B)

¶ 6-200

その全額が損金不算入とされる。）。

　法人は，各事業年度において当該法人に係る国外関連者との間で取引を行った場合には，当該国外関連者の名称及び本店又は主たる事務所の所在地その他の事項を記載した書類（別表17⑷）を当該事業年度の確定申告書に添付しなければならない。

(1) 特殊の関係とは
　(a) 二の法人のいずれか一方の法人が他方の法人の発行済株式の総数又は出資金額（以下「発行済株式等」）の100分の50以上の株式の数又は出資の金額を直接又は間接に保有する関係
　(b) 二の法人が同一の者によってそれぞれその発行済株式等の100分の50以上の株式の数又は出資の金額を直接又は間接に保有される関係

　以下のケースにおいてAとBは特殊の関係にある法人である（％は保有割合）。タックスヘイブン税制（¶6-195）とは保有割合の計算方法は異なる。

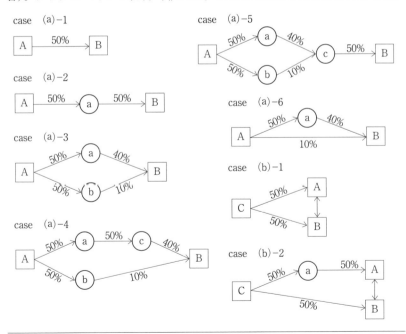

394 CORPORATION TAX

(c)   A relationship in which a director represents (or a number of directors together represent) at least 50% of the directors of one corporation and, concurrently, that director is a director or employee (or those directors are directors or employees) of another corporation.

(d)   A relationship in which one corporation conducts a considerable portion of its business in reliance upon transactions with another corporation, or a relationship in which one corporation procures a considerable portion of the funds necessary for its business activities by borrowing from another corporation, or by receiving guarantees of that corporation.

Note:
The decision as to whether a special relationship exists or not is based upon circumstances as at the time the transaction was conducted.
Stocks which have not been paid up, either wholly or partly, are included as stocks directly or indirectly owned.
Shares held nominally are added to the shares of the real owner.

(2)   "Foreign related transactions" of a foreign corporation subject to Japanese corporation tax means transactions arising from income sources within Japan (see ¶ 4-620) according to the classification of a foreign corporation (see ¶ 6-870). It does not include transactions arising from income exempted or reduced by tax treaties (see ¶ 4-650, ¶ 6-900).

(3)   When a transaction with a foreign related person is carried on through a non foreign-related person, the transaction with the non foreign-related person is treated as a foreign related transaction.

(4)   There are various ways of ascertaining arm's length prices. In the case of sales or purchases of goods, the main methods are:

(i)   The comparable uncontrolled price method (adopting with any necessary modifications the uncontrolled market price for the same or similar goods).

(ii)   The resale price method (taking the price at which the goods are sold by the seller to independent customers (resale price) and subtracting the normal mark-up for the sale by the original vendor).

(iii)   The cost plus method (taking the vendor's cost and adding an appropriate mark-up calculated on a normal profit ratio for the sale by the original vendor and thus for the purchase by the seller).

(iv)   Any other method which is acceptable (income allocation by

¶ 6-200

(c) 当該他方の法人の役員の2分の1以上又は代表する権限を有する役員が，当該一方の法人の役員若しくは使用人を兼務している者又は当該一方の法人の役員若しくは使用人であった者である関係

(d) 当該他方の法人がその事業活動の相当部分を当該一方の法人との取引に依存して行っている関係又は当該他方の法人がその事業活動に必要とされる資金の相当部分を当該一方の法人からの借入れにより，又は当該一方の法人の保証を受けて調達している関係

(注)：外国法人との間に特殊な関係が存在するかどうかの判定は取引を行ったときの現況による。
　　　直接又は間接に保有する株式には，その発行価額の全部又は一部について払込みが行われていないものが含まれる。また，名義株は，その実際の権利者が所有するものとして特殊の関係の有無を判定する。

(2) 外国法人の区分（¶6-870参照）に応じて国内源泉所得（¶4-620，¶6-870参照）を生じさせる取引のある外国法人も本制度の適用がある。ただし，租税条約（¶4-650，¶6-900参照）により軽減又は免除される所得をもたらす取引を含まない。

(3) 法人が，国外関連者との取引を非関連者を通じて行った場合には，当該法人と非関連者間の取引について本制度の適用がある。

(4) 独立企業間価格を算定するには多くの方法がある。商品の販売又は購入については，主な方法は次のとおりである。
　(i) 独立価格比準法（同種又は類似の商品の非支配市場価格に必要な調整を行う。）

　(ii) 再販売価格基準法（商品の買手が特殊の関係にない売手に対して販売した価格〔再販売価格〕から当初の売手の販売のための通常の利潤の額を控除した金額をもってその販売価格とする。）

　(iii) 原価基準法（商品の売手の原価の額に，当初の売手の販売のため又は再販売者の購入のため，通常の利益率により算定する適正な利潤の額を加算する。）

　(iv) その他の認められている方法（費用，固定資産又はその他の要因によ

396   CORPORATION TAX

cost, fixed assets or other factors).

In the case of the provision of services, the same methods as mentioned above apply.

(5)   Tax authorities are authorized to require corporations to submit books or records needed for the calculation of the arm's length price. In this case, if a corporation is required to disclose or submit books, records or copies, it must make an effort to provide them. If a corporation does not submit the required information promptly, the tax authorities will assess the taxable income estimating the arm's length price based on the normal profit ratio, etc. of corporations of the same kind, on the same scale, and similar in other respects.

(6)   Tax authorities are authorized to interrogate or inspect comparable corporations if it is necessary for the calculation of the arm's length price.

(7)   Adjustment with respect to transfer pricing taxation by tax authorities and appeal for the adjustment by tax payers can be made for six years after the time limit for filing the final tax return.

(8)   Due date of payment of back taxes incurred in a transfer pricing tax audits shall be suspended if a company requests negotiations between competent tax authorities under a tax treaty. The company must pledge collateral for the extension period (SM 66-4-2).

Total Cost

¶ 6-205 Taxes and duties

Some taxes which have been paid are deductible and others are not (Law 38).

(1) **Nondeductible taxes:**

(a)   corporation tax (excluding tax on specific funds and interest tax, including delinquency tax and penalty taxes),

(b)   inhabitant tax (prefectural and municipal, excluding the part corresponding to corporation tax on specific pension funds and interest tax),

(c)   delinquency taxes on national and local taxes,

(d)   taxes which can be credited against corporation tax, namely withholding income tax or foreign taxes which can be credited against corporation tax at the option of a taxpayer,

¶ 6-205

法　人　税　397

る所得の配分）

役務の提供については，上記の方法と同等の方法が採用される。

(5)　課税当局は独立企業間価格の算定のために必要とする帳簿，又は書類の提出を求めることができる。この場合において，当該法人は，当該提示又は提出を求められたときは，当該書類若しくは帳簿又はこれらの写しの入手に努めなければならない。

　　法人が要求された情報を遅滞なく提出しなかった場合には，課税当局は，同種，同規模その他同種の条件のもとでその法人の通常の利益率等を基礎として，独立企業間価格を推定して課税所得の更正又は決定をする。

(6)　課税当局は他の比較対象企業に対して独立企業間価格の算定のため質問又は検査をする権限を有する。

(7)　移転価格税制に関する更正及び更正の請求は，法定申告期限から6年間これをすることができる。

(8)　移転価格税制による更正又は決定を受けた者が，租税条約の相手国との相互協議の申立てをした上で申請をしたときは，更正又は決定に係る国税（相互協議の対象となるものに限る。）の納付を猶予する。納税の猶予をする場合には，猶予する金額に相当する担保を徴する（措法66の4の2）。

損　　金

¶6-205　租税公課

損金の額に算入されない租税及び算入される租税の内訳は次のとおりである（法法38）。

(1)　**損金不算入の租税**

　(a)　法人税（退職年金等積立金に対する法人税及び利子税を除き，延滞税及び加算税を含む。）

　(b)　住民税（都道府県民税及び市町村民税をいい，退職年金等積立金に対する法人税及び利子税に相当する税を除く。）

　(c)　国税及び地方税の延滞税

　(d)　法人税額から控除される租税，すなわち，納税者の選択により法人税額から控除し得る源泉所得税及び外国法人税

398   CORPORATION TAX

(e) withholding income tax on the non-assessable income of a foreign corporation,

(f) taxes paid in certain exceptional cases, such as inheritance tax or gift tax paid by a public interest corporation, and

(g) fines, criminal or otherwise.

(2) **Deductible taxes:**

(a) enterprise tax (enterprise tax in a given business year is deductible in computing the amount of ordinary income for the following business year),

(b) excise taxes (national and local),

(c) property taxes (national and local),

(d) interest tax on various national and local taxes, and

(e) various foreign taxes to which the foreign tax credit system does not apply for domestic corporations.

¶ 6-210 Salaries and wages

Salaries and wages paid to employees of a corporation are deductible expenses of the corporation, not only for accounting purposes but also for tax purposes. However, unreasonably high salary paid to an employee who has a special relationship with a director of the corporation is not deductible for tax purposes (Law 36).

Compensation periodically paid to directors and similar highly ranked persons who are not employees of a corporation but who act in the interests of the corporation are also deductible. However, when such compensation is unreasonably high, deductibility is denied for that part which exceeds a reasonable amount. This excess amount is excluded from total costs for tax purposes (Law 34). When the amounts of such compensation have been decided in advance in a shareholders' general meeting or in the articles of association of a corporation, etc., that part of the compensation which exceeds the amount decided is treated as the non-deductible excess. Director's compensation paid by improper means is also not deductible.

The term "compensation" includes not only payments in cash but also any economic benefits granted by whatever name they may be called.

¶ 6-215 Bonuses

Bonuses paid to employees are deductible by the corporation in the business year during which they become due. However, bonuses paid as a

¶ 6-210

(e) 外国法人の総合課税の対象とならない所得の源泉所得税

(f) 公益法人の納付した相続税及び贈与税のような特定の場合に納付される租税及び

(g) 罰金，科料，過料

(2) **損金算入の租税**

(a) 事業税（各事業年度の事業税はその翌事業年度の所得の計算上損金に算入される。）

(b) 消費に対する租税（国税及び地方税）

(c) 財産に対する税（国税及び地方税）

(d) 各種の国税及び地方税に係る利子税

(e) 内国法人について外国税額控除が適用されない外国の租税

¶6-210 給料及び賃金

法人の被用者に支払われる給料及び賃金は企業会計上当然に経費とされるものであり，課税所得計算上も損金として控除される。ただし，その法人の役員と特殊な関係にある被用者の給与で不相当に高額な部分は課税上控除できない（法法36）。

法人の役員及び法人の被用者ではないが法人のために勤務する同様の高度の地位にある者に対して期間ごとに支払われる報酬についても同様である。しかしながら，当該報酬が不相当に高額である場合には，その超過部分の金額については税法上は損金性が否定される（法法34）。当該報酬の金額が株主総会又は会社の定款においてあらかじめ決められている場合には，その決められている金額を超える部分の報酬の金額は損金不算入の超過額として扱われる。また，不正経理により支払われた役員報酬も控除できない。

「報酬」には，いかなる名目により支給されるかを問わず，現金で支払われるもののほかすべての経済的な利益を含む。

¶6-215 賞与

被用者へ支給される賞与は，その支給が法人の利益の処分として支払われるものでない限り，支給の確定した事業年度において控除される。利益処分

400   CORPORATION TAX

distribution of the net profits of a corporation are not deductible because the corporation does not treat them as expenses.

Bonuses paid to directors and similar highly ranked persons are not deductible. When a person has a dual status as an employee and a director of a corporation, that part of the bonus which can reasonably be attributed to that person's status as an employee is deductible.

Remunerations paid by a non-family corporation to its operating directors calculated based on its profits are, however, in principle deducted as expenses provided that they are (1) deducted as expenses for accounting purposes in the accounting year, (2) calculated in accordance with proper procedures such as decision made by the remuneration committees, (3) disclosed in compliance with the securities transaction law, and (4) met further requirements (Law 34).

The term "bonus" includes any non-periodic payments, in cash, in kind or in any other sort of economic benefit including releases from debts, unless they represent retirement allowances. Frequently, some hidden profits are discovered by the Tax Authority and these are considered to have been paid to its directors as bonuses when they are not retained in the corporation.

¶ 6-220 Social insurance premiums

Social insurance premiums, payments to employees' pension funds and similar payments by a corporation are deductible. Beneficiaries of such pension funds, especially employees, are subject to individual income tax at the time of payment of the pension if any legally approved pension funds are concerned, or at the time of payment of premiums if non-approved pension funds are concerned.

¶ 6-225 Retirement allowances

Retirement allowances paid to employees and directors are deductible.

However, with respect to retirement allowances paid to directors and employees who have a special relationship with a director of the corporation, except those which exceed a reasonable amount or are paid (only to directors) as distribution of net profits (Law 34).

¶ 6-230 Entertainment expenses

From accounting periods beginning on or after April 1, 2014, entertainment expenses excess 50% or more of those spent for eat and drink

¶ 6-220

として支払われた賞与は企業が費用として認識しなかったものであるので税法上も企業会計の処理に合わせるものである。

役員及び同様の高度の地位のある者へ支給される賞与は控除されない。

法人の役員であり，かつ，使用人としての二重の地位にある者については，使用人としての職務に合理的に帰属するとされる部分の賞与の金額は控除される。

ただし，法人がその役員に対して支給する利益を基礎として算定される給与のうち，非同族法人が業務を執行する役員に対して支給する給与で，当該事業年度において損金経理がされていること，算定方法につき報酬委員会における決定等の適正な手続きがとられており，かつ，有価証券報告書等で開示されていることその他の一定の要件を満たすものの額は，原則として，損金の額に算入される（法法34）。

「賞与」とは，現金，現物給与，債務の免除益を含むすべての種類の経済的利益で臨時的に支払われる給与であり，退職給与に該当するものを除く。

課税当局により簿外所得がしばしば発見されるが，それらの金額が法人に留保されていない場合には，その役員に対する賞与として支払われたものとされる。

¶6-220　社会保険料

法人が支払う社会保険料，厚生年金基金への掛金及び類似の制度への支払は控除される。当該退職年金に係る被用者の利益は，当該年金積立基金への支払が法律で定められているか又は適格の承認を受けている場合は，年金が被用者へ支払われる際に所得税の対象とされ，当該年金積立基金が承認されていない場合は，雇用者が払込んだ際に被用者に対する所得税課税の対象とされる。

¶6-225　退職給与

被用者及び役員へ支払われる退職給与は控除される。ただし，役員及び役員の特殊関係者に対して支払われる退職給与は，不相当に高額な部分の金額及び利益の分配として支払った金額（役員に対するもののみ）については損金の額に算入されない（法法34）。

¶6-230　交際費

平成26年4月1日以後に開始する事業年度については，それが事業を営むために必要とされるものであっても，支出する交際費等の額のうち接待飲食

402   CORPORATION TAX

are not deductible, even though such expenses are necessary for carrying business (SM 61-4).

However, corporations* whose capital is ¥100 million or less are able to choose to deduct as expenses 100% of entertainment expenses, up until ¥8 million instead of the 50% deduction described as above.

> * This is not applicable to a corporation in 100 percent group if capital of whose parent is ¥500 million or more (see ¶ 6-590 (Transactions within 100% group)).

If entertainment expenses are paid in respect of, and at the discretion of, directors or other corporate officials and the deductibility of those expenses has not been satisfactorily proved, those amounts are deemed to be salaries or bonuses paid to those directors or officials. In such cases, the expenses are deductible as such for corporation tax purposes, but they constitute part of the taxable personal income of those directors and other officials.

Note:
> When the beneficiary of a disbursement is not known, that disbursement is excluded from total cost (R 9-7-20).

¶ 6-235 Contributions paid

Contributions are, in principle, not deductible except in the following cases (Law 37):

(i) Contributions to the national and local government and other designated contributions for public purposes. These contributions are fully deductible.

(ii) Contributions to public interest corporations, public interest trust funds or corporations established by a special law which work for educational or technological development, for the promotion of cultural or social welfare and for other designated purposes. These contributions are deductible up to the limit stated in (iii) below.

(iii) Other contributions, including contributions to political or religious organizations or societies. These contributions (excluding those distributed from net profits) are deductible up to one fourth (half until March 31, 2011) of the amount of the sum of 2.5% of profits plus 0.25% of capital (In the case of public interest corporations see ¶ 6-040).

The term "contribution" is constructed very broadly. It includes all transactions with any person in which a corporation grants any kind of

¶ 6-235

費の額の50％に相当する金額を超える部分の金額は，損金に算入できない。

　ただし，資本金の額が１億円以下の法人*にあっては，800万円までその交際費支出額の100％相当額を損金算入する方法も選択できる（措法61の４）。

　　*資本金の額が５億円以上の法人の100％子法人を除く（¶6-590（完全支配関係がある法人間の取引）参照）。

　支出が役員や従業員の任意に任され，かつ，支出の損金性が十分に証明できないような交際費は，当該役員や従業員に対して支払われる給与又は賞与であるとみなされる場合がある。給与とみなされる場合には法人税の計算上控除される場合もあるが，いずれにしても役員や従業員に対する所得税の課税上は課税所得を構成する。

　（注）：法人が交際費，機密費などの支出を行った場合において，具体的な使途を明らかにしない支出については損金の額に算入されない（法基通９-７-20）。

¶6-235　寄附金

寄附金は，原則として次のとおり控除される（法法37）。

（ⅰ）　国，地方公共団体に対する寄附金及びその他公益目的のための指定寄附金　これらの寄附金は全額控除される。

（ⅱ）　教育又は科学の振興，文化の向上，社会福祉への貢献その他公益の増進に寄与するための公益法人もしくは特定の公益信託又は特別の法律により設立された特定の法人に対する寄附金　これらの寄附金は下記（ⅲ）と同じ限度額の範囲内において控除される。

（ⅲ）　その他の寄附金（宗教団体又は協会への寄附金を含む。）　これらの寄附金（利益処分により支出されるものを除く。）は，所得の金額の2.5％と資本金の0.25％との合計額の４分の１（平成23年度までは２分の１）に相当する金額まで控除される（公益法人等の特例については¶6-040参照）。

「寄附金」は非常に広く解釈されており，法人が何らかの合理的な対価を受領することなく，第三者に対して行うすべての種類の経済的利益の供与を

404 CORPORATION TAX

economic benefit without receiving any reasonable consideration. However, the term does not include any payment which is considered to be:

(a) payment of salaries, bonuses or retirement allowances,

(b) payment of entertainment or advertising expenses, or payment for employees' welfare and the like.

Note:
Donation within 100% group is not treated as expenses at donor, nor income at donee (see ¶ 6-590 (Transactions within 100 percent group)).

¶ 6-240 Bad debt loss

When a corporation proves by the following facts that an account receivable (including loan or other claim) has become worthless, it is allowed to write off the account receivable and charge it to expenses as a bad debt loss (R 9-6-1 to 9-6-3):

(1) The amount to be written off has been determined as a result of a reconstruction plan or special settlement contract or composition which was admissible under legal procedures.

(2) The amount to be written off has been determined as a result of a decision of a creditors' meeting or an agreement between two parties through a bank as intermediary.

(3) The creditor has given a notice of exemption from liabilities to the obligor in anticipation of no recovery.

(4) It is clear that no recovery can be expected because of the financial position of the obligor. However, the value of the securities for the bad debt should be offset against the bad debt loss.

(5) At least one year has elapsed since the suspension of transactions with the obligor, or the cost of collection appears greater than the unsettled account receivable. In these events, the memorandum value must be recorded in the books.

Although the direct write-off of accounts receivable is limited to the above cases, there are reserve procedures which allow the possibility of earlier deductions to some extent. For this purpose, bad debt reserves (¶ 6-360) are permitted.

¶ 6-247 Interest paid to foreign leading shareholders (nondeductible in the case of thin capital)

A counter measure for the tax avoidance caused by a taxpayer paying

¶ 6-240

含む。しかし，次に掲げる金額を除く。

(a)　給与，賞与又は退職給与の支払とされる金額
(b)　交際費，広告宣伝費，被用者への福利厚生費の支払とされる金額

(注)：100％グループ内の内国法人間の寄付については，支出法人において全額損金不算入とするとともに，受領法人において全額益金不算入とする（¶6-590（完全支配関係がある法人間の取引）参照）。

¶6-240　貸倒損失

　法人は，次の事実により債権（貸付金，これに準ずる債権）が回収不能となったことを証明した場合には，その債権を償却し，貸倒損失として損金の額に算入することが認められる（法基通9-6-1～9-6-3）。

(1)　会社更生計画，特別清算に係る協定，法律上の和議の決定があったことにより，切り捨てられることとなった金額

(2)　債権者集会の決定又は銀行のあっせんによる両当事者の合意があったことにより切り捨てられることとなった金額

(3)　債権が回収不能である場合において，債権者が債務者に対して債務免除通知書を送付したとき

(4)　債務者の資産状況からみて，回収不能と見込まれることが明らかになった場合。ただ，回収不能に係る債権の担保物の価額に相当する金額は貸倒損失額から控除しなければならない。

(5)　債務者との取引停止後少なくとも1年を経過し，又は回収費用が債権の金額よりも多額であると見込まれる場合。この場合には，備忘価格（1円）を記帳しなければならない。

　債権の直接償却は上記の場合に限られるが，より早期に損金に計上するための手段が認められている。この目的のために，貸倒引当金（¶6-360）制度が認められている。

¶6-247　国外支配株主等に支払う負債利子（過少資本の場合の損金算入）

　平成4年度の税制で過少資本対策税制が導入された。
　すなわち，法人が国外の支配株主からの借入金が自己資本の3倍を超える

406 CORPORATION TAX

interest on a loan in place of dividends on capital was introduced by the 1992 Tax Reform.

Interest is partly excluded from a corporation's deductible expenses when the corporation has borrowed money exceeding three times the amount of its capital from its leading shareholders (SM 66-5).

A "foreign leading shareholder" means a non-resident or a foreign corporation which can control the corporation in question by owning more than 50% of its capital or keeping a special connection with the corporation.

The nondeductible amount of interest is calculated as follows:

$$
\begin{array}{c}
\text{Total amount of interest} \\
\text{paid to foreign leading} \\
\text{shareholders in the} \\
\text{business year}
\end{array}
\times
\frac{
\begin{array}{c}
\text{Share of the foreign} \\
\text{(X)-leading shareholders*} \times 3**
\end{array}
}{
\begin{array}{c}
\text{Avarage amount of interest bearing} \\
\text{debt in the business year***(X)}
\end{array}
}
$$

> *   The average amount of assets minus the average amount of liabilities (minimum: the corporation's capital amount). Each average amount must be calculated reasonably.
> **   According to the situation, the appropriate ratio which is shown by a corporation may be allowed instead of "3".
> *** The average amount should be calculated reasonably.

A third party loan with foreign related parties' guarantees shall be included in the debt and interests on the loan and the guarantee fees shall be included in the interests.

¶ 6-248   Non-deductible interest paid to related corporations

If amounts of net interests paid to, after deducting interests received from, related corporations are over 50% of adjusted income, the excess amounts cannot be deductible as expenses for the accounting period (SM 66-5-2, 66-5-3).

Valuation of Inventory

¶ 6-250   Need for inventories

Inventories must be taken at the beginning and end of an accounting period when merchandise is produced, purchased or sold.

¶ 6-248

法 人 税　407

場合には，その超過額に対応する負債利子は損金算入しないというものである（措法66の5）。

国外支配株主とは，当該法人の発行済株式の50％以上を直接又は間接に保有する関係又はこれに類する支配関係を有する非居住者又は外国法人である。

損金不算入額は，次の算式により計算される。

$$
\substack{\text{国外支配株} \\ \text{主への支払} \\ \text{利子の総額}} \times \frac{(X)-\text{国外支配株主の資本持分}^{*} \times 3^{**}}{\underbrace{\text{国外支配株主からの利付負債の平均残高}(X)}_{***}}
$$

* 　当該法人の総資産の帳簿価額の平均残高から総負債の帳簿価額の平均残高を控除した残額（最低限資本の金額とされる）。この場合のそれぞれの平均残高の計算方法は合理的なものであれば認められる。
** 　法人が3に代わるべき妥当な比率を示した場合には，修正が認められる。

*** 　利付負債の帳簿価額の平均残高として合理的な方法により計算した金額。

対象となる負債及びその負債の利子には，国外支配株主等が債務の保証をすることにより第三者が資金を提供した場合のその資金に係る負債並びにその負債の利子及び国外支配株主等に支払う債務の保証料が含まれる。

¶6-248　関連者等に係る支払利子等の損金不算入

法人の関連者等への支払利子等（当該関連者等の所得税又は法人税の課税標準となるべき所得に含まれるものを除く。）の額の合計額から一定の受取利子等の額の合計額を控除した残額（以下「関連者純支払利子等の額」）が調整所得金額（当該関連者純支払利子等の額と比較するための基準とすべき所得の金額をいう。）の50％相当額を超える場合には，当該支払利子等の額の合計額のうちその超える部分の金額に相当する金額は，各事業年度の所得の金額の計算上，損金の額に算入できない（措法66の5の2，66の5の3）。

たな卸資産の評価

¶6-250　たな卸の必要性

各事業年度の開始時と終了時において製造，購入又は販売に係る商品のたな卸評価が要求される。

408 CORPORATION TAX

The "inventory" should include all finished and partly finished goods or merchandise, raw materials, supplies and other assets similar to these.

Ordinary income from business operations is determined by deducting the cost of goods sold, which is included in total costs, from sales proceeds, which are included in gross income.

The cost of goods sold is calculated by adding the opening inventory (the inventory at the beginning of the year) to the cost of goods purchased or produced during the year, and deducting from this total the closing inventory (the inventory at the end of the year).

An inventory must conform to accepted accounting practices and it must clearly reflect net income.

¶ 6-255 How to value an inventory

A corporation may select one of the following methods for evaluating inventories (Law 29).

(A) **Cost method.**

   (1)   actual cost method;
   (2)   first-in, first out method;
   (3)   last-in, first out method;
   (4)   weighted-average method;
   (5)   moving-average method;
   (6)   straight average method;
   (7)   most recent purchase price method; or
   (8)   retail inventory method.

   (Last-in, first-out method and straight average method were, however, excluded under the 2009 tax reform from those evaluation methods which could be selected.)

(B) **Cost or market value, whichever is lower.**

   A corporation may use any method other than the above if the Director of the District Tax Office gives special approval for it. The method selected must be used in the valuation of the closing inventory for at least three continuous business years.

   The method of valuation cannot be changed without the tax office's prior approval.

   When a corporation commences business, it should give the tax office written notice of its selected method. In the absence of such notification, the most recent purchase method (A (7)) will be deemed to have

¶ 6-255

「たな卸資産」には，すべての完成品，半製品，商品，原材料，仕掛品その他これらに類する資産を含む。

　事業活動に基づく各事業年度の所得の金額の計算にあたっては，益金となる売上高から控除する損金となる売上原価を計算する必要がある。

　売上原価は，期首たな卸資産（事業年度開始の日におけるたな卸資産）に期中の仕入高又は製造原価を加え，この合計額から期末たな卸資産（事業年度終了の日におけるたな卸資産）を差し引くことにより計算される。

　たな卸は健全な会計慣行に合致し，所得を明らかに反映するものでなければならない。

¶6-255　たな卸資産の評価方法

　法人は，たな卸資産の評価に際し，次のいずれか一つの方法を選定することができる（法法29）。

(A)　原価法

- (1)　個別法
- (2)　先入先出法
- (3)　後入先出法
- (4)　総平均法
- (5)　移動平均法
- (6)　単純平均法
- (7)　最終仕入原価法
- (8)　売価還元法

　（ただし，後入先出法及び単純平均法は，平成21年度の税制改正により，所要の経過措置を講じた上，選定できる評価の方法から除外された。）

(B)　低価法

　しかしながら，法人は税務署長の承認を得ることを条件として，上記以外の特別な評価の方法を選定することができる。

　法人は，期末たな卸資産の評価については少なくとも継続して3年間は選定した評価方法を適用しなければならない。

　法人が新たに事業を開始する場合には，選定した評価方法を書面により税務署へ届け出なければならない。法人からその届出書が提出されない場合，あらかじめ選定した評価方法によらないで評価した場合には，最終仕入原価法（A(7)）により評価される。評価方法を変更しようとする場合には，事業年度開始の日の前日までに税務署長の承認を受けなければならない。

410 CORPORATION TAX

been adopted by the corporation.

When a corporation does not adopt the method selected in advance in a business year, the inventory in that business year should be valued by the recent purchase method.

Depreciation

¶ 6-265 Depreciable assets

The corporation tax law permits the deduction of a reasonable allowance for the exhaustion or wear and tear of depreciable assets, tangible or intangible, within the limits allowed as expenses for the accounting purposes of the corporation (Law 31).

Depreciable tangible assets include all kinds of tangible fixed assets, excluding land, objects of art, etc. For example, buildings, structures, machinery and equipment, vessels, airplanes, vehicles, tools, etc. are depreciable.

Depreciable intangible assets are enumerated in laws and regulations. They include intangible property such as patents, trademarks, mining rights, fishing rights, goodwill, etc.

Some animals and plants used for business operations are treated as depreciable assets.

Methods of depreciation are showed in ¶ 6-270.

However, acquisition cost of minor assets (excluding those on a lease in a foreign country) may be simply deducted as follows.

(1) In the case of an asset whose acquisition cost is less than ¥100,000 per unit;

It may be immediately deducted as expenses in the business year of acquisition (Reg 133).

(2) In the case of an asset whose acquisition cost is less than ¥200,000 per unit (excluding one to which above (1) is applied);

Total cost of assets acquired in the business year may be deductible each business year in equal amount over three years (Reg 133-2).

(3) A small or medium-size corporation can deduct as expenses acquisition cost at lump sum with limitation of ¥3,000,000 for depreciable assets less than ¥300,000 at purchase during April 1, 2006 through March 31, 2012 (SM 67-5).

For deferred assets, see ¶ 6-320 and ¶ 6-325.

¶ 6-265

法　人　税　411

減　価　償　却

¶6-265　減価償却資産

有形及び無形の固定資産の消耗，減耗又は摩滅については法律上合理的な控除が認められている（法法31）。

減価償却費を課税所得計算上損金の額に算入するには企業会計において経費として経理されていなければならない。

有形減価償却資産には土地，芸術作品等の価値の減少しない資産を除くすべての種類の有形固定資産が含まれる。建物，構築物，機械装置，船舶，航空機，車両及び運搬具，工具，器具及び備品が減価償却の対象とされる。

無形減価償却資産は，法令上特別に掲げられている。工業所有権，商標権，鉱業権，漁業権，営業権等の無形資産が含まれる。

事業用の動物や植物には減価償却資産として扱われるものもある。

償却の方法は，¶6-270で述べられているが，少額資産（国外リース資産を除く。）の取得価額については，次のような簡易な方法による控除が認められている。

(1)　取得価額が1単位当たり10万円未満の資産の場合：
資産を取得した事業年度において即時に損金算入することが認められる（法令133）。

(2)　取得価額が1単位当たり20万円未満の資産（上記(1)の適用を受けるものを除く。）の場合：
その事業年度に取得したものの取得価額をまとめて3年にわたり均等額を控除することが認められる（法令133の2）。

(3)　中小企業者等が，平成18年4月1日から平成24年3月31日までの間に，取得価額30万円未満の減価償却資産を取得した場合には，取得価額の全額（ただし，300万円を限度とする。）の損金算入を認める（措法67の5）。

繰延資産については，¶6-320及び¶6-325を参照されたい。

412   CORPORATION TAX

¶ 6-270 Method of depreciation

The depreciation deduction should be computed by one of the following methods:

(a) **Reducing balance method**

The depreciation base is reduced each year by the amount of the depreciation deduction and a uniform rate is applied to the resulting balance. The uniform rate is calculated by taking into account the useful life (¶ 6-290) applicable to the depreciable assets and the residual value, which is legally determined to be 10% of the acquisition costs in the case of tangible assets (Until March 31, 2007).

(b) **Straight line method**

A uniform rate is applied to the acquisition costs of the depreciable assets. The acquisition costs less the residual value are deductible each business year in equal amounts over the useful life applicable to the depreciable assets (Until March 31, 2007).

With regard to the depreciation applicable to the assets acquired after March 31, 2007, residual value concept was abolished. A company can depreciate until residual value of 1 yen. Depreciation ratio under the declining balance method was revised to 2 (2.5 in case an asset was acquired before April 1, 2012) times of the ratio applicable under the straight line method, i.e., 1 divided by statutory useful life. If the amounts of the depreciation expenses in a certain accounting period become smaller than those calculated by dividing residual amounts as of commencement date of the accounting period by remaining useful life, depreciation method must be changed from the declining balance method to the straight line method at that period.

Note:

A corporation which selects declining balance method can continue to use current statutory depreciation rate (2.5 times statutory depreciation rate used for straight line method) if it purchases depreciable assets in the accounting period beginning before April 1, 2012 and ended after April 1, 2012.

(c) **Unit of production method**

This method is applicable only to assets used in the mining industry. The number of metric tons which make up the deposit should be estimated first. Then the acquisition cost of the assets less the residual value (provided that the residual value of mining rights, shafts, drifts, etc. is treated as zero) is divided by the estimated number of tons in the deposit. This quotient is multiplied by the number of tons extract-

¶ 6-270

法 人 税　413

¶6-270　償却の方法
償却の方法には次の方法がある。

(a)　定率法
減価償却資産の取得価額から既に各事業年度において償却費として損金の額に算入された金額を控除した金額を償却の基準として，償却残額に対して一定の償却率を適用する方法である。償却率は減価償却資産の耐用年数（¶6-290）及び法令上定められている残存価額（有形資産については取得価額の10%）を考慮して算出されている（平成19年3月31日まで）。

(b)　定額法
減価償却資産の取得価額に定率（取得価額から残存価額を控除した金額が，減価償却資産に適用される耐用年数期間にわたり毎年同一となる率）を乗じて償却額を計算する方法である（平成19年3月31日まで）。

平成19年4月1日以後に取得する減価償却資産については，残存価額を廃止し，耐用年数経過時点に1円（備忘価額）まで償却できる。定率法の償却率は，定額法の償却率（1／耐用年数）を2（平成24年3月31日以前に取得した資産については2.5）倍した率で，定率法により計算したその事業年度の償却額がその年度開始時の未償却残額を定額法により計算した償却額を下回ることとなったときは，償却方法を定率法から定額法に切り替えて減価償却費を計算する。

（注）：定率法を採用している法人が，平成24年4月1日前に開始し，かつ，同日以後に終了する事業年度において，同日からその事業年度終了の日までの期間内に減価償却資産の取得をした場合には，現行の償却率（定額法の償却率の2.5倍の率）による定率法により償却することを選択できる。

(c)　生産高比例法
この償却方法は鉱業用減価償却資産についてのみ認められる。まず，当該鉱区の採掘予定数量を見積り，次に取得価額から残存価額（鉱業権，坑道等の残存価額を0として取り扱われる。）を控除した金額を採掘予定数量で除する。この一定単位当たりの金額に各事業年度における当該鉱区の採掘数量を乗じる。

この計算結果の金額が各事業年度において償却費として控除できる。

414   CORPORATION TAX

ed during the business year. The result is the depreciation deductible
for the business year.

(d) **Straight line (lease period) method**
The acquisition cost less the residual value of an asset on a lease without title transfer are deductible each business year in equal amount
over its lease period.

(e) **Replacement method**
This is applicable, but only with the consent of a tax office, to rails,
railroad ties etc., which are used in quantities for the same purpose
and replaced regularly. According to this method, 50% of the acquisition costs of the assets installed as initial investment should be depreciated by using the reducing balance or the straight line method at the
discretion of the corporation. Then the acquisition cost of new assets
which replace the discarded old assets is deemed to be the depreciation cost of the initial investment and is deductible accordingly.

(f) **Depreciation according to physical or economic exhaustion**
This applies to cinematography film, fishing nets, and the like, but
only with the approval of the Director of the National Tax Administration Bureau. The depreciation deduction is computed by taking into account physical or economic exhaustion of assets.

(g) **Other methods**
Any other method specially approved by the Director of the District Tax
Office.

¶ 6-275 **Selection of a depreciation method**

A corporation may choose one method for each group of its depreciable
assets or for each office, shop, factory, etc., from among the depreciation
methods outlined in ¶ 6-270 above. The following table shows which method
is applicable to each kind of depreciable asset and which method should be
applied, in principle, when a corporation has not notified a tax office of its
choice:

> **Note:**
> The replacement method and the exhaustion method are, with official
> approval, applicable to certain kinds of assets (see ¶ 6-270(e) and (f)).
> A change in the method of depreciation requires the consent of the Tax
> Authority.

¶ 6-275

法　人　税　415

(d) **リース期間定額法**
　　所有権移転外リース取引に係るリース資産の取得価額から残存価額を控
除した金額をそのリース期間にわたり毎年均等に償却する方法である。

(e) **取替法**
　　この方法は軌条，まくら木その他多量に同一の目的のために同数量ずつ
取り替えられる資産について，税務署長の承認がある場合にのみ適用され
る。この方法によれば，当初の取替資産の取得価額の50％相当額は法人の
選択により定率法又は定額法により償却費として計算される。さらに，使
用に耐えなくなった古い取替資産に代わる新たな資産の取得価額は，当初
の取替資産の償却費とみなされて控除される。

(f) **物理的又は経済的減耗に係る償却方法**
　　この方法は，写真用フィルム，漁網などについて，国税局長の承認を受
けた場合にのみ適用される。減価償却費は，資産の物理的又は経済的減耗
の度合に応じて計算される。

(g) **その他の方法**
　　税務署長の承認を受けたその他の特別な償却方法。

¶6-275　**償却の方法の選定**
　　法人は，減価償却資産の区分及び事業所ごとに上記¶6-270に掲げた償却
方法のいずれか一つを選定することができる。次の表は減価償却資産の種類
ごとに認められる方法及び法人が税務署へ償却方法を届け出なかった場合に
原則として適用される方法を示すものである。

（注）：取替法及び物理的又は経済的減耗による償却方法は，正式の承認を条件として一定種類
　　　の資産（¶6-270(e)及び(f)参照）についてのみ認められる。
　　　償却方法の変更は課税当局の承認を要する。

416   CORPORATION TAX

Kind of assets	Methods applicable	Method applicable when the choice has not been indicated
(a) Tangible assets (excluding (b), (f) & (g))	reducing balance straight line other method specially approved	reducing balance
(b) Buildings acquired on or after April 1, 1998	straight line	straight line
(c) Intangible assets (excluding (d) and (e)), & cattle and fruit-trees	straight line other method specially approved	straight line
(d) Mining rights	unit of production straight line other method specially approved	unit of production
(e) Good will	straight line other method specially approved	straight line
(f) Other assets used for mining industry (excluding (d) and (g))	unit of production reducing balance straight line other method specially approved	unit of production
(g) Assets on a lease	straight line (lease period)	straight line (lease period)

¶ 6-280   Increased depreciation

When machinery or equipment (which is subject to either the reducing balance method or the straight line method) is in operation for significantly more hours in a day than the number which has been taken into account in determining its statutory useful life, an additional amount for depreciation, corresponding to the increase in working hours, may be allowed upon submission of a detailed statement to the tax office (Reg 60).

¶ 6-285   Purchase during business year

If a depreciable asset (except those depreciable by the unit of production method) is placed in service in the middle of a business year, it is only entitled to part of a full business year's depreciation, which is usually calculated on a monthly basis (Reg 59①).

¶ 6-280

法　人　税　417

資産の種類	償却方法	届出がない場合の償却方法
(a) 有形資産 ((b),(f)及び(g)を 除く。)	定率法 定額法 又は承認された 特別な方法	定率法
(b) 建物(平成10年4 月1日以後に取得さ れたもの)	定額法	定額法
(c) 無形資産((d)及び (e)を除く。)並びに 家畜及び果樹	定額法 承認された特別な 方法	定額法
(d) 鉱業権	生産高比例法 定額法又は承認された 特別な方法	生産高比例法
(e) 営業権	定額法又は承認された 特別な方法	定額法
(f) 鉱業用減価償却 資産 ((d)及び(g)を 除く。)	生産高比例法 定率法 定額法 承認された特別な方法	生産高比例法
(g) リース資産	リース期間定額法	リース期間定額法

¶6-280　増加償却

　機械及び装置（定額法又は定率法が選定されているものに限る。）の使用時間が法定耐用年数の計算の基礎となっている平均的な使用時間を超える場合には，当該使用時間超過分に相当する増加償却が税務署へ詳細な書類を提出することにより認められる（法令60）。

¶6-285　事業年度中の中途における取得

　法人が事業年度の中途において減価償却資産を事業の用に供した場合には，生産高比例法以外の償却方法を選定しているものについては月数単位により計算し，事業年度の全月数のうち取得日以後の月数の占める割合に応ずる部分についてのみ控除が認められる（法令59①）。

418   CORPORATION TAX

¶ 6-290 Useful lives

The useful life of many kinds of depreciable assets, tangible or intangible, are legally determined by regulations issued by the Ministry of Finance for this purpose. However, the useful life of secondhand assets could be estimated reasonably by the corporation itself.

If it is difficult to determine the appropriate useful life of a secondhand asset, the useful life is computed using the following formula.

$$\left(\begin{matrix} \text{useful life in the} \\ \text{case of new asset} \end{matrix} - \begin{matrix} \text{used years} \\ \text{of the asset (a)} \end{matrix}\right) + \text{(a)} \times 0.2$$

When a corporation finds that an official useful life is too long because of extraordinary factors, it may apply a shorter useful life, which is reasonable, with the consent of the Director of the National Tax Administration Bureau.

The statutory useful life of selected assets is given in the table at ¶ 6-295.

¶ 6-295 Table: Useful Life of Selected Depreciable Assets

Description of Assets	Useful Life (years)
(1) **Tangible fixed assets other than machinery and equipment**	
Reinforced concrete buildings (for offices)	50
Reinforced concrete buildings (for dwelling houses)	47
Reinforced concrete buildings (for restaurants, theatres)	41
Reinforced concrete buildings (for hotels)	39
Reinforced concrete buildings (for stores)	39
Reinforced concrete buildings (for power plants, garages, stations)	38
Reinforced concrete buildings (for factories)	38
Air conditioners and heaters	15
Elevators	17
Escalators	15
Equipment for fire fighting	8
Structures for railways (rails)	20
Structures for railways (concrete ties)	20
Structures for railways (alarms)	30
Structures for railways (reinforced concrete tunnels)	60
Structures for generation of electricity (reservoirs for water power)	57
Structures for generation of electricity (for steam generation)	41
Structures for generation of electricity (service wires)	30
Tree planting for factory	7
Steel vessels (2,000 tons or more)	
Steel tankers (2,000 tons or more)	
Steel whalers (5,000 tons or more)	
Light metal on alloy boats	9
Strengthened plastic boats	7

¶ 6-290

法 人 税　419

¶6-290　耐用年数

　各種類の減価償却資産の耐用年数は，有形資産又は無形資産のいずれであるかを問わず財務省がこの目的のために公布した省令に基づき法的に定められている。中古資産の耐用年数は，法人自ら合理的に見積ることもできる。中古資産の耐用年数の見積りが困難なときは，次によることが認められる。

$$\substack{中古資産の \\ 耐用年数} = \left(\substack{中古資産が新品である場 \\ 合の耐用年数} - \substack{中古資産の \\ 使用年数(a)} \right) + (a) \times 0.2$$

　法人は，法定耐用年数が何らかの特別の事実に基づき長すぎると認めた場合には，国税局長の承認を条件としてより短期の合理的な耐用年数を適用することができる。

　代表的な資産の法定耐用年数は下表（¶6-295）のとおりである。

¶6-295　代表的な固定資産の耐用年数

減価償却資産	耐用年数（年）
(1)　機械装置以外の有形固定資産	
鉄筋コンクリート建造物（事務所用）	50
同（住宅用）	47
同（飲食店，劇場用）	41
同（ホテル用）	39
同（店舗用）	39
同（発電所用，車庫用，停車場用）	38
同（工場用）	38
冷暖房設備	15
エレベーター	17
エスカレーター	15
消火設備	8
鉄道事業構築物（軌条）	20
同（コンクリート製まくら木）	20
同（信号機）	30
同（鉄筋コンクリート造トンネル）	60
発電用構築物（水力発電用貯水池）	57
同（汽力発電用）	41
同（配電線）	30
鋼船（2,000トン以上）	15
鋼船であるタンカー（2,000トン以上）	13
鋼船である漁船（500トン以上）	12
軽合金船	9
強化プラスチック船	7

420 CORPORATION TAX

Hydrofoils	5
Airplanes (maximum take off weight over 130 tons)	10
Airplanes (over 5.7 tons)	8
Airplanes (others)	5
Helicopters	5
Electronic computers (personal computers, others)	4, 5
Copying equipment	5
Clocks	10
Radio and Television sets	5
Cameras	5
Desks, chairs or cabinets made of metal	15
Typewriters	5
Trucks (for transport businesses)	4
Passenger automobiles (taxis)	4
Motion picture films	2
Plant which is available for hire	2
(2) Machinery and equipment	
Machineries used by food production industries	10
Machineries used by rubber goods production industries	9
Machineries used by business equipments manufacturing industries	7
Machineries used by electric appliance manufacturing industries	7
Machineries used by IT-related equipment manufacturing industries	8
Equipments used at farm	7
Equipments used at forestry	5
Equipments used at fish farm	5
Equipments used by general construction industries	6
Equipments used by heat supply businesses	17
Equipments used by water supply businesses	18
Equipments used by broadcast businesses	6
Equipments used by road transportation businesses	12
Equipments used by warehousing businesses	10
Equipments used by food and drink retail businesses	9
Equipments used by hotel operation businesses	10
Equipments used by restaurant operation businesses	8
(3) Intangible fixed assets	
Patent rights	8
Utility model rights	5
Design rights	7
Rights to trademarks	10
Software (used for sales purposes of copied materials, others)	3, 5
Fishing rights	10
(4) Animals and plants	
Cattle (in principle)	6
Dairy cattle	4
Horses (in principle)	8
Horses (for racing)	4
Pigs	3
Apple plants	29

¶ 6-300 Capital sum recoverable through depreciation

The capital sum recoverable through the depreciation deduction is

¶ 6-300

法　人　税　421

ホーバークラフト	8
航空機（最大離重量130トン超）	10
同（　〃　5.7トン超）	8
同（その他）	5
ヘリコプター	5
電子計算機（パーソナルコンピューター，その他）	4，5
複写機	5
時計	10
金属製の事務机，事務いす及びキャビネット	15
ラジオ，テレビ	5
カメラ	5
タイプライター	5
トラック（運送事業用）	4
乗用車（タクシー）	4
映画フィルム	2
貸付用植物	2

(2) **機械及び装置**

食料品製造業用設備	10
ゴム製品製造業用設備	9
業務用機械器具製造業用設備	7
電気機械器具製造業用設備	7
情報通信機械器具製造業用設備	8
農業用設備	7
林業用設備	5
水産養殖業用設備	5
総合工事業用設備	6
熱供給業用設備	17
水道業用設備	18
放送業用設備	6
道路貨物運送業用設備	12
倉庫業用設備	12
飲食料品卸売業用設備	10
飲食料品小売業用設備	9
宿泊業用設備	10
飲食店用設備	8

(3) **無形固定資産**

特許権	8
実用新案権	5
意匠権	7
商標権	10
ソフトウェア（複写して販売，その他）	3，5
漁業権	10

(4) **生物**

牛（原則）	6
乳用牛	4
馬（原則）	8
競走馬	4
豚	3
りんご樹	29

¶6-300　償却可能限度額

　減価償却を通じて回収し得る資産の価額は，有形固定資産については原則

422 CORPORATION TAX

limited in principle to 95% of the acquisition cost of tangible fixed assets (Reg 61). The remaining 5% may be charged to expenses only when assets are retired or abandoned. However, the remaining 5% of the acquisition cost (excluding memorandum value ¥1) of buildings, structures or equipment of concrete, brick, stone or earth structures may be depreciated equally over the estimated period of years during which such assets seem likely to be still available before abandonment of the assets, if a taxpayer obtains advance approval from the tax office. Depreciation for shafts and any intangible fixed assets may continue to be claimed without the 95% limitation.

With regard to the depreciation applicable to the assets acquired after March 31, 2007, limitation of depreciation (95%) was abolished. A company can depreciate until residual value of 1 yen.

¶ 6-305 Accounting for depreciation

The amount of depreciation deduction for tax purposes should be the same as that for business accounting, asset by asset. However, if the depreciation for business accounting exceeds the limit allowed for tax purposes the excess part is deemed not to be claimed. The excess part of the depreciation for business accounting over the deductible limit for tax purposes may be deducted in subsequent business years within the deductible limit.

If the total amounts of depreciation has not yet been reached to limitation of depreciation described in ¶ 6-300 for tax purposes even after the statutory useful life has passed, the depreciation can be continued.

¶ 6-308 Capital expenditure and maintenance

Expenses for improvements to, or maintenance of, depreciable assets are classified as either capital expenditure or maintenance expenses.

Expenses which extend the useful life or increase the value of a depreciable asset are capital expenditure, and are included in the acquisition cost which is subject to depreciation (Reg 132).

Other expenses are deductible at the time of payment as maintenance expenses.

Considering the difficulty in distinguishing between capital expenditure and maintenance expenses, some simple formulae are adopted (R 7-8-2 to 7-8-5):

¶ 6-305

法　人　税　423

として取得価額の95％に限られる（法令61）。残額の５％は資産を除却又は廃棄したときにおいてのみ費用として損金に算入される。

しかしながら，コンクリート造，ブロック造，石造又は土造の建物，構築物又は装置については，納税者が税務署長よりあらかじめ承認を得ることを条件として，取得価額の残額の５％は当該資産が使用不能となるまで使用しているとみられる各事業年度にわたり１円の備忘価額を残して均等に償却することができる。

坑道及びすべての無形固定資産については，95％の限度額に関係なく減価償却の計上を続けることができる。

なお，平成19年４月１日以後に取得する減価償却資産については，償却可能限度額（原則95％）は廃止され，耐用年数経過時点に１円（備忘価額）まで償却できる。

¶6-305　減価償却の経理

課税上の減価償却費の金額は，資産ごとに経理された会計帳簿上の金額に一致しなければならない。しかし，会計帳簿上の減価償却費が課税上の償却限度額を超える場合には，その超える部分の金額は計上されなかったものとみなされる。会計帳簿上の減価償却費のうち税法上の償却限度額を超える部分の金額は，翌期以降の事業年度において償却限度額の範囲内において控除される。

償却額が法定耐用年数を経過してもなお¶6-300で述べた償却可能限度額に達しない場合には，従来と同一の償却方法及び償却率を適用して償却することができる。

¶6-308　資本的支出及び修繕費

法人が，その所有する減価償却資産について維持管理のために支出した費用は，資本的支出か修繕費かに該当する。

仮にその支出によりその資産の使用可能期間が延長され又はその価値が増加する場合には資本的支出となり，減価償却により費用化される（法令132）。資本的支出に該当しない支出は修繕費とされ支出した事業年度の損金とされる。

資本的支出と修繕費の区別には困難があるのでいくつかの形式的な基準が定められている（法基通７-８-２～７-８-５）。

まず，災害によりき損した資産の原状回復のための支出は修繕費とされる。

424   CORPORATION TAX

The following expenses are treated as maintenance expenses:

(1) Expenses for the restoration of an asset damaged by a disaster.

(2) A small amount of expenses (under 200,000 yen per year) for short-term (within three years) periodic maintenance.

(3) Expenses amounting to less than 600,000 yen or 10% of the acquisition cost of the asset, unless such expenses are clearly recognized as capital expenditure.

Further, a corporation is permitted to treat 30% of its maintenance expenses or 10% of the acquisition cost, whichever is lower, as maintenance expenses, on the condition that it continuously accounts for maintenance expenses in this way.

¶ 6-309 Assets on lease

(Until March 31, 2008)

Generally, assets on lease are depreciated as those of a lender or lessor.

However, a certain lease is regarded as "sale" or "finance activity" for the tax purpose (Reg 136-3).

A certain lease mentioned above includes a lease having the clause of the contract showing no rescission during the lease period, and the borrower or lessee enjoys interests and bears expenses on the asset on lease.

For example, if such lease meets one of following conditions, it will be considered as sale of the asset.

(1) The asset in question should be transferred to the borrower or lessee free or nominal charge at the end or in the middle of the lease period.

(2) The right to buy the asset in question should be granted to the borrower or lessee at a very low price at the end or in the middle of the lease period.

(3) Only borrower or lessee is expected to be the user of the asset in question throughout its useful life, by consulting circumstances (kind, use, placement, etc. of the asset).

(4) A considerable difference between the lease period and the statutory useful life of the asset in question brings any party concerned a remarkable decrease of his corporation tax or income tax.

If such lease meets all of following conditions, it will be regarded as not sale but finance activity.

(1) The asset in question is sold on the condition that the buyer should

¶ 6-309

法　人　税　425

　次に，少額な支出は修繕費とすることが認められる。すなわち，その資産の修理，改良が通常3年以内の間に周期的に行われるものであり，かつ，1事業年度の支出額が20万円未満の場合にこの扱いが認められる。

　さらに，その資産の1回の修理，改良のための支出額が60万円未満で，かつその取得価額の約10％以下である場合には，明らかに資本的支出である場合は別として，修繕費とすることが認められる。

　また，法人がその資産の1回の修理，改良のための支出額の30％とその取得価額の10％とのいずれか少ない金額を修繕費として経理することも継続的に行うことを条件に認められる。

¶6-309　リース資産

（平成20年3月31日まで適用）

　一般的には，リース資産は貸手の資産として償却される。

　しかしながら，一部のリース取引については，課税上，売買又は金融取引として扱われるものがある（法令163の3）。

　そのようなリース取引とは，当該賃貸借契約が賃貸借期間の中途で解除できないものであり，賃借人が当該賃貸借資産に係る利益を享受し，かつ，その使用に伴う費用を負担すべきこととされているものである。

　そして，例えば，このようなリース取引で次の条件のいずれかに該当するものは，当該資産の売買があったものとして扱われる。

　(1)　リース期間の終了の時又はリース期間の中途において，リース資産が無償又は名目的な対価の額で当該賃借人に譲渡されるものであること

　(2)　当該賃借人に対し，リース期間終了の時又はリース期間の中途において，リース資産を著しく有利な価額で買い取る権利が与えられているものであること

　(3)　リース資産の種類，用途，設置の状況等に照らし，リース資産がその使用可能期間中当該賃借人のみ使用すると見込まれるものであること

　(4)　リース期間が当該資産の法定耐用年数と相当の差異があり，当該賃貸人又は賃借人の法人税又は所得税の負担を著しく軽減すると認められるものであること

　また，このようなリース取引で次の条件に該当するものは，金融取引として扱われる。

　(1)　当該資産の譲渡が，当該資産を譲受人が譲渡人に賃貸することを条件

426   CORPORATION TAX

lease it to the seller.
(2) Such sale and lease are practically done as alternative to finance activity (loaning to the seller by the buyer), by considering circumstances (kind of the asset, details of such sale and lease, etc.).
(From April 1, 2008)
(1) A lease transaction with conditions of non-cancelable and full payout is deemed as sale for the corporate tax purposes even if title transfer of its leased asset is not obvious until the end of lease ("Finance Lease without Title Transfer") (Law 64-2).

(2) Under the Finance Lease without Title Transfer, a lessee must depreciate the asset at the Lease Period Straight Line Method. If a lessee deducted rents as expenses, it is deemed as depreciation expenses.
(3) Under the Finance Lease without Title Transfer, a lessor can allocate differences between total rents and costs associated with the lease as income ("Lease Profits") by fixed amounts during the lease period. A lessor can separately allocate 20% of the Lease Profits as interests income calculated based on the Interest (Allocation) Methods.

¶ 6-310 Special depreciation

In addition to ordinary depreciation based on the statutory useful life, which is normally the maximum deduction for a business year, extra depreciation is available as tax incentives to corporations which meet the specified requirements. This extra depreciation is not an investment tax credit but a type of accelerated depreciation. In entering the special depreciation into its books, a corporation may use the same accounting procedures as for ordinary depreciation, i.e. principally, reducing the book value of assets. Since this procedure sometimes makes depreciation accounting unreasonable, a corporation may select a special accounting procedure whereby the special depreciation for a given business year is credited to a special depreciation reserve and over the subsequent seven years (or five years) that reserve is restored to income in seven equal amounts (SM 52-3). When an asset is subject to a special depreciation reserve, ordinary depreciation continues to be claimed as if no special depreciation was claimed.

When a corporation claims less than the special depreciation to which it is eligible in the preceding year, the difference between the maxi-

¶ 6-310

法　人　税　427

に行われたものであること

(2) 当該資産の種類，売買又は賃貸の経緯等の状況に照らし，実質的には融資（譲受人から譲渡人に対する金銭の貸付）と認められるもの

（平成20年4月1日から）

(1) 所有権移転外ファイナンス・リース取引（資産の賃貸借で，賃貸借期間中の契約解除が禁止され，かつ，賃借人が当該資産の使用に伴って生ずる費用を実質的に負担するもののうち，リース開始時においてリース資産の所有権が賃借人に移転することが明らかなもの以外の取引）は，売買取引とみなす（法法64の2）。

(2) 所有権移転外ファイナンス・リース取引の賃借人のリース資産の償却方法は，リース期間定額法（リース期間を償却期間とし，残存価額をゼロとする定額法をいう）とする。賃借人が賃借料として経理した場合も，これを償却費として取り扱う。

(3) 所有権移転外ファイナンス・リース取引の賃貸人は，リース料総額から原価を控除した金額（リース利益額）のうち，受取利息と認められる部分の金額（リース利益額の20％相当額）を利息法により収益計上し，それ以外の部分の金額をリース期間にわたって均等額により収益計上することができる。

¶6-310　特別償却

　通常，各事業年度における減価償却は法定耐用年数に基づく普通償却によるのであるが，これに加えて次に述べる特別償却が租税特別措置法に基づく誘導措置として各々の場合に定められた要件を充足する法人について認められる。これはいわゆる投資税額控除ではなく種々の種類の加速度償却である。この特別償却は，帳簿上では，普通償却と同一の会計手続，すなわち，原則として資産の帳簿価額を減額する方法により行う。この手続では会計上過大な減価償却を行うこととなるため，法人は特定の事業年度における特別償却の金額を特別償却準備金として貸記し，翌期以降7年間（又は5年間）にわたり当該準備金の額を各事業年度において均等に益金に算入するという特別の会計処理手続を選択することができる（措法52の3）。したがって，この期間中は，特別償却準備金の対象となった資産については特別償却が行われなかったものとして，普通償却を継続することになる。

　法人が特別償却の対象資産について特別償却額の全部又は一部を計上しなかった場合には，償却不足額の1年繰越しが認められる（措法52の2）。

　特別償却は，青色申告者に認められる。

　減価償却の特別措置として次のものがある。

428   CORPORATION TAX

mum allowable special depreciation and the special depreciation actually claimed may be carried forward to the following year (SM 52-2).

Special depreciation is allowed to taxpayers who file blue returns.

(1) **Examples of special initial depreciation**

Applicable assets   **Percentage of acquisition cost**

(a) equipment for highly promoting energy saving (SM 42-5)

30%

Note: See ¶ 6-730 (for alternative measures).

(b) specified machinery or equipment acquired by small enterprises (SM 42-6)   30%

Note: See ¶ 6-730 (for alternative measures).

(c) machineries acquired in specified area for national strategy (SM 42-10)   45%, 50% (23%, 25% for buildings)

Note: See ¶6-734 (for alternative measures).

(d) machineries acquired in the international strategic and synthetical special area (SM 42-11)   34%, 40% (17%, 20% for buildings)

Note: See ¶ 6-734 (for alternative measures), ¶ 6-550(2).

(e) machineries acquired and used for certain business in encouraging aria for designated business activating local economics (SM 42-11-2)   40% (20% for buildings)

Note: See ¶ 6-730 (for alternative measures).

(f) buildings acquired in specified local area for economically vitalizing purposes (SM 42-11-3)   15% (25% for certain assets)

Note: See ¶6-730 (for alternative measures).

(g) management improving equipment acquired by certain medium and small sized-corporations (SM 42-12-3)   30%

Note: See ¶ 6-730 (for alternative measures).

(h) designated equipments acquired by small or medium-sized corporations for improving business management (SM 42-12-4)   100%

Note: See ¶ 6-730 (for alternative measures).

(i) equipment using innovative information business (SM 42-12-6) 30%

Note: See ¶ 6-737 (for alternative measures).

(j) qualifying plant or equipment purchased by medium and small-sized corporations and used for the prevention of environmental pollution (listed in a Notification of the MOF) (SM 43①(1))   8%

(k) specified extraordinary labor-efficient steel vessels (SM 43①(2))

16%, 18%

¶ 6-310

法　人　税　429

(1)　初年度特別償却
　　対象資産と特別償却率は，次のとおり。
　(a)　高度省エネルギー増進設備等（措法42の5）

30％

　　　　　（注）：¶6-730（代替措置）参照。
　(b)　中小企業者が取得する特定機械装置（措法42の6）

30％

　　　　　（注）：¶6-730（代替措置）参照。
　(c)　国家戦略特別区域において取得した機械等（措法42の10）

45％，50％（建物は23％，25％）

　　　　　（注）：¶6-734（代替措置）参照。
　(d)　国際戦略総合特別区域内において取得した機械等（措法42の11）

34％，40％（建物は17％，20％）

　　　　　（注）：¶6-734（代替措置），¶6-550⑵参照。
　(e)　地域経済牽引事業の促進区域内において取得した特定事業用機械等
　　　（措法42の11の2）

40％（建物は20％）

　　　　　（注）：¶6-730（代替措置）参照。
　(f)　地方活力向上地域において取得した特定建物（措法42の11の3）

15％（一定のものは25％）

　　　　　（注）：¶6-730（代替措置）参照。
　(g)　特定中小企業者等が取得した経営改善設備（措法42の12の3）

30％

　　　　　（注）：¶6-730（代替措置）参照。
　(h)　中小企業者等が取得した特定経営力向上設備等（措法42の12の4）

100％

　　　　　（注）：¶6-730（代替措置）参照。
　(i)　革新的情報産業活用設備（措法42の12の6）　　　　　　　　30％
　　　　　（注）：¶6-737（代替措置）参照。
　(j)　中小企業者が取得する公害防止用設備（財務大臣告示により指定され
　　　ている。）（措法43①一）　　　　　　　　　　　　　　　　　　8％

　(k)　近代化船（鋼船で一定の設備を備えたもの）（措法43①二）

16％，18％

430   CORPORATION TAX

(l) specified trucks used for training by driving school (SM 43③) 20%

(m) buildings meeting earthquake-proof requirements (SM 43-2①)   25%

(n) facilities requiring special technical criteria (SM 43-2②)   22%, 18%

(o) qualifying assets used for research and development activities located in a designated area (Kansai Cultural Scientific and Research Area) (SM 44)   12% (6% for buildings)

(p) facilities jointly used by cooperative members (SM 44-3)   6%

(q) equipment facilitating smooth information circulation (SM 44-5)
                                                                  15%

(r) buildings, machinery and equipment for manufacturing use, etc. in the following areas: (SM 45①)
   (i) designated under-populated regions   10% (6% for buildings)
   (ii) designated industrial development areas in Okinawa
                                          34% (20% for buildings)
   (iii) designated zones used for international transportation service in Okinawa   50% (25% for buildings)
   (iv) designated areas in Okinawa for activating economy and finances   50% (25% for buildings)
   (v) Okinawa Islands (excluding Okinawa Island)   8% for hotels

(s) following assets used by medical care corporations (SM 45-2)
   designated qualifying medical instruments   12%

(2) **Examples of accelerated depreciation**

Applicable assets   **Rates for normal depreciation**
                                           (Applicable years)

(a) certain manufacturing machinery and equipment used in the following areas (SM 45②)
   (i) designated peninsular areas   32% (48% for buildings) (five years)
   (ii) designated islands areas   32% (48% for buildings) (five years)
   (iii) designated areas in Amami archipelago for promoting development   32% (48% for buildings) (five years)
   (iv) designated mountain villages
                           24% (36% for buildings) (five years)

(b) qualifying plant or other assets acquired by a corporation which employs handicapped persons as not less than 50% of its total workforce (SM 46)   24% (32% for buildings) (five years)

(c) machineries used for promoting approved business reorganization (SM 46-2)   40% (45% for buildings) (five years)

¶ 6-310

法　人　税　431

(l)　自動車教習所が取得する一定の教習用貨物自動車（措法43③）　　20%

(m)　耐震基準適合建物等（措法43の2①）　　25%

(n)　特定技術基準対象施設（措法43の2②）　　22%，18%

(o)　関西文化学術研究都市における研究施設（措法44）

12%（建物は6%）

(p)　共同利用施設（措法44の3）　　6%

(q)　情報流通円滑化設備（措法44の5）　　15%

(r)　次の地域における工業用機械等（措法45①）

　(i)　過疎地域等　　10%（建物は6%）

　(ii)　沖縄の産業高度化地域　　34%（建物は20%）

　(iii)　沖縄の国際物流拠点産業集積地域　　50%（建物は25%）

　(iv)　沖縄の経済金融活性化地域　　50%（建物は25%）

　(v)　沖縄諸島（沖縄島を除く。）　　ホテル用建物8%

(s)　医療機関が使用する次の資産（措法45の2）
　　　特定の医療用機器　　12%

(2)　割増償却（その事業年度の普通償却額を一定割合増加させる制度）

対象資産，割増率及び割増償却期間は，次のとおり。

(a)　次の地域における一定の工業用機械等（措法45②）

　(i)　半島振興対策地域　　32%（建物は48%）（5年間）

　(ii)　離島振興対策実施地域　　32%（建物は48%）（5年間）

　(iii)　奄美群島振興開発特別地域　　32%（建物は48%）（5年間）

　(iv)　山村振興対策地域　　24%（建物は36%）（5年間）

(b)　障害者を50%以上雇用している法人が所有している特定の減価償却資産（措法46）　　24%（建物は32%）（5年間）

(c)　事業再編計画の認定を受けた場合の事業再編促進機械等（措法46の2）

40%（建物は45%）（5年間）

432   CORPORATION TAX

   (d) asset used by business initiated nursery school (SM47)

              12% (15% for buildings) (three years)

   (e) qualifying buildings maintained under city regeneration business
(SM 47-2)   50%, 30% or 10% (five years)

   (f) qualifying goods warehouses (SM 48)   10% (five years)

Deferred Assets

¶ 6-320 Definition and amortization

Expenditures which are properly chargeable to a capital account and recoverable by means of amortization over a period longer than one year are called deferred assets (Law 32). Deferred assets include the following expenditures for tax purposes (Reg 14):

   (a) disbursement in establishing a corporation,

   (b) disbursements in starting a business,

   (c) disbursements in developing a new market, new management system, and the like,

   (d) disbursements in issuing shares,

   (e) disbursements in issuing bonds,

   (f) disbursements paid to a public entity etc. for building or improving public or common facilities,

   (g) premiums paid for rent or use of asset,

   (h) lump-sum allowances or down payments on receiving know-how and the like,

   (i) donations of assets for advertising, and

   (j) disbursements upon receiving service other than above.

The amortization of deferred assets is computed in the same way as the depreciation of intangible assets by applying the straight line method. The useful life applicable to the computation of the deduction for deferred assets is determined by considering the estimated period over which the benefit accruing from those expenditures is enjoyed (Reg 64). For convenience of accounting procedures, deferred assets of less than ¥200,000 per item may be charged as current expenses (Reg 134).

¶ 6-325 Special treatment of certain deferred assets

A corporation may, at its option, deduct in full the following deferred assets in the business year of their disbursement (Reg 64):

¶ 6-320

法 人 税 433

(d) 企業主導型保育施設用資産（措法47）　　　12%（建物は15%）（3年間）

(e) 特定都市再生建築物（措法47の2）　　　50%，30%又は10%（5年間）

(f) 特定営業用倉庫（措法48）　　　　　　　　　　10%（5年間）

繰　延　資　産

¶6-320　定義及び償却
　適正に資産勘定に計上され，かつ，1年超の期間にわたり償却の方法により回収される支出は繰延資産と称される（法法32）。次のものが税法上繰延資産とされている（法令14）。

(a) 創立費
(b) 開業費
(c) 開発費

(d) 株式交付費
(e) 社債等発行費
(f) 公共的施設又は共同的施設の設置又は改良のための負担金

(g) 資産を賃借するための権利金
(h) 役務の提供を受けるための権利金

(i) 贈与した広告宣伝用資産
(j) その他自己が便益を受けるための費用
　繰延資産の償却は，定額法が適用される無形固定資産の減価償却と同様の方法により行われる。繰延資産の償却額の計算の基礎となる償却期間は，当該支出の日からその効果が及ぶ期間を見積ることにより決められる（法令64）。会計処理の便宜上，支出金額が1単位当たり20万円未満のものは，支出した事業年度の損金の額に算入される（法令134）。

¶6-325　特定の繰延資産の特殊取扱い
　次に掲げる繰延資産については，法人の選択により，支出した事業年度において全額控除することができる（法令64）。

434   CORPORATION TAX

(a) disbursements in establishing a corporation,

(b) disbursements in starting a business,

(c) disbursements in developing a new market, new management systems, and the like,

(d) disbursements in issuing shares, and

(e) disbursements in issuing bonds.

If these expenses are not deducted in full in the business year of the disbursement, such expenses may be deducted in subsequent years.

Loss Due to Changes in Book Value

¶ 6-340 Loss due to changes in book value

The computation of taxable net profits usually ignores any change in the book value of the assets held by a corporation, whether or not such a change in book value reflects a change in market value. This principle does not prevent the application of various methods for the valuation of inventory.

Loss due to revaluation of an asset is excluded from total costs for tax purposes (Law 33). However, this principle does not prevent reduction in the book value of assets when they have been severely damaged by floods or earthquakes, etc. or when their value diminishes due to obsolescence, or when a change in book value is necessary under the Corporation Reorganization Law etc.

Loss due to the revaluation of securities is included in total costs only when the market value of the securities falls to one-half of their book value and there is no possibility of recovering their book value at the time of revaluation.

¶ 6-342 Valuation of securities and derivatives at year end

(1) Valuation methods of securities held by corporations at the end of business year are amended as follows (Law 61-3):

(a) Securities held for trading purposes should be assessed according to the market price.

(b) Securities held for other than trading purposes should be assessed according to the cost method. Securities with redemption date and redemption price should be valued by adjusting the differential between the book value of the securities and the redemption price.

¶ 6-340

法　人　税　435

(a)　創立費
(b)　開業費
(c)　開発費

(d)　株式交付費
(e)　社債等発行費
　これらの費用を支出した事業年度において全額控除しない場合には，爾後の年度において控除することができる。

資産の評価損

¶6-340　資産の評価損
　課税所得の計算上，法人の所有する資産の評価換えによる帳簿価額の減少額は，原則として損金の額に算入されない（法法33）。ただし，この原則は，たな卸資産の評価に適用される各種の評価方法の適用を妨げない。
　なお，水害，地震等の災害を受けたことにより著しく損傷した資産，会社更生法その他の法令の適用により評価換えが必要とされた資産，陳腐化した資産については，資産の帳簿価額を減額することが認められる。
　また，有価証券については，その価額が2分の1以下となり回復の見込みがないときにも帳簿価額を減額することが認められる。

¶6-342　有価証券等の事業年度末の評価
(1)　法人が事業年度末に有する有価証券の評価については，次のとおりとする（法法61の3）。
　(a)　売買目的有価証券については，時価法により評価した金額とする。

　(b)　売買目的外有価証券については，原価法により評価した金額とする。
　　なお，償還期限及び償還金額のあるものについては，帳簿価額と償還金額との差額の調整を加えた後の金額により評価した金額とする。

436 CORPORATION TAX

(2) Outstanding derivative trading should be regarded as settled at the end of the business year, and the estimated profit or loss should be reported as profit or loss (Law 61-5).

(3) In the case of derivative trading implemented for the purpose of reducing loss caused by price fluctuation of assets or liabilities, the report of the estimated profit or loss should be deferred (hedging treatment) provided that the derivative trading satisfy certain conditions (Law 61-6, 61-7).

(4) (Short Term Sale Commodity)
A corporation shall evaluate its Short Term Sale Commodity at marker price as of the end of an accounting period and the difference between the market price and book value shall be recorded as profits or losses of the accounting period (Law 61).

¶ 6-345 Credits and debits denominated in foreign currencies

Outstanding credits and debits denominated in foreign currencies at the end of each accounting period should, in principle, be valued by the following exchange rate for tax purposes (Law 61-9):

- Credits and debits—the cost method or the market price, whichever is reported to the Director of the District Tax Office.
- Securities
  Securities held for trading purposes—the market price
  Securities held for non-trading purposes—the cost method or the market price
  Others—the cost method
- Foreign currency—the cost method or the market price

When a corporation has entered into a forward exchange contract with respect to credits or debits, the forward exchange rate applies to that credits or debits. Exchange gains or loss caused by application of a forward exchange rate is included averagely in gross income or total cost of each business year which includes any day during the period the date of a forward exchange contract to the settlement date (Law 61-8, 61-10).

A corporation taking the exchange rate at the date of accrual may apply the exchange rate at the end of the accounting period if the exchange rate at the date of accrual fluctuates remarkably in the accounting period, provided that the corporation changes the book value of the credits and debits denominated in the foreign currency in question calculated by the

¶ 6-345

法　人　税　437

(2)　法人が事業年度末に有する未決済のデリバティブ取引については，事業
年度末に決済したものとみなして計算した利益相当額又は損失相当額を益
金の額又は損金の額に算入する（法法61の5）。
(3)　資産・負債の価額変動による損失を減少させるために行ったデリバティ
ブ取引等のうち一定の要件を満たすものについては，みなし決済による利
益相当額又は損失相当額の計上を繰り延べる等のいわゆるヘッジ処理を行
う（法法61の6，61の7）。

(4)　短期売買商品
　　法人が事業年度末に有する短期売買商品の評価額は時価法により評価し
た金額とし，その評価損益を当該事業年度の損益の額に算入する（法法
61）。

¶6-345　外貨建資産等の換算
　各事業年度終了の時において法人の有する外貨建資産等の金額の円換算額
の計算上，選定することができる換算の方法は，課税上次のとおりである
（法法61の9）。
・外貨建資産等……発生時換算法又は期末時換算法のうち税務署長に届け出
た方法
・外貨建有価証券
　売買目的有価証券……期末時換算法
　売買目的外有価証券……発生時換算法又は期末時換算法
　それ以外……発生時換算法

・外貨預金……発生時換算法又は期末時換算法
　先物外国為替契約が締結されている外貨建資産等については，予約レート
により換算する。この場合に生ずる為替換算損益は，先物外国為替契約の締
結日から決済日までの期間内の事業年度において期間対応で益金又は損金の
額に算入される（法法61の8，61の10）。
　取得時換算法を選定している場合であっても，為替相場が著しく変動した
場合には，帳簿価額の修正を条件に期末時の為替相場によることができる。
　為替相場は，原則として電信売買相場の仲値による。

438   CORPORATION TAX

exchange rate at the end of the accounting period.

The exchange rate for tax purposes means generally the average of telegraphic transfer selling rate and telegraphic transfer buying rate.

Tax-free Reserves

¶ 6-350 General outline

Tax-free reserves include normal reserves and special reserves.

(1) Normal Reserves

A normal reserve is one which is set up to include in the total costs of a business year, estimated expenses or losses which are chargeable to the gross income of the business year.

The following six reserves are accepted for tax purposes.

(a) Bad debts reserves

(b) Reserves for goods returned unsold

(2) Special Reserves

Special reserves are permitted as tax incentives under the Special Taxation Measures Law, and some are similar to normal reserves.

¶ 6-360 Bad debts reserve

When banks, insurance corporations, other similar corporations to those, or medium and small-sized corporations (that is, corporations whose capital is ¥100,000,000 or less and whose parents' capital is not more than ¥500,000,000) credit a certain amount to the bad debts reserve account in a particular business year, the credited amount is deductible, within the following limits (a) and (b), in computing the income of that business year (Law 52, Reg 96):

(a) The amount of confirmed doubtful account receivable as follows;

(1) The amount of the account receivable subject to deferred payment based on a decision to start reorganization procedure, authorization of compulsory composition or special settlement agreement, and the like (excluding a part of amount receivable within five years after such decision, etc. done).

(2) The amount of account receivable unlikely to be recovered in view of the obligor's financial condition or other circumstances.

(3) A half of amount of account receivable (except the amount

¶ 6-350

法　人　税　439

引当金・準備金

¶6-350　概説

　将来支出する費用等の引当額の損金算入が認められる制度として，引当金制度と準備金制度とがある。

(1)　引当金は，企業会計上，費用収益対応の原則からその費用又は損失の発生原因が当期にあり，かつ，その金額が合理的に見積もることのできる場合に，設定することが認められる。

　　課税所得計算上，引当金計上額が損金の額に算入されるのは次の引当金である。

(a)　貸倒引当金

(b)　返品調整引当金

(2)　準備金は，租税特別措置として，一定の政策目的のために，その積立額の損金算入を認める制度である。準備金の中には引当金の性格を有するものがある。

¶6-360　貸倒引当金

　銀行，保険会社その他これらに類する法人及び中小法人等（資本金の額が1億円以下の法人等（資本金の額が5億円以下の法人の100％子法人を除く。））が当該事業年度において損金経理により貸倒引当金勘定に一定の金額を繰り入れた場合には，当該繰入金額は次の(a)及び(b)の金額を限度として当該事業年度の所得の計算上控除される（法法52，法令96）。

(a)　回収の見込みのない次のような債権

　(1)　会社更生計画認可決定，強制和議認可決定，特別清算に係る協定認可その他これらに準ずる事実に基づきその弁済を猶予された金銭債権の額（これらの事実が生じた後5年内に弁済される予定の金額を除く。）

　(2)　債務者の資産状況その他の事情に照らし回収の見込みがないと認められる金銭債権の額

　(3)　会社更生手続開始，和議開始，破産又は特別清算等の申立が生じてい

440   CORPORATION TAX

recovered by warranty, etc.) concerning to a petition to start reorganization procedure, composition, bankruptcy or special settlement, and the like.

(4) A half of amount of account receivable (except the amount recovered by warranty, etc.) financed to a foreign government or a foreign central bank and in the condition of long overdue.

(b) The amount estimated in accordance with actual average percentage of bad debt loss during three years:

$$\begin{array}{c} \text{the accounts receivable outstanding} \\ \text{at the end of the business year} \\ \text{(except those subject to (a))} \end{array} \times \dfrac{\begin{array}{c}\text{average bad debt loss} \\ \text{account during 3 years}\end{array}}{\begin{array}{c}\text{average accounts receivable} \\ \text{outstanding during 3 years}\end{array}}$$

However, the percentages before the reform may be still applied to accounts receivable of a small corporation whose capital amount is less than ¥100 and its average taxable income for three years before the accounting period is ¥150 million or less also (SM 57-10).

The amount credited to the bad debts reserve account should be fully debited at the beginning of the following business year and added to the gross income of that business year.

As a temporary measure, corporations other than banks, insurance corporations, other similar corporations to those, and medium and small-sized corporations may credit 3/4 of bad debt reserve for the accounting period beginning during 2012 financial year, 2/4 for the accounting period beginning during 2013 financial year and 1/4 for the accounting period beginning during 2015 financial year.

¶ 6-385 Reserve for goods returned unsold

The rule for reserve for returned goods unsold was eliminated. However, the current treatment is applicable until the accounting period beginning on or before March 31, 2021 for the corporations which engaged in eligible businesses as described below. Furthermore, transitional measures were given where the corporation could reserve the amounts equivalent to 90% of that of the previous years' reserve for the accounting period beginning April 1 2021 through March 31, 2031.

When a corporation involved in a publishing business or the wholesale of medical supplies, etc., credits a certain amount to a reserve ac-

¶ 6-385

法　人　税　441

る金銭債権の額（担保等により回収されるものを除く。）の２分の１相
当額

(4)　外国の政府あるいは中央銀行に対する金銭債権で長期にわたり弁済が
行われていないものの額（担保等により回収されるものを除く。）の２分
の１相当額

(b)　３年間の平均実績法により計算した金額

$$
\begin{array}{c}\text{期末の貸金残高の合計額}\\ (\text{(a)に係る金額を除く。})\end{array} \times \frac{\text{過去３年間の平均貸倒れによる損失の合計}}{\text{過去３年間の平均期末貸金残高の合計額}}
$$

　ただし，資本金１億円未満の中小法人（当該法人の課税所得（過去３年間
平均）が15億円以下の法人に限る。）は改正前の法定繰入率を継続して適用
できる（措法57の10）。
　貸倒引当金勘定への繰入金額はその翌事業年度の開始の日に全額取り崩し
て益金の額に算入する。
　経過措置として，銀行，保険会社その他これらに類する法人及び中小法人
等以外の法人については，平成23年から平成25年までの間に開始する各事業
年度については，現行法による損金算入限度額に対して，平成24年度は４分
の３，平成25年度は４分の２，平成26年度は４分の１の引当てを認める。

¶6-385　返品調整引当金

　返品調整引当金制度は，平成30年３月31日をもって廃止された。な
お，平成30年４月１日において返品調整引当金制度の対象事業を営む法
人について，平成33年３月31日までに開始する各事業年度については現
行どおりの損金算入限度額による引当てを認めるとともに，平成33
年４月１日から平成42年３月31日までの間に開始する各事業年度につい
ては現行法による損金算入限度額に対して１年ごとに10分の１ずつ縮小
した額の引当を認める等の経過措置がある。

　出版業，医薬品の卸売業等の事業を営む法人が買戻しに係る特約に基づき
買戻しによる損失の見込額として一定の金額を返品調整引当金勘定に繰り入

442   CORPORATION TAX

count for goods returned unsold, in order to provide against future loss from the return of unsold goods on consignment, the credited amount is deductible, as long as the loss is estimated according to recognized methods (Law 53).

(1) Qualifying businesses

(a) publishing

(b) publisher's agent

(c) the manufacture and wholesale of medicines, agricultural chemicals, cosmetics, ready made clothes, records, cassettes or compact discs.

(2) The credited amount is deductible when limited to an amount computed by the following formula:

$$\left(\begin{array}{c} \text{Account receivable from sales of each qualifying} \\ \text{business at the end of the business year in question.} \\ \text{or} \\ \text{Total sales from each qualifying business during the} \\ \text{last two months in the business year in question.} \end{array} \right) \times \begin{array}{l} \text{Average} \\ \text{Sales-returns} \\ \text{Ratio of each} \\ \text{qualifying business} \\ \text{in the two most} \\ \text{recent business years} \end{array}$$

$$\times \begin{array}{l} \text{Sales-profit ratio of each} \\ \text{qualifying business in the} \\ \text{business year in question} \end{array}$$

(3) The amount credited to the account for goods returned unsold should be fully debited at the beginning of the following business year and added to the gross income of that business year.

¶ 6-395   Overseas investment loss reserve

If a domestic corporation acquires and holds particular shares (shown in the second column of the table in ¶ 6-400) of a specified corporation (shown in the first column of the same table) and credits the payment to an overseas investment loss account, the credited amount is deductible provided that such amount is separately calculated for each specified corporation and shares or loans, with the following limitations (SM 55):

(1) The corporation must be a domestic company.

(2) The company must have acquired the stated shares or loans of the specified corporations shown in the table at ¶ 6-400 before March 31, 2012, and must hold such shares or loans until the end of the business year in which they are acquired.

(3) The amount which may be credited may not exceed the proportion shown in the third column of the table in relation to the acqui-

¶ 6-395

法　人　税　443

れた場合には，当該繰入額は法令上定められた方法に基づき予測できる損失である限り控除することができる（法法53）。

(1)　対象となる事業は次のとおりである。
　(a)　出版業
　(b)　出版に係る取次業
　(c)　医薬品，医薬部外品，農薬，化粧品，既製服，蓄音機用レコード，磁気音声再生機用レコード又はデジタル式音声再生機用レコードの製造業及び卸売業
(2)　繰入限度額は，次の算式により計算される。

$$\left(\begin{array}{l}\text{その事業に係る期末売掛金残高又はそ}\\\text{の事業の期末前2カ月間の売上金額}\end{array}\right) \times \begin{array}{l}\text{最近2年間}\\\text{の返品率}\end{array} \times \begin{array}{l}\text{当該事業年度}\\\text{の売買利益率}\end{array}$$

(3)　返品調整引当金勘定への繰入額は，翌事業年度開始の日に全額取り崩して益金の額に算入する。

¶6-395　海外投資等損失準備金

　内国法人が次表第1欄に掲げる特定法人の次表第2欄の株式を取得して保有している場合において，海外投資等損失準備金勘定に積み立てたときは，当該積立額は各特定法人別及びその特定株式等の種類別に区分計算し，かつ，各々の限度額以下であることを条件として，損金に算入することができる（措法55）。

(1)　法人は内国法人でなければならない。
(2)　当該法人は次表に掲げる特定法人の株式を平成24年3月31日前に取得し，これをその取得事業年度終了の日まで保有していなければならない。

(3)　積立額は当該株式の取得価額に対して次表第3欄に掲げる割合を超えることはできない。

444 CORPORATION TAX

sition cost of such shares.

(4) After the reserve has been maintained for five successive years, the amount of reserve multiplied by the number of months of the business year, divided by 60, must be restored to taxable income in succeeding years following the year of reserve accrual.

¶ 6-400 Table for specified corporations

Specified corporations	Specified shares	Ratio
1. Exploitation company	newly issued shares	20%
2. Investment company for exploitation	newly issued shares	20%
3. Exploration company	newly issued shares	50%
4. Investment company for exploration	newly issued shares	50%

Specified corporations are defined as follows:

(1) "Exploitation company" means a corporation whose business is solely for exploration, exploitation and/or extraction of natural resources.

(2) "Investment company for exploitation" means a corporation whose business is solely investment in the exploitation company.

(3) "Exploration company" means a corporation whose business is solely exploration of natural resources.

(4) "Investment company for exploration" means a corporation whose business is solely investment in the exploration company.

¶ 6-432 Reserve for special repairs for specified ships

When a corporation has qualifying assets which require expensive periodical maintenance over a period of several years, and the corporation credits a certain amount to a reserve account for qualifying special repairs in order to provide against future expenditure for such maintenance, the credited amount is deductible (SM 57-8).

(1) Qualifying assets and special repairs

    (a) Ships (over 5 tons gross):

        — Repairs required following periodical inspections under the Ship Safety Law.

¶ 6-400

法　人　税　445

⑷　積立額は爾後 5 年間据置き，据置期間経過後，その準備金の額を60分して当該事業年度の月数を乗じて計算した金額を益金の額に算入する。

¶6-400　特定法人表

法　　　人	株　式　等	割　合
1. 資源開発事業法人	新増資資源株式	20％
2. 資源開発投資法人	新増資資源株式	20％
3. 資源探鉱事業法人	新増資資源株式	50％
4. 資源探鉱投資法人	新増資資源株式	50％

　特定法人の定義は次のとおりである。
⑴　資源開発事業法人とは，天然資源の探鉱，開発又は採取の事業を専ら行う法人及び当該法人に所有されている法人をいう。
⑵　資源開発投資法人とは，資源開発事業法人に専ら投融資する法人をいう。
⑶　資源探鉱事業法人とは，資源開発事業法人のうち，その事業が資源の探鉱の事業に限られている法人をいう。
⑷　資源探鉱投資法人とは，資源探鉱事業法人に対して専ら投融資する法人をいう。

¶6-432　特定船舶に係る特別修繕準備金

　定期的に大修繕を行う必要がある資産の修繕費の見込額として一定の金額を特別修繕準備金勘定に繰り入れた場合には，当該繰入額は損金の額に算入できる（措法57の 8 ）。

⑴　対象となる資産と修繕は次のとおりである。
　⒜　総トン数 5 トン以上の船舶
　　　船舶安全性による定期検査を受けるための修繕

446   CORPORATION TAX

(2)   The credited amount is computed on the basis of 75% of the latest outlay for special repair and the interval between the latest special repair and the next one.

(3)   When special repair expenses are actually paid, they must be debited to the account for special repairs reserves and added to the gross income of the business year in which they are paid.

¶ 6-435 Other miscellaneous special reserves

(1)   Mining companies may set up a "mine prospecting reserve or foreign mine prospecting reserve" and take a deduction each year for additions to that reserve, with the maximum amount of the deduction being equivalent to 12% of the sales proceeds from mineral products, or 50% of the net income arising from such sales, whichever is smaller (in the case of foreign mine prospecting reserves, there is no provision for calculation based on proceeds). This reserve is required to be used for "expenditures in prospecting for mineral deposits or similar expenditures for foreign mineral deposits" (¶ 6-540) within three years after the year of reserve accrual. Otherwise, any unused balance of the reserve must be restored to taxable income at the end of the third year following the year of reserve accrual. Needless to say, these expenditures and depreciation are deductible regardless of the above reserve treatment. This system is comparable to depletion in U.S. tax law (SM 58).

(2)   Used nuclear fuel reprocessing reserves and nuclear plant dismantling reserves are allowed to nuclear power supply companies (SM 57-3, 57-4).

(3)   Unusual accidental loss reserves for fire risks or flood damage risks and unusual accidental loss reserves for atomic damage risks or earthquake risks are allowed to insurance companies, excluding life insurance companies (SM 57-5, 57-6).

(4)   Other kinds of reserves are allowed, e.g. reserve for probable loss incurred by investment into new venture business (SM 55-2), metal mining pollution control reserve (SM 55-5), reserve for prevention of specified disasters (SM 56), specified nuclear energy plant core removal reserve (SM 57-4-2), reserve for the maintenance of the New Kansai International Airport (SM 57-7), reserve for the maintenance of the Chubu International Airport (SM 57-7-2) and reserve

¶ 6-435

法　人　税　447

(2)　繰入限度額は前回の修繕に要した費用の4分の3に相当する金額のうち次の修繕までの期間に含まれる当期の期間に対応する部分の金額である。

(3)　特別修繕準備金の金額は，(2)の修繕のための費用を支出した場合に取り崩して益金の額に算入する。

¶6-435　その他の準備金

(1)　鉱業会社は「探鉱準備金又は海外探鉱準備金」を設け，採掘した鉱物の販売収入金額の12％相当金額と鉱業所得の50％相当額とのいずれか低い金額（海外探鉱準備金については収入金額に係る限度額はない。）を限度として，この準備金として積み立てた金額について損金算入が認められる（措法58）。

　　この準備金は積立て後3年以内に「新鉱床探鉱費又は海外新鉱床探鉱費支出（¶6-540参照）」に充てなければならない。さもなければ，この準備金の未使用残額は準備金を積み立てた年から3年経過後の年の終了の時に益金の額に算入しなければならない。いうまでもないが，このような支出及び減価償却費は上記の準備金の取扱いとは関係なく損金に算入することができる。この制度はアメリカ税法の減耗控除に対比されるものである。

(2)　原子力発電会社については使用済核燃料再処理準備金及び原子力発電施設解体準備金が認められる（措法57の3，57の4）。

(3)　生命保険会社を除く保険会社等については，火災，水害等の危険に係る異常危険準備金，原子力又は地震等の危険に係る異常危険準備金が認められる（措法57の5，57の6）。

(4)　その他，新事業開拓事業者投資損失準備金（措法55の2），金属鉱業等鉱害防止準備金（措法55の5），特定災害防止準備金（措法56），特定原子力施設炉心等除去準備金（措法57の4の2），関西国際空港用地整備準備金（措法57の7），中部国際空港整備準備金（措法57の7の2）及び農業経営基盤強化準備金（措法61の2）が認められている。

448   CORPORATION TAX

for the enforcement of agriculture management infrastructure (SM 61-2).

Exchange, Replacement or Donation of Properties

¶ 6-470 Exchange of property

When a corporation exchanges property ("old property") for other property ("new property"), the fair market value for the new property is included in the gross income for the business year in which the exchange took place. The book value of the old property and the expenses arising from such an exchange are deductible as necessary expenses in the same business year. However, a tax-free exchange is permitted, if certain requirements are met (see ¶ 6-495).

> **Note:**
> The provision of capital in kind is treated as a transfer of assets, and the market value of invested assets must be included in gross income. However, in the case of the incorporation of a subsidiary (split-up), a tax-free provision of capital in kind is permitted (see ¶ 6-600).

¶ 6-475 Replacement of property

When a corporation sells its old property and buys new property, the capital gains derived from the sale of the old property should be included in the income of the business year in which the sale took place.

However, if the book value of the old property is allowed to be applied to the new property under the conditions stated in ¶ 6-495, then the capital gains are not included in net income.

¶ 6-480 Donation received or granted

When a corporation acquires any property as a donation from another corporation or individual, the recipient corporation should include the fair market value of the donated property in its gross income.

When a corporation donates to another corporation or individual, the donor corporation should, in computing its ordinary income, treat the property as if it had been sold for fair market value and the proceeds donated to the recipient corporation or individual. Therefore, capital gains are considered to have been derived from the property, and the amount of the donation may be deducted according to the limits stated in ¶ 6-235 regarding contributions.

¶ 6-470

法 人 税 449

資産の交換，買換え，贈与

¶6-470　資産の交換

　法人が有していた資産（以下「譲渡資産」）を他の資産（以下「取得資産」）と交換した場合には，取得資産の市場価額に基づき当該交換が行われた事業年度の益金の額に算入される。譲渡資産の帳簿価額及び交換に要した費用は交換が行われた事業年度の費用として控除される。しかしながら，一定の要件に合致する場合には，非課税交換が認められる（¶6-495参照）。

> （注）：現物出資は，法人税課税上は現物出資資産の譲渡として扱われる。ただし，一定の要件
> に合致する場合には，非課税扱いとされる（¶6-600参照）。

¶6-475　資産の買換え

　法人が譲渡資産を譲渡し，取得資産を取得した場合には，譲渡資産の譲渡により生ずる譲渡益は当該譲渡が行われた事業年度の所得の金額に加算しなければならない。しかしながら，譲渡資産の帳簿価額が¶6-495で述べる一定の条件のもとで取得資産に引き継がれる場合は，譲渡益は所得金額に含まれないことになる。

¶6-480　贈与

　法人が他の法人又は個人から贈与により資産を取得した場合には，その取得した法人は贈与を受けた資産の市場価額に相当する金額を益金の額に算入しなりればならない。

　法人が他の法人又は個人へ資産を贈与した場合には，その贈与をした法人は当該資産を市場価額で譲渡し，その代金を贈与の相手方である他の法人又は個人へ寄附したものとして所得金額を計算しなければならない。したがって，当該資産から譲渡益が生じたものとされる。また寄附金に相当する額は，寄附金の損金算入限度額（¶6-235参照）以下の金額については損金の額に算入される。

450   CORPORATION TAX

¶ 6-485 Transfer at low price

When a corporation acquires or sells a property at a price lower than its fair market value, treatment similar to that applicable to donations should be applied. As for the seller corporation, the property is deemed to have been sold at a fair market value and capital gains are deemed to have been derived, and the difference between the fair market value and the actual proceeds is deemed to have been donated and is deductible as a contribution within the limits stated in ¶ 6-235.

On the other hand, that difference is also included in the income of the buyer corporation, since it was earned through the transaction.

¶ 6-490 Granting leases without receiving reasonable initial payment

In an urban area in Japan, it is often customary for an initial lump sum payment to be required before a lease of land is granted. If such an initial lump sum was not required and the lessor cannot show reasonable cause therefor then the lessor must treat the sum as if he had received payment and had then donated it to the lessee (see ¶ 6-193).

¶ 6-495 Succession to book value of old property: Special Concession I

In some cases, the application of the book value of old property to new property is permitted for tax purposes, and the recognition of capital gains derived from the alienation of the old property is postponed until the time of the alienation of the new property in the future. The list below indicates some of those cases, but is not exhaustive:

1. Exchange of old fixed assets for new fixed assets if both the old and new assets belong to the same classification and are used for the same purpose and certain other conditions are met (Law 50).
2. Acquisition of fixed assets during the business year which includes the date of selling old assets, or the succeeding business year, and putting the new assets into business use within one year from the date of acquisition. However, the application of this treatment will be limited, for example, to those instances listed below, and capital gains from selling of short-term ownership land subject to special taxation (¶ 6-670) are excluded, and 80% of other capital gains will escape immediate taxation (SM 65-7 to 65-9).

¶ 6-485

法　人　税　451

¶6-485　低額譲渡

　法人が市場価額よりも低い価額で資産を取得し又は譲渡した場合には，贈与に適用されるのと同様の取扱いが適用される。資産を譲渡した法人は，当該資産は市場価額により譲渡したものとみなされるので，その譲渡により譲渡益が生じたものとみなされ，市場価額と実際の譲渡金額との差額は贈与したものとみなされて，当該金額は寄附金として¶6-235に述べる一定限度の範囲内で控除することができるにすぎない。

　他方，資産を購入した法人は，当該差額については取引を通じて稼得したものであり，これを益金に算入する。

¶6-490　借地権等（合理的な権利金を受領しない賃貸借）

　日本の都市地域では，資産の賃貸借を行うに際して権利金を支払うのが通常の慣行とされている。このような権利金を要求せず，かつ，貸貸人が合理的な理由を示さない場合には，賃貸人は通常の権利金を受領し，当該金額を賃借人へ贈与したものと扱われる（¶6-193参照）。

¶6-495　譲渡資産の帳簿価額の引継ぎ：特別措置Ⅰ

　譲渡資産の帳簿価額を取得資産（買換資産）に引き継ぎ，譲渡資産の譲渡により生ずる譲渡益の課税を取得資産が将来譲渡されるときまで繰り延べる措置がある。次にいくつかの例を掲げるが，すべてを網羅しているものではない。

1．交換による取得固定資産と譲渡固定資産が同一の種類のものであり，同一の用途に供され，かつ，その他一定の要件を満たす場合における固定資産の交換（法法50）
2．譲渡資産の譲渡の日を含む事業年度又はその翌事業年度中に代替資産を取得し，その取得資産を取得の日から１年内に事業の用に供する代替資産の取得

　　ただし，この取扱いの適用は例えば次の場合に合致するものに限られる。なお，短期所有土地に係る土地譲渡益重課（¶6-670）の対象となるものには適用されない。また，この特別措置は譲渡益の80％相当額について即時課税をしないというものである（措法65の7～65の9）。

452 CORPORATION TAX

(a) Selling buildings used for offices, factories, stores, warehouses, etc. and sites for these buildings, owned more than 10 years and located in the Greater Tokyo area, Greater Osaka area or Nagoya area, and buying fixed assets (including land) located in other areas.

(b) Selling land, etc. located in the area near the airport and buying fixed assets located outside that area.

(c) Selling land, etc. which has been continuously owned for more than 10 years on January 1 of the year it was sold by a corporation, and buying land etc.

(d) Selling Japanese ships and buying Japanese ships.

(e) Others

3. Acquisition of new fixed assets if purchased with insurance compensation received for the loss of old fixed assets (Law 47).

4. Acquisition of new fixed assets with compensation received for expropriated old property (SM 64, 65).

Capital gain from transfer of certain assets, including those under a non-tax qualified merger, within 100 percent group is taxable by a seller when the assets are sold to outside of the group (see ¶ 6-590 (Transactions within 100 percent group)).

Dividend in kind, including deemed dividend, within 100 percent group is interpreted as a kind of corporate reorganization and taxation on its capital gain incurred by the payment is deferred (see ¶ 6-590 (Transactions within 100 percent group)).

Transfer of shares to issuing company of the shares within 100 percent group is not taxable (see ¶ 6-590 (Transactions within 100 percent group)).

¶ 6-500 Acquisition of fixed assets by subsidy: Special Concession II

When government subsidies or beneficiaries' contributions are granted to a corporation for the construction of certain fixed assets, and the book value of those fixed assets entered in the account books of the corporation has been reduced by the amount of such subsidies or contributions, then those subsidies and contributions are not subject to tax (Law 42 to 44).

¶ 6-500

法　人　税　453

(a)　首都圏，近畿圏又は中部圏の市街化区域内にある，10年を超えて所有
　　　された事業所用建物及びその敷地を譲渡し，それら以外の地域内にある
　　　固定資産（土地を含む。）と買い換える場合

(b)　航空機騒音障害区域内にある土地等を譲渡し，それ以外の区域にある
　　　固定資産と買い換える場合
(c)　法人が，譲渡の年の1月1日において10年を超えて所有していた土地
　　　等を譲渡し，土地等と買い換える場合

(d)　日本船舶を譲渡して日本船舶と買い換える場合
(e)　その他
3．法人の有する固定資産の滅失による損失により支払を受けた保険金によ
　　り新規代替資産を取得する場合（法法47）
4．法人の有する固定資産が収用され，その取得した補償金により代替資産
　　を取得する場合（措法64，65）
　100％グループ内の内国法人間で一定の資産の移転（非適格合併による移
転を含みます。）を行ったことにより生ずる譲渡損益は，その資産のそのグ
ループ外への移転等の時に，その移転を行った法人において計上する（¶6-
590（完全支配関係がある法人間の取引）参照）。
　100％グループ内の内国法人間の現物配当（みなし配当を含む。）について
は，組織再編税制の一環として位置づけ，譲渡損益の計上を繰り延べる（¶
6-590（完全支配関係がある法人間の取引）参照）。
　100％グループ内の内国法人の株式を発行法人に対して譲渡する等の場合
には，その譲渡損益を計上しない（¶6-590（完全支配関係がある法人間の
取引）参照）。

¶6-500　国庫補助金による固定資産の取得：特別措置Ⅱ

　政府が一定の固定資産を取得させるため法人へ補助金又は助成金を交付す
る場合において，当該法人が固定資産の帳簿価額として当該補助金又は助成
金の額に相当する金額を減額した後の金額を記帳したときは，当該法人の所
得の金額の計算上当該補助金又は助成金は課税されない（法法42〜44）。

454   CORPORATION TAX

¶ 6-505 Exemption of capital gains from expropriated property: Special Concession III

If a corporation whose property is expropriated does not acquire another property, any excess of expropriation proceeds over the cost of the property is treated as capital gains. But the taxation of this type of capital gains is mitigated by allowing a deduction of 50 million yen. However, a corporation may choose a deduction of up to 50 million yen or tax deferment by substituting the book value of the expropriated property for the book value of new property acquired in the same business year as the expropriation takes place (see ¶ 6-495). A 20 million yen deduction applies to sales of land to governments or governmental corporations established by the special law in accordance with the Land Adjustment Project and similar projects. A 15 million yen deduction applies to sales of land to persons who develop housing areas where certain requirements are met, and a special deduction of 8 million yen applies to specified land sales by an agricultural corporation. When a taxpayer has a number of expropriations or sales of land each of which could qualify for one of the three types of special deductions for a calendar year, the total deductions to the taxpayer must not exceed 50 million yen for that year (SM 65-2 to 65-6).

Other Deductions

¶ 6-520 Special deduction applicable to capital gain from land purchased in 2009 and 2010

A corporation can deduct ¥10 million from a capital gain generated from transfer of land purchased during January 1, 2009 through December 31, 2010 provided that it will have been owned for 5 years on January 1, of the year during which it is transferred (SM 65-5-2).

¶ 6-525 Special treatment applicable to capital gain from land purchased in 2009 and 2010

A corporation can offset 80% of capital gain generated from sale of land (the "former land") against the price of land purchased (the "latter land") during January 1, 2009 through December 31, 2010 by depreciating value of the latter land provided that the sale of the former land occurred during 10 years from the end of accounting period during which the latter land is purchased. The corporation must notify a competent tax office of the inten-

¶ 6-505

法　人　税　455

¶6-505　収用資産に係る譲渡益の特別控除：特別措置Ⅲ

　法人の資産が収用された場合において他の資産を取得しないときは，取得資産の取得原価を超える収用補償金の額は譲渡益として取り扱われる。しかし，この種の譲渡益については5,000万円の特別措置が認められる。ただし，法人は最高5,000万円までの特別控除を受けるか，あるいは，収用が行われた同一の事業年度において取得した代替資産につき収用資産の帳簿価額を引継ぐ方法による課税の繰延べ（¶6-495）を受けるか，いずれかを選択することができる。土地区画整理その他類似の事業のため政府又は特別の法人に対して土地を譲渡した場合には，2,000万円の特別控除が認められる。一定の要件に合致した住宅地造成業者への土地の譲渡に対して1,500万円の特別控除が認められる。さらに，農業生産法人の特定の土地の譲渡については800万円の特別控除が認められる。納税者が同一暦年においてこれらの三つの特別控除のうちいずれかに該当する土地の収用又は譲渡をした場合には，当該年度の特別控除の合計額は5,000万円を超えないものとされる（措法65の2～65の6）。

その他の控除

¶6-520　平成21年及び22年に取得をした土地の譲渡所得の特別控除

　平成21年1月1日から平成22年12月31日までの間に取得をした土地等で，その年1月1日において所有期間が5年を超えるものを譲渡した場合には，その年中の当該譲渡所得の金額から1,000万円が控除される（措法65の5の2）。

¶6-525　平成21年及び22年に土地の先行取得をした場合の課税の特例

　平成21年1月1日から平成22年12月31日までの期間内に土地等の取得をし，その取得の日を含む事業年度の確定申告書の提出期限までにこの特例の適用を受ける旨の届出書を提出している場合において，その取得の日を含む事業年度終了の日後10年以内にその法人の所有する他の土地等の譲渡をしたときは，その先行取得をした土地等について，他の土地等の譲渡益の80％相当額（土地等が平成22年1月1日から平成22年12月31日までの期間内に先行取得されたものである場合には，60％相当額）を限度として，圧縮記帳がで

456   CORPORATION TAX

tion of application of the treatment until due date of filing of final return of the accounting period in which the latter land is purchased. If the latter land is purchased in calendar year 2010, 60% shall apply instead of the 80%. The treatment shall not apply to land purchased as an inventory (SM 66-2).

¶ 6-540 Expenditures in prospecting for mineral deposits or similar expenditures for foreign mineral deposits

This includes expenditures in prospecting for mineral deposits and depreciation allowances for the machinery and equipment used in prospecting for mineral deposits. This type of expenditure may enjoy a special tax incentive if there is a "mine prospecting reserve or foreign mine prospecting reserve" which has accrued during the past three years (SM 59) (¶ 6-435).

¶ 6-550 Other special deductions or special tax treatment

The following special deductions, etc., are allowed:

(1)   40% of income derived from a designated company in the Okinawa (SM 60).

(2)   A designated corporation which runs specified business in the international strategic and synthetical special area can deduct 20% of taxable income generated from the specified business for 5 years from the establishment date of the corporation instead of special depreciation or special tax deduction (SM 61).

   Note: See ¶ 6-310(1)(c), ¶ 6-735

(3)   A Special Purpose Corporation (TMK) established under the Asset Liquidation Law or an Investment Corporation established under the Investment Corporation Law can deduct dividend paid by it from its taxable amounts provided it fulfills certain requirements under the tax law (SM 67-14, 67-15).

(4)   As for losses incurred by a Nin-i Kumiai or a Tokumei Kumiai, or a silent partnership, excess amounts of losses over the amounts corresponding to the equity amounts in the Kumiai of a corporation participant of the Kumiai (all amounts of the losses in certain cases) shall not be deductible if the participant's responsibility to the NK's debt is limited to the amounts of the equity in substance (SM 67-12).

¶ 6-540

法　人　税　457

きる。土地等が棚卸資産である場合には，本件の適用はない（措法66の２）。

¶6-540　新鉱床探鉱費又は海外新鉱床探鉱費の特別控除

　この特別控除は新鉱床探鉱費の支出を行った場合又は探鉱用機械設備について償却した場合を対象とする。この種の費用については，過去３年間積立てた「探鉱準備金又は海外探鉱準備金」の金額があるときは，課税上特別の優遇措置が受けられる（措法59）（¶6-435）。

¶6-550　その他の特別控除及び所得計算の特例

　その他次のような措置がある。

(1)　沖縄の認定法人に対する所得の40％特別控除（措法60）。

(2)　国際戦略総合特別区域内において，指定を受けた法人が特定の事業を行う場合には，特別償却及び税額控除に代えて，当該法人設立の日から５年間，当該事業に係る所得の20％相当額をその所得から控除できる（措法61）。

　　（注）：¶6-310(1)(c)，¶6-735参照。

(3)　資産流動化法に規定する特定目的会社及び投資法人法に規定する投資法人が支払う利益の配当の額は，税法に定める一定の要件を満たした場合，損金の額に算入できる（措法67の14，67の15）。

(4)　民法組合，匿名組合等の法人組合員の組合損失について，組合債務の責任の限度が実質的に組合資産の額とされている場合等には，当該法人組合員の出資の額を超える部分の金額（一定の場合には組合損失額の全部）は，損金の額に算入しない（措法67の12）。

458   CORPORATION TAX

Net Loss

¶ 6-570 Carry-over and carry-back

If the ordinary income for a given business year shows a net loss, the net loss may, at the option of the corporation, be carried back to the preceding year (Law 80) or carried forward to the ten years (Law 57).

If the corporation elects to carry back the net loss to the business year beginning within one year before the start of the present business year, then the tax, before deducting any tax credits, on ordinary income for the past business year is refunded fully or partially. If the ordinary income for the past business year is equal to or less than the loss carried back then the tax is refunded in full. If the loss carried back is less than the ordinary income for the past business year, a part of the tax for the past business year, namely the tax multiplied by the ratio of the net loss carried back to the ordinary income for the past business year, is refunded (Law 80).

If the corporation does not elect to carry back the net loss, the net loss is carried forward and equivalent amount to 50% (65% for accounting periods beginning on or after April 1, 2015 during March 31, 2017, and 80% for accounting periods beginning on or after April 1, 2012 during March 31, 2015) of the income of the accounting period to which the loss is carried forward is deductible from the income of each business year beginning within ten years (nine years for loss incurred in accounting periods beginning on or before March 1, 2017) after the start of the present business year.

The loss-carried-over provision is only permitted to a corporation which filed a blue tax return for the business year in which the loss was incurred and has continued to file tax returns, either blue or not, for subsequent business years. The loss-carried-back provision is permitted only to a corporation which continuously filed blue tax returns for the business year to which the loss is to be carried back and subsequent business years in which the loss has been incurred (Law 57⑪).

Note:
1. The loss-carried-back provision is not applied to the business years ending during the period from April 1, 1992 to March 31, 2018 (SM 66-13).
2. Net operating losses incurred in a corporation whose capital is ¥100 million or less can be carried back for one year (SM 66-13). This is, however, not applicable to a corporation in 100 percent group if capital of whose parent is ¥500 million or more (see ¶ 6-590 (Transactions within 100 percent group)).

¶ 6-570

法 人 税 459

欠 損 金

¶6-570　欠損金の繰越し及び繰戻し

　法人の一定の事業年度の所得が欠損金額となった場合には，その選択により，欠損金額に相当する金額は前年に繰り戻されるか（法法80）又はその後の10年間繰り越される（法法57）。

　法人が当該事業年度において生じた欠損金額を当該事業年度の開始の日前1年以内に開始する事業年度に繰り戻すことを選択した場合には，当該既往の事業年度における所得に対する法人税の額（税額控除された金額がある場合にはこれを加算した金額とする。）の全部又はその一部について還付を受けられる。既往の事業年度の所得の金額が繰り戻される欠損金額と同額以下である場合には，当該既往の事業年度の税額は全額還付されることとなる。反対に，繰り戻される欠損金額が既往の事業年度の所得の金額よりも少額である場合には，当該既往の事業年度の法人税額の一部，すなわち，既往の事業年度の所得の金額のうちに占める当該事業年度の欠損金額に相当する金額の割合を乗じて計算した金額に相当する法人税額が還付される（法法80）。

　法人が欠損金の繰戻しによる還付を請求しない場合には，各事業年度において生じた欠損金額のうちその繰越控除をする事業年度のその繰越控除前の所得の金額の50％（平成27年4月1日から平成29年3月31日までの間に開始する事業年度においては65％，平成24年4月1日から平成27年3月31日までの間に開始する事業年度においては80％）に相当する額は当該事業年度終了後10年（平成29年3月31日以前に開始する事業年度において生じる欠損金額に関しては9年）以内に開始した事業年度に繰り越され，所得の金額の計算上損金の額に算入される。

　上記の欠損金の繰越しは，欠損金額の生じた事業年度において青色申告書を提出し，かつ，その後において連続して確定申告書（青色であると白色であるとを問わない。）を提出する場合に限り適用される。他方，欠損金の繰戻しは繰り戻す対象となった事業年度から欠損金額が生じた事業年度まで連続して青色申告書を提出した場合に限り適用される（法法57⑪）。

（注）：1．平成4年4月1日から平成30年3月31日までの間に終了する事業年度については，欠損金の繰戻しによる還付制度は適用されない（措法66の13）。

　　　　2．資本金の額が1億円以下の法人等の各事業年度の欠損金額については，前1年間の繰戻還付を認める（措法66の13）。ただし，資本金の額が5億円以上の法人の100％子法人を除く（¶6-590（完全支配関係がある法人間の取引）参照）。

460   CORPORATION TAX

  3. A hundred percent of the loss carried forward of deductible if the capital of the corporation is ¥100,000,000 or less and the corporation is not a subsidiary of a corporation whose capital is more than ¥500,000,000.

  4. Such entities as TMK, J-REIT whose dividends paid can be deductible as expenses can deduct loss carried forward until 100% of income of the accounting period to which the loss is carried forward.

If more than 50% of shares of a deficit corporation are owned directly or indirectly by certain shareholders and the corporation changes its previous line of business within 5 years after the shareholder owns the shares, loss incurred before the change of its line of business can not be carried forward when the corporation meets certain conditions (Law 57-2).

¶ 6-575 Carry-over of accidental loss

When the inventory or fixed assets of a corporation, not including credit and other accounts receivable, are damaged by an earthquake, storm, flood, fire or similar accidental occurrence, the loss suffered from such disasters may be carried forward to the following ten years (nine years for loss incurred in accounting periods beginning on or before March 1, 2017) and equivalent amount to 50% (65% for accounting periods beginning on or after April 1, 2015 during March 31, 2017, and 80% for accounting periods beginning on or after April 1, 2012 during March 31, 2015) of the income of the accounting period to which the loss is carried forward is deductible from income, even though the corporation does not file a blue return (Law 58).

The carry-over of the accidental loss provision is only permitted when a corporation files a tax return accompanied by schedule 7 (a statement of the accidental loss) for the business year in which the accidental loss was incurred, and when the corporation continues to file tax returns for subsequent business years (Law 58⑥).

Note:

  1. A hundred percent of the loss carried forward is deductible if the capital of the corporation is ¥100,000,000 or less and the corporation is not a subsidiary of a corporation whose capital is more than ¥500,000,000.

  2. Such entities as TMK, J-REIT whose dividends paid can be deductible as expenses can deduct loss carried forward until 100% of income of the accounting period to which the loss is carried forward.

¶ 6-580 Deficit covered by directors, shareholders

When competent authorities make decision to start reorganization

¶ 6-575

法　人　税　461

　　3．資本金の額が1億円以下の法人等の各事業年度の欠損金額については，100％に相当
　　　する額の繰越控除を認める。ただし，資本金の額が5億円以上の法人の100％子法人を
　　　除く。
　　4．特定目的会社，投資法人等で，支払配当等の損金算入制度の適用対象となるものに
　　　ついては，現行の控除限度額まで控除できる。

　なお，欠損法人が，特定の株主等によってその発行済株式の総数の50％を
超える数の株式を直接又は間接に保有された場合において，その保有された
日から5年以内に，従来から営む事業を廃止し，かつ，その事業規模を大幅
に超える事業を開始したこと等一定の事由に該当するときは，その該当する
日の属する事業年度前において生じた欠損金額について欠損金の繰越控除制
度を適用しない（法法57の2）。

¶6-575　災害損失の繰越し

　法人のたな卸資産，固定資産（貸付金その他の受取勘定は含まれない。）
が震災，風水害，火災その他の災害により損失を受けた場合には，これら災
害により生じた損失のうち欠損金の部分の金額については，法人が青色申告
書を提出していない場合においても，その繰越控除をする事業年度のその繰
越控除前の所得の金額の50％（平成27年4月1日から平成29年3月31日まで
の間に開始する事業年度においては65％，平成24年4月1日から平成27
年3月31日までの間に開始する事業年度においては80％）に相当する額はそ
の後10年（平成29年3月31日以前に開始する事業年度において生じる欠損金
額に関しては9年）間繰り越して所得の金額の計算上損金の額に算入される
（法法58）。
　この災害損失の繰越しはその損失の生じた事業年度にその損失の金額に関
する明細を記載した確定申告書を提出しており，かつその後においても連続
して確定申告書を提出することを条件に認められる（法法58⑥）。

　（注）：1．資本金の額が1億円以下の法人等の各事業年度の欠損金額については，100％に相当
　　　　　する額の繰越控除を認める。ただし，資本金の額が5億円以上の法人の100％子法人を
　　　　　除く。

　　　　2．特定目的会社，投資法人等で，支払配当等の損金算入制度の適用対象となるものに
　　　　　ついては，現行の控除限度額まで控除できる。

¶6-580　役員，株主からの私財提供

　会社更生法等による手続開始の決定があった場合において，過去の事業年

462   CORPORATION TAX

procedures of a corporation under the Corporation Reorganization Law, and if a net loss carried over from any past business year was covered by special benefits granted by a director or shareholder, etc. to enable the corporation to recover from financial difficulties, the amount of the net loss so covered is deductible in computing the ordinary income of the present business year under certain conditions, even though it is not otherwise allowable (Law 59) (under ¶ 6-570 and ¶ 6-575).

(1)   The deductible net loss is the lower of the following three amounts:

(a)   Any gift of money or property and any debts excused.

(b)   The balance of (i) and (ii) below from the amount of the loss at the end of the business year in which the gift was granted or the debt excused.
(i)   The amount of additional capital at the end of the business year.
(ii)   The amount of net loss (¶ 6-570) and accidental loss (¶ 6-575) which have been deducted from the income.
(c)   The income before applying this item.

(2)   The deduction of this item is only permitted when the corporation files a tax return accompanied by schedule 7 and its certificate of the above mentioned facts.

¶ 6-590 Taxation on transactions within 100 percent group

1. Taxation on transfer of assets within 100 percent group

(1)   Capital gain from transfer of certain assets, including those under a non-tax qualified merger, within 100 percent group is taxable by a seller when the assets are sold to outside of the group.

Note:
100 percent group means a group of companies one of whom owns 100% of shares of other companies directly or indirectly (Law 2).

(2)   Non-tax qualified share exchange within 100 percent group is exempted from requirement for evaluation of assets owned by a subsidiary within 100 percent group under a non-tax qualified share exchange provided that shares of foreign parent corporation is not issued for consideration for the merger.

2. Tax treatment on donation within 100 percent group

Donation within 100 percent group is not treated as expenses at donor,

¶ 6-590

法　人　税　463

度から繰り越された欠損金があり，役員，株主等から財政危機を救うために金銭その他の資産の贈与を受けたときは，当該繰越欠損金が上記¶6-570及び¶6-575の適用を受けない場合においても，当該贈与を受けた金額に相当する欠損金額は当該事業年度の所得の金額の計算上，一定の条件の下で損金に算入される（法法59）。

(1)　損金に算入される金額とは，次の金額のうち最も少ない金額である（法令118）。
　(a)　贈与を受けた金銭その他の資産の額及び債務の免除を受けた金額の合計額
　(b)　贈与又は債務の免除を受けた事業年度の終了のときにおける前事業年度以前の事業年度から繰り越された欠損金額の合計額から次の(i)及び(ii)の金額の合計額を控除した金額
　　(i)　贈与又は債務免除のあった事業年度終了のときにおける資本積立金額
　　(ii)　所得の計算上損金に算入された繰越欠損金（¶6-570）又は災害損失（¶6-575）
　(c)　この規定を適用しないで計算した場合の所得金額
(2)　この規定による欠損金額の損金算入を行う場合には，確定申告書に別表7及びその事実を証する書類を添付しなければならない。

¶6-590　完全支配関係がある法人間の取引
１．100％グループ内の法人間の資産の譲渡取引等
(1)　100％グループ内の内国法人間で一定の資産の移転（非適格合併による移転を含む。）を行ったことにより生ずる譲渡損益は，その資産のそのグループ外への移転等の時に，その移転を行った法人において計上する。
　（注）：100％グループ内の法人とは，完全支配関係（原則として，発行済株式の全部を直接又は間接に保有する関係）のある法人をいう（法法2）。

(2)　100％グループ内の法人間の非適格株式交換等は，非適格株式交換等に係る完全子法人等の有する資産の時価評価制度の対象にはならない。ただし，合併等の対価として一定の外国親法人株式が交付されるものは除く。

２．100％グループ内の法人間の寄付
　　100％グループ内の内国法人間の寄付については，支出法人において全額損金

464　CORPORATION TAX

nor income at donee (Law 25-2, 37).

3. Capital transaction within 100 percent group

(1) Dividend in kind, including deemed dividend, within 100 percent group is interpreted as a kind of corporate reorganization and taxation on the capital gain incurred by the payment is deferred.

(2) When applying dividend received deduction rule to dividend paid within 100 percent group, deduction of interest corresponding to the dividend is not required.

(3) Transfer of shares to issuing company of the shares within 100 percent group is not taxable.

4. Application of special tax treatment to 100 percent group

Special tax treatment, raised as below, applicable to a corporation whose capital is ¥100 million or less shall not be applicable to a corporation in 100 percent group if shares of the corporation is owned by two or more corporations whose capital are ¥500 million or more.

(a) Reduced tax rate (see ¶ 6-060)

(b) Non-application of additional taxation for retained earnings in a family corporation (see ¶ 6-640)

(c) Statutory rate for bad debt reserve

(d) Fixed amount deduction for entertainment expenses (see ¶ 6-230)

(e) Refund of tax by application of loss carry-back (see ¶ 6-570)

Corporate Reorganization
(Corporate Division, Merger, Investment-in-kind, Post-establishment transfer)

¶ 6-600 Tax treatment of corporation

If a corporation transfer its asses to another corporation pursuant to a corporate division, a merger, an investment-in-kind, a dividend in kind or a share transfer ("reorganization"), and the reorganization correspond to a "qualified reorganization" for corporate tax purposes, the recognition of the gains and losses on the transfer of the assets will be deferred.

1. Qualified reorganization (Law 2)

(1) Qualified corporate division

A qualified corporate division is one of he following corporate divisions. It is also required that at the time of corporate division, only

¶ 6-600

法　人　税　465

不算入とし，受領法人において全額益金不算入とする（法法25の2，37）。
3．100％グループ内の法人間の資本関連取引
⑴　100％グループ内の内国法人間の現物配当（みなし配当を含む。）については，組織再編税制の一環として位置づけ，譲渡損益の計上を繰り延べる。
⑵　100％グループ内の内国法人からの受取配当について益金不算入制度を適用する場合には，負債利子控除を適用しない。

⑶　100％グループ内の内国法人の株式を発行法人に対して譲渡した場合，その譲渡損益を計上しない。
4．中小企業向け特例措置の大法人の100％子法人に対する適用
　　資本金の額又は出資金の額が1億円以下の法人（中小企業等）に係る次の制度については，資本金の額若しくは出資金の額が5億円以上の複数の法人に，発行済株式の全部を保有されている子法人には適用しない。

⒜　軽減税率（¶6-060参照）
⒝　特定同族会社の特別税率の不適用（¶6-640参照）

⒞　貸倒引当金の法定繰入率
⒟　交際費等の損金不算入制度における定額控除制度（¶6-230参照）

⒠　欠損金の繰戻しによる還付制度（¶5-570参照）

企業組織再編成
（分割，合併，現物出資，現物分配）

¶6-600　法人における課税の取扱い

　法人が，分割，合併，現物出資，現物分配又は株式移転（以下「組織再編成」）によりその有する資産等を他に移転した場合において，当該組織再編成が適格組織再編成（適格分割，適格合併，適格現物出資，適格現物分配又は適格株式交換）に該当する場合には，各移転資産等の譲渡損益の計上が繰り延べられる。
1．適格分割再編成（法法2）
⑴　適格分割
　　適格分割とは，次のいずれかに該当する分割のうち，分割に伴って分割承継法人の株式のみが交付され，かつ，分割型分割にあっては，分割法人

466 CORPORATION TAX

shares of the transferee corporation should be distributed and in case of a split-up type of corporate division, the shares of the transferee corporation should be distributed in accordance with the percentage ownership of the transferor corporation.

(a) Corporate division in which the transferor corporation and the transferee corporation are in 100% ownership relations

(b) Corporate division in which the transferor corporation and the transferee corporation are in more than 50% but less than 100% ownership relations and also the following conditions are met:

   (i) Main assets and liabilities of the split-up business of the transferor corporation are succeeded to by the transferee corporation.

   (ii) It is expected that approximately 80% or more of the employees of the split-up business of the transferor corporation will be continued to be employed in the succeeded business.

   (iii) It is expected that the transferred business is continued to be operated in the transferee corporation.

(c) Corporate division which is performed for conducting a joint business and meets the following conditions:

   (i) It is expected that the shares of the transferee corporation will be continued to be held.

   (ii) (i), (ii) and (iii) in (b) above

   A joint business is defined as the business where the split-up business of the transferor corporation has relation to one of the businesses of the transferee corporation and the ratios of sales amounts, number of employees or things corresponding to them do not exceed 5 times of each numbers, or some directors of both corporations will become top rank of directors.

(2) Qualified merger and qualified investment-in-kind

A qualified merger and a qualified investment-in-kind are a merger and an investment-in-kind which meet the conditions similar to the qualified corporate division.

(3) Qualified dividend in kind

A qualified dividend in kind is a dividend in kind which meets the following conditions:

Dividend in kind by shares of a Japanese company made within 100 percent group.

¶ 6-600

の株主の持株数に応じて分割承継法人の株式が交付されるものをいう。

(a) 分割法人と分割承継法人とが100％の持分関係である場合の分割

(b) 分割法人と分割承継法人とが50％超100％未満の持分関係である場合
の分割で，次の要件に該当するもの

(i) 分割法人の分割事業の主要な資産及び負債が分割承継法人に引継が
れていること

(ii) 分割法人の分割事業の従業者の概ね80％以上が分割承継法人におい
て引き続き業務に従事することが見込まれていること

(iii) 分割法人の分割事業が分割承継法人において引き続き営まれること
が見込まれていること

(c) 共同事業を行うための分割で，次の要件に該当するもの

(i) 分割により交付された分割承継法人の株式を継続して保有すること
が見込まれていること

(ii) 上記(b)の(i)から(ii)までの要件

共同事業とは，分割法人の分割事業と分割承継法人のいずれかの事業
とが相互に関連性を有するものであることに加え，それぞれの事業の売
上金額，従業者数若しくはこれらに準ずるものの比率が概ね5倍を超え
ないこと又は分割法人と分割承継法人の双方の役員が分割後に分割承継
法人の経営に従事する常務クラス以上の役員となることとの要件に該当
するものをいう。

(2) 適格合併，適格現物出資

適格合併及び適格現物出資とは，適格分割の要件に準ずる要件に該当す
る合併及び現物出資をいう。

(3) 適格現物分配

適格現物分配とは，次の要件に該当する現物分配をいう。

内国法人を現物分配法人とする現物分配のうち，その現物分配により資
産の移転を受ける者がその現物分配の直前において当該内国法人との間
に完全支配関係がある内国法人のみであるもの。

468   CORPORATION TAX

(4) Share exchange or share transfer of a company to establish a new parent company between the company and shareholders of the company and a merger (triangle merger) where a parent company of a merger company issues its shares to shareholders of the merged company under the law are included in a qualified merger (Law 2).

If shareholders of the merged company receive shares of a company in a tax haven country which has no substance, and a merger company in Japan has no substance as well, the merger shall not be classified as a qualified merger even if it meets all of the other requirements (SM 68-2-3).

2. Deferral of recognition of gains and losses

If a corporation transfers its assets pursuant to a qualified corporate division, a qualified merger, a qualified investment-in-kind or a qualified dividend in kind, the book value of the assets can be carried over into the transferee corporation, and gains and losses on the transfer will be deferred (Law 62-2 to 62-4).

Please note that the rule-over treatment on the received shares of the book value of transferred net assets from the transferor pursuant to an investment-in-kind was abolished subsequent to the introduction of the new treatment.

Note:

If a corporation transfers its assets pursuant to a non-qualified corporate division or a non-qualified merger, the corporation must recognize capital gains or losses on the transfer.

However, transfer of certain assets within 100 percent group under a non-tax qualified merger is excluded. Non-tax qualified share exchange within 100 percent group is exempted from requirement for evaluation of assets owned by a subsidiary within 100 percent group under a non-tax qualified share exchange provided that shares of foreign parent corporation is not issued for consideration for the merger (see ¶ 6-590 (Transactions within 100 percent group)).

¶ 6-604 Tax treatment of shareholder

1. Capital gain of share transfer (Law 61-2)

If a shareholder of a transferor corporation or a disappearing corporation only receives shares of a transferee corporation or a surviving corporation pursuant to a split-up type of corporate division or a merger, the recognition of the gains and losses on the transfer of the shares of

¶ 6-604

法 人 税 469

(4) 株式交換又は株式移転制度により子会社となる会社の株式の交換又は移転が行われた場合，及び組織再編成に際し合併法人等の親法人（合併等の直前に合併法人等の発行済株式の全部を直接に保有し，かつ，当該合併等後にその発行済株式の全部を直接に継続して保有することが見込まれる法人をいう。）の株式のみが交付される場合も適格組織再編成に含まれる（法法2）。

ただし，企業グループ内の法人間で行われる合併等のうち，軽課税国に所在する実体のない外国親会社の株式を対価とし，国内の合併法人等にも事業の実体が認められないものは，適格合併等に該当しないこととする（措法68の2の3）。

2. 譲渡損益の計上の繰延べ

適格分割，適格合併，適格現物出資又は適格現物分配による資産等の移転は，帳簿価額による資産等の引継とし，譲渡損益の発生はないものとして取り扱われる（法法62の2〜62の4）。

なお，この措置が講じられたことに伴い，特定の現物出資により取得した有価証券の圧縮記帳制度は廃止された。

(注)：適格分割又は適格合併等に該当しない分割又は合併等による資産等の移転は，時価による資産等の譲渡とし，譲渡益又は譲渡損は，分割型分割又は合併にあってはその前日の属する事業年度，分社型分割にあってはその日の属する事業年度の益金の額又は損金の額とする。

ただし，100％グループ内の内国法人間の非適格合併による一定の資産の移転を除く。また，合併等の対価として一定の外国親法人株式が交付されない場合，当該100％グループ内の法人間の非適格株式交換等を，非適格株式交換等に係る完全子法人等の有する資産の時価評価制度の対象から除外する（¶6-590（完全支配関係がある法人間の取引）参照）。

¶6-604　株主における課税の取扱い

1. 株式の譲渡損益の取扱い（法法61の2）

分割型分割又は合併により，分割法人（又は被合併法人）の株主が分割承継法人（又は合併法人）の株式のみの交付を受けた場合には，旧株（分割法人（又は被合併法人）の株式）の譲渡損益の計上が繰り延べられる。

ただし，合併等により外国親会社の株式が外国法人株主に交付された場

470   CORPORATION TAX

a transferor corporation or a disappearing corporation will be deferred. If a recipient of the shares is a foreign company under the triangle merger, the recipient is subject to capital gain tax on the disposal of shares of the merged company provided that it is subject to tax under the current domestic tax rule. If the recipient has a permanent establishment ("PE") in Japan and the received shares are recorded in the PE, the capital gain taxation shall be deferred until it is disposed from the PE.

2. Deemed dividend (Law 24)

If a shareholder of a transferor corporation or a disappearing corporation receives shares and other assets from a transferee corporation or a surviving corporation pursuant to a non-qualified split-up type of corporate division or a non-qualified merger, the difference between the amounts of the shares and other assets over the amounts corresponding to the reduced capital and capital surplus of the transferor corporation or a disappearing corporation will be treated as deemed dividends. Please note that the deemed dividends treatment without receiving any assets from the corporation by its shareholder was abolished.

¶ 6-607 Others

1. Provision of tax-free reserves

Necessary treatments were added to the provisions of tax-free reserves in accordance with the types of the corporate reorganizations.

2. Anti-tax avoidance provision (Law 57, 132-2)

In addition to the anti-tax-avoidance provisions to prevent the use of the corporate reorganization rules to unreasonably increase the amounts of loss carry forward, a broad anti-tax avoidance provision was adopted.

¶ 6-610 Liquidation (abolished from October 1, 2010)

When a corporation is dissolved and the liquidation procedure has been commenced, tax on ordinary income is not levied for the period after dissolution. However, a corporation should pay tax as if it were not dissolved, because it should make a prepayment of the tax on liquidation income, which is computed in a manner similar to the tax on ordinary income (see ¶ 6-820 to ¶ 6-840). The following points must be kept in mind:

(1) When a corporation is dissolved during a business year, the period

¶ 6-607

合には，その外国法人株主の旧株の譲渡益（日本で課税の対象となる国内
源泉所得に該当するものに限る。）については，課税される。なお，この
取扱いは，外国法人株主が，当該旧株を国内に有する恒久的施設において
管理する間は適用しない。

2．みなし配当の取扱い（法法24）
　　適格分割又は適格合併に該当しない分割型分割（又は合併）により，分
　割法人（又は被合併法人）の株主が交付を受けた分割承継法人（又は合併
　法人）の株式等の価額のうち，資本等の金額を超える部分を原資とする金
　額については，配当とみなされる。
　　なお，資産の交付がない場合のみなし配当課税は廃止された。

¶6-607　その他

1．引当金等
　　その他引当金等の取扱いについて，組織再編成の形態に応じて，所要の
　措置が講じられた。
2．租税回避の防止（法法57，132の2）
　　繰越欠損金等を利用した租税回避の防止規定に加え，組織再編成に係る
　包括的な租税回避防止規定が設けられた。

¶6-610　清算（平成22年10月1日をもって廃止）

　　法人が解散し，清算手段が開始された場合には，解散した事業年度以後に
ついては各事業年度の所得に対する法人税は課されない。しかしながら，法
人は清算所得に対する法人税を予納しなければならず，それは解散しなかっ
たものとして税額を納付するものであり，その計算は各事業年度の所得に対
する法人税の計算方法と類似している（¶6-820〜¶6-840参照）。ただし，
次の点に留意しなければならない。
⑴　法人が事業年度の中途において解散した場合には，課税上，その事業年

472   CORPORATION TAX

from the beginning of that business year to the time of dissolution and the period from the time of dissolution to the end of that business year are deemed to form two independent business years for tax purposes.

(2) In computing the amount of ordinary income for the last business year before the dissolution, deductions for certain kinds of reserve accounts are not allowed.

Consolidated Taxation System

¶ 6-630 Basic rules

1. Scope of applicable corporations and methods of application

    (1) The consolidated taxation system shall be applicable to a group of Japanese companies in which a Japanese company (parent company) directly or indirectly owns 100% ownership of other Japanese companies (subsidiaries).

    (2) The parent company shall be limited to an ordinary corporation or a cooperative association and the subsidiary shall be limited to an ordinary corporation.

    (3) Each group can choose that it would take the system by submitting an application form 3 months before the commencement of an accounting period for which the companies select the application of the consolidated taxation system. If companies would select the system, the companies must take the consolidated taxation methods continuously.

    (4) The parent company shall file the consolidated tax return and pay total taxes to a tax office.

    (5) Each subsidiary shall file its own final return describing its individual income amounts and be jointly responsible for the payments of the total taxes.

    (6) The consolidated accounting period shall be adjusted to meet that of a parent company.

2. Calculations of consolidated income and consolidated tax

    (1) Basic rules for the calculations of consolidated income and consolidated tax

        (a) Consolidated income shall be calculated based on the amount of each company's income and consolidated tax shall be a tax calculated based on the aggregated income.

法　人　税　473

度の開始の日から解散の日までの期間，解散の日の翌日からその事業年度の末日までの期間は，それぞれ独立した事業年度とみなされる。

(2)　解散の日を含む事業年度の所得の金額の計算上，一定種類の引当金・準備金の積立ては認められない。

連結納税制度

¶6-630　基本的な仕組み

1．適用法人，適用方法

(1)　連結納税制度の適用法人は，内国法人である親会社と，その親会社に発行済株式の全部を直接又は間接に保有されるすべての内国法人（100％子会社）とする。

(2)　親会社は普通法人と協同組合等に，100％子会社は普通法人に限る。

(3)　連結納税制度の適用は選択性とし，連結納税制度を選択する場合には，原則として，連結納税制度を適用しようとする事業年度の3ヶ月前までに承認申請書を提出し，その事業年度の開始前に国税庁長官の承認を受けるものとする。また，いったん選択した場合には継続して適用するものとする。

(4)　親会社は，連結所得に対する法人税の申告及び納付を行う。

(5)　連結納税制度の適用を受けた100％子会社は，連結納付責任を負うものとし，連結所得の個別帰属額等を記載した書類を税務署に提出する。

(6)　連結事業年度は，親会社の事業年度に合わせたものとする。

2．連結所得金額及び連結税額の計算

(1)　連結所得金額及び連結税額の計算の基本的な仕組み

　(a)　連結所得金額及び連結税額は，連結グループ内の各法人の個別所得金額を基礎とし，連結グループを一体として計算する。

474   CORPORATION TAX

(b)   The amounts of the consolidated tax shall be allocated to each company based on the percentage of each company's income.

(2)   Internal transactions between companies in a consolidated group
A capital gain or loss of assets derived from internal transactions between companies in a consolidated group shall not be recognized until the assets are transferred to a third party. The assets shall mean fixed assets, land, account receivables, securities and deferred assets (the assets whose book value are less than 10 million yen shall be excluded).

(3)   Prevention against double recognition of profit or loss
When a parent company sells stocks of a consolidated subsidiary or cancels the application of the consolidated taxation system, the book value of the subsidiary's stocks shall be amended properly corresponding to the cancellation.

(4)   Consolidated loss

(a)   Consolidated loss shall be carried forward for 5 years (7 years in case the losses are incurred in accounting periods beginning on and after April 1, 2001).

(b)   Only parent company's loss before the application of the consolidation system shall be included in the consolidated losses.

(c)   When companies or one of the subsidiaries terminate the application of the consolidated taxation system, consolidated loss carried forward shall be taken over by each company in the group based on each attributable loss.

(5)   Tax rates
Corporate tax rates shall be as follows.

(a)   In case that the parent company is an ordinary corporation: 23.2%

(b)   Tax rate applicable to taxable income corresponding to the amounts up to ¥8 million or less (the "reduced rate") in case that its parent is an ordinary corporation and that its capital is ¥100 million or less: 19%

(c)   The reduced rate in case that its parent is a cooperative: 20% (16% for accounting periods ending during April 1, 2012 through March 31, 2015)

Note:
1.   The reduced rate, in case that its parent entity is a specified medical cor-

¶ 6-630

法　人　税　475

(b)　その上で，連結税額を連結グループ内の各法人の個別所得金額又は個別欠損金額を基礎として計算される金額を基にして連結グループ内の各法人に配分する。

(2)　連結グループ内の法人間の取引

連結グループ内の法人間で，資産（固定資産，土地等，金銭債権，有価証券又は繰延資産（これらの資産のうち帳簿価額1,000万円未満のものを除く。））の移転を行ったことにより生ずる譲渡損益は，その資産の連結グループ外への移転等のときに，その移転を行った法人において計上する。

(3)　利益・損失の二重計上の防止

連結納税制度の適用を受けている100％子会社（以下「連結子会社」）の株式を譲渡する場合，連結納税制度の適用を取りやめる場合等には，その譲渡等のときにおいて，その連結子会社の株式の帳簿価額の修正を行う。

(4)　連結欠損金額

(a)　連結欠損金額は，5年間（平成13年4月1日以後に開始した事業年度において生じた欠損金については7年間）で繰越控除する。

(b)　連結納税制度の適用開始前に生じた欠損金額は，親会社の前5年以内に生じた欠損金額等一定のものに限り，連結納税制度のもとで繰越控除できる。

(c)　連結納税制度の適用を取りやめる場合，連結子会社が連結グループから離脱する場合等には，連結欠損金額の個別帰属額をその取りやめる親会社若しくは連結子会社又は離脱する連結子会社に引き継ぐ。

(5)　税率

連結所得に対する法人税の税率は，次のとおりとする。

(a)　親会社が普通法人である場合の税率　23.2％

(b)　親会社が中小法人である場合の軽減税率（年800万円以下の部分）19％

(c)　親会社が協同組合等である場合の軽減税率　20％（平成24年4月1日から平成27年3月31日の間に終了する各事業年度については16％）

(注)：1．親会社が特定の医療法人である場合の軽減税率は20％（平成24年4月1日から平成27年3月31日の間に終了する各事業年度については16％），親会社が特定の協同組合等

476 CORPORATION TAX

poration, is 20% (16% for a accounting periods ending during April 1, 2012 through March 31, 2015), and 22% in case that its parent entity is a specified cooperative.

2. Corporate tax rates applied to an accounting period of ordinary corporations beginning on or after April 1, 2016 during March 31, 2018 are 23.4%.

3. Commencement of the application of the consolidation taxation system, participation to a consolidation group, withdrawal from a consolidation group

   (1) A company shall have a deemed accounting period when it joins in a consolidation group. When the company withdraws from a consolidation group, the beginning of the accounting period during which it withdraws is deemed to be the date of the withdrawal. The company shall not be able to re-enter into the consolidation group for 5 years.

   (2) A company shall evaluate their assets at fair market value when it joins in the consolidation group and shall recognize its capital gain or loss in the accounting period just before the participation. The assets mean fixed assets, land, account receivables, securities and deferred assets (the assets whose book value are less than smaller of 10 million yen or a half amount of its capital and capital surplus shall be excluded.).

   However, the fair market value evaluation shall not be necessary for the following company (In case of a subsidiary, which joins the system, the subsidiaries raised in the following item from (d) to (g) shall not be necessary to make the fair market evaluation.).

   (a) A parent company

   (b) A subsidiary set up by a share transfer

   (c) A 100% subsidiary owned for more than 5 years by a parent company

   (d) A 100% subsidiary set up by a parent company or a 100% subsidiary of the parent company

   (e) A 100% subsidiary owned for more than 5 years by an ex-parent company, which merged into a current parent company under a qualified merger, and becomes a 100% subsidiary of the current parent company

   (f) A company which becomes a 100% subsidiary of a parent com-

¶ 6-630

法　人　税　477

に該当する場合の特別税率は22％とする。

　2．なお，平成28年4月1日から平成30年3月31日の間に開始した各事業年度の普通法人の法人税率は原則23.4％である。

3．連結納税制度の適用開始又は連結グループへの加入，連結グループからの離脱

(1)　連結納税制度の適用を受ける法人又は連結グループに加入する法人については，その適用の開始又は加入の前後でみなし事業年度を設け，その前の期間については単体納税制度又は他の連結グループの連結納税制度のもとで申告納付を行い，その後の期間については連結納税制度のもとで申告納付を行う。

　　連結グループから離脱した法人は，その連結事業年度開始の日に離脱したものとみなし，5年間再加入を認めない。

(2)　連結納税制度の適用開始又は連結グループへの加入に際し，適用開始法人又は加入法人の資産（固定資産，土地等，金銭債権，有価証券又は繰延資産（これらの資産のうちその含み損益が資本等の金額の2分1又は1,000万円のいずれか少ない金額に満たないものを除く。））については，直前の事業年度において，時価評価により評価損益の計上を行う。

　　ただし，次に掲げる法人（加入の場合は，(d)から(g)までに掲げる法人）については，資産の時価評価による評価損益の計上は行わない。

(a)　親会社

(b)　株式移転に係る完全子会社

(c)　親会社に長期（5年超）保有されている100％子会社

(d)　親会社又は100％子会社により設立された100％子会社

(e)　適格合併に係る被合併法人が長期保有していた100％子会社でその適格合併により親会社の100％子会社となったもの等

(f)　法令の規定に基づく株式の買取り等により親会社の100％子会社とな

478   CORPORATION TAX

pany because of the purchase of stocks according to the legal
requirement

(g) A subsidiary, and other subsidiaries owned for more than 5
years by the subsidiary, set up by share for share exchange, if it
meets certain requirement

¶ 6-634 Application of other tax rules to the calculation of consolidated income and consolidated taxes

In principle, a consolidated group shall be treated as one entity for the
purposes of consolidation taxation system. However, certain considerations
shall be taken into account with regard to the application of other tax rules
to the calculation of consolidated income and consolidated taxes, For example, the amounts of dividends paid from consolidated subsidiaries before
deducting attributable interests to the dividends are exempted from taxable
income. Depreciation expenses are separately calculated by each entity.

¶ 6-637 Others

1. Prevention from tax avoidance
   In order to prevent from various tax avoidance structure, comprehensive rules for the prevention shall be introduced into.
2. Other amendments
   Necessary amendments are made to the tax examiner's investigation
   rights and various penalties.
3. Effective date
   The consolidated taxation system shall be applicable to an accounting periods starting on or after April 1, 2002 and closing on or after March 31, 2003.

Undistributed Profits
(for a family corporation)

¶ 6-640 Basic concept

The basis for the tax on undistributed profits is the amount of undistributed profits less the allowance for undistributed profits (Law 67①).

The amount of undistributed profits is computed by applying the following formula to reflect how much is distributable from ordinary income
in a given business year (Law 67③).

¶ 6-634

法　人　税　479

ったもの

⒢　株式交換に係る完全子会社（その完全子会社に長期保有されていた
100％子会社を含む。）で一定の要件を満たすもの

¶6-634　連結所得金額・連結税額の計算に係る諸制度の取扱い

　受取配当については連結グループ内の連結子会社からの受取配当について
負債利子を控除せずその全額を益金不算入とすることとし，減価償却費につ
いては連結グループ内の各法人の個別計算によることとする等，連結所得金
額・連結税額の計算に係る諸制度については，連結グループを一体として要
件の判定や計算等を行うことを基本としつつ，制度の趣旨や技術的な観点も
踏まえて，措置を講ずる。

¶6-637　その他

1．租税回避行為の防止

　多様な租税回避行為に適切に対応するため，包括的な租税回避行為防止規
定等を設ける。

2．その他の整備

　質問検査権，罰則等について所要の整備を行う。

3．適用関係

　連結納税制度については，平成14年4月1日以後に開始し，かつ，平成15
年3月31日以後に終了する事業年度から適用する。

同族会社の留保金課税

¶6-640　基本的考え方

　留保金課税の課税標準は，留保金額から留保控除額を控除した残額であ
る。留保金額は当該事業年度の所得の金額のうちからの配当可能金額を反映
させるため，次の算式を用いて計算する（法法67①）。

480   CORPORATION TAX

Ordinary income + items to be added to ordinary income (¶ 6-645)

– disbursements, the deductibility of which is denied in computing ordinary income (¶ 6-650)

= distributable profits

Distributable profits – distributions (¶ 6-655)   = undistributed profits

Note:
1. The tax on undistributed profits is levied only on a personal family corporation with more than ¥100 million capital. However, additional taxation for retained earnings in a family corporation is applicable to a corporation in 100 percent group if capital of whose parent is ¥500 million or more (see ¶ 6-590 (Transactions within 100% group)).
2. The tax on undistributed profits is levied not on the undistributed profits themselves, but on the undistributed profits less the allowance for undistributed profits (¶ 6-660).
3. The taxation on undistributed profit is not applicable to the following accounting periods of the following corporations (SM 68-2);
   (a) Accounting periods within 2 years after its establishment provided it is a small or medium-size corporation,
   (b) Accounting periods of an authorized corporation under the Law for Encouraging New Business Activities by middle and small-size corporations provided it is performing the business with its authorized plans
4. A small or medium-size corporation (a corporation whose amounts of capital is 100 million or less) is not subject to the taxation on the undistributed profits retained by a family corporation for the periods starting from April 1, 2003 through March 31, 2006 provided that its equity capital ratio (equity capital plus loans from its family owner group divided by gross assets) is 50% or less (SM 68-3-2①(4)).

An example of the tax computation is shown in ¶ 6-775.

¶ 6-645 Items to be added to ordinary income

(1)   The following three items are not included in ordinary income but should be included in computing distributable income (Law 67③):

(a)   dividends received (see ¶ 6-150),

(b)   dividends received from a foreign subsidiary (see ¶ 6-152),

(c)   Donation within 100% group (see ¶ 6-235), and

(d)   certain refunded taxes (see ¶ 6-160).

(2)   The following special deductions are permitted in computing the taxable ordinary income but should not be deducted in computing distributable profits:

(a)   ¥30 or ¥50 million, ¥20 million, ¥15 million, or ¥8 million, as the case may be, as a deduction for the capital gains accruing from the expropriation of properties, etc. (SM 65-2⑨, 65-3⑤, 65-4②, 65-

¶ 6-645

法　人　税　481

〔各事業年度の所得の金額＋左の所得の金額に加算すべき項目（¶6–645）
－所得の金額の計算上損金算入を認められない支出（¶6–650）＝分配可
能所得〕（法法67③）
分配可能所得－支払配当（¶6–655）＝留保金額

(注)：1．留保金課税は資本金の額が1億円超の同族会社（¶3–780，3–790）のみに行われる。
　　　　ただし，資本金の額が5億円以上の法人の100％子法人の場合には，留保金課税が適用
　　　　される（¶6–590（完全支配関係がある法人間の取引）参照）。

　　　2．留保金課税は留保金額そのものに行われるのではなく，留保金額から留保控除額
　　　　（¶6–660）を控除した残額に行われる。

　　　3．同族会社の留保金課税制度について，次の事業年度につき適用しない特例を設ける
　　　　こととする（措法68の2）。
　　　(a)　中小企業者に該当する会社の設立後10年以内の事業年度

　　　(b)　中小企業者の新たな事業活動促進に関する法律の承認事業者の同法の承認計画に
　　　　従って新事業を実施している事業年度

　　　4．平成15年4月1日から平成18年3月31日までの間，自己資本比率（自己資本（同族
　　　　関係者からの借入金を含む。）／総資産）が50％以下の中小法人（資本金1億円以下の
　　　　法人）について，留保金課税を適用しない（措法68の3の2①四）。

　　税額の計算例は，¶6–775に示すとおりである。

¶6–645　各事業年度の所得に加算されるべき項目

(1)　次の3項目は各事業年度の所得の金額には算入されないが，留保金額の
　計算上は加算しなければならない（法法67③）。
　(a)　受取配当（¶6–150参照）
　(b)　外国子会社から受ける配当（¶6–152参照）
　(c)　100％グループ内の法人からの寄付（¶6–235参照）
　(d)　還付を受けた税額のうち特定のもの（¶6 160参照）
(2)　次に掲げる特別控除は課税所得の計算上控除されるが，留保金額の計算
　上は控除できない。

　(a)　資産の収用等又は特定事業の用地買収等の場合の所得の特別控除（措
　　法65の2⑨，65の3⑤，65の4②，65の5③）（¶6–505参照）

482   CORPORATION TAX

5③) (see ¶ 6-505) ;

(b) expenditures in prospecting for new mineral deposits (SM 59) (see ¶ 6-540); and

(c) net loss carried over to the present business year.

¶ 6-650 Disbursements deductible

The following disbursements are often not deductible in computing the amount of ordinary income, but they should be deducted in computing the amount of distributable profits:

(1) corporation tax and inhabitant taxes on ordinary income, and withholding income tax as well as delinquency taxes thereon (see ¶ 6-205);

(2) foreign tax credits (see ¶ 6-205 (2) (e), ¶ 6-740);

(3) fines (see ¶ 6-205(1) (g)); and

(4) contributions, entertainment expenses, bonuses paid to directors, and other kinds of expenses which are not deductible in computing the amount of ordinary income (see ¶ 6-140, ¶ 6-215, ¶ 6-230, ¶ 6-235 etc.).

¶ 6-655 Distributions

Dividends to shareholders payable from the ordinary income of a given business year are deducted in computing the amount of undistributed profits.

¶ 6-660 Allowance for undistributed profits

The basis for tax on undistributed profits is undistributed profits less the allowance for undistributed profits, which is the largest of the following three figures:

(1) (ordinary income + income to be included in distributable income as in ¶ 6-645) 40 (50 in case of middle and small size corporations) %; or

(2) ¥20 million per annum; or

(3) (capital at the end of a business year × 1/4) − (the accumulated retained earnings at the same time).

(4) in case of middle or small size corporations, assets × 30% − equity capital ratio.

¶ 6-650

法 人 税 483

(b) 新鉱床探鉱費等の特別控除（措法59）（¶6-540参照）

(c) 当該事業年度に繰り越された欠損金

¶6-650　控除し得る支出

次に掲げる支出は，各事業年度の所得の計算上は，通常控除できないが，留保金額の計算上は控除することができる。

(1) 各事業年度の所得に対する法人税額及び住民税（道府県民税・市町村民税），源泉所得税並びにこれらに対する延滞税（¶6-205参照）

(2) 外国税額（¶6-205(2)(e)，¶6-740参照）
(3) 罰金（¶6-205(1)(g)参照）
(4) 各事業年度の所得の金額の計算上損金算入が認められない寄附金，交際費，役員賞与及びその他の経費の額（¶6-140，¶6-215，¶6-230，¶6-235等参照）

¶6-655　配当

当該事業年度の所得の金額から支払われる株主への配当の金額は留保金額の計算上控除する。

¶6-660　留保控除額

留保金課税の課税標準は留保金額から，留保控除額として次に掲げる三つの金額のうち最も多い金額を控除したものである。

(1) 当該事業年度の所得等の金額（当該事業年度の所得＋留保所得に含められるもの（¶6-645））の100分の40（中小法人にあっては50）に相当する金額
(2) 年2,000万円
(3) （当該事業年度末の資本金額の100分の25）-（当該事業年度末の利益積立金額）
(4) 中小法人においては，総資産×(30%-自己資本比率)

484   CORPORATION TAX

Special Taxation on Capital Gains from Land

¶ 6-670 Special taxation on capital gains from land or other similar properties

The special taxation stated below has been suspended for capital gains from land transferred from January 1, 1998 to December 31, 2016 (March 31, 2017 for tax rate of 10%) by the 1998 tax reform.

(1) If a corporation other than a non-taxable corporation acquires certain capital gains from its land or other similar properties (hereinafter referred to as land), the gains are subject to 5% additional tax as well as the ordinary corporation tax and the liquidation income tax (SM 62-3).

However, if the land is short-term ownership land, the additional tax rate is raised to 10% (SM 63).

Note:
1. Additional tax rates mentioned above should be applied to capital gains from land transferred on or after January 1, 1996.
2. Short-term ownership land is land which has been owned by a corporation for five years or less.

(2) Capital gains to which additional taxation would apply are as follows:
   (a) Gains from the transfer of land situated in Japan or gains from brokerage of land.
   (b) Gains from the transfer of shares in a corporation, the main properties of which are land.
   (c) Increase in book values due to the revaluation of land caused by the reorganization of a corporation.
   (d) Gains from increases in the book value of any land which is included in the remaining properties of liquidated corporations.

(3) However, gains from sales of inventory land by qualified housing lot suppliers are exempt from 5% additional taxation with some exceptions.

Special taxation on land does not usually apply in the following cases:
   (a) A transfer of land to the national or local governments.
   (b) A transfer of land to the Land Developing Public Corporation or other designated organization whose business requires such a transfer.

¶ 6-670

法　人　税　485

土地譲渡益に対する特別課税

¶6-670　土地その他これに類する資産に係る譲渡益に対する特別課税

> 平成10年度の税制改正により，下記の土地譲渡益に対する特別課税は，平成10年1月1日から平成28年12月31日（10％の税率については平成29年3月31日）までの譲渡については適用されない。

(1) 非課税法人以外の法人が土地又はこれに類する資産（以下「土地等」）を譲渡したことにより譲渡利益金額が生じた場合には，通常の法人税の額のほかに，当該譲渡利益金額に対して5％の税率による追加課税が行われる（措法62の3）。

　　ただし，短期所有土地等の譲渡利益金額に対する税率は10％に引き上げられる（措法63）。

(注)：1．上記の税率は，平成8年1月1日以後の譲渡益について適用されるものである。

　　　2．短期所有土地等とは所有期間が5年以下の土地をいう。

(2)　この土地譲渡重課制度の対象となる譲渡利益とは次のものをいう。

　(a)　日本国内にある土地等の譲渡による利益又は当該土地の売買の仲介に関し受ける報酬
　(b)　その有する資産が主として土地等である法人の株式の譲渡による利益

　(c)　法人の組織の変更に伴う資産の評価換えによる土地等の帳簿価額の増額
　(d)　清算中の法人の土地等に係る残余財産の確定による利益

(3)　ただし，特定のたな卸資産（当該法人が事業の用に供したものを除く。）の譲渡は，5％追加課税の適用除外とされる。また，次に掲げる譲渡行為については，原則として特別税率は適用されない。

　(a)　政府又は地方公共団体への土地等の譲渡
　(b)　土地開発公社その他の指定法人に対する土地等の譲渡でこれらの法人の業務を行うために必要であると認められるもの

486   CORPORATION TAX

(c) A transfer of land by expropriation.

(d) other specific transfers.

Note:
Each special taxation has different tax free transfers respectively.

(4) Additional taxation will be imposed on capital gains calculated as follows:

(a) A capital gain is the amount calculated by deducting the following items from gross receipts on the disposal of land —

(i) the acquisition cost: the book value of the land just before the transfer (excluding interest);

(ii) expenses representing liabilities with respect to the possession and disposal of the land and general administrative expenses, usually calculated on a legal basis using the following prescribed formula but at the option of the taxpayer they can be calculated on an actual basis:

① Liabilities are 6% of the accumulated book value of the land in any business year including the period of the ownership of the land.

② The amount of selling and general administrative expenses is 4% of the accumulated amount of book value of the land of every business year.

Note:
The book value of the land in any business year is the book value at the end of the business year (in case of the business year: the date of transfer) multiplied by the number of months in the business year the land was owned divided by 12.

(b) Special concessions with respect to expropriated land etc. (¶ 6-505) are also allowed. Special concession with respect to succession to book value (¶ 6-495) is allowed only to 5%-additional taxation cases.

(c) The capital gain or loss on land which is subject to an additional taxation cannot be offset against the capital gain or loss on land which is subject to the other special taxations.

Special Taxation of Beneficiary-concealed-disbursement

¶ 6-675 Special taxation of "beneficiary-concealed-disbursement"

A "beneficiary-concealed-disbursement" is expenditure on a beneficiary whose name is kept concealed and its concealment can not be justified. Such expenditure other than by a nontaxable corporation will be subject to

¶ 6-675

（c） 収用による土地等の譲渡

（d） その他特定の譲渡

（注）：適用除外の範囲は，それぞれの重課制度で若干異なる。

(4) 特別税率の課税対象となる譲渡利益金額は次のように計算される。

（a） 譲渡益は土地等の譲渡収入から次の金額を控除した金額である。

（i） 土地等の取得価額：譲渡直前の帳簿価額であり支払利息を含まない。

（ii） 土地等の保有のために要した負債の利子の額及び土地等の譲渡等に要した販売費及び一般管理費：これらは原則として次のとおり法定の方式によって計算されるが，納税者の選択により実額ベースでの計算も認められる。

① 負債の利子の額：土地等の保有期間の各事業年度における土地等の帳簿価額の累積額の6％相当額

② 販売費及び一般管理費の額：土地等の保有期間の各事業年度における土地等の帳簿価額の累計費の4％相当額

（注）：土地等の保有期間の各事業年度における帳簿価額とは，当該各事業年度末における帳簿価額（譲渡事業年度においては譲渡原価）にその事業年度における保有月数を乗じ，これを12で除した金額をいう。

（b） 収用等の場合の特別控除など各種の特別控除等（¶6-505）の適用を受けた金額は控除することができる。さらに，5％追加課税の対象となる譲渡利益金額からは買換えの場合は特例（¶6-495）の適用を受けた金額も控除できる。

（c） 譲渡利益又は譲渡損失は互いに他の重課制度との間で通算できない。

使途秘匿金に対する特別課税

¶6-675 "使途秘匿金"に対する特別課税

使途秘匿金は，支出先が正当な理由なく明らかにされない支出をいう。このような支出（非課税法人による支出を除く。）は，通常の各事業年度の所得に対する法人税に追加して，40％の税率による特別課税の対象となる（措

488   CORPORATION TAX

an additional tax as well as ordinary corporation tax at a rate of 40% on the expenditure (SM 62).

Tax on Ordinary Income and Tax Credits

¶ 6-680 Tax basis for ordinary income
In applying the tax rate, ordinary income should be computed according to ¶ 6-130 to ¶ 6-580.

For a corporation whose capital exceeds ¥100 million, a tax rate of 23.9% is applicable to all of the ordinary income.

For a corporation whose capital amounts to ¥100 million or less, a tax rate of 19% (15%, as a tentative measure, for accounting periods ending during April 1, 2012 through March 31, 2017) is applicable up to ¥8 million to the ordinary income (Law 66①, ②).

¶ 6-690 Tax credits
The six types of credit explained in ¶ 6-700 to ¶ 6-750 may be deducted from the total tax on ordinary income and on undistributed profits. The tax after such deduction is to be paid for a business year by prepayment or final payment.

¶ 6-700 Credit for overpaid tax due to misrepresentation of accounts in financial statement
When the amount of tax reported in a final return for a certain business year has been excessively computed due to a window-dressing, such excess amount of tax may not always be reduced without correction of the accounts in the financial statement of the corporation itself. Even if the accounts are corrected and the excess amount of tax is reduced accordingly, the overpaid tax is not always immediately refunded. At first the overpaid tax is refunded up to the amount of tax which was assessed for the business year beginning within one year before the start of the business year during which the said correction was made. The remainder is then carried forward and credited against the tax on the income of the business year during which the said correction was made and each business year beginning within five calendar years after the start of the business year during which the said correction was made. If certain corporate rehabilitation procedures are taken by a corporation, application of the carry-over rule shall

¶ 6-680

法62)。

各事業年度の所得に対する法人税額及び税額控除

¶6-680　各事業年度の所得に対する法人税の課税標準

　法人税率の適用上，各事業年度の所得は，¶6-130から¶6-580に示すところにより計算される。

　資本の金額が1億円を超える普通法人の税率はすべての所得について23.9％，資本の金額が1億円以下の法人は800万円以下の所得については19％（平成24年4月1日から平成29年3月31日の間に終了する各事業年度については暫定的に15％）の税率が適用される（法法66①，②）。

¶6-690　税額控除

　¶6-700から¶6-750までに説明する6種類の税額控除の金額は，所得に対する法人税額から控除することができる。これらの税額控除後の金額は，各事業年度において中間納付又は確定納付の方法により納付しなければならない。

¶6-700　仮装経理に基づく過大申告の場合の更正に伴う法人税額の控除

　各事業年度の確定申告書に記載された税額が法人の財務諸表の仮装経理に基づき過大となっている場合には，その過大となっている金額は，法人が自ら財務諸表を修正経理しない限り，減額されない。当該経理が修正され当該超過税額が減額されなければならない場合でも，当該過大納付額（仮装経理法人税額）は直ちに還付されるとは限らない。過大納付額は，更正が行われた日の属する事業年度開始の日前1年以内に開始する事業年度の法人税額以下の金額を限度として還付される。次に，残余の過大納付額は，当該更正が行われた日の属する事業年度後5年間に開始する各事業年度に繰り越され，各々の事業年度の所得に対する法人税額から順次控除される。ただし，一定の企業再生事由が生じた場合には，繰越控除制度の適用は終了し，控除未済額は還付される（法法70，134の2）。

490   CORPORATION TAX

be terminated and the overpaid tax shall be refunded (Law 70, 134-2).

¶ 6-710 Income tax credit

Income tax withheld at source from a payment to a corporation may be credited against the tax on ordinary income and on undistributed profits, unless such payment is excluded from gross income, on the condition that schedule 6(1) (Income tax credit statement) is attached to the final return (Law 68).

The income tax credit is computed as follows:

(1)   Deductible income tax on interest from bonds and dividends;

income tax on interest from bonds and dividends

$\times \dfrac{\text{number of months of ownership of the bonds or capital}}{\text{number of months insert on the bonds or the dividends}}$

(2)   Other deductible income tax; the total amount of the income tax

Income tax on uncollected interest or dividends, which is included in gross income, is deductible.

Income tax on dividends from stocks which were transferred, but of which title has not changed yet, is not deductible.

¶ 6-720 Credit for experimental and research expenses

(1)   A corporation can deduct following amounts as tax credit. Maximum amounts of the tax credit are 25% of the amounts of the tax of the accounting period (SM 42-4①).The 25% limitation shall be tentatively increased for accounting periods beginning April 1, 2017 through March 31, 2019 to additional 10% for small or medium-sized corporations, and to additional 0% to 10% in case that the R&D expenses are 10% or more of average sales amounts.
The tax credit rates are as follows.
(a) if fluctuation ratio is more than 5%, 9% +
     (fluctuation ratio – 5%) × 0.3.
(b) if fluctuation ratio is 5% or less, 9% +
     (5% - fluctuation ratio) × 0.1.
(c) if fluctuation ratio is less than 25%, 6%.
The limitation of the tax credit rates is 10% (12% in case of a small and medium-sized corporation). The limitation is 14% (17% in case of a small and medium-sized corporation) for accounting pe-

¶ 6-710

法　人　税　491

¶6-710　所得税額の控除

法人に対する支払で源泉徴収された所得税は，益金の額に算入されている限り，各事業年度の所得に対する法人税の額から控除することができる。この場合，申告書に別表6(1)の添付を要する（法法68）。

所得税額控除額は次のように計算される。

(1)　公社債の利子及び利益の配当等に対する所得税がある場合

$$\text{利子配当等に対} \atop \text{する所得税額} \times \frac{\text{その元本の所有期間の月数}}{\text{利子配当等の計算基礎} \atop \text{となった期間の月数}} = \text{控除所得税額}$$

(2)　(1)以外の所得税がある場合

その全額

益金に計上した未収利子又は未収配当金にかかる所得税についても控除できる。

名義書換え失念株の配当については，所得税額控除の適用はない。

¶6-720　試験研究費の額が増加した場合の法人税額の特別控除

(1)　試験研究費の総額に対し次の控除率による税額控除を認める。ただし，当期の法人税額の25％相当額を限度とする（措法42の4①）。当該25％の限度は，平成29年4月1日から平成31年3月31日の間に開始する事業年度については，中小法人の場合さらに10％，試験研究費が平均売上額の10％超の場合には0～10％上乗せされる。

税額控除率は以下のとおり。

(a)　増減割合が5％超の場合，9％＋（増減割合－5％）×0.3

(b)　増減割合が5％以下の場合，9％－（5％－増減割合）×0.1

(c)　増減割合が25％未満の場合，6％

税額控除率の上限は10％（中小法人の場合12％）。ただし平成29年4月1日から平成31年3月31日の間に開始する事業年度については，14％（中小法人の場合17％）とする。

492   CORPORATION TAX

riods beginning April 1, 2017 through March 31, 2019.

(2)   With regard to joint researches or entrusted researches with universities or national research institutes, a corporation can take tax credit equivalent to 5% of the research expenses in addition to the above tax credit (1)(SM 42-4⑥).

(3)   For small or medium-size corporations, an alternative tax credit is introduced in place of the tax credits (1) and (2) above. The creditable rate is 12% of the total experimental and research expenses. Maximum percentage of the tax credits is 25% of the amount of the tax of the accounting period (SM 42-2③).

(4)   "Experimental and research expenses" are defined as expenses incurred in experimental and research work in order to manufacture products or improve, design or invent techniques. It includes the cost of material, salaries and wages and other related expenses of employees who are engaged exclusively in experimental and research work, as well as a depreciation allowance for machinery and equipment used for such work (SM 42-4⑧).

¶ 6-730 Investment tax credit for specified equipment

When a corporation acquires, produces or constructs qualified plant or equipment which is designed to improve ① equipment for highly promoting energy saving (¶ 6-310(1)(a)), ② specified machinery or equipment acquired by small or medium-sized corporations (¶ 6-310(1)(b)), ③machineries acquired and used for certain business in encouraging aria for designated business activating local economics (¶ 6-310(1)(e)), ④ buildings acquired in specified local area for economically vitalizing purposes (¶ 6-310(1)(f)), management improving equipment acquired by certain small or medium sized corporations (¶ 6-310(1)(g)) or designated equipments acquired by small or midium-sized corporations for improving business management (¶ 6-310(1)(h)) during the designated period, and uses them for its business during that period, an investment tax credit is available. The amount of 7% (4% for ③, 4% in certain cases for ④) of acquisition, production or construction costs or 20% of corporation tax before the tax credit, whichever is the lesser, may be credited against the corporation tax, instead of additional depreciation (SM 42-5 to 42-6, 42-11-2 to 42-11-3, 42-12-3 to 42-12-4).

¶ 6-730

法 人 税 493

(2) 大学，国の試験研究機関等との共同試験研究及びこれらに対する委託試験研究について，上記(1)と合わせてこれらの試験研究に係る試験研究費の額の5％相当額の税額を認める。(措法42の4⑥)。

(3) 中小企業者について，上記(1)及び(2)の税額控除制度の適用に代えて，試験研究費の総額の12％相当額の税額控除を認める。ただし，当期の法人税額の25％相当額を限度とする（措法42の4③)。

(4) 「試験研究費」とは，製品の製造又は技術の改良，考案若しくは発明に係る試験研究のために要する費用をいう。その費用には，その試験研究を行うために要する原材料費，人材費（試験研究の業務に専ら従事する者に係るものに限る。）及び経費（当該業務の用に供される機械設備の減価償却費）を含む（措法42の4⑧)。

¶6-730　一定設備等を取得した場合の法人税額の特別控除

法人が所定の期間内に①高度省エネルギー増進設備（¶6-310(1)(a)），②中小企業者が取得する特定機械装置（¶6-310(1)(b)），③地域経済牽引事業の促進区域内において取得する特定事業用機械等（¶6-310(1)(e)），④地方活力向上地域内の特定建物（¶6-310(1)(f)），⑤特定中小企業者等が取得する経営改善設備（¶6-310(1)(g)）及び中小企業者等が取得する特定経営力向上設備等（¶6-310(1)(h)）を取得し又は製作し若しくは建設し，事業の用に供した場合には，当該設備等の取得価額，製作価額又は建設価額の7％（③については4％，④については一定の場合4％）に相当する金額（税額控除前の法人税額の20％を超えるときは，その20％を限度とする。）を，特別償却に代えて，法人税額から控除することができる（措法42の5～42の6，42の11の2～42の11の3，42の12の3～42の12の4）。

494   CORPORATION TAX

¶ 6-733 Investment tax credit for specified assets in Okinawa

When a corporation acquires, produces or constructs qualified machinery and equipment and building for specified businesses in the tourist attraction promotion zone, the communication industry improvement zone, the industry development zone, the concentrated zone of international physical distribution business or the specified zone for activating economy and finances respectively, and uses them for its business until March 31, 2019, the amount of 15% (8% for buildings) of their acquisition, production or construction costs, or 20% of its corporation tax before the tax credit, whichever is lesser, may be credited against the corporation tax (SM 42-9).

¶ 6-734 Special tax credit applicable to machineries acquired in the specified area for national strategy and the international strategic and synthetical special area

If a designated corporation acquired a certain size of machineries in order to use for the specified business in the specified area for national strategy and the international strategic and synthetical special area, the corporation can deduct 14%, 15%(10%, 12%) (7%, 8% (5%, 6%) for building) of its acquisition cost from its corporate tax (20% of the corporate tax in the maximum) instead of the special depreciation (SM 42-11).

> **Note:** See ¶ 6-310(1)(c), (d), ¶ 6-550(2).

¶ 6-735 Tax credit for increase of employees in specified local area

When a corporation increases five or more employee (two or more in case of a small or medium-sized corporation) in the accounting periods beginning on or after April 1, 2018 through March 31, 2021 and satisfies other conditions, the corporation can deduct the amounts of tax equivalent to ¥300,000 (¥600,000, ¥200,000, 500,000 depending on conditions met) times number of increased employee. The amounts of the tax credit shall be limited to 20% of the corporation tax (SM 42-12).

¶ 6-736 Tax credit for wage increase and capital investment

When a corporation satisfies certain requirements, the corporation can deduct 15% (20% in case that it meets additional requirements) of the increased amounts of wages as tax credit in the accounting periods

¶ 6-733

法　人　税　495

¶6-733　沖縄において一定設備を取得した場合の法人税額の特別控除
　法人が平成31年３月31日までに沖縄の観光振興地域，情報通信産業振興地域，産業高度化地域，国際物流拠点産業集積地域又は経済金融活性化特別地域において，それぞれ所定の事業用の機械装置又は建物を取得，製作若しくは建設し，当該事業の用に供した場合には，その取得価額，製作価額又は建設価額の15％（建物にあっては８％）又は税額控除前の法人税額の20％のいずれか少ない額を法人税額から控除できる（措法42の９）。

¶6-734　国家戦略特別区域又は国際戦略総合特別区域内において機械等を
　　　　取得した場合の法人税額の特別控除
　国家戦略特別区域又は国際戦略総合特別区域において，指定を受けた法人が特定の事業を行うために一定の規模以上の設備を取得した場合には，その取得価額の14％，15％（10％，12％）（建物等については，７％，８％（５％，６％））に相当する額（税額控除前の法人税額の20％を超えるときは，その額を限度とする。）を，特別償却に代えて，法人税額から控除することができる（措法42の11）。

　（注）：¶6-310(1)(c)，(d)，¶6-550(2)参照。

¶6-735　地方活力向上地域等において雇用者の数が増加した場合の法人税
　　　　額の特別控除
　平成30年４月１日から平成33年３月31日までの間に開始する各事業年度において従業員の数が５人以上（中小企業者等については２人以上）増加したこと等一定の要件を満たした場合，増加した数に，条件に応じて，20万円から60万円を乗じた金額相当額の法人税額の特別控除ができる。ただし，税額控除は当期の法人税額の20％を上限とする（措法42の12）。

¶6-736　給与等の引上げ及び設備投資を行った場合等の法人税額の特別控除
　平成30年４月１日から平成33年３月31日までの間に開始する各事業年度において国内雇用者に対して給与等を支給する場合において，一定の要件を満たすときは，給与等支給増加額の15％（一定の上乗せ要件を満たす場合に

496 CORPORATION TAX

beginning on or after April 1, 2018 through March 31, 2021. The amounts of tax credit shall be limited to 20% of the corporation tax (SM42-12-5).

(1) The ratio of the difference between the average wages paid minus the comparable wages paid to the comparable wages paid should be 3% or more.

(2) The ratio of domestic capital investment to the amounts of depreciation should be 90% or more.

¶ 6-737 Tax credit for the acquisition of equipment using innovative IT business

When a corporation approved as users for innovative data business manufactures or acquires devices which has information-sharing system in accounting periods beginning on and after the enforcement of the related law through March 31, 2021, the corporation can deduct 5% (3% in certain cases) of the acquisition cost for tax credit. The amounts of tax credit shall be limited to 20% of the corporation tax (SM42-12-6).

Note: See ¶ 6-310(1)(i).

¶ 6-738 Special treatment for tax credit

If a big corporation, that is, other than small and medium-sized corporations does not satisfy the following criteria, the corporation could not take certain tax credit including that of R&D for the accounting periods beginning on or after April 1, 2018 to March 31, 2021 (SM42-13).

(1) The amounts of average wages paid should be over that of comparable average wages paid.

(2) The ratio of domestic capital investment to the amounts of depreciation should be 10% or more.

¶ 6-740 Credit for foreign taxes

In order to eliminate international double taxation on income, the foreign taxes levied on a Japanese domestic corporation, in the ordinary course of its business, may be credited against Japanese corporation tax. This is called a foreign tax credit (Law 69).

Furthermore, in order to treat investment abroad through a foreign subsidiary in the same manner as investment abroad through a branch, foreign taxes levied on a foreign subsidiary of a Japanese domestic cor-

¶ 6-737

は, 20％) 相当額の法人税額の特別控除ができる。ただし, 控除税額は, 当期の法人税額の20％を上限とする（措法42の12の5）。

(1) 平均給与等支給額から比較平均給与等支給額を控除した金額の比較平均給与等支給額に対する割合が3％以上であること

(2) 国内設備投資額が減価償却費の総額の90％以上であること

¶6-737　革新的情報産業活用設備を取得した場合の法人税額の特別控除

認定革新的データ産業活用事業者が, 生産性向上特別措置法の施行の日から平成33年3月31日までの間に, 情報連携利活用設備を新設又は増設し, その事業の用に供したときは, その取得価額の5％（一定の場合には3％）の税額控除ができることとする。ただし, 税額控除は, 当期の法人税額の20％を上限とする（措法42の12の6）。

(注)：¶6-310(1)(i)。

¶6-738　法人税の額から控除される特別控除額の特例

中小企業者等以外の法人が平成30年4月1日から平成33年3月31日までの間に開始する各事業年度において次のいずれにも該当しない場合には, その事業年度については, 研究開発税制その他の一定の税額控除を適用できないこととする。ただし, その所得の金額が前期の所得の金額以下の一定の事業年度にあっては, 対象外とする（措法42の13）。

(1) 平均給与等支給額が比較平均給与等支給額を超えること

(2) 国内設備投資額が減価償却費の総額の10％を超えること

¶6-740　外国税額控除

所得に対する租税の国際的二重課税を排除するため, 日本の内国法人が, 通常行われる取引において課された外国税額は, 日本の法人税額から控除することができる（法法69）。これは通常の（直接）外国税額控除といわれるものである。

さらに, 外国子会社を通ずる海外投資を海外支店に対する投資と課税上同様に取り扱うため, 日本の内国法人の外国子会社が課された外国税額は日本の親会社が課される日本の法人税額から控除することができる。これは間接

498   CORPORATION TAX

poration may be credited against Japanese corporation tax levied on the Japanese parent corporation. This is called an indirect foreign tax credit. The credit for foreign taxes is granted unilaterally.

¶ 6-745 Foreign tax credit

Any foreign tax levied on the foreign source income of a Japanese domestic corporation may be credited against tax on ordinary income and on undistributed profits within the limits explained below.

If the amount of foreign taxes which has actually accrued in a given business year is over the limit, the foreign tax in excess of the limit may be credited against prefectural inhabitant tax and municipal inhabitant tax on the income of the same business year within 5.0% or 12.3% respectively of the limits applicable to corporation tax. If there still remains any excess foreign tax, that excess amount may be carried forward for the three following years.

On the other hand, if the amount of foreign taxes accruing in a business year does not reach the limit for that business year, the limit for foreign tax credit applicable to the three following years is increased by the shortfall.

The limit of credit for foreign taxes is computed as follows (increased by any shortfall carried over from the preceding business year, as mentioned above):

$$\text{Japanese corporation tax on ordinary income (a)} \times \frac{\text{total income from sources abroad (b)}}{\text{total ordinary income (c)}}$$

In the above formula:

(a) Japanese corporation tax on ordinary income means the tax amount before the deduction of any tax credits.

(b) Total income from sources abroad means the income from sources abroad subject to the tax on ordinary income (other than income from the sale of goods or merchandise not through a fixed place of business in a foreign country). However, the income which is exempted from income tax in the source country is not included in the total income from sources abroad for the purposes of the foreign tax credit.

The definition of the foreign source income (b) above will be changed as follows from accounting periods beginning on or after April 1, 2016 in accordance with the introduction of income attribution approach applicable to a PE of a foreign corporation under the 2014 Tax Reform.

¶ 6-745

法　人　税　499

外国税額控除といわれる。外国税額の控除は相手国との双務的ではなく一方的に認められる。

¶6-745　（直接）外国税額控除

　内国法人の国外源泉所得について課された外国税額は以下に説明する限度額内において各事業年度の所得及び留保金に対する法人税額から控除することができる。

　当該事業年度において実際に納付することとなる外国税額が限度額を超えた場合には，当該限度超過額は，同一事業年度の所得に対する住民税（道府県民税及び市町村民税）から当該年度の法人税控除限度額の5.0％又は12.3％の金額を限度として控除することができる。地方税限度額を超過する外国税額がある場合には，当該限度超過額は引き続く3年以内に開始した各事業年度に繰り越し，その限度額の範囲内で控除することができる。

　他方，当該事業年度において納付することとなる外国法人税の金額が当該事業年度の限度額に達しない場合には，続く3年間に適用される外国税額控除限度額には当該不足額相当額が加算される。

　外国税額控除限度額は次のとおり計算される（上に説明したように，控除限度額には，引き続く事業年度では控除不足額相当額が加算される。）。

$$\text{各事業年度の所得に対する法人税の額(a)} \times \frac{\text{当該事業年度の国外所得金額(b)}}{\text{当該事業年度の所得の金額(c)}}$$

　上記の算式において，
(a)　各事業年度の所得に対する法人税の額とは，すべての税額控除の規定を適用しないで計算した場合の法人税額をいう。
(b)　当該事業年度の国外所得金額とは，各事業年度の所得に対して課税される国外源泉所得金額（国外事業所を通じないたな卸資産の譲渡により生ずる所得は含まない。）である。ただし，外国で課税されない所得の場合には，その全額が除外される。

　上記(b)の規定は，外国法人に対するPE帰属所得概念の導入に伴い，平成28年4月1日以後に開始する事業年度以後から以下のように変更される。

500   CORPORATION TAX

(b) Total income from sources abroad means income attributable
to a foreign PE of the Japanese corporation ("income attributable to a foreign PE"), income derived by usage and holding of
assets located outside of Japan, capital gains derived by sale of
assets located outside of Japan, interests of bonds issued by a
foreign corporation and dividends paid by a foreign corporation,
etc. (Law 694).

Income attributable to a foreign PE is calculated in the same
manner as income attributable to a PE of a foreign corporation
in Japan.

(c) The total ordinary income means the amount of ordinary income, from whatever country it might be derived, without
taking into account any loss in preceding business years carried
over to the present business year.

Foreign tax eligible for foreign tax credit is restricted to those taxes,
national or local, levied abroad on income (not always net income), which are
similar in nature to Japanese corporation tax, excluding delinquency tax and
penalty taxes. However, if the foreign tax rate is considerably higher, the part
of tax which is exceptional is excluded from deductible foreign tax. For example, a corporation tax rate over 35% is deemed to be considerably higher.

Foreign taxes which become due during a given business year are to
be credited against Japanese corporation tax on the income of the same
business year.

If foreign tax is not fully credited against Japanese corporation tax for
the business year in question, the uncredited part is carried over to the
next three business years.

If, in an exceptional case, the foreign taxes which may be credited to
a certain business year within the statutory limit are more than the taxes
on ordinary income and undistributed profits, the balance is refunded.

¶ 6-750 Indirect foreign tax credit (abolished under 2009 tax reform)

When a domestic corporation receives dividends from a subsidiary
which is a foreign corporation, the domestic corporation is deemed by
the following scheme to have itself paid the foreign taxes levied on the
subsidiary. This scheme is based on the assumption that such dividends
were paid after the payment of foreign taxes. Indirect foreign tax credit is

¶ 6-750

法　人　税　501

(b)　当該事業年度の国外所得金額とは，日本法人の国外に有するPEに帰せられる所得（以下「国外PE帰属所得」），国外資産の運用保有所得，国外資産の譲渡所得，外国法人の発行する債券の利子及び外国法人から受ける配当等をいう（法法69④）。

国外PE帰属所得の計算については，原則として外国法人のPE帰属所得の計算に準じて行う。

(c)　当該事業年度の所得金額とは，所得の源泉地国のいかんを問わず，当該事業年度に繰り越された前9年以内の欠損金額の控除の規定を適用しないで計算した場合の所得の金額をいう。

外国税額控除の対象となる外国法人税は，日本の法人税（加算税及び延滞税を除く。）に相当する税であり，外国又はその地方公共団体により法人の所得（純所得に限らない。）を課税標準として課される税に限られる。なお，極めて高い税率で課された部分については，対象とされない。例えば，35％を超える法人税率は極めて高い税率とされる。

当該事業年度において納付することとなる外国法人税は当該事業年度の所得に対する日本の法人税の額から控除することとなる。

当該事業年度において控除しきれない外国法人税は，3年間の繰越しが認められる。

例外的に，当該事業年度において法定の限度額の範囲内で税額控除し得る外国法人税の金額が各事業年度の所得及び留保金に対する法人税の額を超える場合，その超過額は還付される。

¶6-750　間接外国税額控除（平成21年度の税制改正により廃止される。）

内国法人が外国法人である子会社から配当を受領した場合には，当該子会社に対して課された外国法人税は次の考え方により内国法人である親会社自ら納付したものとみなされる。その考え方とは，当該配当が外国税額の納付後に支払われるという仮定の上に立っている。間接外国税額控除は直接外国税額控除と同様の方法により認められる。

502   CORPORATION TAX

allowed in a way similar to ordinary foreign tax credit:

(a) "Foreign subsidiary" means a foreign corporation, not established for any tax consideration, in which a quarter or more of the capital or shares with voting rights were held by the domestic parent corporation for six months before the decision to distribute dividends.

(b) A domestic parent corporation is deemed to derive the income for itself, where both the foreign tax and dividends received were paid out by the subsidiary. Therefore, the portion of the foreign taxes deemed to have been paid by the parent corporation should be included in the taxable ordinary income of the parent corporation in addition to the dividends received. This portion is computed by multiplying the foreign tax by the ratio of the dividends received by the parent corporation to the total dividends paid out by the subsidiary.

Note:

When a foreign subsidiary, as referred to above, receives dividends from its subsidiary which is a foreign corporation (referred to as "indirect foreign subsidiary" in this paragraph), the provision of indirect foreign tax credit may be applied in such a way that the foreign corporation taxes levied on the income of the indirect foreign subsidiary are deemed to be those levied on the foreign subsidiary in a proportion corresponding to dividends received (Law 69⑥ to ⑧).

¶ 6-752 Tax sparing

According to the provisions of tax treaties which have been concluded between Japan and certain the developing countries, Japanese residents, individuals and corporations can claim tax credit against Japanese tax on income, even though the tax amount is exempted or reduced by special tax incentive measures in those developing countries, in the manner as if no special exemption or reduction was provided.

The above foreign tax credit system is called "tax sparing."

The purpose of tax sparing is to provide a tax incentive for foreign investors or corporations through the use of a deemed payment of foreign tax and foreign tax credit system.

Tax sparing is provided in the provisions of tax treaties concluded with the following 17 countries: Ireland, Korea, Zambia, Singapore, Spain, Sri Lanka, Thailand, Philippines, Malaysia, Indonesia, China, Brazil, Bangladesh, Bulgaria, Turkey, Vietnam and Mexico.

¶ 6-752

法　人　税　503

(a)　外国子会社とは，租税負担の軽減を目的として設けた外国法人ではな
く，当該外国法人の株数又は議決権のある株式の総数の100分の25以上に
相当する数の株式が配当等の支払義務の確定する日以前6ヶ月以上引き続
いて親会社により所有されているものをいう。

(b)　内国法人である親会社は，子会社の納付した外国税額及び支払った配当
とも，親会社自ら所得を稼得したものとみなされる。したがって，親会社
が納付したものとみなされる外国法人税に相当する部分の金額は，親会社
の課税所得の計算上，受取配当の金額に加算し，益金の額に算入される。
当該部分の金額は，子会社が支払った配当の総額に親会社が受領する配当
の金額が占める割合を外国法人税額に乗じて計算される。

(注)：内国法人の外国子会社の外国子会社（外国孫会社）の所得に対して課された外国法人税
額のうち外国孫会社が外国子会社に支払う配当に対応する部分の金額は，外国子会社の所
得に対して課される外国法人税の額とみなして上記の間接税額控除の適用が認められる
（法法69⑥〜⑧）。

¶6-752　タックス・スペアリング

わが国と開発途上国との間の租税条約の規定により，わが国の居住者又は
内国法人に対し，開発途上国での租税の減免がなかったとしたら納付したで
あろう租税の額を外国で課された租税の額とみなして外国税額控除を認める
こととしている。

このような外国税額控除はタックス・スペアリングと呼ばれ，開発途上国
における外国企業の租税減免措置が有効に働くよう考慮されている。

次の17カ国との間の租税条約において，タックス・スペアリングが規定さ
れている。

アイルランド，韓国，ザンビア，シンガポール，スペイン，スリランカ，
タイ，フィリピン，ブラジル，マレーシア，インドネシア，中国，バングラ
デシュ，ブルガリア，トルコ，ヴィェトナム及びメキシコ。

504   CORPORATION TAX

¶ 6-755 Credit or deductible expenses: foreign tax

Each corporation has the option of crediting foreign taxes or of treating them as deductible expenses. The option should be exercised on the total amount of foreign taxes on income. Once the expense deduction method is chosen, the right to carry forward the excess tax or shortfall of foreign tax which may be credited (mentioned in ¶ 6-745) is forfeited.

Examples of Computation

¶ 6-770 Computation of tax on ordinary income

Suppose that Company A has earned ordinary income of ¥20,000,000 during its business year April 1, 2018 to March 31, 2019. In addition, Company A has received dividends amounting to ¥2,000,000 which qualify for tax exemption, from which withholding income tax amounting to ¥400,000 has been withheld. Company A is not a family corporation and its capital amounts to ¥50,000,000. Company A's corporation tax liability is as follows:

(1) The tax on ¥8 million bracket of income:
   ¥8,000,000 × 15% = ¥1,200,000
(2) The tax on the other part of (1):
   (¥20,000,000 – ¥8,000,000) × 23.4% = ¥2,808,000
(3) Amounts of corporate tax:
   ¥1,200,000 + ¥2,808,000 = ¥4,008,000
(4) Tax after deducting withholding tax paid:
   ¥4,008,000 – ¥400,000 = ¥3,608,000

¶ 6-775 Computation of tax on undistributed profits

Suppose that Company B, a personal family corporation with paid-in capital of more than ¥100,000,000, has earned ordinary income of ¥30,000,000. It will pay taxes and dividends amounting to ¥8,000,000 in total.

The undistributed profits, therefore, amount to ¥22,000,000. Its accumulated retained earnings before the addition of current earnings at the end of the business year April 1, 2018 to March 31, 2019, amounts to ¥16,000,000.

Company B's tax liability on undistributed profits is as follows:

(1) Undistributed profits: ¥22,000,000
(2) Allowance for undistributed profits (see ¶ 6-660):

¶ 6-755

法 人 税 505

¶6-755　損金算入の外国税

内国法人は，外国法人税を税額控除の対象とするのか，又は損金に算入するのかのいずれかを選択することができる。この選択は所得に対する外国法人税のすべてについて行わなければならない。法人が損金算入の方法を選択した場合には，¶6-745で説明した控除の対象となる限度超過額又は限度不足額の繰越しは認められないこととなる。

計 算 例

¶6-770　各事業年度の所得に対する法人税額の計算

法人Aの平成30年4月1日に開始し，平成31年3月31日に終了する事業年度の所得の金額は20,000,000円と仮定する。さらに，法人Aは受取配当益金不算入の規定が適用される配当2,000,000円を受領し，これに対して400,000円の源泉所得税が差し引かれたものとする。法人Aは同族会社ではなく，その資本金は50,000,000円とする。この場合，法人Aの法人税額の計算は次のとおりである。

(1)　当該事業年度の所得の金額のうち，年800万円に相当する部分の金額に対する税額は　　8,000,000円×15％＝1,200,000円
(2)　(1)以外の部分の金額に対する税額は
　　　　　(20,000,000円－8,000,000円)×23.4％＝2,808,000円
(3)　法人税額は
　　　　　1,200,000円＋2,808,000円＝4,008,000円
(4)　源泉所得税を控除すると
　　　　　4,008,000円－400,000円＝3,608,000円

¶6-775　留保金課税の計算

法人Bは資本金1億円超の同族会社であり，その所得の金額は30,000,000円と仮定する。法人Bは法人税と支払配当との合計額8,000,000円を支払ったものとし，したがって，留保金額は22,000,000円とされる。さらに，法人の平成30年4月1日に開始し，平成31年3月31日に終了する事業年度の末日における利益積立金額（当該事業年度の所得の金額から留保された部分の金額を除く。）は16,000,000円とする。

法人Bの留保金課税の税額計算は次のとおりである。
(1)　留保所得金額　22,000,000円
(2)　留保控除額（¶6-660参照）

506   CORPORATION TAX

(a) 40% of profits, i.e. ¥30,000,000 × 40% = ¥12,000,000
(b) ¥20,000,000 per annum
(c) one quarter of capital minus accumulated
retained earnings, i.e.
¥100,000,000 × 25% − ¥16,000,000 = ¥9,000,000

maximum:
¥20,000,000

(3) Tax base for undistributed profits:
¥22,00,000 − ¥20,000,000 = ¥2,000,000
(4) The tax thereon:
¥2,000,000 × 10% = ¥200,000

Note: See ¶ 6-640, ¶ 6-020.

Return and Payment of Tax on Ordinary Income

¶ 6-800 Interim return, prepayment

An ordinary corporation whose business year is longer than six months should file an interim return as at the end of the first six months of the business year.

The amount of corporation tax to be reported in an interim return is chosen by the corporation from the following two methods:

(a) Tax on ordinary income and tax on undistributed profits for the preceding business year $\quad \times \quad \dfrac{6}{\text{number of months of the preceding business year}}$

(b) Tax on ordinary income computed on the basis of a provisional settlement for the first six month period of the present business year.

A corporation can not file an interim return after the 2011 tax reform if the amount computed according to (a) is ¥100,000 or less or if the amount of tax under the interim return is more than 1/2 of the amount of previous accounting year's tax.

No interim return is required for the first business year of a newly established corporation.

If a corporation has been established by merger or has absorbed another corporation in the preceding business year or in the first six months of the present business year, the tax amount to be reported in an interim return should be adjusted accordingly.

The tax reported on the interim return should be paid to a tax office before the time limit for filing an interim return.

¶ 6-800

法　人　税　507

(a)　所得の金額の40％相当額　30,000,000円×40％＝12,000,000円

(b)　年20,000,000円　　　　　　　　　　　＝20,000,000円

(c)　資本金額の25％相当額から（100,000,000円×25％）
　　利益積立金額を控除した金額　－16,000,000円＝9,000,000円

　　(a)，(b)又は(c)の最も多い金額は20,000,000円

(3)　留保金課税の課税標準　22,000,000円－20,000,000円＝2,000,000円

(4)　同上の税額　2,000,000円×10％＝200,000円

（注）：¶6-640，¶6-020参照。

各事業年度の所得に対する法人税の申告及び納付

¶6-800　中間申告，中間納付

　事業年度が6ヶ月を超える普通法人は，当該事業年度の開始の日以後6ヶ月を経過した日までの期間について中間申告書を提出しなければならない。

　中間申告書に記載すべき法人税額の計算は次の二つの方法のうちいずれかの方法を法人が選択する。

(a)　$前事業年度の所得に対する法人税額 \times \dfrac{6}{当該前事業年度の月数}$

(b)　当該事業年度の最初の6ヶ月の期間の仮決算に基づき計算した所得に対する法人税の額

　上記(a)により算出した法人税額が10万円以下である場合及び仮決算による中間税額が前事業年度の確定法人税額の2分の1を超える場合には，平成23年度より，仮決算による中間申告書は提出できない。

　新たに設立された法人の設立後最初の事業年度については，中間申告書を提出することを要しない。ただし，法人が前事業年度中又は現事業年度中最初の6ヶ月の間に新設合併により又は吸収合併により設立された場合には，所要の調整を行ったうえ，中間申告書を提出しなければならない。

　中間申告書に記載された法人税額は，当該中間申告書の提出期限までに税務署へ納付しなければならない。

　なお，内国法人のうち事業年度開始の時において資本金の額が1億円を超える法人（大法人）の中間申告書の提出については，平成32年4月1日以後に開始する事業年度以後，これらの申告書に記載すべきものとされる事項を

508   CORPORATION TAX

Corporations whose amounts of capital are more than ¥100 million must file its tax returns with using e-Tax systems from the accounting periods beginning on and after April 1, 2020 (Law 75-3).

¶ 6-805 Final return and final payment or refund

A corporation is required to file a final return within two months after the end of its business year, whether or not it has a positive income for that business year.

The ordinary income and corporation tax due on it in the final return are calculated on the basis of the corporation's financial report as approved by the meeting of shareholders.

A final return must be accompanied by the corporation's balance sheet, profit and loss statement, and other documents describing items necessary for calculating its ordinary income, undistributed income and the corporation tax due.

The form of the final return is given at ¶ 6-970.

Corporation tax on ordinary income, undistributed profits and approved pension funds for a business year, minus the amount of prepayment, must be paid to the tax office within two months after the end of the business year.

Refunds from overpayment of the prepayment, tax credits, carry back of net loss to the preceding business year, etc. will be made on request after a final return has been filed.

Corporations whose amounts of capital are more than ¥100 million must file its tax returns with using e-Tax systems from the accounting periods beginning on and after April 1, 2020 (Law 75-3).

¶ 6-810 Special treatment for final return

If a corporation cannot file a final return because the accountant has not finished the audit or for other unavoidable reasons, the time limit for the final return may be postponed for four months (six months after the end of accounting periods) with the approval of the tax authority (Law 75-2).

¶ 6-805

法　人　税　509

電子情報処理組織を使用する方法（e-Tax）により提供しなければならない（法法75の3）。

¶6-805　確定申告，確定納付及び還付

　法人は，事業年度終了の日の翌日から2ヶ月以内に，当該事業年度の所得の金額の有無を問わず，確定申告書を提出しなければならない。確定申告書に記載する各事業年度の所得金額又は法人税額は，株主総会の決議により確定した決算に基づき計算しなければならない。

　確定申告書には，当該事業年度の貸借対照表，損益計算書その他所得金額，留保金額及び法人税額の計算に必要とされるその他の書類を添付しなければならない。

　各事業年度の所得の金額及び退職年金積立金に対する法人税額から，中間納付額を控除した金額を，当該事業年度終了の日の翌日から2ヶ月以内に税務署へ納付しなければならない。

　確定申告書の提出があった場合において，中間納付額，所得税等の税額控除額，欠損事業年度からの欠損金の繰戻し等による過大納付額の還付を請求することができる。

　なお，内国法人のうち事業年度開始の時において資本金の額が1億円を超える法人（大法人）の確定申告書の提出については，平成32年4月1日以後に開始する事業年度以後，これらの申告書に記載すべきものとされる事項を電子情報処理組織を使用する方法（e-Tax）により提供しなければならない（法法75の3）。

¶6-810　確定申告書の提出期限の延長の特例

　法人は，会計監査人の監査が終了していないことその他やむを得ない理由により決算が確定しないため，確定申告書を提出することができない場合には，税務署長の承認を受けて，その提出期限を4ヶ月間（事業年度終了から6ヶ月後まで）延長するよう求めることができる（法法75の2）。

510   CORPORATION TAX

Tax on Liquidation Income
(Special taxation rule for liquidation income was abolished from October 1, 2010.)

¶ 6-820 Liquidation

Where a corporation is dissolved and liquidated, the tax on liquidation income should be paid by:

(1) periodic prepayment for each business year while the corporation still exists during liquidation procedures in the same manner as before the dissolution;

(2) non-periodic prepayment on the occasion of partial distribution of the assets; and/or

(3) final payment immediately before the final distribution of the residual assets.

Tax on liquidation income is levied only on domestic ordinary corporations and cooperatives.

¶ 6-825 Periodic prepayment

A corporation in the process of liquidation is required to file a return and pay corporation tax periodically within two months after the end of each business year, in the same manner as a corporation in operation files a return and makes payments on ordinary income. This is the periodic prepayment of the tax on liquidation income. The amount of the periodic prepayment is computed in the same way as the tax on ordinary income (but not on undistributed profits) with the following exceptions:

(a) no interim return is required;

(b) the amount of the first prepayment is computed for the period between the time of dissolution and the end of the business year during which the dissolution took place;

(c) if in the process of liquidation a partial distribution of assets took place and a non-periodic prepayment was made during the business year, 30% of the distributed assets, which formed neither capital, capital surplus, nor retained earnings at the time of such partial distribution, is credited against the amount of the periodic prepayment for that business year.

¶ 6-820

法　人　税　511

清算所得に対する法人税
（平成22年10月１日から，清算所得課税は廃止され，通常の所得課税に移行された。）

¶6-820　清算
　法人が解散して清算する場合には，清算所得に対する法人税を次により納付しなければならない。
　⑴　清算中の所得に係る予納申告による納付

　⑵　残余財産の一部分配に係る予納申告による納付

　⑶　清算確定申告による納付

　清算確定申告に対する法人税は内国法人（公益法人等を除き，協同組合等を含む。）のみに課される。

¶6-825　清算中の所得に係る予納申告による納付
　清算中の法人は，事業活動を行っている法人が各事業年度の所得につき申告書を提出して納付するのと同様の方法により，事業年度終了の日から２ヶ月以内に，毎期，法人税の申告書を提出して納付しなければならない。これが清算中の所得に対する予納申告に係る納付である。予納申告に係る納付の金額は，次に掲げる例外を除き，各事業年度の所得に対する法人税（留保所得に対する法人税を含まない。）の計算と同様に計算される。

　⒜　中間申告書の提出は必要とされない。
　⒝　最初に予納すべき金額は，解散の日の翌日からその事業年度の末日までの期間について計算される。

　⒞　清算中に残余財産の一部分配が行われ清算中の所得に係る予納申告による納付がなされた場合には，当該一部分配が行われたときの資本金額，資本積立金額又は利益積立金額により構成されない残余財産分配額の30％相当額は当該事業年度の清算中の所得に係る納付税額から控除される。

512   CORPORATION TAX

¶ 6-830 Non-periodic prepayment

When a corporation undergoing liquidation distributes part of its assets, it is required to file a return and make a non-periodic prepayment of the tax on liquidation income before making such a partial distribution, provided that a return and prepayment are not required when the assets are distributed only from capital, capital surplus and retained earnings.

The assets are deemed to be distributed first, from capital or capital surplus; secondly, from retained earnings at the time of the partial distribution; and then, thirdly, from the remainder.

The tax is computed as if the partial distribution was the final distribution of the residual assets.

¶ 6-835 Final payment

A corporation undergoing liquidation is required to file a final return and make a final payment of the tax on liquidation income immediately before the final distribution of residual assets. If the final distribution does not take place within one month after the final confirmation of the net residual assets, the corporation is required to file a final return and make a final payment within one month after the final confirmation of the net residual assets.

¶ 6-840 Taxation on liquidation income

The basis for the tax on liquidation income is the amount of liquidation income, that is:

$$\begin{pmatrix} \text{Distributable} \\ \text{residual assets} \end{pmatrix} + \begin{pmatrix} \text{Nondeductible} \\ \text{disbursement} \end{pmatrix} - \begin{cases} \text{Capital and capital surplus and} \\ \text{retained earnings at the time} \\ \text{of the dissolution (opening of} \\ \text{liquidation proceedings)} \end{cases}$$

The main nondeductible disbursements to be added to distributable residual assets are:

(i)   corporation tax on liquidation income, additional taxes and delinquency tax thereon;

(ii)   inhabitant taxes related to (i);

(iii)   withholding income tax;

(iv)   enterprise tax on liquidation income;

(v)   revaluation tax; and

(vi)   contributions considered unnecessary for liquidation.

The result is the liquidation income, to which 27.1% tax rate applies.

¶ 6-830

法　人　税　513

¶6-830　残余財産の一部分配に係る予納申告に係る納付

　清算中の法人が残余財産の一部の分配をしようとする場合には，当該残余財産が資本金額，資本積立金額又は利益積立金額の合計額を超えるときは，分配のつど，その分配の日の前日までに残余財産の一部分配に係る予納申告書を提出し，かつ，その税額を納付しなければならない。

　分配しようとする残余財産は，(1)資本金額又は資本積立金額，(2)一部分配が行われたときの利益積立金額，(3)その他の部分，から順次分配されるものとみなされる。

　その税額は残余財産の全部を分配する場合と同様の方法により計算される。

¶6-835　清算確定申告による納付

　清算中の法人がその残余財産の最後の分配をしようとする場合には，その最後の分配の日の前日までに清算確定申告書を提出し，その税額を納付しなければならない。ただし，残余財産の最後の分配の日の1ヶ月前に，残余財産が確定した場合には，当該法人はその確定の日の翌日から1ヶ月以内に清算確定申告書を提出し，その税額を納付しなければならない。

¶6-840　清算所得に対する課税

　清算所得に対する法人税の課税標準は清算所得であり，次のように計算される。

$$\begin{pmatrix} 分配可能な残 \\ 余財産の価額 \end{pmatrix} + \begin{pmatrix} 残余財産の価 \\ 額への算入額 \end{pmatrix} - \begin{pmatrix} 解散時（清算手続開始）における資本 \\ 金額，資本積立金額及び利益積立金額 \end{pmatrix}$$

　分配可能な残余財産の価額への算入額のうち主なものは次のとおりである。

(i)　清算所得に対する法人税，これに係る加算税及び延滞税

(ii)　上記(i)に係る住民税

(iii)　源泉所得税

(iv)　清算所得に対する事業税

(v)　再評価税及び

(vi)　清算に必要とされない寄附金

　上記の計算結果が清算所得であり，27.1％の税率が適用される。ただし，

514   CORPORATION TAX

This rate is reduced to 20.5% for cooperatives.

Income tax credit is deducted from the tax resulting from the application of the tax rates. The balance after such deductions is the tax on liquidation income. The tax to be paid in the final payment is the tax on liquidation income so computed, less periodic and non-periodic prepayments. If the balance shows a figure below zero, the overpayment is refunded.

¶ 6-845 When merged in the course of liquidation

When a corporation in the process of liquidation is merged and absorbed by another corporation, the taxes paid in may periodic or non-periodic prepayments are not refunded or credited.

Tax on Specific Funds
(The Taxation is Suspended from April 1, 1999 until March 31, 2017)

(The tax qualified pension fund regime was abolished from April 1, 2002 and a new pension fund agreement is not treated as a tax qualified agreement. Existing agreements are, however, treated as tax qualified pension fund agreements until March 31, 2012.)

¶ 6-855 Interim return and final return

(1) A corporation carrying on approved pension business, employees' welfare pension business or employees' assets formation business whose business year is longer than six months should file an interim return before the end of the first eight months of the business year, with respect to the term of the first six months of that business year.

The tax reported on the interim return must be paid to a tax office before the time limit for filing an interim return.

(2) A corporation carrying on business as mentioned in (1) above is required to file a final return within two months after the end of its business year.

Tax on specific funds of a business year, less the amount of prepayment on the interim return of the business year, must be paid to the tax office before the time limit for filing a final return.

¶ 6-845

法　人　税　515

協同組合等については20.5％の軽減税率が適用される。

　所得税額は法人税率適用後の法人税額から控除される。当該税額控除後の残額が清算所得に対する法人税額である。清算確定申告による納付額は，法人税額から清算中の所得に係る予納申告による納付額及び残余財産の一部分配に係る予納額を控除した金額とされる。差引マイナスとなる場合には，当該税額は還付される。

¶6-845　清算中の法人の合併

　清算中の法人が他の法人に合併された場合には，清算中の予納額（清算中の所得に係る予納申告による納付額及び残余財産の一部分配に係る予納申告による納付額）は還付又は税額控除されない。

退職年金等積立金に対する法人税
（平成11年4月1日から平成29年3月31日まで課税なし。）

　（なお，適格退職年金制度は，平成14年3月31日において廃止され，平成14年4月1日以後は，原則として新たな契約の締結は適格退職年金契約として認められないこととなった。ただし，現に締結されている適格退職年金制度については，平成24年3月31日までに限り経過的に存続することとされている。）

¶6-855　中間申告及び確定申告

(1)　適格退職年金業務，厚生年金基金業務又は勤労者財産形成業務を行う法人でその事業年度が6ヶ月を超えるものは，当該事業年度の最初の6ヶ月間につき8ヶ月終了するまでに中間申告をしなければならない。

　中間申告税額は，中間申告期限までに税務署へ納付しなければならない。

(2)　上記(1)の業務を行う法人は事業年度終了後2ヶ月以内に確定申告をしなければならない。

　退職年金等積立金に対する法人税（中間納付額控除後）は確定申告期限までに税務署へ納付しなければならない。

516   CORPORATION TAX

Other Procedural Matters

¶ 6-860 Corrections, determination, penalty taxes, tax disputes

(1) See ¶ 5-740 to ¶ 5-820 for correction of returns, determination of tax liability, penalty taxes, tax disputes and information returns, as these matters are common to both assessment income tax and corporation tax.

(2) Statutory correctable periods of corporate tax calculation by tax authorities were extended as follows (GL 70).

    (a) Correctable periods applicable to losses shall be extended from five years to ten years. The revision shall apply to losses incurred in accounting periods beginning on and after April 1, 2017.

    (b) Correctable periods applicable to income other than evasion cases shall be extended from three years to five years. The revision shall apply to the income of which filing due date is on April 1, 2004 or after.

Foreign Corporations

Taxation principle applied to a foreign corporation was changed, under the 2014 tax reform, from an entire income approach to an attributable income approach in line with the OECD Model Tax Convention amended in 2010. This change will be effective from accounting periods beginning on or after April 1, 2016 (see detail in ¶ 6-920).

¶ 6-870 Tax implication of a foreign corporation applicable on or after 2016 fiscal year

1. Scope of Japan source income (based on attributable income approach) (Law 138)

    (1) Income attributable to a PE in Japan of a foreign corporation is classified as one of Japan source income. Income derived from an investment into a third country by the PE become taxable in Japan after the change of the current law regardless of whether or not such income is taxed in the third country.

    (2) Japan source income which is not attributable to a PE in Japan

¶ 6-860

法 人 税 517

その他の手続

¶6-860　更正，決定，加算税，不服申立て

(1)　更正，決定，加算税，不服申立て，資料の提出などについては申告所得税と法人税とも共通する事項であるので，¶5-740〜¶5-820を参照されたい。

(2)　なお，法人税に係る更正の期間制限については，平成16年度の税制改正において，次のとおり見直しが行われた（通則法70）。

(a)　欠損金に係る更正の期間制限を10年に延長する。この改正は平成29年4月1日以後に開始した事業年度において生じた欠損金額について適用する。

(b)　脱税以外の場合の過少申告に係る更正の期間制限を5年（現行3年）に延長する。この改正は平成16年4月1日以後に法定申告期限等が到来する法人税について適用する。

外　国　法　人

　外国法人に対する課税原則は，平成26年の税制改正により，従来のいわゆる「総合課税」に基づく課税関係から，平成22年改訂後のOECDモデル租税条約に沿った「帰属主義」に見直された。改正後の規定は平成28年4月1日以後に開始する事業年度から適用される（詳細は¶6-920参照）。

¶6-870　平成28年度から適用される外国法人の課税関係

1．（帰属主義の概念に基づく）国内源泉所得の範囲（法法138）

(1)　外国法人が日本に有する恒久的施設（Permanent Establishment（以下「PE」）に帰せられる所得（以下「PE帰属所得」）が，国内源泉所得の一つとされた。PEが外国から収受する投資所得は，帰属主義においては日本で課税される。

(2)　PE帰属所得以外の国内源泉所得については，PE帰属所得とは分離して，

518   CORPORATION TAX

of a foreign corporation ("income not attributable to a PE") is subject to taxation separately from income attributable to the PE and taxed effectively in the same manner as Japan source income earned by a foreign corporation without a PE in Japan (Law 142-9).

(3) Scope of capital gains treated as Japan source income is limited to capital gains from sale of real estate located in Japan, shares in a corporation holding real estate located in Japan, etc., which is identical with the entire income approach.

(4) Certain Japan source income (interests, dividends, royalties, etc.) which was subject to corporation tax under the entire income approach if a foreign corporation has a PE in Japan, is not subject to corporation tax under the attributable income approach. The income is only subject to withholding tax under the attributable income approach.

2. Income attributable to a PE

(1) Income attributable to a PE in Japan of a foreign corporation should be calculated based on the assumption that the PE were a separate and independent corporation from its head office and other branches (Law 138).

(2) Intra-entity dealings (Law 138)

(a) In calculating income attributable to a PE, profits or losses derived from intra-entity dealings should be recorded.

(b) The transfer pricing rules should be applied to intra-entity dealings (SM 66-4-3).

(c) Provisions of start-up funds from a head office to its PE and profit distribution from a PE to its head office should be treated as capital transactions.

(d) Deemed payments of interests from a PE to its head office under intra-entity dealings should not be subject to Japanese withholding tax.

(3) Calculation of income attributable to a PE (Law 142)

(a) The rule, where mere purchase of goods or merchandise by a PE for its head office does not generate any profits, was abolished.

(b) Reasonable allocation to a PE of costs and expenses commonly incurred for both the PE and its head office should be admitted as expenses of the PE.

(c) When a PE is sold, capital gains or losses incurred from the sale should be recognized as income attributable to the PE (Law 138).

¶ 6-870

法 人 税 519

Non-PE外国法人が得る国内源泉所得と同様に課税される（法法142の9）。

⑶　国内源泉所得とされる国内資産譲渡所得の範囲については，従来と同様，国内不動産，国内不動産関連株式等，日本にPEを有しない外国法人（以下「Non-PE外国法人」）において課税対象となる資産の譲渡に限る。

⑷　総合課税のもとでは法人税の課税対象とされていたその他の国内源泉所得（例えば，利子，配当，使用料等）については，源泉課税で課税関係が完了する。

2．PE帰属所得
⑴　PE帰属所得は，PEが本店等から分離・独立した企業であると擬制した場合に当該PEに帰せられる所得とする（法法138）。

⑵　PEと本店等との間の内部取引（法法138）
　⒜　PE帰属所得の算定においては，PEと本店等との間の内部取引について損益を認識する。
　⒝　内部取引に対し移転価格税制等の規定を適用する（措法66の4の3）。

　⒞　本店からPEへの支店開設資金の供与やPEから本店への利益送金等については，資本等取引として擬制する。

　⒟　PEから本店等に対する内部支払利子等のみなし支払に関しては，源泉課税を行わない。

⑶　PE帰属所得の計算（法法142）
　⒜　PEが本店等のために行う単なる購入活動からは所得が生じないものとする単純購入非課税の取扱いは，廃止する。
　⒝　本店等で行う事業とPEで行う事業に共通する費用を合理的な基準でPEに配賦した場合には，PEにおける費用として認める。

　⒞　PEが外部に譲渡される場合には，その譲渡による所得はPE帰属所得とする（法法138）。

520   CORPORATION TAX

(d) If a PE is closed, built-in gains or losses in PE's assets should be recognized as income attributable to the PE in the accounting period during which the PE is closed (Law 142-4).

(4) Limitation on deductibility on interest expenses (Law 142-4)
When capital of a PE in Japan of a foreign corporation is less than the capital to be attributed to the PE if the PE were separate and independent corporation from its head office, and the PE makes payment of interest, including intra-entity dealings of interest, on a debt incurred by the business of the PE, the interest corresponding to deficient capital should not be deductible in the calculation of the PE's attributable income.

(5) Application of thin-capitalization rule
The thin-capitalization rule is no longer applied to a PE in Japan of a foreign corporation in accordance with the introduction of the new interest deduction limitation rule as described above in (4).

3. Tax base (Law 141), Tax losses carried-forward (Law 142)

(1) "Income attributable to a PE" and "Income not attributable to a PE" is taxed separately. Tax losses incurred in one category should not be utilized to offset income in the other category.

(2) A foreign corporation without a PE is subject to taxation on "Income not attributable to a PE". Tax is calculated based on the income after deducting loss carried-forward from the income.

4. Foreign tax credits (Law 144-2)

(1) A foreign tax credit system applicable to a foreign corporation with a PE is newly introduced since income derived in a third country will be included in taxable income in Japan under the attributable income approach.

(2) Creditable foreign tax
(a) The creditable foreign tax is the tax which is imposed by a third country and attributable to a PE.
(b) If the foreign tax exceeds the amount calculated using the reduced tax rate under the tax treaty between Japan and the third country, the excess portion is not creditable. The portion, however, can be deducted as expenses for calculating the income.

¶ 6-870

法 人 税 521

(d) PEが閉鎖等に伴ってPEに該当しないこととなる場合には，その該当しないこととなる直前のPEに帰せられる資産（以下「PE帰属資産」）の時価評価損益を，PEの閉鎖等の日の属する事業年度のPE帰属所得として認識する（法法142の4）。

(4) PEの支払利子控除制限（法法142の4）

PEの自己資本相当額が，PEが本店等から分離・独立した企業であると擬制した場合に帰せられるべき資本（以下「PE帰属資本」）の額に満たない場合には，PEにおける支払利子総額（PEから本店等への内部支払利子及び本店等からPEに費用配賦された利子を含む。）のうち，その満たない部分に対応する金額について，PE帰属所得の計算上，損金の額に算入しない。

(5) 過少資本税制の適用

資本の配賦に基づいてPEの支払利子の損金算入を制限する上記(4)の措置の導入に伴い，PEにおいて損金算入される支払利子を算定する上で，過少資本税制は適用しない。

3．課税標準（法法141），繰越欠損金（法法142）

(1) PEを有する外国法人の課税標準は，PE帰属所得とPE帰属所得以外の国内源泉所得（以下「PE非帰属国内源泉所得」）とに区分し，これらを通算しない。繰越欠損金についても，それぞれに係る繰越欠損金を区分し，それぞれの所得からのみ控除する。

(2) Non-PE外国法人の課税標準は，PE非帰属国内源泉所得とする。税額の計算は，当該PE非帰属国内源泉所得から繰越欠損金を控除した額に税率を乗じて計算する。

4．外国法人のPEに係る外国税額控除（法法144の2）

(1) 外国法人のPEが本店所在地国以外の第三国で得た所得がPE帰属所得として日本の課税対象となることに伴い，PEのための外国税額控除制度を設ける。

(2) 控除の対象となる外国法人税

(a) 控除の対象となる外国法人税は，外国法人に対して本店所在地国以外の第三国で課された外国法人税のうちPEに帰せられるものとする。

(b) PEが第三国から得る所得について第三国で課された外国法人税に関し，外国税額控除の対象とする金額は，その課された外国法人税のうち日本と第三国との間の租税条約に定める限度税率によって計算される金額を限度とする。なお，当該租税条約に定める限度税率を超える部分については，PE帰属所得の計算上，損金の額に算入する。

522   CORPORATION TAX

5. Declaration of income (Law 144-3 to 144-8)

 (1) It is required for a foreign corporation with a PE in Japan to file a corporation tax return to declare income attributable to a PE and income not attributable to a PE.

 (2) It is required for a foreign corporation without a PE to file a corporation tax return to declare income not attributable to a PE, if any.

6. Anti-tax avoidance provision (Law 147-2)

An anti-tax avoidance provision similar to that applied to a Japanese family corporation is newly introduced. Under the provision, the Tax Authorities would be able to impute tax base of income attributable to a PE of a foreign corporation if the Tax Authorities consider that admission of intra-entity dealings of the foreign corporation would result in an improper decrease of corporation tax burden of the foreign corporation.

¶ 6-875 Classification of foreign corporations (Info: tax treatments before the 2014 tax reform)

 Foreign corporations, that is corporations which do not have their head office in Japan, are classified into the following four types for tax purposes (Law 141):

 (1) Foreign corporations carrying on business through a branch office, factory, mine or other fixed place of business situated in Japan; the term "fixed place of business" does not include any facilities established solely for purchasing or storing goods, or solely for advertising, supplying information, conducting research or other such activities of an auxiliary nature.

 (2) Foreign corporations carrying on business not through permanent establishments stated in (1), but through:

  (a) undertaking construction, installation, or assembly activities in Japan for longer than one year or supervising such activities undertaken in Japan for longer than one year; or

  (b) an agent (other than an independent agent) in Japan who:

   (i) has, and habitually exercises, the authority to conclude contracts (excluding contracts only for purchases of goods) for or on behalf of a foreign corporation (excluding cases such as an airline company selling tickets for other airline companies

¶ 6-875

法　人　税　523

5．申告（法法144の3〜144の8）
⑴　PEを有する外国法人については，事業年度ごとにPE帰属所得及び法人
　税の課税対象となるPE非帰属国内源泉所得に係る法人税の申告書を提出
　する。
⑵　Non-PE外国法人については，法人税の課税対象となるPE非帰属国内源
　泉所得を有する場合にのみ，当該PE非帰属国内源泉所得に係る法人税の
　申告書を提出する。
6．適正な課税の確保（法法147の2）
　　外国法人のPE帰属所得及び税額の計算に関し，同族会社の行為計算否
　認規定に類似した租税回避防止規定を設ける。

¶6-875　外国法人の区分（参考：平成26年の税制改正以前の取扱い）
　外国法人，すなわち日本国内に本店を有しない法人は，課税上，次の四つ
に分類される（法法141）。

⑴　支店，事務所，工場，鉱山その他事業を行う一定の場所を日本国内に有
　する外国法人
　　この場合，「事業を行う一定の場所」には，資産を購入し又は保管する
　業務のためにのみ使用する場所，広告宣伝，情報の提供，市場調査その他
　その事業の遂行にとって補助的な機能を有する事業上の活動を行うために
　のみ使用する場所は含まれないものとされる。
⑵　上記⑴に掲げる恒久的施設は通じないが，次に掲げるものを通じて事業
　を行う外国法人
　⒜　国内において1年を超えて施設，すえ付け，組立てその他の作業又は
　　その作業の指揮監督の役務の提供

　⒝　日本における次のような代理人（独立の地位を有する代理人等を除く。）
　　⒤　外国法人のためにその事業に関し契約（資産を購入するための契約
　　　を除く。）を締結する権限を有し，かつ，これを常習的に行使する者
　　　（航空会社が他の航空会社の航空券を代理人として発売するような者
　　　は除く。）

524   CORPORATION TAX

as their agent),

    (ii) habitually maintains a stock of goods in Japan from which he or she regularly fills orders and delivers goods on behalf of a foreign corporation, or

    (iii) habitually conducts important activities for securing orders, such as negotiating with customers for or on behalf of a foreign corporation.

(3) Foreign corporations not carrying on business as stated above in (1) or (2) but having the following items of income:

  (a) profits from a business of arranging technical services or performances of public entertainers in Japan;

  (b) rent, etc. for the use of real estate and the like property in Japan;

  (c) income from assets situated in Japan which is not subject to Japanese withholding income tax;

  (d) capital gains accruing from the alienation of assets situated in Japan. Capital gains accruing to a foreign corporation are subject to Japanese corporation tax only in the following cases, if it does not carry on business as stated in (1) or (2):

    (i)   sale of real estate situated in Japan,

    (ii) cutting or sale of timber situated in Japan,

    (iii) sale of shares in a domestic corporation bought for cornering purposes,

    (iv) sale of the majority interest in the capital of a domestic corporation under certain conditions;

(If a foreign corporation sells stocks or units of a Japanese corporation whose 50% or more of assets are real estates, the capital gains shall be included in the income subject to corporate taxes.)

(If stocks or units of a Japanese corporation are owned by a foreign corporation through a Nin-i Kumiai ("NK"), or a partnership, or an entity similar to a NK (including a foreign entity corresponding to a NK), stocks or units owned by other participants of the NK shall be included in the ownership ratio of the foreign corporation when judging 25% ownership for the purposes of capital gain taxation similar to business transfer. However, if it meets certain requirement such that it is an

¶ 6-875

(ⅱ) 外国法人のために顧客の通常の要求に応ずる程度の数量の資産を保管し，かつ，当該資産を顧客の要求に応じて引き渡す者

(ⅲ) 外国法人のために常習的にその事業に関し契約を締結するための注文の取得，協議など重要な部分をする者

(3) 上記(1)又は(2)に掲げた事業は営んでいないが，次に掲げる種類の所得を有する外国法人
(a) 国内において人的役務の提供（科学技術などの専門的知識の提供又は芸能人など）を主たる内容とする事業に係る対価
(b) 国内にある不動産の保有による家賃などの所得

(c) 日本の源泉所得税の対象とならない国内にある資産からの所得

(d) 日本国内にある資産の譲渡により生ずる所得
「譲渡により生ずる所得」は，法人が(1)又は(2)に掲げる事業を営んでいない限り，次に掲げる所得以外の所得については日本の法人税を課されない。
(ⅰ) 国内にある不動産の譲渡による所得
(ⅱ) 国内にある山林の伐採又は譲渡による所得
(ⅲ) 内国法人の発行する特定の株式の譲渡による所得

(ⅳ) 内国法人の発行する株式の譲渡による所得

（外国法人が，国内にある不動産が総資産の50％以上である法人が発行する株式等を譲渡をした場合，当該譲渡による所得を申告納税の対象となる国内源泉所得の範囲に加える。）

（外国法人に係る事業譲渡類似株式等の譲渡益課税に係る所有割合25％の判定上，外国法人が民法組合等（外国におけるこれらに類するものを含む。）を通じて内国法人の株式等を所有する場合，当該民法組合等の他の組合員を加える。ただし，当該組合が投資事業有限責任組合で，かつ当該外国法人が有限責任組合員である等一定の条件を満たす場合には，他の組合員の所有割合は判定に含まない。）

526   CORPORATION TAX

investment business limited partnership and the foreign corporation is a limited partner of it, other partners' ownership ratio is not required to aggregate for the judgment purpose.)

(e) miscellaneous items of income of minor importance from sources in Japan enumerated in a Cabinet Order.

(4) Foreign corporations not falling into the above categories.

¶ 6-880 Income assessable (Info: tax treatments before the 2014 tax reform)

Class (4) corporations, according to the categories defined in ¶ 6-870 (4) above, are not subject to corporation tax because their tax liability has been fully settled through withholding income tax.

Class (3) corporations are subject to corporation tax only with regard to the income enumerated in ¶ 6-870 (3) (a) to (e). Tax liability with regard to the other income enumerated in ¶ 4-620 (1) to (4) and (8) to (17) is finally settled through withholding income tax.

Class (2) corporations are subject to corporation tax on:

(a) the income derived from a business in Japan as stated in ¶ 6-870 (2);

(b) the income enumerated in ¶ 6-870 (3); and

(c) the income enumerated in ¶ 4-620 (1) to (4) and (8) to (17) in so far as that is attributable to a business in Japan.

Class (1) corporations defined in ¶ 6-870 (1) are subject to corporation tax on their entire income from sources in Japan.

¶ 6-885 Allocation of profits to Japanese sources (Info: tax treatments before the 2014 tax reform)

When a corporation carries on business both inside and outside Japan, the income derived from the business is called domestic business income if derived from source inside Japan, and foreign business income if derived from sources outside Japan, according to the following criteria (Reg 176):

(1) If a corporation merely purchases goods or merchandise in Japan and sells them abroad, the whole profits from such a sale is foreign business income. If a corporation merely purchases goods or merchandise outside Japan and sells them inside Japan, the whole

¶ 6-880

(e)　政令で定める日本国内源泉のその他の所得

(4)　上記(1)，(2)及び(3)以外の外国法人

¶6-880　課税所得の範囲（参考：平成26年の税制改正以前の取扱い）

　上記(4)の法人は，そのすべての納税義務が源泉所得税を通じて処理されるために法人税の納税義務の対象とならない。

　上記(3)の法人は¶6-870(3)に掲げた所得についてのみ法人税の納税義務の対象となる。¶4-620(1)～(4)及び(8)～(17)に掲げたその他の所得は源泉所得税の対象となる。

　上記(2)の法人は，

(a)　¶6-870(2)に掲げた国内において行う事業から生ずる所得，

(b)　¶6-870(3)に掲げた特定の所得並びに，

(c)　¶4-620(1)～(4)及び(8)～(17)に掲げた所得についてはその所得が国内において行う事業に帰せられたものである限り，それぞれ法人税の納税義務の対象となる。

　上記(1)の法人は，すべての国内源泉所得について法人税の納税義務の対象となる。

¶6-885　所得の国内源泉所得への配分（参考：平成26年の税制改正以前の取扱い）

　法人が国内及び国外の双方にわたって事業を行う場合には，当該事業からの所得は次の区分に従い国内において行う事業から生ずる国内源泉所得と国外において行う事業から生ずる国外源泉所得とに区分される（法令176）。

(1)　その法人が国内において譲渡を受けたたな卸資産につき国外で譲渡する場合には，当該譲渡により生ずるすべての所得は国外源泉所得とする。また，その法人が国外において譲渡を受けたたな卸資産につき国内で譲渡する場合には，当該譲渡により生ずるすべての所得は国内源泉所得とする。

528   CORPORATION TAX

profits from such a sale are domestic business income.

(2) If a corporation manufactures goods or merchandise wholly or partly in Japan and sells them abroad, the income derived from such a sale is allocated between domestic business income and foreign business income, just as if the goods or merchandise had been manufactured by a domestic corporation, and were purchased by a foreign corporation in a transaction at arm's length, and sold abroad. If a corporation manufactures goods or merchandise wholly or partly abroad and sells them in Japan, the income derived from such sales is allocated similarly.

(3) If a corporation engages in activities within Japan such as construction, installation or assembly, the income derived from such activities is treated as domestic business income, even though the contract was concluded or labor and materials were procured abroad.

(4) The income from sea transportation is allocated between domestic business income and foreign business income on the basis of revenue from outgoing passengers and cargo. The income from air transportation is allocated on the basis of factors such as receipts, expenditures, value of fixed assets, etc.

(5) The income attributable to insurance contracts concluded through a place of business in Japan or an agent in Japan is domestic business income.

(6) If publishing or broadcasting companies perform advertising activities in Japan for any other person, the income derived therefrom is domestic business income.

(7) If a corporation engages solely in auxiliary activities in Japan, such as advertising, liaison, etc., for its business carried on abroad, no domestic business income is attributed to such auxiliary activities.

(8) If money is raised through a branch office of a foreign corporation located in Japan and put to the use of its head office situated abroad, no domestic business income is deemed to accrue. On the other hand, if money is raised through the head office of a foreign corporation located abroad and put to the use of its branch office located in Japan, interest, etc., received thereon is treated as domestic income, while expenses incurred abroad for raising money, such as interest paid on deposits at the head office, are deductible in computing the amount of domestic business income. This principle

¶ 6-885

(2) その法人が国内において全部又は一部を製造し，その製造により取得したたな卸資産を国外において譲渡する場合，当該譲渡により生ずる所得のうち，当該製造に係る業務を国内業務とし，当該譲渡に係る業務を国外業務とし，他の者との間において通常の取引の条件に従って他の者へ譲渡されたものとした場合における国内業務に係る国内源泉所得と国外業務に係る国外源泉所得とに区分する。法人が国外において全部又は一部を製造したたな卸資産を国内において譲渡する場合には，当該譲渡により生ずる所得は上記の原則により配分される。

(3) その法人が国内において建設，すえ付けその他の作業を施行する場合には，当該作業により生ずる所得は，その契約の締結又は当該作業に必要な人員又は資材の調達を国外において行ったとしても，すべて国内源泉所得として取り扱われる。

(4) 国際航空又は海運の事業を行う場合には，船舶による運送の事業にあっては旅客又は貨物の乗船又は船積みに係る収入金額を基準とし，航空機による運送の事業にあっては国内又は国外業務に係る収入金額，経費，固定資産の価額など所得の発生要因を基準として，国内源泉所得と国外源泉所得とに分類する。

(5) その法人が損害保険又は生命保険の事業を行う場合には，国内にある営業所又は代理人を通じて締結した保険の契約に基因する所得は国内源泉所得とする。

(6) その法人が出版又は放送の事業を行う場合において他の者のために広告に係る事業を行うときは，国内において行われる広告に係る収入金額を国内源泉所得とする。

(7) 法人が広告，市場調査等の国外で行われる事業の補助的機能の行為を国内において行う場合には，当該補助的機能を有する行為に帰属する所得は国内源泉所得とされない。

(8) 法人の国内にある支店を通じて資金を調達し，国外にあるその本店においてその資金を貸し出す場合には，当該調達による所得は国内源泉所得とはみなされない。他方，法人の国外にある本店を通じて資金を調達し，国外にある支店においてその資金を貸し出す場合には，当該貸出による所得（利子）は国内源泉所得とされる。この場合，本店における預金に係る支払利息など当該資金の調達のために国外において生じた経費は国内源泉所得の金額の計算上控除される。この原則は資金のみならず，産業的施設等にも適用される。

530   CORPORATION TAX

is applicable not only to money, but also to industrial assets, etc.

(9) If a foreign corporation makes a loan, an investment, etc. to other foreign customers abroad through a branch, an office or other permanent establishment in Japan, the income raised from such activities is domestic business income to the extent that it is attributable to such branch, etc.

¶ 6-900 Concessions under tax treaties (corporation tax)

Japan has tax treaties with the following countries listed:

Australia, Austria, Bangladesh, Belgium, Brazil, Brunei, Bulgaria, Canada, Chile, China, Czech, Denmark, Egypt, Fiji, Finland, France, Germany, Hong Kong, Hungary, India, Indonesia, Ireland, Israel, Italy, Korea, Kuwait, Latvia, Luxembourg, Malaysia, Mexico, New Independent States, New Zealand, Norway, Oman, Pakistan, Poland, Portugal, Qatar, Romania, Russia, Saudi Arabia, Singapore, Slovakia, Slovenia South Africa, Spain, Sri Lanka, Sweden, Switzerland, Thailand, the Netherlands, the Philippines, Turkey, U.S.A., United Arab Emirates, United Kingdom, Vietnam, Zambia.

Further, there are tax treaties between Bahamas, Bermuda, British Virgin Irelands, Cayman Islands, Guernsey, Isle of Man, Jersey, Liechtenstein, Macao, Panama, Samoa for mainly information exchange purpose.

¶ 6-900

(9)　その法人が国内にある支店，事務所その他の恒久的施設を通じて外国の
　　顧客へ資金の貸出又は投資をした場合には，当該行為から生ずる所得は当
　　該恒久的施設に帰属する限りにおいて国内で行う事業から生ずる所得とさ
　　れる。

¶6-900　租税条約による特例（法人税）

わが国が締結した租税条約の相手国は次のとおりである。

アイルランド，アメリカ，アラブ首長国連邦，イギリス，イスラエル，イタリア，
インド，インドネシア，ヴェトナム，エジプト，NIS諸国，オーストラリア，
オーストリア，オマーン，オランダ，カナダ，カタール，韓国，クウェート，
サウジアラビア，ザンビア，シンガポール，スイス，スウェーデン，スペイン，
スリ・ランカ，スロヴァキア，スロベニア，タイ，チェコ，中国，チリ，
デンマーク，ドイツ，トルコ，ニュージーランド，ノールウェー，パキスタン，
ハンガリー，バングラデシュ，フィジー，フィリピン，フィンランド，ブラジル，
フランス，ブルガリア，ブルネイ，ベルギー，ポーランド，ポルトガル，香港，
マレーシア，南アフリカ，メキシコ，ラトビア，ルーマニア，ルクセンブルク，
ロシア

なお，その他，英領バージン諸島，ガーンジー，ケイマン諸島，サモア，
ジャージー，パナマ，バハマ，バミューダ，マカオ，マン島，リヒテンシュ
タインとの間に情報交換規定を主体とした租税条約を締結している。

532

CHAPTER 7

INHERITANCE TAX AND GIFT TAX

	Paragraph
Chart: Computation of Inheritance Tax	¶ 7-005
Structure of Inheritance Tax and Gift Tax	¶ 7-010

Inheritance Tax

Taxpayer and Taxable Property	¶ 7-100
Computation of Inheritance Tax	¶ 7-250
Valuation of Properties	¶ 7-550
Return and Payment	¶ 7-600

Gift Tax

Taxpayer and Taxable Property	¶ 7-760
Tax Basis and Rates	¶ 7-840
Return and Payment	¶ 7-900

第 7 章
相続税及び贈与税

相続税の計算……………………………………………………… ¶7-005
相続税と贈与税の構成…………………………………………… ¶7-010
相続税
　納税義務者及び課税財産………………………………………… ¶7-100
　相続税の計算……………………………………………………… ¶7-250
　財産の評価………………………………………………………… ¶7-550
　申告及び納付……………………………………………………… ¶7-600
贈与税
　納税者及び課税財産……………………………………………… ¶7-760
　課税標準及び税率………………………………………………… ¶7-840
　申告及び納付……………………………………………………… ¶7-900

534   INHERITANCE TAX AND GIFT TAX

¶ 7-005 Chart: Computation of Inheritance Tax

Heir A	Heir B	Legatee C	
Inherited assets (Gross)	Inherited assets (Gross)	Assets devised or bequeathed (Gross)	(¶ 7-270 to ¶ 7-320)
(+)	(+)	(+)	
Property treated as acquired by inheritance	Property treated as acquired by inheritance	Property treated as acquired by devise or bequest	(¶ 7-270)
(–)	(–)	(–)	
Exempt properties	Exempt properties	Exempt properties	(¶ 7-290)
(–)	(–)	(–)	
Liabilities succeeded to	Liabilities succeeded to	Liabilities taken over	(¶ 7-330)
(+)	(+)	(+)	
Assets gifted within preceding 3 years	Assets gifted within preceding 3 years	Assets gifted within preceding 3 years	(¶ 7-280)
(=)	(=)	(=)	
Net assets inherited (a)	Net assets inherited (b)	Net assets devised or bequeathed (c)	
Aggregated Net Taxable Assets			(¶ 7-340)
(–)			
Basic Estate Allowance			(¶ 7-340, ¶ 7-350)
(=)			
Aggregated Net Assets after Allowance			(¶ 7-360)
Statutory share attributable to heir A	Statutory share attributable to heir B		
(Application of the tax rate)			
Tax amount (A)	Tax amount (B)		(¶ 7-370)
Total tax amount			

(Prorating on the basis of (a), (b) and (c) over net taxable assets)

Prorated tax amount for A	Prorated tax amount for B	Prorated tax amount for C	(¶ 7-380)
(+)	(+)	(+)	
Surtax, if any	Surtax, if any	Surtax, if any	(¶ 7-390)
(–)	(–)	(–)	
Tax credits	Tax credits	Tax credits	(¶ 7-400)
(=)	(=)	(=)	
Tax payable by heir A	Tax payable by heir B	Tax payable by legatee C	

See also ¶ 7-260.

¶ 7-005

¶7-005 相続税の計算（¶7-260参照）

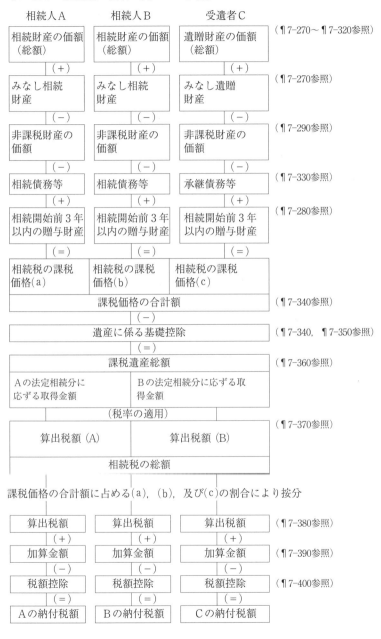

536   INHERITANCE TAX AND GIFT TAX

Structure of Inheritance Tax and Gift Tax

¶ 7-010 Basic structure

Japanese inheritance tax and gift tax are based on the theory that these kinds of taxes should be considered as special components of the comprehensive individual income tax system which finds the individual's obligation to pay tax by examining the increase in his net assets during a given period. In other words, these two taxes have the function of supplementing the individual income tax system in a customary sense. An increase in net assets resulting from an inheritance, bequest, devise, etc. is really a form of net assets increase, but it is treated separately from the usual increase of net assets due to its particular nature.

Inheritance tax is levied on the increase in net assets of an individual resulting from an inheritance, bequest or devise. Gift tax is levied on the increase in net assets of an individual resulting from a donation from other individuals, whereas a donation from a corporation is subject to income tax as occasional income.

¶ 7-020 Liability of administrator or executor

The administrator or executor of the estate of a decedent has no obligation to pay inheritance tax. Under Civil Code, the properties are deemed to have been acquired retroactively by heirs or legatees at the time of death, no matter how long the interval between the time of death and the time of the actual distribution. Heirs and legatees have an obligation to file a return and pay the tax jointly or severally, while the administrator or executor is not required to file a return or to pay inheritance tax.

¶ 7-030 Taxation on non-juridical organizations or public interest corporations

If an individual makes a bequest, devise or gift to a non-juridical organization that has a representative or administrator (¶ 3-140), that organization is deemed to be an individual and subject to inheritance tax or gift tax (except the case where corporation tax is levied on the properties devised to the organization). However, the rate of gift tax is applied not to the total amount of the gifts received in a year, as in the case of individuals, but to each gift received from each individual donor (Law 66①).

¶ 7-010

相続税と贈与税の構成

¶7-010　基本的仕組み

　日本の相続税及び贈与税は，一定期間における純資産の増加いかんにより納税額を定める所得税（総合課税）制度の特殊要素として捉えるべきであるとの理論に立って構成されている。換言すれば，この二つの租税は通常の意味で所得税を補完する機能を有している。相続・遺贈等による純資産の増加は純資産増加の一形態ではあるが，その特殊な性格により通常の純資産の増加とは切り離して扱われる。

　相続税は相続・遺贈を原因とする個人の純資産の増加に対して課されるものである。他方，贈与税は他人からの贈与を原因とする個人の純資産の増加に対して課されるものであるが，法人からの贈与には一時所得として所得税が課される。

¶7-020　遺産管理人，遺言執行人の責任

　被相続人の遺産管理人又は遺言執行人は相続税を納付すべき責任を負うものではない。日本の民法上は，死亡時点と実際の遺産分割の時点とがいかに離れていても，財産は死亡時に遡って相続人・受遺者が取得したものとみなされている。従って，相続人・受遺者は，共同して若しくは別々に，申告し納税する義務を負うが，遺産管理人・遺言執行人には申告する義務もなければ相続税を納付する義務もない。

¶7-030　人格のない社団・財団又は公益法人に対する課税

　個人が代表者又は管理者の定めのある人格のない社団・財団（¶3-140参照）に対し遺贈又は贈与を行った場合，これらの社団又は財団は個人とみなされ，そのような社団・財団に対して相続税又は贈与税が課せられる（ただし，遺贈に係る財産について法人税が課税された場合を除く。）。その場合の贈与税の税率は，個人の場合のごとくその年中に取得した受贈額の合計に対してではなく，贈与者の各々から取得した各受贈額に対して適用される（相法66①）。

　個人が公益法人（¶6-040参照）に対して遺贈又は贈与を行った場合，こ

538   INHERITANCE TAX AND GIFT TAX

The same principle applies when an individual makes a bequest, devise or gift to a public interest corporation (¶ 6-040), thereby causing the inheritance tax or gift tax which would otherwise be levied on a legator's or donor's relatives, or other persons connected with them, to be unreasonably reduced.

¶ 7-031 Taxation on Designated General Incorporated Association

Where the decedent is a director of a general incorporated association which meets one of the conditions below ("Designated General Incorporated Association" or "DGIA"), the net asset of DGIA divided by the number of the family directors (including the decedent) at the time of the death will be deemed bequest from the decedent to DGIA which will be subject to inheritance tax (Law 66-2).

    (1)   The number of the family directors consists more than half of the total directors immediately before the commencement of succession

    (2)   The number of the family directors have consisted more than half the total directors for 3 years or more during the last 5 years before the commencement of succession.

In case DGIA is subject to inheritance tax, the gift tax already levied on the property gifted to DGIA will be credited against the inheritance tax.

The amendment will be applicable to the death of director of general incorporated association on and after April 1, 2018. As for general incorporated association established before April 1, 2018, however, the amendment will be applicable on and after April 1, 2021, and the period before April 1, 2018 is excluded in calculation of the period of more than half concerning (2) mentioned above (Supplementary Provision 43).

¶ 7-040 Denial of transactions or entries of family corporations

If the Tax Authority finds that a certain transaction or book-entry by a family corporation (¶ 3-780) unreasonably reduces the burden of inheritance tax or gift tax on its shareholders, their relatives, or other persons specially connected with them, then the Tax Authority is entitled to deny such a transaction or book-entry and levy taxes on an adjusted tax basis (Law 64).

¶ 7-031

相続税及び贈与税　539

れにより遺贈者又は贈与者の親族その他これらの者と特別の関係のある者の相続税又は贈与税が不当に減少する結果となるときには，同様の考え方が適用される。

¶7-031　特定一般社団法人等に対する課税

　一般社団法人等の理事である者が死亡した場合で，その一般社団法人等が次の要件のいずれかを満たす特定一般社団法人等に該当する場合は，その特定一般社団法人が，相続開始の時におけるその法人等の純資産額をその死亡時における同族理事（被相続人を含む。）の数で除して計算した金額に相当する金額を被相続人から遺贈により取得したものとみなして，当該特定一般社団法人等に相続税を課する（相法66の2）。

(1)　相続開始の直前における同族理事数が総理事数の2分の1を超えること。

(2)　相続開始前5年以内において，同族理事数の割合が総理事数の2分の1を超える期間の合計が3年以上であること。

　但し，特定一般社団法人等に相続税が課される場合には，その相続税の額から，贈与等により取得した財産について既に当該特定一般社団法人等に課税された贈与税等の額を控除する。

　平成30年4月1日以後の一般社団法人等の理事の死亡に係る相続税について適用する。但し，同日前に設立された一般社団法人等については，平成33年4月1日以後の相続に適用し，平成30年3月31日以前の期間は上記(2)の2分の1を超える期間に該当しないものとする（附則43）。

¶7-040　同族会社の行為又は計算の否認

　同族会社（¶3-780参照）の行為又は計算が，その株主又はその親族その他これらの者と特別の関係がある者の相続税又は贈与税の負担を不当に減少させる結果となると認められる場合においては，税務署長はその行為又は計算を否認し，適正な課税標準による課税を行うことができる（相法64）。

540   INHERITANCE TAX AND GIFT TAX

¶ 7-050 Tax treaty

Japan has concluded a tax treaty with the U.S.A. in order to avoid double taxation on estates, inheritances and gifts.

INHERITANCE TAX

Taxpayer and Taxable Property

¶ 7-100 Scope of tax liability

An heir or legatee who received property as the following is liable to inheritance tax at the time of the decedent's death on or after April 1, 2018, if he or she (Law 1-3).

(1) has domicile in Japan either who;
  (a) is not temporary resident, or
  (b) is temporary resident (except the decedent is temporary resident or non-resident.)
(2) has not domicile in Japan, where;
  (a) the heir has Japanese nationality, and the decedent had domiciled in Japan anytime during ten years before the decedent's death.
  (b) the heir has not Japanese nationality (except the decedent is temporary resident or non-resident.).
(3) has domicile in Japan who received property situated in Japan (except (1) as above)
(4) has not domicile in Japan who received property situated in Japan (except (2) as above)
(5) has not Japanese nationality who received property situated in Japan from non-resident decedent.

¶ 7-105 Taxpayer

Inheritance tax is levied on individuals, or deemed individuals including non-juridical organizations, public interest corporations, or Designated General Incorporated Associations that acquire property from any inheritance, bequest or devise including gifts on donor's death. Therefore, the following persons are subject to inheritance tax (Law 1).

(1) **Heirs**

A decedent's heirs are his or her spouse and blood relatives as pre-

¶ 7-050

相続税及び贈与税　541

¶7-050　租税条約

相続及び贈与に対して二重課税を排除するため，日本は米国と租税条約を締結している。

相　続　税

納税義務者及び課税財産

¶7-100　納税義務の範囲

平成30年4月1日以降に相続又は遺贈で財産を取得した個人で，被相続人の死亡時において次のいずれかに該当する者は，相続税を納める義務がある（相法1の3一，二，三，四）。

(1)　日本に住所を有する者で，以下に該当する者

　(a)　一時居住者でない個人

　(b)　一時居住者である個人（被相続人が一時居住者又は非居住者である場合を除く。）

(2)　日本に住所を有せず，以下に該当する者

　(a)　日本国籍を有する者で，被相続人又は相続人等が相続開始前10年以内のいずれかの時において日本国内に住所を有していたことがある場合

　(b)　日本国籍を有しない者（被相続人が一時居住者又は非居住者を除く。）

(3)　日本にある財産を取得した個人で住所を有する者（(1)に掲げる者を除く。）

(4)　日本にある財産を取得した個人で住所を有しない者（(2)に掲げる者を除く。）

(5)　日本国籍を有しない非居住者が，非居住被相続人より国内財産を取得した場合

¶7-105　納税義務者

相続税は，相続又は遺贈（死因贈与を含む。）によって財産を取得した個人又は個人とみなされる人格なき社団，公益法人等（¶7-030），特定一般社団法人等（¶7-031）に課税され，次の者は相続税の納税義務がある（相法1）。

(1)　相続人

相続人は，被相続人の配偶者及び被相続人と一定の血族関係がある者で

542   INHERITANCE TAX AND GIFT TAX

scribed by the Civil Code.

An embryo or a fetus is assumed to have been born at the time of the inheritance. However not applicable if stillborn (Civil Code 886).

An heir loses his or her right to inherit if that person kills intentionally or intends to kill the decedent or an heir with a higher priority (Civil Code 891).

A presumed heir loses his or her right to inherit if the Court of Family Affairs judge to exclude that person from the inheritance for the claim of the decedent (Civil Code 892, 893).

An adopted child can be an heir in the same matter as a natural child. See ¶ 7-355 for the details of definitions for heirs.

(2) **Legatees**

A legatee is an individual who acquires inherited property by bequest.

A bequest is the grant of property without compensation under directions in the decedent's will.

Bequests are classified as either inclusive bequests or specified bequests.

An inclusive bequest is one under which the distributed properties are not specified by the decedent's will. The legatee under an inclusive bequest takes a share with other heirs.

A specified bequest is one under which the distributed properties are specified by the decedent's will.

(3) **Beneficiaries of gift contracts effective by the death of a donor**

A beneficiary of a gift contract is an individual who is endowed with property under a contract that becomes effective on the death of the donor.

Gift tax is levied on gifted properties. Inheritance tax is levied, however, if the gift contract is effective by the death of the donor. Gift contracts differ from bequests because bequests are unilateral legal acts by the legator as opposed to bilateral agreements between donors and beneficiaries.

(4) **Designated General Incorporated Associations**

General incorporated associations which fall under Designated General Incorporated Associations.

¶ 7-110 **Domicile**

The definition of domicile is practically the same definition as the one given for income tax. For the purposes of inheritance tax, a domicile is defined as the principal base of the taxpayer's living. However, this defini-

¶ 7-110

ある。

　胎児は，相続の場合にはすでに生まれたものとみなされる。しかし，死
体で生まれたときにはこの適用はない（民法886）。

　相続人となるべき者が故意に被相続人又は相続の先順位者を殺し，又は
殺そうとして刑に処せられた場合などは相続権を失う（民法891）。

　推定相続人が被相続人の請求により家庭裁判所において廃除の審判を受
けた場合には，その者は相続権を失う（民法892，893）。

　相続については，養子も実子と同様相続人となる。相続人の定義の詳細
については，¶7-355を参照のこと。

(2)　受遺者

　受遺者とは遺贈によって財産を取得した者のことである。遺贈とは，遺
言によって財産を他人に無償で与えることである。

　遺贈には，包括遺贈と特定遺贈がある。包括遺贈とは，財産を特定しな
いでする遺贈のことで，包括遺贈を受けた者は，相続人と同じく遺産の分
割に参加する。特定遺贈とは，遺言により，特定の財産を遺贈することで
ある。

(3)　死因贈与による受贈者

　死因贈与による受贈者とは，被相続人が生前において贈与契約をし，そ
の効力が死亡を原因として生ずるようにしておく場合のその財産の受贈者
のことである。

　贈与財産については贈与税が課されるのであるが，死因贈与については
相続税が課されることとなる。贈与は贈与者と受贈者の契約であるのに対
し，遺贈は遺贈者の単独行為である点が異なる。

(4)　特定一般社団法人等

　特定一般社団法人等に該当する一般社団法人等

¶7-110　住所

　住所の意義は所得税法上の住所とほぼ同じである。すなわち，相続税法上
の住所とは，納税義務者の生活の本拠をいうのであるが，これは客観的事実
によって判断され，何人も同時に二つ以上の住所はないものとされる。

544   INHERITANCE TAX AND GIFT TAX

tion is objective and does not consider the case of anyone possessing more than one domicile at the same time.

Furthermore, those who have left Japan temporarily, e.g., for the purposes of studying or business, are deemed to have a domicile in Japan.

¶ 7-120 Situs of properties

It is an especially important question for a taxpayer who is domiciled abroad whether or not a certain property was situated in Japan at the time of death. The law (Law 10) provides that:

(1) tangible assets, including real property, are considered to be situated where the assets actually are, except that ships or aircraft are considered to be situated in the country of registration;

(2) mining concession rights are considered to be in the country where the mining lot is situated;

(3) fishing concession rights are considered to be in the country to whose shores the concession is nearest;

(4) the right to a deposit with a bank and similar claims are considered to be situated in the country where the office in which the deposit was made is situated;

(5) insurance proceeds are considered to be situated in the country where the head offices or principal place of business of the insurance carrier, etc. associated with said insurance policy, or the place of business, etc. at which said policy is administered, or other similar such place of business is situated;

(6) retirement allowances and other similar such compensation are considered to be situated in the country where the address, head offices or principal place of business of the person making payment of said compensation is situated;

(7) the right to a loan is considered to be situated in the country where the borrower is domiciled or has its head office;

(8) securities such as shares, debentures, etc. are considered to be situated in the country where the issuer of the securities has its head office (Japanese national or local bonds are considered to be situated in Japan); in the case of Depositary Receipts such as ADR, EDR, they are situated in the country where the original shares are situated;

(9) the rights to joint operation trusts or securities investment trusts

¶ 7-120

相続税及び贈与税　545

　したがって，例えば勉学・商用等で一時的に日本を離れる者の住所は日本にあるものとされる。

¶7-120　財産の所在

　特に国外に住所を有する納税者にとっては，ある一定の財産が被相続人の死亡時において日本に所在するものか否かは重要な問題である。相続税法によると以下の財産の所在地は次のとおりである（相法10）。

⑴　動産又は不動産は，その動産又は不動産が現実にある所に所在するものとされ，船舶又は航空機は，登録した国にあるものとされる。

⑵　鉱業権は，鉱区が所在する国にあるものとされる。

⑶　漁業権は，漁場に最も近い沿岸の属する国にあるものとされる。

⑷　金融機関に対する預貯金等は，預貯金の受入れをした営業所が所在する国にあるものとされる。

⑸　保険金は，その保険金の契約に係る保険会社等の本店又は主たる事務所（日本に事務所がない場合は，契約に係る事務を行う営業所等，その他これらに準ずるもの。次号において同じ。）が所在する国にあるものとされる。

⑹　退職手当金等，その他これらに準ずる給与は，その給与を支払った者の住所又は本店若しくは主たる事務所が所在する国にあるものとされる。

⑺　貸付金債権は，債務者の住所又は本店が所在する国にあるものとされる。

⑻　株式若しくは社債等の有価証券は，当該有価証券の発行法人の本店が所在する国にあるものとされ（日本の国債又は地方債は日本にあるものとされる。），ADR，EDR等の預託証券については，当該預託証券に係る株式の発行法人の本店が所在する国にあるものとされる。

⑼　合同運用信託又は証券投資信託に関する権利はこれらの信託の引受をし

546   INHERITANCE TAX AND GIFT TAX

are considered to be situated in the country where the office of the business is situated;

(10) patent and other industrial intangible rights are considered to be situated in the country where the right is registered;

(11) copyrights and neighboring rights are considered to be situated in the country where the publisher's place of business, etc. is located;

(12) other rights regarding business are considered to be situated in the country where the office of the business is situated;

(13) other rights or properties are considered to be situated in the country where the decedent was domiciled.

¶ 7-130 Modification by Japan-U.S. Inheritance Tax Convention

The general principle on the situs of assets is described in ¶ 7-120. However, in a case where the Japan-U.S. Inheritance Tax Convention (see ¶ 7-050) is to be applied, the location of assets is modified. Article III of the Convention reads:

(1) If a decedent at the time of his death or a donor at the time of the gift was a national of, or domiciled in, the United States, or if a beneficiary of a decedent's estate at the time of such decedent's death or beneficiary of a gift at the time of the gift was domiciled in Japan, the situs at the time of the transfer of any of the following property or property rights shall, for the purpose of the imposition of the tax and for the purpose of the credit authorized by Article V, be determined exclusively in accordance with the following rules:

(a) Immovable property or rights therein (not including any property for which specific provision is otherwise made in this Article) shall be deemed to be situated at the place where the land involved is located.

(b) Tangible movable property (including currency and any other form of money recognized as legal tender in the place of issue and excepting such property for which specific provision is otherwise made in the Article) shall be deemed to be situated at the place where such property is physically located, or, if in transit, at the place of destination.

(c) Certain investments in debts (including bonds, promissory notes, bills of exchange, bank deposits and insurance, except

¶ 7-130

た営業所が所在する国にあるものとされる。

⑽　特許権等の工業所有権は，その権利が登録された国にあるものとされる。

⑾　著作権等の著作隣接権は，出版する営業所が所在する国にあるものとされる。

⑿　その他の事業上の権利は，当該事業に係る営業所が所在する国にあるものとされる。

⒀　その他の財産は，被相続人が住所を有していた国にあるものとされる。

¶7-130　日米相続税条約による修正

　財産の所在地に関する一般原則は，¶7-120で述べたとおりであるが，日米相続税条約（¶7-050参照）が適用される場合には，財産の所在地は修正される。同条約の第3条では次のように規定されている。

⑴　被相続人がその死亡のときに若しくは贈与者がその贈与のときに合衆国の国籍を有し若しくは合衆国内に住所を有していた場合，又は被相続人の遺産の受益者がその被相続人の死亡のときに若しくは贈与の受益者がその贈与のときに日本国内に住所を有していた場合には，これらのときにおける次に掲げる財産又は財産権の所在地，租税の賦課及び第5条によって認められる税額控除については，専ら次に定めるところに従って決定されるものとする。

　(a)　不動産又は不動産に関する権利（本条において他に特別の規定があるものを除く。）は，その不動産に係る土地の所在地にあるものとする。

　(b)　有体動産（通貨及び発行地で法貨として認められているすべての種類の貨幣を含み，本条において他に特別の規定がある財産を除く。）は，それが現実にある場所にあるものとし，運送中である場合には，目的地にあるものとする。

　(c)　債権（債券，約束手形，為替手形，銀行預金及び保険証券を含み，債券その他の流通証券で持参人払式のもの及び本条において他の特別の規

548   INHERITANCE TAX AND GIFT TAX

bonds or other negotiable instruments in bearer form and such debts for which specific provision is otherwise made in the Article) shall be deemed to be situated at the place where the debtor resides.

(d) Certain investments in shares or debts of a corporation shall be deemed to be situated at the place under the laws of which such corporation was created or organized.

(e) Ships and aircraft shall be deemed to be situated at the place where they are registered.

(f) Goodwill as a trade, business or professional asset shall be deemed to be situated at the place where the trade, business or profession to which it pertains is carried on.

(g) Patents, trade-marks, utility models and designs shall be deemed to be situated at the place where they are registered (or used, if they are not registered).

(h) Copyrights, franchises, rights to artistic and scientific works and rights or licenses to use any copyright material, artistic and scientific works, patents, trade-marks, utility models or designs shall be deemed to be situated at the place where they are exercisable.

(i) Mining or quarrying rights or mining leases shall be deemed to be situated at the place of such mining or quarrying.

(j) Fishing rights shall be deemed to be situated in the country in whose government's jurisdiction such rights are exercisable.

(k) Any property for which provision is not hereinbefore made shall be deemed to be situated in accordance with the laws of the contracting State imposing the tax solely by reason of the situs of property within such State, but if neither of the contracting States imposes the tax solely by reason of the situs of property therein, then any such property shall be deemed to be situated in accordance with the laws of each contracting State.

(2) The application of the provisions of paragraph (1) of this Article shall be limited to the particular property, and any portion thereof, which without such provisions would be subjected to the taxes of both contracting States or would be so subjected except for a specific exemption.

¶ 7-130

定がある債権を除く。）は，債務者が居住する場所にあるものとする。

(d) 法人の株式又は法人に対する出資は，その法人が設立され，又は組織された準拠法が施行されている場所にあるものとする。

(e) 船舶及び航空機は，それらが登録されている場所にあるものとする。

(f) 営業上，事業上又は専門職業上の資産としてののれんは，その営業，事業又は専門職業が営まれている場所にあるものとする。

(g) 特許権，商標権，実用新案権及び意匠権は，それらが登録されている場所（登録されていない場合には，それらが行使される場所）にあるものとする。

(h) 著作権，地域的独占権（フランチャイズ），芸術上又は学術上の著作物に対する権利及び著作権のある著作物，芸術上若しくは学術上の著作物，特許発明，商標，実用新案若しくは意匠を使用する権利又はこれらの使用を許諾された地位は，それらを行使することができる場所にあるものとする。

(i) 鉱業権若しくは租鉱権又は採石権は，採鉱又は採石が行われる場所にあるものとする。

(j) 漁業権は，その権利の行使について管轄権を有する国にあるものとする。

(k) 前各号に規定されていない財産は，いずれか一方の締約国が自国内に財産があることのみを理由として租税を課する場合には，その締約国の法令で定めている場所にあるものとし，また，いずれの締約国も自国内に財産があることのみを理由として租税を課するのではない場合には，各締約国の法令で定めている場所にあるものとする。

(2) 本条(1)の規定は，特定の財産及びその一部分で同項の規定がなければ両締約国によって租税が課せられるもの（諸控除がなければ租税が課せられることとなるものを含む。）についてのみ，適用する。

550   INHERITANCE TAX AND GIFT TAX

Computation of Inheritance Tax

¶ 7-250 History

The ability to pay inheritance tax is attributed to the increase in the net assets of an individual resulting from an inheritance, bequest or devise. Therefore, the amount of inheritance tax to be paid by each heir or legatee should be computed quite separately from the others on the basis of each individual's increase in net assets. Such a theoretically consistent system was actually effective before 1958, but under such a system heirs or legatees were tempted to consult with each other and to evade the tax by pretending that the estate was divided evenly among them, so that the high progressive rate might not be applied. It was very troublesome for the Tax Authority to penetrate their arrangements and uncover the truth.

The present system was introduced in 1958 in order to remedy this form of evasion.

¶ 7-260 Outline of computation

Inheritance tax to be paid by each heir or legatee is computed by the following seven steps (see ¶ 7-005 and ¶ 7-410):

(1)   Ascertain all the assets subject to inheritance tax with respect to each heir or legatee (¶ 7-270 to ¶ 7-320) and evaluate each asset (¶ 7-550). In computing net taxable assets, the amount of the funeral expenses shared and the liabilities succeeded to by an heir or legatee (¶ 7-330) are to be deducted from the sum of his gross assets. The value of assets gifted from the decedent within three years before his or her death should be added (¶ 7-280).

(2)   Total the net taxable assets acquired by all heirs and legatees (total of net taxable assets), then deduct the "basic estate allowance" (¶ 7-350) from that total (¶ 7-340); the balance is called the "aggregated net assets after allowance".

(3)   Divide the aggregated net assets after allowance to each heir at law in accordance with the statutory shares, as if the decedent had not left any will (¶ 7-360).

(4)   Apply the progressive tax rate to the statutory shares of each heir, then aggregate all the tax amounts of each heir or legatee resulting from the application of the tax rate (¶ 7-370).

¶ 7-250

相続税及び贈与税　551

相続税の計算

¶7-250　沿革

　相続税の担税力は相続又は遺贈による個人資産の増加に求められる。したがって，相続人又は受遺者が納付すべき相続税は，各人の個人資産の増加を基礎として，各人別に計算されるべきことになる。昭和33年まではこのような理論的体系によっていたが，このような体系の下では，相続人又は受遺者は通謀して累進課税を免れるためにあたかも遺産を均等に分割したかのように仮装することにより脱税を図ることになる。現行制度（¶7-005）は，この種の脱税を防止するため，昭和33年に導入されたものである。

¶7-260　計算の概略

　各相続人又は受遺者が納付すべき相続税は，次の7段階に従って計算される（¶7-005及び¶7-410参照）。

(1)　各相続人又は受遺者につき相続税の課税財産のすべてを確認し（¶7-270～¶7-320），各財産の評価を行う（¶7-550）。相続税の課税価格を計算する際，その者が負担した葬式費用及びその者が承継した債務（¶7-330）をその者の課税財産から控除し，一方，その者が被相続人から相続開始前3年以内に贈与を受けた財産の価額を加算する（¶7-280）。

(2)　各相続人及び受遺者の相続税の課税価格を合計し（課税価格の合計額）（¶7-340），この合計額から「遺産に係る基礎控除」を控除する（¶7-350）。その残額を「課税遺産総額」という。

(3)　課税遺産総額から，被相続人が遺言しなかったものと仮定して，各法定相続人の法定相続分に応ずる取得金額を算出する（¶7-360）。

(4)　各法定相続人の法定相続分に応ずる取得金額に累進税率を乗じ，各法定相続人に係る算出税額を合計して，「相続税の総額」を出す（¶7-370）。

552   INHERITANCE TAX AND GIFT TAX

(5) Prorate the aggregated tax resulting from the application of the tax rate in proportion to the net taxable assets actually acquired by each heir or legatee (¶ 7-380).

(6) Add a 20% surtax to the tax, prorated in accordance with (5), if the successor is not the decedent's spouse, parent or child (¶ 7-390).

(7) Deduct credit for gift tax paid, credit for a spouse, credit for a minor, credit for chain successions, credit for a handicapped person and credit for foreign taxes (¶ 7-400), from the tax amount.
An example of computation is shown in ¶ 7-410.

¶ 7-270 Cases treated as inheritances, bequests or devises

The below economic benefit acquired by a person from a decedent is deemed to have been acquired through an inheritance if the person is an heir, or through a bequest or devise if the person is not an heir.

(1) Insurance proceeds or other similar proceeds received as a result of the decedent's death, if the premiums for the life insurance or the designated casualty insurance contracts were paid by the decedent (Law 3①(1)).

However, if any part of insurance premium relating to the insurance contracts is paid by other than the decedent, amount subject to this rule shall be calculated based on below formula.

$$\text{(amount of insurance proceeds)} \times \frac{\text{(premiums paid by the decedent)}}{\text{(premiums paid by the decedent + premiums paid by others)}}$$

That part of an insurance proceeds which corresponds to the share of the premiums paid by the beneficiary is not regarded as a benefit acquired by the inheritance, or by the bequest or devise (R 3-38).

The premiums paid by the decedent are taken as the total amount that has been paid under the terms of the insurance contract. The exempt amount of the premiums is not included in the premiums paid. The premiums paid through cross entry with loans and accrued premiums are included (R 3-13).

(2) Retirement allowances, payments for meritorious services or other similar payments including a lump sum payment from an approved pension fund, etc. are regarded as benefits from an inheritance,

¶ 7-270

相続税及び贈与税　553

(5)　相続税の総額を，各相続人又は受遺者の課税価格の割合により按分する（¶7-380）。

(6)　相続財産を取得した者が被相続人の配偶者及び一親等の血族以外の者である場合には，(5)により按分した税額にその20％に相当する金額を加算する（¶7-390）。

(7)　贈与税額控除，配偶者に対する相続税の軽減，未成年者控除，相次相続控除，障害者控除，及び外国税額控除を行う（¶7-400）。

計算の具体例は¶7-410に示す。

¶7-270　みなし取得財産

被相続人から受けた下記の経済的利益は，取得者が相続人であれば相続により，また，取得者が相続人以外の者であれば遺贈により，それぞれ取得したものとみなされる。

(1)　被相続人が生命保険・損害保険契約の保険料を負担し，被相続人の死亡により取得した保険金（相法3①一）

当該保険契約に係る保険料のうち，被相続人以外の者が負担した部分があるときは，次の算式により計算した金額。

$$\frac{保険金 \times 被相続人の支払った保険料等}{被相続人が支払った保険料等 + 被相続人以外の者が支払った保険料等}$$

保険料の一部を保険金受取人自身が負担している場合は，その部分に対応する保険金額は相続又は遺贈により取得した財産とみなされない（相基通3-38）。

被相続人が負担した保険料は，保険契約に基づき払い込まれた保険料の合計額によるが，保険料の払込みの免除があった場合にはその額は保険料には含まれず，また，振替貸付けによる保険料の払込み又は未払保険料があった場合にはその額を加算した金額による（相基通3-13）。

(2)　被相続人の死亡により，相続人等が被相続人に支給されるべきであった退職手当金，功労金その他これらに準ずる給与（適格退職金契約等による一時金又は年金の給付金を含む。）で，被相続人の死亡後3年以内に支給

554   INHERITANCE TAX AND GIFT TAX

bequest or devise, as long as the payments are paid and agreed to be paid within 3 years after the death of the decedent (Law 3①(2)). Condolence money and money for wreaths, or expenses paid to a bereaved family by an employer of the decedent, are treated as follows (R 3-20).

(a)   When the death of the decedent was employment related —
The total amount of condolence money and money for wreaths and funeral expenses is treated as condolence money up to an amount equivalent to 3 years' regular salary at the time of death, excluding bonuses. The excess of that amount is treated as a taxable retirement allowance.

(b)   When the death of the decedent was not employment related —
The total amount of condolence money, etc. paid by the employer of the decedent is treated as condolence money up to an amount equivalent to one half of the regular salary at the time of death. The excess of that amount is treated as a taxable retirement allowance.

The term "retirement allowance" means any money or goods, regardless of their ostensible purpose, paid by an employer for the services of a decedent employee (R 3-18).

It should be noted that any salary or bonus actually paid after the death of a decedent but which fell due for payment or which was agreed to be paid before the death is not a retirement allowance but an inherited asset (R 3-32, 3-33).

(3)   At an inception of inheritance, among those insurance contract right which policyholder is someone other than the decedent, if an event insured against have not taken place, any portion of insurance premium paid by the decedent (Law 3①(3)).

(4)   At an inception of inheritance, among those pension benefits contract right which policyholder is someone other than the decedent, if an event set against such pension payment have not taken place, the portion of insurance premium paid by the decedent (Law 3①(4)).

Where a policyholder is the person who has paid its insurance premium, such insurance right is part of inheritance asset (R 3-42).

(5)   Among pension benefits or lump-sum payment which heirs receive based on whole life annuity with guaranteed installment, the portion

¶ 7-270

相続税及び贈与税　555

が確定し支給を受けた給与（相法3①二）

　被相続人の死亡によって被相続人の雇用主から遺族が受ける弔慰金，花輪代，葬祭料などについては，次のように取り扱われる（相基通3-20）。

(a)　被相続人の死亡が業務上の死亡である場合

　その雇用主から受ける弔慰金，花輪代，葬祭料等の合計額のうち，被相続人の死亡当時における賞与以外の普通給与の3年分に相当する金額までは弔慰金とし，それを超える部分の金額を退職手当金等に該当するものとして課税する。

(b)　被相続人の死亡が業務上の死亡でない場合

　その雇用主から受ける弔慰金等の合計額のうち，被相続人の死亡当時における普通給与の半年分は弔慰金とし，それを超える部分を退職手当金等に該当するものとして課税する。

　退職手当金等とはその名義のいかんにかかわらず，実質上被相続人の生前の役務の対価として支給される金品をいう（相基通3-18）。

　生前受けるべきであった賞与や支払期が死亡後に到来した給与は，退職手当金等ではなく，本来の相続財産であることに注意を要する（相基通3-32, 3-33）。

(3)　相続開始時に，まだ保険事故が発生していない生命保険契約で，被相続人以外の者が当該契約の契約者である場合，当該契約に関する権利のうち被相続人が負担した保険料に相当する部分（相法3①三）

(4)　相続開始時に，まだ定期金給付事由が発生していない定期金給付契約で，被相続人以外の者が当該契約の契約者である場合，当該契約に関する権利のうち被相続人が負担した保険料に相当する部分（相法3①四）

　契約者と保険料の負担者が同一人であるときは当該保険料の負担者の本来の相続財産となる（相基通3-42）。

(5)　保証期間付終身年金契約に基づいて相続人等が取得する定期金又は一時金のうち，被相続人が負担した保険料に相当する部分（相法3①五）

556   INHERITANCE TAX AND GIFT TAX

which the decedent has paid its insurance premium (Law 3①(5)).

(6) An heir's non-contractual right to receive pension benefit or lump-sum payment because of the decedent's death (Law 3①(6)).

(7) Amount received deemed as gift accordance with ¶ 7-850 within 3 years of inception of inheritance.

¶ 7-275 Benefits treated as a bequest or devise

In the following cases, the benefits are deemed to have been acquired by a bequest or devise:

(1) Distributed assets

A distribution of an inherited asset under the Civil Code 958-3① is regarded as an acquisition of the equivalent amount by a bequest (Law 4).

(2) Other benefits

In the following cases, the beneficiary or the assignee of property is regarded as the legatee.

(a) Where property of a decedent is sold to another person at an unreasonably low price pursuant to directions in the decedent's will (Law 7).

(b) Where debts are excused by a decedent, or another's debts are paid, pursuant to directions in the decedent's will (Law 8).

(c) Where a benefit is granted by the decedent without payment or at an unreasonably low cost pursuant to directions in the decedent's will, other than as outlined in case (a) or case (b) (Law 9).

¶ 7-276 Bequests and Devises of Trust Interests

(1) Persons who become beneficiaries, etc. of a trust without paying fair consideration shall be deemed to have acquired an interest in the trust by bequest or devise in the following instances:

(a) If the trust is to take effect and said person is to become a beneficiary, etc. of the trust upon the death of the trustor (Law 9-2①).

(b) If a person becomes a new beneficiary, etc. of a trust with existing beneficiaries, etc. pursuant to the death of one or more persons who were formerly beneficiaries, etc. of said trust (Law 9-2②).

¶ 7-275

相続税及び贈与税　557

(6)　被相続人の死亡により，相続人等が定期金又は一時金を取得する権利
　　で，契約に基づく以外のもの（相法3①六）
(7)　相続開始3年以内に，被相続人から¶7-850に述べるような贈与を受け
　　たものとみなされたもの

¶7-275　遺贈により財産を取得したとみなされる場合

　　次の場合の便益等は遺贈により取得したものとみなされる。

(1)　分与財産

　　民法第958条の3第1項に規定される相続財産の分与を受けた者は，そ
　　の分与時の財産の時価に相当する金額を被相続人から遺贈により取得した
　　ものとみなされる（相法4）。

(2)　その他

　　次に掲げる場合には，その譲渡を受けた者又はその利益を受けた者が遺
　　贈を受けたものとみなされる。
　(a)　遺言により著しく低い価額の対価で財産の譲渡が行われた場合（相法
　　　7）

　(b)　遺言により対価を支払わないで，又は著しく低い価額で債務の免除，
　　　引受け又は第三者のためにする債務の弁済による利益を受けた場合（相
　　　法8）
　(c)　(a)及び(b)以外の場合で対価を支払わないで又は著しく低い価額で利益
　　　を受けた場合で，その行為が遺言によりされたとき（相法9）

¶7-276　信託に関する権利の遺贈

(1)　適正な対価を負担せず，信託の受益者等となる者は，以下の信託につい
　　ては，信託に関する権利を遺贈により取得したとみなされる。

　(a)　委託者の死亡により信託の効力が生じ，信託の受託者等となる場合
　　　（相法9の2①）

　(b)　受益者等の存する信託で受益者等であった者の死亡により新たに受益
　　　者等となる場合（相法9の2②）

558   INHERITANCE TAX AND GIFT TAX

- (c) If an existing beneficiary, etc. of the trust receives an additional interest in the trust pursuant to the death of one or more of the other beneficiaries, etc. of said trust (Law 9-2③).
- (d) If a distribution of remaining assets is received upon termination of the trust pursuant to the death of the beneficiaries, etc. (Law 9-2④).

(2) In the case of a successive beneficiary trust, etc., a beneficiary that acquires an interest in the trust upon the death of a beneficiary, etc. without paying fair consideration shall be deemed to have acquired said interest in said trust by bequest or devise. In the event that restrictions are imposed with respect to benefits under said trust, said restrictions shall be deemed not to exist (Law 9-3①).

(3) In the case of a trust that has no beneficiaries, etc., if the trust comes into effect and a relative of the trustor becomes a beneficiary, etc. upon the death of the trustor, or a relative of the trustor receives a distribution of remaining assets upon the termination of said trust, the trustee shall be deemed to have acquired an interest in the trust from the trustor by bequest or devise (Law 9-4①).

(4) If all of the beneficiaries, etc. of a trust die and a relative of the trustor or a decedent beneficiary becomes a beneficiary, etc., the trustee of said trust shall be deemed to have acquired the interest in the trust from the decedent beneficiary by bequest or devise (Law 9-4②).

(5) In cases (3) and (4) above, the amount of corporate income taxes assessed against said trustee shall be deducted against the amount of the inheritance taxes imposed upon said trustee (Law 9-4④).

¶ 7-280 Gift before death

If a decedent made gifts to an heir or legatee within three years before death or if a heir or legatee selected the unified gift-and-inheritance tax system (¶ 7-896), these gifts are added to the taxable assets inherited, devised or bequeathed. When a spouse has deducted the spouse allowance for gift tax from these gifts (¶ 7-840), only the balance should be added. In return, the amount of gift tax thereupon is credited against inheritance tax (¶ 7-400).

¶ 7-280

(c) 受益者等の存する信託で，一部の受益者等が死亡により既存の受益者等が新たに利益を受ける場合（相法9の2③）

(d) 受益者等の死亡により信託が終了し，信託の残余財産の給付を受ける場合（相法9の2④）

(2) 受益者連続型信託等において，受益者等の死亡により，信託に関する権利を適正な対価を負担せずに取得した受益者は，信託に関する権利を遺贈により取得したものとみなされる。なお，信託の受益に関する制約が付されているものについては，この制約は付されていないものとみなされる（相法9の3①）。

(3) 受益者等が存しない信託において，委託者の死亡により効力が発生し，委託者の親族が受益者等になる時，又は信託終了時に委託者の親族が残余財産を給付される場合，受託者は委託者より信託に関する権利を遺贈により取得したものとみなされる（相法9の4①）。

(4) 受益者等が存する信託において，受益者等の死亡により受益者が不在になった場合に，委託者又は死亡した受益者の親族が受益者等になる時，その信託の受益者は死亡した受益者より信託に関する権利を遺贈により取得したものとみなされる（相法9の4②）。

(5) 上記(3)，(4)において，受託者が課される相続税額については，その受託者に課された法人税額を控除する（相法9の4④）。

¶7-280　生前贈与

　被相続人が相続開始前3年以内に，相続人・受遺者に対して贈与していた場合又は相続人が贈与税の相続時精算課税制度（¶7-896）を選択していた場合，その贈与財産は相続税の課税価格に算入される。配偶者が贈与税の配偶者控除を受けていた場合（¶7-840），控除額の価額のみを算入する。その代わり，当該贈与に係る贈与税は相続税から控除する（¶7-400）。

560   INHERITANCE TAX AND GIFT TAX

¶ 7-290   Exempt properties

The following properties are excluded from gross taxable assets for the purposes of inheritance tax (Law 12①):

(1) Burial plots and tombs.

(2) Property which is acquired for religious, charitable, scientific, educational or social welfare purposes and which is for public use. An individual who acquires property which is exempt under the above provision, may not grant any unusual benefits to an affiliated person. A non-juridical organization that acquires property which is exempt should not be managed arbitrarily (Reg 2).

If a person engaged in social welfare activities does not actually use the exempt property for these activities within 2 years from the date of acquisition, the property will be added to taxable assets (Law 12②).

If an heir or a legatee contributes an inherited or bequeathed asset to the national government, or to a municipality or an approved social welfare organization before the due date for payment of inheritance tax the contributed asset is exempt. Money paid to an approved welfare trust is also exempt (SM 70①, ③).

(3) Benefits from a mentally or physically handicapped persons mutual aid plan.

Benefits paid from a mentally or physically handicapped persons mutual aid plan approved under municipal ordinance and managed by a municipality are exempt from inheritance tax.

A mutual aid plan will be approved under a municipal ordinance if its members consist of supporters of mentally or physically handicapped persons, and the supporters contribute premiums to the municipality which pays grants for supporting mentally and physically handicapped persons. The plan should meet the requirements of the income tax ordinance article 20 paragraph 2 (Reg 2-2).

(4) Insurance payments or other similar payments received by heirs. The following amount is exempt with regard to each heir:

$$\text{¥5,000,000} \times \text{number of heirs at law}^{\text{Note}} \times \frac{\text{amount received by the taxpayer heir}}{\text{total amount received by all heirs}}$$

Note:
As for the inclusion of adopted children in the number of legal heirs, see ¶ 7-355. If the total amount received by all heirs does not exceed the amount

¶ 7-290

相続税及び贈与税　561

¶7-290　相続税の非課税財産
相続税法上，以下の財産は課税価格に算入しない（相法12①）。

(1)　墓所等
(2)　宗教，慈善，学術，その他公益を目的とする事業を行う者が取得した財産で，その公益事業の用に供することが確実なもの

　　公益事業を行う者が個人であるときは，特別関係者に特別の利益を与えないこと，また，人格のない社団等であるときには，その事業の運営が特定の者の意思によってなされていないことなどの条件がある（相令2）。

　　公益事業を行う者がその財産を取得した日から2年以内に，現実にその公益事業の用に供していないときには課税価格に算入される（相法12②）。

　　また，相続人又は受贈者が相続又は遺贈により取得した財産を，相続税の申告期限までに，国若しくは地方公共団体又は一定の公益法人等に贈与した場合の贈与財産や一定の特定公益信託の信託財産とするために支出した金額についても，非課税としている（措法70①，③）。

(3)　心身障害者共済制度に基づく給付金の受給権

　　精神若しくは身体に障害のある者（以下「心身障害者」という。）又はその者を扶養する者が，条例の規定により地方公共団体が心身障害者に関して実施する共済制度に基づいて支給される給付金を受ける権利。

　　非課税の適用がある共済制度は，地方公共団体の条例において心身障害者を扶養する者を加入者とし，その加入者が地方公共団体に掛金を納付し，地方公共団体が心身障害者の扶養のための給付金を定期に支給することを定めている制度で，所得税法施行令第20条第2項各号に掲げる要件を備えているものに限られる（相令2の2）。

(4)　相続人の取得した生命保険金のうち，次の算式によって計算した金額までの金額

$$（500万円×法定相続人の数）^{(注)} × \frac{その相続人の受け取った保険金の合計額}{相続人全員の受け取った保険金の合計額}$$

（注）：被相続人の養子がいる場合には，¶7-355を参照のこと。
　　　相続人全員の受け取った保険金の合計額が「500万円×法定相続人の数」以下である場

562   INHERITANCE TAX AND GIFT TAX

of "¥5,000,000 × number of heirs at law", the total amount received by each heir is exempt.

(5)   Retirement allowances or other similar payments paid to heirs.

The following amount is exempt with regard to each heir:

$$\text{¥5,000,000} \times \begin{array}{c} \text{number of} \\ \text{heirs at law} \end{array} \times \frac{\text{amount received by the taxpayer heir}}{\text{total amount received by all heirs}}$$

Note:

If the total amount received by all heirs does not exceed the amount of "¥5,000,000 × number of heirs at law", the total amount received by each heir is exempt.

Again, in counting the number of legal heirs, none are assumed to have renounced their inheritance. As for the inclusion of adopted children in the number of legal heirs, see ¶ 7-355.

¶ 7-300   Special rules for valuation of small-scale housing lots

Among assets an individual received through inheritance or bequest, for those real estate which either an ancestor or family member of an ancestor has used continuously until the date of inheritance tax return due date for business or residential purpose, accordance with below classification, certain amount shall be reduced against taxable value of such assets (SM 69-4).

(1)   Qualifying land

(a)   Designated business purpose land

Business purpose land received by the family member of the decedent through inheritance or bequest, which had been used for business excluding rental one, being used continuously for the business as well as owned by the family member until the due date of the inheritance tax return.

(b)   Designated residential purpose land

Residential land which had been used for the decedent's own residence, received through inheritance or bequest by the spouse or family member who had lived with the decedent, being dwelling in the house until the due date of the inheritance tax return.

Where the family member who had not lived with the decedent received the land through inheritance or bequest, provided that there was no heir lived with the decedent and the heir had not lived in his or her own house for the 3 years before the commencement of succession, the land continuously owned

¶ 7-300

相続税及び贈与税　563

合には，各相続人の受け取った保険金の全額が非課税となる。

(5)　相続人が支給を受けた退職手当金等のうち，次の算式によって計算した
　金額までの金額

$$（500万円×法定相続人の数）× \frac{その相続人の支給を受けた退職手当金等の合計額}{相続人全員の支給を受けた退職手当金等の合計額}$$

　(注)：相続人全員が支給を受けた退職手当金等の合計額が「500万円×法定相続人の数」以下
　　である場合には，各相続人が支給を受けた退職手当の全額が非課税となる。
　　　法定相続人の数は相続放棄がなかったものとした場合に法定相続人となるべき者の数に
　　よる。被相続人の養子がいる場合には，¶7-355を参照のこと。

¶7-300　小規模宅地等についての相続税の課税価格の特例
　個人が相続又は遺贈により取得した財産のうち，当該相続の開始直前ま
で，被相続人若しくは被相続人と生計を一にしていた被相続人の親族の事業
又は居住の用に供されていた以下の宅地等で，相続税の申告期限まで所有又
は居住又は事業を継続している場合には，この適用を受けることが出来る
（措法69の4）。

(1)　特例対象宅地
　(a)　特定事業用宅地等
　　　被相続人等の貸付事業を除く事業の用に供されていた宅地等を，被相
　　続人の親族が相続又は遺贈により取得し，申告期限までその事業を営
　　み，所有している宅地等

　(b)　特定居住用宅地等
　　　被相続人等の居住の用に供されていた宅地等を，被相続人の配偶者若
　　しくは被相続人と同居していた親族が相続又は遺贈により取得し，申告
　　期限まで引き続きその家屋に居住し，所有している宅地等
　　　被相続人と同居していない親族が相続又は遺贈により取得する場合，
　　同居の相続人がおらず，相続開始前3年以内にこの相続人又はその配偶
　　者の所有する家屋に居住したことがなく，相続税の申告期限まで所有し
　　ている宅地等

564   INHERITANCE TAX AND GIFT TAX

until the due date of the inheritance tax return.

(c) Designated family corporation business purpose land
Residential land which was used for business of the designated corporation excluding rental one, the family member of the decedent is a director of the corporation who received the land through inheritance or bequest, as well as owned until the due date of the inheritance tax return.

(d) Rental business purpose land
Business purpose land received by the family member of the decedent through inheritance or bequest, which had been used for the rental business, being used continuously for the business as well as owned by the family member until the due date of the inheritance tax return. Certain limitations shall apply.

(2) Deduction ratio in inheritance tax base:

(a) 80% deduction up to 240 square meters for certain residential purpose land (up to 330 square meters effective January 1, 2015)

(b) 80% deduction up to 400 square meters for certain business purpose land except for rental purpose

(c) 80% deduction up to 730 square meters if the land falls under both (a) and (b) categories (effective January 1, 2015)

(d) 50% deduction up to 200 square meters for rental purpose land

(3) Applied conditions

(a) Treatment for double family residence
Residential real estate which is structurally separated for double family, in which the decedent and the heir relatives by different livelihood who has acquired the portion of the residential land, are eligible for the special rule of small-scale housing lots altogether.

(b) Treatment for nursing home admission
Where the decedent has been in nursing home, the residential land which had been used for residential purpose for the decedent before the admission of such facility is eligible for the special rule of small-scale housing lots, if the following

¶ 7-300

相続税及び贈与税　565

(c)　特定同族会社事業用宅地等

　　一定の法人の貸付事業を除く事業の用に供されていた宅地等で，被相続人の親族がその法人の役員であり，その親族が相続又は遺贈により取得し，申告期限まで所有している宅地等

(d)　貸付事業用宅地等

　　被相続人等の貸付事業の用に供されていた宅地等を，被相続人の親族が相続又は遺贈により取得し，貸付事業を申告期限までに引き継ぎ貸付事業を営み，所有している宅地等

(2)　減額割合
　　次の区分に応じて定める割合が，課税価格から減額される。

(a)　居住用宅地等のうち，240㎡（平成27年1月1日以後の相続又は遺贈は330㎡）までの部分の80%

(b)　不動産貸付用以外の事業用の宅地のうち，400㎡までの部分の80%

(c)　宅地等の全てが前(a)及び(b)である場合には，それぞれの適用対象面積330㎡及び400㎡の合計730㎡まで完全併用が認められる（平成27年1月1日以後の相続又は遺贈について適用）。

(d)　不動産貸付用宅地のうち，200㎡までの部分の50%

(3)　適用要件

(a)　二世帯住宅の取り扱い

　　構造上区分のある二世帯住宅に，被相続人及び生計別の親族が居住し，その親族が相続又は遺贈により取得した宅地等のうち，被相続人及びその親族が居住していた分に対応する宅地等のすべてを特例の対象とすることができる。

(b)　老人ホーム入所時の取り扱い

　　被相続人が老人ホームへ入所していた場合，次の要件を満たす時は，被相続人が老人ホーム入所前にまでに居住の用に供されていた宅地等も，この適用を受けることが出来る。

566   INHERITANCE TAX AND GIFT TAX

conditions are met:

① The decedent entered the nursing home because of nursing care necessity.

② The real estate has not been provided for rental purpose.

(c) Treatment for the heir not residing in his or her own house who inherited the designated residential purpose land

Where the decedent had not spouse nor heir to have lived with, the heir or the spouse who had not lived in his or her own house may be qualified for the special tax measurement.

However, it is not qualifying if he or she lived in a house which was owned by the relative within the third degree, or by the family corporation having special relationship with the relative, or if he or she owned the residence in which the family member lived at the time of the commencement of succession.

¶ 7-311 Inheritance tax payment deferral on unlisted shares

When a management successor obtains those voting stocks of unlisted shares certified by the minister of economy, trade and industry through inheritance, the payment of the inheritance tax amount equivalent to 80% of the taxable value of voting stock (limited to two third (2/3) of SME's total issued and outstanding voting shares owned by a person, including those voting shares held at the inception of inheritance) may be deferred until death of a person, subject to the person submitting collateral equivalent to such tax amount and filing a tax return before the due date.

However, failure to meet business continuance requirements in management succession period (5 years after the due date of the tax return) will lead to tax liability for all or some of the deferred inheritance tax with interest tax (SM 70-7-2).

¶7-312   Special measurement for inheritance tax payment deferral on unlisted shares

Where the company submits a special succession plan to the governor of prefecture until March 31, 2023, the special successor received unlisted shares from the special approved successor company from the deceased representative director of the said company through inheritance, the total inheritance tax otherwise imposed on the received shares will be deferred until the death of the special successor.

¶ 7-311

相続税及び贈与税　567

① 被相続人に介護が必要なために入所したものであること

② 当該家屋が貸付等の用途に供されていないこと

(c) 持ち家に居住していない者が特定居住用宅地等を相続する場合の取扱い

　　被相続人に配偶者及び他の同居の相続人がおらず，相続開始前３年以内にこの相続人又はその配偶者の所有する家屋に居住したことがない場合は特例を受けられる。

　　しかし，相続開始前３年以内に，その親族の３親等内の親族又はその親族と特別の関係のある法人が所有する家屋に居住した事があるか，又は相続開始時にその親族が居住している家屋を過去に所有した事がある場合は適用されない。

¶7-311　非上場株式等についての相続税の納税猶予

　経営承継相続人が相続等により，経済産業大臣の認定を受ける非上場会社の議決権株式等を取得した場合は，その経営承継相続人が納付すべき相続税額のうち，議決権株式等（相続開始から既に保有していた議決権株式等を含めて，その中小企業者の発行済議決権株式等の総数等の３分の２に達するまでの部分に限る。）に係る課税価格の80％に対応する相続税額については，担保を提供して期限内申告書を提出すれば，その経営承継相続人等の死亡の日まで，納税が猶予される。

　但し，経営承継期間（申告期限後５年以内）に，事業継続要件を満たすことが出来なくなった場合には，納税が猶予されていた相続税の全部又は一部と利子税を併せて納付しなければならない（措法70の７の２）。

¶7-312　非上場株式等についての相続税の納税猶予の特例

　特例承継計画を平成35年３月31日までに都道府県知事に提出した会社で，特例後継者が相続等により，特例認定承継会社の代表権を有していた者から，その特例認定承継の非上場株式等を取得した場合は，その取得した全ての非上場株式等に係る相続税の全額について，特例後継者の死亡の日等までに納税が猶予される。

　但し，経営承継期間（申告期限後５年以内）に，事業継続要件を満たすことが出来なくなった場合には，やむを得ない理由がある場合を除き，猶予さ

568   INHERITANCE TAX AND GIFT TAX

However, the failure to meet the business continuity conditions during the management succession period (5 years from the due date of the tax return), except for unavoidable reason, will lead to tax payment along with interest tax of all or some of the deferred inheritance tax,

The deferred inheritance tax may be exempted from taxation in case of the death of the special successor, as well as exemption qualified donation after the management succession period, the bankruptcy, transfer or liquidation of the company (SM 70-7-6).

¶ 7-315 Special provision for deferral of inheritance tax payment on farmlands

If an heir acquires farmland through either inheritance or bequest from a legatee who was in business of farming, and continues such farming business on the farmland acquired, under certain conditions, inheritance taxes against the farm investment value exceeding the farmland acquired may be deferred as long as the farm business is continued on this farmland. The tax deferral is also applicable to lend certain acquired urban farmlands. Where the farmland under the deferral measure of inheritance tax payment was established with sectional surface rights, it will continue to be eligible for the purpose of the tax deferral. The amount of tax deferral may be exempted from taxation if any of the following applies (SM 70-6).

(1) In cases where an heir who utilized this special provision passes away.

(2) In cases where an heir who utilized this special provision gifts all of the subject farmland prior to his/her death to a successor of the farm business in one lump.

(3) In cases where an heir who utilized this special provision continued the farm business for twenty (20) years at an urbanization area farmland.

However, any farmland acquired by gift which is subject to unified gift/inheritance tax system would not qualify for this special provision.

¶ 7-316 Special provision for inheritance tax payment deferral on forests

When a timber management successor obtains forests located in the designated forest management plan through inheritance or devise, and the successor continues forest management practice, the payment of the

¶ 7-315

相続税及び贈与税　569

れている相続税の全部又は一部と利子税を併せて納付しなければならない。

　一方，納税が猶予されている相続税は，特例後継者の死亡の他，経営承継期間の経過後に免除対象贈与を行った場合，会社の破産，会社の譲渡・解散があったなどの場合は納税が免除される（措法70の7の6）。

¶7-315　農地等の相続税の納税猶予の特例

　農業を営んでいた被相続人から相続人が，農地等を相続または遺贈によって取得して農業を営む場合には，一定の要件の下にその主とした農地等の農業投資価格を超える価格に対する相続税については，その取得した農地等について農業を継続する限り，その納税は猶予される。更に，取得した特定の都市農地を貸し付けた場合でも，その納税は猶予される。又，納税猶予を受けている農地等に区分地上権の設定があった場合でも，引き続き耕作等を行うときは，納税猶予は継続される。

　この納税猶予税額は，次のいずれかに該当することになったときに免除される（措法70の6）。

(1)　特例の適用を受けた相続人が死亡した場合

(2)　特例の適用を受けた相続人が特例農地等の全部を農業の後継者に生前一括贈与した場合

(3)　特例の適用を受けた相続人が市街化区域内農地で農業を20年間継続した場合

　なお，相続時精算課税に係る贈与によって取得した農地等については，この特例の適用を受けることはできない。

¶7-316　山林についての相続税の納税猶予

　林業経営相続人が，相続又は遺贈により，特定森林経営計画に存する山林を被相続人から一括して取得した場合において，その林業経営相続人が引き続き施業を継続していくときは，その山林に係る課税価格の80％に対応する相続税額は，その林業経営相続人の死亡の日まで，その納税を猶予する（措

570   INHERITANCE TAX AND GIFT TAX

inheritance tax amount equivalent to 80% of the taxable value of the forests may be deferred until death of the successor (SM 70-6-4).

¶ 7-317 Special provision for inheritance tax payment deferral on equity interest in medical corporations

Where heir acquires equity interest in a medical corporation which has equity of share holders through inheritance or bequest and that the medical corporation is certified medical corporations at the due date of inheritance tax return, the payment may be deferred until the end of transfer period to a medical corporation without equity of share holders, on condition that security has been provided. Where the heir refuses succession of all the equity interest during the transfer period, the deferred tax payment shall be exempted (SM 70-7-8).

¶ 7-318 Inheritance tax deferral for designated art works

Where individual who had entrusted designated art works with museum in accordance with the approved preservation utilization plan, deceased, and the successor of the bailment who received the designated art works through inheritance or bequest continues the bailment based on the bailment contract, 80% of the taxable amount of the designated art works will be deferred under the condition of collateral.

If the successor of the bailment deceased, the designated art works are donated to the deposited museum, or the art works are ruined by natural disaster, the deferred tax will be exempted (SM 70-6-7).

¶ 7-320 Property situated abroad

If both an heir or a legatee and the decedent had never domiciled in Japan for the last ten years before the commencement of the inheritance, the heir or the legatee will not be liable to inheritance tax on property situated abroad.

¶ 7-330 Deduction for inherited liability

If an heir or legatee domiciled in Japan succeeds to liabilities or pays expenses for the funeral of the decedent, then the amount of such liabilities or expenses is deductible in computing the net taxable assets which he or she has acquired (Law 13).

If an heir or legatee is not domiciled in Japan at the time of the death,

¶ 7-317

法70の6の4）。

¶7-317　医療法人の相続税の納税猶予

　個人が持分の定めのある医療法人の持分を相続又は遺贈により取得した場合において，その医療法人が相続税の申告期限において認定医療法人であるときは，担保の提供を条件に，持分の定めのない医療法人への移行期間満了までその納税を猶予する。また，移行期間内に当該相続人が持分の全てを放棄した場合には，猶予額を免除する（措法70の7の8）。

¶7-318　特定の美術品についての相続税の納税猶予

　個人が認定保存活用計画に基づき特定美術品を美術館に寄託した場合において，その者が死亡し，その特定美術品を相続又は遺贈により取得した寄託相続人が，その寄託契約に基づき寄託を継続したときは，担保の提供を条件に，その特定美術品に係る課税価格の80％に対応する相続税の納税を猶予する。

　寄託相続人が死亡した場合，寄託先美術館へその特定美術品の贈与した場合，又は自然災害によるその特定美術品の滅失があった場合には，猶予税額を免除する（措法70の6の7）。

¶7-320　国外財産

　被相続人等及び相続人等がともに相続開始前10年以内に日本に住所を有したことがない場合で，相続人等が取得した被相続人等の死亡時に国外にあった財産については，相続税は課されない。

¶7-330　債務控除

　日本に住居を有する相続人又は受遺者が被相続人の債務を承継して又は葬式費用を負担した場合には，この債務額又は費用はその者の課税価格の計算上控除する（相法13）。

　また，日本に住所を有しない相続人又は受遺者については，その者の取得した国内財産に係る承継債務のみを控除する。

572 INHERITANCE TAX AND GIFT TAX

only those liabilities which are closely connected with assets received which are situated in Japan are deductible.

The following conditions apply.

(1) Qualifying debts of the decedent are those that existed at the time of the decedent's death.

(2) The provision applies to heirs and legatees of inclusive bequests.

(3) The deductible amount of a debt is that which belongs to an heir or a legatee's share, or that part of a debt that is designated to a particular heir or legatee.

(4) The debts should be certain.

Note:

1. The amount of a debt which belongs to an heir or a legatee's share means that person's actual share of the inherited or bequeathed debt. If the heir or legatee's share is not yet settled, that person takes an assumed statutory share (R 13-3). The tax liabilities of a decedent are included in the above mentioned debts.

2. A decedent's funeral expenses are inevitable and will effect the amount of inherited assets. They are not debts belonging to the decedent and they do not exist at the time of the decedent's death. However, funeral expenses are deductible (R 13-4).

   Examples of funeral expenses are:

   (a) Expenses for the burial, cremation or transportation of remains at or before the funeral.

   (b) Gifts for attendants at the funeral which are proper according to the occupation, and position etc. of the decedent.

   (c) Expenses in addition to those in (a) or (b) which are normally connected with funerals.

   (d) Expenses for locating a body or transporting a corpse or remains.

¶ 7-340 Aggregation of net taxable assets and aggregated net taxable assets after allowance

The net taxable assets acquired by all heirs and legatees should be aggregated as the first step of the computation. This aggregated amount is called "the aggregated net taxable assets".

Then the basic estate allowance (see ¶ 7-350) is deducted from the aggregated net taxable assets. The amount of this balance is called "the aggregated net taxable assets after allowance".

There are some special treatments to mitigate the tax burden in computing the amount of net taxable assets for the defined portions of land that have been used for business or residence by the decedent or an heir who has lived with the decedent in the same household (see ¶ 7-300).

¶ 7-340

相続税及び贈与税　573

債務控除には次の条件が必要である。
(1)　控除できる債務は，被相続人の債務で相続開始の際，現に存するもので
ある。
(2)　債務控除ができる者は，相続人と包括受遺者及び相続人である受遺者で
ある。
(3)　控除金額は，相続又は遺贈（包括遺贈及び相続人に対する遺贈に限る。）
により承継した債務又は限定された債務で，その者の負担に属する部分の
金額である。
(4)　その債務は確実と認められたものに限られる。

　　（注）：1．その者の負担に属する金額とは，相続，包括遺贈又は被相続人からの相続人に対す
　　　　　　る遺贈によって財産を取得した者が実際に負担する金額をいうのであるが，負担する
　　　　　　金額が確定していないときは，法定相続分又は包括遺贈の割合に応じて負担する金額
　　　　　　をいう（相基通13-3）。債務には公租公課が含まれる。

　　　　　　2．葬式費用は，本来被相続人が負担している債務ではなく，また相続開始当時に現存
　　　　　　する債務でもないが，相続開始時に必然的に伴う葬式の費用の負担は，相続財産取得
　　　　　　の一つの条件ないし前提であり，また相続財産そのものが担っている負担と考えられ
　　　　　　るので，控除が認められている。
　　　　　　　　葬式費用とは次のようなものをいう（相基通13-4）。
　　　　　(a)　埋葬，火葬，納骨及び遺骸，遺骨の回送その他これらの処置に要した費用
　　　　　(b)　葬式に際し施与した金品で，被相続人の職業，財産その他の事情に照らして相当
　　　　　　程度と認められるものに要した費用
　　　　　(c)　(a)(b)に掲げるもののほか，葬式の前後に生じた出費で通常葬式に伴うものと認め
　　　　　　られるもの
　　　　　(d)　死体の捜索，又は死体，遺骨の運搬に要した費用

¶7-340　課税価格の合計額と課税遺産総額

　各相続人及び受遺者ごとの課税価格は，いったん合計されなければならな
い。その総額を「課税価格の合計額」と呼ぶ。
　しかる後，この課税価格の合計額から遺産に係る基礎控除額（¶7-350参
照）を控除する。この残額を「課税遺産総額」という。
　各相続人が取得した財産のうち被相続人又は被相続人と生計を一にしてい
た被相続人の親族の事業の用又は居住の用に供されていた宅地等のうち一定
の割合については，課税価格計算の特例が設けられている（¶7-300参照）。

574   INHERITANCE TAX AND GIFT TAX

¶ 7-350 Basic estate allowance

The basic estate allowance was amended effective from January 1, 2015 as the following (Law 15①):

$$¥30,000,000 + (¥6,000,000 × number of the legal heirs)$$

Note:
For the application of the basic estate allowance, abandonment of the right of inheritance is ignored. Therefore, the number of legal heirs includes heirs who abandon the inheritance (Law 15②, ③).

¶ 7-355 Special treatment for adopted children as to the basic estate allowance for children

If the decedent had adopted children, the following number of adopted children can be counted as legal heirs for estate allowances:

(1)   Where the decedent has one natural child.................................. one

(2)   Where the decedent has no natural children .... two

However, if application of this provision reduces the burden of inheritance tax unreasonably, the director of the tax office can exclude the adopted children as legal heirs, for the calculation of inheritance tax (Law 63).

For the application of this provision, the following persons are regarded as natural children of a decedent (Law 15③, Reg 3-2).

(1)   A child adopted by special adoption provided for under the Civil Code.

(2)   A natural child of a decedent's spouse who became an adopted child of the decedent.

(3)   Special adopted child of a decedent's spouse who became the decedent's adopted child after the marriage between the decedent and that spouse.

(4)   Lineal descendants of any decedent natural child, adopted child or lineal descendants who had a right to an inheritance, and any lineal descendants of any natural child, adopted child or lineal descendant who lost their right to an inheritance.

Special adoption provided for under the Civil Code 817-2 is an adoption approved by the Court of Family Affairs and acts to cease the relationship by blood.

The following conditions apply to special adoption.

(a)   Adoptive parents should be married and both should become

¶ 7-350

相続税及び贈与税　575

¶7-350　遺産に係る基礎控除額

　平成27年１月１日以後に開始した相続又は遺贈により取得した財産に係る基礎控除額は，次の算式で計算した金額である（相法15①）。

　　　3,000万円＋600万円×法定相続人の数^(注)

（注）：遺産に係る基礎控除額を計算する場合の法定相続人の数は，原則として，相続を放棄した人があっても，その放棄がないとした場合の相続人の数をいう（相法15②，③）。

¶7-355　養子がある場合の特例

　被相続人に養子があるときは，上記の法定相続人の数に含める養子の数については，次に掲げる場合の区分に応じて，それぞれ次に掲げる人数までとなる。

(1)　被相続人に実子がある場合　　１人

(2)　被相続人に実子がない場合　　２人

　なお，１人又は２人の養子を法定相続人の数に算入することが，相続税の負担を不当に減少させる結果となると認められる場合には，税務署長は，その養子の数を法定相続人の数に算入しないで相続税の課税価格及び相続税額を計算することができることとされている（相法63）。

　なお，この場合において，次に掲げる者は実子とみなされる（相法15③，相令３の２）。

(1)　民法上の特別養子縁組による養子となった者

(2)　配偶者の実子で被相続人の養子となった者

(3)　被相続人との婚姻前に被相続人の配偶者の特別養子縁組による養子となった者でその婚姻後に被相続人の養子となった者

(4)　実子若しくは養子又は直系卑属が相続開始以前に死亡し，又は相続権を失ったため相続人となったその者の直系卑属

　特別養子とは，実方の血族との親族関係が終了する養子縁組で，家庭裁判所が成立させるものをいう（民法817の２）。

　縁組の成立要件は，次のとおりである。

(a)　養親は婚姻している者に限られ，夫婦がともに養親となることを要す

576   INHERITANCE TAX AND GIFT TAX

adoptive parents.

(b)   Adoptive parents should not be younger than 25 years.

(c)   The adopted child should be younger than 6 years at the time of the application for judgement being filed with the Court of Family Affairs.

¶ 7-360 Amount of assets according to the statutory share of inheritance

The aggregated net taxable assets after allowance should be divided among all the heirs at law in accordance with their statutory shares, assuming the decedent left no will and the estate was distributed among the heirs according to the provisions of the Civil Code other than Article 904-2.

(1)   The following assumptions are made under the Civil Code:

   (a)   The spouse of the decedent is always considered an heir.

   (b)   The following persons become heirs in the following order together with the spouse:

   (i)   The natural children of the decedent (including the natural children of a predecedent heir).

   (ii)   Lineal ascendants by blood of the decedent.

   (iii) The decedent's own brothers and sisters (including the natural children of a predecedent heir).

(2)   Some examples of the application of the law concerning statutory shares are given below:

   (a)   When the heirs are the children (including the natural children of a predecedent heir) and the spouse, the statutory share of the children (including natural children of a predecedent heir) is 1/2, and the statutory share of the spouse is 1/2.

   (b)   When the heirs are the parents and the spouse, the statutory share of the parents is 1/3, and the statutory share of the spouse is 2/3.

   (c)   When the heirs are the brothers and sisters and the spouse, the statutory share of the brothers and sisters is 1/4, and the statutory share of the spouse is 3/4.

   (d)   If there are two or more heirs who have the same priority, the statutory share of each is equal.

The share of a half-brother or half-sister is one half of the share of a full brother or full sister of the decedent (Civil Code 900(4)).

¶ 7-360

る。
　(b)　養親となる者は，25歳以上の者でなければならない。
　(c)　養子となる者は，縁組の審判の申立のときにおいて，原則として6歳未満でなければならない。

¶7-360　法定相続分に応じた各人の取得金額

　課税遺産総額は，被相続人が遺言をしなかったものとして，その遺産を民法第904条の2以外の相続分に関する規定に基づき，法定相続人の間で分割したと仮定して，各法定相続人ごとに法定相続分に応じた取得金額に分割する。

(1)　民法上，相続順位は次のとおりである。
　(a)　被相続人の配偶者は，常に相続人となる。
　(b)　次に掲げる者は，次の順序で配偶者とともに相続人になる。

　　(i)　被相続人の子（代襲相続人を含む。）

　　(ii)　被相続人の直系尊属
　　(iii)　被相続人の兄弟姉妹（代襲相続人を含む。）

(2)　これらの法定相続人の法定相続分は次のとおりである。

　(a)　法定相続人が子（代襲相続人を含む。）及び配偶者である場合，子（代襲相続人を含む。）の法定相続分は2分の1とし，配偶者の法定相続分も2分の1である。

　(b)　法定相続人が両親及び配偶者である場合，両親の法定相続分は3分の1，配偶者の法定相続分は3分の2である。

　(c)　法定相続人が兄弟姉妹及び配偶者である場合，兄弟姉妹の法定相続分は4分の1，配偶者の法定相続分は4分の3である。

　(d)　同一順位の法定相続人が2人以上いる場合，各人の法定相続分は均等とされる。
　　また，父母の一方だけを同じくする兄弟姉妹は，父母の双方を同じくする兄弟姉妹の相続分の半分である（民法900四）。

578   INHERITANCE TAX AND GIFT TAX

¶ 7-370   Tax rates and total amount of inheritance tax

The tax rates shown in the right hand column apply to the statutory share of each heir (Law 16). The tax amount of each heir should be aggregated. This aggregated amount is the "total amount of inheritance tax".

The inheritance tax rate table effective from January 1, 2015 is as the following:

Taxable amount		Tax rate
Over	But not over	%
(¥)	— (¥) 10,000,000	10%
10,000,000	30,000,000	15%
30,000,000	50,000,000	20%
50,000,000	100,000,000	30%
100,000,000	200,000,000	40%
200,000,000	300,000,000	45%
300,000,000	600,000,000	50%
600,000,000		55%

¶ 7-380   Tax payable by each heir and legatee

The total amount of inheritance tax should be prorated to the actual heirs and/or the legatees in the proportion of their actual shares to aggregated net taxable assets. The actual share of each heir or legatee is the net taxable assets of each heir or legatee (Law 17).

This prorated tax is to be paid by each heir or legatee, unless the additions or deductions stated in ¶ 7-390 to ¶ 7-400 are necessary.

¶ 7-390   Surtax on inheritance tax

A surtax on inheritance tax is levied when an heir or legatee is not a decedent's child by blood (if no child is able to inherit because of prior death or other reason, the decedent's grandchild by blood, and so on), a decedent's parent by blood, or spouse (Law 18).

The surtax amounts to 20% of the amount of the prorated inheritance tax as stated in ¶ 7-380, with the limitation that the amount of inheritance tax including surtax cannot exceed 70% of the heir's net taxable assets.

¶ 7-400   Tax credits

Five kinds of tax credits may be credited, in the following priority,

¶ 7-370

相続税及び贈与税　579

¶7-370　税率及び相続税の総額

　法定相続人の法定相続分に応じた取得金額を次表の左欄に掲げる金額に区分して，それぞれの右欄に掲げる税率を適用し，各人の税額を合計する（相法16）。この合計した金額を「相続税の総額」という。

相続税の税率（課税標準は，各法定相続人の法定相続に応じた取得金額）

　平成27年1月1日以後に開始した相続又は遺贈により取得した財産に係る相続税については，次表の税率を適用する。

法定相続分に応ずる取得金額		税　率
—	1,000万円以下の金額	10%
1,000万円を超え	3,000万円　〃	15%
3,000万円　〃	5,000万円　〃	20%
5,000万円　〃	1億円　〃	30%
1億円　〃	2億円　〃	40%
2億円　〃	3億円　〃	45%
3億円　〃	6億円　〃	50%
6億円を超える金額		55%

¶7-380　各相続人・受遺者の相続税額

　相続税の総額は，実際の相続人及び受遺者に対して，課税価格の合計額に対する各人の課税価格の割合に応じて，按分する（相法17）。

　この按分税額が，¶7-390～¶7-400に述べる税額の加減算が必要のない相続人の納付すべき税額となる。

¶7-390　相続税の加算

　相続人及び受遺者が，被相続人の一親等の血族（一親等の血族である者の代襲相続人を含む。）及び配偶者以外の者である場合には，その者については相続税の加算がなされる（相法18）。

　加算金額は，¶7-380で述べたその者の按分税額の20%である。ただし，按分税額と加算金額の合計は，その者の課税金額の70%を超えないものとされる。

¶7-400　税額控除

　¶7-380及び¶7-390で述べた相続税の算出税額から以下の5種類の税額控

580   INHERITANCE TAX AND GIFT TAX

against the inheritance tax calculated in ¶ 7-380 and ¶ 7-390 (R 21-3).

(1) **Credit for gift tax paid**

    (a) If heirs or legatees who inherited assets from a decedent, or received them as a bequest, had been donated other assets by the decedent within three years before the decedent's death, the value of the donated assets should be included in the net taxable assets (see ¶ 7-280). Therefore, both inheritance tax and gift tax may be levied.

        However, in order to avoid double taxation, the amount of the gift tax levied on such gifts may be deducted from the amount of the inheritance tax.

        (i) The donated assets should be valued at their current market price at the time of acquisition, before deduction of the basic allowance (R 19-1).

        (ii) "Three years before the decedent's death" means a term taken from the day of the decedent's death going back 3 years to the same day of that year (R 19-2).

        (iii) If a spouse allowance for gift tax purposes was applicable to the donated assets, the amount of the allowance is not treated as applicable to donated assets (Reg 4).

        (iv) Exempt gifts, including gifts for severely handicapped persons, provided for in ¶ 7-870, should not be added to taxable assets.

    (b) In case where a taxpayer selects the unified system for gift tax purposes (¶ 7-896) and if he/she becomes the heir or legatee of the decedent donor, inheritance tax computed on the aggregated amount of properties gifted under the unified system and other properties inherited, devised or bequeathed should be payable after applying the tax credit of the aggregated gift tax amount which had been paid under the unified system. Uncreditable excess gift tax amount, if any, will be refunded. For inheritance tax purposes, the properties gifted under the unified system are valued at their fair market value at the time of the gift.

(2) **Credit for a spouse**

    Where the heir is the spouse of the decedent, the tax payable by the spouse is the excess amount of (i) over (ii). If (ii) is greater than (i), the spouse has no tax liability.

    (i) the tax payable by the spouse after credit for gift tax paid.

¶ **7-400**

除があり，この順序によって控除する（相基通21-3）。

⑴ 贈与税額控除

(a) ¶7-280で述べたとおり，相続又は遺贈により財産を取得した者が，相続開始前3年以内に被相続人からの贈与により財産を取得している場合には，相続税法上，その贈与財産の価額を相続税の課税価格に算入することになっている。この限りにおいては，贈与税と相続税とが二重に課されることになる。

そこで，この間の調整を図るため，相続税の課税価格に算入される贈与財産に係る贈与税を，相続税の算出税額から控除する。

(i) 「贈与財産の価額」とは，その財産を贈与により取得したときにおける時価により評価した贈与税の基礎控除前の価額をいう（相基通19-1）。

(ii) 「相続の開始前3年以内」とは，その相続開始の日から遡って3年目の応当日からその相続開始の日までをいう（相基通19-2）。

(iii) 贈与を受けた財産について贈与税の配偶者控除の適用がある場合には，その贈与を受けた財産のうち配偶者控除額相当部分は贈与を受けなかったものとされる（相令4）。

(iv) 非課税とされる贈与財産（特別障害者に対する贈与税の非課税適用部分（¶7-870参照）も含む。）は，加算の対象とはならない。

(b) 納税者が贈与税の相続時精算課税制度（¶7-896）を選択した場合において，当該制度に係る贈与者からの相続があったときは，当該制度の対象とされた贈与財産の累計額と相続財産とを合算した額に対する相続税額から，既に支払った本制度による贈与税額を控除する。控除しきれない場合には，還付を受けることができる。相続財産と合算する贈与財産の価額は，贈与時の時価とする。

⑵ 配偶者に対する相続税額の軽減

相続人が配偶者である場合，配偶者が納付すべき相続税は，(i)が(ii)を超過する場合の差額である。(ii)が(i)を超える場合には，配偶者が納付すべき相続税額はない。

(i) 贈与税額控除後の配偶者の納付すべき税額

582   INHERITANCE TAX AND GIFT TAX

(ii) the amount of aggregated tax multiplied by the following ratio:

$$\text{ratio} = \frac{\{(a) \text{ or } (b) \text{ whichever is greater}\} \text{ or } (c) \text{ whichever is smaller}}{\text{aggregated net taxable assets}}$$

   (a) the statutory share of the aggregated net taxable assets for the spouse

   (b) ¥160 million

   (c) the net taxable assets (actual acquired only) of the spouse

This credit is not applicable to the tax on the property which was concealed or misrepresented by a spouse, if an heir other than the spouse inherits the property (Law 19-2⑤).

For application of this credit, the spouse must be the legitimate spouse, so that common-law marriage cannot apply (R 19-2-2).

For this credit to apply, the inheritance tax return (including any return to be filed after the due date or any amendment return) must be filed with all necessary items and prescribed evidence attached. A copy of the census register, a copy of the attachment sheet of the census register, any agreement on the distribution of inherited assets and a copy of the will, etc. are required to be attached to the return.

If the inheritance tax return was filed without application of the spouse credit, because the assets were not divided by the due date, but the spouse credit should have applied following a change in the inheritance tax due to the distribution of assets, an amendment return may be filed or a correction to reduce tax may be requested of the tax office (Law 31, 32 (1), 32(6)).

(3) Credit for a minor

Where an heir has not reached 20 years of age by the time of the decedent's death, the credit for a minor may be deducted from the tax, unless the heir was domiciled abroad. The amount of credit for a minor is ¥100,000 multiplied by the number of years which would pass before the minor reaches 20 years of age. However, if such an heir inherited from another person in the past and had already enjoyed the benefit of the credit for a minor, that heir cannot again enjoy this credit.

If a decedent was a U.S. citizen or had a domicile in the U.S. at the time of death, special measures under the Japan-U.S. Inheritance Tax Convention apply.

This credit also is applicable to the following legal heirs (R 19-3-2, 19-3-3).

   (a) A legal heir who is regarded as an adult under a provision of the

¶ 7-400

相続税及び贈与税　583

(ii)　相続税の総額に次の割合を乗じて算出した金額

$$\frac{\left(\begin{array}{l}\text{課税価格の合計額に配偶者の法定}\\\text{相続分を乗じて計算した金額又は}\\\text{1億6,000万円のいずれか多い方の金額}\end{array}\right)\text{と}\left(\begin{array}{l}\text{配偶者の課税価格}\\\text{（実際取得額）}\end{array}\right)\text{とのいずれか}\atop\text{少ない金額}}{\text{相続税の課税価格の合計額}}$$

　　ただし，配偶者が仮装又は隠ぺいしていた財産を配偶者以外の相続人が取得した場合には，当該仮装又は隠ぺいしていた財産に伴い増加する税額については税額軽減措置を適用しない（相法19の2⑤）。

　　配偶者に対する相続税額の控除を受けることができる配偶者は，婚姻の届出をした者に限られるから，いわゆる内縁関係にある者は含まれない（相基通19の2-2）。

　　この軽減措置は，相続税の申告書（期限後申告書及び修正申告書を含む。）を提出し，かつ，その申告書に必要な事項の記載と一定の書類の添付がある場合に限り適用される。申告書に添付すべき書類は，戸籍の謄本及び戸籍の付票の写し，遺産分割協議書や遺言書の写し等である。

　　期限内には未分割で申告しているので，期限後に分割された財産について配偶者軽減を受けることにより相続税額が異なる場合には修正申告又は更正の請求を行う（相法31，32一，32六）。

(3)　未成年者控除

　　相続人・受遺者（日本に住所を有しないものを除く。）が相続開始時において20歳未満である場合，その者の算出税額から未成年者控除を行うことができる。未成年者控除額は，10万円にその者が20歳に達するまでの年数を乗じて得た金額である。ただし，その者が既に相続等による未成年者控除を受けている場合，既に受けた未成年者控除額を控除した後の金額となる。

　　被相続人が米国籍を有し，又は米国に住所を有していたときは，日米相続税条約により，特例が認められている。

　　この控除は次の法定相続人にも適用される（相基通19の3-2，19の3-3）。

(a)　民法753条の規定により成年に達したとみなされる者で20歳未満の者

584 INHERITANCE TAX AND GIFT TAX

Civil Code 753 but has not reached 20 years of age.

(b) A fetus is regarded as an heir under art. 886 of the Civil Code, provided that the fetus is born. In this case the credit is ¥2 million.

If the credit exceeds the inheritance tax liability of the minor, the excess can be credited against the inheritance tax liability of the minor's guardian (Law 19-3).

(4) Credit for a handicapped person

Where an heir or legatee is a handicapped person, as defined in the Regulations, and that heir or legatee is domiciled in Japan, the amount calculated as follows may be deducted from the tax (Law 19-4):

$$\left\{ ¥100,000 \text{ or } \begin{pmatrix} ¥200,000 \text{ for a severely} \\ \text{handicapped person} \end{pmatrix} \times \begin{pmatrix} \text{number of years before the} \\ \text{heir reaches 85 years of age} \end{pmatrix} \right\}$$

A handicapped person is (Reg 4-4):

(a) a person defined as such under the Individual Income Tax Law Regulation 10①(1) through (5) and (7);

(b) a person defined as such under the Individual Income Tax Law Regulation 10①(6) with the approval of the director of a public welfare office.

If the credit exceeds the inheritance tax liability of the handicapped person, the excess, like the credit for a minor, can be credited against the inheritance tax liability of the handicapped person's guardian (Law 19-4③).

(5) Credit for chain successions

A credit for chain successions is granted to the heirs of a succession (the second succession), when the decedent had paid inheritance tax on the succession within the preceding 10 years (the first succession).

The amount credited for an heir is:

$$A \times \frac{C}{B - A} \left[\text{not exceeding} \times \frac{100}{100} \right] \times \frac{D}{C} \times \frac{10 \text{ years} - E}{10 \text{ years}}$$

A: Inheritance tax levied on the decedent at the first succession.

B: Amount of assets succeeded to by the decedent at the first succession.

C: Amount of total assets succeeded to by all the heirs and legatees at the second succession.

D: Amount of total assets succeeded to by the heir.

E: The number of years between the first and the second succes-

¶ 7-400

相続税及び贈与税　585

(b) 民法886条の規定により相続について既に生まれたものとされる胎児（この場合，未成年者控除は，200万円となる。）

　未成年者控除の金額がその控除を受ける者について算出した相続税額を超える場合は，その超える部分の金額は未成年者控除を受ける者の扶養義務者の相続税額から控除できる（相法19の3）。

(4) 障害者控除

　日本に住所を有する相続人・受遺者が政令で定める障害者である場合，次の金額を算出税額から控除することができる（相法19の4）。

$$10万円（特別障害者である場合には20万円）× \frac{その者が85歳に達するまでの年数}{}$$

　障害者の範囲は次のとおり（相令4の4）。

(a) 所令10①一～五，七に掲げる者

(b) 所令10①六に掲げる者で福祉事務所長の認定を受けた者

　障害者控除についても，控除しきれなかった金額があれば，未成年者控除と同様，その障害者の扶養義務者の相続税額から控除する（相法19の4③）。

(5) 相次相続控除

　被相続人がその者の相続（第2次相続）開始前10年以内の相続（第1次相続）により相続税を納付していた場合，その者の相続人について相次相続控除を行うことができる。

　各相続人の相次相続控除額は次のとおりである。

$$A × \frac{C}{B-A} \left(\frac{100}{100} を限度とする \right) × \frac{D}{C} × \frac{10年-E}{10年}$$

A…第1次相続に係る当該被相続人の相続税額

B…当該被相続人が第一次相続により承継した純資産の価額

C…第2次相続によって，各相続人及び受遺者が承継した純資産の合計額

D…第2次相続によって，各相続人が承継した純資産の価額

E…第1次相続から第2次相続までの間の年数

586   INHERITANCE TAX AND GIFT TAX

sion.

In the above formula the tax amount of 'A' does not include interest tax, delinquency tax, penalty tax for a short return, penalty tax for no return and heavy penalty tax.

If the above formula (10 years – E) is a fraction of a year it is raised to one year (Law 20(3)).

(6) **Credit for foreign taxes.**

According to Japanese law (as described in ¶ 7-120), properties situated abroad are subject to Japanese inheritance tax if an heir is domiciled in Japan. However, it is quite possible for a foreign country, state or province, or local authority to levy estate or inheritance taxes on the same property.

This kind of international double taxation may be eliminated unilaterally by a credit for foreign taxes (Law 20-2).

Foreign inheritance and estate taxes may be credited against Japanese inheritance tax up to a certain limit. This limit is computed as follows:

$$\text{Amount of Japanese inheritance tax (after credit for chain successions)} \times \frac{\text{Value of the net taxable assets situated abroad}}{\text{Total value of the net taxable assets on a global basis}}$$

The exchange rate of a foreign currency for the credit amount is the telegraphic selling rate of the amount of foreign tax on the due date. The telegraphic selling rate at the date of remittance may also be applicable, at the taxpayer's option, so long as the remittance is not excessively delayed (R 20-2-1).

¶ 7-410 Example of computation of inheritance tax

Case:

(1) Mr. X had his domicile in Japan and died in June, 2015.

(2) Mr. X had assets valued at ¥590 million and liabilities amounting to ¥90 million at the time of his death.

(3) Mr. X had a brother. In the past, Mr. X and his brother succeeded to the estate of their father valued at ¥300 million net in December, 2011 on an equal share basis and paid inheritance tax amounting to ¥43 million each (i.e. there was a three-year interval between the first succession and the second succession).

(4) Mr. X married 26 years ago and had two children, Mr. A and Mr.

¶ 7-410

Aの税額は，利子税，延滞税，過少申告加算税，無申告加算税及び重加算税に相当する税額を控除した金額による。また，上の式（10年－E）で計算される年数に1年未満の端数があるときは，その端数は1年として計算する（相法20三）。

(6) 外国税額控除

　¶7-120で述べたとおり，相続人・受遺者が日本に住所を有している場合には，その者が取得した国外財産に対しても日本の相続税が課される。他方，外国政府及びその地方公共団体は当該財産に対して相続税に相当する税を課すことができる。この種の国際二重課税は最終的には外国税額控除によって排除される（相法20の2）。

　外国相続税額は一定の限度内において日本の相続税から控除することができる。控除限度額は次のとおりである。

$$\text{相次相続控除後の相続税額} \times \frac{\text{国外財産の価格}}{\text{相続又は遺贈により取得した財産の総額}}$$

　控除される外国税額は，その納付すべき日における電信売相場により邦貨に換算する。ただし，送金が著しく遅れる場合を除き，国内から送金する日の電信売相場によることができる（相基通20の2-1）。

¶7-410　相続税の計算例
事実：
(1) X……被相続人（日本に住所を有し，相続開始の日は平成27年6月。）
(2) Xの遺産……総額5億9,000万円，負債額は9,000万円

(3) 第1次相続……Xには弟が1人いる。Xと弟は平成23年12月に父から純相続財産3億円を平等に相続し，各々4,300万円の相続税を納付した。
　　（第1次相続と第2次相続との間の年数は3年である。）

(4) Xは26年前に結婚し，2人の子（A及びB）がいる。Xは遺言をし，その

588   INHERITANCE TAX AND GIFT TAX

B. He left a will declaring that Mrs. X should get one-half of the estate and each of the children one-quarter.

A picture valued at ¥20 million was to be separated from the estate and bequeathed to Mr. T who was a friend of Mr. X.

(5) Mr. A was 21 years old and Mr. B was 14 years old at the time of Mr. X's death.

(6) Mr. X made a gift, worth ¥40 million, to Mrs. X in July, 2013 and Mrs. X paid gift tax thereon amounting to ¥17,200,000.

(7) Mr. X paid premiums for life insurance and Mrs. X received the insurance payments amounting to ¥350 million. These insurance receipts should not be included in the estate mentioned in (4) above, according to Mr. X's will.

Computation:

(1) Value of the net assets acquired by each heir or legatee:

Mr. T		¥20,000,000
Mrs. X	¥350,000,000 (insurance) – ¥15,000,000 (exempt) =	¥335,000,000
	¥40,000,000 (gift made within preceding 3 years)	¥40,000,000
	(¥590,000,000 – ¥90,00,000 – ¥20,000,000) × 1/2	¥240,000,000
	Total	¥615,000,000

Mr. A	(¥590,000,000 – ¥90,000,000 – ¥20,000,000) × 1/4 =	¥120,000,000
Mr. B	(¥590,000,000 – ¥90,000,000 – ¥20,000,000) × 1/4 =	¥120,000,000

(2) Total net assets ¥875,000,000

Less basic estate allowance

(¥30,000,000 + ¥6,000,000 × 3) ¥48,000,000

Aggregated net assets after allowance ¥827,000,000

(3) Divide the aggregated net assets after allowance into the statutory shares of each heir:

statutory share of Mrs. X (1/2 under the Civil Code)	¥413,500,000
statutory share of Mr. A (1/2 × 1/2 = 1/4 under the Civil Code)	¥206,750,000
statutory share of Mr. B (1/2 × 1/2 = 1/4 under the Civil Code)	¥206,750,000
	¥827,000,000

(4) Application of tax rate

for	Mrs. X's statutory share	¥164,750,000
	Mr. A's statutory share	¥66,037,500
	Mr. B's statutory share	¥66,037,500
	Total	¥296,825,000

(5) Proration of total tax amount from (4)

¶ 7-410

相続税及び贈与税　589

　妻に遺産の2分の1，2人の子に各々4分の1を与えるものとするが，絵画（2,000万円）は別途Xの友人Tに遺贈するとしている。

(5)　Xの相続開始日現在，子Aは21歳，子Bは14歳である。

(6)　Xは平成25年7月，妻に4,000万円の贈与をしており，妻は1,720万円の贈与税を納付している。

(7)　Xは生命保険料を自ら支払っており，妻が生命保険金3億5,000万円を受け取っている。Xの遺言によれば，当該生命保険金は(4)に述べた遺産総額に含めないものとされている。

計算：

(1)　各相続人，受遺者の相続税の課税価額　　　　　　　　　　　　　　　（円）

友人T		20,000,000
妻	350,000,000（生命保険金）－15,000,000（非課税部分）	335,000,000
	40,000,000（前3年以内の贈与）	40,000,000
	（590,000,000－90,000,000－20,000,000）×½	240,000,000
		615,000,000
子A	（590,000,000－90,000,000－20,000,000）×¼	120,000,000
子B	（590,000,000－90,000,000－20,000,000）×¼	120,000,000

(2)　各相続税の課税価額の合計額　　　　　　　　　　　　875,000,000
　　（減）　遺産に係る基礎控除額（30,000,000＋6,000,000×3）　48,000,000
　　課税遺産総額　　　　　　　　　　　　　　　　　　　827,000,000

(3)　課税遺産総額の法定相続分

妻		413,500,000
子A	（1－½）×⅓＝¼	206,750,000
子B	（1－½）×½＝¼	206,750,000
		827,000,000

(4)　税率の適用

妻の法定相続分に係る相続税	164,750,000
子A	66,037,500
子B	66,037,500
相続税の総額	296,825,000

(5)　相続税の総額の按分

590   INHERITANCE TAX AND GIFT TAX

for Mr. T	¥20,000,000	0.02	
for Mrs. X	¥615,000,000	0.70	
for Mrs. A	¥120,000,000	0.14	
for Mr. B	¥120,000,000	0.14	
Total	¥875,000,000	1.00	
for Mr. T	¥292,150,000	× 0.02 =	¥5,936,500
for Mr. X	¥292,150,000	× 0.70 =	¥207,777,500
for Mr. A	¥292,150,000	× 0.14 =	¥41,555,500
for Mr. B	¥292,150,000	× 0.14 =	¥41,555,500
			¥296,825,000

(6) Surtax and tax credits —

for Mr. T: ¥5,936,500

    Surtax (¥5,936,500 × 0.2 = ¥1,187,300)   ¥1,187,300

                                                     ¥7,123,800

                                    (tax due from Mr. T)

for Mrs. X: ¥207,777,500

    Credit for gift tax   ¥17,200,000 (a)

    Credit for spouse

$$¥296,825,000 \ \times \ \frac{875,000,000 \times 1/2}{875,000,000} \ = \ ¥148,412,500 \ (b)$$

(The numerator is ¥875,000,000 × 1/2 or ¥615,000,000 (value actually acquired), whichever is smaller.)

Credit for chain succession:

$$¥43,000,000 \ \times \ \frac{¥835,000,000}{¥300,000,000 \times 1/2 - ¥43,000,000} \ \text{(not exceeding 1.00)}$$

$$\times$$

$$\frac{¥575,000,000}{¥835,000,000} \ \times \ \frac{7 \text{ (years)}}{10 \text{ (years)}} \ = \ ¥20,727,545 \ (c)$$

total of credit (a) + (b) + (c)   ¥186,340,044

¥207,777,500 − ¥186,340,004   =   ¥21,437,400 (round off under ¥100)

                                        (tax due from Mrs. X)

for Mr. A: ¥41,555,500

    Credit for chain successions

$$¥43,000,000 \ \times \ (1.00) \times \frac{¥120,000,000}{¥835,000,000} \ \times \ \frac{7 \text{ (years)}}{10 \text{ (years)}} \ = \ ¥4,325,748$$

¥41,555,500 − ¥4,325,748 =   ¥37,229,700 (round off under ¥100)

¶ 7-410

相続税及び贈与税　591

	（相続税の課税価額）	按分割合	按分税額
T	20,000,000	0.02	5,936,500
妻	615,000,000	0.70	207,777,500
子A	120,000,000	0.14	41,555,500
子B	120,000,000	0.14	41,555,500
	875,000,000	1.000	296,825,000

(6) 相続税の加算及び税額控除

T：按分税額　　　　　　　　　　　　　　　　5,936,500

相続税の加算　$5,936,500 \times 0.2 = 1,187,300$　　1,187,300

　　　　　　　　　　　　　　　　　　　　　　7,123,800

　　　　　　　　　　　　　　　　　　　　（納付税額）

妻：按分税額　　　　　　　　　　　　　　　207,777,500

税額控除

贈与税額控除額　　　　　　　　　17,200,000　（イ）

配偶者の税額軽減額

$$296,825,000 \times \frac{875,000,000 \times \frac{1}{2}}{875,000,000} = 148,412,500 \quad （ロ）$$

分子は，875,000,000×½又は実際に取得した
価格615,000,000のいずれか低い方の額

相次相続控除額

$$43,000,000 \times \left(\frac{835,000,000}{300,000,000 \times \frac{1}{2} - 43,000,000} \geqq 1 \right)$$

$$\times \frac{575,000,000}{835,000,000} \times \frac{7 \, 年}{10 年} = 20,727,544 \quad （ハ）$$

（イ）+（ロ）+（ハ）　　　　　　　186,340,044

$207,777,500 - 186,340,004 =$　21,437,400

（納付税額100円未満切捨て）

子A：按分税額　　　　　　　　　　　　　　41,555,500

相次相続控除額

$$43,000,000 \times 1 \ \times \frac{120,000,000}{835,000,000} \times \frac{7 \, 年}{10 年} = 4,325,748$$

$$41,555,500 - 4,325,748 = 37,229,700$$

592   INHERITANCE TAX AND GIFT TAX

(tax due from Mr. A)

for Mr. B: ¥41,555,500
Credit for a minor:
¥100,000 × (20 – 14) years =   ¥600,000
Credit for chain successions:
the same as for Mr.A   ¥4,325,748
total of credits   ¥4,925,748
¥41,555,000 – ¥4,925,748 =   ¥36,629,700 (round off under ¥100)

(tax due from Mr. B)

¶ 7-420 Forms of inheritance tax return

The following forms are samples of the usual tax return forms for inheritance tax.

Ⓐ

¶ 7-420

（納付税額100円未満切捨て）

子B：按分税額   41,555,500

　　　税額控除

　　　　未成年者控除額100,000×(20−14)年＝600,000（イ）

　　　　相次相続控除額（Aと同じ）   4,325,748（ロ）

　　　　（イ）＋（ロ）   ＝4,925,748

　　　　41,555,500−4,925,748   ＝36,629,700

（納付税額100円未満切捨て）

¶7-420　相続税の申告書

参考までに，相続税の申告書の主要フォームを掲げておく。

594   INHERITANCE TAX AND GIFT TAX

¶ 7-450 Form 1: Inheritance Tax Return

To Director,

_____ District Taxation Office

Date of submission _____

Date of death _____

	Total	Acquirer of property
Name	Decedent's Name_____	
Date of birth (Age)		
Residence and phone number		
Occupation		
Relationship with decedent Cause of acquisition	Circle either Inheritance or bequest	[ ] Inheritance/bequest Gift under unified gift/ inheritance tax system

				Total	Acquirer of property
Taxable amount	Value of acquired property (Form 11 ③)	①			
	Value of property applied to unified gift/inheritance tax system	②			
	Debt and funeral expense (Form13-3 ⑦)	③			
	Net value acquired (① + ② – ③)	④			
	Value of gift within 3 years before the inheritance which is taxable at calendar year basis (Form 14-1 ④)	⑤			
	Net taxable assets (④ + ⑤)	⑥			
Tax amount	Number of heirs at law & basic estate allowance		Number of heirs ⒝		← Fill in the same number and amount as Form2 ②
	Aggregated tax amount	⑦			← Fill in the same amount as Form2 ⑧
	Ratio (⑥/Ⓐ)	⑧		1.00	
	Prorated tax amount (⑦ × ⑧)	⑨			
	Tax amount calculated by special concession	⑩			
	Surtax for those other than decedent's child, parent or spouse (Form 4-1 ⑤)	⑪			
Tax amount payable	**Tax Credit(s) for** Gift tax paid (Form 4 ⑬)	⑫			
	Spouse (Form 5)	⑬			
	Minor (Form 6-1)	⑭			
	Handicapped (Form 6-2)	⑮			
	Chain successions (Form 7)	⑯			
	Foreign taxes (Form 8)	⑰			
	Total	⑱			
	Difference ((⑨ + ⑪ – ⑱) or (⑩ + ⑪ – ⑱)	⑲			
	Gift tax paid under unified gift/ inheritance tax system (Form 11-2 ⑧)	⑳		00	00
	Tax amount payable	㉑			

¶ 7-450

相続税及び贈与税 595

¶7-450

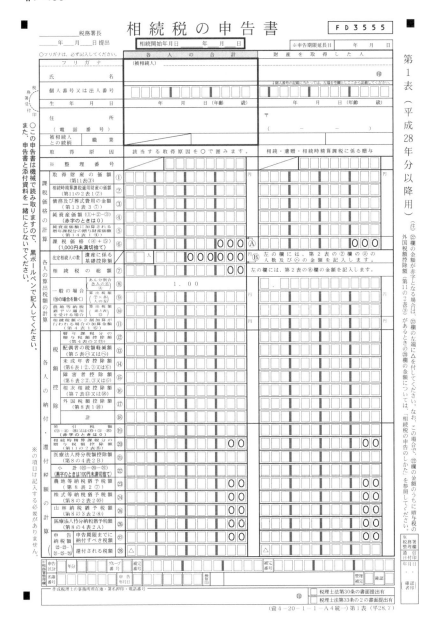

596   INHERITANCE TAX AND GIFT TAX

¶ 7-455 Form 2: Computation of Aggregate Inheritance Tax
(where none of the acquirers are "farming heirs")

		Decedent's Name
①Total Amount of Net Taxable Assets (from Form 1, ⑥, Ⓐ)	②Basic Estate Allowance (to Form 1, Ⓑ)	③Total Amount of Net Taxable Assets after Basic Estate Allowance (① − ②)

④Heirs at law		⑤ Statutory share	Computation of Amount of Aggregated Tax	
Name	Relationship with decedent		⑥Amount of Statutory Share of Each Heir (③ × ⑤)	⑦Tax Amount (⑥ × Tax Rate ⑨ − ⑩) (see Tax Table)
			¥ ,000	¥
			¥ ,000	¥
			¥ ,000	¥
			¥ ,000	¥
			¥ ,000	¥
			¥ ,000	¥
			¥ ,000	¥
TOTAL		1	¥ ,000	⑧ (to Form 1, ⑦) ¥ 00

Tax Table
(thousand yen)

(a)	10,000 or less	30,000 or less	50,000 or less	100,000 or less	200,000 or less	300,000 or less	600,000 or less	over 60,000
(b)	10%	15%	20%	30%	40%	45%	50%	55%
(c)	–	500	2,000	7,000	17,000	27,000	42,000	72,000

(a): Amount of statutory share of each heir
(b): Tax rate
(c): Subtraction
Note: Tax amount = (a) × (b) − (c)

¶ 7-455

相続税及び贈与税　597

¶7-455

相続税の総額の計算書　被相続人　

第2表（平成27年分以降用）

この表は、第1表及び第3表の「相続税の総額」の計算のために使用します。
なお、被相続人から相続、遺贈や相続時精算課税に係る贈与によって財産を取得した人のうちに農業相続人がいない場合は、この表の⑧欄及び⑩欄並びに⑨欄から⑪欄までは記入する必要がありません。

○この表を修正申告書の第2表として使用するときは、④欄には修正申告書第1表の⑭欄の⑥④の金額を記入し、⑥欄には修正申告
○第3表の1の⑭欄の⑥④の金額を記入します。

① 課税価格の合計額	② 遺産に係る基礎控除額	③ 課税遺産総額
ⓘ（第1表⑥Ⓐ）　　　　　円 ,000	Ⓑの法定相続人の数 3,000万円＋（600万円× Ⓑ 人）＝ Ⓐ 万円	㊁ （ⓘ－Ⓐ）　　　　　円 ,000
（第3表⑥Ⓐ）　　　　　円 ,000	Ⓑの人数及びⒶの金額を第1表Ⓑへ転記します。	（㊀－Ⓐ）　　　　　,000

④ 法定相続人（(注)1参照）		⑤ 左の法定相続人に応じた法定相続分	第1表の「相続税の総額⑦」の計算		第3表の「相続税の総額⑦」の計算	
氏　名	被相続人との続柄		⑥ 法定相続分に応ずる取得金額（㊁×⑤）(1,000円未満切捨て)	⑦ 相続税の総額の基となる税額 下の「速算表」で計算します。	⑨ 法定相続分に応ずる取得金額（㊁×⑤）(1,000円未満切捨て)	⑩ 相続税の総額の基となる税額 下の「速算表」で計算します。
			円 ,000	円	円 ,000	円
			,000		,000	
			,000		,000	
			,000		,000	
			,000		,000	
			,000		,000	
			,000		,000	
法定相続人の数 Ⓐ　人		合計 1	⑧ 相続税の総額（⑦の合計額）(100円未満切捨て) 00		⑪ 相続税の総額（⑩の合計額）(100円未満切捨て) 00	

(注)1　④欄の記入に当たっては、被相続人に養子がある場合や相続の放棄があった場合には、「相続税の申告のしかた」をご覧ください。
2　⑧欄の金額を第1表⑦欄へ転記します。財産を取得した人のうちに農業相続人がいる場合は、⑧欄の金額を第1表⑦欄へ転記するとともに、⑪欄の金額を第3表⑦欄へ転記します。

相続税の速算表

法定相続分に応ずる取得金額	10,000千円以下	30,000千円以下	50,000千円以下	100,000千円以下	200,000千円以下	300,000千円以下	600,000千円以下	600,000千円超
税　率	10%	15%	20%	30%	40%	45%	50%	55%
控除額	－ 千円	500千円	2,000千円	7,000千円	17,000千円	27,000千円	42,000千円	72,000千円

この速算表の使用方法は、次のとおりです。
⑥欄の金額×税率－控除額＝⑦欄の税額　　　⑨欄の金額×税率－控除額＝⑩欄の税額
例えば、⑥欄の金額30,000千円に対する税額（⑦欄）は、30,000千円×15％－500千円＝4,000千円です。

○連帯納付義務について
相続税の納税については、各相続人等が相続、遺贈や相続時精算課税に係る贈与により受けた利益の価額を限度として、お互いに連帯して納付しなければならない義務があります。

第2表(平28.7)　　　　　　　　　　　　　　　　　　　　　　　　　　　　　　　（資4－20－3－A4統一）

598 INHERITANCE TAX AND GIFT TAX

¶ 7-465 Form 4: "Surtax for those other than decedent's child, parent or spouse"

Name of Applicant					
Tax amount before tax credit	①				
Fill in if there is change about relationship with decedent	Value of property applied unified gift/ inheritance tax system after the applicant became decedent's child, parent or spouse	②			
	Value of property (Form 1 ①, ②, ⑤)	③			
	Tax not applied to surtax (① × ② ÷ ③)	④			
Surtax (① × 0.2) if ②~⑤ applied ((①–⑤) × 0.2)		⑥			

To Form 1, ⑪

¶ 7-465

相続税及び贈与税　599

¶7-465

相 続 税 額 の 加 算 金 額 の 計 算 書

被相続人

第4表（平成28年分以降用）

1　相続税額の加算金額の計算

この表は、相続、遺贈や相続時精算課税に係る贈与によって財産を取得した人のうちに、被相続人の一親等の血族（代襲して相続人となった直系卑属を含みます。）及び配偶者以外の人がいる場合に記入します。

なお、相続や遺贈により取得した財産のうちに、租税特別措置法第70条の2の3（直系尊属から結婚・子育て資金の一括贈与を受けた場合の贈与税の非課税）第10項第2号に規定する管理残額がある人は、下記「2　加算の対象とならない相続税額の計算（管理残額がある場合）」を作成します。

（注）一親等の血族であっても相続税額の加算の対象となる場合があります。詳しくは「相続税の申告のしかた」をご覧ください。

加算の対象となる人の氏名						
各人の税額控除前の相続税額 （第1表⑨又は第1表⑩の金額）	①	円	円	円	円
相続開始の時において被相続人の養子となっている人のうち被相続人の直系卑属に該当しない人でかつ、その人の相続税の課税価格に算入された贈与財産の価額に変更があった場合に記入します。	被相続人の一親等の血族であった期間内にその被相続人から相続時精算課税に係る贈与によって取得した財産の価額	②	円	円	円	円
	被相続人から相続、遺贈や相続時精算課税に係る贈与によって取得した財産などで相続税の課税価格に算入された財産の価額 （第1表①＋第1表②＋第1表⑤）	③				
	加算の対象とならない相続税額 （①×②÷③）	④				
管理残額がある場合	加算の対象とならない相続税額 （下記「2」の⑬の金額）	⑤	円	円	円	円
相続税額の加算金額 （①×0.2） ただし、上記②～⑤の金額がある場合には、 （（①-④-⑤）×0.2）となります。		⑥	円	円	円	円

（注）　1　相続時精算課税適用者である孫が相続開始の時までに被相続人の養子となった場合は、「相続時精算課税に係る贈与を受けている人で、かつ、相続開始の時までに被相続人との続柄に変更があった場合」には含まれませんので②欄から④欄までの記入は不要です。

　　　　2　各人の⑥欄の金額を第1表のその人の「相続税額の2割加算が行われる場合の加算金額⑪」欄に転記します。

600   INHERITANCE TAX AND GIFT TAX

"Tax credit for Gift tax paid under calendar year taxation"

	Name of Applicant					
For the year which includes the date of inheritance	Total amount of gifts received	①				
	Value to be added to Net Taxable Assets of gift from decedent	②				
	Gift tax for the year	③				
	Gift tax credited (③ × ② ÷ ①)	④				
	District Taxation Office to which gift tax return was filed					
For the 1st preceding year	Total amount of gifts received	⑨				
	Value to be added to Net Taxable Assets of gift from decedent	⑩				
	Gift tax for the year	⑪				
	Gift tax credited (⑪ × ⑩ ÷ ⑨)	⑫				
	District Taxation Office to which gift tax return was filed					
For the 2nd preceding year	Total amount of gifts received	⑬				
	Value to be added to Net Taxable Assets of gift from decedent	⑭				
	Gift tax for the year	⑮				
	Gift tax credited (⑮ × ⑭ ÷ ⑬)	⑯				
	District Taxation Office to which gift tax return was filed					
Gift tax credited in total (④ + ⑧ + ⑫ + ⑯)		⑰				

To Form 1, ⑫

¶ 7-465

相続税及び贈与税　601

暦年課税分の贈与税額控除額の計算書

被相続人

第4表の2（平成28年分用）

　この表は、第14表の「1　純資産価額に加算される暦年課税分の贈与財産価額及び特定贈与財産価額の明細」欄に記入した財産のうち相続税の課税価格に加算されるものについて、贈与税が課税されている場合に記入します。

	控除を受ける人の氏名				
	贈与税の申告書の提出先	税務署	税務署	税務署	税務署
相続開始の年の前年分（平成27年分）	被相続人から暦年課税に係る贈与によって租税特別措置法第70条の2の5第1項の規定の適用を受ける財産（特例贈与財産）を取得した場合				
	相続開始の年の前年中に暦年課税に係る贈与によって取得した特例贈与財産の価額の合計額 ①	円	円	円	円
	①のうち被相続人から暦年課税に係る贈与によって取得した特例贈与財産の価額の合計額（贈与税額の計算の基礎となった価額）②				
	その年分の暦年課税分の贈与税額（裏面の「2」参照）③				
	控除を受ける贈与税額（特例贈与財産分）（③×②÷①）④				
	被相続人から暦年課税に係る贈与によって租税特別措置法第70条の2の5第1項の規定の適用を受けない財産（一般贈与財産）を取得した場合				
	相続開始の年の前年中に暦年課税に係る贈与によって取得した一般贈与財産の価額の合計額（贈与税の配偶者控除後の金額）⑤	円	円	円	円
	⑤のうち被相続人から暦年課税に係る贈与によって取得した一般贈与財産の価額の合計額（贈与税額の計算の基礎となった価額）⑥				
	その年分の暦年課税分の贈与税額（裏面の「3」参照）⑦				
	控除を受ける贈与税額（一般贈与財産分）（⑦×⑥÷⑤）⑧				
相続開始の年の前々年分（平成26年分）	贈与税の申告書の提出先	税務署	税務署	税務署	税務署
	相続開始の年の前々年中に暦年課税に係る贈与によって取得した財産の価額の合計額（贈与税の配偶者控除後の金額）⑨	円	円	円	円
	⑨のうち被相続人から暦年課税に係る贈与によって取得した財産の価額の合計額（贈与税額の計算の基礎となった価額）⑩				
	その年分の暦年課税分の贈与税額 ⑪	00	00	00	00
	控除を受ける贈与税額（⑪×⑩÷⑨）⑫				
相続開始の年の前々々年分（平成25年分）	贈与税の申告書の提出先	税務署	税務署	税務署	税務署
	相続開始の年の前々々年中に暦年課税に係る贈与によって取得した財産の価額の合計額（贈与税の配偶者控除後の金額）⑬				
	⑬のうち相続開始の日から遡って3年前の日以後に贈相続人から暦年課税に係る贈与によって取得した財産の価額の合計額（贈与税額の計算の基礎となった価額）⑭				
	その年分の暦年課税分の贈与税額 ⑮	00	00	00	00
	控除を受ける贈与税額（⑮×⑭÷⑬）⑯				
	暦年課税分の贈与税額控除額計（④+⑧+⑫+⑯）⑰	円	円	円	円

（注）各人の⑰欄の金額を第1表のその人の「暦年課税分の贈与税額控除額⑫」欄に転記します。

第4表の2（平28.7）

（資4-20-5-3-A4統一）

602   INHERITANCE TAX AND GIFT TAX

¶ 7-480 Form 14: Value to be added to Net Taxable Assets of gifts within the 3 years before the death of the decedent

Name of acquirer who received gift from decedent	Date of gift	Assets gifted				Spouse allowance applied, if any	Value to be added to Net Taxable Assets ③(① − ②)
		Kind	Situs	Quantity	① Value		

Name of acquirer				④Total
Value to be added to his/her Net Taxable Assets				

To Form 1, ⑤

¶ 7-480

相続税及び贈与税　603

¶7-480

純資産価額に加算される暦年課税分の
贈与財産価額及び特定贈与財産価額
出資持分の定めのない法人などに遺贈した財産
特定の公益法人などに寄附した相続財産・
特定公益信託のために支出した相続財産

の明細書

被相続人	

第14表（平成27年分以降用）

1　純資産価額に加算される暦年課税分の贈与財産価額及び特定贈与財産価額の明細

　この表は、相続、遺贈や相続時精算課税に係る贈与によって財産を取得した人（注）が、その相続開始前3年以内に被相続人から暦年課税に係る贈与によって取得した財産がある場合に記入します。

（注）　被相続人から租税特別措置法第70条の2の3（直系尊属から結婚・子育て資金の一括贈与を受けた場合の贈与税の非課税）第10項第2号に規定する管理残額以外の財産を取得しなかった人は除きます（相続時精算課税に係る贈与によって財産を取得している人を除く。）。

番号	贈与を受けた人の氏名	贈与年月日	相続開始前3年以内に暦年課税に係る贈与を受けた財産の明細					②①の価額のうち特定贈与財産の価額	③相続税の課税価格に加算される価額（①－②）
			種類	細目	所在場所等	数量	①価額		
							円	円	円
1		・・							
2		・・							
3		・・							
4		・・							
贈与を受けた人ごとの③欄の合計額	氏名	（各人の合計）							
	④金額	円		円		円		円	円

上記「②」欄において、相続開始の年に被相続人から贈与によって取得した居住用不動産や金銭の全部又は一部を特定贈与財産としている場合には、次の事項について、「（受贈配偶者）」及び「（受贈財産の番号）」の欄に所定の記入をすることにより確認します。

（受贈配偶者）　　　　　　　　　　　　　　　　　（受贈財産の番号）

　私□□□については贈与税の課税価格に算入します。

　なお、私は、相続開始の年の前年以前に被相続人からの贈与について相続税法第21条の6第1項の規定の適用を受けていません。

（注）　④欄の金額を第1表のその人の「純資産価額に加算される暦年課税分の贈与財産価額⑤」欄及び第15表の㉗欄にそれぞれ転記します。

604   INHERITANCE TAX AND GIFT TAX

Valuation of Properties

¶ 7-550   Evaluation of assets

To ascertain the net taxable assets subject to inheritance tax for each heir or legatee, the taxpayer must evaluate each asset acquired from the decedent, including each asset deemed to have been acquired through inheritance, bequest or devise (¶ 7-270) other than assets exempt from inheritance tax (¶ 7-290). Details of the evaluation of assets are stipulated in the Inheritance and Gift Tax Act and in Evaluation Rulings issued by the National Tax Administration. Assets should be valued, in principle, at their fair market value at the time of the decedent's death, and the fair market value is as follows:

(1) **Land for residence**

(a) Land for residence in major cities.

The fair market value of land for the decedent's own use as an office or factory in major cities is evaluated on the basis of the road tax rating (AR 13). In this case, "land for residence" is not limited to land for residence; there is only one valuation category for land for residence. In summary, the computation is as follows:

$$\left(\begin{array}{l} \text{the amount of road-tax-} \\ \text{rating per 1 m}^2 \text{ of land space} \end{array} \right) \times \left(\begin{array}{l} \text{the number of m}^2 \text{ of land} \\ \text{space in each lot} \end{array} \right)$$

(b) Land for residence in other areas.

Land for residence in other areas is valued according to the rate provided by the National Tax Administration Bureau for the tax base of the fixed asset tax (see ¶ 2-360), the ratio varying for each area (AR 21, 21-2). Special treatments apply to small-scale land up to 330 or 400 square meters (see ¶ 7-300).

(2) **Agricultural land**

(a) Land used by the owner.

The value of agricultural land is calculated by multiplying the value of the land set forth for the purposes of fixed asset tax by a certain amount. If the fields can be used as a residential site, the value of land for residences in the neighboring area is considered to be the value (AR 37 to 40).

¶ 7-550

相続税及び贈与税　605

財産の評価

¶7-550　相続財産の評価

　各相続人及び受遺者の相続税の課税価額を決定するには，非課税財産（¶7-290）を除き，各人が被相続人から取得した個々の財産（みなし取得（¶7-270）を含む。）を評価しなければならない。

　財産評価の詳細は，相続税法及び評価通達に定められているが，原則として，財産評価は相続開始日の時価によるものとされている。各財産に係る時価を例示すれば，以下のとおりである。

(1)　**宅地**

　(a)　主要都市に所在する宅地

　　主要都市にある土地で被相続人が自宅，事務所，工場等の用地にしていたものは路線価方式により評価される（評基通13）。この場合，宅地とは自宅の居住用土地に限られず，土地の評価上の一区分にすぎない。

　　具体的には，その計算は次のとおり。

$$\begin{pmatrix} 1\,\text{㎡当たりの} \\ \text{路線価の価格} \end{pmatrix} \times \begin{pmatrix} 1\,\text{区画ごとの} \\ \text{地積である㎡数} \end{pmatrix}$$

　(b)　その他の地域にある宅地

　　その他の地域にある宅地は固定資産税（¶2-360参照）の評価額に国税局が定める一定の倍率を乗じて計算したものである（評基通21, 21-2）。

　　なお，330㎡又は400㎡までの小規模宅地については，特例がある（¶7-300参照）。

(2)　**田畑**

　(a)　自用地

　　固定資産税評価額に一定の倍率を乗じて計算する。ただし，宅地などに転用できる田畑については，付近の宅地の価額に比準して計算する（評基通37～40）。

606   INHERITANCE TAX AND GIFT TAX

   (b) Tenant rights (AR 42).

     Value of land × ratio of the value of tenant's rights to the value of the land.

   (c) Leased land (AR 41).

     Value of land – (Value of land × ratio of the value of tenant's rights to the value of the land).

(3) Forests

The value of forests is calculated by multiplying the value of the land set forth for the purposes of fixed asset tax by a certain amount. If the forest is located in a city area, the value of land for residence in a neighboring area is considered to be the value (AR 45).

(4) House for residence

   (a) The value of a house is calculated by multiplying the value of the house set forth for the purposes of property tax by a certain amount (at present 1.0) (AR 89).

   (b) Leased house (AR 93).

     Value of house – (Value of house × ratio of the value of tenant's rights to the value of the house).

(5) Leasehold and so on

Method of calculation:

   (a) Leasehold (AR 27)—

     value of land × ratio of leasehold to land value*

      *This ratio is provided by the National Tax Bureau. Evaluation of leasehold is effective within the area where leasehold is transacted as a custom.

   (b) Leased residential site (AR 25)—

     value of land – value of leasehold

   (c) Residential lot with rental house (AR 26)—

     value of land – (value of land × ratio of leasehold value to land value* × ratio of the value of tenant rights to the value of the house)

      *If there is no custom to transact leasehold, this ratio is deemed to 20%.

   (d) Tenant rights (AR 94)—

     (value of house × ratio of the value of tenant rights to the value of the house*)

      *This ratio is provided by the National Tax Bureau. Evaluation of tenant rights is effective within the area where tenant rights are transacted as premium money.

¶ 7-550

相続税及び贈与税　607

(b)　賃借権（耕作権）（評基通42）
　　　自用地の価額×賃借権（耕作権）の割合

(c)　貸付地（評基通40）
　　　自用地の価額－（自用地の価額×賃借権割合）

(3)　山林

固定資産税評価額に一定の倍率を乗じて計算する。ただし，市街地にある山林については，付近の宅地の価額に比準して計算する（評基通45）。

(4)　家屋

(a)　家屋の価額は，1棟の家屋ごとに，その家屋の固定資産税評価額に一定の倍率（現行は1.0）を乗じて計算した金額によって評価する（評基通89）。
(b)　貸家（評基通93）
　　　自用地の価額－（自用家屋の価額×借家権割合）

(5)　土地の上に存する権利等

計算方法：
(a)　借地権（評基通27）
　　　借地権の目的となっている宅地の自用地価額×借地権割合 (注)
(注)：借地権割合は国税局長が定める。借地権の取引慣行のある地域に限り借地権の価額を評価する。
(b)　貸宅地（評基通25）
　　　自用地価額－借地権の価額
(c)　貸家建付地（評基通26）
　　　自用地価額－（自用地価額×借地権割合 (注) ×借家権割合）
(注)：借地権の取引慣行のない地域にある宅地については，この割合を20／100とする。

(d)　借家権（評基通94）
　　　家屋の価額×借家権割合 (注)
(注)：借家権割合は国税局長が定める。権利金等の名称で借家権の取引慣行のある地域に限り借家権の価額を評価する。

608   INHERITANCE TAX AND GIFT TAX

(6) **Stock**

The value of stock is calculated for each description of stock as follows.

(a) Listed stock (AR 169)—

The value is the lowest of the following:

(i) the last price of the stock at the market session on the date of the decedent's death; or

(ii) the lowest of the monthly average price of the stock during the preceding three months including the date of the decedent's death.

(b) Semi-public stock (AR 174)—

The average of the comparative value of a similar company and the value published by a daily newspaper on the date of the decedent's death.

(c) Unlisted stock

The unlisted stock is valued using Basic Method where the beneficiary belongs to family shareholder group in the family corporation, or Dividend Return Method in cases other than above.

① Basic Method (AR 178 to 186-3)

Basic Method classifies large company, medium company and small company based on the table below.

(i) Classification of company

Company class	Description of classification		Net asset per book (number of employees)	Annual turnover
Large Company	The number of employees is 70 or over and meets one of the category prescribed right	Wholesales	¥2 billion or more (except company with employees of 35 or less)	¥3 billion or more
		Retail/ Service	¥1.5 billion or more (except company with employees of 35 or less)	¥2 billion or more
		Other businesses	¥1.5 billion or more (except company with employees of 35 or less)	¥1.5 billion or more
Medium Company	The number of employees is less than 70 (except Large Company)	Wholesales	¥70 million or more (except company with employees of 5 or less)	¥200 million or more but less than ¥3 billion
		Retail/ Service	¥40 million or more (except company with employees of 5 or less)	¥60 million or more but less than ¥2 billion
		Other businesses	¥50 million or more (except company with employees of 5 or less)	¥80 million or more but less than ¥1.5 billion

¶ 7-550

相続税及び贈与税　609

(6)　**株式**

株式の価額は，その銘柄の異なるごとに，次に掲げる区分に従い，その1株ごとに評価する。

(a)　上場株式（評基通169）

その株式が上場されている証券取引所の公表する課税時期の最終価格又は課税時期の属する月以前3カ月間の毎日の最終価格の各月ごとの平均額のうち最も低い方の価額

(b)　気配相場のある株式（評基通174）

日刊新聞に掲載されている課税時期の価格と類似業種比準価額によって計算した価額との平均額

(c)　取引相場のない株式

取引相場のない株式の評価額を算定するには，相続又は贈与で株式を取得した株主が当該株式の発行会社の同族会社は原則的評価方式で，それ以外の株主は配当還元方式により評価する。

①　原則的評価方式（評基通178～186-3）

原則的評価方式は，評価する株式を発行する会社の規模により大会社，中会社，小会社に区分され，それぞれの方式で評価する。

(ⅰ)　会社の区分

区分	区分の内容		簿価総資産価額及び従業員数	年取引金額
大会社	従業員数が70人以上で右のいずれかに該当する会社	卸売業	20億円以上（従業員数が35人以下の会社を除く。）	30億円以上
		小売・サービス業	15億円以上（従業員数が35人以下の会社を除く。）	20億円以上
		卸売業，小売・サービス業以外	15億円以上（従業員数が35人以下の会社を除く。）	15億円以上
中会社	従業員数が70人未満で右のいずれかに該当する会社（大会社に該当する場合を除く。）	卸売業	7,000万円以上（従業員数が5人以下の会社を除く。）	2億円以上30億円未満
		小売・サービス業	4,000万円以上（従業員数が5人以下の会社を除く。）	6,000万円以上20億円未満
		卸売業，小売・サービス業以外	5,000万円以上（従業員数が5人以下の会社を除く。）	8,000万円以上15億円未満

610   INHERITANCE TAX AND GIFT TAX

Small Company	The number of employees is less than 70	Wholesales	Less than ¥70 million or number of employees 5 or less	Less than ¥200 million
		Retail/ Service	Less than ¥40 million or number of employees 5 or less	Less than ¥60 million
		Other businesses	Less than ¥50 million or number of employees 5 or less	Less than ¥80 million

(ii) Valuation

Valuation of unlisted stocks under Basic Method is either Comparable Similar Business Model which compares with market price of listed stock in the similar business using 3 factors such as amount of dividend, profit and net book value, or Net Asset Value Model which evaluates property for inheritance tax purpose by subtracting liabilities and constructive corporation tax relating to corporation taxes.

Large Company stock is valued by the Comparable Similar Business Model or Net Asset Value Model, whichever is smaller.

Medium Company stock is valued by the combination of Comparable Similar Business Model and Net Asset Value Model.

Small Company stock is valued by the combination of Comparable Similar Business Model and Net Asset Value Model or Net Asset Value Model, whichever is smaller.

[Calculation of Comparable Similar Business Model]

$$A \times \left[\frac{\frac{b}{B} + \frac{c}{C} + \frac{d}{D}}{3} \right] \times \boxed{\text{ratio}} \times \frac{e}{¥50}$$

Where

[A]=Price of listed stock in similar business

[b]=Dividend per share of the Company

[c]=Profit per share of the Company

[d]=Net book value per share of the Company

[e]=Statutory capital per share in the Company

[B]=Dividend per share in similar business

[C]=Profit per share in similar business

[D]=Net book value per share in similar business

ratio=0.7 (Large Company), 0.6 (Medium Company), 0.5 (Small Company)

¶ 7-550

小会社	従業員数が70人未満で右のいずれにも該当する会社	卸売業	7,000万円未満又は従業員数が5人以下	2億円未満
		小売・サービス業	4,000万円未満又は従業員数が5人以下	6,000万円未満
		卸売業，小売・サービス業以外	5,000万円未満又は従業員数が5人以下	8,000万円未満

(ii) 評価方式

　　取引相場のない株式は，上場している類似業種の株式を基に，評価する会社の1株当たりの配当金額，利益金額及び簿価純資産価額の三つを比準する類似業種比準方式と，会社の財産を相続税評価額で評価し，その評価した資産から負債や評価差額に対する法人税額相当額を控除する純資産価額方式により評価する。

　　大会社は類似業種比準方式と純資産価額方式により計算したいずれか低い金額により評価する。

　　中会社は類似業種比準方式と純資産価額方式の評価方法を併用して評価する。

　　小会社は純資産価額方式と類似業種比準方式及び純資産価額方式の評価方法を併用して計算した金額のいずれか低い金額により評価する。

　　【類似業種比準価額方式　計算式】

$$A \times \left[\frac{\dfrac{b}{B} + \dfrac{c}{C} + \dfrac{d}{D}}{3} \right] \times \boxed{斟酌率} \times \frac{e}{50円}$$

　　上記算式中の「A」，「b」，「c」，「d」，「e」，「B」，「C」，「D」及び斟酌率は，それぞれ次による。

　　「A」＝類似業種の株価

　　「b」＝1株当たり評価会社の配当金額

　　「c」＝1株当たり評価会社の利益金額

　　「d」＝1株当たり評価会社の純資産価額

　　「e」＝1株当たり評価会社の資本金等の額

　　「B」＝1株当たり類似業種の配当金額

　　「C」＝1株当たり類似業種の利益金額

　　「D」＝1株当たり類似業種の簿価純資産価額

　　斟酌率＝大会社0.7，中会社0.6，小会社0.5

612 INHERITANCE TAX AND GIFT TAX

② Dividend return method (AR 188-2)

The stock which was obtained by someone who is not a family shareholder is evaluated by a special method regardless of the size of the company. The dividend return method is a method used to evaluate the value of the shares with the dividend amount of one year received by owning the stocks. A principal was reduced at a fixed interest rate (10%).

(7) **Investments**

(a) A partnership, a limited partnership or a limited liability company is valued in the manner prescribed in (6) (c) above (AR 194).

(b) A medical care corporation is valued in the manner prescribed in (6) (c) above and the computation outlined in (6) (c) (i) is modified as follows (AR 194-2):

$$A \times \frac{\dfrac{C'}{C} + \dfrac{D'}{D}}{2} \times 0.7^*$$

* In case of medium or small corporation, 0.6 or 0.5 respectively.

(8) **Bonds**

(a) Interest-bearing bonds are valued by adding the accrued interest for the term to the issued par value, and deducting the withholding tax payable on the interest. If the issued par value exceeds the indicator price or the fair market price, that price is adopted instead of the issued par value (AR 197-2).

(b) Discount bonds are valued by adding the accrued profits for the term to the issued par value. If this value exceeds the indicator price or fair market price that price is taken as the value (AR 197-3).

(c) Convertible bonds are valued in the same manner as interest-bearing bonds. If the stock price exceeds the converted price, the stock price is adopted (AR 197-5).

(9) **Evaluation of a beneficiary certificate of loan trust** is made by adding accrued profits to the principal and deducting the withholding tax and charges on the investment (AR 198).

(10) **Beneficiary certificates of securities investments** are trusts valued at the standard price appearing in the daily press (AR 199).

(11) **Deposits** are valued by adding the accrued interest to the principal, and deducting the withholding tax on the investment. Accrued inter-

¶ 7-550

相続税及び贈与税　613

② 配当還元方式（評基通188-2）

同族株主以外の株主が取得した株式については，その株式の発行会社の規模にかかわらず，特例的な評価方式の配当還元方式で評価する。配当還元方式は，その株式を所有することによって受け取れる1年間の配当金額を，一定の利率（10％）で還元して元本である株式の価額を評価する方式である。

(7) **出資**

(a) 合名会社，合資会社又は有限会社に対する出資の価額は，(6)(c)に準じて評価する（評基通194）。

(b) 医療法人の出資の価額は，(6)(c)に準じて評価するが，(6)(c)(i)の計算式は，次の算式とされる（評基通194-2）。

$$A \times \frac{\dfrac{C'}{C} + \dfrac{D'}{D}}{2} \times 0.7^{(注)}$$

（注）中会社又は小会社の場合にはそれぞれ0.6又は0.5。

(8) **公社債**

(a) 利付債については，発行価額に利払期未到来分の源泉所得税相当額控除後の既経過利息を加えた額により評価する。

ただし，発行価額が取引価格，気配の金額を超えるときは，発行価額に代えて取引価格又は気配の金額を用いる（評基通197-2）。

(b) 割引債については，発行価額に既経過償還差益を加えた額により評価する。

ただし，その価額が取引価格，気配の金額を超えるときは，取引価格，気配の金額とする（評基通197-3）。

(c) 転換社債については，利付債の方法により評価する。ただし，株式の価額が転換価格を超えるときは株式の価額に比準して評価する（評基通197-5）。

(9) **貸付信託受益証券**については，元本の額に既経過収益の額を加え，源泉税相当額と買取手数料を控除した額により評価する（評基通198）。

(10) **証券投資信託受益証券**については，日刊新聞に掲載された基準価額による（評基通199）。

(11) **預貯金**は預入残高に既経過利子を加え源泉税相当額を控除した額により評価する。この場合既経過利子は，課税時期現在で解約するとした場合の

614   INHERITANCE TAX AND GIFT TAX

est is computed at the time of the inheritance as if the investment was cancelled (AR 203).

(12) **Loans, credit sales and advance payments**, etc. are valued as the total of principals and accrued interest (AR 204).

(13) **Bills receivable** are valued as follows (AR 206):

   (a) A bill which has matured or will mature within 6 months of the inheritance, is valued at its par value.

   (b) In all other cases, the value is the redeemed amount, if the bill was discounted at the time of the inheritance.

(14) **Household furnishings** are valued as if they were bought under existing conditions (AR 129).

(15) **Arts and curios** are valued by reference to similar sales or on the advice of specialists (AR 135).

(16) **Automobiles** are valued in the manner prescribed in (14) above (AR 129).

(17) **Telephone subscription rights** are valued at their fair market price or the standard price at the time of the inheritance (AR 161).

(18) **Golf club memberships** are valued as follows (National Tax Agency Direct Tax Department Property Tax Division Notification 3-3, 1973):

   (a) Membership by a shareholding

      (i)   A membership right with quotation is valued at 70% of the fair market price.

      (ii) A membership right without quotation is valued in the same manner as stock.

   (b) Membership by a shareholding and payment of an entrance fee.

      (i)   A membership right with quotation is valued at 70% of fair market price after deducting the entrance fee. In this case the entrance fee is computed as a redeemable amount if this is possible at the time of the inheritance. If the entrance fee is to be refunded after the inheritance, the computation for the entrance fee is discounted at standard compound interest per year for the period from the time of the inheritance to the refund.

      (ii) A membership right without quotation is divided into the share portion and the entrance fee portion for valuation purposes. The share portion is valued in the same manner as stock. The entrance fee portion is valued in the same manner

¶ 7-550

相続税及び贈与税　615

利率により計算した金額とする（評基通203）。

⑿　**貸付金，売掛金，仮払金等の貸付金債権**は，元本と既経過利息の合計額により評価する（評基通204）。

⒀　**受取手形**は次の価額により評価する（評基通206）。
　(a)　支払期限が到来したもの，又は課税時期から6カ月内に到来するもの：券面額
　(b)　(a)以外のもの：課税時期において割引したとき回収できる金額

⒁　**家庭用財産**は，その財産をその状態で買うとした場合の価額による（評基通129）。

⒂　**書画・骨とう等**は，類似品の売買実例価額や専門家の意見などを参考として評価する（評基通135）。

⒃　**自動車**は，⒁と同様に評価する（評基通129）。

⒄　**電話加入権**は，相続開始の日の取引価額又は標準価額による（評基通161）。

⒅　**ゴルフ会員権**は，会員権の態様に応じ，次のように評価する（昭48直資3-3）。
　(a)　株主でなければ会員となれない会員権
　　(ⅰ)　取引相場のあるものは，課税時期の通常の取引価格の70％に相当する金額により評価する。
　　(ⅱ)　取引相場のないものは，株式の評価方法によって評価する。

　(b)　株主であり，かつ，入会金等を支払わなければ会員となれない会員権
　　(ⅰ)　取引相場のあるものは，株式の価額については，課税時期における通常の取引価額から入会金等を控除した金額の70％相当額により評価する。課税時期において直ちに返還を受けられる入会金等については，返還を受けられる金額により評価する。また，課税時期から一定の期間経過後に返還を受けられる入会金等については，返還を受けられる金額を，その課税時期から返還を受ける日までの期間に応ずる基準年利率による複利現価の額によって評価する。

　　(ⅱ)　取引相場のないものの場合には，株式の価額は株式の評価方法に従い，入会金等については，(ⅰ)により評価する。

616   INHERITANCE TAX AND GIFT TAX

as the valuation of the entrance fee in (i) above.

(19) **Goodwill** is valued as the smaller of the following (AR 165, 166).

   (a)   The amount of surplus profitability for a period (usually 10 years) discounted at standard compound interest per year for the term.
   (b)   The amount of net income of the previous year. If the business is well known, the value is triple the amount of net income.

(20) **The right to receive an annuity or similar payments** shall be valuated as below, depending upon either an event set against such payment has taken place or not.

   (a)   An annuity or similar payments right's valuation amount shall be the largest of either one of below if an event set against such payment has taken place (Law 24).
       (i)   Amount equivalent to cancellation refund
       (ii)   If able to receive lump-sum payment instead of fixed annuity, amount equivalent to such lump-sum payment
       (iii)   Amount calculated based on guaranteed yields
   (b)   An annuity or similar payments right's valuation amount shall be the amount equivalent to refund if an event set against such payment has not taken place (Law 25).

Return and Payment

¶ 7-600 Return

An inheritance tax return should be filed by any taxpayer described in ¶ 7-105. When the total net taxable assets as stated in ¶ 7-340 exceed the total basic estate allowance, this balance is the taxpayer's tax obligation after deducting tax credits (not including the credit for a spouse). The return should be filed with the tax office in the district that had jurisdiction over the residence of the decedent at the time of death. It should be filed within ten months after the taxpayer learns of the death (Law 27, revised by Law No. 16, March 31, 1992, applicable to inheritances on and after January 1, 1996).

If a taxpayer proposes to leave Japan, without retaining domicile or residence in Japan, within that six-month period, that taxpayer must file a return before leaving the country.

¶ 7-600

相続税及び贈与税　617

⒆　**営業権**は，次の(a)及び(b)のうちいずれか低い金額により評価する（評基通165，166）。

　(a)　超過利益金額の営業権の持続年数（原則として，10年）に応ずる基準年利率による複利現価の額

　(b)　前年の所得の金額（著名なものはその3倍）

⒇　**定期金に関する権利**は，給付事由が発生しているか否かで，次のように評価する。

　(a)　給付事由が発生している定期金に関する権利の評価額は，次のいずれか多い金額とする（相法24）。

　　(ⅰ)　解約返戻金相当額

　　(ⅱ)　定期金に代えて一時金の給付を受けることができる場合には，当該一時金相当額

　　(ⅲ)　予定利率等を基に算出した金額

　(b)　給付事由が発生していない定期金に関する権利の評価額は，原則として返戻金相当額とする（相法25）。

申告及び納付

¶7-600　申告

　¶7-105に該当する納税者で，¶7-340の課税価格の合計額が遺産に係る基礎控除額を超えており，配偶者に対する税額軽減以外の諸税額控除後の納付すべき相続税額のある者は，相続のあったことを知った日の翌日から10カ月以内に，相続税の申告書を被相続人の納税地を所轄する税務署に提出すべきことになっている（相法27，平成4年3月31日法律第16号改正，平成8年1月1日以後の相続に適用）。

　納税者がその期間内に住所又は居所を有しなくなるときは，出国するときまでに申告書を提出しなければならない。

618   INHERITANCE TAX AND GIFT TAX

¶ 7-620 Payment

A taxpayer should fully pay his or her inheritance tax within the time limits mentioned in ¶ 7-600 above, unless he or she leaves Japan within that period. All heirs and legatees are jointly and severally responsible for paying the tax, although their responsibility is limited to the value of the net assets they individually acquired from the decedent.

However, the joint and several obligations shall not apply (Law 34), where:

(1) Five years have passed since the filing deadline of the inheritance tax.

(2) The taxpayer is allowed for a postponement of the tax payment.

(3) The taxpayer is applied to a tax payment grace.

If there are any reasons that a taxpayer is unable to pay the tax in a lump-sum, it is permissible for the taxpayer to make installment payments (subject to the payment of interest for deferred payment). The following table shows the conditions that apply, e.g. the provision of collateral.

percentage of deferrable immovable properties	applicable tax	deferrable	interest	special rate (d)
75% or more	Inheritance tax for the portion of immovable properties	20 years (a)	3.6% per year	0.8%
	Inheritance tax for the portion of other than immovable properties	10 years	5.4% per year	1.3%
50% or more, and less than 75%	Inheritance tax for the portion of immovable properties	15 years (b)	3.6% per year	0.8%
	Inheritance tax for the portion of other than immovable properties	10 years	5.4% per year	1.3%
less than 50%	Inheritance tax for the portion of other than immovable properties	5 years (c)	6.0% per year	1.4%

(a) If the permitted deferrable tax is less than ¥2,000,000, the deferrable term will not exceed the number of years calculated by the following formula (SM 70-9①):

permitted deferrable tax /¥100,000 = deferrable years

(b) If the deferrable tax is less than ¥1,500,000, the deferrable term will not exceed the number of years calculated by the following formula (Law 38 ①, ②):

deferrable tax / ¥100,000 = deferrable years

(c) If the deferrable tax is less than ¥500,000, the deferrable term will not exceed the number of years calculated by the following formula (Law 38 ①, ②):

deferrable tax / ¥100,000 = deferrable years

If the tax is less than ¥50,000 and the period of installment payment is not longer than 3 years, collateral will not be required (Law 38④).

(d) Special rate applied as of January 1, 2016.

¶ 7-620

相続税及び贈与税　619

¶7-620　納付

　納税者は出国する場合を除き，申告期限（¶7-600）以内に相続税を全額納付しなければならない。各相続人，受遺者は，自己が被相続人から当該相続，遺贈により受けた利益を限度として，相続税の全額につき連帯して納付する責任を負う。

　ただし，次の場合には相続税の連帯納付義務が解除される（相法34）。

(1)　申告期限から5年を経過した場合

(2)　納税義務者が延納の許可を受けた場合

(3)　納税義務者が納税猶予の適用を受けた場合

　金銭による一括納付ができない事由がある場合には，担保を提供する等一定の要件により，以下のとおり延納が認められる。

区　　分		延納期間（最長）	利子税	特例割合(d)
不動産等の価額が75％以上の場合	不動産等の価額に対応する税額	20年(a)	年3.6％	0.8％
	その他の財産の価額に対応する税額	10年	年5.4％	1.3％
不動産等の価額が50％以上75％未満の場合	不動産等の価額に対応する税額	15年(b)	年3.6％	0.8％
	その他の財産の価額に対応する税額	10年	年5.4％	1.3％
不動産等の価額が50％未満の場合	その他の財産の価額に対応する税額	5年(c)	年6.0％	1.4％

(a)　支払期限が到来したもの，又は課税時期から6カ月内に到来するもの：券面額

　　延納許可税額が200万円未満であるときには，次により計算される年数が限度とされる（措法70の9①）。

　　延納許可税額／￥100,000＝最長延納年数

(b)　延納税額が150万円未満であるときは，次により計算される年数が限度とされる（相法38①，②）。

　　延納税額／￥100,000＝最長延納年数

(c)　延納税額が50万円未満であるときは，次により計算される年数が限度とされる（相法38①，②）。

　　延納税額／￥100,000＝最長延納年数

　　なお，延納税額が50万円未満で，かつ，延納期間が3年以下である場合には，担保の提供を要しない（相法38④）。

(d)　特例割合は，平成28年1月1日現在の「延納特例基準割合」1.8％で計算している。

620   INHERITANCE TAX AND GIFT TAX

Inheritance tax on timber falling under an afforestation plan is treated in order to prolong the deferrable term of payments and to reduce the interest rate (SM 70-7①). The interest charged on deferred tax payable on land which is located in a woods preservation area is also treated in order that it may be reduced (SM 70-8①).

The taxpayer may elect to pay the tax in kind, such as in public bonds, real estate, debentures, shares, etc., rather than in cash, under certain conditions.

The value of assets for payment in kind is their taxable value. The value can be revised by the relevant tax office if the fair market value of the asset has significantly changed at the time of payment (Law 43①).

If the taxpayer inherits land for agriculture, etc., the tax can be deferred on certain conditions.

¶ 7-630 Correction, penalty taxes, tax disputes, etc.

See ¶ 5-740 for correction of returns, determination of tax liability, penalty taxes, delinquency taxes, tax disputes, etc., as these matters are the same for both assessment income tax and inheritance tax.

GIFT TAX

Taxpayer and Taxable Property

¶ 7-760 Taxpayer for gift tax liabilities

The taxpayer for the gift tax is the individual who acquires properties through gifts (not including devises or bequests) from another individual. If an individual acquires gifts from a corporation, this individual should pay individual income tax instead of gift tax on the acquisitions.

A gift is a contract that is concluded by declaration of a donor's intention to give property to another person without compensation and by the donee's acceptance (Civil Code 549).

A gift by a verbal contract with no written document can be withdrawn. However, the executed portion of a gift contract cannot be withdrawn (Civil Code 550).

A gift contract between a married couple can be withdrawn anytime during the marriage so long as the withdrawal does not infringe the right of a third party (Civil Code 754).

¶ 7-630

相続税及び贈与税　621

　計画伐採に係る森林計画立木部分の税額については延納期間の延長及び利子税の軽減等の措置がある（措法70の7①）。また，緑地保全地区等内の土地に係る税額の延納については利子税の軽減措置がある（措法70の8①）。

　また，納税者は，一定の要件の下に，金銭によらず，公債，不動産，社債及び株式等による物納を選択することができる。

　物納財産の収納価額は，課税価格計算の基礎となったその財産の価額による。ただし，収納のときまでにその財産の状況に著しい変化が生じた場合は，税務署長は収納のときの現況によって財産の収納価額を定めることができる（相法43①）。

　相続人が農地等を相続して農業を営む場合には，一定の要件の下に納税が猶予される。

¶7-630　更正等，加算税及び争訟

　これらについては，原則として，申告所得税における取扱いと同じであるので，¶5-740を参照されたい。

贈　与　税

納税者及び課税財産

¶7-760　納税者

　贈与（遺贈を除く。）により他の個人から財産を取得した個人が，贈与税の納税者である。個人が法人から贈与を受けた場合には，贈与税ではなく，所得税が課せられる。

　贈与とは，当事者の一方が，自己の財産を無償で相手方に与えるという意思を表示し，相手方がこれを承諾することによって成立する契約である（民法549）。

　書面によらない，単なる口頭の贈与は，当事者が取り消すことができる。ただし，既に履行が終わった部分については取り消すことができない（民法550）。

　夫婦間の契約は婚姻中いつでも夫婦の一方から取り消すことができる。ただし，第三者の権利を害することはできない（民法754）。

　人格のない社団等又は公益法人については，¶7-030に述べたと同じように，例外的に贈与税が課せられる場合がある。

622   INHERITANCE TAX AND GIFT TAX

In some cases, non-juridical corporations and public interest corporations are subject to gift tax (see ¶ 7-030).

¶ 7-761 Scope of tax liability

A done who received property as the following is liable to gift tax at the dime of the donation on or after April 1, 2018, if he or she (Law 1-4);

(1) has domicile in Japan either who
  (a) is not temporary resident, or
  (b) is temporary resident (except the donor is temporary resident or non-resident.)
(2) who has not domicile in Japan, where;
  (a) the donee has Japanese nationality, and the donor had domiciled in Japan anytime during ten years before the gift.
  (b) the donee has not Japanese nationality (except the donor is temporary resident or non-resident.).
(3) has domicile in Japan who received property situated in Japan (except (1) as above)
(4) has not domicile in Japan who received property situated in Japan (except (2) as above)
(5) has not Japanese nationality who received property situated in Japan from non-resident donor.
    However, where the long stay individual (who have had domicile in Japan for more than 10 years during the last 15 years without Japanese nationality) donates foreign property within 2 years from the departure from Japan, and he or she re-enters to have domicile in Japan again, such donation shall be liable to gift tax.

¶ 7-780 Taxable property

When a taxpayer of gift tax is domiciled in Japan at the time of the gift or has Japanese nationality (except for the case where both the person who acquires properties and the person who gifts them have never been domiciled in Japan within five years before the time of the gift), the entire property is subject to gift tax, wherever the property may be situated (unlimited taxpayers). Donee who has not Japanese nationality will be also unlimited taxpayer if the donor has a domicile in Japan at the time of the gift (Law 1-4(1), (2)). As for a taxpayer who does not fall in above-mentioned

¶ 7-761

相続税及び贈与税　623

¶7-761　納税義務の範囲

　平成30年4月1日以降に贈与で財産を取得した個人で，その財産を取得した時において次のいずれかに該当する者は，贈与税を納める義務がある（相法1の4一，二，三，四）。

(1)　日本に住所を有する者で，以下に該当する者
　(a)　一時居住者でない個人
　(b)　一時居住者である個人（贈与者が一時居住者又は非居住者である場合を除く。）

(2)　日本に住所を有せず，以下に該当する者
　(a)　日本国籍を有する者で，贈与者又は受遺者が贈与開始前10年以内のいずれかの時において日本国内に住所を有していたことがある場合
　(b)　日本国籍を有しない者（贈与者が一時居住又は非居住を除く。）

(3)　日本にある財産を贈与された個人で住所を有する者（(1)に掲げる者を除く。）

(4)　日本にある財産を贈与された個人で住所を有しない者（(2)に掲げる者を除く。）

(5)　日本国籍を有しない非居住者が，非居住贈与者より国内財産を取得した場合※
　※但し，日本に長期滞在した者（過去15年以内に10年超日本に住所が有り，継続して日本国籍無し）が，出国後2年以内の内に行う国外財産の贈与については，出国後2年以内に再び国内に住所を戻した場合には，その国外財産も贈与税の課税対象になる。

¶7-780　課税財産

　贈与税の納税義務者が，贈与を受けたときに国内に住所を有している場合又は日本国籍を有する場合（受贈者及び贈与者がともに贈与前5年以内に日本国内に住所を有したことがない場合を除く。）又は日本国籍を有していない場合（贈与者が贈与をした時に日本に住所を有していた場合に限る。）には，財産の所在地のいかんを問わず，全贈与財産につき納税義務を負う（相法1の4一，二）。上記の範疇に属さない納税義務者は，国内に所在する財産についてのみ納税義務を負う（相法1の4三）。財産の所在地については，¶7-120を参照されたい。

624   INHERITANCE TAX AND GIFT TAX

category, only the property which is situated in Japan is subject to gift tax (Law 1-4(3)) (see ¶ 7-120 for location of property).

Gifted properties acquired by an heir or a legatee within one year before the inheritance, are not levied with gift tax but with inheritance tax (Law 21-2④). If the heir or legatee does not acquire any property by the inheritance, gift tax is levied on the gifted property (R 21-2-3).

A distribution of property following a divorce, is not regarded as a gift. If the value of the distributed property is excessive or the distribution causes evasion of gift tax or inheritance tax, that property should be regarded as an acquisition by gift (R 9-8).

Tax Basis and Rates

¶ 7-840 Computation of gift tax

Gift tax is computed and levied annually. The tax is computed by the following steps:

(1)   Ascertain the total value of properties acquired by a taxpayer through gifts from other individuals in a calendar year (¶ 7-850, ¶ 7-860). Valuation of property is covered by the same principles as stated in ¶ 7-550.

Land and houses, etc. that are acquired as gifts with compensation, or through an onerous transaction between individuals, are valued at their fair market price. If the original acquisition price of land or a newly-built house of the donor or the assignor is acceptable as the fair market price at the time of the gift, such original acquisition price is adopted as the value (National Tax Agency Direct Tax Department Property Tax Division Evaluating Notification 5, March 29, 1989, and National Tax Agency Direct Tax Department Property Tax Division Notification 2-204).

(2)   Deduct the basic allowance for gift tax and the spouse allowance for gift tax from the annual taxable value ascertained in Step (1) mentioned above.

(a)   The basic allowance for gift tax is ¥1,100,000 (SM 70-2-3).

(b)   The spouse allowance for gift tax is the value of a residential house acquired by gift from a taxpayer's spouse or the money acquired similarly for purchasing such a house. This allowance

¶ 7-840

相続開始の年に被相続人からの贈与により取得した財産の価額は，相続税が課税されるから，贈与税の対象とならない（相法21の2④）。しかし，その被相続人から相続又は遺贈により，財産を取得しなかった場合は，贈与により取得した財産について贈与税が課税される（相基通21の2-3）。離婚等に伴う財産の分与による財産の取得は贈与とされないが，その分与額が過当と認められる場合又は贈与税，相続税のほ脱を図ると認められる場合は贈与により取得した財産となる（相基通9-8）。

課税標準及び税率

¶7-840　贈与税の計算

贈与税は暦年ごとに計算して申告する。納付税額の計算は以下のとおりである。

(1)　一暦年に納税義務者が他の個人から贈与により取得した財産の価額の合計額を計算する（¶7-850，¶7-860）。財産の評価については，¶7-550に述べたと同じ原則が適用される。

なお，土地等及び家屋等のうち，負担付贈与又は個人間の対価を伴う取引により取得したものの価額は，その取得時における通常の取引価額によって評価する。ただし，贈与者又は譲渡者が取得又は新築した土地等又は家屋等の取得価額が課税時期における通常の取引価額に相当すると認められる場合には，取得価額に相当する金額によって評価する（平成元年3月29日直評5，直資2-204）。

(2)　贈与税の基礎控除額及び配偶者控除額を，上記の課税価額から控除する。

(a)　贈与税の基礎控除額は，60万円である（相法21の5）が，平成13年1月1日以後に贈与により取得した場合には特例により，取得価格から110万円を控除する（措法70の2の3）。

(b)　贈与税の配偶者控除は，以下(i)(ii)を条件として，配偶者が贈与により居住用不動産を取得した場合又は居住用不動産を購入するための金銭を取得した場合に認められる。

626   INHERITANCE TAX AND GIFT TAX

is applicable under the following conditions:

(i)   The residential house should have been used as a dwelling by the spouse, and should be expected to be used continuously as a dwelling.

(ii) It is deductible only once in a taxpayer's life as a spouse of a donor with a maximum of ¥20,000,000.

Moreover, the allowance is deductible only if a taxpayer has held the status of spouse to the donor for twenty years or longer (Law 21-6).

(3) Apply the tax rate to the amount resulting from Step (2) (Law 21-7) (¶ 7-880).

(4) Deduct any credit for foreign taxes from the tax resulting from Step (3) (Law 21-8) (¶ 7-890).

¶ 7-850 Benefits treated as gifts

If the following cases, each person is deemed to acquire property as a gift.

(1) Mr. A is deemed to acquire property from Mr. B through a gift (Law 4 to 9).

(a) When Mr. A receives compensation or other payments from a life insurance contract, the premiums for which Mr. B paid in the past.

(b) When Mr. A receives annuities or other payment from an annuity contract which was wholly or partially bought by Mr. B.

(c) When Mr. A buys property from Mr. B at an unreasonably low price.

The background of the transaction and the relationship of the persons concerned, etc. will be taken into consideration when assessing the reasonableness of the price. Then, it can be determined whether the transaction can be deemed a gift or not. If the compensation for the transfer of a land or a house is less than the fair market price, the compensation is regarded as an unreasonably low price, so long as the market price is not falling (National Tax Agency Direct Tax Department Property Tax Division Evaluating. Notification 5, March 29, 1989, and National Tax Agency Direct Tax Department Property Tax Division Notification 2-204).

¶ 7-850

(i)　居住用不動産にあっては，その者の居住の用に供し，かつ，その後
　　　引き続き居住の用に供する見込みであること

　(ii)　金銭にあっては，その金銭をもって居住用不動産を取得してこれを
　　　その者の居住の用に供し，かつ，その後引き続き居住の用に供する見
　　　込みであること
　　　　配偶者控除は，2,000万円を限度として，同一の配偶者からは生涯に
　　　一度認められるものである。また，この控除は，贈与者と20年以上の
　　　婚姻関係のある配偶者についてのみ認められる（相法21の6）。
(3)　上記諸控除後の金額を課税標準として，税率（¶7-880）を適用する
　　（相法21の7）。
(4)　上記税額から，外国税額控除（¶7-890）を行う（相法21の8）。

¶7-850　みなし贈与
　以下の場合には各人が贈与により財産を取得したものとみなされる。

(1)　個人Aは個人Bから贈与によって財産を取得したものとみなされる（相
　　法4～9）。
　(a)　Bが保険料を支払った生命保険契約によりAが保険金を取得した場合

　(b)　Bが掛金を支払った定期金給付契約によりAが定期金を取得した場合

　(c)　AがBから著しく低い価額で財産の譲渡を受けた場合
　　　　著しく低い価額かどうかは，個々の取引について取引の事情，取引当
　　　事者間の関係等を総合勘案し，実質的に贈与を受けたと認められる金額
　　　があるかどうかにより判定するが，土地又は家屋の取引においては，そ
　　　の取引における対価の額がその取引に係る土地又は家屋の取得価額を下
　　　回る場合には，その土地又は家屋の価額が下落したことなど合理的な理
　　　由があると認められるときを除き，著しく低い価額に当たるものとされ
　　　る（平成元年3月29日直評5，直資2-204）。

628   INHERITANCE TAX AND GIFT TAX

(d)   When Mr. A is discharged from a debt to Mr. B without reasonable repayment, or is discharged from a debt to a third person by Mr. B's action, unless Mr. A is in financial difficulties.

(e)   When Mr. A receives any other kind of benefit through the sacrifice of Mr. B (Law 9, R 9-2 to 9-4).

Examples:

(i)   Warrants for new stock are underwritten by a child nominally.

(ii)   A parent and a child set up a family corporation. Whereas the child makes investment in money, the parent makes investment with extremely under-estimated non-cash assets that resultingly means transfer of latent property to the child.

(iii)   A transfer of the ownership of fixed property or stock, etc. without compensation, or the acquisition of fixed property or stock, etc. under the name of another person (R 9-9). If these transactions are executed for an obvious reason without the intention of making a gift, or executed by mistake or oversight, these transactions are not treated as gifts so long as ownership is restored to the original owner before the due date of gift tax (National Tax Agency Direct Tax Department Inquiry Division Notification 22, 1964).

(f)   When Mr. B makes a contribution to a public interest corporation from which Mr. A is in a position to enjoy a special benefit, unless the corporation itself pays gift tax as mentioned in ¶ 7-030.

¶ 7-851   Gifts of Trust Interests

(1)   Persons who become beneficiaries, etc. of a trust without paying fair consideration shall be deemed to have acquired an interest in the trust by gift in the following instances:

(a)   If the trust is to take effect and said person is to become a beneficiary, etc. (Law 9-2①).

(b)   If a person becomes a new beneficiary, etc. of a trust with existing beneficiaries, etc. (Law 9-2②).

(c)   If an existing beneficiary, etc. of the trust receives an additional interest in the trust pursuant to the absence of one or more persons who were formerly beneficiaries, etc. of said trust (Law 9-2③).

¶ 7-851

相続税及び贈与税　629

(d)　AがBに対する債務の免除を受け，又は第三者に対する債務について
Bによる債務引受・第三者弁済により債務を免れた場合。ただし，Aが
資力を喪失している場合を除く。

(e)　AがBからその他の経済的利益を受けた場合（相法9，相基通9-2，9
-3，9-4）
例えば次のものがある。

(i)　新株の引受権を子供名義で引き受けさせる場合

(ii)　親と子で同族会社を設立し，親が財産を非常に低く評価して現物出
資し，子は現金出資する方法で，結果的に会社の含み資産を子供に贈
与する場合

(iii)　不動産，株式等の名義変更があった場合において対価の授受が行わ
れていないとき，及び，他の者の名義で新たに不動産，株式等を取得
したとき（相基通9-9）。この場合において，その取得が贈与の意思
に基づくものでなく，他のやむを得ない一定の理由に基づいて行われ
た場合又は過誤等に基づき，又は軽率にされた場合には，原則として
贈与税の申告又は更正決定前に名義を改めたときに限り，贈与がなか
ったものとして取り扱われる（昭和39年5月23日直審22通達）。

(f)　Bが公益法人等に対して財産を贈与し，当該公益法人等からAがこれ
に特別の利益を受ける場合。ただし，当該公益法人等が自ら贈与税を納
付すべき場合（¶7-030）を除く。

¶7-851　信託に関する権利の贈与

(1)　適正な対価を負担せず，信託の受益者等となる者は，以下の信託につい
ては，信託に関する権利を贈与により取得したとみなされる。

(a)　信託の効力が生じ，信託の受託者等となる場合（相法9の2①）

(b)　受益者等の存する信託で，新たに受益者等となる場合（相法9の2②）

(c)　受益者等の存する信託で，一部の受益者等が不在になった時，既存の
受益者等が新たに利益を受ける場合（相法9の2③）

630   INHERITANCE TAX AND GIFT TAX

(d) If a distribution of remaining assets is received upon termination of the trust (Law 9-2④).

(2) In the case of a successive beneficiary trust, etc., a beneficiary that acquires an interest in the trust without paying fair consideration shall be deemed to have acquired said interest in said trust by gift. In the event that restrictions are imposed with respect to benefits under said trust, said restrictions shall be deemed not to exist (Law 9-3①).

(3) In the case of a trust that has no beneficiaries, etc., if the trust comes into effect and a relative of the trustor becomes a beneficiary, etc. or a relative of the trustor receives a distribution of remaining assets upon the termination of said trust, the trustee shall be deemed to have acquired an interest in the trust from the trustor by gift (Law 9-4①).

(4) If all of the beneficiaries, etc. of a trust not to exist and a relative of the trustor or a decedent beneficiary becomes a beneficiary, etc., the trustee of said trust shall be deemed to have acquired the interest in the trust from the decedent beneficiary by gift (Law 9-4②).

(5) In the case of a trust has no beneficiaries, etc., if a relative of the trustor becomes a beneficiary after the trust is formed said trust, the beneficiary shall be deemed to have acquired an interest in the trust by gift (Law 9-5).

(6) In cases (3) and (4) above, the amount of corporate income taxes assessed against said trustee shall be deducted against the amount of the inheritance taxes imposed upon said trustee (Law 9-4④).

¶ 7-860 Exempt gifts

Gift tax is not levied on the following items (Law 21-3):

(1) Gifts from a corporation (income tax and inhabitant tax are levied on these gifts as a kind of income).

(2) Gifts between persons who have a legal responsibility to support each other, unless the gift is made for a purpose other than support or livelihood.

(3) Donations to a person carrying on activities for religious, charitable, scientific, educational, or social welfare purposes.

(4) Gifts of money or goods that are designated by the Minister of Finance as a prize for notable contributions to art and science or subsidies for specially valuable study of art and science from a public trustee designated by the Minister of Finance, and subsidies from specific

¶ 7-860

相続税及び贈与税　631

(d)　受益者等の存する信託が終了し，信託の残余財産の給付を受ける場合（相法9の2④）

(2)　受益者連続型信託等において，信託に関する権利を適正な対価を負担せずに取得した受益者は，信託に関する権利を贈与により取得したものとみなされる。なお，信託の受益に関する制約が付されているものについては，この制約は付されていないものとみなされる（相法9の3①）。

(3)　受益者等が存しない信託の効力が生ずる場合において，委託者の親族が受益者等になる時，又は信託終了時に委託者の親族が残余財産を給付される場合は，受託者等は委託者より信託に関する権利を贈与により取得したものとみなされる（相法9の4①）。

(4)　受益者等が存する信託において受益者等が不在になった場合に，委託者又は前受益者の親族が受益者等になる時，その信託の受託者は前受益者より信託に関する権利を贈与により取得したものとみなされる（相法9の4②）。

(5)　受益者等が存しない信託等において，信託契約時に存しない者が受益者等となる場合で，受益者等が委託者の親族である時は，その受益者は信託に関する権利を個人から贈与により取得したものとみなされる（相法9の5）。

(6)　上記(3)，(4)において，受託者が課される贈与税額については，その受託者に課された法人税額を控除する（相法9の4④）。

¶7-860　贈与税の非課税財産
次の財産には贈与税は課せられない（相法21の3）。

(1)　法人から贈与により取得した財産（ただし，所得税・住民税が課せられる。）

(2)　扶養義務者から贈与により取得した財産で，生活費等に充てられるもの

(3)　宗教・慈善・学術その他公益を目的とする事業を行う者が贈与により取得した財産

(4)　学術に関する顕著な貢献を表彰するものとして又は顕著な価値がある学術に関する研究を奨励するものとして財務大臣の指定する特定の公益信託から交付された金品で財務大臣の指定するもの及び学生や生徒に対する学費の支給を行うことを目的とする特定の公益信託から交付された金品

632   INHERITANCE TAX AND GIFT TAX

public trustees to students or pupils for supporting their educational expenses.

(5) The right to receive a grant from a mutual aid fund for disabled persons.

(6) Contributions to a candidate for an election under the Public Service Election Law provided the conditions stated in that law are satisfied.

(7) Gifts from a person who died in the same year, if the acquisition of property is subject to inheritance tax as stated in ¶ 7-280.

(8) Condolence money, money for wreaths, seasonal gifts, congratulatory gifts, etc. that are necessary for social reasons and commonly accepted (R 21-3-10).

¶ 7-870 Exempt gifts for severely handicapped persons

If a severely handicapped person receives as a gift from an individual, a right to receive benefits from a trust according to a special plan for such persons, the first ¥60 million of such amount is exempt (¥30 million for severely handicapped persons without special disabilities), provided a declaration of a tax-exempt trust gift for the handicapped person is filed.

Two or more declarations of tax-exempt trust gifts for handicapped persons can be filed up to the overall ceiling amount of ¥60 million (¥30 million for severely handicapped persons without special disabilities). These declarations are filed through only one specific branch of only one specific trust bank (Law 21-4).

¶ 7-875 Gift tax exemption of fund used to acquire residential property

A recipient who received fund used to acquire residential property as a gift during January 1, 2015 through December 31, 2021 from lineal ascendant, and entered into an agreement relating to the acquisition of the residential houses in until December 31, 2021. If below requirements are met, gift tax be exempted accordance with each limitation as specified (SM 70-2).

(1) Requirement of qualified recipient
    (a) Must be a taxpayer with unlimited tax liability
    (b) 20 years of age or over at January 1 of year received the gift
    (c) Entire amount of fund for acquisition of residential property received as gift is used to acquire a residential property or for ex-

¶ 7-870

相続税及び贈与税　633

(5)　心身障害者共済制度に基づく給付金の受給権

(6)　公職選挙法の適用を受ける選挙における公職の候補者が受けた贈与で公職選挙法に定める要件を満たすもの

(7)　被相続人から相続開始の年に贈与により取得した財産で，相続税の課税価額に算入されるもの（ただし，相続税が課せられる（¶7-280）。）

(8)　個人から受ける香典，花輪代，年末年始の贈答，祝物又は見舞等の金品で社交上必要と認められるもので，社会通念上相当と認められるもの（相基通21の3-10）

¶7-870　特別障害者に対する贈与税の非課税

特定障害者が，個人から当該特定障害者を受益者とする特定障害者扶養信託契約に基づいて，信託の利益を受ける場合，その価格のうち6,000万円（特定障害者のうち特別障害者以外の者については3,000万円）までの金額は贈与税の課税を受けない。ただし，障害者非課税信託申告書を提出しなければならない。

非課税信託申告書はこの信託受益権の価額が6,000万円（特定障害者のうち特別障害者以外の者については3,000万円）に達するまで，二以上の提出ができるが，いずれも一の信託銀行の一の営業所等においてのみ提出できる（相法21の4）。

¶7-875　住宅取得等資金の贈与税の非課税

平成27年1月1日から平成33年12月31日までの間に，直系尊属から住宅取得資金の贈与を受け，その住宅用家屋の取得に係る契約を平成33年12月31日までに締結した受贈者は，下記の要件に該当する場合にはそれぞれの限度額について贈与税が非課税となる（措法70の2）。

(1)　適用を受けるための受贈者の要件
　(a)　無制限納税義務者である。
　(b)　贈与を受けた年の1月1日において，20歳以上である。
　(c)　贈与を受けた年の翌年3月15日までに，住宅取得資金の全額を充て住宅の取得若しくは増改築等をする。

634   INHERITANCE TAX AND GIFT TAX

tension renovation by March 15 of following year when gift was received.

(d)   To live in the residential property by March 15 of following year when gift was received.

(e)   Total income of the year which gift is received must not exceed 20 million yen.

(f)   Residential house with the floor space of at least 50 square meters and not exceeding 240 square meters (if the recipient is a victim of the Great East Japan Earthquake, the ceiling cap does not apply).

(2)   Tax exemption ceiling

① Cases not subject to 10% consumption tax

Contract date	2015	January 2016– March 2020	April 2020– March 2021	April 2021– December 2021
Energy saving, Earthquake resistance, Barrier-free house	15 million yen	12 million yen	10 million yen	8 million yen
None of the above	10 million yen	7 million yen	5 million yen	3 million yen

② Cases subject to 10% consumption tax

Contract date	April 2019– March 2020	April 2020– March 2021	April 2021– December 2021
Energy saving, Earthquake resistance, Barrier-free house	30 million yen	15 million yen	12 million yen
None of the above	25 million yen	10 million yen	7 million yen

(3)   Effective period

Until December 31, 2021.

¶ 7-876 Exemption on lump sum gift of educational funds from lineal ascendants

Where a lineal ascendant transfers lump-sum donation to donee who is under 30 years of old for purpose to secure educational cost in the form of trust, etc. in the designated financial institution from April 1 2013 to

¶ 7-876

相続税及び贈与税　635

(d)　贈与を受けた年の翌年 3 月15日までに，その家屋に居住する。

(e)　贈与を受けた年の合計所得が2,000万円以下である。

(f)　住宅用家屋の床面積は50m²以上240m²以下である（東日本大震災の被災者は上限なし。）。

(2)　非課税の限度額
①　消費税10%の課税を受けないケース

契約日	平成27年	平成28年 1 月〜平成32年 3 月	平成32年 4 月〜平成33年 3 月	平成33年 4 月〜平成33年12月
省エネ・耐震バリアフリー住宅	1,500万円	1,200万円	1,000万円	800万円
上記以外	1,000万円	700万円	500万円	300万円

②　消費税10%の課税を受けるケース

契約日	平成31年 4 月〜平成32年 3 月	平成32年 4 月〜平成33年 3 月	平成33年 4 月〜平成33年12月
省エネ・耐震バリアフリー住宅	3,000万円	1,500万円	1,200万円
上記以外	2,500万円	1,000万円	700万円

(3)　適用期限
　平成33年12月31日までとする。

¶7-876　直系尊属から教育資金の一括贈与を受けた場合の贈与税の非課税

　受贈者（30歳未満の者に限る。）の教育資金に充てるために，その直系尊属が金銭等を金融機関に信託等をした場合には，拠出された金銭等の額のうち受贈者 1 人につき1,500万円（学校等以外の者に支払われる金銭については，500万円を限度とする。）までの金額に相当する部分の価額については，

636   INHERITANCE TAX AND GIFT TAX

March 31, 2019, up to ¥15,000,000 per donee (¥5,000,000 for payment to other than schools, etc.) will be exempt for gift tax purpose (SM 70-2-2).

Qualified educational fee is determined by the Minister of Education, Culture, Sports, Science and Technology as the following:
  (1) Enrollment fee, etc. paid to schools, etc.
  (2) Certain educational payment to other than school, etc. (Including commuting costs and expenses of a study abroad)

¶ 7-877 Exemption on lump sum gift for marriage and childcare funds from lineal ascendants

When a lineal ascendant (donor) transfer the lump sum donation to child/grandchild (age between 20 above to 50 below only) for marriage, pregnancy, childbirth, and childcare in the designated financial institution from April 1, 2015 to March 31, 2019, up to ¥10 million of donation per donee, inheritance tax is waived (SM 70-2-3).

However, when the child/grandchild reaches the age of 50, the bank account will be terminated and if there is account balance left, it will be subjected to gift tax.

Before the termination of the bank account and the donor passed away, the account balance will be count as his/her heritage.

¶ 7-880 Special provision for gift tax payment deferral on equity interest in medical corporations

Where an equity interest holder in a medical corporation which has equity of share holders refuse his/her interest and that the other interest holder becomes subject to gift tax, the gift tax payment may be deferred until the end of the transfer period if it is a certified medical corporation, on condition that security has been provided. Where the other equity holder in the medical corporation refuses all the equity interest during the transfer period, the deferred tax payment shall be exempted (SM 70-7-5).

¶ 7-881 Gift tax payment deferral on unlisted shares

In cases where a donee, who is also a successor, acquires through gift, all of the unlisted shares of stock from a family member (however, limited to a maximum of two thirds (2/3) of the total issued voting shares including those held by donee prior to receiving this gift) who operates a non-public company certified by the minister of economy, trade and industry, the full

¶ 7-877

平成25年４月１日から平成31年３月31日までの間に拠出されるものに限り，贈与税を課さないこととする（措法70の２の２）。

尚，教育資金とは，文部科学大臣が定める次の金銭をいう。

(1) 学校等に支払われる入学金その他の金銭
(2) 学校等以外の者に支払われる金銭のうち一定のもの（通学定期代，留学渡航費等を含む。）

¶7-877　直系尊属から結婚・子育て資金の一括贈与を受けた場合の贈与税の非課税

平成27年４月１日から平成31年３月31日までの間に直系尊属（贈与者）が，子・孫（20歳以上50歳未満の者に限る。）等の名義で金融機関の口座等に結婚，妊娠，出産，育児に必要な資金を拠出した場合，各子・孫ごとに1,000万円までの金額に相当する部分の価額については，贈与税を課さないこととする（措法70の２の３）。

ただし，子・孫が50歳に達する日に口座等は終了し，終了時に口座残高があれば，その時点で贈与税を課税する。

また，口座終了前に贈与者が死亡し，口座に残高がある場合は，贈与者の相続財産に加算する。

¶7-880　医療法人の贈与税の納税猶予

持分の定めのある医療法人の出資者が，持分を放棄したことにより他の出資者に贈与税が課される場合において，その医療法人が認定医療法人であるときは，担保の提供を条件に，持分の定めのない医療法人への移行期間満了までその納税を猶予する。また，移行期間内に当該他の出資者が持分の全てを放棄した場合には，猶予額を免除する（措法70の７の５）。

¶7-881　非上場株式等についての贈与税の納税猶予

後継者である受贈者が，経済産業大臣の認定を受けた非上場会社を経営していた親族から，贈与によりその保有株式等の全部（贈与前から既に後継者が保有していたものを含めて，発行済議決権株式の総数等の３分の２に達するまでの部分を上限とする。）を取得した場合，担保を提供して期限内申告書を提出すれば，猶予対象株式等の贈与にかかる贈与税の全額が猶予され

638   INHERITANCE TAX AND GIFT TAX

amount of the gift tax payment from this gift of shares that qualify for deferral may be deferred, subject to a person submitting collateral equivalent to such tax amount and filing a tax return before the due date.

However, failure to meet business continuance requirements in management succession period (5 years after the due date of the tax return) will lead to tax liability for all or some of the deferred gift tax with interest tax (SM 70-7).

¶ 7-882 Special measurement for gift tax payment deferral on unlisted shares

Where the company submits a special succession plan to the governor of prefecture until March 31, 2023, the special successor received unlisted shares from the special approved successor company from the representative director of the said company through donation, the total gift tax otherwise imposed on the received shares will be deferred until the end of the management donation succession period.

However, the failure to meet the business continuity conditions during the management donation succession period, except for unavoidable reason, will lead to tax payment along with interest tax of all or some of the deferred gift tax,

The deferred gift tax may be exempted from taxation in case of the death of the donor or donee, as well as exemption qualified donation after the management succession period, the bankruptcy, transfer or liquidation of the company (SM 70-7-5).

¶ 7-885 Special provision for deferral of gift tax payment on farmlands

When an individual who has engaged in farming business donates his/her farmland to the qualified person who meets the following conditions, and he/she files the gift tax return before the due date with providing collateral, the gift tax will be deferred until the death of the donor. The tax deferral is also applicable to lend certain acquired urban farmlands (SM 70-4).

(1) The person is heir apparent

(2) The person is eighteen (18) years old or over at the day of donation

(3) The person has been engaged in farming business for at least three (3) years before the day of donation

¶ 7-882

相続税及び贈与税　639

る。
　但し，経営承継期間（申告期限後5年以内）に，事業継続要件を満たすことが出来なくなった場合には，納税が猶予されていた贈与税の全部又は一部と利子税を併せて納付しなければならない（措法70の7）。

¶7-882　非上場株式等についての贈与税の納税猶予の特例

　特例承継計画を平成35年3月31日までに都道府県知事に提出した会社で，特例後継者が贈与等により，特例認定承継会社の代表権を有していた者から，その特例認定承継の非上場株式等を一定数取得した場合は，その取得した全ての非上場株式等に係る贈与税の全額について，特例経営贈与承継期間終了まで納税が猶予される。
　但し，特例経営贈与承継期間に，事業継続要件を満たすことが出来なくなった場合には，やむを得ない理由がある場合を除き，猶予されている贈与税の全部又は一部と利子税を併せて納付しなければならない。
　一方，納税が猶予されている贈与税は，贈与者又は受贈者の死亡，経営承継期間の経過後に免除対象贈与を行った場合，会社の破産，会社の譲渡・解散があったなどの場合は納税が免除される（措法70の7の5）。

¶7-885　農地等を贈与した場合の贈与税の納税猶予

　農業を営む個人がその農業の用に供している農地を，下記要件を満たした受贈者へ贈与した場合，担保を提供し期限内申告書を提出すれば，その贈与税について贈与者の死亡の日まで，納税は猶予される。又，取得した特定都市農地を貸し付けた場合でも，その納税は猶予される（措法70の4）。

(1)　推定相続人であること
(2)　贈与日において，18歳以上であること

(3)　贈与日前3年以上農業に従事していたこと

640   INHERITANCE TAX AND GIFT TAX

(4) The person starts to operate the farm management after donation without delay

(5) The person is qualified farmer

¶ 7-890 Tax rates

The taxable amount after deduction of the basic allowance and the spouse allowance should be apportioned according to the amount shown in the left hand column of the table (except for unified gift/inheritance tax system). Then the tax rate shown in the right hand column is applied to each portion of the taxable amount. These partial amounts of tax should be totaled to determine the gross amount of gift tax (Law 21-7).

Rate of Gift Tax

Taxable amount		Tax rate
Over	But not over	%
(¥) — (¥)	2,000,000	10%
2,000,000	3,000,000	15%
3,000,000	4,000,000	20%
4,000,000	6,000,000	30%
6,000,000	10,000,000	40%
10,000,000	15,000,000	45%
15,000,000	30,000,000	50%
30,000,000		55%

¶ 7-891 Special tax rate for donee who is 20 years of age or above on gift acquired from lineal ascendants

The special gift tax rate may be applied where donee is 20 years of age or above who acquires gift from his/her lineal ascendants (except for unified gift/inheritance tax system), effective from January 1, 2015 as the following (SM 70-2-4):

¶ 7-890

(4)　贈与を受けた後，速やかに農業経営を行うこと

(5)　認定農業者等であること

¶7-890　税率
　贈与により取得する財産で，相続時精算課税制度の対象とならないものは，基礎控除額及び配偶者控除を控除した後の贈与額の課税価格を，次表の左欄に掲げる金額に区分して，それぞれの金額に同表の右欄に掲げる税率を適用して計算した金額が贈与税の額となる（相法21の7）。

贈与税の税率

金　　　　　　額		税　　率
—	200万円以下の金額	10%
200万円を超え	300万円　〃	15%
300万円　〃	400万円　〃	20%
400万円　〃	600万円　〃	30%
600万円　〃	1,000万円　〃	40%
1,000万円　〃	1,500万円　〃	45%
1,500万円　〃	3,000万円　〃	50%
3,000万円を超える金額		55%

¶7-891　20歳以上の者が直系尊属から贈与を受けた贈与税の税率の特例
　平成27年1月1日以後の贈与により取得する財産で，20歳以上の者が直系尊属から贈与により取得した財産で，相続時精算課税制度の対象とならないものは，下記の税率を適用することができる（措法70の2の4）。

642   INHERITANCE TAX AND GIFT TAX

Taxable amount		Tax rate
Over	But not over	%
(¥) — (¥)	2,000,000	10%
2,000,000	4,000,000	15%
4,000,000	6,000,000	20%
6,000,000	10,000,000	30%
10,000,000	15,000,000	40%
15,000,000	30,000,000	45%
30,000,000	45,000,000	50%
45,000,000		55%

¶ 7-892 Credit for foreign taxes

The amount of foreign taxes similar in character to Japanese gift tax may be deducted from the amount of Japanese gift tax on the same principles as stated for inheritance tax in ¶ 7-400, Item (6).

¶ 7-893 Unified gift/inheritance tax system

A taxpayer (acquirer) can choose the unified gift/inheritance tax system instead of the ordinary gift tax system. Under the unified system, a taxpayer will pay gift tax on gifted properties. However, at the time of inheritance, the gift tax can be credited from the inheritance tax by calculating based on aggregated amount of the gifted properties and other inherited properties (Law 21-9).

(1) Qualified taxpayer

The unified system is available only to taxpayer (donee) of 20 years of age or above who is a presumptive heir (or successor in stirpes) to his/her parent or grandparent (donor) who is 60 years of age or above.

(2) Application procedure

To select the unified system, the taxpayer (acquirer) must attach an application for the unified system to the gift tax return and file the return with the tax office during February 1 through March 15 of the following year the taxpayer acquired the first gift.

(3) Qualified properties, etc.

There is no limitation to the type of properties, amount or number of gifts to apply the unified system.

¶ 7-892

金　　　　　　　　額		税　　率
—	200万円以下の金額	10%
200万円を超え	400万円　〃	15%
400万円　〃	600万円　〃	20%
600万円　〃	1,000万円　〃	30%
1,000万円　〃	1,500万円　〃	40%
1,500万円　〃	3,000万円　〃	45%
3,000万円　〃	4,500万円　〃	50%
4,500万円を超える金額		55%

¶7-892　外国税額控除

¶7-400(6)に述べたところと同一の考え方により，日本の贈与税に相当する外国贈与税額は，日本の贈与税額から控除される。

¶7-893　相続時精算課税制度

受贈者は，原則的な贈与税制度に代えて，贈与時に贈与財産に対する贈与税を支払い，その後の相続時にその贈与財産と相続財産とを合計した価額を基にした相続税額から，既に支払った贈与税を控除することにより，贈与税・相続税を通じた納税を選択することができる（相法21の9）。

(1)　適用対象者

本制度の適用対象となる贈与者は60歳以上の親又は祖父母，受贈者は20歳以上の子である推定相続人（代襲相続人を含む。）又は孫とする。

(2)　適用手続

本制度を選択しようとする受贈者（子）は，その選択に係る最初の贈与を受けた年の翌年2月1日から3月15日までの間に所轄税務署長に対してその旨の届け出を贈与税の申告書に添付することにより行わなければならない。

(3)　適用対象財産等

贈与財産の種類，金額，贈与回数には，制限がない。

644   INHERITANCE TAX AND GIFT TAX

(4) Computation of tax
   (a) Computation of gift tax
        Once a taxpayer (child) selects the unified system, he/she should
        file a gift tax return with respect to the properties gifted by the
        donor (his/her father or mother) and pay gift tax computed based
        on the aggregated amount of properties that have been gifted by
        the donor since the year of unified system selection. The gift tax
        for the unified system should be computed separately from gift tax
        on properties that do not fall under the unified system.
        For the unified system purposes, a special allowance of ¥25 million
        is applicable instead of the ordinary basic allowance of ¥1,100,000.
        This special allowance is deductible from the aggregated gifted
        amount in the year of the unified system selection and the
        following years. If the aggregated gifted amount exceeds the
        special allowance of ¥25 million, a fixed tax rate of 20% applies to
        the remainder to calculate the gift tax.
        For other types of gift tax, standard calculation will be performed.
   (b) Computation of inheritance tax
        The taxpayer (acquirer: child) who selects the unified system
        will pay inheritance tax computed in the ordinary manner on
        the aggregate amount of properties gifted and other properties
        inherited, devised or bequeathed from the donor (decedent:
        father or mother). However, the aggregate gift tax which had been
        paid under the unified system is creditable from the inheritance
        tax amount. Remainder of the gift tax will be refunded. For
        inheritance tax purposes, the properties gifted under the unified
        system are valued at their fair market value at the time of the gift.
(5) Exception relating to fund used to acquire residential property
     If a presumptive heir child or over receives fund to acquire residential
     property from a parent as gift and use such fund to obtain residen-
     tial property which meets certain requirement, or land to be used to
     build such residence, or use such fund for extension renovation, then
     resides in the resident by March 15th of following year when gift is
     received, even if such gift is from a parent below age of 60 years old,
     such gift shall be treated as an exception (SM 70-3).
     However, this exception only applies to such fund as gift received dur-
     ing January 1, 2003 through December 31, 2021.

¶ 7-893

相続税及び贈与税　645

⑷　税額の計算
　⒜　贈与税額の計算
　　　本制度の選択をした受贈者（子）は，本制度に係る贈与者（親）から
　　の贈与財産について贈与時に申告を行い，他の贈与財産と区分して，選
　　択をした年以後の各年にわたるその贈与者（親）からの贈与財産の価額
　　の合計額を基に計算した本制度に係る贈与税を支払わなければならな
　　い。
　　　この場合，原則的な基礎控除額110万円は適用されず，代わりに贈与
　　財産の価額の累計額から複数年にわたり利用できる特別控除額2,500万
　　円が適用される。贈与財産の価額の累計額が2,500万円を超える部分に
　　対して，一律20％の税率を乗じた贈与税を納付しなければならない。
　　　本制度外の贈与については，これを区分し，原則的な贈与税制度に基
　　づいて贈与税額を計算する。

　⒝　相続税額の計算
　　　本制度の選択をした受贈者（子）は，本制度に係る贈与者（親）から
　　の相続時に，本制度に基づく贈与財産の累計額と相続財産とを合算し原
　　則的な相続税制度に基づいて計算した相続税額から，既に支払った本制
　　度による贈与税額を控除する。控除しきれない場合には，還付を受ける
　　ことができる。相続財産と合算する贈与財産の価額は，贈与時の時価と
　　する。

⑸　住宅取得資金に係る特例
　　　20歳以上で推定相続人である子が親から住宅取得資金の贈与を受け，一
　　定の要件を満たす家屋あるいは住宅の新築等に先行してその敷地の用に供
　　される土地等の取得又は増改築の費用に充て，その家屋にその資金を取得
　　した日の属する年の翌年３月15日までに居住した場合には，60歳未満の親
　　からの贈与でも，本制度の対象とされる（措法70の３）。
　　　なお，この特例は平成15年１月１日から平成33年12月31日までの間にさ
　　れた贈与により取得した住宅取得資金について適用される。

646   INHERITANCE TAX AND GIFT TAX

Return and Payment

¶ 7-900 Return

A gift tax return should be filed during February 1 through March 15 of the following year at the tax office in the district where the taxpayer is domiciled (or is resident, if not domiciled in Japan). If leaving Japan without retaining domicile or residence in Japan, the taxpayer must file a return before leaving Japan.

¶ 7-910 Payment

Gift tax should be paid within the period of filing a return. If it is difficult for the taxpayer to pay the tax in a lump sum, and the total is more than ¥100,000, the taxpayer may be permitted to make installment payments for up to 5 years with interest of 6.6% per year. However, some conditions are required, such as supplying security to support the tax liabilities.

Payment in kind is never permitted.

The donor and the donee are jointly and severally responsible for paying the gift tax.

A scheme for the special installment payment of tax related to land used for agriculture has been introduced.

¶ 7-915 Correction

Correction with respect to gift tax can be made by the tax authorities for six years after filing the tax return.

¶ 7-920 Return form for gift tax

The form for the gift tax return is shown below for reference.

¶ 7-900

相続税及び贈与税　647

申告及び納付

¶7-900　贈与税の申告

　贈与税の申告書は，贈与を受けた翌年の2月1日から3月15日までの間に，納税地の税務署に提出しなければならない。納税者が出国するときは，出国の日までに申告書を提出しなければならない。

¶7-910　納付

　贈与税は，贈与税の申告期限までに納付しなければならない。一括納付が困難である場合には，当該贈与税額が10万円を超える場合には，担保を提供する等一定の条件のもとに，5年以内の延納（年6.6%の利子税がかかる。）が認められる。

　贈与税については物納は認められない。

　財産を贈与した者は，自己が贈与した財産に係る贈与税の部分について，連帯納付の責任を負う。

　農地に関しては，特別に納税の猶予の制度が認められている。

¶7-915　更正

　贈与税に関する更正は，決定申告期限から6年間これをすることができる。

¶7-920　贈与税の申告書

　参考までに，贈与税の申告書のフォームを掲げておく。

648   INHERITANCE TAX AND GIFT TAX

Gift Tax Return

To Director of ——————— District Taxation Office

Date of submission ————————————————

Residence	
Name	
My Number	
Date of birth	

		Donor	Details of property acquired					Date of acquisition
			Kind	Sub-item	Description	Quantity	Unit Price	
			Situr			Fixed asset tax value	Adjustment	Value
I Annual Taxation	**Gift from lineal ascendant**	Address					yen	yen
		Name | relation				yen		
		Date of birth						
		Address					yen	yen
		Name | relation				yen		
		Date of birth						
		Subtotal taxable amount					①	
	Gift from other donor	Address					yen	yen
		Name | relation				yen		
		Date of birth						
		Address					yen	yen
		Name | relation						
						yen		
		Date of birth						
		Subtotal taxable amount					②	
		Spouse allowance: The first time application of spouse allowance/ Amount used for acquisition of residential property ——— yen					③	
		Total taxable amount (① + ② - ③)					④	
		Basic allowance					⑤	1,100,000
		Adjusted total taxable amount (④ – ⑤)					⑥	,000
		Tax amount on ⑥					⑦	
		Foreign tax credit					⑧	
		Tax credit for interest in medical corporation					⑨	
		Tax amount payable (⑦ – ⑧ – ⑨)					⑩	
II Unified Gift/ Inheritance Taxation		Total taxable amount calculated by each specified donor					⑪	
		Total tax amount calculated by each specified donor					⑫	
III Aggregation		Aggregated taxable amount (① + ② + ⑪)					⑬	
		Aggregated tax amount payable (⑩ + ⑫)					⑭	00
		Deferred taxes amount					⑮~⑰	00
		Tax amount to be paid (⑭ – ⑮ – ⑯ – ⑰)					⑱	00

¶ 7-900

相続税及び贈与税　649

平成□□年分贈与税の申告書（兼贈与税の額の計算明細書）　ＦＤ４７２６

第一表（平成28年分以降用）

住宅取得等資金の非課税の申告は申告書第一表の二又は第一表の三と、相続時精算課税の申告は申告書第二表と、一緒に提出してください。

（資5-10-1-1-A4統一）

650

CHAPTER 8

CONSUMPTION TAX

	Paragraph
Outline of the Consumption Tax	¶ 8-010
Taxable Transactions	¶ 8-030
Non-taxable Transactions	¶ 8-070
Tax Exemption	¶ 8-170
Taxpayer	¶ 8-230
Place for Tax Payment	¶ 8-310
Taxable Period	¶ 8-360
Time of Transfer of Assets, etc.	¶ 8-390
Tax Base	¶ 8-490
Tax Rate	¶ 8-510
Tax Credits and Other Adjustments	¶ 8-530
Special Exceptions for Government and the Like	¶ 8-700
Filing Tax Returns and Payment of Tax	¶ 8-750
Others	¶ 8-790

第 8 章
消　費　税

消費税の概要……………………………………………………	¶ 8–010
課税対象…………………………………………………………	¶ 8–030
非課税……………………………………………………………	¶ 8–070
免税………………………………………………………………	¶ 8–170
納税義務者………………………………………………………	¶ 8–230
納税地……………………………………………………………	¶ 8–310
課税期間…………………………………………………………	¶ 8–360
資産の譲渡等の時期……………………………………………	¶ 8–390
課税標準…………………………………………………………	¶ 8–490
税率………………………………………………………………	¶ 8–510
税額控除等………………………………………………………	¶ 8–530
国等に対する特例………………………………………………	¶ 8–700
申告及び納付……………………………………………………	¶ 8–750
その他……………………………………………………………	¶ 8–790

652   CONSUMPTION TAX

Outline of the Consumption Tax

¶ 8-010 Characteristics of the consumption tax

(1) **To be borne widely by consumers**

Unlike the individual excise taxes in which particular products and services are subject to taxation, the consumption tax is categorized as an indirect tax in which almost every domestic transaction and every transaction for the import of foreign goods except for financial transactions, capital transactions, medical services, welfare services and education services, will be subject to taxation at the rate of 6.3% (Together with the effective local consumption tax rate of 1.7%, the total effective tax rate is 8%).

Note:

Tax rate will increase to 7.8% after October 2019 (together with local consumption tax rate 2.2%, total effective tax rate will be 10%).

As Japan's economic situation will be taken into consideration prior to the implementation of those consumption tax rate increase, there may be an option of ceases those tax rate increase if necessary (October 2016, consumption tax reform).

(2) **To be borne by consumers only, in order to eliminate multiple taxation**

The consumption tax is so structured as to be passed on ultimately to consumers by addition to the price of products sold and services provided by an enterprise.

It is also designed to eliminate multiple taxation at each stage of manufacture and distribution by allowing for the credit of consumption tax on purchases against that on sales.

(3) **Measures to facilitate calculation of tax**

(a) Allowing for tax-exempt enterprises (see ¶ 8-250 to ¶ 8-280): An enterprise whose taxable sales amount is not more than ¥10 million for the base period (the year two years prior to the current year for an individual enterprise, the fiscal year two fiscal years prior to the current fiscal year for a corporation) is a tax-exempt enterprise except the enterprise making the election to be a taxable enterprise.

¶ 8-010

消　費　税　653

消費税の概要

¶8-010　消費税の性格
(1)　消費に広く薄く負担を求める税
　消費税は，特定の物品やサービスに課税する個別消費税とは異なり，消費に広く薄く負担を求めるという観点から，金融取引，資本取引，医療，福祉及び教育の一部を除き，ほとんどすべての国内取引や外国貨物（輸入取引）を課税対象として，6.3％（地方消費税（1.7％）を合わせると8％）の税率で課税される間接税である。

　　(注)：平成31年10月以降7.8％（地方消費税2.2％と合わせると10％）に税率引上げが行われる。
　　　　　ただし，消費税率引上げの前に経済状況等を総合的に勘案して，消費税率引上げが停止されることもある（平成28年11月，消費税法改正）。

(2)　消費者に転嫁し，税の累積を排除する仕組み
　消費税は，事業者に負担を求めるのではなく，税金分は事業者の販売する物品やサービスの価格に上乗せされ，次々と転嫁され，最終的には消費者に負担を求める税である。
　また，生産，流通の各段階で二重，三重に税が課されることのないよう，売上げに係る消費税額から仕入れに係る消費税額を控除し，税が累積しないような仕組みが採られている。

(3)　事務負担の軽減措置等
　　(a)　免税事業者制度（¶8-250〜¶8-280参照）　基準期間（個人事業者は前々年，法人は前々事業年度）の課税売上高が1,000万円以下の事業者は，選択により課税事業者になる場合を除き，免税事業者になる。

654   CONSUMPTION TAX

Note:
> This measure will not apply for the enterprise whose taxable sales amount is more than ¥10 million for the period from January 1 through June 30 of the previous year for individual enterprises, the period of the first half of the previous business year etc. for corporations.

(b) Simplified tax system (see ¶ 8-680): An enterprise whose taxable sales amount is not more than ¥50 million for the base period can make election to apply the simplified tax system in which the tax liability is calculated on the basis of the taxable sales amount only.

(c) Purchase tax credit calculated from accounting records (see ¶ 8-610): Consumption tax paid by a taxpayer as a component of purchase cost, which may be credited against the tax component of sales by the taxpayer, may be calculated from sales records and invoices.

¶ 8-020 Basic structure

(1) **Basic formula to calculate tax** (see ¶ 8-490 to ¶ 8-590)

The basic formula for calculating the tax is as follows:

$$\text{Tax due} = \begin{pmatrix} \text{total amount of} \\ \text{consumption tax} \\ \text{on sales} \\ (6.3\% \text{ of taxable sales}) \end{pmatrix} - \begin{pmatrix} \text{total amount of} \\ \text{consumption tax} \\ \text{on purchases} \\ (6.3\% \text{ of taxable purchases}) \end{pmatrix}$$

Note:
> Together with an effective local consumption tax rate of 1.7%, the total effective tax rate is 8%.

(2) **Taxable transactions** (see ¶ 8-030 to ¶ 8-060)

Taxable transactions are domestic transactions and transactions for the import of foreign goods.

(a) Domestic transactions: Domestic transactions in which consideration is paid for the transfer or lease of assets or the provision of services for business purposes will be subject to taxation.

(b) Import transactions: Foreign goods received or removed from a bonded area in Japan will be subject to taxation.

(c) Electronic commerce: Such as distribution of electronic book, music, advertisement etc., provided by foreign entities.

Note:
> Apply after Oct. 2015 (2015 tax reform)

¶ 8-020

消　費　税　655

(注)：前年1月から6月の課税売上高が1,000万円を超える個人事業者及び前事業年度開始の日から6カ月間の課税売上高が1,000万円を超える法人等については，この制度は適用されない。

(b)　簡易課税制度（¶8-680参照）　　基準期間の課税売上高が5,000万円以下の事業者については，課税売上高のみに基づいて納付税額を計算する簡易課税制度を選択することができる。

(c)　帳簿書類による前段階控除（仕入税額控除）（¶8-610参照）　　仕入れに係る消費税額の計算は，帳簿上の記録，納品書及び請求書等を基に行うことができる。

¶8-020　消費税の基本的仕組み

(1)　**納付税額の一般的な計算方法**（¶8-490～¶8-590参照）

課税期間の納付すべき消費税額は，次の算式により算出する。

$$納付税額 = \begin{bmatrix} 売上げに係る消費税額 \\ （課税売上高 \times 6.3\%） \end{bmatrix} - \begin{bmatrix} 仕入れに係る消費税額 \\ （課税仕入高 \times 6.3\%） \end{bmatrix}$$

(注)：地方消費税（1.7%）を合わせると8%となる。

(2)　**課税取引**（¶8-030～¶8-060参照）

消費税の課税の対象となる取引は，次の国内取引及び輸入取引である。

(a)　国内取引　　国内において事業者が行った資産の譲渡等，つまり，国内において事業者が事業として対価を得て行う資産の譲渡，資産の貸付け及び役務の提供を課税の対象とする。

(b)　輸入取引　　保税地域から引き取られる外国貨物を課税の対象とする。

(c)　電子商取引　　国外事業者が行う電子書籍，音楽，広告の配信などの電子商取引

(注)：平成27年10月から施行（平成27年度税制改正）。

656 CONSUMPTION TAX

(3) **Non-taxable transactions** (see ¶ 8-070 to ¶ 8-165)

Transactions which are deemed not to be properly taxable by their nature are categorized as non-taxable transactions. Further, education services, medical services and welfare services under certain conditions are non-taxable transactions according to the Government's policy. However, the number of such non-taxable transactions is very limited because the basic concept of the consumption tax requires the tax burden to be spread over a wide range.

(4) **Tax exempt transactions** (see ¶ 8-170 to ¶ 8-220)

Consumption tax requires consumers to bear tax on products and services consumed in Japan, so that export transactions, international communications and international transportation services are exempt from consumption tax (export tax exemption).

(5) **Taxpayer** (see ¶ 8-230 to ¶ 8-245)

Tax payer	Domestic transactions: Enterprises (individual enterprises and corporations) conducting taxable transactions.
	Note: This includes governments, local municipalties, public interest corporations and non-juridical organizations. Non-residents and foreign corporations are subject to taxation when conducting taxable transactions in Japan.
	Import transactions: Individuals and corporations removing foreign goods from a bonded area.
	Note: Not only enterprises but also individuals who import goods as consumers must pay the tax.

(6) **Tax base** (see ¶ 8-490 to ¶ 8-500)

Tax base	Domestic transactions: The consideration paid for taxable transactions (excluding consumption tax, but including individual excise taxes such as liquor tax and gasoline tax.)
	Import transactions: Transaction amount of taxable foreign goods (tax base for customs purposes (C.I.F.) + individual excise taxes + customs duties).

¶ 8-020

(3) **非課税取引**（¶8-070〜¶8-165参照）
　消費に負担を求める税としての性格上，課税の対象とすることが相当でないものは，非課税とされている。また，特別の政策的な配慮に基づき，医療，福祉及び教育の分野の一定のものは非課税とされているが，この政策的配慮に基づく非課税取引は，消費全般に広く薄く負担を求めるというこの税の性格上，極めて限定されている。

(4) **免税取引**（¶8-170〜¶8-220参照）
　消費税は，国内において消費される商品やサービスについて負担を求めるものであるから，課税事業者が輸出取引や国際通信，国際運輸等のいわゆる輸出類似取引を行う場合には，消費税が免除される（輸出免税）。

(5) **納税義務者**（¶8-230〜¶8-245参照）

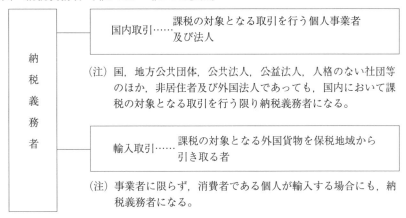

(6) **課税標準**（¶8-490〜¶8-500参照）

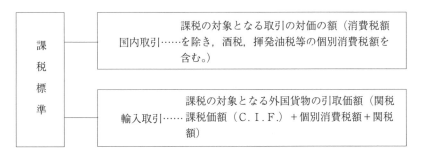

658   CONSUMPTION TAX

(7) **Tax rate** (see ¶ 8-510 to ¶ 8-520)

The tax rate is a uniform rate of 6.3%.

Note:
Together with an effective local consumption tax rate of 1.7%, the total effective tax rate is 8%.

(8) **Purchase tax credit** (see ¶ 8-530 to ¶ 8-680)

To avoid multiple taxation, the tax component of purchases may be credited against tax on sales at each stage of manufacture or distribution, where payers of the consumption tax are enterprises supplying products or providing services, or those receiving foreign goods or removing them from a bonded area.

(9) **Place for tax payment** (see ¶ 8-310 to ¶ 8-355)

(a) Domestic transactions:

(i)   Place for tax payment by an individual enterprise—

* For an individual domiciled in Japan: the said domicile.

* For an individual resident in Japan without domicile: the place of residence.

* For an individual having an office etc. in Japan without either domicile or residence: the location of the said office etc. (where the individual has two or more offices, the main office's location).

(ii) Place for tax payment by a corporation—

* For a domestic corporation: the location of its head or main office.

* For a foreign corporation having its office etc. in Japan: the location of the said office etc. (where the foreign corporation has two or more offices etc. the location of the main office).

(b) Import transactions:

The location of the bonded area from which the foreign goods are removed.

(10) **Taxable period** (see ¶ 8-360 to ¶ 8-380)

(a) General rules:

(i)   The taxable period for individual enterprises is the calendar year from January 1 through December 31.

(ii) The taxable period for a corporation is its business year.

(b) Exceptions:

¶ 8-020

消費税　659

⑺　**税率**（¶8-510～¶8-520参照）
税率は，6.3％の単一税率である。
(注)：地方消費税（1.7％）を合わせると8％となる。

⑻　**仕入税額控除**（¶8-530～¶8-680参照）
消費税は，財貨やサービスを提供する事業者及び外国貨物を引き取る者を納税義務者とするものであるが，生産・流通の各段階で二重，三重に税が課されることのないように仕入れに係る消費税額を売上げに係る消費税額から控除する仕組みがとられている。

⑼　**納税地**（¶8-310～¶8-355参照）
　(a)　国内取引
　　(i)　個人事業者の納税地
　　　＊　国内に住所を有する場合は，住所地とする。
　　　＊　国内に住所を有せず，居所を有する場合は，居住地とする。
　　　＊　国内に住所及び居所を有せず，事務所等を有する場合は，事務所等の所在地（2以上ある場合は主たるものの所在地）とする。

　　(ii)　法人の納税地
　　　＊　内国法人の場合は，本店又は主たる事務所の所在地とする。
　　　＊　内国法人以外の法人で国内に事務所等を有する法人の場合は，事務所等の所在地（2以上ある場合は主たるものの所在地）とする。

　(b)　輸入取引
　　外国貨物の引取りに係る保税地域の所在地とする。

⑽　**課税期間**（¶8-360～¶8-380参照）
　(a)　原則
　　(i)　個人事業者については，1月1日から12月31日までの期間（暦年）とする。
　　(ii)　法人については，事業年度とする。
　(b)　課税期間の特例

660   CONSUMPTION TAX

By filing an application with the director of the tax office, a taxpayer can shorten the taxable period to one month or in the following manner:

(i)   In the case of individual enterprises—
From January to March, April to June, July to September, and October to December.

(ii) In the case of a corporation whose business year exceeds three months—
The corporation's business year divided into three-month periods.

(11) **Filing tax returns and tax payment** (see ¶ 8-750 to ¶ 8-780)

(a) Domestic transactions:

(i)   The final tax return must be filed and the tax must be accounted for to the tax office within two months after the end of the taxable period. If there is any deficiency in crediting the consumption tax amount on purchases, or the tax amount payable in an interim tax return against the tax amount on sales in the final tax return, such amount will be refunded.

(ii) Three-monthly (monthly) interim return must be filed in the case where the annual consumption tax of the previous taxable period exceeds ¥4,000,000 (¥48,000,000) and six-monthly interim return must be filed in the case where the consumption tax of the previous taxable period exceeds ¥480,000.

(b) Import transactions:

Those who receive or remove taxable foreign goods from a bonded area must file a tax return with the director of the relevant customs office and pay tax at the time the goods are removed. In this case, an extension is allowed for up to 3 months if an application for extension of the time limit for payment is submitted and if security is provided.

(12) **Bookkeeping obligations** (see ¶ 8-800)

Enterprises (except tax-exempt enterprises) must keep records of the following matters in their books:

(a) Transfers of assets, etc.

(b) Taxable purchases.

(c) The removal of taxable foreign goods from bonded areas.

¶ 8-020

消　費　税　661

　　税務署長に届出書を提出することにより，課税期間を1月又は次のように短縮することができる。

　　(i)　個人事業者の場合　1〜3月，4〜6月，7〜9月，10〜12月

　　(ii)　法人（その事業年度が3月を超える法人に限る。）の場合　事業年度をその開始の日以後3月ごとに区分した期間

⑾　**申告及び納付**（¶8-750〜¶8-780参照）
　(a)　国内取引
　　(i)　課税期間終了後2月以内に確定申告書を提出し，納付する（確定申告）。なお，確定申告に際し，仕入れに係る消費税額又は中間納付額の控除不足額がある場合には，還付される。

　　(ii)　前課税期間の年税額が48万円を超える場合は，6月（400万円を超える場合は3月，4,800万円を超える場合は毎月）ベースの中間申告をしなければならない。

　(b)　輸入取引
　　課税貨物を保税地域から引き取る者は，その引取りのときまでに申告書を提出し，引取りに係る消費税額を納付しなければならない。この場合，納期限延長申請書を提出し，かつ，担保を提出したときには，最長3月間の納期限の延長が認められる。

⑿　**記帳義務等**（¶8-800参照）
　事業者（免税事業者等を除く。）は，帳簿を備え付けて，これに次の事項を記録し，かつ，その帳簿を保存しなければならない。
　(a)　資産の譲渡等
　(b)　課税仕入れ
　(c)　課税貨物の保税地域からの引取り

662   CONSUMPTION TAX

Taxable Transactions

¶ 8-030 Taxation on domestic transactions

Transfers of taxable assets, etc. conducted by enterprises in Japan are subject to the consumption tax (Law 4①). "Transfers of taxable assets, etc." means transfers of assets, leases of assets and the provision of services which are conducted for consideration and as a business by the enterprises, but the term does not include non-taxable transactions provided for under Art. 6① (Law 2①(8), 5①).

¶ 8-040 Definitions

The terms used in ¶ 8-030 above are defined as follows:

(1) **Definition of "enterprise"**

"Enterprise" means individual enterprises (individuals doing business) and corporations, regardless of whether they are residents or non-residents (Law 2①(4)).

(2) **Definition of "business"**

"Business" means a course of action in which similar acts are repeated, but the scale of the business is not considered in the definition.

The definition of "business" is included in order to provide rules for non-business activities which are not subject to taxation, such as where an individual conducts sales as a consumer (for instance, when a person transfers a non-business asset such as a television for private use).

Transfers and leases of assets as well as the provision of services accompanied by and related to business activities are included in the transfers of assets, etc. conducted as a business (for instance, transfers of disused articles).

(3) **Definition of "conducted for consideration"**

"Conducted for consideration" means receiving consideration for a supply of goods or provision of services. Therefore, gifts of assets, leases of assets without charge are not subject to taxation (R 5-1-2).

Examples of payments which are not in consideration for transfers of assets, etc. are: insurance money paid by an insurance company or a mutual aid association; dividends; distributions of a surplus; dona-

¶ 8-030

消 費 税 663

課 税 対 象

¶8-030　国内取引の課税対象
　消費税の課税の対象としては，まず，国内において事業者が行う課税資産の譲渡等がある（消法4①）。この場合の課税資産の譲渡等とは，事業として対価を得て行われる資産の譲渡，資産の貸付け（資産に係る権利の設定その他他の者に資産を使用させる一切の行為を含む。）及び役務の提供で，消法第6条第1項（（非課税））の規定により非課税とされるもの以外のものをいう（消法2①八，5①）。

¶8-040　定義
　¶8-030で使用されている用語の定義は，以下のとおりである。
(1)　事業者の意義
　事業者とは，個人事業者（事業を行う個人）及び法人をいい，その個人事業者又は法人が居住者であるか非居住者であるかを問わない（消法2①四）。

(2)　「事業として」の意義
　「事業」とは，同種の行為を反復，継続，独立して行うことをいうのであるが，このようなものであれば，その規模を問わないというのが基本的な考え方である。
　「事業として……」と限定されているのは，個人事業者が消費者の立場で資産の譲渡等を行う場合（例えば，家庭で使用していたテレビ等の非事業用資産を譲渡する場合）には，課税の対象としないという趣旨である。
　また，事業に付随して対価を得て行われる資産の譲渡及び資産の貸付け並びに役務の提供は，資産の譲渡等に含まれるのであるが，例えば，事業活動の一環として，又はこれに関連して行われるものがこれに該当する（例えば不用品の譲渡等）。

(3)　「対価を得て行われる」の意義
　「対価を得て行われる」とは，反対給付として対価を得ることをいうのである。したがって，単なる資産の贈与，資産の無償貸付けは，課税の対象とはならない（不課税取引）（消基通5-1-2）。
　資産の譲渡等の対価に該当しないものには，保険金，共済金，利益の配当，剰余金の分配，寄付金，祝金，見舞金等がある。

664   CONSUMPTION TAX

tions and gifts of money as an expression of sympathy or congratulation, etc.

(4) **Definition of "assets"**

The term "assets" means any asset which is the object of a transaction (transfer or lease). Therefore, rights and intangible assets are included as well as tangible assets such as inventory assets and fixed tangible assets (R 5-1-3).

(5) **Determination of a domestic transaction**

Whether a transaction is conducted in Japan or not is determined by (a) the place where the asset is located, in the case of a transfer or lease of assets, or (b) the place where the service is provided, in the case of the provision of services (see ¶ 8-050).

(6) **Definition of "transfer of assets"**

"Transfer of assets" means any transfer of assets to another party in which the identity of the assets is preserved.

Therefore, in the case of reclamation work under the Public Area Reclamation Law, compensation is paid for extinguishing or decreasing the value of fishery rights, and this does not fall into the category of transfer of assets.

When considering a transfer of assets, the reason for the transfer is not taken into account even, for example, when the assets are transferred in satisfaction of the other party's debts or when they are transferred under the procedure of compulsory conversion into money.

(7) **Definition of "lease of assets"**

A "lease of assets" includes the creation of a right regarding the assets or any act allowing another party use of assets (Law 2②).

(a) "Creation of a right regarding assets" means, for instance, creation of superficies or servitium regarding land, creation of rights to use industrial properties (i.e. patents, utility models, designs and trademarks) or the creation of a right to publish a book (R 5-4-1).

(b) "Allowing another party use of assets" means allowing others to use real estate, intangible property or other rights, and the following are examples of consideration for these acts:

(i) Rent for land or houses.

(ii) Leasing fees for construction machinery, automobiles or

¶ 8-040

消　費　税　665

(4)　**資産の意義**
　「資産」とは，取引（譲渡，貸付け）の対象となる一切の資産をいうから，棚卸資産又は固定資産のような有形資産に限らず，権利その他の無形資産も含まれる（消基通5-1-3）。

(5)　**国内取引の判定**
　資産の譲渡等が国内において行われたかどうかは，その取引が，資産の譲渡又は資産の貸付けである場合にあっては，その資産の所在していた場所が，また，役務の提供である場合にあっては，その役務の提供が行われた場所が，それぞれ国内であるかどうかによって判定する（¶8-050参照）。

(6)　**資産の譲渡の意義**
　「資産の譲渡」とは，資産につきその同一性を保持しつつ，他人に移転させることをいうのである。
　したがって，例えば公有水面埋立法の規定に基づく公有水面の埋立てをする場合に，漁業権又は入漁権の消滅又はこれらの価値の減少の対価として補償金が授受されるが，このような場合の権利の消滅又は価値の減少は，一般に資産の譲渡に該当しない。
　また，資産の譲渡は，その原因を問わないから，例えば，他の者の債務の保証を履行するために資産を譲渡する場合又は強制換価手続により換価された場合でも，その譲渡又は換価は，資産の譲渡に該当する。

(7)　**資産の貸付けの意義**
　「資産の貸付け」には，資産に係る権利の設定その他他の者に資産を使用させる一切の行為が含まれる（消法2②）。
　(a)　「資産に係る権利の設定」とは，例えば土地に係る地上権若しくは地役権，工業所有権（特許権，実用新案権，意匠権及び商標権をいう。）に係る実施権若しくは使用権又は著作物に係る出版権の設定をいう（消基通5-4-1）。

　(b)　「他の者に資産を使用させる」とは，不動産，無体財産権その他の権利を他人に使用させることをいい，これの対価に該当するものとしては，例えば，次のようなものがある。
　　(ⅰ)　土地，建物の賃貸料
　　(ⅱ)　建設機械，自動車，事務用機械等のリース料

666   CONSUMPTION TAX

business machines.

(iii) Interest on loans.

(iv) Rent or charges for rented warehouses or safe-deposit boxes.

(v) Fees for the use of intangible property such as patents, copyrights, etc.

Note:
Rent for land and interest on loans are non-taxable.

(c) The following are examples of "acts allowing use of assets" (R 5-4-2).

(i) Use, provision or instruction of industrial properties, etc. (i.e. patents, utility models, designs and trademarks, and the rights to apply and use these properties).

(ii) Reproduction, presentation, broadcast, exhibition, screening, translation, arrangement (of music), dramatization, cinematization of a work or any other act which allows a work to be used or performed.

(iii) Use, provision or instruction of an original work sufficiently made up for repetitious use for production or other operation but not an object of industrial property, etc. (i.e. an original idea or method about special material, prescription, machinery, tools or manufacturing process, etc., or similar technologically valuable know-how, knowledge and design).

(8) **Definition of the "provision of services"**

"Provision of services" means rendering services, for example, construction work, repairs, transportation, storage, printing, advertising, brokerage, entertainment, technical assistance, furnishing information, performing, writing and service facilities where a service based on intellectual knowledge or skills is provided, including services provided by attorneys, public accountants, tax accountants, writers, athletes, film directors and Shogi (chess) players (R 5-5-1).

(9) **Acts similar to the "transfer of assets, etc."**

The following acts are included in "transfer of assets, etc." (Reg 2):

(a) transfers of assets as gifts which are made out of an obligation;

(b) investments in kind (by non-cash assets);

(c) entrustment of assets to the corporate taxation trust under certain conditions;

(d) succession or transfer of pecuniary credits such as loans (ex-

¶ 8-040

消　費　税　667

 (iii) 貸付金の利息
 (iv) 貸倉庫料，貸金庫使用料
 (v) 特許権，著作権等の無体財産権の使用料

(注)：(i)の土地の賃貸料，(iii)の貸付金の利息は非課税である。

(c) 「資産を使用させる一切の行為」とは，例えば次のものをいう（消基
通5-4-2）。
 (i) 工業所有権等（特許権，実用新案権，意匠権及び商標権並びにこれ
らの権利に係る出願権及び実施権をいう。）の使用，提供又は伝授

 (ii) 著作物の複製，上演，放送，展示，上映，翻訳，編曲，脚色，映画
化その他著作物を利用させる行為

 (iii) 工業所有権等の目的になっていないが，生産その他業務に関し繰り
返し使用し得るまでに形成された創作（特別の原料，処方，機械，器
具，工程によるなど独自の考案又は方法についての方式，これに準ず
る秘けつ，秘伝その他特別に技術的価値を有する知識及び意匠等をい
う。）の使用，提供又は伝授

(8)　役務の提供の意義

 「役務の提供」とは，例えば，土木工事，修繕，運送，保管，印刷，広
告，仲介，興行，技術援助，情報の提供，便益，出演，著述その他のサービ
スを提供することをいい，弁護士，公認会計士，税理士，作家，スポーツ選
手，映画監督，棋士等によるその専門的知識，技能等に基づく役務の提供も
これに含まれる（消基通5-5-1）。

(9)　資産の譲渡等に類する行為

 「資産の譲渡等」には，次に掲げる行為が含まれる（消令2）。
 (a) 負担付き贈与による資産の譲渡
 (b) 金銭以外の資産の出資
 (c) 法人課税信託の委託者がその有する資産を信託する場合等一定の信託
に係る一定の資産の移転等
 (d) 貸付金その他の金銭債権の譲受けその他の承継等（包括承継を除く。）

668   CONSUMPTION TAX

cept general succession); and

(e)   radio or television broadcasting which is conducted by collecting a reception fee.

Note:

Where the right of ownership or other right of an enterprise is expropriated under the Compulsory Purchase of Land Act or other law, and the enterprise acquires compensation for the right from the person who acquires the right, the transaction will be included in transfers of assets which are conducted for consideration (Reg 2②).

(10) Scope of deemed transfer

Consumption Tax is levied on transfers of assets, etc. which are conducted for consideration and as a business by enterprises. Transfers of assets, etc., without consideration are not subject to taxation. On the other hand, however, as it is a tax on consumption, the following cases only are subject to taxation (Law 4④):

(a)   the private use or consumption of inventory assets or of assets other than inventory assets which have been used for business purposes by individual enterprises; and

(b)   the transfer of assets by a corporation as a gift to its directors (directors are those stipulated in Art. 2 (15) of the Corporation Tax Act).

¶ 8-050   Determination of domestic transactions

As transfers of assets, etc. conducted "in Japan" (domestic transactions) are subject to taxation, transactions are not subject to taxation if they are conducted outside of Japan. Whether it is a domestic transaction or not depends on whether the following place is located in Japan or not (Law 4③).

(1) Transfers or leases of assets

In principle, a transfer or lease is deemed to be conducted in the place where the assets are located at the time of the transaction. However, the place of transfer of the following assets is deemed to be the place mentioned, as at the time of the transaction (Reg 6①).

(a)   Ships (registered ships only)—the place of the agency at which the ship was registered.

But in the case where a resident leases a ship other than of Japanese nationality (a ship registered in Japan), or a non-resident transfers or leases a ship of Japanese nationality—the place of

¶ 8-050

消　費　税　669

(e)　受信料を徴収して行われるラジオ，テレビ等の送信

(注)：事業者が，土地収用法その他の法律の規定に基づいてその所有権その他の権利を収用され，かつ，当該権利を取得する者から当該権利の消滅に係る補償金を取得した場合には，対価を得て資産の譲渡を行ったものとされる（消令2②）。

⑽　みなし譲渡の範囲

　消費税の課税対象は，事業者が事業として対価を得て行う資産の譲渡等であり，無償で行う資産の譲渡等は課税対象とならないが，消費に負担を求める税としての性格上，次の場合に限り，課税の対象となる（消法4④）。

(a)　個人事業者が棚卸資産又は棚卸資産以外の資産で事業の用に供していたものを家事のために消費し又は使用した場合

(b)　法人が資産をその役員（法人税法第2条第15号に規定する役員をいう。）に対して贈与した場合

¶8-050　国内取引の判定

　「国内において」行った資産の譲渡等を課税対象とすると規定されていることから，国外で行われる資産の譲渡等は課税対象外となるが，国内における取引か否かは，次に掲げる場所が国内であれば国内取引となる（消法4③）。

⑴　資産の譲渡又は貸付け

　原則として，取引時の資産の所在場所。ただし，次に掲げる資産については，取引時における次に掲げる場所（消令6①）。

(a)　船舶（登録を受けたものに限る。）　船舶の登録をした機関の所在地。ただし，居住者が行う日本船舶（国内において登録を受けた船舶）以外の船舶の貸付け及び非居住者が行う日本船舶の譲渡又は貸付けにあっては，譲渡又は貸付けを行う者の住所地（住所又は本店若しくは主たる事務所の所在地）

670   CONSUMPTION TAX

domicile (domicile or the place where the head or main office is situated) of the transferor or lessor.

(b) Ships other than those mentioned in (a) above—the place of the transferor's or lessor's office through which the transfer or lease is made.

(c) Aeroplanes—the place of the agency at which the aeroplane was registered. Aeroplanes not registered—the place of the transferor's or lessor's office through which the transfer or lease is made.

(d) Mining rights, other rights regarding mines or stone-quarrying rights, etc.—the place of the mining area or the quarry.

(e) Patents, utility models, designs, trademarks, rights to use circuits, nursery right—the place of the agency at which these rights were registered. When a right is registered in two or more countries—the place of domicile of the assignor or lessor.

(f) Copyrights (including printing rights, associated and similar rights) or production methods using special technology (know-how) and similar property—the place of domicile of the assignor or lessor.

(g) Goodwill, fishery rights or common piscatorial rights—the place of domicile of the person doing business with respect to these rights.

(h) Securities (except shares in golf clubs etc.)—the place where the securities were located.

(i) National bonds, prefectural or municipal bonds, or debentures, etc. which are registered—the place of the agency at which they are registered.

(j) Interests in juridical persons such as general partnerships, limited partnerships or limited liability companies—the place of the head or main office of such juridical person.

(k) Pecuniary credits—the place of the creditor's office through which the pecuniary credit is assigned.

(l) Shares in golf club etc.—the place where the golf club etc. is located.

(m) Assets other than the above whose location is not clear—the place of the transferer's or lessor's office through which the transaction is conducted.

¶ 8-050

(b) (a)に掲げる船舶以外の船舶　譲渡又は貸付けを行う者の譲渡又は貸付けに係る事務所等（事務所，事業所その他これらに準ずるもの）の所在地
(c) 航空機　航空機の登録をした機関の所在地。登録を受けていない航空機にあっては，譲渡又は貸付けを行う者の譲渡又は貸付けに係る事務所等の所在地

(d) 鉱業権若しくは租鉱権又は採石権等　鉱業権に係る鉱区若しくは租鉱権に係る租鉱区又は採石権等に係る採石場の所在地
(e) 特許権，実用新案権，意匠権，商標権，回路配置利用権又は育成者権　これらの権利の登録をした機関の所在地。同一の権利について2以上の国において登録をしている場合には，これらの権利の譲渡又は貸付けを行う者の住所地
(f) 著作権（出版権及び著作隣接権その他これらに準ずる権利を含む。）又は特別の技術による生産方式（いわゆるノウ・ハウ）及びこれらに準ずるもの　これらのものの譲渡等又は貸付けを行う者の住所地

(g) 営業権又は漁業権若しくは入漁権　これらの権利に係る事業を行う者の住所地

(h) 有価証券（ゴルフ場利用株式等を除く。）　有価証券が所在していた場所
(i) 登録国債等　登録国債等の登録をした機関の所在地

(j) 合名会社等法人の出資者の持分　持分に係る法人の本店又は主たる事務所の所在地

(k) 金銭債権　金銭債権に係る債権者の譲渡に係る事務所等の所在地

(l) ゴルフ場利用株式等　ゴルフ場その他の施設の所在地

(m) 上記以外の資産でその所在していた場所が明らかでないもの　譲渡又は貸付けを行う者の譲渡又は貸付けに係る事務所等の所在地

672   CONSUMPTION TAX

(2) Provision of services

In principle, the place where the service is provided (Reg 6②) with the exception of the following services.

(a) International transportation—either the place of departure, forwarding, or arrival (if any of these is in Japan, it is a domestic transaction).

(b) International communication—either the place the communication was sent or received.

(c) International mail—either the place of forwarding or distributing of mail.

(d) Insurance—the place of the office of the insurance company (excluding the agent for the contract) granting the insurance contract.

(e) Provision and design of information—the place of the office of the person providing the service through which the information is provided or designed.

(f) Provision of services such as research, planning or advice requiring special knowledge of science or technology with respect to the construction or manufacture of buildings or plants for mining and manufacturing industries—the place where most of the materials necessary for the construction of manufacture are supplied.

(g) Provision of services other than the above for which the place where the service is rendered is not clear—the place of the office of the person providing the service through which the service is rendered.

(3) Others

Loans for interest (including acquisition of interest-bearing national bonds, etc.), making deposits or discounting bills, etc.—the place of the office of the person performing the act through which the service is provided (Reg 6③).

¶ 8-060 Taxation on foreign goods removed from a bonded area

(1) Object of taxation

Foreign goods (goods imported from foreign countries and goods

¶ 8-060

消　費　税　673

(2)　**役務の提供**

　役務の提供については，原則としては，その役務の提供が行われた場所が国内にあれば国内取引となる（消令6②）。

　ただし，次に掲げるものについては，それぞれ次に掲げる場所が国内にある場合には，その役務の提供は，国内取引に該当する。

　(a)　国内及び国内以外の地域にわたって行われる旅客又は貨物の輸送　出発地若しくは発送地又は到着地

　(b)　国内及び国内以外の地域にわたって行われる通信　発信地又は受信地

　(c)　国内及び国内以外の地域にわたって行われる郵便　差出地又は配達地

　(d)　保険　保険に係る事業を営む者（保険契約締結の代理をする者を除く。）の保険契約の締結に係る事務所等の所在地

　(e)　情報の提供又は設計　情報の提供又は設計を行う者の情報の提供又は設計に係る事務所等の所在地

　(f)　専門的な科学技術に関する知識を必要とする調査，企画，立案等に係る役務の提供で，建物，鉱工業生産施設等の建設又は製造に関するもの　その建設又は製造に必要な資材の大部分が調達される場所

　(g)　上記以外の役務の提供で国内及び国内以外の地域にわたって行われる役務の提供その他役務の提供が行われた場所が明らかでないもの　役務の提供を行う者の役務の提供に係る事務所等の所在地

(3)　**その他**

　利子を対価とする金銭の貸付け（利子を対価とする国債等の取得等を含む。），預貯金の預入・手形の割引等　これらの行為を行う者のこれらの行為に係る事務所等の所在地（消令6③）。

¶8-060　保税地域から引き取られる外国貨物に対する課税

(1)　**課税の対象**

　保税地域から引き取られる外国貨物（外国から本邦に到着した貨物及び輸

674   CONSUMPTION TAX

permitted for export) removed from a bonded area are subject to consumption tax (Law 4②). The term "foreign goods" is not limited to goods sold for consideration, all goods removed from a bonded area are subject to taxation, regardless of the business activity or whether the removal was for consideration.

(2) **Cases of deemed removal**

When foreign goods are consumed or used in a bonded area, such goods are deemed to have been removed from the bonded area by the person who consumed or used them at the time of consumption or use. The following foreign goods are not subject to taxation (Law 4⑤, Reg 7):

(a) Foreign goods consumed or used as raw materials of taxable foreign goods (other than those which are non-taxable under Law 6②).

(b) Foreign goods consumed or used by competent government officials in accordance with the law (for inspection purposes, etc.).

Non-taxable Transactions

¶ 8-070 **Domestic transactions**

Transfers of assets, etc. conducted in Japan, which are discussed in ¶ 8-075 to ¶ 8-163 are not taxable (Law 6①, Table 1, Reg 8 to 16).

¶ 8-075 **Transfers and leases of land (including rights attaching to land)**

(1) While "land" does not usually include fixed assets, such as timber, which may be the object of a separate transaction, garden trees, stone walls and other garden arrangements (including pavilions, pantheons and other facilities attaching to gardens) which are transferred en bloc with housing land (except houses, buildings and attached facilities to houses or buildings) are included in "land" (R 6-1-1).

"Rights attaching to land" means rights with respect to the use or profitable utilization of land such as superficies, leases servitium, the right to permanent tenancy, the right to cultivate, etc. It excludes mining rights, quarrying rights and rights to use hot springs (R 6-1-2).

Leases attaching to land include, for example, leases of superficies

¶ 8-070

消　費　税　675

出の許可を得た貨物）には，消費税が課税される（消法4②）。

　保税地域から引き取られる外国貨物については，国内において事業者が行った資産の譲渡等の場合のように，「事業として対価を得て行われる……」ものには限られないから，保税地域から引き取られる外国貨物に係る対価が無償であっても，また保税地域からの外国貨物の引取りが事業として行われないものであっても，いずれも課税の対象となる。

⑵　**引取りとみなす場合**

　保税地域において，外国貨物が消費又は使用された場合には，その消費又は使用をした者がその消費又は使用をしたときに，その外国貨物をその保税地域から引き取るものとみなして消費税が課税される。ただし，次の場合には課税対象とはならない（消法4⑤，消令7）。

　⒜　その外国貨物が課税貨物（消費税法第6条第2項により非課税とされるもの以外の外国貨物をいう。）の原料又は材料として消費又は使用される場合
　⒝　法律の規定により権限のある公務員が収去した外国貨物をその権限に基づいて消費又は使用する場合等

非　課　税

¶8-070　国内取引

　国内において行われる資産の譲渡等のうち，¶8-075〜¶8-163に掲げるものは，非課税とされる（消法6①，別表1，消令8〜16）。

¶8-075　土地（土地の上に存する権利を含む。）の譲渡及び貸付け

⑴　「土地」には，立木その他独立して取引の対象となる土地の定着物は含まれないが，その土地が宅地である場合には，庭木，石垣，庭園（庭園に附属する亭，庭内神し（祠）その他これらに類する附属設備を含む。）その他これらに類するもののうち宅地と一体として譲渡するもの（建物及びその附属施設を除く。）は含まれる（消基通6-1-1）。

　　「土地の上に存する権利」とは，地上権，土地の賃借権，地役権，永小作権等の土地の使用収益に関する権利をいい，鉱業権，土石採取権及び温泉利用権は，これに含まれない（消基通6-1-2）。

　　土地の上に存する権利の貸付けには，例えば，地上権の貸付け，賃借権の転貸がこれに該当する。

676   CONSUMPTION TAX

and sub-leases.

(2) The following "leases of land" are taxable (Reg 8):

   (a) Short term leases

        Leases of land for a period of less than one month are taxable
        (R 6-1-4).

   (b) Use of facilities attached to land

        The use of facilities attached to land, such as buildings, baseball
        grounds, swimming pools and tennis courts are excluded from
        the definition of a lease of land and are taxable, even though the
        use of facilities brings about a "lease of the land" (R 6-1-5).

Note:
   1. When an enterprise permits another to use its land as a parking lot for
       cars or bicycles and the land has no improvements such as a prepared
       surface, fences, partitions or buildings for the use as a parking lot, that
       right to use the land constitutes a lease.
   2. When a lease of buildings includes other facilities or services attached to
       the use of land, the total consideration is treated as payment for a lease
       of buildings, etc., even if the consideration is divided into an amount for a
       lease of buildings, etc., and an amount for lease of the land.

¶ 8-080 Transfers of securities and payments prescribed in the Foreign Exchange and Trade Law

(1) Non-taxable "securities" include:

   (a) Securities prescribed under Art. 2 of the Securities Transaction
        Tax Law:

        (i)   national, prefectural or municipal bonds, debentures, con-
              vertible bonds and bonds with warrants (to subscribe for
              shares);

        (ii) investment securities issued by corporations established by
              special legislation, such as the Bank of Japan;

        (iii) stock certificates;

        (iv) beneficiary certificates of securities investment trusts;

        (v)   beneficiary certificates of loan trusts;

        (vi) securities identified in (i) to (v) above, and issued by foreign
              countries or foreign corporations; and

        (vii) shares without issued share certificates, warrants, or rights
              relating to underwriting of the stock issue.

   (b) Other securities such as:

¶ 8-080

消　費　税　677

(2)　「土地の貸付け」の中で課税されるのは，次の場合である（消令8）。
　(a)　一時的に使用させる場合
　　　契約貸付期間が1月に満たない土地の貸付けは課税される（消基通6-1-4）。
　(b)　施設の利用に伴い土地を使用させる場合
　　　例えば，建物，野球場，プール又はテニスコート等の施設の利用が土地の使用を伴うことになるとしてもこれは土地の貸付けから除かれ，課税される（消基通6-1-5）。

　（注）：1．事業者が駐車場又は駐輪場として土地を利用させた場合において，その土地につき
　　　　　　駐車場又は駐輪場としての用途に応じる地面の整備又はフェンス，区画，建物の設置
　　　　　　等をしていないとき（駐車又は駐輪にかかる車輌又は自転車の管理をしている場合を
　　　　　　除く。）は，その土地の使用は，土地の貸付けに含まれる。
　　　　　2．建物その他施設の貸付け又は役務の提供（「建物の貸付等」という。）に伴って土地
　　　　　　を使用させた場合において，建物の貸付け等に係る対価と土地の貸付けに係る対価と
　　　　　　に区分しているときであっても，その対価の額の合計額が当該建物の貸付け等に係る
　　　　　　対価の額となることに留意する。

¶8-080　有価証券等の譲渡並びに外国為替及び外国貿易法に規定する支払手段の譲渡

(1)　非課税の対象となる有価証券等の範囲は，次のとおりである（消基通6-2-1）。
　(a)　証券取引法第2条に規定する有価証券

　　(i)　国債証券，地方債証券，社債券，転換社債券及び新株引受権付社債券

　　(ii)　日本銀行その他の特別の法律により設立された法人の発行する出資証券
　　(iii)　株券
　　(iv)　証券投資信託の受益証券
　　(v)　貸付信託の受益証券
　　(vi)　外国又は外国法人の発行する有価証券で(i)〜(v)の性質を有するもの

　　(vii)　株券の発行がない株式，株式の引受けによる権利，新株引受権

　(b)　有価証券に類するもの

678   CONSUMPTION TAX

    (i)   national, prefectural or municipal bonds, or debentures registered under legislation concerning national bonds or rules relating to the registration of debentures, etc. (including bonds issued by entities other than corporations under special laws) and similar foreign bonds;

    (ii) interests in general partnerships, limited partnerships or limited liability companies, the interests of union members in Kyodo Kumiai or membership interests and interests in other corporations;

    (iii) mortgage securities (including similar foreign securities); and

    (iv) pecuniary credit such as loans, deposits, accounts receivable (including negotiable certificates of deposit and commercial paper) (R 6-2-1).

Note:
Bills of lading, warehouse bonds and membership rights in golf courses, etc. in the form of shares or deposits are excluded from these non-taxable securities (R 6-2-2).

(2) Payments prescribed in Art. 6① to ⑦ of the Foreign Exchange and Trade Law cover the following, which excludes those for collection and sales (Reg 9③, ④ and R 6-2-3):

    (a) Bills of exchange issued by banks, and legal currency.

    (b) Checks (including traveller's checks), bills of exchange, postal money orders and letters of credit.

    (c) Promissory notes.

    (d) Payments similar to (a) to (c) above.

    (e) Payment by qualified electric or magnetic cards, etc.

    (f) Special drawing rights (SDRs) under the Agreement of the International Monetary Fund.

¶ 8-090 Lease of assets with interest

A lease of assets or provision of services with interest or the like, such as the following, are non-taxable (R 6-3-1).

(1) Interest on national, prefectural or municipal bonds, debentures, convertible bonds, bonds with warrants, loans, deposits and special drawing rights (SDRs) under the International Monetary Fund.

(2) Guarantee fees for credit.

(3) Trust remuneration for joint operation trusts or bond investment

¶ 8-090

消　費　税　679

(i)　国債に関する法律又は社債等登録法の規定により登録された国債，地方債及び社債（会社以外の法人が特別の法律により発行する債券を含む。）並びにこれらに類する外国の債券

(ii)　合名会社，合資会社又は有限会社の社員の持分，協同組合等の組合員又は会員の持分その他法人の出資者の持分

(iii)　抵当証券（これに類する外国の証券を含む。）

(iv)　貸付金，預金，売掛金その他の金銭債権（譲渡性預金証書及びコマーシャルペーパーを含む。）

(注)：なお，船荷証券，貨物引換証又は倉庫証券は，これに含まれない。また，株式，出資若しくは預託形態によるゴルフ会員権等もこれに含まれない（消基通6-2-2）。

(2)　外国為替及び外国貿易法第6条の第1項から第7項に規定されている支払手段等とは次のものをいい，収集品及び販売用のものはこれに含まれない（消令9③，④，消基通6-2-3）。
(a)　銀行券，政府紙幣，小額紙幣及び硬貨
(b)　小切手（旅行小切手を含む），為替手形及び郵便為替，信用状
(c)　約束手形
(d)　(a)～(c)に掲げるもののいずれかに類するもので，支払のために使用することができるもの
(e)　一定の電子的又は電磁的支払手段
(f)　国際通貨基金協定に規定する特別引出権（SDR）

¶8-090　利子を対価とする資産の貸付け等

非課税となる利子を対価とする貸付金等の範囲は，概ね次のものを対価とする資産の貸付け又は役務の提供となる（消基通6-3-1）。
(1)　国債，地方債，社債，転換社債，新株引受権付社債，貸付金，預金，貯金，国際通貨基金協定に規定する特別引出権（SDR）の利子

(2)　信用の保証料
(3)　合同運用信託又は公社債投資信託（株式又は出資に対する投資として運

680   CONSUMPTION TAX

trusts (limited to trusts in which funds are not invested in shares and capital).

(4) Insurance premiums (excluding portions corresponding to administration expenses for approved pension plans etc.).

(5) Dividends distributed by joint operation trusts, securities investment trusts or special public interest trusts.

(6) Payments from mutual funds or term deposits, or profit from mutual financing contracts.

(7) Interest on mortgage securities.

(8) The difference between the issued price and the redemption price of bonds (including interest-bearing bonds) of which the issued price is under face value.

(9) Discount fees for bills and notes.

(10) The difference between the purchase price and par value of pecuniary credits or advance payments.

(11) Commission on installment sales prescribed under Art. 2① of the Installment Sales Law, loan-related sales prescribed under Art. 2② and installment sales promotion prescribed under Art. 2③ (limited to those where the amount is clearly described in the contract).

(12) Interest or guarantee fees in the case of transfers of assets according to a method similar to installment sales but this is limited to the amount which is described in the contract.

(13) Lending fees for securities (including registered national, prefectural and municipal bonds, and debentures, but excluding rights to use golf facilities).

(14) Mortgage guarantee fees.

(15) Premiums for mutual insurance, etc. (excluding portions corresponding to administration expenses for approved pension plans, etc.).

(16) Amounts equivalent to interest or insurance premiums in trusts leasing movable or immovable property with special provision for transferring the property for the amount of undepreciated balance at the time of termination of the leasing period (limited to those cases where the amount equivalent to interest and insurance premiums is clearly distinguished in the contract).

(17) Amounts equivalent to interest or insurance premiums of rent of financial lease (limited to those cases where the amount equivalent to interest and insurance premiums is clearly described in the contract).

¶ 8-090

用しないものに限られる。）の信託報酬

⑷　保険料（適格退職年金契約等に係る事務費部分は除かれる。）

⑸　合同運用信託，証券投資信託又は特定公益信託等の収益の分配として分配される分配金
⑹　相互掛金又は定期積金の給付補填金及び無尽契約の掛金差益

⑺　抵当証券の利息
⑻　割引債（利付債も含まれる。）の償還差益

⑼　手形の割引料
⑽　金銭債権の買取り又は立替払に係る差益

⑾　割賦販売法第2条第1項に規定する割賦販売，同法第2条第2項に規定するローン提携販売及び同条第3項に規定する割賦購入あっせんの手数料（契約においてその額が明示されているものに限られる。）

⑿　割賦販売等に準ずる方法により資産の譲渡等を行う場合の金利又は保証料相当額（契約においてその額が明示されている部分に限られる。）

⒀　有価証券（登録された国債，地方債及び社債を含み，ゴルフ場利用株式等は除かれる。）の賃貸料

⒁　物上保証料
⒂　共済掛金（適格退職年金契約に係る事務費部分を除く。）等

⒃　動産又は不動産の貸付けを行う信託で，貸付期間の終了時に未償却残額で譲渡する旨の特約が付けられたものの金利及び保険料相当額（金利及び保険料相当額が契約において明確に区分されているものに限られる。）

⒄　いわゆるファイナンス・リースに係るリース料のうち，金利及び保険料相当額（契約において利子又は保険料の額として明示されている部分に限られる。）

682   CONSUMPTION TAX

Note:

1. Interest on advance payment is included in "non-taxable leases of assets with interest", since the advance payment is similar to a loan in its economical substance (R 6-3-5).
2. Agency commission or other commission for services, such as damage assessment or investigation, etc. on behalf of insurance companies, etc., which is received by insurance agencies is taxable (R 6-3-2).
3. Premiums for mutual insurance borne by members of bodies, organized not only under law but also voluntarily, are included in non-taxable premiums for mutual insurance (R 6-3-3).

¶ 8-100 Transfers of postage stamps and others

(1) Non-taxable transfers of postage stamps, other postal materials and stamps for stamp tax are limited to transfers conducted by the national or municipal government and transfers at designated places such as post offices, postage stamp shops or stamp (for stamp tax) shops. Transfers of stamps at non-designated places (so-called transfers of collections of postage stamps) are taxable (Table 1 (4), R 6-4-1).

(2) Non-taxable postage stamps and other postal materials are those listed below (R 6-4-2):

(a) postage stamps;

(b) post cards (issued by the government);

(c) postal letters;

(d) postal envelopes for forwarding cash;

(e) packing materials for parcels; and

(f) prepaid cards for (a) to (e) above.

¶ 8-110 Transfers of exchange checks, etc.

Transfers of exchange checks, etc. are non-taxable (Table 1 (4), Reg 11).

"Exchange checks, etc." are instruments presenting the right to claim supply of goods regardless of the name of them such as merchandise bonds (exchange checks) or gift certificates, and instruments presenting the right to claim provision of services or lease of goods.

"Instrument presenting the right to claim" means an instrument in which the preparer or the obligor of the instrument promises to supply or lease certain goods, or to provide certain services to the bearer upon exchange of the instrument, regardless of whether the bearer is inscribed or uninscribed, or the preparer and the obligor are the same or not (R 6-4-3).

Note:

Requests for release of goods issued by their owner to a warehouse keeper

¶ 8-100

消　費　税　683

（注）：1．前渡金等の利子のように経済的実質が貸付金であるものに係る利子は，非課税である利子を対価とする資産の貸付けに該当する（消基通6-3-5）。

2．保険代理店が収受する役務の提供に係る代理店手数料又は保険会社等の委託を受けて行う損害調査や鑑定等の役務の提供に係る手数料は，課税資産の譲渡等に係る対価に該当する（消基通6-3-2）。

3．非課税とされる共済掛金には，法令等により組織されている団体等のほか，任意の互助組織による団体の構成員が負担する共済掛金が含まれる（消基通6-3-3）。

¶8-100　国が行う郵便切手類又は印紙の譲渡

(1)　非課税とされる郵便切手類又は印紙の譲渡は，国又は地方公共団体が行う譲渡及び簡易郵便局又は郵便切手類販売所若しくは印紙売りさばき所における譲渡等一定の場所における譲渡に限られるから，これら以外の場所における郵便切手類又は印紙の譲渡（いわゆる収集品たる郵便切手類等の譲渡等）は，非課税とはならない（別表1四，消基通6-4-1）。

(2)　非課税となる郵便切手類とは次のものをいう（消基通6-4-2）。

(a)　郵便切手
(b)　官製葉書
(c)　郵便書簡
(d)　現金封筒
(e)　小包郵便包装物品
(f)　(a)～(e)の給付を受けることができるプリペイドカード

¶8-110　物品切手等の譲渡

物品切手等の譲渡は非課税である（別表1四，消令11）。

物品切手等とは，商品券その他名称のいかんを問わず，物品の給付請求権を表彰する証書（物品切手）及び役務の提供又は物品の貸付けにかかる請求権を表彰する証書をいう。

「～の請求権を表彰する証書」とは，証書の所持人に対してその作成者又は給付義務者がこれと引換えに一定の物品の給付若しくは物品の貸付け又は特定の役務の提供をすることを約する証書をいい，記名式であるかどうか，又はその証書の作成者と給付義務者とが同一であるかどうかは問わない（消基通6-4-3）。

（注）：資産の寄託者が倉庫業者あてに作成する出庫依頼書又はこれらに類する文書は，物品切手等に該当しない。

684   CONSUMPTION TAX

are excluded from exchange checks, etc.

Cards for obtaining goods (including transport tickets) or services through vending machines, etc. and cards similar to these are included in exchange checks, etc. Therefore, prepaid cards such as telephone cards and Orange Cards are included in exchange checks, etc.

¶ 8-120 Services rendered by the government, local governments public corporations, and public interest corporations

Certain fees received by the government, or local government, by corporations listed in table 3, and by persons designated or appointed by the government or local governments according to legislation are not taxable (R 6-5-1). This includes the following:

(1) Fees paid for the following services when the provision of the services and collection of the fees are provided for by legislation:

   (a) registrations, patents, licenses, permissions, sanctions, approvals, recognitions, identifications and designations;

   (b) inspections, examinations and training;

   (c) certification;

   (d) delivery, renewal, revision, perusal and duplication of official documents;

   (e) settlements of disputes such as trials;

   (f) issuing passports;

   (g) arbitration, delivering judgements and other determinations;

   (h) delivery, renewal, revision, perusal and duplication of documents similar to official documents (including medals, marks, etc.); and

   (i) settlements of objections and requests for reconsideration, etc.

(2) Fees paid for registration, recognition, identification, designation, inspection, examination and training (hereinafter referred to as "registration, etc.") when carried out according to legislation and when the collection of the fees is not provided for by legislation:

   (a) registration, etc. which is required by legislation as a requisite to obtain or to retain a qualification, such as attorneys-at-law, or to practice using the qualification;

   (b) registration, etc. of assets which is required by legislation as a requisite to dealings with those assets, such as exportation;

¶ 8-120

消　費　税　685

　自動販売機等により物品（乗車券等を含む。）の譲渡又はサービスの給付
を受けるためのカードその他これに類するものは，物品切手等に該当する。
したがって，テレフォンカードやオレンジカード等のいわゆるプリペイドカ
ードは物品切手等に該当する。

¶8-120　国，地方公共団体，公共法人，公益法人等が法令に基づき徴収する手数料等に係る役務の提供

　国，地方公共団体，法別表第三に掲げる法人その他法令に基づき国若しく
は地方公共団体の委託又は指定を受けた者が徴収する手数料等で法別表
((国，地方公共団体等が行う役務の提供)) の規定により非課税とされている
ものは，次のものである（消基通6-5-1）。

(1)　法令に基づいて行われる次に掲げる事務の手数料，特許料，申立料その
　他の料金（手数料等）で，その徴収について法令に根拠となる規定がある
　もの
　(a)　登記，登録，特許，免許，許可，認可，承認，認定，確認及び指定
　(b)　検査，検定，試験，審査，及び講習
　(c)　証明
　(d)　公文書の交付（再交付及び書換交付を含む。），更新，訂正，閲覧及び
　　謄写
　(e)　裁判その他の紛争の処理
　(f)　旅券の発給
　(g)　裁定，裁決，判定及び決定
　(h)　公文書に類するもの（記章，標識その他これらに類するものを含む。）
　　の交付（再交付及び書換交付を含む。），更新，訂正，閲覧及び謄写

　(i)　異議申立て，審査請求その他これらに類するものの処理
(2)　法令に基づいて行われる登録，認定，確認，指定，検査，検定，試験，
　審査及び講習（登録等）で法令に手数料等の徴収の根拠となる規定がない
　もののうち，次に掲げる登録等の手数料等

　(a)　法令において，弁護士その他の法令に基づく資格を取得し，若しくは
　　維持し，又はその資格に係る業務若しくは行為を行うための要件とされ
　　ている登録等
　(b)　法令において，輸出その他の行為を行う場合にはその対象となる資産
　　又は使用する資産について登録等を受けることが要件とされている登録
　　等

686   CONSUMPTION TAX

    (c)   registration, etc. where a certain standard is required, or use of a certain name is prohibited, by legislation and the registration, etc. states that the asset meets the standard;

    (d)   registration, etc. which has to be carried out as a legal obligation; and

    (e)   certification and delivery, renewal, revision, perusal and duplication of official documents and similar documents (except those services which do not fall within (a) to (d) above).

(3) Handling fees, etc. collected by the government or local governments according to legislation for failure to pay fees or amounts assessed, etc.

(4) Handling fees, etc. collected by the certain indipendent state-run institutions according to legislation.

¶ 8-130 International postal services and foreign exchange services

(1) **Non-taxable services**

The following international postal services are not taxable:

    (a)   services for overseas postal money orders, overseas mail transfers;

    (b)   services for foreign exchange and issuance of payment overseas (letters of credit, traveller's checks, etc.); and

    (c)   services provided by a monetary exchange issuing traveller's checks.

(2) **Taxable services**

The following foreign exchange services are taxable (Reg 13):

    (a)   acting as an intermediary or agency for residents to obtain negotiable certificates of deposit from non-residents or for non-residents to obtain such certificates from residents;

    (b)   acting as an intermediary or agency for residents to obtain commercial papers from non-residents and for non-residents to obtain such securities from residents; and

    (c)   acting as custodian of securities, jewellery, etc. for non-residents.

¶ 8-140 Medical services

(1) **Non-taxable medical services**

The following medical services are non-taxable (Table 1 (6)):

¶ 8-130

消　費　税　687

(c)　法令において，登録等により一定の規格に該当するものとされた資産
でなければ一定の規格についての表示を付し，又は一定の名称を使用す
ることができないこととされている登録等

(d)　法令において，登録等を受けることが義務付けられている登録等

(e)　証明，公文書及び公文書に類するものの交付（再交付及び書換交付を
含む。），更新，訂正，閲覧及び謄写（(a)から(d)までに該当しない登録等
に係るものを除く。）

(3)　国又は地方公共団体が，法令に基づき行う他の者の徴収すべき料金，賦
課金その他これらに類するものの滞納処分について，法令に基づき他の者
から徴収する手数料等

(4)　一定の独立行政法人等が法令に基づき徴収する手数料

¶8-130　国際郵便為替及び国際郵便振替の役務の提供並びに外国為替業務及び両替業務としての役務の提供

(1)　非課税取引

非課税とされる国際郵便為替等の役務の提供の範囲は，次のとおりである。

(a)　外国郵便為替，外国郵便振替の役務の提供

(b)　外国為替取引及び対外支払手段（信用状，旅行小切手）の発行に係る
役務の提供

(c)　両替商が行う旅行小切手の発行に係る役務の提供

(2)　課税取引

外国為替業務関係のうち，次のものは課税の対象となる（消令13）。

(a)　譲渡性預金証書の居住者による非居住者からの取得又は非居住者によ
る居住者からの取得に係る媒介，取次ぎ又は代理に係る業務

(b)　コマーシャルペーパーの居住者による非居住者からの取得又は非居住
者による居住者からの取得に係る媒介，取次ぎ又は代理に係る業務

(c)　非居住者のために行う有価証券，貴金属その他の物品の保護預り業務

¶8-140　医療の給付その他これらに類するものに係る医療

(1)　非課税となる医療等

非課税となる医療等の範囲は，概ね次のとおりである（別表１六）。

688   CONSUMPTION TAX

(a) medical treatment provided, or for which specified medical care expenses, family medical care expenses or special medical care expenses are receivable, under the Health Insurance Law or National Health Insurance Law, etc.;

(b) medical services provided and medical treatment for which specified medical care expenses and medical care expenses are receivable, and medical treatment using medical facilities for aged persons who are entitled to receive medical treatment for the aged, under the Health Law for the Aged;

(c) medical services provided or for which medical expenses are receivable under the Disabled Persons Welfare Law, medical services provided under the Mental Health Law, medical services provided or for which medical expenses are receivable under the National Assistance Law and medical services provided, or for which medical expenses are receivable under the Law Concerning Medical Treatment for Victims of the Atomic Air Raids;

(d) medical services for which medical expenses are receivable under the Law concerning Compensation for Victims of Environment Pollution;

(e) medical treatment provided, or for which medical expenses are receivable under the Worker's Compensation Insurance Law; medical services provided, or for which medical expenses are receivable where the medical services are provided as a labor welfare project under the same law; medical treatment for which compensation for injury is paid to the victim under the Automobile Accident Compensation Security Law; and

(f) other similar medical services or treatment, such as medical services for which financial assistance is granted under the School Health Law; medical services for children provided, or for which medical expenses are receivable under the Health Law for Mothers and Children; and medical services or treatment the expense of which is totally or partly borne by the government or a local government according to their policies.

(2) **Taxable medical services**

The following medical services are taxable:

(a) fees for a hospital room (less the amount covered by insurance under the Health Insurance Act);

¶ 8-140

消　費　税　689

(a)　健康保険法，国民健康保険法等の規定に基づく療養の給付及び特定療養費，療養費，家族療養費又は特別療養費の支給に係る療養

(b)　老人保健法の規定に基づく医療及び特定療養費又は医療費の支給に係る療養並びに老人医療受給対象者に係る施設療養

(c)　身体障害者福祉法の規定に基づく更生医療の給付及び更生医療に要する費用の支給に係る医療，精神保健法の規定に基づく医療，生活保護法の規定に基づく医療扶助のための医療の給付及び医療扶助のための金銭給付に係る医療並びに原子爆弾被爆者の医療等に関する法律の規定に基づく医療の給付及び医療費又は一般疾病医療費の支給に係る医療

(d)　公害健康被害の補償等に関する法律の規定に基づく療養の費用の支給に係る療養

(e)　労働者災害補償保険法の規定に基づく療養の給付及び療養の費用の支給に係る療養並びに同法の規定による労働福祉事業として行われる医療の措置及び医療に要する費用の支給に係る医療，自動車損害賠償保障法の規定による損害賠償の支払を受けるべき被害者に対するその支払に係る療養

(f)　その他これらに類するものとしての例えば学校保健法の規定に基づく医療に要する費用の援助に係る医療，母子保健法の規定に基づく養育医療の給付又は養育医療に要する費用の支給に係る医療等，国又は地方公共団体の施策に基づきその要する費用の全部又は一部を国又は地方公共団体により負担される医療及び療養（いわゆる公費負担医療）

(2)　**課税の対象となる医療**
医療のうち課税の対象となるのは，概ね次のものである。
(a)　特別の病室の提供のうち，いわゆる差額ベッド代部分

690   CONSUMPTION TAX

   (b)   fees for dental care (less the amount covered by insurance);

   (c)   that part of the fee charged for a patient's first visit to a designated University Hospital, etc. not covered by insurance;

   (d)   fees for special meals at hospitals (less amounts covered by insurance);

   (e)   dental charges not covered by insurance; orthopedic treatment not covered by insurance;

   (f)   acupuncture, moxa cautery treatment not covered by insurance.

   (g)   preventive injections, medical check-ups, medical advice, health education; and

   (h)   services provided under the Social Insurance Law (sterilization, sanitization, cleaning and repair of bed clothes or equipment used for nursery care, meal supply or medical examination).

¶ 8-150 Transfers of assets, etc. involving social welfare services provided under the Social Welfare Services Law, etc.

The following transfers of assets, etc. involving social welfare services provided under the Social Welfare Services Law, etc. are non-taxable. However, transfers of assets, etc. carried out as activities of industrial workshops, mentioned below in (1)(d),(e),(g), and (2)(g) are taxable (Table 1 (7)).

(1) **First-class Social Welfare Services.**

   (a)   Businesses operating aid facilities, rehabilitation facilities and other facilities for providing the poor with relief as stipulated in the National Assistance Law.

   (b)   Businesses operating infant homes, homes for mothers and children, homes for dependent, neglected or abused children, homes for mentally handicapped children, facilities for physically handicapped children, facilities for severely handicapped children, facilities for the short term treatment of children with emotional problems or juvenile reformatories as stipulated in the Child Welfare Law.

   (c)   Businesses operating homes for the aged, special homes for the aged and low-cost housing for the aged as stipulated in the Welfare Law for the Aged.

   (d)   Businesses operating rehabilitation facilities, treatment facilities, welfare homes or industrial workshops for disabled per-

¶ 8-150

消　費　税　691

(b)　歯科治療差額部分

(c)　指定された大学病院等での初診の保険給付以外の部分

(d)　特別注文食の給食料との差額部分

(e)　歯科自由診療，保険対象外の整形施術

(f)　保険対象外のはり，きゅう施術

(g)　予防接種，健康診断，健康相談，健康教育

(h)　社会保険診療に係る受託事業（看護，給食，検査，寝具設備に係る消毒，洗濯又は修理）

¶8-150　社会福祉事業法等に規定する社会福祉事業等として行われる資産の譲渡等

社会福祉事業法等に規定する次の社会福祉事業等に係る資産の譲渡等は，非課税とされる。ただし，これらのうち(1)の(d)，(e)，(g)及び(2)の(g)の事業のうち授産施設等を経営する事業において，授産作業に基づき行われる資産の譲渡等は課税対象とされている（別表1七）。

(1)　第一種社会福祉事業

(a)　生活保護法にいう救護施設，更生施設その他生計困難者を無料又は低額な料金で収容して生活の扶助を行うことを目的とする施設を経営する事業及び生計困難者に対して助葬を行う事業

(b)　児童福祉法にいう乳児院，母子寮，養護施設，精神薄弱児施設，精神薄弱児通園施設，盲ろうあ児施設，虚弱児施設，肢体不自由児施設，重症心身障害児施設，情緒障害児短期治療施設又は教護院を経営する事業

(c)　老人福祉法にいう養護老人ホーム，特別養護老人ホーム又は軽費老人ホームを経営する事業

(d)　身体障害者福祉法にいう身体障害者更生施設，身体障害者療護施設，身体障害者福祉ホーム又は身体障害者授産施設を経営する事業

692   CONSUMPTION TAX

sons as stipulated in the Disabled Persons Welfare Law.

(e) Businesses operating rehabilitation facilities or industrial workshops for mentally deficient persons as stipulated in the Welfare Law for Mentally Deficient Persons.

(f) Businesses operating rescue homes as stipulated in the Anti-Prostitution Act.

(g) Businesses operating public pawnshops or industrial workshops or businesses for providing the poor with interest-free or low-interest loans.

(2) **Second-class Social Welfare Services.**

(a) Businesses providing the necessaries of life or money for, or giving counsel to, the poor.

(b) Businesses providing home help service, day home help service or short stay service, businesses operating maternity homes, nursery schools or welfare facilities for children or businesses giving child-welfare counsel as stipulated in the Child Welfare Law.

(c) Businesses providing home help service, businesses operating welfare facilities for mothers and children and businesses providing similar home help service for families of fathers and children as stipulated in the Mother and Child and Widow Welfare Law.

(d) Businesses providing home help service, day home help service or short stay service and businesses operating day home service center for the aged, short-stay facilities for the aged or welfare centers for the aged as stipulated in the Welfare Law for the Aged.

(e) Businesses providing home help service, day home help service or short stay service and businesses operating welfare centers for disabled persons, facilities for manufacturing equipment for disabled persons and facilities for providing information for visually and/or auditorially handicapped persons or businesses giving rehabilitation counselling as stipulated in the Disabled Persons Welfare Law.

(f) Businesses providing home help service or short stay service or businesses assisting the daily life of mentally deficient persons or giving rehabilitation counsel as stipulated in the Welfare Law

¶ 8-150

消　費　税　693

(e)　精神薄弱者福祉法にいう精神薄弱者更生施設又は精神薄弱者授産施設を経営する事業

(f)　売春防止法にいう婦人保護施設を経営する事業

(g)　公益質屋又は授産施設を経営する事業及び生計困難者に対して無利子又は低利で資金を融通する事業

(2)　第二種社会福祉事業

(a)　生計困難者に生活必需品や金銭を与え又は生活の相談に応ずる事業

(b)　児童福祉法にいうホームヘルパー，デイサービス，ショートステイ事業及び助産施設，保育所，児童厚生施設経営事業又は児童福祉相談事業

(c)　母子及び寡婦福祉法にいうホームヘルパー事業，母子福祉施設経営事業及び同種の父子家庭へのホームヘルパー事業

(d)　老人福祉法にいうホームヘルパー，デイサービス，ショートステイ事業及び老人デイサービスセンター，老人ショートステイ施設又は老人福祉センターを経営する事業

(e)　身体障害者福祉法にいうホームヘルパー，デイサービス，ショートステイ事業及び身体障害者福祉センター，補装具製作施設，視聴覚障害者情報提供施設を経営する事業又は更生相談事業

(f)　精神薄弱者福祉法にいうホームヘルパー，ショートステイ事業又は精神薄弱者地域生活援助事業及び更生相談事業

694   CONSUMPTION TAX

for Mentally Deficient Persons.

(g)   Businesses operating rehabilitation facilities (including industrial workshops) for the mentally handicapped as stipulated in
the Mental Health Law.

(h)   Businesses renting simple houses to or providing free or low-
cost lodgings for the poor; Businesses providing free or low-cost
medical treatment for the poor.

(i)   Businesses providing free or low-cost facilities for health care
for the aged, as stipulated in the Health Law for the Aged, for
low or no charge.

(j)   Settlement work (various activities for the betterment or improvement of life of needy neighborhood inhabitants such as
setting up settlement houses for those inhabitants).

(k)   Supplementary businesses to the businesses listed in (a) to (j)
and (1)(a) to (g) above.

(3)   **Transfers of assets, etc. conducted as businesses similar to
social welfare services.**

For example, meal delivery services for the aged or bathing services
for the aged provided by buses equipped with bathrooms.

¶ 8-155 Midwifery services, burial services and the transfer or lease of equipment for disabled persons

The following transfers of assets, etc. are non-taxable:

(1)   transfers of assets, etc. with respect to midwifery services (i.e. provision of services ranging from testing for pregnancy to hospital treatment and testing after delivery including artificial abortion) (Table 1
(8));

(2)   burial and cremation services (Table 1 (9))

(3)   transfers or leases of equipment with special properties, structures
or functions for disabled persons (Table 1 (10)), for example, artificial
limbs, wheelchairs, crutches, artificial eyes, braillewriters, hearing
aids or remodelled automobiles.

¶ 8-160 School tuition, entrance fees and textbooks

(1)   The tuition, entrance fees, fees for facilities or equipment or fees for
issuing a diploma, etc. described below are non-taxable (Table 1 (11)):

¶ 8-155

消　費　税　695

(g)　精神保護法にいう精神障害者社会復帰施設を経営する事業

(h)　生計困難者のため無料又は低額で簡易住宅を貸し付け又は宿泊所等を利用させる事業，生計困難者のために無料又は低額な料金で診療を行う事業

(i)　生計困難者に対して，無料又は低額な費用で老人保健法にいう老人保健施設を利用させる事業

(j)　隣保事業（隣保館等の施設を設け，その近隣地域における福祉に欠けた住民を対象として，無料又は低額な料金でこれを利用させる等，当該住民の生活の改善及び向上を図るための各種の事業を行うものをいう。）

(k)　(a)～(j)及び(1)の(a)～(g)の事業に関する連絡又は助成を行う事業

(3)　社会福祉事業に類する事業として行われる資産の譲渡等

　例えば在宅老人に給食を届けるサービス又は風呂設備を備えたバスによる在宅老人への入浴サービスがこれに当たる。

¶8-155　助産，埋葬に係る資産の譲渡等及び身体障害者用物品の譲渡及び貸付け

　次の資産の譲渡等は非課税である。

(1)　助産に係る資産の譲渡等（医師又は助産師等による妊娠検査から出産後の入院検査までの間の役務の提供等をいい，人工妊娠中絶を含む。）（別表1八）

(2)　埋葬及び火葬に係る埋葬料及び火葬料を対価とする役務の提供（別表1九）

(3)　身体障害者の使用に供するための特殊な性状，構造又は機能を有する物品の譲渡，貸付等（別表1十）

　　例えば，義肢及び装具，車いす，歩行補助つえ，義眼，点字器，補聴器及び改造自動車等がこれに当たる。

¶8-160　教育施設の授業料又は入学金等を対価とする役務の提供及び教科用図書の譲渡

(1)　非課税の対象となる学校教育の範囲は，次のとおりであり，授業料，入学金，施設設備費及び学籍証明等手数料を対価とする部分が非課税とされ

696   CONSUMPTION TAX

(a) education services provided at schools as stipulated in the School Education Law;

(b) education services provided at professional schools as stipulated in the School Education Law;

(c) educational services satisfying certain conditions provided at other schools as stipulated in the School Education Law; and

(d) educational services satisfying certain conditions provided at certain independent administrative institutions, or at technical education universities as stipulated in the Professional Capacity Development Law.

(2) Textbooks:

Transfers of textbooks stipulated in the School Education Law (authorized textbooks, etc.) are non-taxable (Table 1 (12)).

¶ 8-163 Rent for houses

Rent for houses (except temporary rent) is non-taxable (Table 1 (13)).

A building for residence is taxable if it is rented for non-residential purposes such as for offices or shops. If meals are provided in boarding houses or dormitories, the charge for board is taxable even if it is included in the rent.

¶ 8-165 Foreign goods

The following foreign goods removed from a bonded area are non-taxable (Law 6②):

(1) securities, etc. listed in ¶ 8-080;

(2) postage stamps;

(3) other stamps;

(4) exchange checks, etc. defined in ¶ 8-110;

(5) equipment for disabled persons; and

(6) textbooks.

Tax Exemption

¶ 8-170 Export tax exemption

Transfers of taxable assets, etc. conducted by enterprises (except tax exempt enterprises (¶ 8-250)) in Japan which qualify as export transac-

¶ 8-163

消　費　税　697

ている（別表1十一）。
(a)　学校教育法に規定する学校を設置する者が当該学校における教育として行う役務の提供
(b)　学校教育法に規定する専修学校を設置する者がその専修学校の高等課程，専門課程又は一般課程における教育として行う役務の提供
(c)　学校教育法に規定する各種学校を設置する者がその各種学校における一定の要件に該当する教育として行う役務の提供
(d)　一定の独立行政法人である文教研修施設又は職業能力開発促進法に規定する職業訓練大学校等がその施設における一定の要件に該当する教育として行う役務の提供

(2)　非課税とされる教科用図書
　　学校教育法に規定する教科用図書（検定済教科書等）の譲渡は，非課税とされている（別表1十二）。

¶8-163　住宅の貸付け
　住宅の貸付け（一時的に貸し付ける場合を除く。）は非課税とされる（別表1十三）。
　住宅用に建築された建物であっても，事務所用，店舗用など居住用以外の目的で賃貸する場合は課税対象となる。また，下宿・独身寮において食事の提供がある場合には，食事提供部分は課税対象となる。

¶8-165　外国貨物
　保税地域から引き取られる外国貨物のうち次のものは，非課税とされる（消法6②）。
(1)　有価証券等（¶8-080に掲げられているもの）
(2)　郵便切手類
(3)　印紙，証紙
(4)　物品切手等（¶8-110に掲げられているもの）
(5)　身体障害者用物品
(6)　教科用図書

免　　　税

¶8-170　輸出免税
　事業者（¶8-250の免税事業者を除く。）が国内において行う課税資産の譲渡等のうち，輸出取引等（¶8-190に掲げられているもの）に該当するもの

698   CONSUMPTION TAX

tions (¶ 8-190) are tax-exempt (Law 7).

Export sales are not subject to consumption tax. The consumption tax component included in the purchase cost is creditable against the taxpayer's consumption tax liability, so that all export activities are tax-free. In a non-taxable transaction, on the other hand, the consumption tax component of the purchase cost cannot be credited.

¶ 8-180 Required conditions for export tax exemption

The export tax exemption is only available for transfers of assets, etc. which fulfill all of the following conditions (R 7-1-1).

(1) The transfers of assets, etc. are conducted by taxable enterprises (enterprises other than those which are exempt from the obligation of paying consumption tax under Art. 9① (tax exemption for small enterprises)).

(2) The transfers of assets, etc. are conducted in Japan.

(3) The transfers of assets, etc. qualify as transfers of taxable assets, etc. That is, where Art. 31① and ② (the special rule with respect to purchase tax credit for the export, etc. of non-taxable assets) does not apply.

(4) The transfers of assets, etc. qualify as one of the transactions listed in Art. 7①.

(5) The transfers of assets, etc. are certified to qualify as one of the transactions listed in Art. 7①.

¶ 8-190 Scope of export tax exemption

The following transactions qualify for the export tax exemption (R 7-2-1):

(1) transfers or leases of assets from Japan (typical export);

(2) transfers or leases of foreign goods (excluding (1));

(3) international transportation of passengers and cargo;

(4) transfers or leases of ships and aeroplanes for the transportation of passengers and cargo between foreign countries, or between a foreign country and Japan (hereinafter referred to as "ships etc. used for overseas service") (limited to transfers or leases for enterprises conducting shipping or airline transportation services, or leases of ships (hereinafter referred to as "a shipping enterprise, etc."));

(5) repair services for ships, etc. used for overseas service provided upon

¶ 8-180

については，消費税が免除される（消法7）。

輸出免税については，その売上げについて消費税が課されない一方，仕入れに係る消費税額は控除できるので，全く税負担を負わないこととなる。

これに対して非課税は，その売上げについて消費税が課されないが，仕入れに係る消費税額の控除ができないので，両者はその性格を異にする。

¶8-180　輸出免税の要件

資産の譲渡のうち，輸出免税の規定が適用されるのは，次の要件を満たしているものに限られる（消基通7-1-1）。

(1)　その資産の譲渡等は，課税事業者（消費税法第9条第1項（（小規模事業者に係る納税義務の免除））の規定により消費税を納める義務が免除される事業者以外の者）によって行われるものであること

(2)　その資産の譲渡等は，国内において行われるものであること

(3)　その資産の譲渡等は，消費税法第31条第1項及び第2項（（非課税資産の輸出等を行った場合の仕入れに係る消費税額の控除の特例））の適用がある場合を除き，課税資産の譲渡等に該当するものであること

(4)　その資産の譲渡等は，消費税法第7条第1項各号に掲げるものに該当するものであること

(5)　その資産の譲渡等は，消費税法第7条第1項各号に掲げるものに該当することにつき，証明がなされたものであること

¶8-190　輸出免税の範囲

免税の対象となる輸出等取引の範囲は，次のとおりである（消基通7-2-1）。

(1)　本邦からの輸出として行われる資産の譲渡又は貸付け（典型的な輸出のことである。）

(2)　外国貨物の譲渡又は貸付け（(1)に該当するものを除く。）

(3)　国内及び国内以外の地域にわたって行われる旅客若しくは貨物の輸送

(4)　外航船舶等（専ら国内及び国外の地域にわたって又は国外の地域の間で行われる旅客又は貨物の輸送の用に供される船舶又は航空機をいう。）の譲渡若しくは貸付け（船舶運航事業，船舶貸渡業又は航空運送事業を営む者（船舶運航事業者等）に対して行われるものに限られる。）

(5)　外航船舶等の修理で船舶運航事業者等の求めに応じて行われるもの

700   CONSUMPTION TAX

the request of a shipping enterprise, etc.;

(6) transfers or leases of containers used for the transportation of cargo between foreign countries, or between a foreign country and Japan, by shipping enterprises, etc. and repair services for such containers provided upon the request of a shipping enterprise, etc.;

(7) services provided for shipping enterprises, etc. such as piloting guidance, assistance for entry to and departure from ports or for the provision of facilities for entry to and departure from ports, anchorage or hardstanding and other similar services;

(8) services such as stevedoring, transportation, storage, tallying or inspection of foreign goods;

(9) international communication and postal services;

(10) transfers or leases of intangible assets to non-residents, such as mining rights, industrial rights (including know-how), copyright, goodwill, etc.; and

(11) services provided to non-residents except the following:

   (a) transport and storage services for assets located in Japan;

   (b) meals and accommodation services in Japan; and

   (c) services available in Japan which are similar to the above (a) and (b).

¶ 8-200 **Tax exemption for commodities sold at export shops**

Sales by export shops are tax-exempt when the goods (except expendables such as food, drinks, cigarettes, medicine, cosmetics, film and batteries) are for the daily use of non-residents and purchased by them in the prescribed manner outlined in (2) below (Law 8①, Reg 18①).

"Export shop" means a shop managed by an enterprise with the approval of the director of the tax office with jurisdiction over the place where the enterprise must pay tax (Law 8⑥).

(1) **Requirements**

   (a) Commodities transferred must be tax-exempt.

   (b) Sales must be made in the designated manner at an export shop.

   (c) Purchasers must be non-residents.

(2) **Procedure**

   Non-residents must present their passports when purchasing commodities at an export shop and their passports will receive a "Record of Purchase of Consumption-Tax-Exempt for Export". Non-residents

¶ 8-200

消　費　税　701

(6)　専ら本邦と外国又は外国と外国との間の貨物の輸送の用に供されるコンテナーの譲渡，貸付けで船舶運航事業者等に対するもの又はそのコンテナーの修理で船舶運航事業者等の求めに応じて行われるもの

(7)　外航船舶等の水先，誘導，入出港若しくは離着陸の補助又は入出港，離着陸，停泊若しくは駐機のための施設の提供に係る役務の提供その他これらに類する役務の提供で船舶運航事業者等に対して行われるもの

(8)　外国貨物の荷役，運送，保管，検数，鑑定等の役務の提供

(9)　国内と国外との間の通信又は郵便

(10)　鉱業権，工業所有権（ノウ・ハウを含む。），著作権，営業権等の無体財産権の譲渡又は貸付けで非居住者に対して行われるもの

(11)　非居住者に対して行われる役務の提供で次に掲げるもの以外のもの
　(a)　国内に所在する資産に係る運送又は保管
　(b)　国内における飲食又は宿泊
　(c)　(a)及び(b)に掲げるものに準ずるもので，国内において直接便益を享受するもの

¶8-200　輸出物品販売場において譲渡する物品の免税

　輸出物品販売場を経営する事業者が，非居住者に対し通常生活の用に供する物品（食品類，飲料類，たばこ，薬品類及び化粧品類，並びにフィルム，電池その他の消耗品を除く。）で，輸出するため所定の方法により購入されるものの譲渡を行った場合には消費税が免除される（消法8①，消令18①）。
　この場合の「輸出物品販売場」とは，事業者が経営する販売場で，納税地の所轄税務署長の許可を受けた販売場をいう（消法8⑥）。

(1)　免税要件
　(a)　譲渡に係る物品が免税対象物品であること
　(b)　輸出物品販売場において所定の方法により販売されること
　(c)　免税で購入する者が非居住者であること

(2)　免税手続
　非居住者は，輸出物品販売場において物品を購入する際，旅券等を提示し，これに購入の事実を記載した「輸出免税物品購入記録票」のはり付けを受けるとともに，購入後輸出するものであることを記載した「購入者誓約

702   CONSUMPTION TAX

must then submit a "Covenant of Purchaser of Consumption-Tax-Exempt of Ultimate Export" stating that the commodities are for ultimate export from Japan and will not be disposed of in Japan, and then the commodities will be delivered.

¶ 8-210 Approval and cancellation of approval for export shop

(1) Approval: Enterprises which wish to open an export shop must obtain approval from the director of the tax office with jurisdiction over the place where the enterprise must pay tax. Such approval is available only if all the required conditions are satisfied (Law 8⑥).

(2) Cancellation: The director of the tax office can cancel the approval of an export shop if the enterprise which manages the export shop fails to meet certain conditions.

¶ 8-220 Tax exemptions under the Special Taxation Measures Law, etc.

(1) **Exemption for transfers of commodities loaded onto ships, etc. on overseas service**

Where an enterprise transfers or removes designated goods from a bonded area with the approval of the director of the customs office with jurisdiction over the port or airport, for loading onto and for use on a ship or aeroplane which is on overseas service and which carries the Japanese flag, such transfer or removal is deemed to be an export or loading onto a ship or aeroplane carrying a foreign flag, and is tax-exempt (SM 85, Reg 45).

(2) **Exemption for transfers of taxable assets for foreign embassies and legations**

Where an enterprise transfers taxable assets, etc. to foreign embassies or legations situated in Japan, or to ambassadors etc. accredited to operate in Japan, and the foreign embassies or legations, or the accredited ambassadors etc., purchase or take a lease of the taxable assets (or are provided with services in the required manner) as a necessary part of carrying out their duties, such transfer of taxable assets, etc. is tax-exempt (SM 86).

(3) **Exemptions for transfers of assets to navy exchanges etc.**

Transfers are tax-exempt when an enterprise transfers goods

¶ 8-210

消　費　税　703

書」を事業者に提出し，その物品の引渡しを受けることとなる。

¶8-210　輸出物品販売場の許可及び取消し
(1)　輸出物品販売場の許可
　輸出物品販売場を開設しようとする事業者は，その経営する販売場につい
て納税地を所轄する税務署長の許可を受けなければならない。輸出物品販売
場に係る許可は，一定の要件のすべてを満たしている場合に限り与えられる
（消去8⑥）。
(2)　輸出物品販売場の許可の取消し
　税務署長は，輸出物品販売場を経営する事業者が一定の要件に該当するこ
ととなった場合には，輸出物品販売場に係る許可を取り消すことができる。

¶8-220　租税特別措置法

(1)　外航船舶等に積み込む物品の譲渡等に係る免税
　酒類その他の指定物品の譲渡を行う事業又は指定物品を保税地域から引き
取る者が，本邦の外航船又は本邦の国際航空機に船用品又は機用品として，
積み込もうとする港の所在地の所轄税関長の承認を受けた指定物品を譲渡
し，又は保税地域から引き取る場合には，輸出又は外国の船舶若しくは航空
機への積込みとみなして，消費税が免除される（措法85，措令45）。

(2)　外国公館等に対する課税資産の譲渡等に係る免税
　事業者が，本邦にある外国の大使館等又は本邦に派遣された大使等に対し
課税資産の譲渡等を行った場合において，その外国の大使館等又は派遣され
た大使等が，外交，領事その他の任務を遂行するために必要なものとして，
一定の方法により，その課税資産を譲り受け，若しくは借り受け，又は役務
の提供を受けるときは，消費税が免除される（措法86）。

(3)　海軍販売所等に対する物品の譲渡に係る免税
　事業者が，日本国とアメリカ合衆国との間の相互協力及び安全保障条約第

704   CONSUMPTION TAX

which are purchased by military personnel, or by civilian personnel, and their families, from a navy exchange post or exchange post stipulated in Art. 15① (a) of the Agreement under Article VI of the Treaty of Mutual Cooperation and Security between Japan and the United States of America, regarding Facilities and Areas and the Status of United States Armed Forces in Japan.

(4) **Exemptions for transfers of assets, etc. for U.S. Armed Forces**
Where an enterprise transfers goods purchased by the United States Armed Forces or its officially approved supply agency for the use of the U.S. Armed Forces, or by an individual or corporate contractor for construction, maintenance or management services provided for the U.S. Armed Forces and for photographic film or plate and gasoline purchased by such contractor to carry out its project, such a transfer is tax-exempt provided the enterprise keeps a certificate issued by the competent authority of the U.S. Armed Forces showing that the transferred taxable assets are for the use of the U.S. Armed Forces.

Taxpayer

¶ 8-230 Taxpayer for domestic transactions
A taxpayer for a domestic transaction is an enterprise (including nonresidents and foreign corporations) which transfers taxable assets, etc. (Law 5①). An enterprise is an individual enterprise or a corporation (Law 2①), and a non-juridical organization qualifies as an enterprise by being deemed to be a corporation (Law 3).

¶ 8-240 Taxpayer removing foreign goods from a bonded area
Taxpayers removing foreign goods from a bonded area are those who receive and remove taxable foreign goods (Law 5②). The term includes individuals as consumers.

¶ 8-245 Taxpayer for a joint enterprise, etc.
Taxpayers for transfer of assets, etc., taxable purchase or removal of foreign goods conducted by a joint enterprise are the members of the joint enterprise, corresponding to the ratio of their holdings or the ratio of their share in the profits (R 1-3-1). For consumption tax purposes, each member

¶ 8-230

消　費　税　705

6条に基づく施設及び区域並びに日本国におけるアメリカ合衆国軍隊の地位に関する協定第15条第1項(a)に規定する海軍販売所又はピー・エックスに対して，同協定第1条に規定するアメリカ合衆国軍隊の構成員及び軍属並びにこれらの家族が輸出する目的でこれらの機関から購入する物品で一定のものを譲渡する場合には，その物品の譲渡については，消費税が免除される。

(4)　**合衆国軍隊等に対する資産の譲渡等に係る免税**

　事業者が，合衆国軍隊若しくは合衆国軍隊の公認調達機関が合衆国軍隊の用に供するために購入するもの又は個人契約者若しくは法人契約者がその建設等契約に係る建設，維持又は運営のみの事業の用に供するために購入するもので合衆国軍隊の用に供されるもの及びその事業を行うためにこれらの者が購入する写真用フィルム，乾板又は揮発油等を譲渡等する場合において，その譲渡した課税資産が合衆国軍隊の用に供するものであることにつき，合衆国軍隊の権限ある官憲が発給する証明書を保存している場合には，消費税が免除される。

納税義務者

¶8-230　国内取引に係る納税義務者

　国内取引についての納税義務者は，課税資産の譲渡等を行った事業者（非居住者，外国法人を含む。）とされている（消法5①）。事業者とは，個人事業者及び法人をいい（消法2①），人格のない社団等は，法人とみなされることにより事業者に該当することとなる（消法3）。

¶8-240　保税地域から引き取られる外国貨物に係る納税義務者

　保税地域から引き取られる外国貨物に係る納税義務者は，課税貨物を保税地域から引き取る者（消費者たる個人を含む。）とされている（消法5②）。

¶8-245　共同事業等に係る納税義務者

　共同事業に属する資産の譲渡等若しくは課税仕入れ又は外国貨物の引取りに係る納税義務者は，当該共同事業の持分の割合又は利益の分配割合に対応する当該共同事業の構成員である（消基通1-3-1）。なお，共同事業に係る消費税の納付については，納税義務者である各構成員が連帯して納税義務を

706   CONSUMPTION TAX

of a joint enterprise is jointly and severally liable for payment of tax (GL 9).

A taxpayer for an anonymous association business is the operator of the business (R 1-3-2).

¶ 8-250 Tax exemption for small-scale enterprises

Where the amount of taxable sales of an enterprise in its base period is not more than ¥10 million, the enterprise will be exempt from tax on the transfer of taxable assets, etc. during the taxable period (tax-exempt enterprise) (Law 9①).

In this case, "base period" means: ① the year two years prior to the current year for an individual enterprise; and ② the business year two business years prior to the current business year for a corporation. (For corporations whose base period is less than one year, the base will be the period resulting from combining all business years that commenced during the one-year period beginning on the day two years before the first day of the current business year.) (Law 2①(14)).

If the amount of taxable sales of an enterprise in the base period becomes more than ¥10 million, and if the amount of taxable sales of an enterprise which does not elect to be a taxable enterprise becomes not more than ¥10 million, the enterprise must file a report stating that fact to the director of the tax office with jurisdiction over the place where the enterprise must pay tax (Law 57).

> Note:
> 1. If the amount of taxable sales of an enterprise in the taxable period is not more than ¥10 million and in the base period is more than ¥10 million, the enterprise will not be exempt from consumption tax in the taxable period (R 1-4-1).
> 2. Individuals and corporations are exempt from tax during their first and second business years, because there are no taxable sales for the relevant base periods (R 1-4-6). (This is not applied in the case as mentioned in #3, #5, #6 below.)
> 3. Against the #2 above, it is not exempt from tax during its first and second business years, if the share capital of the corporation is ¥10 million or more at the beginning of the business year when there are no relevant base periods (Law 12-2).
> 4. If the base period is not one year, the judgment whether the taxable sales becomes more than ¥10 million should be made by taking the figures of taxable sales in the base period proportioned to one year basis (Law 9②(2)).
> 5. The enterprise whose taxable sales amount is more than ¥10 million for the period from January 1 through June 30 of the previous year for individuals, the period of the first half of the previous business year, etc. for

¶ 8-250

消　費　税　707

負う（通則法9）。

　匿名組合の事業に係る納税義務者は，営業者である（消基通1-3-2）。

¶8-250　小規模事業者に係る納税義務の免除

　基準期間における課税売上高が1,000万円（免税点）以下の事業者（免税事業者）は，その課税期間の課税資産の譲渡等について，納税義務が免除される（消法9①）。

　この場合，「基準期間」とは，①個人事業者の場合には，その年の前々年を，②法人の場合には，その事業年度の前々事業年度（その前々事業年度が1年未満の法人は，その事業年度開始の日の2年前の日の前日から同日以後1年を経過する日までの間に開始した各事業年度を合わせた期間）をいう（消法2①十四）。

　課税期間の基準期間における課税売上高が1,000万円を超えることとなった事業者及び課税期間の基準期間における課税売上高が1,000万円以下となった課税選択事業者以外の事業者は，その旨を所轄税務署長に届け出なければならない（消法57）。

（注）：1．その課税期間における課税売上高が1,000万円以下の場合であっても，基準期間における課税売上高が1,000万円を超えているときは，その課税期間については消費税の納税義務は免除されない（消基通1-4-1）。

　　　　2．個人事業者の新規開業年とその翌年，法人の設立事業年度とその翌事業年度は，基準期間の課税売上高がないので免税となる（消基通1-4-6）（下記3，5，6を除く。）。

　　　　3．上記2にかかわらず，基準期間のない法人のその事業年度開始の日において資本金が1,000万円以上である場合については，その事業年度の納税義務は免除されない（消法12の2）。

　　　　4．基準期間が1年でない法人については，基準期間の売上高を1年に按分して1,000万円を超えるかどうかの判定をする（消法9②二）。

　　　　5．前年1月から6月の課税売上高が1,000万円を超える個人事業者及び前事業年度開始の日から6カ月間の課税売上高が1,000万円を超える法人等については，その事業年度の納税義務は免除されない（消法9の2）。

708   CONSUMPTION TAX

corporations, is not exempt from consumption tax in the taxable period (Law 9-2).

6. In case of newly established corporation governed by the controlling shareholder (holds more than 50% of share), and when the taxable sales amount of that controlling shareholder or relative corporations of that controlling shareholder is more than ¥500 million, exempt from tax while it does not have a base period (Law 12-3) (apply after April 1, 2014).

¶ 8-260 Election to be a taxable enterprise

An enterprise can elect to become a taxable enterprise by filing an "Application for Election to be Taxable Enterprise" with the director of the tax authority with jurisdiction over the place where the enterprise must pay tax, stating that the rules for taxpayer exemption do not apply.

The election becomes effective from the taxable period following the taxable period in which the application was made. For enterprises commencing operations and those succeeding to a business by inheritance, merger or certain corporate division, which had been operated by an enterprise, which had effectively filed the application, the election becomes effective from the current taxable period (Law 9④).

Once such an election has been made, it cannot be cancelled unless an "Application to Reverse the Election to be a Taxable Enterprise" has been filed on or after the first day of the taxable period commencing two years after the election was made (except for discontinuing businesses) (Law 9⑤, ⑥).

¶ 8-265 Restriction for becoming tax exempted enterprise for certain period when adjustment tax on the purchase certain fixed assets required under considerable change of its taxable sales ratio (see ¶8-650, ¶8-680)

(1) For individual, under certain circumstances it is restricted to become tax exempted enterprise for the period when adjustment tax on the purchases certain fixed assets should be required under considerable change of taxable sales ratio (Law 9⑦).

(2) For corporation, under certain circumstances it is restricted to become tax exempted enterprise for the period when adjustment tax on the purchases certain fixed assets should be required under considerable change of taxable sales ratio (Law 12-2②).

¶ 8-260

消　費　税　709

6．他の者により支配されている新設法人で，かつ，他の者及び他の者の関係法人のうちいずれかの基準期間に相当する期間の課税売上高が5億円を超えている場合には，基準期間が無い事業年度についても納税義務は免除されない（消法12-3）（平成26年4月1日以降適用）。

¶8-260　課税事業者の選択

　事業者は，所轄税務署長に対し，納税義務の免除の規定の適用を受けない旨の消費税課税事業者選択届出書を提出することができ，課税事業者になることができる。

　なお，この届出の効力は，消費税課税事業者選択届出書を提出した日の属する課税期間の翌課税期間（新たに事業を開始した場合若しくは相続，合併又は吸収分割によりこの届出を行っていた事業者の事業を承継した場合にあっては，その課税期間）から生ずる（消法9④）。

　また，消費税課税事業者選択届出書を提出した事業者は，事業廃止の場合を除き，課税選択によって課税事業者となった初めての課税期間の初日から2年を経過する日の属する課税期間の初日以後でなければ，その適用をやめようとする旨の消費税課税事業者選択不適用届出書を提出することができない（消法9⑤，⑥）。

¶8-265　調整対象固定資産がある場合の免税事業者成りの制限（¶8-650，¶8-680参照）

(1)　調整対象固定資産についての仕入れに係る消費税の調整の対象となるべき課税期間において，課税事業者選択不適用について制限される（消法9⑦）。

(2)　調整対象固定資産についての仕入れに係る消費税の調整の対象となるべき課税期間において，小規模免税事業者の適用を受けない新設法人が免税事業者になることについて制限される（消法12の2②）。

710   CONSUMPTION TAX

¶ 8-270   Calculation of amount of taxable sales

The "amount of taxable sales in the base period" means the balance after deducting the total amount of refund of consideration for sales (excluding tax) from the total amount of consideration for the transfer of taxable assets, etc. (excluding tax) in the base period. (For a corporation whose base period is less than one year, the calculation is converted proportionately to an amount that corresponds to one year.) (Law 9②).

"Transfer of taxable assets, etc. in the base period" includes transfers of assets etc. which are exempt from consumption tax (see ¶ 8-170 to ¶ 8-220), and those which are deemed to be transfers of assets (see ¶ 8-040(10)). Deductions are not allowed for bad debts (R 1-4-2).

If an enterprise operates different kinds of businesses or operates from two or more places of business, the amount of taxable sales in the base period is the total amount of consideration for all transfers of taxable assets, etc. from all of its businesses and from all of its places of business (R 1-4-4).

¶ 8-280   Special exceptions

(1)   Special exceptions for inheritance

Whether or not an enterprise succeeding to a business by inheritance qualifies as a tax-exempt enterprise is determined by the following factors.

(a)   For the year in which the inheritance occurs (for the period from the day following the date of inheritance to December 31 of that year)—if either the amount of taxable sales of the heir who succeeds to the deceased's business by inheritance, or the amount of taxable sales of the deceased in the base period for the year in which the inheritance occurs, exceeds ¥10 million, the heir will not be a tax-exempt enterprise (Law 10①).

(b)   For the year following the year in which the inheritance occurs and the year after that—if the total of the heir's amount of taxable sales and the deceased's amount of taxable sales in the base period exceeds ¥10 million, the heir will not be a tax-exempt enterprise (Law 10②).

(c)   Special exception for calculation of the deceased's amount of taxable sales—in special cases, the deceased's amount of taxable sales is determined by the following factors:

(i)   where two or more heirs succeed to the deceased's business

¶ 8-270

消　費　税　711

¶8-270　課税売上高の計算等

　免税事業者に該当するかどうかを判定する場合の「基準期間における課税売上高」とは，基準期間中の課税資産の譲渡等の対価の額（税抜き）の合計額から売上げに係る対価の返還等の金額（税抜き）の合計額を控除した金額（基準期間が1年でない法人については，その金額を1年分に換算した金額）をいう（消法9②）。

　基準期間中の課税資産の譲渡等には消費税が免除される場合（¶8-170〜¶8-220参照）及び資産のみなし譲渡の規定により資産の譲渡とみなされる場合（¶8-040⑽参照）の資産の譲渡等を含む。なお，貸倒れがあっても，その分は控除されない（消基通1-4-2）。

　一の事業者が異なる種類の事業を行う場合又は二以上の事業所を有している場合であっても，それらの事業又は事業所における課税資産の譲渡等の対価の額の合計額により基準期間における課税売上高を算定する（消基通1-4-4）。

¶8-280　相続等があった場合の特例

(1)　相続があった場合の特例

　相続があった場合に，相続により事業を承継した相続人が免税事業者に該当するかどうかの判定については，次による。

　(a)　相続があった年（相続のあった日の翌日からその年の12月31日まで）……相続により被相続人の事業を承継した相続人又はその被相続人の相続があった年の基準期間における課税売上高のうちいずれかが1,000万円を超える場合，その相続人について免税の規定は適用されない（消法10①）。

　(b)　相続のあった年の翌年及び翌々年……その相続人の基準期間における課税売上高とその被相続人の基準期間における課税売上高との合計額が1,000万円を超える場合には，その相続人は，免税事業者に該当しない（消法10②）。

　(c)　被相続人の課税売上高の計算の特例
　　　相続について特殊な事情がある場合の基準期間における被相続人の課税売上高は次による。
　(i)　二以上の事業場を有する被相続人の事業を二以上の相続人が各事業

712   CONSUMPTION TAX

which has more than one business place and the business is divided for each heir by the unit of each business place—the deceased's amount of taxable sales for the inherited business place in the base period (Reg 21①).

(ii) where there are two or more heirs and the inherited properties are not divided—the product of the deceased's taxable sales amount in the base period multiplied by the successor's statutory shares (R 1-5-5) (see ¶ 7-360).

(2) **Special exception for corporate mergers**

Whether a transferee (or new) corporation succeeding to a business by merger qualifies as a tax-exempt enterprise is determined as follows.

(a) For the business year in which the merger occurs (on and after the date of merger)—if either the amount of taxable sales of the transferee corporation or the amount of taxable sales of each transferor (or old) corporation in the base period exceeds ¥10 million, the transferee corporation will not be a tax-exempt enterprise (Law 11①).

(b) For the business year following the business year in which the merger occurs and the business year after that—if the sum of the transferee corporation's amount of taxable sales in the base period added to the total of the transferor corporation's amount of taxable sales for the corresponding period exceeds ¥10 million, the transferee corporation will not be a tax-exempt enterprise (Law 11②).

(3) **Special exception for split-up of a corporation**

Special tax rules apply if the old corporation manages the new corporation substantially after the split-up of a corporation. Whether the old corporation and the new corporation qualify as tax-exempt enterprises is determined by the following factors (Law 12).

(a) For the business year in which the split-up occurs (commencing from the date of the split-up)—if the old corporation's amount of taxable sales in the base period exceeds ¥10 million, the new corporation is not a tax-exempt enterprise.

(b) For the business years following the initial business year (the following business year in the case of the old corporation) in which the split-up occurs—if the new corporation satisfies the

¶ 8-280

消　費　税　713

　　　場ごとに分割して承継した場合…相続した事業場に係る基準期間における被相続人の課税売上高（消令21①）

　　(ii)　二以上の相続人がおり，かつ，相続財産の分割が実行されるまでの間…被相続人の基準期間における課税売上高にその相続人の法定相続割合（¶7-360参照）を乗じた金額（消基通1-5-5）

(2)　法人の合併があった場合の特例

　合併があった場合に，合併により事業の承継等をした合併法人が免税事業者に該当するかどうかの判定については，次による。

　　(a)　合併があった事業年度（合併があった日以降分）……合併により被合併法人の事業を承継した合併法人及びその各被合併法人の基準期間における課税売上高のうちいずれかが1,000万円を超える場合には，その合併法人は，免税事業者に該当しない（消法11①）。

　　(b)　合併があった事業年度の翌事業年度及び翌々事業年度……その合併法人の基準期間の課税売上高とその各被合併法人におけるその合併法人の基準期間に対応する期間の課税売上高との合計額が1,000万円を超える場合には，その合併法人は，免税事業者に該当しない（消法11②）。

(3)　法人の分割があった場合の特例

　法人が分割された場合に，分割親法人及び分割子法人が免税事業者に該当するかどうかの判定については，次による（消法12）。

　この場合，納税義務の免除の特例の対象となる法人の分割とは，分割親法人が分割子法人を実質的に支配している場合のみをいう。

　　(a)　分割があった事業年度……分割親法人の基準期間における課税売上高が1,000万円を超える場合には，分割子法人は，その設立の日の属する事業年度においては免税事業者に該当しない。

　　(b)　分割があった事業年度の翌事業年度（分割親法人については翌々事業年度）以後の各事業年度……各事業年度の基準期間の末日において分割子法人が特定要件のすべてに該当する場合において，分割子法人の基準

714   CONSUMPTION TAX

necessary conditions on the last day of the base period of each business year, and the sum of the new corporation's amount of taxable sales in the base period added to the old corporation's amount of taxable sales in that same period exceeds ¥10 million, the new corporation is not a tax-exempt enterprise. If the sum of the old corporation's amount of taxable sales in the base period and the new corporation's taxable sales amount in the same period exceeds ¥10 million, the old corporation is not a tax-exempt enterprise.

"The necessary conditions" are:

(i)   that the old corporation and the person specially connected with it must hold all of the issued shares or 50% or more of the investments of the new corporation, and

(ii) that all, or almost all, of the business conducted by the new corporation must be the same kind of business as that conducted by the old corporation.

¶ 8-290 Principle of taxation of the actual performer

Where a transfer of assets, etc. is conducted in the name of the holder of the title deed and the beneficiary is some party other than the holder, the beneficiary is deemed to conduct that transfer of assets, etc (Law 13).

The beneficiary is deemed to be the person who is the actual owner of the business (R 4-1-1).

The owner of a business conducted by relatives who live together is presumed to be the person who is the predominant decision maker regarding the administrative policy of the business (R 4-1-2).

¶ 8-300 Tax liability of trust funds

A beneficiary of trust is deemed to own the assets of the trust and make the assets deals (Law 14①).

However, it is not applied to the assets and the assets deals of the jointly investment trust, the corporate taxable trust, the pension trust, the specified public interest trust.

Note:
The assets deals include transferring of assets, purchasing of taxable assets, removing taxable assets from a bonded area.

¶ 8-290

期間における課税売上高と分割親法人における分割子法人の基準期間に対応する期間の課税売上高との合計額が1,000万円を超えるときは，その分割子法人は免税事業者に該当せず，また，分割親法人の基準期間における課税売上高と分割子法人における分割親法人の基準期間と対応する期間の課税売上高との合計額が1,000万円を超えるときは，その分割親法人は免税事業者に該当しない。

特定要件とは，次のものをいう。

(i) 分割子法人の発行済株式の総数又は出資金額の50％以上を分割親法人とその特殊関係者が所有していること

(ii) 分割子法人の行う事業の全部又は相当部分が，分割親法人の行う事業と同種のものであること

¶8-290　実質行為者課税の原則

　資産の譲渡等を行った者が単なる名義人であって，その対価を享受せず，他の者が享受しているときは，その享受する者が資産の譲渡等を行ったものとみなされる（消法13）。

　この場合において，資産の譲渡等に係る対価を享受する者がだれであるかにより，その事業を経営していると認められる者（事業主）が判定される（消基通4-1-1）。

　生計を一にしている親族間における事業に係る事業主は，その事業の経営方針の決定につき支配的影響力を有すると認められる者と推定される（消基通4-1-2）。

¶8-300　信託財産に係る納税義務

　信託の受益者はその信託の信託財産に属する資産を有するものとみなし，かつ，その信託財産に係る資産等取引はその受益者が行う資産等取引とみなす（消法14①）。

　ただし，集団投資信託，法人課税信託，退職年金信託，特定公益信託等の信託財産に属する資産及びその資産等取引を除く。

　（注）：資産等取引とは，資産の譲渡等，課税仕入れ及び課税貨物の保税地域からの引取りをいう。

716   CONSUMPTION TAX

If it is the corporate taxable trust, the trust is subject to the consumption tax by each trusted assets and trustee's own assets. In the case each trusted assets and trustee's own assets should be deemed as separated ones (Law 15①).

Place for Tax Payment

¶ 8-310 Individual enterprise

(1) **Principle**

The place for tax payment by an individual enterprise is as follows (Law 20, Reg 42):

(a) For an individual domiciled in Japan—the said domicile.

(b) For an individual resident in Japan without domicile—the place of residence.

(c) For an individual having an office etc. in Japan without either domicile or residence—the location of the said office etc. (where the individual has two or more offices, the main office's location).

(d) For an individual who has been covered by (a) or (b) above, but who leaves the place of domicile or residence and does not have an office etc. in Japan, and whose relatives reside continuously at the former place for tax payment—the former place for tax payment.

(e) For an individual who does not fall into the cases (a) to (d) above and receives consideration from a lease of real estate or a right on real estate, or the creation of a right regarding mines— the place where the said real estate, etc. is located.

(f) For an individual who had a place for tax payment according to (a) to (e) above, but who ceases to fall into these categories—the same place for tax payment as before the change in circumstances.

(g) For an individual who does not fall into the cases (a) to (f) above, and performs an act with respect to the consumption tax such as filing a return or making notification—the place chosen by the individual.

(h) For an individual who does not fall into the cases (a) to (g) above—the place within the jurisdiction of Kojimachi Tax Office.

(2) **Special exception**

When an application has already been made under Art. 16③ and ④ of the Income Tax Law for a special exception regarding the place

¶ 8-310

消　費　税　717

　法人課税信託の受託者は，各法人課税信託の信託資産等及び固有資産等ごとにそれぞれ別の者とみなす（消法15①）。

納　税　地

¶8-310　個人事業者の納税地
(1)　原則
　個人事業者の納税地は次の区分に応じ，それぞれ次に掲げる場所である（消法20，消令42）。
- (a)　国内に住所を有する場合　その住所地
- (b)　国内に住所を有せず，居所を有する場合　その居住地

- (c)　国内に住所及び居所を有せず，事務所等を有している場合　その事務所等の所在地（その事務所等が二以上ある場合には，主たるものの所在地）
- (d)　(a)又は(b)により納税地を定められていた者が国内に住所及び居所を有しないこととなった場合において，国内に事務所等を有せず，かつ，その納税地とされていた場所にその者の親族等が引き続き又はその者に代わって居住しているとき　従来の納税地
- (e)　(a)～(d)に該当しない場合で，不動産，不動産上の権利，採石権の貸付け又は租鉱権の設定による対価を受ける場合　不動産等の所在地

- (f)　(a)～(e)のいずれにも該当しないこととなった場合　直前の納税地

- (g)　(a)～(f)に該当しない者が申告又は届出等をする場合　その者が選択した場所

- (h)　(a)～(g)に該当しない場合　麹町税務署の所轄区域内の場所

(2)　特例
　所得税法第16条第3項又は第4項（（納税地の特例））に定める納税地の特例に関する書類を提出して，居所地又は事務所等の所在地を納税地としてい

718　CONSUMPTION TAX

for income tax payment (for income tax purposes), the application is deemed to cover consumption tax as well (Law 21①, ②).

In the case of inheritance, the place for tax payment by the heir with respect to transfers of assets, etc. conducted by the deceased is the place for tax payment by the deceased.

¶ 8-320　Corporation

The place for tax payment by a corporation is as follows (Law 22, Reg 43).

(1)　For a corporation having its head office or main office in Japan (a domestic corporation)—the location of the said office.

(2)　For a foreign corporation having its office etc. in Japan—the location of the said office etc. (where the foreign corporation has two or more offices etc. the location of the main office).

(3)　For a foreign corporation which does not fall within category (2) above and receives consideration from leasing real estate—the place where the said real estate is located.

(4)　For a foreign corporation which has been covered by category (2) or (3) above, but has ceased to fall into either category—the same place for tax payment as before the change in circumstances.

(5)　For a foreign corporation which does not fall into categories (2) to (4) above, and performs an act with respect to the Consumption Tax such as filing a return or making a notification—the place chosen by the corporation.

(6)　For a foreign corporation which does not fall into categories (2) to (5) above—the place within the jurisdiction of the Kojimachi Tax Office.

¶ 8-330　Designation of place for tax payment

If it is clear that the place for tax payment by an individual enterprise or a corporation according to the regulations is not a suitable place considering the location of transfer of assets, etc., the director of a competent Regional Tax Bureau (or the Commissioner of the National Tax Administration Agency, if the place for tax payment is outside the jurisdiction of the Regional Tax Bureau) can designate another suitable place for tax payment (Law 23①, Reg 44).

¶ 8-340　Change of place for tax payment

When the place for tax payment is changed, the enterprise must is-

¶ 8-320

消　費　税　719

るときは，消費税においてもその居所地等が納税地とされる（消法21①，②）。

　なお，相続があった場合には，被相続人の資産の譲渡等に係る納税地は，相続人の納税地ではなく，被相続人の納税地とされている。

¶8-320　法人の納税地

　法人の納税地は，次の区分に応じ，それぞれ次に掲げる場所である（消法22，消令43）。

(1)　国内に本店又は主たる事務所を有する法人（内国法人）の場合　その本店又は主たる事務所の所在地

(2)　内国法人以外の法人で国内に事務所等を有する法人の場合　その事務所等の所在地（二以上ある場合には主たるものの所在地）

(3)　(2)に該当しない外国法人が国内にある不動産の貸付けによる対価を受ける場合　対価に係る資産の所在地

(4)　外国法人が(2)及び(3)のいずれにも該当しないこととなった場合　直前の納税地

(5)　(2)～(4)以外の外国法人が申告又は届け出等をする場合　その外国法人が選択した場所

(6)　(2)～(5)に該当しない外国法人の場合　麹町税務署管内の場所

¶8-330　納税地の指定

　個人事業者又は法人の納税地が，資産の譲渡等の状況からみて消費税の納税地として不適当であると認められる場合には，その納税地の所轄国税局長（指定される納税地が，所轄国税局長の管轄区域外の地域にある場合には，国税庁長官）は，適当とする納税地を指定することができる（消法23①，消令44）。

¶8-340　納税地の異動

　事業者は，その資産の譲渡等に係る消費税の納税地に異動があった場合に

720   CONSUMPTION TAX

sue a Notice of Change of Place for Tax Payment to the directors of the tax offices with jurisdiction over both the old and new places for tax payment (Law 25, MO 14).

¶ 8-350 Place for tax payment for foreign goods removed from a bonded area

The place for tax payment with respect to foreign goods removed from a bonded area is the place in which the bonded area is located (Law 26).

¶ 8-355 Place for tax payment in special cases

If a non-resident makes a tax-exempt purchase at an export shop in the following circumstances, the place for tax payment is as follows (Law 27).

(1) Where the non-resident does not export the goods until the day of departure from Japan—the place of departure.

(2) Where the non-resident becomes a resident without exporting the goods—the place of his or her domicile or residence at the time of becoming a resident.

(3) Where the non-resident transfers the goods in Japan with or without the approval of the director of the tax office—the place where the goods were located at the time of the approval or transfer, respectively.

Taxable Period

¶ 8-360 Taxable period for individual enterprises

(1) **Principle**

The taxable period for individual enterprises is from January 1 through December 31 of each year (Law 19①(1)). Even if they start or discontinue their business during a year, the taxable period is from January 1 through December 31 of the year (R 3-1-1, 3-1-2).

(2) **Special exception**

Individual enterprises may shorten their taxable periods to each month or from January 1 through March 31, from April 1 through June 30, from July 1 through September 30, and from October 1 through December 31 by filing a Notification for Election of Special Exception for Taxable Period with the director of the tax office with jurisdiction over the place for tax payment (Law 19①(3)).

¶ 8-350

消　費　税　721

は，遅滞なく，納税地異動届出書により，異動前の納税地の所轄税務署長及び異動後の所轄税務署長に対してその旨を届け出なければならない（消法25，消規14）。

¶8-350　保税地域から引き取られる外国貨物に係る納税地

保税地域から引き取られる外国貨物に係る納税地は，その保税地域の所在地である（消法26）。

¶8-355　特別な場合の納税地

非居住者が輸出物品販売場において免税で購入した物品を譲渡した場合等の納税地は，次のとおりである（消法27）。

(1)　その非居住者がその物品を，本邦から出国する日までに輸出しない場合
　　出国の際の出港地

(2)　その非居住者がその物品を輸出しないまま居住者となる場合
　　居住者となるときにおける住所又は居所の所在地

(3)　その非居住者が，税務署長の承認を受け又は受けずに国内においてその物品を譲渡した場合
　　その承認又は譲渡があったときにおけるその物品の所在地

課　税　期　間

¶8-360　個人事業者の課税期間

(1)　**原則**

個人事業者の課税期間は，1月1日からその年の12月31日までの期間である（消法19①一）。

年の中途において，事業を開始した場合又は廃止した場合であっても，課税期間は，1月1日から12月31日となる（消基通3-1-1，3-1-2）。

(2)　**特例**

納税地の所轄税務署長に対し消費税課税期間特例選択届出書を提出することにより，各月又は1月1日から3月31日まで，4月1日から6月30日まで，7月1日から9月30日まで，10月1日から12月31日までの各3月の期間を一の課税期間とすることができる（消法19①三）。

722 CONSUMPTION TAX

¶ 8-370 Taxable period for corporations

(1) Principle

The taxable period for corporations is their business year (Law 19① (2)). The business year as defined in Chapter V of the Corporation Tax Law and "deemed business year" may also constitute a taxable period (Law 2①(13)).

(2) Special exception

Corporations may divide their taxable period into monthly or three-monthly periods beginning on the first day of the business year. A Notification for Election of Special Exception for Taxable Period must be filed with the director of the tax office with jurisdiction over the place for tax payment (Law 19①(4), 19①(4-2)).

¶ 8-380 Special exception for taxable period

The taxable period can be shortened, effective from the period following the period in which a notification to do so is filed (three-monthly period discussed in ¶ 8-360 (2) or ¶ 8-370 (2)). When the 'special exception' rule applies, the day before the first day of the first shortened period is deemed to be the end of a taxable period (Law 19②).

An enterprise applying for this special exception must continue to employ the shortened taxable period and cannot file a Notification for Revocation of Special Exception for Taxable Period before the first date of the period which contained the date of two years after the effective date of the Election of Special Exception for Taxable Period (except where the business is discontinued) (Law 19⑤).

Time of Transfer of Assets, etc.

¶ 8-390 General rule

The following paragraphs (¶ 8-400 to ¶ 8-440) set out, in principle, the rules regarding the time of transfer of assets, etc. except for cases where the rules for special exception for the time of transfer of assets, etc. by long term installment sales (¶ 8-450), by long term contracts (¶ 8-470) or regarding small-scale enterprises (¶ 8-475) apply.

¶ 8-400 Time of transfer of inventory assets

The time of transfer of inventory assets is the date of delivery (R 9-1-1).

¶ 8-370

消　費　税　723

¶8-370　法人の課税期間
(1)　原則
　法人の課税期間は，その法人の事業年度である（消法19①二）。
　この場合の事業年度とは，法人税法第1編第5章《事業年度》に規定する事業年度をいうのであるから，《みなし事業年度》についても同様に適用されることになる（消法2①十三）。
(2)　特例
　法人は，納税地の所轄税務署長に対して消費税課税期間特例選択届出書を提出することにより，その事業年度をその開始の日以後1月又は3月ごとに区分した各期間を一の課税期間とすることができる（消法19①四，19①四の二）。

¶8-380　課税期間の特例の適用
　課税期間の短縮の特例は，届出書を提出した日の属する¶8-360の(2)又は¶8-370の(2)の期間の翌期間から適用でき，この適用を受けた場合には，適用開始の日の前日までを一の課税期間とみなして確定申告等をすることとなる（消法19②）。
　なお，この課税期間の特例の適用を受けた事業者は，事業廃止の場合を除きその特例の効力が生ずる日から2年を経過する日の属するこれらの規定に定める期間の初日以後でなければ，消費税課税期間特例選択不適用届出書を提出することはできない（消法19⑤）。

資産の譲渡等の時期

¶8-390　通則
　資産の譲渡等の時期は《長期割賦販売等（¶8-450），長期工事の請負（¶8-470）及び小規模業者（¶8-475）に係る資産の譲渡等の時期の特例等》の規定の適用を受ける場合を除き，原則としてそれぞれ次に掲げるとおりとなる。

¶8-400　棚卸資産の譲渡の時期
　棚卸資産の譲渡については，その引渡しの日とされている（消基通9-1-1）。

724   CONSUMPTION TAX

(1) The date of delivery is the day which enterprises would select from among reasonable dates as the date of delivery based on the nature of the assets and the terms of the contract of sale, such as the date of shipment, the date of inspection by the counterparty, the date when the counterparty can use them, and the date when the sales quantities would be confirmed by meterreading etc. If the inventory assets consist of land or rights attached to land, and the date of delivery is not clear, the date of delivery is treated as being the earlier of the following:

   (a) the date on which the enterprise would have received most of the sale price (usually more than 50%); or

   (b) the date on which the enterprise would have made an application for registration of a change of proprietary rights (including delivery to the counterparty of the documents necessary to apply for registration) (R 9-1-2).

(2) Time of transfer of inventory assets by consignment sales.

    The date of a consignment sale of inventory assets is treated as being the date on which the consignees would transfer them. However, if sales statements for the consigned goods are drawn up for each sale, the enterprise can select, consistently, the date of arrival of the statements as the date of transfer of inventory assets (R 9-1-3).

¶ 8-410 Time of transfer of assets, etc. by contract for work

In principle, the transfer of assets, etc. by contract for work is considered to be carried out when all the materials have been delivered to the other party, or on the date when all services have been completed for a contract which does not involve products (R 9-1-5).

¶ 8-420 Time of transfer of fixed tangible assets, etc.

The time of transfer of fixed tangible assets is, in principle, the date of delivery. However, in the case of fixed tangible assets such as land or buildings, enterprises can select the date of the coming into effect of contracts of transfer as the time of transfer (R 9-1-13). The mode of determining the date of delivery of fixed tangible assets also applies to that of inventory assets (R 9-1-13 Note).

¶ 8-410

消　費　税　725

(1)　棚卸資産の引渡しの日がいつであるのかについては，例えば，出荷した日，相手方が検収した日，相手方において使用収益ができることとなった日，検針等により販売数量を確認した日等，その棚卸資産の種類及び性質，その販売に係る契約の内容等に応じてその引渡しの日として合理的であると認められる日のうち，事業者が継続して棚卸資産の譲渡を行ったこととしている日によるものとされている。

この場合において，その棚卸資産が，土地又は土地の上に存する権利であり，その引渡しの日がいつであるかが明らかでないときは，次に掲げる日のうちいずれか早い日にその引渡しがあったものとすることができる。

(a)　代金の相当部分（概ね50％以上）を収受するに至った日

(b)　所有権移転登記の申請（その登記の申請に必要な書類の相手方への交付を含む。）をした日（消基通9-1-2）。

(2)　委託販売による資産の譲渡の時期

棚卸資産の委託販売に係る委託者における資産の譲渡をした日は，その委託品について受託者が譲渡した日となる。ただし，その委託品についての売上計算書が売上げのつど作成されている場合において，事業者が継続してその売上計算書の到着した日を棚卸資産の譲渡をした日としているときは，その日とすることができる（消基通9-1-3）。

¶8-410　請負による資産の譲渡等の時期

請負による資産の譲渡等の時期については，原則として，物の引渡しを要する請負契約にあってはその目的物の全部を完成して相手方に引き渡した日，物の引渡しを要しない請負契約にあってはその約した役務の全部を完了した日とされている（消基通9-1-5）。

¶8-420　固定資産の譲渡の時期

固定資産の譲渡の時期は，原則として，その引渡しがあった日とされている。しかし，その固定資産が土地，建物その他これらに類する資産である場合において，事業者がその固定資産の譲渡に関する契約の効力発生の日を資産の譲渡の時期としているときは，その日とすることができる（消基通9-1-13）。固定資産の引渡しの日がいつであるかについては，棚卸資産の引渡しの日の例による（消基通9-1-13（注））。

726   CONSUMPTION TAX

¶ 8-425 Time of transfer of industrial property etc.

(1) The date of transfer or creation of the right to use industrial property is the date of the coming into effect of contracts for transfer or creation of the right to use. However, if the contract comes into effect only upon registration, enterprises can select the date of registration as the date of transfer of the industrial property etc. (R 9-1-15).

(2) Time of transfer of assets, etc. by the transfer of know-how, and involving a lump-sum payment or a down payment, is the date of full disclosure of the know-how. When the disclosure is to be conducted in lots and the lump-sum or down payment paid in corresponding lots then, the date of disclosure shall be treated as the date of the transfer of the assets (R 9-1-16).

¶ 8-430 Time of transfer of securities

The time of transfer of securities is, in principle, the date of delivery (R 9-1-17).

¶ 8-440 Time of transfer of assets, etc. for consideration such as interest

(1) Interest: The amount of interest accrued from loans, deposits and securities is the amount which accrues in the taxable period according to the manner and period over which the said interest is calculated. However, if an enterprise is not a financial enterprise or an insurance enterprise, and if the due date of interest comes periodically within less than a year, the date of transfer can be the due date of interest on condition that the enterprise consistently applies this manner (R 9-1-19).

(2) Rent: The date of the transfer of assets, etc. for rent received on a regular basis, such as monthly, is the due date under the contract. However, if the amount of rent is not defined because of a dispute (except a dispute regarding the increase or decrease of rent), and if the payment of rent is not made during the taxable period, the date of transfer can be the date on which the amount of rent is defined after the settlement of the dispute, regardless of whether the lessee deposits the money or not (R 9-1-20).

¶ 8-425

消　費　税　727

¶8-425　工業所有権等の譲渡の時期

(1)　工業所有権等の譲渡又は実施権の設定については，その譲渡又は設定に関する契約の効力発生日に行われたものとなる。ただし，その譲渡又は設定に関する契約の効力が登録により生ずることとなっている場合で，事業者が，その登録日によっているときは，その日とすることができる（消基通9‐1‐15）。

(2)　ノウ・ハウの設定契約に際して支払を受ける一時金又は頭金を対価とする資産の譲渡等の時期は，そのノウ・ハウの開示を完了した日となる。ただし，ノウ・ハウの開示が2回以上にわたって分割して行われ，かつ，その一時金又は頭金の支払がほぼこれに見合って分割して行われることとなっている場合には，その開示をした日に資産の譲渡等があったものとなる（消基通9‐1‐16）。

¶8-430　有価証券の譲渡の時期

有価証券の譲渡の時期は，原則としてその引渡しがあった日とされている（消基通9‐1‐17）。

¶8-440　利子等を対価とする資産の譲渡等の時期

(1)　利子等を対価とする資産の譲渡等

貸付金，預金，貯金又は有価証券（以下「貸付金等」という。）から生ずる利子の額は，その利子の計算期間の経過に応じその課税期間に係る金額をその課税期間の資産の譲渡等の対価の額とすることとされている。ただし，主として金融及び保険業を営む事業者以外の事業者は，その有する貸付金等（その事業者が金融及び保険業を兼業する場合には，当該金融及び保険業に係るものを除く。）から生ずる利子で，その支払期日が1年以内の一定の期間ごとに到来するものの額につき，継続してその支払期日の属する課税期間の資産の譲渡等の対価の額とすることができる（消基通9‐1‐19）。

(2)　使用料等を対価とする資産の譲渡等

資産の賃貸借契約に基づいて月ごと等年以下の期間を単位として支払を受ける使用料等の額（前受けに係る額を除く。）を対価とする資産の譲渡等の時期は，その契約又は慣習によりその支払を受けるべき日とされている。ただし，その契約について係争（使用料等の額の増減に関するものを除く。）があるためその支払を受けるべき使用料等の額が確定せず，その課税期間においてその支払を受けていないときは，相手方が供託したかどうかにかかわらず，その係争が解決して当該使用料等の額が確定しその支払を受けることとなる日とすることができる（消基通9‐1‐20）。

728   CONSUMPTION TAX

(3) Royalties: The relevant date is considered to be when the amount of
     the royalty is established (R 9-1-21).

¶ 8-450 Special exception for the time of transfer of assets, etc. by long term installment sales

If an enterprise conducts long term installment sales of inventory assets or services and keeps accounts for all the long term installment sales
on an installment basis so as to attract the provisions of Art. 63① of the
Corporation Tax Law or Art. 65① of the Income Tax Law, installments the
due dates of which do not fall within the taxable period to which the day
of the long term installment sales belongs (except those actually received
in the taxable period) are deemed not to be transfers conducted in the taxable period, and are deductible from the consideration received for inventory assets or services in the taxable period (Law 16①).

The installments deducted according to the provision mentioned
above, are deemed to be transfers of assets, etc. conducted in each succeeding taxable period in which their payment becomes due. (Those
already received in previous taxable periods are deemed to be transfers
of assets, etc. conducted in each previous taxable period, and those for
which payment has not become due but has been received in the taxable
period are deemed to be transfers of assets, etc. conducted in that taxable
period.), so long as the accounting method of installment basis is applied
consistently (Law 16②, Reg 31).

(1) **Definition of long term installment sales.**

"Long term installment sales" are certain sales of goods or services conducted under a regular contract which stipulates that the
consideration is to be paid in installments (R 9-3-3).

(2) **Treatment where the installment basis is not applied, etc.**

If an enterprise does not keep its accounts on the installment basis or ceases to apply this special exception in a taxable period, the
uncollected balance of installments is deemed to be a transfer of assets, etc. conducted within the taxable period (Reg 32).

(3) **Treatment of a taxable enterprise which becomes a tax-exempt
     enterprise, and vice versa.**

If a taxable enterprise becomes a tax-exempt enterprise or a tax-

¶ 8-450

消　費　税　729

(3)　工業所有権等の使用料を対価とする資産の譲渡等

工業所有権等又はノウ・ハウを他の者に使用させたことにより支払を受ける使用料の額を対価とする資産の譲渡等の時期は，その額が確定した日とされている（消基通9-1-21）。

¶8-450　長期割賦販売等に係る資産の譲渡等の時期の特例

棚卸資産又は役務の長期割賦販売等を行った事業者が，所得税法第65条第1項又は法人税法第63条第1項の適用を受けるため長期割賦販売等をしたすべての棚卸資産又は役務に係る対価につき延払基準の方法により経理しているときは，賦払金のうち長期割賦販売等をした日の属する課税期間中にその支払期日が到来しないもの（その課税期間中に支払を受けたものを除く。）は，その課税期間において資産の譲渡等を行わなかったものとみなして，その課税期間における棚卸資産又は役務に係る対価の額から控除することができる（消法16①）。

控除した額は，延払基準の方法による経理が継続される限り，賦払金の支払期日が到来する各課税期間（その課税期間前に既に支払を受けたものはその課税期間前の各課税期間，また，翌課税期間以後に支払期日が到来するものでその課税期間中に支払を受けたものはその課税期間）において資産の譲渡等が行われたものとみなされる（消法16②，消令31）。

(1)　長期割賦販売等の意義

この特例の適用がある長期割賦販売等とは，月賦，年賦その他の賦払の方法により対価の支払を受けることを定型的に定めた約款に基づき行われる一定の販売又は提供をいう（消基通9-3-3）。

(2)　延払基準を適用しなかった場合等の取扱い

延払基準の方法により経理がされなかった場合又は特例の適用を受けないこととした場合には，その経理をしなかった又は特例の適用を受けないこととした課税期間における割賦未収金については，その課税期間において資産の譲渡等が行われたものとみなされる（消令32）。

(3)　免税事業者となった場合等の取扱い

課税事業者が免税事業者となった場合又は免税事業者が課税事業者となった場合には，その免税事業者となった又は課税事業者となった課税期間にお

730　CONSUMPTION TAX

exempt enterprise becomes a taxable enterprise during a taxable period, the balance of uncollected installments in the taxable period is deemed to be a transfer of assets, etc. conducted on the day before the first day of the taxable period (Reg 33).

¶ 8-470　Special exception for the time of transfer of assets, etc. under long-term contracts

If an enterprise transfers assets, etc. under long-term contracts and keeps its accounts on the "percentage of completion" basis, as stipulated by Art. 66①, ② of the Income Tax Law or Art. 64①, ② of the Corporation Tax Law, it is possible to treat the same percentage of transfers of assets, etc. as falling within the taxable period to which the end of the business year (December 31 of the year in case of an individual enterprise) belongs, when the certain percentage of proceeds are included in gross income, according to the "percentage of completion" basis (Law 17①, ②).

In the case where an enterprise delivers the assets to which this basis applies, the amount of consideration which has already been taxed shall be deducted from the amount of consideration for the transfer of the assets under long-term contracts (Law 17③).

(1) **Definition of a long-term contract.**

　　A "long-term contract" is a contract which satisfies conditions of Art. 66①, ② of the Income Tax Law or Art. 64①, ② of the Corporation Tax Law (Law 17①, ②).

(2) **Treatment where the "percentage of completion" basis is not applicable, or other cases.**

　　Regarding on contracts satisfying the condition of Art. 66② of the Income Tax Law or Art. 64② of Corporation Tax Law, if during any business year an enterprise does not keep its accounts according to the "percentage of completion" basis, or certain circumstances arise and there seems to be a loss in respect of the long-term contracts, this special rule does not apply in the taxable period to which the end of the relevant business year belongs.

¶ 8-475　Special exception for the time of transfer of assets, etc. in relation to small-scale enterprises, etc.

In the case of an individual enterprise which keeps its accounts on a cash basis in the manner stipulated by Art. 67 of the Income Tax Law, the

¶ 8-470

消　費　税　731

ける割賦未収金については，その課税期間の初日の前日において資産の譲渡等が行われたものとみなされる（消令33）。

¶8-470　長期工事の請負に係る資産の譲渡等の時期の特例

　長期工事の請負に係る契約に基づき資産の譲渡等を行った者が，所得税法第66条第1項，第2項又は法人税法第64条第1項，第2項に規定する工事進行基準の方法により経理しているときは，これらの収入金額が計上された事業年度の終了の日（個人事業者の場合には，その年の12月31日）の属する課税期間において，その部分の資産の譲渡等を行ったものとすることができる（消法17①，②）。

　また，この適用を受ける目的物の引渡しを行った場合には，既に課税処理された部分に係る対価の額の合計額をその目的物に係る長期工事の請負に係る対価の額から控除する（消法17③）。

(1)　長期工事の意義

　長期工事とは，所得税法第66条第1項，第2項又は法人税法第64条第1項，第2項に規定するものをいう（消法17①，②）。

(2)　工事進行基準を適用しなかった場合等の取扱い

　所得税法第66条第2項又は法人税法第64条第2項に規定する工事について，工事進行基準により経理しなかった場合又は長期工事の請負につき損失が生ずると見込まれるに至った事由が生じた場合には，その経理しなかった事業年度又はその事由が生じた事業年度の終了の日の属する課税期間以降はこの特例の適用はできない。

¶8-475　小規模事業者に係る資産の譲渡等の時期の特例

　所得税法第67条に規定する現金主義の適用を受ける個人事業者の資産の譲渡等及び課税仕入れを行った時期は，対価を収受した日及び費用を支払った日とすることができる（消法18①）。

732   CONSUMPTION TAX

time of transfer of assets, etc. and of conducting the taxable purchase can be the date of receiving the consideration, or the date of payment (Law 18①).

Tax Base

¶ 8-490 Domestic transactions

The tax base for domestic transactions is the amount of consideration for the transfer of assets, etc. (Law 28①).

(1) **Amount of consideration for the transfer of assets, etc.**

"The amount of consideration for the transfer of assets, etc." does not include consumption tax and includes the amount of cash or goods other than cash, right or other economic benefit which is received, or should be received, as consideration for the transfer of assets, etc. (Law 28①).

The value of goods other than cash, rights or other economic benefits is the value at the time when the goods or rights are received, or the benefit is given (Reg 45①).

(2) **Deemed amount of consideration for the transfer of assets, etc.**

The value of assets when they are transferred, consumed or gifted in the following cases shall be the amount of consideration for the transfer.

(a) The transfer of assets by a corporation to its directors at an extremely low price compared with their market value (Law 28①).

(b) The consumption of inventory assets and other business assets for private use by an individual enterprise (Law 28②(1)).

(c) The gift of assets by a corporation to its directors (Law 28②(2)).

Note:
In the case of (b) or (c) above, it is possible to treat the amount as the tax base on condition that the amount exceeds the purchase price of the asset and 50% of the fair market value (R 10-1-18).

(3) **Special rules**

In the case of special types of transfer, etc. listed below, the amounts indicated are the amounts of consideration (Reg 45②).

(a) Transfer of asset in order to make a payment in substitution—the amount of debt which is discharged by the payment in substitution (In case the value of the asset transferred exceeds the amount of debt discharged and the difference is refunded, the difference shall be added to the amount of debt.).

(b) Transfer of asset in the form of gift which bears an obligation—

¶ 8-490

消　費　税　733

課　税　標　準

¶8-490　国内取引
　国内取引に係る消費税の課税標準は，課税資産の譲渡等の対価の額である（消法28①）。

(1)　課税資産の譲渡等の対価の額
　「課税資産の譲渡等の対価の額」とは，事業者が課税資産の譲渡等につき対価として収受し，又は収受すべき一切の金銭又は金銭以外の物若しくは権利その他経済的な利益の額をいい，課税資産の譲渡等について課されるべき消費税に相当する額を含まない（消法28①）。

　また，金銭以外の物又は権利その他経済的な利益の額は，その物若しくは権利を取得し，又はその利益を享受するときにおける価額である（消令45①）。

(2)　課税資産の譲渡等の対価の額とみなされる額
　次に掲げる場合には，その資産の譲渡，消費又は使用若しくは贈与のときにおける価額が課税資産の譲渡等の対価の額とみなされる。
- (a)　法人が資産をその役員に対してその資産の価額に比し著しく低い対価により譲渡した場合（消法28①）
- (b)　個人事業者が棚卸資産又は棚卸資産以外の資産で事業の用に供していたものを家事のために消費し，又は使用した場合（消法28②一）
- (c)　法人が資産をその役員に対して贈与した場合（消法28②二）

　(注)：上記(b)又は(c)の場合，その資産の仕入値を下回らず，かつ，通常売価の概ね50％以上相当額としても差し支えない（消基通10-1-18）。

(3)　特則
　次に掲げる譲渡等の場合には，次に掲げる金額が譲渡等の対価の額となる（消令45②）。
- (a)　代物弁済による資産の譲渡
　　代物弁済により消滅する債務の額（その代物弁済により譲渡される資産の価格がその債務の額を超える額に相当する金額につき支払を受ける場合は，その支払を受ける金額を加算した金額）

- (b)　負担付き贈与による資産の譲渡

734   CONSUMPTION TAX

the amount of the obligation.

(c)   Investment of non-cash asset in stocks—the fair market value of the stocks when they are acquired by the investment.

(d)   Exchange of asset—the fair market value of the asset when it is acquired by the exchange (If the price of the asset transferred exceeds that of the asset acquired, and the difference is paid to the transferor, the difference shall be added to the price of the asset acquired.

If the price of the asset acquired exceeds that of the asset transferred, and the transferor paid the difference to the transferee, the difference shall be deducted from the price of the asset acquired.).

(4)   **Treatment of individual excise taxes**

"The amount of consideration for the transfer of assets, etc." includes liquor tax, tobacco tax, gasoline tax, petroleum coal tax, petroleum gas tax, etc. but does not include diesel oil delivery tax, golf course tax and bathing tax, because the taxpayers of the latter taxes are the users. If the amount of tax is not clearly distinguished from the amount of consideration, the tax is included in the amount of consideration (R 10-1-11).

(5)   **Treatment where the land and the buildings are transferred as a whole**

When the taxable assets and the assets other than the taxable assets are transferred as a whole, the amount of consideration for the transfer of taxable assets and that of assets other than taxable assets should be reasonably distinguished.

In the case of the land and the buildings, however, the amount of consideration can be calculated by the rules stipulated by the income tax law or the corporate tax law (R 10-1-5).

(6)   **Treatment where the amount of consideration is not determined**

When the amount of consideration for the transfer of assets, etc. is not determined by the end of the taxable period, the amount should be estimated reasonably. If the amount determined later is different from the estimated amount, the difference should be adjusted at the taxable period in which the amount of consideration is determined (R 10-1-20).

¶ 8-490

負担付き贈与に係る負担の価額に相当する金額

(c) 金銭以外の資産の出資

出資により取得する株式（出資を含む。）の取得のときにおける価額に相当する金額

(d) 資産の交換

交換により取得する資産の取得のときにおける価額（その交換により譲渡する資産の価額と交換により取得する資産の価額との差額を補うための金銭を取得する場合はその取得する金銭の額を加算した金額とし，その差額を補うための金銭を支払う場合はその支払う金銭の額を控除した金額とする。）

(4) **個別消費税の取扱い**

譲渡等の対価の額には，酒税，たばこ税，揮発油税，石油石炭税，石油ガス税等が含まれるが，軽油引取税，ゴルフ場利用税及び入湯税は，利用者等が納税義務者となっており，対価の額に含まれない。ただし，これらの税額に相当する金額について明確に区分されていない場合は，対価の額に含まれる（消基通10-1-11）。

(5) **土地と建物を一括譲渡した場合の取扱い**

課税資産と課税資産以外の資産とを一括して譲渡した場合には，それぞれの資産の譲渡に係る対価の額について合理的に区分しなければならないのであるが，土地，建物等を一括譲渡した場合においては，それぞれの対価の額につき，所得税又は法人税の特例計算による取扱いによる区分をしているときはその区分によることができる（消基通10-1-5）。

(6) **譲渡等に係る対価が未確定の場合の取扱い**

資産の譲渡等を行った場合において，その資産の譲渡等をした日の属する課税期間の末日までに，その対価の額が確定していないときは，同日の現況によりその金額を適正に見積もる。この場合において，その後確定した対価の額が見積額と異なるときは，その差額はその確定した日の属する課税期間における資産の譲渡等に係る対価の額に加算し，又は当該対価の額から減算する（消基通10-1-20）。

736   CONSUMPTION TAX

¶ 8-500 Import transaction

The tax base for taxable foreign goods removed from a bonded area is the total of the following three items (Law 28③):

(1) the tax base for customs duties (i.e. C.I.F. Price);

(2) individual excise taxes which are levied when the taxable foreign goods are removed from a bonded area; and

(3) customs duties.

> **Note:**
> "Individual excise taxes" include liquor tax, tobacco tax, gasoline tax, local road tax, petroleum gas tax and petroleum coal tax.

Tax Rate

¶ 8-510 Tax rate

(1) The tax rate for consumption tax is a uniform rate of 6.3% (Law 29).

> **Note:**
> Together with an effective local consumption tax rate of 1.7%, the total effective tax rate is 8%.

(2) In accordance with the tax rate increase to 7.8% (together with an effective local consumption tax rate 2.2%, the total effective tax rate is 10%) from October 1, 2019, reduced tax rate (6.3%, together with effective local consumption tax rate 1.7%, the total effective tax rate is 8%) is introduced for "drinks and foods excluding alcohol and those served at restaurants" and "newspaper subscription fees" (October 2016, consumption tax reform).

Tax Credits and Other Adjustments

¶ 8-530 Purchase Tax Credit

Where a taxable enterprise makes a taxable purchase (see ¶ 8-600) in Japan or removes taxable foreign goods from a bonded area, the total consumption tax amount on the purchase, and on the foreign goods during the taxable period, is credited against the consumption tax amount on the tax base in the taxable period during which the taxable purchase is made or the taxable foreign goods are removed from a bonded area (Law 30①).

> **Note:**
> 1. Purchase tax credit is not available to a tax-exempt enterprise.

¶ 8-500

消　費　税　737

¶8-500　輸入取引

保税地域から引き取られる課税貨物に係る消費税の課税標準は，次の金額の合計額である（消法28③）。

(1)　関税の課税価格（いわゆるC.I.F.価格）

(2)　課税貨物の保税地域からの引取りに課されるべき個別消費税

(3)　関税

(注)：個別消費税とは，酒税，たばこ税，揮発油税，地方道路税，石油ガス税及び石油石炭税をいう。

税　　率

¶8-510　税率

(1)　消費税の税率は，6.3％の単一税率である（消法29）。

(注)：地方消費税（1.7％）と合わせると8％となる。

(2)　平成31年10月1日の税率7.8％（地方消費税2.2％と合わせると10％）への引上げに伴い，飲食料品（酒類，外食を除く。）及び新聞の定期購読料について軽減税率（6.3％，地方消費税1.7％と合わせると8％）が適用されることとなった（平成28年11月，消費税法改正）。

税額控除等

¶8-530　仕入れに係る消費税額の控除

課税事業者が，国内において課税仕入れ（¶8-600参照）を行った場合又は保税地域から課税貨物の引取りを行った場合には，その課税仕入れを行った日又は課税貨物の引取りを行った日の属する課税期間の課税標準額に対する消費税額（売上げに係る消費税額）から，当該課税期間中に国内において行った課税仕入れに係る消費税額及びその課税期間中に保税地域から引取った課税貨物について課された又は課されるべき消費税額（課税仕入等の税額）の合計額を控除する（消法30①）。

(注)：1.　仕入れに係る消費税額の控除は，納税義務を免除された小規模事業者には適用されない。

738   CONSUMPTION TAX

2. An individual enterprise which starts a new business and a newly established corporation other than taxable enterprise cannot claim purchase
tax credits, unless the enterprise elects to be a taxable enterprise (R 11-
1-7) (see ¶ 8-250).

¶ 8-540 Computation of consumption tax amount on taxable purchase

The consumption tax amount on a taxable purchase is computed as
follows (Law 30①):

$$\text{Amount of taxable purchase} \times \frac{6.3}{108} \left[\text{Together with the local consumption tax amount on a taxable purchase, } \frac{8}{108} \right]$$

¶ 8-545 Computation of purchase tax credit where the taxable sales ratio is 95% and over

If all transfers of assets, etc. conducted in a taxable period are transfers of taxable assets, etc., the whole tax amount on taxable purchases,
etc. is creditable.

If an enterprise conducts transfers of taxable assets, etc. and transfers of assets, etc. other than transfers of taxable assets, etc. (hereinafter
referred to as "transfers of other assets, etc."), in principle, only the tax
amount on the taxable purchases, etc. corresponding to the transfer of
taxable assets, etc. is creditable. However, if the taxable sales ratio (see ¶
8-580) of the enterprise is 95% and over, the whole tax amount on taxable
purchases etc. is creditable as if the enterprise had conducted only transfers of taxable assets, etc (Law 30①).

Note:
Apply only for enterprises whose taxable sales amount is not exceed ¥500
million for the taxable period (for a corporation whose taxable period is less
than one year, the calculation is converted proportionately to an amount that
corresponds to one year), otherwise the amount of consumption tax on taxable purchases, etc. is calculated as same as ¶8-550 below (apply for a taxable period beginning after April 1 2012).

¶ 8-550 Computation of purchase tax credit where the taxable sales ratio is less than 95%

Where the taxable sales ratio during the taxable period is less than
95%, the amount of consumption tax on taxable purchases and taxable foreign goods which are necessary for transfers of taxable assets, etc. is cal-

¶ 8-540

消　費　税　739

　　2．新たに事業を開始した個人事業者又は新たに設立した法人（課税事業者となる事業
　　　者を除く。）は，課税事業者を選択しない限り，仕入税額控除は適用されない（消基
　　　通11-1-7）（¶8-250参照）。

¶8-540　課税仕入れに係る消費税額の計算

　課税仕入れに係る消費税額は，次の算式により計算する（消法30①）。

$$課税仕入れに係る支払対価の額 \times \frac{6.3}{108}（地方消費税を合わせると \frac{8}{108}）$$

¶8-545　課税売上割合が95％以上の場合の仕入税額控除の計算

　その課税期間中に行った資産の譲渡等が課税資産の譲渡等のみである場合
には，課税仕入れ等の税額の全額が仕入税額控除の対象とされる。

　また，課税資産の譲渡等と課税資産の譲渡等以外の資産の譲渡等（以下
「その他の資産の譲渡等」という。）がある場合には，本来課税資産の譲渡等
に対応する課税仕入れ等の税額のみが仕入税額控除の対象とされるのである
が，その課税期間の課税売上割合（¶8-580参照）が100分の95以上であると
きには，課税資産の譲渡等のみを行っている場合と同様に，課税仕入れ等の
税額の全額を控除することができる（消法30①）。

　（注）：その課税期間の課税売上高が5億円（その課税期間が1年に満たない場合には，その金
　　　　額を1年分に換算した金額）以下の事業所のみに適用され，課税売上高が5億円を超える
　　　　事業者は次の¶8-550と同様に計算することとなる（平成24年4月1日以降開始する課税
　　　　期間から適用）。

¶8-550　課税売上割合が95％に満たない場合の仕入税額控除の計算

　その課税期間における課税売上割合が95％に満たない場合の控除税額の計
算は，課税資産の譲渡等を行うために要する課税仕入れ及び課税貨物に係る
部分の消費税額として¶8-560～¶8-570に掲げる場合に応じ，それぞれによ
り計算した金額とする（消法30②）。

740   CONSUMPTION TAX

culated using the following itemized or proportional methods (¶ 8-560 to ¶ 8-570) respectively (Law 30②).

> **Note:**
> Even if an enterprise has approval from the director of the tax office to use the substitutional ratio (see ¶ 8-590) instead of the taxable sales ratio, the substitutional ratio cannot be used. The taxable sales ratio should be used to determine whether the taxable sales ratio is less than 95% or not (R 11-5-9).

¶ 8-560 Itemized method

Where taxable purchases, and taxable foreign goods removed from a bonded area (hereinafter called "taxable purchase, etc.") during the taxable period, can be classified into the following items, the amount of purchase tax credit is computed by using the itemized method shown below (Law 30②(1)):

① transfer of taxable assets, etc. only;

② transfer of other assets, etc. only;

③ transfer of taxable assets, etc. and other assets, etc. in common.

Computation:

$$\begin{bmatrix} \text{consumption tax} \\ \text{amount on } ① \end{bmatrix} + \begin{bmatrix} \text{consumption tax} \\ \text{amount on } ③ \end{bmatrix} \times \begin{bmatrix} \text{taxable sales ratio} \\ \text{or substitutional ratio} \\ \text{(see ¶ 8-590)} \end{bmatrix}$$

(1) Taxable purchases, etc. for transfers of taxable assets, etc. include, for example, the following taxable purchases (R 11-2-12):

   (a) taxable assets transferred as they are;

   (b) materials, packages, wrapping paper, machinery and equipment, tools, fixtures, etc. consumed or used only in the manufacture of taxable assets;

   (c) warehouse charges, carriage, advertisement expenses, commission and sub-contract expenses with regard to the taxable assets.

(2) Taxable purchases, etc. for transfers of other assets, etc. means taxable purchase merely for non taxable sales that include, for example, expenses for development of land for sales (R 11-2-15).

¶ 8-570 Proportional method

In cases where a taxable purchase, etc. cannot be classified as above (¶ 8-560), the amount of purchase tax credit is computed by using the proportional method as follows (Law 30②(2)):

¶ 8-560

消　費　税　741

(注)：課税売上割合が95％に満たないか否かの判定は，事業者が課税売上割合に準ずる場合（¶8-590参照）について税務署長の承認を受けている場合であってもその準ずる割合によることはできず，課税売上割合を用いる（消基通11-5-9）。

¶8-560　個別対応方式

その課税期間中の課税仕入れ及び課税貨物（以下「課税仕入等」という。）につき，次のように区分ができる場合には，次の算式により計算される（消法30②一）。

① 課税資産の譲渡等にのみ要するもの
② その他の資産の譲渡等にのみ要するもの
③ 課税資産の譲渡等とその他の資産の譲渡等に共通して要するもの

（算式）

$$\left(\begin{array}{c}①に係る\\消費税額\end{array}\right) + \left(\begin{array}{c}③に係る\\消費税額\end{array}\right) \times \left(\begin{array}{c}課税売上割合又は\\同割合に準ずる割合（¶8-590参照）\end{array}\right)$$

(1) 課税資産の譲渡等にのみ要するものとは，例えば，次に掲げるものの課税仕入れ等がこれに該当する（消基通11-2-12）。
　(a) そのまま他に譲渡される課税対象譲渡資産
　(b) 課税対象資産の製造用にのみ消費し，又は使用される原材料，容器，包紙，機械及び装置，工具，器具，備品等

　(c) 課税対象資産に係る倉庫料，運送費，広告宣伝費，支払手数料又は支払加工賃等

(2) その他の資産の譲渡等のみに要するものとは，非課税資産の譲渡のためにのみ必要な課税仕入れをいい，例えば，販売用の土地の造成費用の支出等がこれに該当する（消基通11-2-15）。

¶8-570　一括比例配分方式

課税仕入れ等が¶8-560のように区分できない場合には，次の算式により計算した金額となる（消法30②二）。

742   CONSUMPTION TAX

consumption tax amount on taxable purchase, etc. ×   taxable sales ratio

An enterprise, which calculates purchase tax credit by using the itemized method, may select to apply the proportional method instead. Once an enterprise selects to use the proportional method, it is required to apply this method continuously during the taxable period beginning on the first day of the taxable period during which the enterprise selected to use this method through to the day on which two years elapses from that day (Law 30⑤).

¶ 8-580 Taxable sales ratio

The taxable sales ratio is the ratio of the total amount of consideration for transfers of assets etc., conducted in Japan during the taxable period, to the total amount of consideration for transfers of taxable assets etc., also conducted in Japan, during the taxable period (Law 30⑥).

The amount of consideration for transfers of assets, etc. and taxable assets, etc. does not include the consumption tax amount. It is the amount arrived at after deducting refunds etc. of consideration for sales (including refunds, etc. of consideration for export transactions) (Reg 48①). That amount includes the amount of consideration for export transactions, and excludes that for transactions conducted outside Japan (R 11-5-4).

Calculation of the taxable sales ratio:

$$\text{Taxable sales ratio} = \frac{\text{Total amount of consideration for transfers of taxable assets, etc. conducted in Japan during the taxable period}}{\text{Total amount of consideration for transfers of assets, etc. conducted in Japan during the taxable period}}$$

Note:
The taxable sales ratio cannot be calculated for each branch or department, etc. individually (R 11-5-1).

(1) Amounts not included in the denominator

The amount of consideration paid for the following transfers is not to be included in the denominator in calculating the taxable sales ratio (Reg 48②):

(a) transfers of means of payment, such as money, checks, etc;

(b) transfers of monetary assets acquired in consideration of trans-

¶ 8-580

$$課税仕入等の税額 = \begin{pmatrix} その課税期間中の課税仕入れ及び \\ 課税貨物に係る税額の合計額 \end{pmatrix} \times \begin{matrix} 課税売 \\ 上割合 \end{matrix}$$

　なお，個別対応方式により控除税額を計算できる事業者が，選択により比例配分方式により計算することもできるが，この方法を選択した場合には，この方法により計算することとした課税期間の初日から同日以後2年を経過する日までの間に開始する課税期間までの間は継続して適用しなければならない（消法30⑤）。

¶8-580　課税売上割合

　課税売上割合とは，その課税期間中の国内における資産の譲渡等の対価の額の合計額に占めるその課税期間中の国内における課税資産の譲渡等の対価の額の合計額の割合をいう（消法30⑥）。

　この場合，資産の譲渡等の対価の額及び課税資産の譲渡等の対価の額は，いずれも消費税を含まない金額であり，また，それぞれ売上げに係る対価の返還等の金額（輸出取引に係る対価の返還等の金額を含む。）を控除した金額である（消令48①）。

　課税売上割合は，国内取引に係る資産の譲渡等に基づき計算することとされているから，資産の譲渡等の対価の額又は課税資産の譲渡等の対価の額には，輸出取引に係る対価の額は含まれ，国外取引に係る対価の額は含まれない（消基通11-5-4）。

課税売上割合の計算：

$$課税売上割合 = \frac{\begin{matrix} その事業者がその課税期間中において行った \\ 課税資産の譲渡等の対価の額の合計額 \end{matrix}}{\begin{matrix} その事業者がその課税期間中において行った \\ 資産の譲渡等の対価の額の合計額 \end{matrix}}$$

　(注)：課税売上割合の計算は，事業所単位又は事業部単位等で行うことはできない（消基通11-5-1）。

(1)　資産の譲渡等に含まれない金額

　次に掲げる資産の譲渡等の対価の額は，課税売上割合の計算上，資産の譲渡等の対価の額には含めない（消令48②）。

(a)　通貨，小切手等の支払手段の譲渡

(b)　資産の譲渡等の対価として取得した金銭債権の譲渡

744   CONSUMPTION TAX

fers of assets, etc;

(c) transfers of government bonds, local government bonds, negotiable certificate deposits, etc. on condition that they will be bought back within a year ("gensaki" transactions).

(2) **Amounts to be partially included in the denominator**

Where an enterprise transfers certain securities, commercial papers or negotiable certificates of deposit, etc. (other than those referred to above in (1)(c)), 5% of the amount of consideration must be included in the denominator (Reg 48⑤).

(3) **Loss on redemption of government bonds**

If there is any loss upon redemption of government bonds, etc., the amount of loss must be deducted from the denominator (Reg 48⑥).

(4) **Treatment of exported non-taxable assets etc.**

In the case where an enterprise exports non-taxable assets or exports assets for its own use, it is deemed to export taxable assets (Law 31). However, this rule does not apply if the exported assets are securities, means of payment, mortgage securities or monetary assets.

(5) **Treatment of transfer of assets without consideration**

Where an enterprise transfers assets without consideration and the transfer is not subject to the consumption tax, the fair market value of the assets is not included in the denominator or the numerator, even if the fair market value of the assets should be included in the gross income under the Corporation Tax Law.

¶ 8-590 Substitutional ratio for the taxable sales ratio

In the case where an enterprise calculates the amount of purchase tax credit by the itemized method, it may use the substitutional ratio for the taxable sales ratio, starting from the taxable period during which it obtained permission to do so from the director of the tax office.

If an enterprise wants to stop using the substitutional ratio, it must file a notification with the director of the tax office by the end of the taxable period (Law 30③).

(1) **Calculation of the substitutional ratio for the taxable sales ratio**

The substitutional ratio for the taxable sales ratio must be calculated by using reasonable factors, such as the number of employees

¶ 8-590

消　費　税　745

　　(c)　国債，地方債，譲渡性預金証書等の条件付売買（１年未満の現先取引）

(2)　一部分の金額を資産の譲渡等の金額とするもの

　事業者が一定の有価証券，コマーシャルペーパー又は譲渡性預金等（上記(1)(c)に掲げるものを除く。）を譲渡した場合には，その有価証券等の譲渡の対価の額の５％に相当する金額を分母に計上する（消令48⑤）。

(3)　償還差損が生ずる国債等

　国債等について償還差損が生ずる場合には，課税売上割合の計算上その償還差損は資産の譲渡等の対価の額から控除する（消令48⑥）。

(4)　非課税資産の輸出等の取扱い

　非課税資産の輸出を行った場合又は自己使用のための資産の輸出を行った場合においても，消費税法第31条（（非課税資産の輸出等を行った場合の仕入れに係る消費税額の控除の特例））の規定により課税資産の輸出を行ったものとみなされる。ただし，輸出される資産が非課税規定に該当する有価証券，支払手段，抵当証券及び金銭債権である場合には，この規定の適用はない。

(5)　無償譲渡の取扱い

　無償譲渡をしたことにより，課税されていないものがある場合には，法人税法上は収益に計上すべきものであっても，消費税においては分子，分母には計上しない。

¶8-590　課税売上割合に準ずる割合

　個別対応方式により仕入控除税額を計算する場合には，税務署長の承認を受けた日の属する課税期間以後は課税売上割合による按分に代えて課税売上割合に準ずる割合を用いることができる。

　課税売上割合に準ずる割合の適用をやめようとする場合には，事業者はその課税期間の末日までに税務署長に届出書を提出しなければならない（消法30③）。

(1)　課税売上割合に準ずる割合の算出方法

　課税売上割合に準ずる割合は，使用人の数又は従事割合，消費又は使用する資産の価額又は使用割合その他課税非課税共通用のものの性質に応ずる合

746   CONSUMPTION TAX

involved in, the level of manpower committed to, the amount of assets consumed or used for, or the ratio of using the assets for each taxable or non-taxable business activity (R 11-5-7).

(2) **Scope of application**

In the case of applying the substitutional ratio for taxable sales ratio, it is not necessary to apply only one ratio. It is possible to classify enterprises by type of business, type of expenses or place of business, etc. and use a different ratio in each case (R 11-5-8).

¶ 8-600 **Definition of a taxable purchase**

A "taxable purchase" is made when an enterprise receives taxable assets by transfer or lease, or receives services (excluding services for salaries, etc. stipulated by Art. 28① of the Income Tax Law) as part of its business from another person. This definition applies only where the transfer or lease of taxable assets, or provision of services by the other person itself qualifies as a "transfer of taxable assets, etc.", on the assumption that it is conducted as a business by the other person except where the consumption tax is exempt according to the provisions of the export tax exemption, etc. (Law 2①(12)).

(1) **Scope of a taxable purchase**

(a) Contribution in kind.

Contribution by cash does not qualify as a taxable purchase. Contribution in kind, however, qualifies as a taxable purchase if the purchase of the asset constitutes a taxable purchase or involves the removal of taxable foreign goods from a bonded area (R 11-2-17).

(b) Travelling expenses, hotel charges or daily allowances.

Travelling expenses, hotel charges or daily allowances given to employees by an enterprise qualify as taxable purchases to the extent of the sums which are usually necessary for the trip (R 11-2-1).

Note:

Travelling expenses, etc. for overseas trips usually do not qualify as taxable purchases.

(c) Commutation allowances.

Commutation allowances given to an employee by an enterprise qualify as taxable purchases to the extent of the sums which are

¶ **8-600**

消　費　税　747

理的な基準により算出する（消基通11-5-7）。

(2)　適用範囲

　課税売上割合に準ずる割合を適用する場合には，その事業者について同一の割合を適用する必要はなく，事業の種類，費用の種類又は事業場の異なるごとに区分して異なった割合を用いることができる（消基通11-5-8）。

¶8-600　課税仕入れの意義

　課税仕入れとは，事業者が，事業として他の者から課税資産を譲り受け，若しくは借り受け，又は役務の提供（所得税法第28条第1項に規定する給与等を対価とする役務の提供を除く。）を受けること（その他の者が事業としてその資産を譲り渡し，若しくは貸し付け，又はその役務の提供をしたとした場合に課税資産の譲渡等に該当することとなるもので，輸出免税等の規定により消費税が免除されるもの以外のものに限る。）をいう（消法2①十二）。

(1)　課税仕入れの範囲

　(a)　現物による寄附

　　　金銭による寄附は課税仕入れに該当しないが，資産（現物）を贈与した場合のその資産の取得が課税仕入れ又は保税地域からの課税貨物の引取りに該当するときは，その課税仕入れは，仕入税額控除の対象となる（消基通11-2-17）。

　(b)　出張旅費，宿泊費，日当

　　　事業者がその使用人等に支給する出張旅費，宿泊費，日当のうち，その旅行について通常必要であると認められる部分の金額は，課税仕入れに係る支払対価に該当する（消基通11-2-1）。

　　(注)：海外出張のために支給する旅費等は原則として課税仕入れに該当しない。

　(c)　通勤手当

　　　事業者が役員又は使用人等に支給する通勤手当のうち，その通勤に通常必要であると認められる部分の金額は課税仕入れに係る支払対価に該

748   CONSUMPTION TAX

usually necessary for the commutation (R 11-2-2).

(d) Payment in kind.

Where an enterprise gives assets other than money to its directors or employees, the purchase costs of the assets should be
determined as taxable purchases or non taxable purchase, regardless of whether the payment in kind is liable to assessment
income tax as employment income (R 11-2-3).

(e) Remuneration paid to salesmen, etc.

Remuneration or fees paid to salesmen, collectors, metermen
and the like do not qualify as taxable purchases to the extent
of the sums which are subject to assessment income tax as employment income (R 11-2-5).

(f) Membership fees or union duties.

Membership fees paid to groups of fellow businessmen or union
duties do not qualify as taxable purchases, unless the receipts of
the fees or duties by the groups or the unions qualify as "transfers of taxable assets, etc." (R 11-2-6).

(2) **Time of taxable purchase**

The amount of consumption tax payable on taxable purchases
conducted in the taxable period is subject to purchase tax credit. The
date of the taxable purchase is ordinarily the date of transfer or lease
of the assets, or the date on which services were rendered and it is
decided in the manner described in "Time of Transfer of Assets, etc."
(R 11-3-1) (¶ 8-390 to ¶ 8-470).

¶ 8-610 Prerequisite for application of purchase tax credit

A prerequisite for the application of purchase tax credit is the keeping of books and bills, etc. with respect to purchase tax credits in the
taxable period. If these books or bills, etc. are not kept, the amount of
consumption tax payable on a taxable purchase or removal of taxable foreign goods from a bonded area is not creditable. It is creditable, however,
if an enterprise proves that a disaster or other unavoidable circumstance
caused the absence of books or bills, etc. (Law 30⑦).

Note:
Purchase tax credit is not applicable when an enterprise spends the money
on an entertainment or secret expense account, etc. and the purpose for
which the money is spent is not clear (R 11-2-23).

¶ 8-610

消　費　税　749

当する（消基通11-2-2）。

(d) 現物給付

　　事業者が役員又は使用人等に金銭以外の資産を給付した場合，その給付が給与として所得税の課税の対象とされるか否かにかかわらず，その現物給付に係る資産の取得の態様で課税仕入れに該当するかどうか判断される（消基通11-2-3）。

(e) 外交員等の報酬

　　外交員，集金人，電力量計等の検針人その他これらに類する者に対して支払う報酬又は料金のうち給与所得に該当する部分については，課税仕入れには該当しない（消基通11-2-5）。

(f) 会費，組合費等

　　事業者がその同業者団体，組合等に支払った会費又は組合費等については，その同業者団体，組合等における会費又は組合費等の受領が，課税資産の譲渡等に係る対価の受領に該当しないときは，事業者のその会費又は組合費等の支払も課税仕入れに該当しない（消基通11-2-6）。

(2) **課税仕入れの時期**

　仕入税額控除の対象となるのは，その課税期間中に行った課税仕入れに係る消費税額である。課税仕入れがいつ行われたかの判断は原則として，資産の譲り受け，借り受け又は役務の提供を受けたのがいつかによるが，これについては「資産の譲渡等の時期」（¶8-390〜¶8-470）の取扱いに準ずる（消基通11-3-1）。

¶8-610　仕入税額控除の適用要件

　その課税期間の課税仕入れ等の税額の控除に係る帳簿及び請求書等の保存があることが適用要件とされており，それらの保存のない課税仕入れ又は課税貨物に係る税額については，税額控除の適用がない。

　ただし，災害その他やむを得ない事情によって，保存をすることができなかったことを事業者において証明した場合は，この限りでない（消法30⑦）。

(注)：事業者が交際費，機密費等の名義をもって支出した金銭でその費途が明らかでないものについても仕入税額控除の適用を受けることができない（消基通11-2-23）。

750   CONSUMPTION TAX

(1) **Scope of books**

Books, for the purposes of purchase tax credits, are those recording the items listed in each of the following cases (Law 30⑧).

   (a)   Taxable purchase—
   (i)   name or title of the other party;
   (ii)   date of conducting taxable purchase;
   (iii)   contents of assets or services; and
   (iv)   amount of consideration.

   (b)   Removal of taxable foreign goods from a bonded area—
   (i)   date of removing taxable foreign goods from the relevant bonded area;
   (ii)   contents of the taxable foreign goods; and
   (iii)   amount of consumption tax and local consumption tax or the total amount of these taxes.

(2) **Scope of bills, etc.**

Bills, etc., for the purposes of purchase tax credits, are the documents listed in each of the following cases (Law 30⑨).

   (a)   Taxable purchase—

   Bills, invoices or other similar documents reporting the following items:

   (i)   name or title of the enterprise making the documents;
   (ii)   date of conducting the taxable purchase;
   (iii)   contents of the assets or services;
   (iv)   amount of consideration (including consumption tax amount and local consumption tax amount); and
   (v)   name or title of the enterprise receiving the documents.

   (b)   Removal of taxable foreign goods from a bonded area—

   Documents which certify import permission for the taxable foreign goods, granted by the director of the relevant customhouse to the enterprise which removes taxable foreign goods from the bonded area. The documents must contain the following particulars:

   (i)   director of the customhouse which has jurisdiction over the relevant bonded area;
   (ii)   date on which the taxable foreign goods could be removed

¶ 8-610

消　費　税　751

(1)　帳簿の範囲

　課税仕入れ等の税額の控除に係る帳簿とは，その課税仕入れ等の税額が次のいずれかに該当するかに応じ，それぞれ次の事項を記録した帳簿をいう（消法30⑧）。

　(a)　課税仕入れに係るものである場合

　　(ⅰ)　課税仕入れの相手方の氏名又は名称

　　(ⅱ)　課税仕入れを行った年月日

　　(ⅲ)　課税仕入れに係る資産又は役務の内容

　　(ⅳ)　課税仕入れに係る支払対価の額

　(b)　保税地域から引き取った課税貨物に係るものである場合

　　(ⅰ)　課税貨物を保税地域から引き取った年月日

　　(ⅱ)　課税貨物の内容

　　(ⅲ)　課税貨物の引取りに係る消費税額及び地方消費税額又はその合計額

(2)　請求書等の範囲

　課税仕入れ等の税額の控除に係る請求書等とは，次の区分に応じそれぞれ次に掲げる書類をいう（消法30⑨）。

　(a)　課税仕入れに係るものである場合

　　事業者に対し課税資産の譲渡等を行う他の事業者が交付する請求書，納品書その他これらに類する書類又は事業者がその行った課税仕入れにつき作成する仕入明細書，仕入計算書その他これらに類する書類で次に掲げる事項が記録されたもの

　　(ⅰ)　書類の作成者の氏名又は名称

　　(ⅱ)　課税資産の譲渡等を行った年月日

　　(ⅲ)　課税資産の譲渡等の対象とされた資産又は役務の内容

　　(ⅳ)　課税資産の譲渡等の対価の額（消費税額及び地方消費税額を含む。）

　　(ⅴ)　書類の交付を受けるその事業者の氏名又は名称

　(b)　保税地域から引き取った課税貨物に係るものである場合

　　課税貨物を保税地域から引き取る事業者がその地域の所在地を所轄する税関長から交付を受けるその課税貨物の輸入の許可があったことを証する書類その他の一定の書類で次に掲げる事項が記録されたもの

　　(ⅰ)　保税地域の所在地を所轄する税関長

　　(ⅱ)　課税貨物を保税地域から引き取ることができることとなった年月日

752   CONSUMPTION TAX

from the bonded area;

(iii) contents of the taxable foreign goods;

(iv) amount of tax base, consumption tax amount and local consumption tax amount; and

(v) name or title of the enterprise receiving the documents.

(3) From April 1, 2021, The Invoice-based method will be introduced, and under this method, keeping qualified invoice is required to apply purchase tax credit.

From April 1, 2017 to March 31, 2021, simple methods can be applied as interim measures (2016 tax reform).

¶ 8-620 Adjustment of the amount of purchase tax credit in case of refund etc. of consideration for purchase

Where an enterprise returns goods or is given an allowance or rebate with respect to a taxable purchase conducted in Japan, and hence receives a refund etc. of the consideration for the purchase (i.e. a refund of all or part of the consideration for the taxable purchase, or a reduction of all or part of liabilities such as accounts payable with respect to the taxable purchase), the amount of consumption tax paid on the refund, etc. must be deducted from the tax amount on the taxable purchase for the purposes of purchase tax credit for the taxable period in which the refund etc. of consideration is received (Law 32①).

If there is any amount which cannot be deducted, such amount is deemed to be the consumption tax amount on the transfer of taxable assets, etc. and is added to the consumption tax amount on the tax base in that taxable period (Law 32②).

(1) **Scope of refund, etc. of consideration for purchase**

(a) Dispatch money—

Dispatch money received by an enterprise from a marine transportation company in respect of transportation by ship qualifies as a refund, etc. of consideration for purchase (R 12-1-1).

(b) Sales promotion money—

Sales promotion money received by an enterprise from a supplier qualifies as a refund, etc. of consideration for purchase (R 12-1-2).

(c) Disbursement according to the degree of utilization—

Disbursement received by an enterprise according to the

¶ 8-620

消　費　税　753

　　(iii)　課税貨物の内容
　　(iv)　課税貨物に係る消費税の課税標準である金額及び引取りに係る消費
　　　　税額及び地方消費税額
　　(v)　書類の交付を受ける事業者の氏名又は名称
(3)　平成33年4月1日からインボイス制度が導入され，適格請求書等の保存
　が仕入税額控除の要件とされることとなった。
　　平成29年4月1日から平成33年3月31日までは経過措置として簡素な方
　法によることができることとなった（平成28年度税制改正）。

¶8-620　仕入れに係る対価の返還等を受けた場合の控除税額の調整

　事業者が，国内において行った課税仕入れにつき返品をし，又は値引若し
くは割戻しを受けたことにより仕入れに係る対価の返還等があった場合に
は，仕入控除税額の計算に当たっては，その対価の返還等を受けた日の属す
る課税期間における課税仕入れ等の税額の合計額から，その課税期間におい
て仕入れに係る対価の返還等を受けた金額に係る消費税額の合計額を控除す
る（消法32①）。

　この場合，控除しきれない金額があるときは，その控除しきれない金額を
課税資産の譲渡等に係る消費税額とみなして，その課税期間の課税標準額に
対する消費税額に加算する（消法32②）。

(1)　対価の返還等の範囲
　(a)　船舶の早出料
　　　事業者が海上運送事業を営む事業者から船舶による運送に関連して支
　　払を受ける早出料は，仕入れに係る対価の返還等に該当する（消基通12-
　　1-1）。
　(b)　販売奨励金等
　　　事業者が販売促進の目的で取引先から金銭により支払を受ける販売奨
　　励金等は，仕入れに係る対価の返還等に該当する（消基通12-1-2）。

　(c)　事業分量配当金
　　　事業者が，協同組合から支払を受ける法人税法第60条の2第1項

754   CONSUMPTION TAX

amount of the purchase from a cooperative according to the degree of utilization, as stipulated in Art. 60-2①(1) of the Corporation Tax Law, qualifies as a refund, etc. of consideration for purchase (R 12-1-3).

(d) Purchase discount—

Purchase discount given to an enterprise because, for example, the amount due is paid in advance before the date of payment, qualifies as a refund, etc. of consideration for purchase (R 12-1-4).

(e) Exemption of liabilities—

Even in the case where an enterprise is exempted from all or part of its liabilities, such as accounts payable, in respect of a taxable purchase, such exemption of liabilities does not qualify as a refund, etc. of consideration for purchase (R 12-1-7).

(2) **Time of refund, etc. of consideration**

(a) A purchase rebate is treated as having been received in the following taxable periods respectively (R 12-1-10).

(i) For a purchase rebate assessed according to the purchase amount or quantity, where the assessment basis has been declared plainly by contract or otherwise—the taxable period to which the date of transfer of assets, etc. connected with the purchase belongs.

(ii) For a purchase rebate other than (i) (i.e. rebate given at seller's discretion)—the taxable period to which the day of notification of the rebate to the purchaser belongs.

(b) Where the purchase rebate is reserved by the transferor of assets, etc. as guarantee money, etc. until the time of cancellation of a franchise agreement, or in case unforeseen circumstances, such as a calamity, arise, or until a period of at least five years passes, as specified under the contract with the transferor, the purchase rebate is generally treated as being received in the taxable period to which the day of actual receipt (including offsetting account payable, etc.) belongs. However, the recipient of a purchase rebate may treat it as being received on the day of the purchase of the inventory assets or the day on which the recipient received information from the transferor regarding the rebate (R 12-1-11).

¶ 8-620

第1号の事業分量配当金のうち課税仕入れの分量等に応じた部分の金額は，仕入れに係る対価の返還等に該当する（消基通12-1-3）。

(d) 仕入割引
　仕入れに係る対価をその支払期日よりも前に支払ったこと等を基因として支払を受ける仕入割引は，仕入れに係る対価の返還等に該当する（消基通12-1-4）。

(e) 債務免除
　事業者が課税仕入れの相手方に対する買掛金その他の債務の全部又は一部について債務免除を受けた場合においても，その債務免除は，仕入れに係る対価の返還等に該当しない（消基通12-1-7）。

(2) **対価の返還等の時期**
(a) 仕入割戻しを受けた時期は，次の区分に応じ，次に掲げる課税期間とする（消基通12-1-10）。
　(i) その算定基準が購入価額又は数量によっており，かつ，その算定基準が契約その他の方法により明示されている仕入割戻し
　　資産の譲渡等を受けた日の属する課税期間

　(ii) (i)に該当しない仕入割戻し
　　その仕入割戻しの金額の通知を受けた日の属する課税期間

(b) 仕入割戻しの金額につき資産の譲渡等を受ける相手方との契約により特約店契約の解約，災害の発生等特別な事実が生ずるときまで又は5年を超える一定の期間が経過するまでその相手方に保証金等として預けることとしている場合には，一定の場合を除き現実に支払（買掛金等への充当を含む。）を受けた日の属する課税期間の仕入割戻しとされる。ただし，棚卸資産を購入した日の属する課税期間又はその相手方から通知を受けた日の属する課税期間に仕入割戻しを受けたものとして処理しても差し支えない（消基通12-1-11）。

756   CONSUMPTION TAX

(3) **Consumption tax paid on refund, etc.**

Consumption tax paid on a refund etc. of consideration for a purchase is computed as follows:

Refund etc. of consideration for purchase ×

(4) **Method of deduction**

The methods of deducting the consumption tax paid on a refund etc. of consideration for a purchase from the tax amount on a taxable purchase are as follows (Law 32①)—

(a) In the case where the taxable sales ratio in the taxable period is 95% or over (i.e. where Art. 30② is not applied)—consumption tax on the refund etc., received in the same taxable period as the consideration for the purchase, is deducted from the total tax amount on the taxable purchase in that taxable period (Law 32①(1)).

(b) In the case where the taxable sales ratio in the taxable period is less than 95%, and consumption tax on the purchase is computed by the itemized method (the method stipulated in Law 30②(1))—

(i)   Consumption tax paid on the refund etc., received in the same taxable period as the consideration for the taxable purchase necessary only for the transfer of taxable assets, etc., is deducted from the total tax amount on the taxable purchase necessary only for the transfer of taxable assets, etc (Law 32①(2)).

(ii) The product of the consumption tax paid on the refund etc., received in the same taxable period as the consideration for taxable purchase commonly necessary for a transfer of taxable assets etc. and a transfer of other assets etc. multiplied by the taxable sales ratio, is deducted from the product of the total of the consumption tax amount on the taxable purchase commonly necessary for the transfer of taxable assets etc. and the transfer of other assets etc. multiplied by the taxable sales ratio (Law 32①(2)).

(c) In the case where the taxable sales ratio is less than 95% and consumption tax amount for purchase is computed by the proportional method (the method stipulated in Law 30②(2))—the

¶ 8-620

消　費　税　757

(3)　仕入れに係る対価の返還等を受けた金額に係る消費税額

　仕入れに係る対価の返還等を受けた金額に係る消費税額とは，当該支払対価の額につき返還を受けた金額又は減額を受けた債務の額に105分の4を乗じて計算した金額をいう。

(4)　控除の方法

　仕入れに係る対価の返還等を受けた金額に係る消費税額を課税仕入れ等の税額から控除する方法は，次のとおりである（消法32①）。

(a)　その課税期間における課税売上割合が95％以上の場合（消法30②の適用がない場合）

　　その課税期間の課税仕入れ等の税額の合計額から，その課税期間において仕入れに係る対価の返還等を受けた金額に係る消費税額の合計額を控除する（消法32①一）。

(b)　その課税期間における課税売上割合が95％に満たない場合で，仕入れに係る消費税額を個別対応方式で計算している場合（消法30②一に定める方法による場合）

　(i)　課税資産の譲渡等にのみ要する課税仕入れ等の税額の合計額から，課税資産の譲渡等にのみ要する課税仕入れにつきその課税期間において仕入れに係る対価の返還等を受けた金額に係る消費税額の合計額を控除する（消法32①二）。

　(ii)　課税資産の譲渡等とその他の資産の譲渡等に共通して要する課税仕入れ等の税額の合計額に課税売上割合を乗じて計算した金額から，課税資産の譲渡等とその他の資産の譲渡等に共通して要する課税仕入れにつきその課税期間において対価の返還等を受けた金額に係る消費税額の合計額に課税売上割合を乗じて計算した金額を控除する（消法32①二）

(c)　その課税期間における課税売上割合が95％に満たない場合で，仕入れに係る消費税額を一括比例配分方式により計算している場合（消法30②二に定める方法による場合）

758   CONSUMPTION TAX

product of the total of the consumption tax paid on the refund, etc., received in the taxable period as the consideration for the taxable purchase multiplied by the taxable sales ratio, is deducted from the product of the total tax amount on the taxable purchase multiplied by the taxable sales ratio (Law 32①(3)).

¶ 8-630 **Tax credit in case of refund etc. of consideration for sales**

Where a taxable enterprise makes a refund etc. of consideration for sales due to the return of goods, allowances or rebates with respect to the transfer of taxable assets, etc. conducted in Japan, the consumption tax paid on the refund etc. is creditable against the total consumption tax on the tax base in the taxable period in which the refund etc. is made (Law 38).

(1)   **Definition of refund etc. of consideration for sales**

A refund etc. of consideration for sales means a refund of all or part of the consideration, inclusive of tax, or a reduction of all or part of liabilities such as accounts payable due to the return of goods, allowances or rebates with respect to the transfer of taxable assets, etc. conducted in Japan.

(2)   **Computation of creditable amount**

The amount available as a credit is computed as follows:

$$\text{Refunded amount of tax-inclusive consideration or amount of reduced liabilities} \times \frac{6.3}{108} \left[\text{Together with the local consumption tax, } \frac{8}{108}\right]$$

(3)   **Condition for application of the rule**

This rule is not applicable to a refund etc. of consideration for sales of which accounting records are not kept by the enterprise, except where it is proved by the enterprise that it was impossible to do so because of a disaster or other uncontrollable circumstance (Law 38②).

(4)   **Computation for blanket rebate**

If a combined rebate was paid for the transfer of taxable assets etc. and the transfer of other assets etc., the amount paid is to be divided in a rational manner into two parts corresponding to each transfer (R 14-1-5).

(5)   **Time of rebate**

A sales rebate is treated as being made in a particular taxable period according to the following rules (R 14-1-9).

¶ 8-630

消　費　税　759

　課税仕入れ等の税額の合計額に課税売上割合を乗じて計算した金額か
ら，その課税期間において仕入れに係る対価の返還等を受けた金額に係
る消費税額の合計額に課税売上割合を乗じて計算した金額を控除する
（消法32①三）。

¶8-630　売上げに係る対価の返還等をした場合の消費税額の控除

　課税事業者が，国内において行った課税資産の譲渡等について返品，値引
き又は割戻しにより，売上げに係る対価の返還等を行った場合には，対価の
返還を行った日の属する課税期間の課税標準額に対する消費税額から対価の
返還等の金額に係る消費税額を控除する（消法38）。

⑴　売上げに係る対価の返還等の意義

　売上げに係る対価の返還等とは，国内において行った課税資産の譲渡等に
ついて，返品を受け又は値引き若しくは割戻しをしたことによる課税資産の
譲渡等の税込対価の額の全部若しくは一部の返還又は売掛金その他の債権の
額の全部又は一部の減額をいう。

⑵　控除額の計算

　対価の返還等に係る消費税額として控除する額の計算は次により行う。

$$\text{返還した税込対価の額又は}\atop\text{減額した債権の額} \times \frac{6.3}{108}\left(\text{地方消費税を合わせると}\frac{8}{108}\right)$$

⑶　適用要件

　本措置は，売上げに係る対価の返還等について，その明細を記録した帳簿
を保存していない場合には適用されない。ただし，災害その他やむを得ない
事情により保存をすることができなかったことを証明した場合には，この限
りではない（消法38②）。

⑷　一括割戻しの場合の計算

　課税資産の譲渡等とその他の資産の譲渡等について一括して割戻しを行っ
たときは，それぞれの資産の譲渡等に係る部分の割戻金額を合理的に区分し
て計算する（消基通14-1-5）。

⑸　売上げ割戻しの時期

　売上げ割戻しの時期は，次の区分に応じ，それぞれに定める課税期間とさ
れる（消基通14-1-9）。

760   CONSUMPTION TAX

(a) For a sales rebate which is assessed according to the sales amount or sales quantity, and the assessment basis has been declared plainly to the other party by contract or otherwise, the relevant taxable period is the one in which the date of the transfer of taxable assets etc. falls. However, if enterprises consistently treat rebates as having been made in the taxable period in which the date of notification or payment of the rebates fall, such treatment is acceptable.

(b) For sales rebates other than (a), the relevant taxable period is the one in which the date of notification or payment of the rebate falls. However, if the making of the sales rebate and its assessment basis have been decided internally by the enterprise but not communicated to the other party until the end of each taxable period, and if the enterprise records the amount computed as an account payable in the taxable period and notifies the other party of it by the time limit for submitting the final return, such treatment is acceptable provided that it is applied consistently.

¶ 8-640   Tax credit for bad debt loss

Where an enterprise transfers taxable assets etc. in Japan, and if certain matters arise with respect to the account receivable, with the result that all or part of it becomes uncollectable, the consumption tax amount on the uncollectable tax-inclusive consideration is creditable against the total consumption tax on the tax base in the taxable period when the credit becomes uncollectable (Law 39).

(1)   Computation of creditable amount

The amount allowed as a credit is computed as follows (Law 39①):

$$\text{Amount of uncollectable tax-inclusive consideration} \times \frac{6.3}{108} \left[\text{Together with the local consumption tax, } \frac{8}{108} \right]$$

In this case, if a bad debt loss is incurred on the transfer of taxable assets, etc. or on the transfer of other assets, etc., the loss must be divided, item by item, before the above computation is made. However, if it is difficult to divide it item by item, the enterprise may prorate the loss on the basis of the amount of each account receivable (R 14-2-3).

¶ 8-640

消　費　税　761

(a) 割戻しの基準が販売価額又は販売数量によっており，かつ，その基準が契約その他の方法により相手方に明示されている売上げ割戻し

課税資産の譲渡等をした日の属する課税期間。なお，売上げ割戻しの金額の通知又は支払をした日の属する課税期間に売上げ割戻しがあったこととすることもできるが，この場合は，その取扱いを継続する必要がある。

(b) (a)以外の売上げ割戻し

その売上げ割戻しの金額の通知又は支払をした日の属する課税期間。なお，各課税期間終了の日までに，その課税資産の譲渡等の対価の額について売上げ割戻しを支払うこと及びその売上げ割戻しの算定基準が内部的に決定している場合には，その基準により計算した金額をその課税期間において未払金として計上するとともに確定申告期限までに相手方に通知することによりその課税期間に売上げ割戻しがあったこととすることもできるが，この場合は，その取扱いを継続する必要がある。

¶8-640　貸倒れに係る消費税額の控除

課税事業者が国内において課税資産の譲渡等を行った場合において，その相手方に対する売掛金その他の債権について一定の事実が生じたためその全部又は一部の領収をすることができなくなったときは，その領収することができなくなった税込対価の額に係る消費税額の合計額を，その課税期間の課税標準額に対する消費税額から控除する（消法39）。

(1)　控除額の計算方法

控除額の計算は次により行う（消法39①）。

$$\text{貸倒れに係る税込対価の額} \times \frac{6.3}{108} \left(\text{地方消費税を合わせると} \frac{8}{108}\right)$$

なお，課税資産の譲渡等に係る売掛金等とその他の資産の譲渡等について貸倒れがあった場合は，原則としてこれらを区分したうえで計算し，これらを区分することが困難な場合には，それぞれに係る売掛金等の額の比により計算することができる（消基通14-2-3）。

762   CONSUMPTION TAX

(2) **Bad debt losses eligible for tax credit**

Bad debt losses eligible for tax credit are those arising in the following ways (Law 39①, Reg 59, MO 18).

(a) Where credit has been cut off due to the approval of a reorganization scheme.

(b) Where credit has been cut off due to the approval of a reformation scheme under the Civil Reformation Act.

(c) Where credit has been cut off due to admission of arrangements with respect to special liquidation under the Companies Act.

(d) Where credit has been cut off due to the approval of a reorganization scheme under the special laws of reorganization of financial institutions.

(e) Where it is clear that full repayment of the debt cannot be made, having regard to the financial status and solvency of the debtor with respect to the credit.

(f) Where credit has been cut off following deliberation and agreement between the parties concerned, which is not a reorganization procedure prescribed by law, such as:

　(i)   deliberation and agreement by the creditors' meeting which settles the debt on a rational basis; or

　(ii) agreement with the contents similar to (i) concluded through the deliberation between the parties concerned, which is mediated by a third party such as an administrative body or a financial institution.

(g) Where the debtor has continually exceeded his credit limit and is deemed to be insolvent, and the enterprise has relinquished its claim and has notified the debtor of that fact by letter.

(h) Where the following facts have arisen with the debtor, and the enterprise has calculated the bad debt loss by deducting the memorandum value from the amount of the credit:

　(i)   one year or more has passed since the enterprise had suspended business with the debtor, who had been its continuous business acquaintance, because the financial condition and solvency of the debtor had worsened;

　(ii) where the total amount of credits against debtors in a particular region is less than the travelling or other expenses necessary for collecting such a sum, and no repayment has been

¶ 8-640

消　費　税　763

(2)　控除の対象となる貸倒れ

　本措置の対象となる貸倒れは，次の事実が生じたため税込価額の全部又は一部の領収ができなくなったものである（消法39①，消令59，消規18）。

- (a)　更生計画認可の決定により債権の切捨てがあったこと

- (b)　民事再生法の規定による再生計画認可の決定により債権の切捨てがあったこと
- (c)　会社法の規定による特別清算に係る協定の認可により債権の切捨てがあったこと
- (d)　金融機関等の更生手続の特例等に関する法律の規定による更生計画認可の決定により債権の切捨てがあったこと

- (e)　債権に係る債務者の財産の状況，支払能力等からみてその債務者が債務の全額を弁済できないことが明らかであること

- (f)　法令の規定による整理手続によらない関係者の協議決定で次に掲げるものにより債権の切捨てがあったこと

　- (i)　債権者集会の協議決定で合理的な基準により債務者の負債整理を定めているもの
　- (ii)　行政機関又は金融機関その他の第三者のあっせんによる当事者間の協議により締結された契約でその内容が(i)に準ずるもの

- (g)　債務者の債務超過の状態が相当期間継続し，その債務を弁済できないと認められる場合において，その債務者に対し書面により債務の免除を行ったこと
- (h)　債務者について次に掲げる事実が生じた場合において，その債務者に対して有する債権につき，事業者がその債権の額から備忘価額を控除した残額を貸倒れとして経理したこと
　- (i)　継続的な取引を行っていた債務者につきその資産の状況，支払能力等が悪化したことにより，その債務者との取引を停止したとき以後1年以上経過した場合

　- (ii)　事業者が同一地域の債務者について有するその債権の総額がその取立てのために要する旅費その他の費用に満たない場合において，その債務者に対し支払を督促したにもかかわらず弁済がないとき

764   CONSUMPTION TAX

made in spite of the enterprise pressing the debtor to do so.

¶ 8-650 Adjustment of consumption tax amount on purchase of fixed assets subject to adjustment in case of considerable change in taxable sales ratio

These provisions relate to where a taxable enterprise which has conducted a taxable purchase of fixed assets subject to adjustment, or removed taxable foreign goods qualified as fixed assets subject to adjustment from a bonded area, and computed the consumption tax on the purchase by the proportional method (including the case where the full tax amount on the taxable purchase of the assets subject to adjustment was credited under Art. 30①) and the enterprise holds such assets on the last day of the third-year taxable period.

The third-year taxable period is the taxable period in which three years elapse from the first day of the taxable period in which the assets subject to adjustment were purchased or removed from the bonded area. If the average taxable sales ratio in the third-year taxable period has changed considerably when compared to the taxable sales ratio of the taxable period of the purchase, the consumption tax on the purchase is adjusted in the third-year taxable period (Law 33).

(1) **Scope of fixed assets subject to adjustment**

Fixed assets subject to adjustment include buildings, structures, machinery and equipment, ships and vessels, aeroplanes, automobiles and vehicles, tools, furniture and fixtures, mining rights, and other assets, where the tax-excluded purchase cost of one unit of such assets is 1 million yen or more (Reg 5).

(2) **Average taxable sales ratio**

The average taxable sales ratio is the ratio which the total amount of consideration for the transfer of taxable assets, etc. conducted in Japan in each taxable period, from the taxable period of the purchase to the third-year taxable period, bears to total amount of consideration for the transfer of assets, etc. conducted in Japan in the same taxable periods (Law 33②, Reg 53③).

(3) **Considerable change**

The taxable sales ratio is considered to have "changed considerably" in the following cases.

¶ 8-650

消　費　税　765

¶8-650　課税売上割合が著しく変動した場合等の調整対象固定資産についての仕入れに係る消費税額の調整

　課税事業者が国内において調整対象固定資産の課税仕入れを行い，又は調整対象固定資産に該当する課税貨物を保税地域から引き取り，かつ，比例配分法により仕入れに係る消費税額を計算した場合（消法30①によりその調整対象固定資産に係る課税仕入れ等の税額の全額が控除された場合を含む。）において，その者が，当該調整対象固定資産の仕入れ等の課税期間の開始の日から３年を経過する日の属する課税期間（第３年度の課税期間）の末日においてその調整対象固定資産を保有しており，かつ，第３年度の課税期間における通算課税売上割合が仕入れ等の課税期間における課税売上割合に対して著しく変動したときは，第３年度の課税期間において仕入れに係る消費税額を加減算する方法により調整する（消法33）。

(1)　調整対象固定資産の範囲

　調整対象固定資産とは，建物，構築物，機械及び装置，船舶，航空機，車両及び運搬具，工具，器具及び備品，鉱業権その他の資産で一取引単位についての購入価額（税抜き）が100万円以上のものをいう（消令5）。

(2)　通算課税売上割合

　通算課税売上割合とは，仕入れ等の課税期間から第３年度の課税期間までの各課税期間において国内で行った資産の譲渡等の対価の合計額のうちに国内で行った課税資産の譲渡等の対価の合計額の占める割合をいう（消法33②，消令53③）。

(3)　著しく変動した場合

　課税売上割合が著しく変動した場合等とは，次の場合をいう。

766　CONSUMPTION TAX

(a)　Cases of considerable increase (Reg 53①):

Case where $\dfrac{A-B}{B} \geqq \dfrac{50}{100}$ and $A-B \geqq \dfrac{5}{100}$

A:　average taxable sales ratio
B:　taxable sales ratio in the taxable period of the purchase

(b)　Cases of considerable decrease (Reg 53②):

Case where $\dfrac{B-A}{B} \geqq \dfrac{50}{100}$ and $B-A \geqq \dfrac{5}{100}$

A, B:　same definitions as (a) above.

(4)　Method of adjustment

(a)　In the case of considerable increase, the amount computed as follows must be added to the consumption tax amount on the purchase in the third-year taxable period.

$$\left[C \times A \right] - \left[C \times B \right]$$

A, B:　the same definitions as (3)(a).
C:　consumption tax amount on the taxable purchase of fixed assets subject to adjustment.

(b)　In the case of considerable decrease, the amount computed as follows must be deducted from the consumption tax amount on the purchase in the third-year taxable period. And if there is any amount which cannot be deducted, such amount must be added to the consumption tax amount for the tax base in the third-year taxable period.

$$\left[C \times B \right] - \left[C \times A \right]$$

A, B, C:　Same definitions as (a) above.

¶ 8-660　Adjustment of consumption tax on purchase in case of diversion of fixed assets, subject to adjustment, from taxable business use to non-taxable business use

(1)　Where a taxable enterprise has conducted a taxable purchase of fixed assets subject to adjustment, or has removed taxable foreign goods qualifying as fixed assets subject to adjustment from a bonded area,

¶ 8-660

消　費　税　767

(a)　著しく増加した場合（消令53①）

$$\frac{A-B}{B} \geqq \frac{50}{100} \text{かつ} A-B \geqq \frac{5}{100} \text{の場合をいう。}$$

　　A：通算課税売上割合
　　B：仕入れ等の課税期間における課税売上割合

(b)　著しく減少した場合（消令53②）

$$\frac{B-A}{B} \geqq \frac{50}{100} \text{かつ} B-A \geqq \frac{5}{100} \text{の場合をいう。}$$

　　A，B：(a)の定義に同じ。

(4)　調整の方法

　調整の方法は，次のとおりである。

(a)　課税売上割合が著しく増加した場合

　次により計算した金額を第3年度の課税期間の仕入れに係る消費税額に加算する。

　　$(C \times A) - (C \times B)$

　　A，B：(3)(a)の定義に同じ

　　C：調整対象固定資産の課税仕入れに係る消費税額

(b)　課税売上割合が著しく減少した場合

　次により計算した金額を第3年度の課税期間の仕入れに係る消費税額から控除し，なお控除しきれない金額がある場合には，その金額を第3年度の課税期間の課税標準額に対する消費税額の合計額に加算する。

　　$(C \times B) - (C \times A)$

　　A，B，C：(a)の定義に同じ

¶8-660　課税業務用調整対象固定資産を非課税業務用に転用した場合の調整

(1)　課税事業者が，国内において調整対象固定資産の課税仕入れを行い又は調整対象固定資産に該当する課税貨物の引取りを行い，かつ，その課税仕入れ又は課税貨物に係る課税仕入れ等の税額（調整対象税額）につき課税

768   CONSUMPTION TAX

and has computed the consumption tax on the purchase with respect to the tax amount to be adjusted (the tax amount on the taxable purchase or the taxable foreign goods) by the itemized method, treating the taxable purchase, etc. as necessary only for transfers of taxable assets, etc., and if the enterprise diverted the fixed assets subject to adjustment to the use of the business for the transfer of other assets within three years from the date of the purchase, the following consumption tax amount must be deducted from the consumption tax amount on the purchase in the taxable period in which the date of the diversion falls (Law 34①).

   (a) In the case where the assets are diverted in the period from the day of the purchase through to the day when one year elapses from that day (first year)—an amount equivalent to the tax amount to be adjusted (the whole of the tax amount already credited).

   (b) In the case where the assets are diverted from the day following the last day of the period specified in (a) above through to the day when one year elapses from that day (second year)—an amount equivalent to 2/3 of the tax amount to be adjusted.

   (c) In the case where the assets are diverted from the day following the last day of the period specified in (b) above through to the day when one year elapses from that day (third year)—an amount equivalent to 1/3 of the tax amount to be adjusted.

(2) If there is any amount which cannot be deducted, such amount must be added to the consumption tax amount on the tax base in the taxable period in which the date of diversion falls (Law 34②).

¶ 8-670 Adjustment where a tax-exempt enterprise changes to a taxable enterprise and vice versa

(1) **Change from a tax-exempt to a taxable enterprise:**

    If the inventory assets owned on the day before the date of change include some inventory assets with respect to the taxable purchases etc. in tax-exempt periods, the consumption tax amount on such inventory assets qualifies for purchase tax credit in the taxable period in which the tax-exempt enterprise changes to a taxable enterprise (Law 36①).

    This adjustment is also applied to the case where a taxable enter-

¶ 8-670

資産の譲渡等にのみ要するものとして個別対応方式（消法30②一の方法）
により仕入れに係る消費税額を計算した場合において，調整対象固定資産
を仕入れ等の日から３年以内にその他の資産の譲渡等に係る業務の用に転
用したときは，転用した日が次の期間のいずれに属するかにより，次に定
める消費税額を，転用した日の属する課税期間の仕入れに係る消費税額か
ら控除する（消法34①）。

(a) 仕入れ等の日から同日以後１年を経過する日までの期間

仕入税額控除済みの税額

(b) (a)の期間の末日の翌日から同日以後１年を経過する日までの期間

(a)の税額の３分の２相当額

(c) (b)の期間の末日の翌日から同日以後１年を経過する日までの期間

(a)の税額の３分の１相当額

(2) 調整の結果，仕入れに係る消費税額から控除してなお控除しきれない金
額がある場合には，その金額を，転用した日の属する課税期間の課税標準
額に対する消費税額に加算することにより調整する（消法34②）。

¶8-670　免税事業者が課税事業者となる場合等の調整

(1)　課税事業者となる場合

　免税事業者が課税事業者となる日の前日において所有する棚卸資産のう
ち，納税義務が免除されていた期間中の課税仕入れ等に係るものがあるとき
は，その棚卸資産に係る消費税額は，課税事業者となった課税期間の課税仕
入れ等の税額とみなして仕入税額控除の対象とする（消法36①）。

　なお，課税事業者である相続人又は合併法人が免税事業者である被相続人
又は被合併法人の所有する棚卸資産で納税義務が免除されている期間中の課
税仕入れ等に係るものを承継した場合にも同様に消費税額の調整を行うこと

770   CONSUMPTION TAX

prise succeeds to the business of a tax-exempt enterprise by inheritance or by merger (Law 36③, ④).

This adjustment can be applied only when the enterprise keeps records of the details of inventory assets with respect to the taxable purchases etc. (Law 36②, ④).

(2) **Change from a taxable to a tax-exempt enterprise:**

If the inventory assets owned on the day before the date of change include some inventory assets with respect to taxable purchases etc. in the taxable period in which the day before the date of change falls, the consumption tax amount on such inventory assets does not qualify as the tax amount on taxable purchases etc. in that taxable period (Law 36⑤).

If an enterprise had chosen the simplified tax system (¶ 8-250) in the taxable period before the taxable period in which it had elected the rule of tax exemption for small-scale enterprises, this adjustment does not apply (R 12-6-4).

¶ 8-680 Special credit for small and medium-sized enterprises (simplified tax system)

For taxable enterprises whose amount of taxable sales in the base period is ¥50 million or less, and which file a Notification for Election of Simplified Tax System with the director of the tax office with jurisdiction over the place for tax payment, the consumption tax on purchases for purchase tax credit purposes is deemed to be the product of the consumption tax on the tax base of the taxable period (after crediting the consumption tax paid on the refund, etc. of consideration for sales (see ¶ 8-630)) multiplied by the deemed purchase ratio (Law 37).

(1) **Deemed purchase ratio (Reg 57①, ⑤)**

Sales have to be divided into the following categories for which each deemed purchase ratio is applicable:

(a) First-class businesses 90%

"First-class businesses" means wholesalers (businesses where enterprises sell goods purchased from others to other enterprises without changing the property or the form of the goods).

(b) Second-class businesses 80%

"Second-class businesses" means retailers (businesses

¶ 8-680

消　費　税　771

とされている（消法36③，④）。

　この調整は，課税仕入れ等に係る棚卸資産の明細を記録した書類を保存することを適用要件としている（消法36②，④）。

⑵　免税事業者となる場合

　課税事業者が免税事業者となった日の前日において所有する棚卸資産のうち，その前日の属する課税期間中の課税仕入れ等に係るものがあるときは，その棚卸資産に係る消費税額は，当該課税期間の課税仕入れ等の税額に含めない（消法36⑤）。

　この調整は，事業者が，小規模事業者に係る納税義務の免除の規定（¶8-250参照）の適用を受けることとなった課税期間の初日の前日の属する課税期間において，簡易課税制度の適用を受ける場合には適用されない（消基通12-6-4）。

¶8-680　中小事業者等の控除の特例（簡易課税制度）

　課税事業者が，基準期間における課税売上高が5,000万円以下である課税期間について，消費税簡易課税制度選択届出書を所轄税務署長に提出した場合には，実際の仕入れに係る消費税額を計算することなく，その課税期間の課税標準額に対する消費税額（売上げに係る消費税額）からその課税期間の売上げに係る対価の返還等の金額に係る消費税額の合計額を控除した残額に一定の率（みなし仕入率）を乗じた金額を仕入れに係る消費税額とみなして控除することができる（消法37）。

⑴　みなし仕入率（消令57①，⑤）

　事業者は次の事業ごとに売上げを区分し，それぞれの売上げについてそれぞれ次のみなし仕入率を適用して控除税額を計算する。

　⒜　第一種事業……………………………………………………………90％
　　　第一種事業とは，卸売業（他の者から購入した商品をその性質及び形状を変更しないで他の事業者に対して販売する事業）をいう。

　⒝　第二種事業……………………………………………………………80％
　　　第二種事業とは，小売業（他の者から購入した商品をその性質及び形

772   CONSUMPTION TAX

where enterprises sell goods purchased from others without changing the property or the form of the goods, excluding first-class businesses).

Note:
After October 1, 2019, businesses of producing agricultural and fishery products of edible will be included (2018 tax reform).

(c)   Third-class businesses 70%

"Third-class businesses" include businesses of agriculture, forestry, fishery, mining, construction, manufacture (including manufacturing retailers), and electricity, gas, heat or water supply businesses, excluding first-class and second-class businesses, and businesses of providing services for consideration (such as processing fees).

Note:
After October 1, 2019, businesses of producing agricultural and fishery products of edible will be excluded (2018 tax reform).

(d)   Fourth-class businesses 60%

"Fourth-class businesses" are businesses other than first, second, third and or fifth-class businesses. Restaurants is classified as this category.

(e)   Fifth-class businesses 50%

"Fifth-class businesses" include transportation, communication, financial or insurance and service industry (excluding restaurants) other than first, second and or third class businesses.

(f)   Sixth-class businesses 40%

"Sixth-class businesses" means real estate business.

(2)   **Effective taxable period**

The simplified tax system is effective from the taxable period following the taxable period during which the election is made. However, for enterprises which commenced the relevant businesses or succeeded to them by inheritance or merger, the system is effective from the taxable period which includes the date of election or succession. There are some restrictions with respect to the effective taxable period for a parent company and its subsidiary which is set up under the rule of "division of corporation by specified investment" (Law 37① and Reg 55, 56).

¶ 8-680

状を変更しないで販売する事業で第一種事業以外のもの）をいう。

(注)：平成31年10月1日以降，食用の農水産物を生産する事業も含む（平成30年度税制改正）。

(c) 第三種事業‥‥‥‥‥‥‥‥‥‥‥‥‥‥‥‥‥‥‥‥‥‥‥‥‥‥‥‥‥70％

　　第三種事業とは，農業，林業，漁業，鉱業，建設業，製造業（製造小売業を含む。），電気業，ガス業，熱供給業及び水道業をいい，第一種事業又は第二種事業に該当するもの及び加工賃その他これに類する料金を対価とする役務の提供を行う事業を除く。

(注)：平成31年10月1日以降，食用の農水産物を生産する事業を除く（平成30年度税制改正）。

(d) 第四種事業‥‥‥‥‥‥‥‥‥‥‥‥‥‥‥‥‥‥‥‥‥‥‥‥‥‥‥‥‥60％

　　第四種事業とは，第一種事業，第二種事業，第三種事業及び第五種事業以外の事業をいう。飲食店業がこれに該当する。

(e) 第五種事業‥‥‥‥‥‥‥‥‥‥‥‥‥‥‥‥‥‥‥‥‥‥‥‥‥‥‥‥‥50％

　　第五種事業とは，運輸通信業，金融保険業，サービス業（飲食店業を除く。）をいい，第一種事業，第二種事業及び第三種事業以外の事業をいう。

(f) 第六種事業‥‥‥‥‥‥‥‥‥‥‥‥‥‥‥‥‥‥‥‥‥‥‥‥‥‥‥‥‥40％

　　第六種事業とは，不動産業をいう。

(2) 対象課税期間

　簡易課税制度は，その選択の届出を行った日の属する課税期間の翌課税期間以後の課税期間について適用される。ただし，新たに事業を開始した場合若しくは相続又は合併によりこの選択の届出を行っていた事業者の事業を承継した場合にあっては，その課税期間から適用される。なお，「特定出資による法人の分割」に係る分割親法人と分割子法人については，対象課税期間について制限が加えられている（消法37①，消令55，56）。

774   CONSUMPTION TAX

(3) **Restriction for applying the rule for certain period when adjustment tax on purchase certain fixed assets required under considerable change of its taxable sales ratio.**

Certain taxable enterprise should be restricted to apply this rule for certain period when adjustment tax on purchase certain fixed assets should be required under considerable change of its taxable sales ratio (Law 37②, ③).

(4) **Duration of effect**

The effect of a Notification for Election of Simplified Tax System lasts for the duration of the taxable period during which a Notification for Revocation of Simplified Tax System is filed (Law 37⑥).

(5) **Revocation of simplified tax system**

In the event of an enterprise, which has elected to apply the simplified tax system, ceasing to elect at will or discontinuing its business, the enterprise must file a Notification for Revocation of Simplified Tax System (Law 37④).

Enterprises electing to apply this system, however, must maintain it for at least two years from the starting date of the first applicable taxable period in all cases except where the business is discontinued (Law 37⑤).

Special Exceptions for Government and the Like

¶ **8-700 Special exceptions regarding the business unit**

While various rules apply to a corporation as one business unit, if the government or a local government conducts operations under general accounts or special accounts, the operations under each account are deemed to be those conducted by a separate corporation for the purpose of the tax. In this case, operations under special accounts the purpose of which is to conduct transfers of assets, etc. only for general accounts are deemed to be included in the general accounts (Law 60①).

¶ **8-710 Special exceptions regarding the time of transfer of assets, etc.**

The accounting system for the government or a local government is totally different from that for private corporations, where revenue and expenses are recorded by cash basis under the rules regarding budget

¶ 8-700

消　費　税　775

⑶　調整対象固定資産の税額調整期間による制限

　一定の課税事業者が調整対象固定資産についての仕入れに係る消費税の調整の対象となるべき課税期間について簡易課税制度の適用が制限される（消法37②，③）。

⑷　届出書の効力存続期間

　この選択の届出の効力は，消費税簡易課税制度選択不適用届出書の提出があった日の属する課税期間の末日の翌日以後から失われる（消法37⑥）。

⑸　簡易課税制度の不適用

　簡易課税制度の適用を受けている事業者が，その適用を任意にやめようとする場合又は事業を廃止した場合は，消費税簡易課税制度選択不適用届出書を提出しなければならない（消法37④）。

　なお，簡易課税制度の適用を受けた場合には，事業を廃止した場合を除き，その適用を受けることとなった最初の課税期間の初日から2年を経過する日の属する課税期間（課税期間が1年の場合には翌課税期間）の初日以後でなければ，この選択不適用の届出書を提出することはできない（消法37⑤）。

国等に対する特例

¶8-700　事業単位についての特例

　法人については，法人ごとに一の事業単位として法が適用されるが，国又は地方公共団体の一般会計に係る業務として行う事業又は特別会計を設けて行う事業については，一般会計又は特別会計ごとに一の法人が行う事業とみなして法が適用される。ただし，特別会計を設けて行う事業であっても，「専ら当該特別会計を設ける国又は地方公共団体の一般会計に対して資産の譲渡等を行う特別会計」については，一般会計に係る業務として行う事業とみなされている（消法60①）。

¶8-710　国又は地方公共団体についての資産の譲渡等の時期の特例

　国又は地方公共団体の会計は，予算決算及び会計令又は地方自治法施行令の規定によりその歳入及び歳出の所属会計年度が定められ，これらの規定では歳入は収納基準による。また，歳出は支払基準によることとされる等，一般の民間企業とは異なる会計処理が行われている。

776   CONSUMPTION TAX

and accounting systems.

Transfers of assets, etc. conducted by the government or a local government are regarded as having been made at the end of the fiscal year in which consideration must be received. As for taxable purchases or the removal of taxable foreign goods from a bonded area, it is regarded that they are conducted at the end of the fiscal year in which the expenses must be paid (Law 60②, Reg 73).

¶ 8-720 Special exceptions regarding the time of transfer of assets, etc. for public service corporations and the like

The special exceptions regarding the time of transfer of assets, etc. (see ¶ 8-710 above) also apply to the corporations listed in Table 3 of the Consumption Tax Law if their accounting procedures as prescribed by a law, certificate of incorporation, articles of association, statute or by-law are similar to that of the government or local government, and if the application of special exceptions is approved by the director of the tax office (Law 60③, Reg 74).

¶ 8-730 Special exceptions regarding the purchase tax credit
(1) Special exception for general accounts

In the case of general accounts of the government or a local government, the consumption tax amount on the tax base in the taxable period is equal to the total amount of consumption tax on the taxable purchases, etc. (Law 60⑥). Therefore, no tax is payable or refundable.

(2) Special exceptions for special account etc.

Where the government or a local government undertakes a project through special accounts, or a corporation listed in Table 3 of the Consumption Tax Law (such as a public service corporation), or a non-juridicial organization has "specific revenue" in the taxable period, special rules apply for the computation of purchase tax credit. The creditable tax amount is computed as the ordinary creditable tax amount less the tax amount on the taxable purchases, etc. corresponding to the specific revenue (Law 60④).

(a) Cases where the adjustment is required:

If the total amount of special revenue is more than 5% of the sum of the total consideration for the transfer of assets, etc. and the total amount of specific revenue, an adjustment of purchase

¶ 8-720

消　費　税　777

　このため，国又は地方公共団体が行った資産の譲渡等については《《歳入の会計年度所属区分》）等の規定によりその対価を収納すべきこととされる会計年度の末日において行われたものとし，課税仕入れ及び課税貨物の保税地域からの引取りについては，《《歳出の会計年度所属区分》）等の規定によりその費用の支払をすべきこととされる会計年度の末日において行われたものとすることができる（消法60②，消令73）。

¶8-720　国又は地方公共団体に準ずる法人についての資産の譲渡等の時期の特例

　消費税法別表第三に掲げる法人のうち，法令又はその法人の定款，寄附行為，規則若しくは規約に定める会計の処理の方法が国又は地方公共団体の会計の処理の方法に準ずるものが，税務署長の承認を受けた場合には，国又は地方公共団体と同様に，資産の譲渡等の時期について，特例規定が適用される（消法60③，消令74）（¶8-710参照）。

¶8-730　仕入税額の控除の特例

(1)　一般会計に係る特例

　国又は地方公共団体の一般会計については，仕入税額控除の特例として，その課税期間の課税標準額に対する消費税額と課税仕入れ等に係る消費税額その他の控除することができる消費税額の合計額とは同額であるものとみなされる（消法60⑥）。したがって，これらの一般会計では納付税額，還付税額ともに発生することはない。

(2)　特別会計等に係る特例

　国若しくは地方公共団体の特別会計，消費税法別表第三に掲げる公共法人若しくは公益法人又は人格のない社団等の特定収入がある課税期間については，その課税期間の課税標準額に対する消費税額から控除することができる課税仕入れ等の税額の合計額は，通常の計算により算出した課税仕入れ等の税額の合計額から，特定収入に係る課税仕入れ等の税額を控除した残額とする特例規定が設けられている（消法60④）。

(a)　仕入控除税額の調整が必要な場合

　　資産の譲渡等の対価の額の合計額に特定収入の合計額を加算した金額のうちに特定収入の合計額の占める割合が5％を超える場合には，仕入控除税額を調整する。

778   CONSUMPTION TAX

tax credit is required.

However, even if the percentage is more than 5%, and if the above organization applies the rule of "special exception for purchase tax credit for small and medium sized enterprises" to the computation of consumption tax on the purchase, such adjustment is not required.

(b) Meaning of "specific revenue":

"Specific revenue" means revenue other than consideration received for the transfer of assets, etc. The following are examples of specific revenue: taxes, subsidies, grants, burden charges, money transferred from other accounts (general accounts or other special accounts), donations, dividends for investments, insurance money, compensation for damages, etc.

¶ 8-740 Special exceptions regarding the time limit for filing tax returns

As regards the time limit for filing final or interim returns for the government or local governments (provided that they undertake projects through special accounts), or corporations listed in Table 3 of the Consumption Tax Law (limited to those which obtained approval to apply the 'special exception' rule from the director of the tax office)—the words "within 2 months" in the general rules (¶ 8-750, ¶ 8-760) are replaced as follows (Law 60⑧, Reg 76):

(1) Government—"within 5 months"

(2) Local governments (excluding (3))—"within 6 months"

(3) Corporations managed by local governments to which the provision of "Settlement of account" of Local Public Management Corporation Law applies—"within 3 months"

(4) Corporations which obtain the approval from the director of the tax office—"within the specified period approved by the director of the tax office, but not exceeding 6 months"

Filing Tax Returns and Payment of Tax

¶ 8-750 Final returns

Taxable enterprises must file final returns within 2 months from the day after the end of the taxable period. However, if there have been no

消　費　税　779

　　ただし，この割合が5％を超える場合であっても，国若しくは地方公
共団体の特別会計，消費税法別表第三に掲げる公共法人若しくは公益法
人又は人格のない社団等が，その課税期間の仕入れに係る消費税額の計
算について《《中小事業者の仕入れに係る消費税額の控除の特例》》の規
定の適用を受けている場合には，このような仕入控除税額の調整はする
必要がない。
　(b)　特定収入の意義
　　　特定収入とは，資産の譲渡等の対価としての収入以外の対価性のない
収入をいい，例えば，租税，補助金，交付金，負担金，他会計（一般会
計又は他の特別会計）からの繰入金，寄付金，出資に対する配当金，保
険金，損害賠償金等がこれに該当する。

¶8-740　申告期限についての特例

　国若しくは地方公共団体の特別会計又は消費税法別表第三に掲げる法人で
税務署長の承認を受けたものの中間申告書及び確定申告書の提出期限につい
ては，通常の「2月以内」（¶8-750，¶8-760参照）とあるのは，次に掲げ
る期間内とされる（消法60⑧，消令76）。

(1)　国　　　　　　　　　　　　　　　　5月以内
(2)　地方公共団体（(3)に掲げるものを除く。）　6月以内
(3)　地方公営企業法の《《決算》》の規定の適用を受ける地方公共団体の経営
　する企業　　　　　　　　　　　　　3月以内

(4)　税務署長の承認を受けた法人　　　　6月以内で税務署長が承
　　　　　　　　　　　　　　　　　　　　認する期間

申告及び納付

¶8-750　確定申告

　課税事業者は，課税期間の末日の翌日から2月以内に確定申告書を提出
し，その申告に係る消費税額を納付しなければならない。

780   CONSUMPTION TAX

transfers of taxable assets, etc. or all transfers of assets, etc. are qualified as tax exempt, and if there is no refund of consumption tax on any purchase, a return is not required (Law 45①).

Final returns must be filed by each enterprise as a unit. No division or branch of an enterprise is allowed to file an independent return (for exceptions see ¶ 8-700 above.).

The following items must reported in a final return.

(1) Amount of tax base.

(2) Consumption tax amount on the tax base.

(3) Total of the following consumption tax amounts to be credited against the amount (2) above:

    (a) consumption tax on purchases;

    (b) consumption tax on refunded consideration for sales;

    (c) consumption tax corresponding to bad debt loss; and

    (d) marginal tax credit.

(4) Excess or short amount after crediting the amount (3) against (2).

(5) Excess or short amount after deducting interim payment from (4).

(6) Details for calculating the above amounts.

¶ 8-760 Interim returns

(1) Monthly interim returns

Enterprises of which tax amount payable for previous taxable period exceeds ¥48 million, must file an interim tax return on monthly basis and pay the amount equivalent to basically one twelfth of tax amount of previous taxable period (Law 42①).

(2) Three-monthly interim returns

Enterprises of which tax amount payable for previous taxable period exceeds ¥4 million, must file an interim tax return on three-monthly basis and pay the amount equivalent to basically a quarter of tax amount of previous taxable period (Law 42④).

(3) Six-monthly interim returns

Enterprises of which tax amount payable for previous taxable period exceeds ¥480,000, must file an interim tax return on six-monthly basis and pay the amount equivalent to basically a half of tax amount of previous taxable period (Law 42⑥).

¶ 8-760

消　費　税　781

　ただし，課税資産の譲渡等がない場合又は課税資産の譲渡等のすべてが免税の対象となる場合で，かつ，仕入れに係る消費税額の控除不足額がないときは，申告義務はない（消法45①）。

　確定申告書は，事業者単位で提出することとされ，事業部単位又は本支店等ごとに提出することは認められていない（¶8-700参照）。

　確定申告書の記載事項は，次の事項である。

(1)　課税標準額
(2)　課税標準額に対する消費税額
(3)　(2)の合計額から控除されるべき次の消費税額の合計額

　　(a)　仕入れに係る消費税額
　　(b)　売上げに係る対価の返還等をした金額に係る消費税額
　　(c)　貸倒れに係る消費税額
　　(d)　限界控除税額
(4)　(2)の消費税額から(3)の消費税額を控除した残額又は控除不足額
(5)　(4)の額から中間納付額を控除した残額又は控除不足額
(6)　(1)～(5)に掲げる金額の計算の基礎その他の事項

¶8-760　中間申告

(1)　毎月ベースの中間申告

　直前の課税期間（1年分）の確定消費税額が4,800万円を超える事業者は，毎月中間申告をし，原則として前年確定税額の12分の1額を納付しなければならない（消法42①）。

(2)　3月ベースの中間申告

　直前の課税期間（1年分）の確定消費税額が400万円を超える事業者は，3月毎に中間申告をし，原則として前年確定税額の4分の1額を納付しなければならない（消法42④）。

(3)　6月ベースの中間申告

　直前の課税期間（1年分）の確定消費税額が48万円を超える事業者は，6月毎に中間申告をし，原則として前年確定税額の2分の1額を納付しなければならない（消法42⑥）。

782   CONSUMPTION TAX

(4) **Enterprises which have not obligation to file an interim tax return**

Enterprises of which tax amount payable for previous taxable period less than ¥480,000; have no obligation to file an interim tax return, may file an interim tax return on six-monthly basis and pay the amount equivalent to a half of tax amount of previous taxable period with submission of a notification (Law 42⑧) (Apply after April 1, 2014).

(5) **Where no interim return required**

No interim tax returns mentioned in (1) through (3) above are required:

(a) for the first taxable period of individual enterprises;

(b) for the first taxable period of newly established corporations (except for incorporation through merger).

(6) **Failure to meet time limit**

Where an enterprise which should file an interim tax return has not done so within the time limit, the enterprise is deemed to have filed it with payable tax amount stated in (1) through (3) above (Law 44).

¶ 8-770 Refund of consumption tax on purchase

When the consumption tax on the tax base is less than the consumption tax on purchase, etc., the short amount can be refunded upon the filing of a final return, or by correction (Law 52①, 54①).

Interest on the refund becomes payable for the period from the day listed below to the day on which the determination of payment is made.

(i) In the case of a final return filed within the due date — the day following the due date of filing.

(ii) In the case of a final return filed after the due date or with an application for refund — the day following the end of the month on which the return was filed (the day following the day on which 2 months elapse after the end of the taxable period, if the final return with an application for refund was filed before the day on which 2 months elapse after the end of the taxable period).

¶ 8-775 Refund of interim consumption tax

Where the consumption tax after crediting the consumption tax on purchase, etc. is less than the interim consumption tax, the short amount can be

¶ 8-770

消　費　税　783

⑷　**中間申告義務のない事業者**
　直前の課税期間の消費税額が48万円以下（中間申告義務のない事業者）
は，届出書を提出することにより，6月毎に中間申告をし，前年確定税額
の2分の1額を納付することができる（消法42⑧）（平成26年4月1日以降適
用）。

⑸　次の課税期間については，⑴～⑶の中間申告をする必要はない。

　⒜　個人事業者が事業を開始した最初の課税期間
　⒝　新設法人（合併によるものを除く。）の最初の課税期間

⑹　中間申告書を提出すべき事業者が，これを提出期限までに提出しなかっ
　た場合には，⑴～⑶に記述した額を納付税額とする中間申告書が提出され
　たものとみなされる（消法44）。

¶8-770　仕入れに係る消費税額の控除不足額の還付
　課税標準額に対する消費税額が，仕入れに係る消費税額等に満たない場合
には，その満たない金額について，確定申告書を提出すること又は更正によ
り還付される（消法52①，54①）。
　なお，還付金には，次に掲げる日から支払決定をする日までの期間につい
て還付加算金が付される。
　（i）　期限内申告書……その提出期限の翌日

　（ii）　期限後申告書及び還付請求申告書……申告書が提出された日の属する
　　　月の末日（還付を受けるための申告書が課税期間終了後2月を経過する
　　　日前に提出された場合は，2月を経過する日）の翌日

¶8-775　中間納付額の還付
　仕入れに係る消費税額等を控除した後の消費税額が，中間納付額に満たな
い場合には，その満たない金額について，確定申告書を提出すること又は更

784   CONSUMPTION TAX

refunded upon the filing of a final return, or by correction (Law 53① and 55①, ②).

If the delinquency tax was imposed on the interim tax, it is also refunded (Law 53②, 55③). Interest on the refund becomes payable for the period (excluding the late filing period) from the day of paying the interim tax (the due date of payment, in the case of paying the tax before the due date) to the day on which the determination of payment is made (Law 53③, 55④).

¶ 8-780 Tax return for foreign goods removed from a bonded area

(1) Tax return and payment

Persons intending to remove taxable foreign goods from a bonded area must file a tax return reporting the name and quantity of the foreign goods, the amount of tax base and the consumption tax amount with the director of the customhouse. Tax must be paid by the time of removal, except in the case where the removal is exempted from consumption tax under a provision of other legislation or a treaty (Law 47①, 50①).

(2) Extension of the time limit for tax payment

Where the tax return has been filed, if an application for extension of the time limit for payment is submitted and if security is provided, an extension of time is allowed for up to 3 months (Law 51①).

Regardless of the provisions of Art. 511 mentioned above, if an application for extension of the time limit for tax payment is submitted with respect to the total consumption tax amount on the taxable foreign goods to be removed in a particular month and if security is provided by the end of the previous month, an extension of the time limit for tax payment is allowed for up to 3 months from the day following the end of that particular month (Law 51②).

Others

¶ 8-790 Submission of notification

An enterprise must notify the competent director of the tax office immediately in the following cases:

¶ 8-780

消　費　税　785

正等により還付される（消法53①，55①，②）。

　この場合，還付される中間納付額について納付した延滞税があるときは，あわせて還付される（消法53②，55③）。また，還付金には，中間納付の日（納期限前納付については納期限）から支払決定をする日までの期間（期限後申告の場合の申告期限の翌日から申告書提出までの期間を除く、更正や決定の場合もこれに準ずる。）について還付加算金が付される（消法53③，55④）。

¶8-780　保税地域から引き取られる外国貨物についての申告及び納付

(1)　確定申告及び納付

　課税貨物を保税地域から引き取ろうとする者は，免税の場合を除き，課税貨物の品名，数量，課税標準額，消費税額を記載した申告書を税関長に提出し，その貨物を保税地域から引き取るときまでに消費税を納付しなければならない（消法47①，50①）。

(2)　納期限の延長

　確定申告書を提出した場合において，納期限延長申請書を提出し，かつ，担保を提供したときは3月以内の納期限の延長が認められる（消法51①）。

　なお，その月の前月末日までに，その月に引き取ろうとする課税貨物に課される消費税の合計額に関し，納期限延長申請書を提出し，かつ，担保を提供したときはその月の末日の翌日から3月以内の納期限の延長が認められる（消法51②）。

そ　の　他

¶8-790　届出書の提出等

　事業者は，次に掲げる場合に該当することとなったときは，納税地を所轄する税務署長に対してその事実を速やかに届け出なければならない。その届出書は，次の表のとおりである。

786 CONSUMPTION TAX

	Case where notification is required	Person required to issue notification	Title of the notification
1	Taxable sales in the base period exceed ¥10 million	The enterprise	Notification of Taxable Enterprise (Schedule 21)
2	Taxable sales in the base period become ¥10 million or less (Taxable enterprise becomes tax-exempt enterprise)	The enterprise	Notification of Non-taxpayer (Schedule 23)
3	Taxable enterprise discontinues business	The enterprise	Notification of Discontinuance of Business (Schedule 24)
4	Person as a taxable enterprise	The heir of the individual enterprise	Notification of Death of Individual Enterprise (Schedule 25)
5	Corporation as a taxable enterprise ceases to exist due to merger	The transferee corporation	Notification of Cessation of Existence of Corporation by Merger (Schedule 26)

¶ 8-800 Bookkeeping obligation

(1) Taxable enterprises must record the following matters in good order and clearly in their books and maintain them in hand for 7 years at the place for tax payment or the office, etc. where the business is conducted (Law 58, Reg 71). If certain necessary conditions are fulfilled, records for periods more than 5 years before can be maintained on microfilm.

Particulars to be recorded

 (a) Matters regarding transfer of assets, etc. —
  (i) Name or title of the other party to the transfer of assets, etc.
  (ii) Date of transfer of assets, etc.
  (iii) Description of asset or conduct of service provided.
  (iv) Amount including tax.
 (b) Matters regarding refund, etc. of consideration for sales —
  (i) Name or title of person who receives refund, etc. of consideration.
  (ii) Date of refund etc.
  (iii) Description of refund etc.
  (iv) Amount of refund etc.
 (c) Matters regarding refund etc. of consideration for purchases —
  (i) Name or title of person who pays refund etc. of consideration.
  (ii) Date of refund etc.
  (iii) Description of refund etc.
  (iv) Amount of refund etc.

¶ 8-800

区分	届出書を提出しなければならない場合	提出すべき者	提　出　書
1	基準期間における課税売上高が1,000万円を超えることとなった場合	その事業者	消費税課税事業者届出書（取通別紙第21号様式）
2	基準期間における課税売上高が1,000万円以下となった場合（課税事業者が免税事業者となった場合）	その事業者	消費税の納税義務者でなくなった旨の届出書（取通別紙第23号様式）
3	課税事業者が事業を廃止した場合	その事業者	事業廃止届出書（取通別紙第24号様式）
4	課税事業者が死亡した場合	その死亡した個人事業者の相続人	個人事業者の死亡届出書（取通別紙第25号様式）
5	課税事業者である法人が合併により消滅した場合	その合併に係る合併法人	合併による法人消滅届出書（取通別紙第26号様式）

¶8-800　記帳義務

(1) 課税事業者は，帳簿を備え付けて，これに次の事項を整然と，かつ，明瞭に記録し，その帳簿を 7 年間，納税地又はその事業に係る事務所等の所在地に保存しなければならない。

なお，一定の要件を満たす場合には，5 年経過後の期間について，マイクロフィルムにより保存することができる。

(a) 資産の譲渡等に関する事項
  (i) 資産の譲渡等の相手方の氏名又は名称
  (ii) 資産の譲渡等を行った年月日
  (iii) 資産の譲渡等に係る資産又は役務の内容
  (iv) 税込価額
(b) 売上げに係る対価の返還等に関する事項
  (i) 対価の返還等を受けた者の氏名又は名称
  (ii) 対価の返還等をした年月日
  (iii) 資産の譲渡等に係る対価の返還等の内容
  (iv) 対価の返還等をした金額
(c) 仕入れに係る対価の返還等に関する事項
  (i) 対価の返還等をした者の氏名又は名称
  (ii) 対価の返還等を受けた年月日
  (iii) 仕入れに係る対価の返還等の内容
  (iv) 対価の返還等を受けた金額

788   CONSUMPTION TAX

    (d) Matters regarding refund of consumption tax on taxable foreign goods under provisions of other legislation —

        (i) Customhouse in which jurisdiction the bonded area is situated.

        (ii) Date of removal.

        (iii) Description of taxable foreign goods.

        (iv) Refunded tax amount.

    (e) Matters regarding bad debts loss —

        (i) Name or title of contractor of bad debt.

        (ii) Date of occurrence.

        (iii) Description of assets or content of services with respect to bad debts.

        (iv) Amount of bad debts loss.

(2) For retailers and food service industries, the name of the other party to the transfer of assets, etc. can be omitted.

(3) As regards transfers of assets, etc. for cash by retailers and other similar industries conducting transfers of assets, etc. to many and unspecified persons, the total sum of sales for cash of taxable assets, etc. and transfers of assets, etc. other than transfers of taxable assets, etc. respectively can be recorded on a daily basis instead of matters regarding transfers of assets, etc.

(4) Enterprises applying the simplified tax system can omit to record matters regarding the refund, etc. of consideration for purchases and matters regarding the refund of consumption tax on taxable foreign goods under provisions of other legislation.

¶ 8-810 Succession to obligations of filing returns, etc.

In case of inheritance, the heirs succeed to the deceased's obligations of filing returns and bookkeeping. In case of a merger, the transferee corporation succeeds to the similar obligations of the transferer corporation (Law 59).

The heirs must succeed to obligations of filing returns regardless of whether the heirs have succeeded to the business of the deceased or not.

¶ 8-820 Right to make inquiry and inspection

The officials of the National Tax Administration, Regional Tax Bureau, National Tax Office and Customhouses can interrogate consumption tax payers or persons regarded as consumption tax payers and inspect their books and documents.

¶ 8-810

消　費　税　789

　(d)　課税貨物に係る消費税額につき他の法律の規定により受けた還付に関
　　　する事項
　　　(ⅰ)　保税地域の所轄税関
　　　(ⅱ)　引取りを行った年月日
　　　(ⅲ)　課税貨物の内容
　　　(ⅳ)　還付を受けた金額
　(e)　貸倒れに関する事項
　　　(ⅰ)　貸倒れの相手方の氏名又は名称
　　　(ⅱ)　貸倒れがあった年月日
　　　(ⅲ)　貸倒れに係る課税資産の譲渡等に係る資産又は役務の内容

　　　(ⅳ)　貸倒れとなった金額
(2)　小売業，飲食業等については，資産の譲渡等の相手方及び対価の返還等
　　を受けた者の氏名又は名称を省略することができる。
(3)　小売業その他これに準ずる事業で不特定かつ多数の者に資産の譲渡等を
　　行う事業者の現金売上げに係る資産の譲渡等については，資産の譲渡等に
　　関する事項に代えて，課税資産の譲渡等と課税資産の譲渡等以外の資産の
　　譲渡等に区分した日々の現金売上げのそれぞれの総額によることができ
　　る。

(4)　簡易課税制度を適用している事業者は，仕入れに係る対価の返還等を受
　　けた事項及び課税貨物につきその他の法律の規定により還付を受けた事項
　　については，帳簿への記載を省略することができる。

¶8-810　申告義務等の承継

　相続の場合には相続人は被相続人の申告及び記帳及び帳簿保存の義務を，
合併の場合には合併法人は被合併法人の申告及び記帳及び帳簿保存の義務
を，それぞれ承継する（消法59）。
　なお，相続人については，その相続人が相続により被相続人の事業を承継
したかどうかを問わず，申告義務を承継する。

¶8-820　質問検査権

　国税庁，国税局，税務署及び税関の当該職員は，消費税の納税義務がある
者及び納税義務があると認められる者等に対して質問し，帳簿書類等を検査
することができる。

790

CHAPTER 9

LOCAL TAX etc.

	Paragraph
Individual Inhabitant Taxes	¶ 9-010
Corporation Inhabitant Tax	¶ 9-180
Individual Enterprise Tax	¶ 9-340
Corporation Enterprise Tax	¶ 9-460
Fixed Assets Tax (City Planning Tax)	¶ 9-580
Enterprise Establishment Tax	¶ 9-760
Social Insurance	¶ 9-860
Labor Insurance	¶ 9-880

第 9 章
地 方 税 等

個人住民税	……………………………………………………	¶9–010
法人住民税	……………………………………………………	¶9–180
個人事業税	……………………………………………………	¶9–340
法人事業税	……………………………………………………	¶9–460
固定資産税（都市計画税）	………………………………	¶9–580
事業所税	………………………………………………………	¶9–760
社会保険	………………………………………………………	¶9–860
労働保険	………………………………………………………	¶9–880

792   LOCAL TAX etc.

Individual Inhabitant Taxes

¶ 9-010 Taxpayer

Two individual inhabitant taxes are levied—a prefecture inhabitant tax and a municipal inhabitant tax. Individual inhabitant tax is levied on the following (Law 24, 39, 294, 318):

(1) individuals domiciled in the municipality as of January 1st of each year—per capita levy and per income levy;

(2) individuals who have their house, office or place of business in the municipality but are not domiciled there as of January 1st of each year —per capita levy.

Individuals mentioned above are liable for both municipal inhabitant tax and prefectural inhabitant tax.

"Individuals who are domiciled in the municipality" means individuals who have been recorded in the municipal "Inhabitant Basic Roll Book", except those individuals who are recorded in that book because their occupations require them to be apart from their family. In the latter case, domicile is determined by the central vital factors of the individual's daily life.

¶ 9-030 Per capita levy

The standard amounts of per capita levy in a year are shown in the table below (Law 38, 310):

Prefectural	Municipal	Total
standard ¥1,000	standard ¥3,000	standard ¥4,000

Note:
1. The "standard tax rate" is the usual rate of tax levied by local tax entities.
2. Per capita levy is taxed for every individual in general, but not collected from: (i) individuals who have no income; (ii) individuals who are welfare recipients; (iii) taxpayers under a certain income amount (for example, ¥1,610,000, in the case of a family composed of a taxpayer, a spouse who is entitled to the spouse allowance and two dependants) (Law 24-5, 295).
3. During the period from the year 2014 to 2023, ¥500 additional per capita levy will levy on both prefectural and municipal. These total per capita levy will be ¥5,000 (Surtaxes for Reesustraction Funding).

¶ 9-010

地　方　税　等　793

個人住民税

¶9-010　納税義務者

個人住民税は個人に対する道府県民税と市町村民税の総称であり，その納税義務者は次に掲げる者である（地法24，39，294，318）。

(1)　各年1月1日現在において市町村内に住所を有する個人……均等割額と所得割額の合算額
(2)　各年1月1日現在において市町村に事務所，事業所，又は家屋敷を有する個人でその市町村内に住所を有しない個人……均等割額

上記の個人は市町村税たる住民税を課税されるとともに，その市町村の属する道府県に対しても道府県税たる住民税が同時に課税される。

なお，「市町村内に住所を有する個人」とは，原則としてその市町村の住民基本台帳に記録されている者をいうが，勤務先の関係で家族と離れて居住している者等については，本人の日常生活等の実情をみて住所を設定することとされている。

¶9-030　均等割額の課税

個人住民税の均等割額は定額であり，その標準税率は次のとおりである（地法38，310）。

道府県住民税	市町村住民税	計
標準税率	標準税率	標準税率
1,000円	3,000円	4,000円

(注)：1．標準税率とは地方団体が通常よるべき税率である。
　　　2．均等割はすべての個人を対象とするが，（イ）前年中に所得を有しなかった者，（ロ）生活扶助を受けている者及び（ハ）所得額が一定金額（例えば，家族構成が本人，控除対象配偶者，扶養親族2名の場合には，1,610,000円）以下の納税者に対しては非課税とされる（地法24の5，295）。
　　　3．平成26年度から平成35年度までの間について，道府県民税，市町村民税ともに500円ずつ引き上げられ，均等割額の合計は5,000円となる（復興特別税）。

794   LOCAL TAX etc.

¶ 9-050 Per income levy—income computation

Income in the preceding year is taken as the tax basis for the income levy. The income is the taxpayer's "ordinary income amount", "forestry income", and "retirement income" and accordingly, interest income which is subject to withholding income tax only under the income tax law is not included (Law 32, 313).

Income is computed as it is done for national income tax (see ¶ 5-090), except where local tax laws stipulate otherwise (Law 32, 313).

Non-taxable income under income tax law (see ¶ 5-070) is non-taxable under local tax law as well. The privileges attached to blue returns (see ¶ 5-160), such as the deduction of salary or wages paid to family members, are also extended under the individual income levy. The main points of difference between income tax law and the individual income levy are these.

(1) Dividend income and capital gain from stock can be excluded from the tax basis for the income levy by election. In this case, dividend income and capital gain from stock is subject to only per dividend levy and per stock capital gain levy.

(2) Domestic source income which accrued while an individual was non-resident is taxed separately under national income tax but is subject to global taxation, inclusive of all other income, under local inhabitant tax.

(3) Carry back of net loss is not recognized by local inhabitant tax (Law 32, 313).

But, taxpayers having less than a certain income amount (for example, ¥1,720,000 when the family is composed of the taxpayer, a spouse who is entitled to spouse allowance, and two dependants) is not taxable (LS 3-3).

¶ 9-080 Per income levy—deductions and allowances

Various deductions and allowances recognized in individual inhabitant tax are similar to those under national income tax, and are allowed according to the circumstances of each case.

The amounts of deduction and allowance are different from income tax (Law 34, 314-2). The following table (¶ 9-090) shows such differences.

¶ 9-050

地　方　税　等　795

¶9-050　所得割額の課税（所得の計算）

　所得割額とは前年の所得に対する比例税額であり，その所得とは地方税法に規定されている総所得金額，退職所得金額及び山林所得金額である。したがって，所得税法上源泉分離課税の対象となる利子所得は含まれない（地法32，313）。

　この場合の所得金額の計算方法は，地方税法で特別の定めをする場合を除くほか，所得税に関する法令の規定の例（¶5-090参照）によって行われる。したがって，収入金額の計算，必要経費の計算，損益通算等については，原則として所得税の例によるものである（地法32，313）。

　地方税法上の所得金額の計算上，所得税法上の非課税所得（¶5-070参照）は非課税とされ，青色事業専従者などの青色申告の特典（¶5-160参照）はそのまま適用されるが，所得税の例と異なる主なものは次のとおりである。

(1)　配当割、譲渡所得割の導入により，配当所得もしくは株式等の譲渡所得については，選択により，所得に算入しないことができる。この場合には，配当所得もしくは株式等の譲渡所得は配当割課税もしくは株式等譲渡割課税のみで課税関係は終了する。

(2)　所得税で分離課税とされた非居住者期間中の国内源泉所得は，住民税では他の所得と総合して課税される。

(3)　所得税では，純損失の繰戻し還付制度が設けられているが，住民税では認めていない（地法32，313）。

　ただし，所得金額が一定金額（例えば，家族構成が本人，控除対象配偶者及び扶養親族2名の場合には1,720,000円）以下の納税者については非課税とされる（地法附3の3）。

¶9-080　所得割額の課税（所得控除）

　個人住民税でも所得税と同じく納税者の人的事情を考慮して各種の所得控除が認められているが，所得税との相違点は次のとおりである（地法34，314の2）。

796   LOCAL TAX etc.

¶ 9-090 Comparison of income tax and income levy

Deduction and allowances	Income tax (national)	Income levy (prefectural and municipal)
1. Deduction for accidental loss	¶ 5-320	the same
2. Deduction for medical expenses	¶ 5-330	the same
3. Deduction for social insurance premiums	¶ 5-340	the same
4. Deduction for contributions to Small Enterprises Mutual Aid Plan	¶ 5-350	the same
5. Deduction for life insurance premiums		
1) general life insurance	(limit ¥50,000) ¶ 5-370	not over ¥15,000 ...... 100% not over ¥40,000 .... 50% in excess of ¥40,000 .. 25% (limit ¥35,000)
2) private pension insurance	(limit ¥50,000)	not over ¥15,000 ...... 100% not over ¥40,000 .... 50% in excess of ¥40,000 .. 25% (limit ¥35,000)
6. Deduction for earthquake insurance premiums	¶ 5-380	(a) if the insured term is 10 years or longer .... limit ¥10,000 (b) 50% of earthquake insurance premiums .... limit ¥25,000 ((a)+(b): limit ¥25,000)
7. Allowance for spouse	¥380,000 ¶ 5-410	limit ¥330,000 (¥380,000 for age 70 and over) vary to income of taxpayer
8. Special allowance for spouse	(limit ¥380,000) ¶ 5-412	(limit ¥330,000) vary to income of taxpayer and spanse
9. Allowance for dependant (Student) (Aged)	¥380,000 (¥630,000) (¥480,000) ¶ 5-420	¥330,000 (¥450,000) (¥380,000)
10. Allowance for physically handicapped person	¥270,000 ¶ 5-430	¥260,000
11. Allowance for a widow or widower	¥270,000 ¶ 5-450	¥260,000
12. Allowance for a working student	¥270,000 ¶ 5-460	¥260,000
13. Basic allowance	¥380,000 ¶ 5-470	¥330,000

¶ 9-090

地　方　税　等　797

¶9-090　各種の所得控除に係る所得税と所得割額の比較

	国税（所得税）	地方税
1.　雑損控除	¶5-320参照	同じ
2.　医療費控除	¶5-330参照	同じ
3.　社会保険料控除	¶5-340参照	同じ
4.　小規模企業共済掛金控除	¶5-350参照	同じ
5.　生命保険料控除		
(1) 一般の生命保険	¶5-370参照 （最高50,000円）	15,000円以下　　全額 40,000円以下　　½ 40,000円超　　　¼ （最高35,000円）
(2) 個人年金保険	（最高50,000円）	15,000円以下　　全額 40,000円以下　　½ 40,000円超　　　¼ （最高35,000円）
6.　地震保険料控除	¶5-380参照	(a) 保険期間10年以上のもの 　　最高10,000円 (b) 地震保険料 　　最高25,000円 　　((a)＋(b)：最高25,000円)
7.　配偶者控除	¶5-410参照 380,000円	納税者の所得額等により異なる。 最高330,000円（70歳以上，最高 380,000円）
8.　配偶者特別控除	¶5-412参照 （最高380,000円）	納税者及び配偶者の所得額により 異なる。 最高330,000円
9.　扶養控除一般	¶5-420参照 380,000円	330,000円
（学生）	（630,000円）	（450,000円）
（老人）	（480,000円）	（380,000円）
10.　障害者控除	¶5-430参照 270,000円	260,000円
11.　寡婦（寡夫）控除	¶5-450参照 270,000円	260,000円
12.　勤労学生控除	¶5-460参照 270,000円	260,000円
13.　基礎控除	¶5-470参照 380,000円	330,000円

798   LOCAL TAX etc.

Note:
After the year 2021 (2018 tax reform)

Amount of total income	Individual income tax	Individual inhabitant tax
¥24,000,000 and under	¥480,000	¥430,000
¥24,500,000 and under	¥320,000	¥290,000
¥25,000,000 and under	¥160,000	¥150,000
more than ¥25,000,000	NIL	NIL

Note:
1. The same definitions of "spouse" and "dependant" apply for income tax and income levy purposes (see ¶ 5-410, ¶ 5-420).
2. When total deductible amount of both (b) and (c) is more than ¥25,000, deductible amount is limited to ¥25,000.
3. The deduction for dependents (up to 15 years old) is abolished from 2012 for local tax purposes.
4. The additional part of deduction for the specified dependents (between 16 and 18 years) is abolished from 2012 for local tax purposes.

¶ 9-100 Income levy—computation of tax amount

The taxable income for income levy purposes is calculated by deducting: the offset of losses suffered in each category of income, carried over net loss, and the deductions and allowances (mentioned above) from the taxable amounts of ordinary income, retirement income and forestry income (Law 32, 313).

Long-term and short-term capital losses from the sale of land etc. can't be allowed to deduct from income amount other than capital gains from the sale of land etc. and carry forward for the succeeding calendar year.

Capital losses from the sale of listed-stock can be allowed to carry forward for the succeeding calendar year. And also, capital losses of open stock investment funds can be allowed.

Carry-forward of long-term capital loss on replacement of residential property is applicable until December 31, 2011.

The tax amount for income levy purposes is calculated at the following standard tax rate for taxable income (Law 35, 314-3).

(Tax Rate)

Income	Income levy		
	prefectural	municipal	total
Flat	4%	6%	10%

¶ 9-100

地　方　税　等　799

（注）：平成33年分以降（平成30年度税制改正）

	（国　税）	（住民税）
合計所得2,400万円以下	480,000円	430,000円
2,450万円以下	320,000円	290,000円
2,500万円以下	160,000円	150,000円
2,500万円超	なし	なし

（注）：　1．配偶者控除又は扶養控除の適用対象となる者の要件は，所得税及び所得割とも同じ
　　　　　　である（¶5-410，¶5-420参照）。
　　　　　2．長期損害保険料控除額と地震保険料控除額を併用する場合，控除額はあわせて最高
　　　　　　25,000円とする。
　　　　　3．平成24年度分から15歳以下の扶養控除が廃止される。
　　　　　4．平成24年度分から特定扶養親族のうち，年齢16歳以上19歳未満の者に係る扶養控除
　　　　　　の上乗せ分が廃止される。

¶9-100　所得割の課税（税額の計算）

　総所得金額，退職所得金額及び山林所得金額から各種所得間での損失の通
算，繰越損失及び前記の所得控除を差し引いた後の金額がそれぞれ課税所得
となる（地法32，313）。

　土地，建物等の長期譲渡所得の金額又は短期譲渡所得の金額の計算上生じ
た損失の金額については，その他の所得との相殺は認められない。また，翌
年以降の繰越しを認めない。

　上場株式等の譲渡所得の金額の計算上生じた損失の金額は，繰越控除を認
める。また，公募株式投資信託の受益証券の譲渡所得に係る損失の金額につ
いても繰越控除を認める。

　居住用財産の買換え等の場合の譲渡損失の繰越控除が平成23年12月31日ま
で適用される。

　所得割の額は課税所得に対して次に掲げる標準税率を乗じて計算する（地
法35，314の3）。

〔税率〕

所得区分　　　　　　　　　　　　　　所得割

（単位千円） 一律	道府県民税 4%	市町村民税 6%	合計 10%

800   LOCAL TAX etc.

Example computation

Taxable ordinary income: ¥3,000,000
Prefecture inhabitant tax: ¥120,000 (¥3,000,000 × 4%)
Municipal inhabitant tax: ¥180,000 (¥3,000,000 × 6%)
Total   ¥300,000

Tax credits

The amounts available as tax credits against the income levy are as follows:

(i)   The housing loan tax credit

Taxpayers who are allowed to apply the housing loan tax credit after 2009 for national income tax purposes, and uses for living the house from the year 2009 to June 2018, can credit the specified amount against inhabitant tax the following year, if they could not have been fully deducted the housing loan tax credit from national income tax.

Tax reduction is limited to the 5% of taxable income amount (maximum: 97.5 thousand yen, 7% of taxable income amount (maximum: 136.5 thousand ten) for the year after 2014) (LS 5-4-2).

(ii) Dividend credits

A taxpayer who has received dividend income from a domestic corporation is entitled to credit the amounts of dividend income multiplied by the following dividend credit ratios (LS 5).

When taxable ordinary income is ¥10,000,000 or under:

Prefecture inhabitant tax 1.2%
Municipality inhabitant tax 1.6%
                                                        (total)   2.8%

When taxable ordinary income is over ¥10,000,000

Prefecture inhabitant tax 0.6%
Municipality inhabitant tax 0.8%
                                                        (total)   1.4%

(iii) Foreign tax credits

If the amounts of income tax (both national and local taxes on income) levied by a foreign country are over the limitation amounts of income tax credits, the excess amounts may be allowed as credits against the income levy to the extent of 12% of the limitation amounts of income tax credits against prefecture inhabitant tax, and 18% of the limitation amounts of income tax against municipal inhabitant tax

¶ 9-100

地　方　税　等　801

（計算例）　課税所得金額　3,000,000円
　　道府県民税　3,000,000円×4％＝　120,000円
　　市町村民税　3,000,000円×6％＝　180,000円
　　合計　　　　　　　　　　　　　　300,000円

（税額控除）
　上記の算出税額から控除し得る税額控除の金額は次のとおりである。

(ⅰ)　住宅借入金等特別税額控除
　　平成21年分以後の所得税において住宅借入金等特別税額控除の適用がある者（平成21年1月から平成31年6月までに入居した者に限る。）のうち，当該年分の住宅借入金等特別税額控除額から当該年分の所得税額を控除した残額があるものについては，翌年度分の個人住民税において，当該残額に相当する額（当該年分の所得税の課税総所得金額等の額に100分の5を乗じて得た額（最高9.75万円），平成26年4月以降は100分の7を乗じて得た額（最高13.65万円）を限度とする。）を減額する（地方附5の4の2）。

(ⅱ)　配当控除
　　納税者が内国法人から配当所得を受領した場合には，納税者はその配当所得の金額に次の配当控除率を乗じた金額を控除することができる（地法附5）。

区　　　　　分		配　当　控　除　率
課税総所得金額 1,000万円以下	道府県民税	1.2％
	市町村民税	1.6％
1,000万円超	道府県民税	0.6％
	市町村民税	0.8％

(ⅲ)　外国税額控除
　　外国で課された所得税等の額のうち所得税の控除限度額を超える額があるときは，所得税等の控除限度額の道府県民税については12％，市町村民税については18％を限度として所得割の額から控除する（地法37の3，314の8，地令7の19，48の9の2）。

802   LOCAL TAX etc.

(Law 37-3, 314-8 and Reg 7-19, 48-9-2).

(iv) Adjusted credit

In order to adjust the tax burden increase arising from the difference between the personal deductions for national income tax purposes and those for local inhabitant tax purposes, an individual may deduct the following amount against his income levy of inhabitant tax (Law 37, 314-6).

(1)   If a taxable income amount for inhabitant tax purposes is ¥2,000,000 or less, 5% of the following amount, whichever is the smaller, is creditable.

(a): Difference between personal deductions for income tax purposes and those for inhabitant tax purposes

(b): Taxable income amount for inhabitant tax purposes

(2)   If taxable income amount for inhabitant tax purposes is over ¥2,000,000, the following amount, whichever is the greater, is creditable.

(a): (Difference between personal deductions for income tax purposes and those for inhabitant tax purposes – (Taxable income amount for inhabitant tax purposes – ¥2,000,000)) × 5%

(b): ¥2,500

(v)   Donation credit

In case of donation to a local government or any of certain specified organizations, the specific amount can be deducted from the individual inhabitant tax (Law 37-2, 314-7).

(1)   Donation to a local government (so called hometown tax payment)

Total of (a) and (b) below

(a) (amount donated to a local government –¥2,000) × 10%

(b) (amount donated to a local government –¥2,000)   × (90%– 0 to 40% (the limit rate of income tax applicable to the donor))

Note:
1. Up to 10% of per income levy amount
   Up to 20% per income levy amount after the year 2016 (2015 tax reform)
2. The limit rate of income tax is the highest of plural tax rates apply for calculating an income tax.

(2)   Donation to prefectural Community Chest in donor's domicile or to local chapter of Japan Red Cross in donor's domicile

(Amount donated –¥2,000) × 10%

(3)   Donation qualified by local government for deduction

¶ 9-100

地 方 税 等 803

(iv) 調整控除

　　所得税と個人住民税の人的控除額の差に基づく負担増を調整するため，所得割額から次の額を減額する（地方37，314の 6 ）。

(1) 個人住民税の課税所得金額が200万円以下の者

　　(a)と(b)のいずれか小さい額の 5 ％

　　(a)　人的控除額の差の合計額

　　(b)　個人住民税の課税所得金額

(2) 個人住民税の課税所得金額が200万円を超える者

　　(人的控除額の差の合計額 －(個人住民税の課税所得金額－200万円))
　　× 5 ％

　　　　ただし，この額が2,500円未満の場合は，2,500円とする。

(v) 寄附金控除

　　地方自治体や一定の団体等に寄附した金額がある場合，次の額が所得割額から控除される（地法37の 2 ，314の 7 ）。

(1)　地方自治体に対する寄附（いわゆるふるさと納税）

　　(a)と(b)の合計額

　　(a)　(地方自治体に対する寄附金額－2,000円)×10％

　　(b)　(地方自治体に対する寄附金額－2,000円)×(90％－0～40％（寄附者に適用される所得税の限界税率))

　　(注)： 1 ．所得割額の 1 割が上限。

　　　　　　平成28年度分以降は 2 割が上限（平成27年度税制改正）。

　　　　 2 ．所得税の限界税率とは，所得税を計算する場合における最も高い税率をいう。

(2)　住宅地の都道府県共同募金会及び住所地の日本赤十字社に対する寄附

　　(寄附金額－2,000円)×10％

(3)　各地方自治体が条例により指定した控除対象寄附金

804   LOCAL TAX etc.

 (a) Donation qualified by prefectural government of donor's domicile (deducted from the prefectural inhabitant tax amount)

  (Amount donated –¥2,000) × 4%

 (b) Donation qualified by municipal government of donor's domicile (deduct from the municipal inhabitant tax amount)

  (Amount donated –¥2,000) × 6%

Note:

> The upper limit of deductable donation is 30% of the total income in the total of (1) (2) (3).

¶ 9-101 Carry-forward of capital loss on the sale of residential property

If a taxpayer sells his house or land owned for more than 5 years and used for his residential purpose for the period from January 1, 2004 to December 31, 2013, to the extent that there are capital losses generated from the sale of residential property, the amount of capital losses can be carried forward for the succeeding 3 years and allowed to deduct from income amount if the certain conditions are satisfied.

¶ 9-110 Per dividend levy

Dividend from specified listed stock paid to stockholders is subject to per dividend levy as follows.

Taxable items

- Dividend income on listed stocks, etc.
- Allocations on public-issue securities
- Investment trust earnings, etc.

Tax rates

January 1, 2004 to December 31, 2013	3%
January 1, 2014 or later	5%

(1) No filing of returns is required to the extent that dividend is subject to per dividend levy.

(2) If a taxpayer filed a tax return, dividend is subject to income levy and tax amount of per dividend levy can be deducted from tax amount of income levy.

¶ 9-101

地 方 税 等 805

(a) 住所地の都道府県が指定した控除対象寄附金（都道府県民税額から控除）

(寄附金額－2,000円)× 4 %

(b) 住所地の市区町村が指定した控除対象寄附金（市区町村民税額から控除）

(寄附金額－2,000円)× 6 %

(注)：控除対象となる寄附金の限度額は(1)から(3)を合わせて総所得金額等の30%。

¶9-101　特定の居住用財産の譲渡損失の繰越控除等

　個人が，平成16年1月1日から平成25年12月31日までの間にその有する家屋又は土地等でその年1月1日において所有期間が5年を超えるものの当該個人の居住の用に供しているものの譲渡をした場合において，当該譲渡の日の属する年に当該譲渡資産に係る譲渡損失の金額があるときは，一定の要件の下で，その譲渡損失の金額についてその年の翌年以後3年内の各年分の総所得金額等からの繰越控除を認める。

¶9-110　道府県民税配当割の課税

　上場株式等の配当等については，他の所得と分離して配当割が課税される。

(課税対象)

・上場株式等の配当等

・公募証券投資信託の収益の分配に係る配当等

・特定投資法人の投資口に係る配当等

(税率)

平成16年1月1日〜平成25年12月31日	3 %
平成26年1月1日以後	5 %

(1) 納税者は申告を要しない。

(2) 納税義務者が申告をした場合には，所得割により課税し，所得割額から配当割額相当額を控除する。

806   LOCAL TAX etc.

¶ 9-111 Per stock capital gain levy

Capital gain generated from stock transaction in the designated account subject to withholding tax by election is subject to per stock capital gain levy as follows.

January 1, 2004 to December 31, 2013	3%
January 1, 2014 or later	5%

(1) No filing of returns is required to the extent that stock capital gain is subject to per stock capital gain levy.

(2) If a taxpayer filed a tax return, stock capital gain is subject to income levy and tax amount of per stock capital gain levy can be deducted from tax amount of income levy.

¶ 9-120 Separate taxation

(1) **Interest income**

Interest income (excluding non-taxable interest under the national income tax law and interest received by foreign corporations or non-residents) is separately subject to 5% withholding tax as the interest levy of prefecture inhabitant tax (Law 23, 24, 71-6). A specified part of the revenue from this tax is transferred to the municipality.

(2) **Retirement income**

If an individual selects separate withholding income tax treatment on retirement income under the national income tax law (see ¶ 4-340), retirement income under the local tax law is separately subject to withholding inhabitant tax at the rate of 90% of the usual rate mentioned above (Law 50-2 to 50-6, 328 to 328-16 and LS 7).

In this case, the retirement income is taxed separately from other income by the prefecture and the municipality which govern the taxpayer's domicile as of January 1st of the year in which the retirement income is received.

Note:
For the retirement income to be paid after Jan 1, 2013, this 10% tax credit measure will be abolished and will levy full amount of individual inhabitant tax (introduced by 2012 tax reform).

(3) **Business income etc. from a short-term capital gain on land etc. (LS 33-3, 33-4)**

The amount of tax for business income etc. from land etc. is (a) or (b) below whichever is larger (The provision is not applicable to a capital

¶ 9-111

地　方　税　等　807

9-111　道府県民税株式譲渡所得割の課税
　源泉徴収選択適用の特定口座内の株式等の譲渡益について株式譲渡所得割が課税される。

平成16年1月1日～平成25年12月31日	3 %
平成26年1月1日以後	5 %

⑴　納税者は申告を要しない。

⑵　納税義務者が申告をした場合には，所得割により課税し，所得割額から配当割額相当額を控除する。

¶9-120　分離課税
⑴　利子所得
　利子所得（所得税法上の非課税利子，非居住者及び外国法人が支払を受ける利子などを除く。）については，道府県民税利子割として5％の税率により特別徴収（分離課税）される（地法23，24，71の6）。
　その税収の一部は道府県から市町村へ交付される。

⑵　退職所得
　個人が所得税法上「退職所得に対する源泉分離課税（¶4-340参照）」を選択した場合には，退職所得に対する住民税^(注)は通常税率の90％相当額の税率により特別徴収（分離課税）される（地法50の2～50の6，328～328の16，地法附7）。
　この場合，その所得は他の所得と分離して，退職金を受領した年の1月1日現在の住所地の道府県及び市町村により課税される。

(注)：平成25年1月1日以後に支払われる退職金には，この10％の税率軽減の適用は廃止され，通常の個人住民税率で課税される（平成24年度税制改正）。

⑶　短期所有土地等に係る事業所得等（地法附33の3，33の4）
　土地等に係る事業所得等については次の金額のうち，いずれか多い金額により課税される（平成10年1月1日から平成25年12月31日までは適用なし。）。

808   LOCAL TAX etc.

gain between January 1, 1998 through December 31, 2013):

(a) taxable business income etc. on land etc. × 12% (prefecture tax 4.8%, and municipality tax 7.2%); or

(b) normal tax amounts for global taxation calculated at the normal tax rate × 110%

(4) **Long-term capital gains on land etc. (LS 34)**

Tax rate for sale 5%

(prefectural inhabitant tax 2.0% and municipal tax 3.0%)

Note:

1. Capital gains from sales of land etc. which will contribute to promoting the supply of good quality housing (LS 34-2):
    • Tax rate for sales:
    capital gains after special deduction are not more than ¥20,000,000....4%
    (prefectural inhabitant tax 1.6% and municipal tax 2.4%)
    capital gains after special deduction are over ¥20,000,000....................5%
    (prefectural inhabitant tax 2.0% and municipal tax 3.0%)

2. Capital gains from residential house and land (LS 34-3):
    • Tax rate for sales:
    capital gains after special deduction of not more than ¥60,000,000......4%
    (prefectural inhabitant tax 1.6%, and municipality tax 2.4%)
    capital gains after special deduction of more than ¥60,000,000.............5%
    (prefectural inhabitant tax 2.0%, and municipality tax 3.0%)

3. When a taxpayer enjoys other special treatments, a taxpayer is not permitted to apply this special treatment.

4. With regard to the sale of the land purchased in 2009 or 2010 after ownership of the land for at least 5 years, a taxpayer can apply the special tax deduction up to 10 million yen to the profit gains from the sale of the land.

(5) **Short-term taxable capital gains on land etc. (LS 35)**

The amount of tax is as follow:

taxable short-term capital gains × 9%

(prefectural inhabitant tax 3.6% and municipal tax 5.4%)

However, 5% (prefectural inhabitant tax 2.0% and municipal tax 3.0%) of the taxable amount of short-term capital gains derived from land etc. transferred to the National or Local governments.

(6) **Capital gains etc. from stock or shares (LS 35-2)**

Capital gains etc. of stocks from the sale are subject to local inhabitant tax at the rate of 5%.

(prefectural inhabitant tax 2.0% and municipal tax 3.0%)

Capital gains of listed stocks from the sale are taxed as follows.

January 1, 2004 to December 31, 2013	10%
	(income tax 7%, local inhabitant tax 3%)

¶ 9-120

地　方　税　等　809

(a) 土地等に係る課税事業所得等に対して
　　道府県民税4.8%　市町村民税7.2%　合計12.0%
(b) 総合課税として通常税率により計算された税額に対して
　　110%相当額

(4) **土地等に係る長期譲渡所得（地法附34）**
　　特別控除後の譲渡益　　5 ％（道府県民税 2 ％，市町村民税 3 ％）

　　(注)：1．優良住宅地の供給促進に係る土地等の譲渡益（地法附34の 2 ）
　　　　　　　特別控除後の譲渡益2,000万円以下の部分 4 ％（道府県民税1.6%，市町村民税2.4%）
　　　　　　　特別控除後の譲渡益2,000万円超の部分 5 ％（道府県民税2.0%，市町村民税3.0%）
　　　　　2．居住用財産の長期譲渡所得（地法附34の 3 ）
　　　　　　　特別控除後の譲渡益が6,000万円以下の部分 4 ％（道府県民税1.6%，市町村民税2.4%）
　　　　　　　特別控除後の譲渡益が6,000万円超の部分 5 ％（道府県民税2.0%，市町村民税3.0%）
　　　　　3．収用交換等により代替資産等を取得した場合の課税の特例，換地処分等に伴い資産
　　　　　　を取得した場合の課税の特例その他の課税の繰延措置並びに収用交換等の5,000万円特
　　　　　　別控除，特定土地区画整理事業等のための2,000万円特別控除，特定住宅地造成事業等
　　　　　　のための1,500万円特別控除，農地保有合理化等のための800万円特別控除及び居住用財
　　　　　　産の3,000万円特別控除を適用した場合には，この軽減税率の特例は適用しない。
　　　　　4．個人が，平成21年 1 月 1 日から平成22年12月31日までの間に取得をした国内にある
　　　　　　土地等で，その 1 月 1 日において所有期間が 5 年を超えるものの譲渡をした場合には，
　　　　　　その年中の当該譲渡に係る長期譲渡所得の金額から1,000万円（当該長期譲渡所得の金
　　　　　　額が，1,000万円に満たない場合には，当該長期譲渡所得の金額）を控除する。

(5) **土地等に係る短期譲渡所得（地法附35）**
　　次の税率による。
　　課税短期譲渡所得金額に対して，9 ％（道府県民税3.6%，市町村民税
5.4%）。
　　ただし，国等に対する譲渡については，次の税額による。
　　譲渡益の 5 ％（道府県民税 2 ％，市町村民税 3 ％）

(6) **株式等に係る譲渡所得等（地法附35の 2 ）**
　　株式等に係る譲渡所得等については，譲渡所得金額に対して 5 ％（道府
県民税 2 ％，市町村民税 3 ％）の税率により課税される。
　　上場株式等及び公募株式投資信託の受益証券の譲渡所得等については，
株式等の課税所得金額に対して，次の税率により課税される。

| 平成16年 1 月 1 日〜平成25年12月31日 | 10％（所得税 7 ％，住民税 3 ％） |

810   LOCAL TAX etc.

Note:
1. The amount of loss derived from the case, where the corporation issuing stocks deposited in a designated control account have ended to the liquidation and the economic value of the stock issued by the corporation becomes worthless, is deemed to be capital loss from the disposition of the stock and can be applied to the special treatment described in ¶ 5-256(8) (LS 35-2-2).
2. A resident taxpayer who acquired stocks of qualified ventures by investing capital in cash is entitled to enjoy special treatments at the time of the disposal of the stocks under the certain conditions (LS 35-3).

(7) **Capital gains from commodity futures trading (LS 35-4)**

A certain capital gains arise from commodity futures trading are subject to local tax at the rate of 5% (prefectural inhabitant tax 2.0% and municipal tax 3.0%) separate from other income.

Capital losses arise from commodity futures trading are deemed not to arise.

To the extent that there are capital losses generated from commodity or stock futures trading, the amount of capital losses can be carried forward for the succeeding 3 years and allowed to deduct from capital gains generated from commodity or stock futures trading under the specified conditions(LS 35-4-2).

(8) **Inhabitant tax rate applied to separate taxation**

Unless otherwise specified tax rate applied to separate taxation is 10% (prefecture tax 4.0% and municipal tax 6.0%) as same as tax rate applied to comprehensive taxation.

¶ 9-130 Tax exemption on dividends and capital gains from listed stock etc. (NISA)

After January 2014, dividends and capital gains from listed stock etc. held or transferred from the tax exempt account (up to 1 million yen a year, maximum 5 million yen for 5 years) established with a financial instruments business operator will be excluded from taxation (LS 35-3-2).

¶ 9-140 Return and payment

A "notification of inhabitant tax assessment" is issued generally by the tax office. Due tax must be paid directly by the taxpayer. However, salary income is subject to withholding tax.

(1) **Return**

Individual taxpayers are required to file the inhabitant tax return with

¶ 9-130

地 方 税 等 811

(注)：1．特定管理株式を発行した株式会社に清算結了等の事実が生じ，当該特定管理株式の
　　　　価値を失ったことによる損失の金額については，譲渡損失とみなして，譲渡所得等の
　　　　課税の特例を適用することができる（地法附35の２の２）。
　　　２．特定中小会社の株式を払込みにより取得をした居住者等については，一定の要件の
　　　　下に，当該株式に係る譲渡所得等の特例を適用することができる（地法附35の３）。

(7)　**商品先物取引に係る事業所得又は雑所得（地法附35の４）**

　　商品先物取引による所得で一定のものについては，他の所得と分離して
５％（道府県民税２％，市町村民税３％）の税率により課税される。

　　商品先物取引による損失の金額は生じなかったものとみなされる。

　　平成15年１月１日以後に商品先物取引又は有価証券等先物取引に係る差
金等決済をしたことにより生じた損失の金額のうちに，一定の要件の下
で，その控除しきれない金額についてその年の翌年以後３年内の各年分の
商品先物取引又は有価証券等先物取引に係る雑所得等の金額から繰越控除
を認める（地法附35の４の２）。

(8)　**分離課税等に係る個人住民税の税率**

　　分離課税等に係る都道府県分と市町村分の税率は，別途定めがある場合
のほか総合課税と同様の（道府県民税４％，市町村民税６％）である。

¶9-130　少額上場株式等に係る配当・譲渡益等の非課税措置（NISA）

　　平成26年１月以降，証券会社や銀行に設定した上場株式等の保有のための
「非課税口座（年間100万円限度で最大５年間で500万円)」内の上場株式等の
配当，譲渡益が非課税となる（地法附35の３の２)。

¶9-140　申告及び納付

　　個人住民税の申告及び納付は，給与所得者とその他の一般納税者とではそ
の方法が異なり，給与所得者の住民税は給与の支払者が特別徴収し，その他
の一般納税者は納税通知書の交付を受けて直接納付する。

(1)　**申告**

　　納税義務者は一定の事項を記載した住民税申告書を１月１日現在の住所地

812   LOCAL TAX etc.

the municipal tax office governing their place of domicile as of January 1 by March 15 (Law 45-2, 317-2).

But if a taxpayer is a salary income earner with no income other than salary income, he or she is not required to submit a tax return.

> **Note:**
> Taxpayers with income, other than salary income, of ¥200,000 or under need not file an individual income tax return, but are required to file an individual inhabitant tax return.

If an individual taxpayer has filed an income tax return to a national taxation office (see ¶ 5-720), the taxpayer is deemed to have filed an inhabitant tax return (Law 45-3, 317-3).

(2) **Payment**

Taxpayers other than salary income earners will be issued a "notification of inhabitant tax assessment" by the inhabitant tax office concerned. The tax due should be paid in four equal installments in June, August and October of the given year and in January of the following year in accordance with the notification (Law 319, 320).

If the taxpayer pays the total amount of the four equal installments by June of the given year, the taxpayer is qualified to receive a refund of a specified percentage of the amount paid in advance (Law 321).

(3) **Salary income earner**

The payer of salary income and the withholding agent of withholding income tax (see ¶ 4-230) is required to submit an information return for salary income paid to the salary income earner (the same form as the notification of withholding income tax issued to a receiver) describing the amount of salary income and other items paid in the preceding year. The return must be submitted to the inhabitant tax office administering the salary income earner's place of domicile by January 31 of that year (Law 317-6).

The payer of salary income and the withholding agent of withholding income tax (see ¶ 4-230) is required to submit salary payment report with regard to an employee leaving an employer at the middle of the year with local tax office.

An inhabitant tax office calculates the individual inhabitant tax amounts payable by each salary income earner, and gives notice to the withholding agent not later than May 31.

The withholding agent is required to withhold inhabitant tax through 12 months, from June of each year to May of the following year, and is required to pay the tax withheld to the inhabitant tax office not later than

¶ 9-140

の市町村長に3月15日までに提出しなければならない。

ただし，給与所得者であり，給与所得以外の所得がなかった者は提出を要しない（地法45の2，317の2）[注]。

> [注]：所得税法上給与所得以外の所得が20万円以下の場合には確定申告書の提出を要しないが，住民税の申告書は提出することが必要である。

なお，納税義務者が所得税の確定申告書を税務署長に提出した場合には（¶5-720参照），同じ日に住民税の申告書も提出したものとみなされる（地法45の3，317の3）。

(2)　納付

納税義務者は，住民税の申告書を提出した市町村長から納税通知書の交付を納期限前10日前までに受けて，これに基づき6月，8月，10月及び翌年の1月の4回に分けて，均等割額と所得割額との合計額をそれぞれ4分の1ずつを納付する（地法319，320）。

納税義務者が4分割の年税額をその年の6月に一括して前納した場合には，支払額の一定割合の報奨金を受け取ることができる（地法321）。

(3)　給与所得者

給与所得の支払者であり，所得税の源泉徴収義務のある者（¶4-230参照）は，前年中に支払った給与の金額その他の事項を記載した"給与支払報告書（源泉徴収票と同じ。）"を給与所得者の住所地の市町村長に1月31日までに提出しなければならない（地法317の6）。

給与の支払をする者で所得税法の規定により源泉徴収義務のあるものについて，当該給与の支払を受けている者のうち給与の支払を受けなくなったものがある場合に給与支払報告書を提出する義務がある。

当該市町村課税当局は給与所得者の住民税額を計算して特別徴収義務者へ5月末日までに通知し，特別徴収義務者はその年の6月から翌年5月までの12カ月間にわたり毎月給与の支払の際に住民税額を差し引き，その翌月10日までに市町村課税当局へ納入しなければならない（地法321の5）。

なお，所得税の源泉徴収のような税額の計算及び年末調整の手続は必要とされない。

814   LOCAL TAX etc.

the 10th of the following month (Law 321-5). It is noted that year end adjustment of withholding tax is not required.

¶ 9-160 Assessment and tax disputes

Procedures for tax assessment and tax disputes are the same as for
self-assessment income tax (see ¶ 5-740 to ¶ 5-820).

Corporation Inhabitant Tax

¶ 9-180 Taxpayer

Corporation inhabitant tax, like individual inhabitant tax, includes a
prefecture tax and a municipality tax on corporations. It is levied on the
following corporations (Law 24, 294):

(i)   a corporation which has its office or place of business during
the business year in a municipality—per capita levy and per
corporation tax levy; and

(ii)   a corporation which does not have its office or place of business in a municipality, but maintains a dormitory, club or
similar facility there—per capita levy.

Accordingly, if a corporation has its head office in Chiyoda-ward,
Tokyo, and has a branch office in Kita-ward, Osaka, the corporation is
taxed by both municipalities on per capita levy and per corporation tax levy.

An organization which does not have a juridical personality, but has
its own representative or administrator, is deemed to be a corporation, and
is subject to corporation inhabitant tax on profits accruing from profits-
making business (Law 24, 294).

A corporation designated as a public interest corporation (see ¶ 6-040) is
taxed by per capita levy and corporation tax levy on profits accruing to it from
profit-making business in a similar way to corporation tax law (Law 24, 294).

Note:
A foreign corporation without any facilities is deemed to have its office, etc.
in the municipality where it is doing business (Law 24, 294).

¶ 9-200 Per capita levy

The amounts of per capita levy in a business year are fixed amounts.
The standard tax rate varies according to capital amounts and the number
of employees (Law 52, 312).

¶ 9-160

地　方　税　等　815

¶9-160　賦課及び不服審査

賦課及び不服審査の手続は申告所得税と同様である（¶5-740〜¶5-820参照）。

法人住民税

¶9-180　納税義務者

法人住民税は法人に対する道府県民税と市町村民税との総称であり，その納税義務者は次に掲げる者である（地法24，294）。

(i)　市町村内に事務所又は事業所を有する法人──均等割額と法人税割額の合算額

(ii)　市町村内に寮，宿泊所，クラブその他これらに類する施設を有する法人でその市町村内に事務所又は事業所を有しないもの──均等割額

したがって，法人が東京都千代田区内に本店事務所を有し，大阪市北区に支店事務所を有している場合には，その法人は双方の道府県及び市町村から均等割額と法人税割額の課税がなされる。

また，法人格を有しない社団又は財団で代表者又は管理人の定めがあり，かつ収益事業を行うものについては，法人とみなされ，法人住民税が課税される（地法24，294）。

公益法人（¶6-040参照）は法人税法における場合と同じく，収益事業からの所得に対して，均等割と法人税割とが課税される（地法24，294）。

(注)：外国法人については，その事業が行われる場所をもってその事業所又は事務所とする（地法24，294）。

¶9-200　均等割額の課税

法人住民税の均等割額は定額であり，その標準税率は，事業年度末日現在の資本金等の額及び従業者数に応じて，それぞれ次の金額とされている（地法52，312）。

816   LOCAL TAX etc.

Standard rate   (amount per annum)

Capital amount	Prefectural inhabitant tax	Municipal inhabitant Tax	
	Standard tax rate	Number of Employees in the municipality	Standard tax rate
¥10,000,000 or less	¥20,000	50 or less, exceeding 50	¥50,000 ¥120,000
(more than) (or less) ¥10,000,000 ~ 100,000,000	¥50,000	50 or less, exceeding 50	¥130,000 ¥150,000
¥100,000,000 ~ 1,000,000,000	¥130,000	50 or less, exceeding 50	¥160,000 ¥400,000
¥1,000,000,000 ~ 5,000,000,000	¥540,000	50 or less, exceeding 50	¥410,000 ¥1,750,000
¥5,000,000,000 or more	¥800,000	50 or less, exceeding 50	¥410,000 ¥3,000,000

Note:
1. "Capital amounts" means the total of capital amounts and capital surplus (see ¶ 6-080). In a mutual corporation, it means the amount of net assets. In a public corporation, the tax rate for capital amounts of ¥10,000,000 or less in the first column is applied.
2. Municipal tax authorities may tax up to 120% of the tax amounts mentioned above.
3. With respect to a corporate taxpayer located in 23 ward of Tokyo (metropolitan), the tax rates for the per capita levy of corporation inhabitant tax are as follows:

Per capita levy

Capital amounts		Employee numbers	Per capita levy
over ¥5,000,000,000		over 50	¥3,800,000
over ¥1,000,000,000 or under ¥5,000,000,000		over 50	¥2,290,000
over ¥5,000,000,000		or under 50	¥1,210,000
over ¥1,000,000,000 or under ¥5,000,000,000		or under 50	¥950,000
over ¥100,000,000 or under ¥1,000,000,000		over 50	¥530,000
over ¥100,000,000 or under ¥1,000,000,000		or under 50	¥290,000
over ¥10,000,000 or under ¥100,000,000		over 50	¥200,000
over ¥10,000,000 or under ¥100,000,000		or under 50	¥180,000
	or under ¥10,000,000	over 50	¥140,000
	or under ¥10,000,000	or under 50	¥70,000

¶ 9-220 Per corporation tax levy (tax base)

The tax base for the corporation tax levy is the amount of the national

地　方　税　等　817

（標準課税）

資本金等の額	道府県民税	市　町　村　民　税	
	標準税率	当該市町村における従業員数	標準税率
1,000万円以下	20,000円	50人以下 50人超	50,000円 120,000円
1,000万円超～1億円以下	50,000円	50人以下 50人超	130,000円 150,000円
1億円超～10億円以下	130,000円	50人以下 50人超	160,000円 400,000円
10億円超～50億円以下	540,000円	50人以下 50人超	410,000円 1,750,000円
50億円超	800,000円	50人以下 50人超	410,000円 3,000,000円

　（注）：1．「資本金等の額」とは，資本金の額と資本積立金との合計額である。相互会社では純
　　　　　資産額を表わし，公益法人は資本金等の額が1,000万円以下として税率が適用される。
　　　　2．市町村の課税当局は上記の市町村の標準税率による税額に1.2倍までの税額（制限税
　　　　　率）を課税し得る。このため，市町村により若干の課税額の差異がある。
　　　　3．東京都23区では，道府県民税と市町村民税とを合わせて，次のように課税している。

（東京都の実例）

資本金等の額	従業員数	均等割の金額
50億円超	50人超	3,800,000円
50億円超	50人以下	1,210,000円
10億円超　50億円以下	50人超	2,290,000円
10億円超　50億円以下	50人以下	950,000円
1億円超　10億円以下	50人超	530,000円
1億円超　10億円以下	50人以下	290,000円
1,000万円超　1億円以下	50人超	200,000円
1,000万円超　1億円以下	50人以下	180,000円
1,000万円以下	50人超	140,000円
1,000万円以下	50人以下	70,000円

¶9-220　法人税割額（課税標準）

　法人住民税の法人税割額の課税標準は，原則として法人税法の規定により

818   LOCAL TAX etc.

corporation tax. The different points of calculation to be considered are as follows.

(i)   The tax base for corporate inhabitant tax is the national corporation tax amount before making deductions such as income tax credits (see ¶ 6-710), foreign tax credits (see ¶ 6-740), but after deducting credits for experimental and research expenses (see ¶ 6-720), credits for an increased amount of imports (see ¶ 6-735) and credits for human investment expenses (see ¶ 6-736), if qualified for such credit (Law 23, 292).

(ii)   If a corporation carried back its net loss to the preceding year and received a tax refund under the provisions of the corporation tax law, it may carry forward the tax refund to the succeeding seven years in accordance with inhabitant tax law (Law 53, 321-8).

(iii) The term "corporation tax amounts" does not include penalty tax (see ¶ 5-750), interest tax or delinquency tax (see ¶ 5-730).

Note:
Local tax authorities can see and make copies of the documents for correction or determination made by the national tax office (Law 63, 325).

¶ 9-240 Per corporation tax levy (tax rates)

The standard tax rate is as follows (Law 51, 314-4):

Prefectural inhabitant tax	Municipal inhabitant tax	Total
3.2%	9.7%	12.9%
(4.2%)	(12.1%)	(16.3%)

The maximum tax rate is shown in ( ). Almost all prefectures apply the maximum tax rate in practice.

For example, a Tokyo tax authority applied the following tax rate:

Capital amount is more than ¥100,000,000 or

Corporation tax amount is more than ¥10,000,000 .... 16.3%

The other corporation 12.9%

Note:
This tax levied on undistributed profits of foreign subsidiaries (see ¶ 6-190).

¶ 9-260 Per corporation tax levy (tax amounts)

The amount payable as inhabitant tax is, for the purposes of the per corporation tax levy, calculated by multiplying corporation tax by the tax

¶ 9-240

計算した法人税額であるが，次の点において異なる。

(i) 課税標準である法人税額は所得税額控除（¶6-710参照），外国税額控除（¶6-740参照）などの税額控除前の税額であるが，中小企業等の試験研究費に係る法人税額の特別控除（¶6-720参照），製品輸入額が増加した場合の法人税額の特別控除（¶6-735参照），中小企業者等の教育訓練費に係る法人税額の控除等（¶6-736参照），一定の特別控除の適用がある場合はこれらについて控除した後の税額である（地法23，292）。

(ii) 法人が法人税法上欠損金の繰戻しによる法人税額の還付を受けた場合には，地方税法上では還付された法人税額を7年間にわたり繰越控除して計算する（地法53，321の8）。

(iii) 法人税額には，法人税に係る利子税，延滞税（¶5-730参照）及び各種加算税（¶5-750参照）の額を含めない。

(注)：地方税課税当局は税務署の更正決定に関する書類を閲覧し，記録することができる（地法63，325）。

¶9-240　法人税割額（税率）

法人税割額の標準税率は次のとおりである（地法51，314の4）。

道府県民税	市町村民税	合計
3.2%	9.7%	12.9%
(4.2%)	(12.1%)	(16.3%)

制限税率は上記（　）内に示しているが，ほとんどの道府県が適用している。例えば，東京都では，次の税率により課税している。

資本金の額が1億円超又は
法人税額が年1,000万円超の法人 ……16.3%
その他の法人 ………………………………12.9%

(注)：外国子会社の未分配所得（¶6-190参照）についても法人税割額が課される。

¶9-260　法人税割（税額）

納税義務者は，法人税額を課税標準として前記税率を乗じて算定した法人税割から次に掲げる税額控除を差し引くことができる（地法53，321の8）。

820   LOCAL TAX etc.

rates mentioned above (¶ 9-240). The following tax credits are allowed (Law 53, 321-8):

(i) Foreign tax credits—

If the amount of tax (both national and local tax on income) levied by a foreign country exceeds the limitation of tax credits allowed against national corporation tax, the excess amount is creditable against the inhabitant corporation tax levy, subject to a limitation of 5.0% of the excess amount against prefectural tax or 12.3% of the excess amount against municipal tax (see ¶ 6-745).

(ii) Tax overpaid due to misrepresentation of accounts in financial statements—

If the national tax authorities correct incorrect accounting treatment, the tax overpaid for the year in which the correction was made is refunded (see ¶ 6-700). The amount of tax refunded is deducted by the local tax authorities from the amounts of the corporation tax levy in the five following years (Law 53, 321-8).

(iii) Donation credits (so called enterprise hometown tax payment)

In case of donation to certain projects listed in a plan certified under the Local Revitalization Act, the specific amount (20% of donated amount, up to 20% of Corporation Inhabitant Tax) can be deducted from the Corporation Inhabitant Tax (2016 tax reform).

¶ 9-280 Separate taxation

Separate taxation like individual inhabitant tax is not applied to corporate inhabitant tax. If corporate taxpayers are taxed at the special additional tax rate of 5 or 10% on capital gains from land according to corporation tax law (see ¶ 6-670), corporate taxpayers are taxed on the aggregate corporation tax amount including the tax amounts calculated at the special additional tax rates, under local tax laws (Law 23, 292).

¶ 9-300 Return and payment

A corporation is required to file a return with, and pay tax to, a prefectural tax office in the case of prefectural inhabitant tax, and a municipal tax office in the case of municipal inhabitant tax (Law 53, 321-8).

The time limits for filing returns or making payment are the same as in the case for corporation tax (¶ 6-800, ¶ 6-805, ¶ 6-810).

¶ 9-280

地　方　税　等　821

⒤　外国税額控除

　　外国税額のうち国税の控除限度額（¶6-745参照）を超える額があると
きは，国税の控除限度額の5.0％を道府県民税の限度額として，その12.3％
を市町村民税の限度額として税額控除する。

⒥　仮装経理に伴う過大申告

　　仮装経理に伴う過大申告について法人税額の減額更正が行われた場合
（¶6-700参照），その過大申告税額は減額更正のあった事業年度開始の日
から5年以内に開始する各事業年度の法人税割の額から順次控除する（地
法53，321の8）。

⒦　寄附金控除（いわゆる企業版ふるさと納税）

　　地方公共団体が行う認定地方創生事業に対する寄附金額の一部（寄附金
額の20％，税額の20％を上限）が税額控除されることとされた（平成28年
度税制改正）。

¶9-280　分離課税

　　個人住民税のような分離課税はない。

　　なお，法人が法人税法上，土地又はその他の資産の譲渡所得について5％
又は10％の特別税率により課税された場合（¶6-670参照），その法人は地方
税法に従い土地重課を含む全税額が課税の対象とされる（地法23，292）。

¶9-300　法人住民税の申告及び納付

　　法人は道府県知事に対し道府県民税の申告書を提出して納付し，また，市
町村長に対し市町村民税の申告書を提出して納付しなければならない（地法
53，321の8）。

　　申告期限及び納付期限は，法人税の場合と同じである（¶6-800，¶6-
805，¶6-810）。また，法人税法の規定により，申告書の提出期限の延長を

822   LOCAL TAX etc.

An extension for filing a corporate inhabitant tax return is allowed for a corporation whose corporate tax return is allowed to be extended under corporate tax law provided that an application for an extension is filed with the governor of the relevant prefecture and municipality (Law 53, 321-8).

A taxpayer filing an amended return with national tax authorities, or a taxpayer who is assessed after a correction or determination by national tax authorities when the corporation tax amount is short, is required to file an amended corporation inhabitant tax return and make payment within the time limits for paying corporation tax (Law 53, 321-8).

When a tax liability is overstated in a final return, the taxpayer is entitled to request the local tax authority to refund the amount overpaid, up to one year from the time limit for filing the return (Law 20-9-3).

¶ 9-320 Large corporation (divided corporation tax levy)

If a corporate taxpayer has its office or place of business in two or more prefectures or two or more municipalities, the corporation tax levy to be paid to each prefecture or municipality is determined by prorating the total tax amount on the basis of the number of employees on the last day of the business year in the office or place of business located in each prefecture or municipality (Law 57, 321-13).

Individual Enterprise Tax

¶ 9-340 Taxpayer

Individual enterprise tax (enterprise tax on individuals) is levied on persons who carry on the categories of business listed below (¶ 9-360 to ¶ 9-400). The tax is levied by the prefecture tax office governing the place of business (Law 72-2).

If the individual does not have a specific place of business, the location of the vital interest of the business is deemed to be the place of business for the purpose of determining domicile.

¶ 9-360 Category I business
Scope

This category includes almost all kinds of mercantile business activity such as retail or wholesale trade, manufacturing, money-lending, transportation, hotel, restaurants, etc.—37 kinds.

¶ 9-320

地　方　税　等　823

認められている法人については，その旨を道府県知事に届け出ることにより法人住民税の提出期限も延長される（地法53，321の8）。

　なお，法人税の修正申告書の提出，更正，決定により，不足税額が生じることとなった場合は，法人税額を納付すべき日までに，法人住民税の増加した税額を申告納付しなければならない（地法53，321の8）。

　また，過大税額が生じた場合には，申告期限から1年以内に更正の請求をすることができる（地法20の9の3）。

¶9-320　住民税額の分割

　二以上の市町村又は道府県において事務所又は事業所を有する法人については，各市町村又は道府県に納付すべき法人税割額は課税標準となる法人税額をその事務所又は事業所の各事業年度の末日現在の従業員の数に按分して分割して算定される（地法57，321の13）。

個人事業税

¶9-340　納税義務者

　個人事業税（個人に対する事業税）は，次に掲げる種類の事業を営む個人に対して事務所又は事業所所在の道府県課税当局により課される（地法72の2）。

　なお，事務所又は事業所を設けないで事業を行う場合には，事業者の住所（又は居所）のうちその事業と最も関係の深いものが事務所又は事業所とみなされる。

¶9-360　第一種事業

（範囲）

　第一種事業は，物品販売業，製造業，金銭貸付業，運送業，旅館業，飲食店業など商工業のほとんどのすべての事業であり，37種ある。

824   LOCAL TAX etc.

Tax rate

5% of the income. Mining industry and forest industry are not subject to enterprise tax.

¶ 9-380 Category II business
Scope
This category includes primitive industries such as fishing, the livestock industry and charcoal-making, but excludes businesses operated mainly by family workers.

Tax rate

4% of the income — 3 kinds.

¶ 9-400 Category III business
Scope
As a general rule, this category includes all professionals such as physicians, dentists, lawyers, certified accountants, certified tax accountants and hairdressers — 30 kinds.

Tax rate

5% of the income (3% of the income for professionals such as masseurs, masseuses etc.).

¶ 9-410 Taxable income
The taxable income of an individual enterprise tax is the amount of business income earned during the previous year. If an individual enterprise taxpayer discontinues business in the middle of a year, taxable income is the aggregate of the previous year's business income and business income earned from January 1 until the date of discontinuance of the business of the current year (Law 72-49-7).

¶ 9-420 Calculation of income
(1)   The tax base for enterprise tax on individuals is the income derived in the preceding year, computed in the same way as real-estate income or business income (see ¶ 5-130) as defined for income tax purposes, with some minor exceptions.

Accordingly, categories of income other than real-estate income or business income categorized under income tax law are not taxable (Law 72-49-8).

¶ 9-380

地　方　税　等　825

（税率）
　所得の5％
なお，鉱業，林業からの所得は事業税が非課税とされている。

¶9-380　第二種事業
（範囲）
　水産業，畜産業，薪炭製造業などの原始産業に属するもので，主として自家労力を用いて行うもの以外のもので，3種ある。

（税率）
　所得の4％

¶9-400　第三種事業
（範囲）
　医業，歯科医業，弁護士業，公認会計士業，税理士業，理容業などの自由業で，30種ある。

（税率）
　所得の5％
ただし，あんま等の所得について3％

¶9-410　課税標準
　個人事業税の課税標準は前年中のその個人の行う事業の所得である。年の途中で事業を廃止した場合は，前年の所得と，本年1月1日から事業廃止の日までの事業の所得を課税標準とする（地法72の49の7）。

¶9-420　所得の算定方法
(1)　個人事業税の課税標準である所得は，若干の例外を除くほか，前年分の所得税の事業所得及び不動産所得の計算の例（¶5-130参照）によって算定する。したがって，所得税法上の所得分類における事業所得及び不動産所得以外の所得は課税されない（地法72の49の8）。

826   LOCAL TAX etc.

(2) In computing the tax base, a "proprietor's allowance", amounting to ¥2,900,000 per year, is deductible (Law 72-49-10).

(3) Various deductions or allowances under income tax law (for example, allowances for a spouse or dependant, deductions for medical expenses, etc.) are not deductible from enterprise tax. Tax credits are also not deductible (Law 72-49-8).

(4) Enterprise tax is limited to domestic business. The income derived from foreign business is not subject to enterprise tax (Law 72-49-9). Accordingly, when an individual who has a main place of business in Japan and a place of business (office, factory, mine or other fixed place of business) in a foreign country, carries on business both inside and outside Japan, the foreign business income attributed to the fixed place of business situated in the foreign country is not subject to enterprise tax.

If separation of foreign income from total income is difficult, the taxpayer may calculate foreign income according to the ratio of the number of employees employed in each fixed place.

If a taxpayer is taxed foreign income tax on domestic income, the foreign income tax is deducted from his domestic income.

(5) The following tax treatments accepted under income tax law are not applicable under local tax law for the purposes of enterprise tax (Law 72-49-8):

   (i) the deduction for a blue return in the case of a taxpayer filing a blue form return.

   (ii) in the case of a taxpayer filing a blue return, the limitation on the deduction for salaries or wages paid to family members (see ¶ 5-160(3)(a));

   Under enterprise tax law the deduction allowed for salaries or wages paid to family members is limited to either: (a) the actual amount of salaries or wages paid to family members engaged in the taxpayer's business, in the case of a taxpayer filing a blue return form or (b) in the case of other taxpayers, the lesser of ¥500,000 per family member (¥860,000 for a spouse) or the amount of business income divided by the number of family members plus one (Law 72-49-8).

   (iii) in the case of a taxpayer filing a blue return, the carry-back of the net loss to the preceding calendar year (see ¶ 5-280);

   (iv) separate taxation on business income from capital gains from

¶ 9-420

地　方　税　等　827

(2) 課税標準の計算上，年290万円の事業主控除を所得から控除し得る（地法72の49の10）。

(3) 所得税の計算の例による各種の所得控除（例えば，配偶者控除，扶養控除，医療費控除）は事業税では認められない。税額控除も同じである（地法72の49の8）。

(4) 個人事業税の対象は国内の事業に限られ，したがって，国外の事業から生ずる所得については課税されない（地法72の49の9）。

国内に主たる事業所を有し，国外にその事業が行われる場所（支店，工場，鉱山その他の事業所）を有する個人が国内及び国外の双方にわたって事業を営む場合には，国外の事業所に帰属する外国事業の所得金額は事業税の課税対象とはされない。

この場合，所得金額の総額から国外の事業に帰属する所得を分割することが困難な場合には，納税者は従業員数で按分して計算する。なお，国内所得について外国の租税が課された場合には，その税額は必要経費に算入される。

(5) 所得税法上認められている次の課税の取扱いは，事業税の課税所得の算定上では認められない（地法72の49の8）。

(i) 青色申告者である場合の青色申告控除

(ii) 青色申告者である場合の家族従事者に対する支払給与の控除（¶5-160(3)(a)参照）

なお，個人事業税における事業専従者控除は，青色申告者については所得税で青色専従者給与として認められた金額，白色申告者については専従者1人につき50万円（配偶者の場合は86万円）と事業所得の金額を専従者の数に1を加えた数で除した額のうち，いずれか低い金額である（地法72の49の8）。

(iii) 青色申告者である場合の損失の繰戻し（¶5-280参照）

(iv) 土地の譲渡に係る事業所得の分離課税（¶5-550参照）

828   LOCAL TAX etc.

land or other property (see ¶ 5-550);

(v)   payment from the social insurance medical foundation etc.

¶ 9-440 Return and payment

The taxpayer is required to file a return with the prefectural tax office for the area in which his head office is located by March 15 of the tax year.

For taxpayers who have offices or places of business in more than one prefecture, each prefecture levies enterprise tax on such individuals by prorating the total tax amount on the basis of the number of employees in each prefecture. The taxpayer is required to file a return with the prefectural tax office for the area in which the head office is located by March 15 of the tax year, unless a return for assessment income tax has already been filed with a national tax office (Law 72-55).

Enterprise tax on individuals must be paid in equal instalments twice a year, in August and November of each tax year, on receipt of notification from the prefecture (Law 72-51). If the business is terminated during a given year, a taxpayer is required to file a tax return within one month from the date of discontinuance.

Corporation Enterprise Tax

¶ 9-460 Taxpayer

(1)   Corporate enterprise tax is levied on all corporations (different from individual enterprise tax), except those which engage in agriculture or mining (Law 72-2).

(2)   The tax is levied by the prefecture tax office for the area where the head office, branch office, factory or other kind of business place (permanent establishment) of the corporation is located. Accordingly, corporations which have their office or fixed place of business in two or more prefectures should pay the enterprise tax to each prefecture (Law 72-48).

(3)   Foreign corporations with property in Japan but which do not carry on business in Japan are not subject to enterprise tax (Law 72-2).

(4)   Non-juridical organizations which have representatives or managers and operate profit-making business, are deemed to be corporations and are taxed corporate enterprise tax.

Public interest corporations (see ¶ 6-040) are taxed on those profits ac-

¶ 9-440

⒱　社会保険診療報酬の収入金額

¶9-440　申告及び納付
　二以上の道府県に事務所又は事業所を有する個人事業者については，これらの所在する道府県から従業員数に応じて按分された個人事業税が課される。納税者は，税務署長に対して所得税の確定申告書を提出している場合を除き，課税年の３月15日までに主たる事務所の所在地の道府県知事に対して申告書を提出しなければならない（地法72の55）。
　個人事業税は，道府県からの通知に基づき，その年の８月と11月の２回に分けて均等額を納付しなければならない（地法72の51）。
　なお，年の中途において事業を廃止した場合には，廃止から１月以内に申告書を提出しなければならない。

法人事業税

¶9-460　納税義務者
⑴　法人事業税は，農業，鉱業及び林業の例外を除き，すべての事業（この点において個人事業税と異なる。）を行う法人に課税される（地法72の２）。

⑵　この税は，法人の本店事務所，支店事務所，工場その他の事業所（恒久的施設）の所在する道府県により課税される。
　したがって，二以上の道府県に事務所又は事業所を設けて事業を行う法人には，それぞれの道府県に事業税を分割して納付しなければならない（地法72の48）。

⑶　ただし，外国法人で単に日本国内に資産を有するのみで事業を行わないものは事業税の納税義務者とはならない（地法72の２）。
⑷　法人でない社団又は財団で代表者又は管理人の定めがあり，かつ，収益事業を営むものは法人とみなされ，法人事業税の規定が適用される。公益法人は収益事業からの所得について課税され非収益事業からの所得については課税されない（地法72の２）。

830   LOCAL TAX etc.

cruing from profit-making business, but not on other income (Law 72-2).

¶ 9-480 Tax base and tax rate (Law 72-24-7, LCS 2)

Standard corporate enterprise tax rates are as follows.

(1) Corporations doing business as electric power suppliers, gas suppliers
or insurers.. 0.9% of their gross proceeds

(2) Other corporations:

(a) Ordinary corporations with capital amounts over ¥100,000,000

The income up to ¥4,000,000 annually	1.6%
The income over ¥4,000,000 and up to 8,000,000 annually	2.3%
The income over ¥8,000,000 annually	3.1%
Per value added	0.72%
Per capital	0.3%

Note:
After the year 2015, tax rate will be reduced in accordance with expansion of size-based corporation tax.

The year 2014	4.3%
Current	3.1%
After the year 2016	0.7%

(2015 tax reform)
(see ¶9-570)

(b) Ordinary corporations with capital amounts of ¥100,000,000 or less

The income up to ¥4,000,000 annually	3.4%
The income over ¥4,000,000 and up to ¥8,000,000 annually	5.1%
The income over ¥8,000,000 annually	6.7%

(c) Special corporations

The income up to ¥4,000,000 annually	3.4%
The income over ¥4,000,000 annually	4.6%

Note:
1. The above rates are standard rates; prefectures may tax up to a ceiling of 110% above standard rates.
2. "Income" means ordinary income and liquidation income (see ¶ 6-005).
3. Corporations with capital amounts of ¥10,000,000 or more and offices or factories located in three or more prefectures are not allowed to apply to preferential tax rate.

(3) Donation credits (so called enterprise hometown tax payment)

In case of donation to certain projects listed in a plan certified under the Local Revitalization Act, the specific amount (10% of donated amount, up to 20% [15% after the year 2017] of Corporation Enterprise Tax) can be deducted from the Corporation Enterprise Tax (2016 tax

¶ 9-480

地 方 税 等　831

¶9-480　課税標準及び税率（地法72の24の7，地法特2）

法人事業税の標準税率は次のとおりである。

(1)　電気供給業，ガス供給業及び保険業を営む法人にあっては，収入金額の0.9%

(2)　その他の事業を営む法人

(a)　資本金の額又は出資金の額1億円超の普通法人の所得割の標準税率

年400万円以下の所得	1.6%
年400万円超年800万円以下	2.3%
年800万円超の所得及び清算所得	3.1%
付加価値割の税率	0.72%
資本割の税率	0.3%

(注)：平成27年度以降外形標準課税の拡大に伴い法人事業税の所得割の税率が引き下げられる。

平成26年度	4.3%
現行	3.1%
平成28年度以降	0.7%

（平成27年度税制改正）

（¶9-570参照）

(b)　資本金1億円以下の普通法人等の所得割の標準税率

年400万円以下の所得	3.4%
年400万円超年800万円以下	5.1%
年800万円超の所得及び清算所得	6.7%

(c)　特別法人の所得割の標準税率

年400万円以下の所得	3.4%
年400万円超の所得及び清算所得	4.6%

(注)：1．上記の税率は標準税率であり，道府県はその税率の110%相当の制限税率により課税し得る。

2．「所得」とは，通常の所得及び清算所得（¶6-005参照）を示す。

3．3以上の都道府県に事務所又は事業所を設けて事業を行う法人のうち資本金1,000万円以上であるものの所得割に係る税率については，軽減税率の適用はない。

(3)　寄附金控除（いわゆる企業版ふるさと納税）

地方公共団体が行う認定地方創生事業に対する寄附金額の一部（寄附金額の10%，税額の20%（平成29年度以降は15%）を上限）が税額控除されることとされた（平成28年度税制改正）。

832   LOCAL TAX etc.

reform).

¶ 9-500 Gross proceeds taxation

(1) Taxable gross proceeds of electric power suppliers or gas suppliers are the gross proceeds from their business after deducting government subsidies, capital gains from fixed assets, insurance received, and dividends or capital gain from stocks (Law 72-24-2).

(2) Taxable gross proceeds of life insurers or damages insurers are computed on the gross proceeds from their gross premiums received multiplied by a specified percentage based on the kind of insurance, for example, 24% in case of individual insurance and 25% in case of vessel insurance (Law 72-24-2).

¶ 9-520 Income taxation

(1) Income subject to enterprise tax is the ordinary income or liquidation income in each accounting period as per corporation tax laws and special tax measures, with some exceptions. Accordingly, privileges of blue return is applicable (¶ 6-056), and the undistributed profits of foreign corporations (tax haven counter measure, ¶ 6-195) are taxed in the same way as under corporation tax laws (Law 72-12, 72-23).

(2) The main differences between enterprise tax and corporation tax with regard to the tax base are as follows:

(a) Enterprise tax is levied on "ordinary income" and "liquidation income". However, in addition to those forms of income, "undistributed profits" of domestic corporations and "approved pension funds" are subject to tax for corporation tax purposes (¶ 6-005).

(b) When a Japanese domestic corporation has a permanent establishment abroad, the portion of its profit which is attributable to that permanent establishment is excluded from the tax basis for enterprise tax, but is not excluded for the purpose of corporation tax.

(c) Enterprise tax can be deducted in computing taxable income or taxable profits for both corporation tax and enterprise tax purposes in the following business year, but corporation tax is not so deductible.

(d) For electric power suppliers, gas suppliers and insurance businesses, the net profits system of taxation is not used. Instead, the gross proceeds are taken as the tax basis for enterprise tax.

¶ 9-500

地　方　税　等　833

¶9–500　収入金額課税

(1)　電気供給業及びガス供給業の課税収入金額は，事業からの収入金額の総額から政府からの補助金，固定資産の売却による収入金額，保険金，受取利息，受取配当，有価証券の売却による収入金額その他の収入金額を控除した金額である（地法72の24の2）。

(2)　生命保険又は損害保険事業の課税収入金額は，受取収入保険料である収入金額から保険の区分に応じた一定割合，例えば，生命保険24％，船舶保険25％，を乗じて算定する（地法72の24の2）。

¶9–520　所得金額課税

(1)　事業税の所得は，若干の例外はあるものの原則として法人税法及び租税特別措置法上の各事業年度の通常の所得及び清算所得である。

したがって，青色申告の特典（¶6–056）はそのまま事業税における所得の計算に適用され，外国会社の留保金額（タックスヘイブン対策税制）は法人税法と同じく課税される（地法72の12, 72の23）。

(2)　課税標準に関する事業税と法人税の主要な相違点は，次のとおりである。

　(a)　事業税は，各事業年度の所得及び清算所得に対して課税される。しかしながら，法人税の場合には，これらのもの以外に，留保金額及び適格退職年金積立額に対しても課税される（¶6–005）。

　(b)　日本の内国法人が国外に恒久的施設を有する場合には，その恒久的施設に帰属する所得は，事業税の課税標準の計算上は除外されるが，法人税の計算上は除外されない。

　(c)　事業税の額は，法人税及び事業税の課税標準の計算上は翌事業年度において損金に算入されるが，法人税の額は損金に算入されない。

　(d)　電気供給業，ガス供給業，保険業については，事業税の課税標準として純利益課税方式は採られておらず，これに代えて，収入金額がとられている。

834   LOCAL TAX etc.

(e) Deductions for overseas technical service transactions (¶ 6-530), and/ or overseas investment loss reserves (¶ 6-395), are not applicable.

(f) Gross income from the social insurance fund is not subject to enterprise tax.

(g) Carrying back of net losses is not allowed.

(h) Foreign tax credit is not allowed. Foreign taxes levied on Japanese sourced income are deductible from taxable income.

¶ 9-540 Division basis for two or more prefectures

Corporations which have their offices or factories in two or more prefectures should file a return for prefecture tax to the tax authorities in the area where both the offices and the factories are located. Enterprise tax is payable to each prefecture by prorating the income applied to each bracket on the basis of both the number of employees and offices or factories (Law 72-48).

Instead of the basis of both the number of employees and offices or factories, the basis of the value of fixed assets is applied for electric power, gas supply, warehousing and railroad business.

In case of a manufacturing company with capital amounting to ¥100 million or more, the number of factory employees multiplied by 1.5.

Example for a non-manufacturing business is as follows:

1. Conditions

	number		taxable income
	employees	offices	
Office A	50	1	X
Total	100	10	1,000

2. Calculation

$$X = \left[1,000 \times \frac{1}{2} \times \frac{50 \text{ employees}}{100 \text{ employees}} \right] + \left[1,000 \times \frac{1}{2} \times \frac{1 \text{ office}}{10 \text{ offices}} \right]$$

$$X = 300 \text{ (taxable income of office A)}$$

Note:
"Employees" means the number of persons who receive salary or wages or similar payments from the corporation.

¶ 9-540

地　方　税　等　835

(e)　技術等海外取引に係る所得の特別控除（¶6-530），海外投資等損失準備金（¶6-395）は適用されない。

(f)　社会保険診療報酬基金からの収入金額は事業税の対象とならない。

(g)　欠損金の繰戻還付の適用はない。

(h)　外国税額控除の適用はない。しかし，国内源泉所得に課された外国税額については，損金算入する。

¶9-540　二以上の道府県に対する分割基準

　二以上の道府県に事務所，工場等を有する法人は，従業員数及び事務所数などの比によりその課税標準額を分割し，これに基づいて算出した税額を各道府県に対して申告納付しなければならない（地法72の48）。

　しかしながら，電気供給業，ガス供給業，倉庫業，鉄道事業にあっては，この従業員数及び事務所数に基づく按分計算方式は，固定資産の価額等の方式に置き替えられる。

　また，資本金1億円以上で製造業を営む法人にあっては，工場の従業員数を1.5倍する。

　非製造業の場合の計算例

1．状　況

| | 数 | | 課税所得 |
	従業員	事務所	
A事務所	50	1	X
合　　計	100	10	1,000

2．計算式

$$X = (1{,}000 \times \frac{1}{2}) \times \frac{50人}{100人} + (1{,}000 \times \frac{1}{2}) \times \frac{1事務所}{10事務所}$$

$$= 300円　（A事務所の課税所得）$$

　(注)：従業員数とは，法人から給料，賃金その他これに類する給付を受けている者の数をいう。

836   LOCAL TAX etc.

¶ 9-560 Return and payment

As with corporation tax, a corporation is required to file a final return for enterprise tax within two months after the end of its business year, whether or not it has a positive income for that business year.

An extension for filing an enterprise tax return is allowed for a corporation, whose corporate tax return is allowed, subjected to the approval of the relevant prefecture (Law 72-25, 72-28).

A corporation whose business year is longer than six months should file an interim return at the end of the six months of the business year. The tax reported on the interim return should be paid to a prefecture tax office before the limit for filing the interim return (Law 72-26).

The tax amount described on the return must be paid to the prefectural tax office for the area in which the office or the fixed place of business is located by due date to file (Law 72-25, 72-26, 72-28).

¶ 9-570 Size-based corporate taxation

A corporation with capital exceeding ¥100,000,000 is subjected to a size-based corporate taxation designed to cover 1/4 of corporation enterprise tax revenue (Law 72-2).

(1) Tax base consists of profits, capitals and other value added items such as wages, interest and rentals (Law 72-12, 72-14 to 72-24).

(2) Special measures to reduce tax burden for corporations with high proportion of wages in their value added and those with significant amount of capital are taken.

(3) Tax rates are as follows:

Per income   : 1.6% to 3.1% (¶ 9-480)
Per value added   : 0.72%
Per capital   : 0.3%

Note:
Size-based corporate taxation will be expanded to twice in this coming two years (2015 tax reform).

¶ 9-560

地　方　税　等　837

¶9-560　申告及び納付

　法人税と同様に，法人はその事業年度の所得金額が赤字であっても，当該事業年度終了後 2 カ月以内に事業税の確定申告書を提出しなければならない。また，法人税法の規定により申告期限の延長を認められる法人については，道府県知事の承認を得て法人事業税の延長が認められる（地法72の25，72の28）。

　事業年度の期間が 6 カ月を超える法人にあっては，当該事業年度の開始の日以後 6 カ月を経過した日までの期間について中間申告書を提出しなければならない（地法72の26）。

　申告書に記載された事業税額は，当該申告書の提出期限までに事務所又は事業所所在地の道府県へ納付しなければならない（地法72の25，72の26，72の28）。

¶9-570　外形標準課税

　資本金 1 億円超の法人を対象として，外形基準の割合を 4 分の 1 とする外形標準課税制度が適用される（地法72の 2 ）。

(1)　課税標準は所得金額のほか，資本等，付加価値額，の金額である（地法72-12，72-14〜72-24）。
(2)　報酬給与額が多額な法人に対しては税負担の軽減を図る措置がとられている。

(3)　税率は以下のとおりである。
　　所得割　　：1.6％〜3.1％（¶9-480）
　　付加価値割：0.72％
　　資本割　　：0.3％

　（注）：外形標準課税は 2 年間で 2 倍に拡大される（平成27年度税制改正）。

838   LOCAL TAX etc.

The year 2014

per value added 0.48%	per income 7.2%*
per capital 0.2%	

1   :   3

Current

per value added 0.72%	per income 6.0%*
per capital 0.3%	

3   :   5

After the year 2016

per value added 1.2%	per income 3.6%*
per capital 0.5%	

5   :   3

*included local special corporate tax.

Fixed Assets Tax (City Planning Tax)

¶ 9-580 Taxpayer

Fixed assets tax is paid on land, buildings, ships, aircraft or any other kind of depreciable assets by the registered owner as of January 1 of each year (Law 341, 343). "Registered owner" means the person registered as the owner of the property in the registration book maintained by a national juridical office.

Accordingly, if a person had sold land to a third person but had not changed its registration before January 1 of the relevant year, the old owner is liable for payment of this tax.

Automobiles or other vehicles which are subject to automobile tax or light automobile tax are not subject to this tax.

¶ 9-600 Tax entity

Fixed assets tax is levied by the municipality (town, city) on property

¶ 9-580

地　方　税　等　839

平成26年度

付加価値割 0.48%	所得割 7.2%＊
資本割 0.2%	

1　：　3

現行

付加価値割 0.72%	所得割 6.0%＊
資本割 0.3%	

3　：　5

平成28年度以降

付加価値割 1.2%	所得割 3.6%＊
資本割 0.5%	

5　：　3

＊地方法人特別税を含む。

固定資産税（都市計画税）

¶9–580　納税義務者

　固定資産税は，土地，家屋，船舶，航空機及びその他の減価償却資産について，各年の1月1日現在の所有名義人に対して課税される（地法341，343）。「所有名義人」とは，登記所の登記簿上の当該資産の所有者として登記されている者をいう。

　したがって，土地等を第三者へ売却し，当該年度の1月1日前までに所有権移転登記していない場合には，旧所有者が納税義務者となる。

　しかし，自動車税及び軽自動車税の対象となる自動車及びその他の車両については課税対象とされない。

¶9–600　課税主体

　固定資産税は，原則として固定資産（課税資産）の所在する市町村が課す

840   LOCAL TAX etc.

located in the municipality (Law 342).

Large scale depreciable assets tax is levied by the municipality and the prefecture according to the tax base for this tax. For example, in the case of a municipality having a population of 200,000 or more, that part of the tax base of 4,000,000,000 yen or under is taxed by the municipality and amounts over 4,000,000,000 yen are taxed by the prefecture (Law 349-4, 740).

¶ 9-620 Taxable fixed assets

Fixed assets tax is levied on all kinds of land, buildings (houses, shops, factories, electricity generating plants, warehouses (excluding gardens)). The following are treated as depreciable assets (Law 341):

(1)   assets used for business;

(2)   tangible assets excluding trees;

(3)   assets that are subject to depreciation for the corporation or the individual income tax purposes (¶ 6-265).

However, minor assets are not subject to property tax, provided that acquisition cost is immediately deducted as expenses in the business year of acquisition.

Buildings for a school, church, shrine or temple are not taxable.

¶ 9-640 Tax base — general rules

The tax base for fixed assets tax is fair market value. In practice, land or buildings are taxed on the basis of their value assessed by the municipality. Municipalities appraise the fair market value of land and buildings every three years (Law 341).

The fair market value of land is evaluated on the basis of the comparison to the real dealing price method; the fair market value of a building is evaluated on the basis of the rebuilding price method.

2018 is the year for new appraisal (Law 349). The appraisal value of 2018 will be continued in 2019 and 2020. However, simple modification of this appraisal value in 2019 and 2020 was accepted under the introduction of special treatment.

Municipalities determine new appraisal values according to the result of field audits by appraisal members, and the comparative method for the dealing price of similar assets.

The assets' values are registered in the fixed assets register book (Law 404 to 411).

¶ 9-620

地　方　税　等　841

る（地法342）。

　大規模の償却資産は一の納税義務者が所有するこの税の課税標準額に従っ
て市町村とその市町村を包括する道府県によって課税される。例えば，人口
200,000人以上の市にあっては，課税標準額が40億円以下の部分については
市により，40億円を超える部分の金額についてはその市を包括する道府県に
より，課税される（地法349の4，740）。

¶9-620　課税固定資産

　固定資産税は，納税義務者が毎年1月1日（賦課期日）現在において所有
しているすべての土地，家屋（住家，店舗，工場，発電所，倉庫を含み，庭
園を除く。）及び次の償却資産（構築物，機械装置，車両，工具，器具，備
品等）に対して課される（地法341）。
　(1)　事業の用に供している資産であること
　(2)　有形資産であること
　(3)　法人税法及び所得税法上減価償却の対象となる資産であること（¶6-
　　　265）
　ただし，一括損金算入した少額資産については固定資産税の対象となる資
産ではない。
　しかし，学校，教会，神社，寺院の建物は非課税とされる。

¶9-640　課税標準（原則）

　固定資産税の課税標準は適正な時価である。実務上では，土地，家屋につ
いては市町村の定める評価額に基づいて課税される。市町村は3年に一度，
土地及び建物の評価額を改訂する（地法341）。
　土地の適正な時価は売買実例価格を基準とし，家屋の適正な時価は再建築
価格を基準として評価される。
　平成30年度は基準年度に当たるので新評価額が決められる（地法349）。
　基準年度（平成30年度）の価格は3年間据え置くこととされているが，平
成31年度及び平成32年度には，簡易な方法により価格の修正ができるとされ
ている。
　土地及び家屋については，市町村の固定資産評価員が実地調査した結果に
基づいて，類似資産の価格に比準する価格により新価格が決められる。
　市町村は基準年度の3月末日までに課税台帳に評価額を登録する（地法404
～411）。
　納税義務者は毎年4月1日から20日までの間市町村役場においてその新評
価額が登録された固定資産課税台帳を縦覧することができる（地法416）。納
税義務者がその評価額に不服がある場合には，市町村役場へ審査の申出をす

842   LOCAL TAX etc.

Taxpayers can see the fixed assets register book on new appraisal values from April 1 to April 20 of each year in the municipality office (Law 416). If a taxpayer is not satisfied with the assessed value, the taxpayer may request the municipality office to reinvestigate the assessed value (Law 432).

Depreciable assets are not subject to registration, and taxpayers should file returns containing their appraisal value of their own assets by January 31 of the assessment year (Law 383). The municipality may determine the appraisal value on the basis of acquisition price according to the result of audits by appraisal members by the end of March of the assessment year (Law 410).

¶ 9-660 Tax base as exception

(1) Land for residential use

The tax base, that is, the taxable value of land for residential use is one-third (for fixed assets tax purpose) and two-thirds (for city planning tax purpose) of the appraisal value determined above (Law 349-3-2, 702-3).

(2) Small land for residential use

The taxable value of land of up to 200 m^2 is one-sixth (for fixed assets tax purpose) and one-third (for city planning tax purpose) of the appraisal value determined as mentioned above (Law 349-3-2, 702-3).

(3) Specified depreciable assets

The taxable value of vessels for international service, for example, is one-sixth or one-fifth of the appraisal value (Law 349-3).

(4) Newly constructed housing

The tax amount of newly constructed housing (constructed before March 31, 2020) of specified squares or prices is reduced by one-half over three years (LS 15-6).

(5) Newly constructed high buildings

The tax amount of newly constructed buildings (constructed before March 31, 2020) having three or more floors for housing is reduced by one-half over five years (LS 15-6).

(6) House improvement for free of barriers

When a qualified resident finishes making home improvements to make houses free of barriers from April 1, 2007 to December 31, 2020, by taking a specified procedure, the tax amount of housing with a free of barriers is reduced by one-third on the year following the year of completion of home improvement (LS 15-9).

¶ 9-660

ることができる（地法432）。

　他方，償却資産については登記の対象とならず，所有資産について１月31日までに評価額に関する申告書を提出しなければならない（地法383）。市町村は固定資産評価額の実地調査の結果を考慮し，取得価額を基準として評価額を３月末日までに決定する（地法410）。

¶9-660　課税標準の特例

(1)　住宅用地

　専ら個人の居住の用に供する家屋の敷地に対する固定資産税の課税標準は上記評価額の３分の１の額とされ，都市計画税の課税標準は，上記評価額の３分の２の額とされる（地法349の３の２，702の３）。

(2)　小規模住宅用地

　住居１戸の住宅用地が200㎡以下の場合には，固定資産税の課税標準は上記評価額の６分の１の額とされ，都市計画税の課税標準は，上記評価額の３分の１の額とされる（地法349の３の２，702の３）。

(3)　特殊な償却資産

　例えば，外航船舶については評価額の６分の１及び５分の１の額が課税標準とされる（地法349の３）。

(4)　新築住宅

　一定の要件を満たしている新築住宅（平成32年３月31日までに新築されたもの）に係る税額は３年度間２分の１に軽減される（地法附15の６）。

(5)　中高層耐火住宅

　新築の地上階数３以上の中高層耐火住宅（平成32年３月31日までに新築されたもの）に係る税額は５年度間２分の１に軽減される（地法附15の６）。

(6)　バリアフリー改修工事を行った住宅

　一定の居住者が，その者の居住の用に供する家屋について一定のバリアフリー改修工事を平成19年４月１日から平成32年12月31日までの間に完了したときは，一定の手続により，当該住宅に係る固定資産税の税額を３分の１減額する（地法附15の９）。

844   LOCAL TAX etc.

(7) Adjustment of proportional allotment on very tall buildings for residential use

After April 2017, proportional allotment on condominium of newly built and sold very tall buildings (more than 60 meter high) will be revised according to the trend of transaction prices; higher tax burden for high floors lower for lower floors (Law 352-2).

¶ 9-680 Tax burden adjustment

Increases in land dealing prices in recent years were remarkable, and taxpayers would have had difficulty paying this tax based on the market value of the land located in the Tokyo, Osaka or Nagoya areas. As a result, municipalities have adopted an assessment value which is different from the appraisal value. This system is called the "tax burden adjustment". These adjustment measures are described below.

To prevent a rapid increase in tax liabilities, a maximum amount for the fixed assets tax and the city planning tax on land for residential use from 2006 is computed by multiplying the previous year's tax amount by the tax burden adjustment ratio, which is stipulated in accordance with the percentage of the previous year's appraisal value to the given year's (LS 17 and others).

(1) Land for commercial use

Tax burden level*	Burden adjustment rate Tax base amount
Over 70%	70% Market value × 70%
60% or more, 70% or less	100% Tax base amount of previous year × 100%
Less than 60%	Tax base amount of previous year + current year value × 5% However, tax base amount of current year is more than 60% of current year market value, current year tax base amount comes to 60% of current year market value and if current year market base amount is less than 20% of current year market value, current year tax base amount comes to 20% of current year market value.

* Tax burden level is computed as follows.
= Previous year tax base amount / Current year value × 1/6 (1/3)

¶ 9-680

(7) タワーマンションの税額負担の調整

　平成29年4月以降に売買契約が始まる60メートル以上の新築タワーマンションの税額按分方法を取引価額の傾向に応じ，高層階は高額に低層階は低額となるよう調整する（地法352の2）。

¶9-680　負担調整措置

　最近土地の取引価格の高騰が著しいため，東京，大阪及び名古屋圏に所在する土地の時価評価額に基づいて固定資産税を納付する納税者は負担が過大なものとなっている。

　そこで，市町村は評価額とは異なる課税標準を採用しており，この措置を「租税負担調整措置」と呼んでいる。

　この負担調整措置の内容は次のとおりである。

　租税負担の急激な増加を防止する見地から，平成18年度から宅地等に係る固定資産税の額は，前年度課税標準額の当該年度の評価額に対する割合の区分に応じて定める次表に掲げる負担調整率を前年度の税額に乗じて求めた額を限度とするものである（地法附17ほか）。

(1)　商業地

負　担　水　準　の　区　分	負　担　調　整　率
70％超	70％ 価格×70％
60％以上70％以下	100％ 前年度課税標準額×100％
60％未満	前年度の課税標準額に，当該年度の評価額の5％を加えた額を課税標準とする。 ただし，当該額が，評価額の60％を上回る場合には，60％相当額とし，評価額の20％を下回る場合には20％相当額とする。

　「負担水準」は，以下の算式により求められる。

＝前年度課税標準額／当該年度価格

846   LOCAL TAX etc.

(2) Land for residential use

Adjustment for tax burden will be continuously taken for 3 years in accordance with increase ratio (introduced by 2015 tax reform).

Tax burden level*	Burden adjustment
100% or more	No adjustment Market value × 1/6 (1/3)
90% or more	Previous year tax base amount + current year market value × 1/3(1/6) × 5% However, if tax base amount of current year is more than one third (or one-sixth) of current year market value, current year tax base comes to one-third (or
Less than 90%	one-sixth) of current year market value and if tax base amount of current year is less than 20% of one-third (or one-sixth) of current year market value, current year tax base comes to 20% of one-third (or one-sixth) of current year market value.

* Tax burden level is computed as follows.

= Previous year tax base amount / Current year value × 1/6 (1/3)

(3) Land for farm land

Adjustment for tax burden will be continuously taken in accordance with increase ratio as same as current base.

Note:

1. The above ratios for land for residential use are also applicable to farm land located in the city planning zones of Tokyo, Osaka or Nagoya.

2. For other farm land, the following tax burden adjustment ratio is applied from 2009 to 2011 (LS 19).

Tax burden level*	Burden adjustment rate
90% or more	102.5%
80% or more, less than 90%	105%
70% or more, less than 80%	107.5%
Less than 70%	110%

* Tax burden level is computed as follows.

= Previous year tax base amount / Current year value

3. Various temporary measures are applied.

¶ 9-700 Tax rate

The standard annual tax rate is 1.4% (Law 350).

Fixed assets tax is not levied if a taxpayer owns less than the following amount of fixed assets located in the same municipality (Law 351):

¶ 9-700

地　方　税　等　847

(2)　住宅用地

　負担水準に応じた負担調整措置を3年延長する（平成27年度税制改正）。

負担水準の区分	負　担　調　整
100％以上	本則課税標準額 （価格×1／6又は1／3）
90％以上	前年度の課税標準額に，本則課税標準額の5％を加えた額を課税標準とする。 ただし，当該額が，本則課税標準額を上回る場合には本則課税標準額相当額とし，本則課税標準額の20％を下回る場合には20％相当額とする。
90％未満	

　「負担水準」は，以下の算式により求められる。

＝前年度課税標準額／当該年度価格×1／6（1／3）

(3)　農地

　一般農地に対する固定資産税の負担調整措置は，現行と同様とする（下記（注）参照）。

　(注)：1．東京，大阪及び名古屋都市圏の市街化区域農地については上記宅地等に係る負担調整率を適用する。

　　　　2．その他の農地については平成21年度以降平成23年度までの固定資産税及び都市計画税について次の負担調整率を適用する（地法附19）。

負 担 水 準 の 区 分	負担調整率
90％以上	102.5％
80％以上90％未満	105％
70％以上80％未満	107.5％
70％未満	110％

　　　　　「負担水準」は，以下の算式により求められる。

　　　　　＝前年度課税標準額／当該年度価格

　　　　3．その他種々の経過措置が設けられている。

¶9-700　税率

　標準税率は1.4％である（地法350）。

　同一市町村の区域内に同一人が所有する固定資産税の課税標準額が次の額未満の場合には，固定資産税が免除される（地法351）。

848   LOCAL TAX etc.

Land	300,000 yen
Buildings	200,000 yen
Depreciable assets	1,500,000 yen

¶ 9-720 Payment

The fixed assets tax is paid in four installments in April, July and December of the taxation year, and February of the following year.

¶ 9-730 Information disclosure system on Fixed assets tax (City planing tax)

In line with an introduction of Information disclosure system on fixed assets tax (City planning tax), leaseholder or tenants can read the amount of fixed assets tax (City planning tax) of land or house they are leasing.

¶ 9-740 City planning tax

The city planning tax is levied on land and buildings located in an area, where a city planning scheme is in effect, as an additional tax to the fixed assets tax.

The tax rate is 0.3% of the value of the land and buildings (Law 702-4).

Enterprise Establishment Tax

¶ 9-760 Tax authority

Enterprise establishment tax is levied by large cities such as Tokyo, Osaka, Nagoya, Hiroshima, Fukuoka, Sapporo, Sendai, Yokohama, Kawasaki, Kyoto, Kobe, Kitakyuushu and other cities with a population of more than 300,000 and designated by Cabinet order.

The revenue from this tax is assigned to special aid of the cities (Law 701-30, 701-31).

¶ 9-780 Taxpayer

The taxpayer is the person who carries on business in an enterprise establishment located in one of the tax entities mentioned above, and the building contractor for newly built enterprise establishments located in the tax entities (Law 701-32).

地　方　税　等　849

　　土地　30万円：家屋　20万円：償却資産　150万円

¶9-720　納付
　固定資産税は課税年度の 4 月, 7 月及び12月並びに翌年度の 2 月に 4 分割して納付する（地法362）。

¶9-730　情報開示制度
　固定資産税の情報開示制度が整備され，借地人・借家人が固定資産税や都市計画税を閲覧することができる。

¶9-740　都市計画税
　都市計画税は固定資産税の付加税として，市街化区域に所在する土地及び家屋に対して課税される。
　年税率は土地及び家屋の評価額の0.3％である（地法702の 4 ）。

事　業　所　税

¶9-760　課税主体
　事業所税は東京，大阪，名古屋，広島，福岡，札幌，仙台，横浜，川崎，京都，神戸，北九州などの大都市及び人口30万人以上の政令指定都市により課税される。
　この税の収入は市の特別財源に充てられる（地法701の30, 701の31）。

¶9-780　納税義務者
　納税義務者は上記課税主体区域内に所在する事業所を設けて事業を営む者及び新築の事業所の建築主である（地法701の32）。

850   LOCAL TAX etc.

¶ 9-800 Tax base and tax rate

The tax amounts consist of:

(a) an assets levy of 600 yen per square metre of floor space; and

(b) a number of employees levy of 0.25% of the gross wage amounts paid by the enterprise (Law 701-40, 701-42).

When the floor space is not more than 1,000m^2 or the number of employees is not more than 100 persons, the establishment is free from this tax.

The tax amounts are calculated per calendar year for individual enterprises, and per business year for corporate enterprises.

"Number of employees" includes directors, and excludes employees aged 60 years or more. However, the age of excluded employees will be increased step by step.

¶ 9-820 Exemptions and deductions

Buildings for schools, hospitals, kindergartens, employee's dormitories or welfare facilities and electricity generating plant are exempt from this tax.

Buildings for hotels, inns and agricultural cooperatives are levied one-half of the tax amounts mentioned above (Law 701-41).

¶ 9-840 Return and payments

When the buildings are already established, corporations are required to file a return and pay the tax amounts within two months after the end of the business year. Individuals are required to file a return and pay the tax amounts by March 15 of the following year (Law 701-46, 701-47).

¶ 9-800

地　方　税　等　851

¶9-800　課税標準及び税率

税額は次の合計額である（地法701の40，701の42）。

(a)　資産割…床面積 1 平方メートル当たり600円

(b)　従業者数割…当該企業の支払給与総額の0.25％

　　　　ただし，床面積が1,000平方メートル以下の場合又は従業者数が100人以下の場合には，資産割又は従業者数割が免除される（地法701の40，701の42）。

事業所税の税額は個人事業者については暦年，法人事業者については事業年度により計算され，「従業者」には役員を含み，60歳以上の従業者を除くこととしている。ただし，その年齢を段階的に引き上げることとしている。

¶9-820　免除及び軽減

学校，病院，幼稚園，社員寮，社員厚生施設及び発電所用の建物は事業所税が非課税とされる。ホテル，旅館，農業協同組合用の建物は上記税額の 2 分の 1 相当額が課税される（地法701の41）。

¶9-840　申告及び納付

建物が既設のものである場合には，法人事業者は事業年度終了後 2 カ月以内に申告書を提出し，納付しなければならないし，個人事業者については翌年 3 月15日までに申告書を提出し，納付しなければならない（地法701の46，701の47）。

852   LOCAL TAX etc.

Social Insurance
(General Principle as of April 1, 2018)

¶ 9-860 Health insurance and employees' pension insurance

The social insurance program in Japan consists of medical care insurance, pension insurance and labor insurance.

Medical care insurance is divided into Health Insurance for employees and National Health Insurance for the self-employed. Pension insurance is likewise divided into Employees' Pension Insurance for employees and National Pension Insurance for the self-employed (those who take part in the employees' pension scheme at the same time join the national pension scheme by way of a basic pension).

For labor insurance see ¶ 9-880.

Health Insurance is a system of paying medical care benefits and allowances to the employees of business firms and their families when they are taken ill or are injured, give birth to babies, or die.

The Employees' Pension Insurance System aims to guarantee a stable life to the employees of firms and their families by paying them benefits when the employees retire, are disabled due to illness or injury, or in the event of their death.

Every individual who meets the prescribed conditions is expected to participate in these systems as an insured person, regardless of nationality.

(1) **Covered place of work**

The Health Insurance and the Employees' Pension Insurance are applied to the employees at their respective places of work, such as companies and factories. The establishment to which the insurance systems are applied is referred to as a "covered place of work". Private enterprises regularly employing more than five employees are compulsorily covered places of work, and are obliged to join the systems.

Any establishment run by a juridical person is compulsorily covered by the systems if it regularly employs one or more workers.

These places of work are responsible for the procedures for participation and for the payment of premiums.

All employees of the covered place of work are expected to join the systems and become insured persons (over 75 years of age under the Health Insurance and over 70 years of age under the Employees' Pension

¶ 9-860

地　方　税　等　853

社　会　保　険
（平成30年 4 月 1 日現在の一般原則）

¶9-860　健康保険及び厚生年金保険

　日本の社会保険制度は医療保険，年金保険及び労働保険から成り立っている。

　医療保険はさらに被用者対象の健康保険と自営業者対象の国民健康保険に分かれ，同様に年金保険も被用者対象の厚生年金保険と自営業者対象の国民年金に分かれる（なお，「基礎年金」の関係では厚生年金の加入者が同時に国民年金の加入者でもあるという仕組みになっている。）。

　ここでは，健康保険と厚生年金保険を取り上げることとする。また労働保険については後で述べる（¶9-880）。

　健康保険は会社などで働く人及びその家族が病気にかかったりけがをしたとき，あるいは出産，死亡といった事態が起こったときに必要な医療給付を行ったり，手当金を支給したりするものである。

　また，厚生年金保険は同じく会社で働く人の退職（老齢），障害，死亡，などの事故に対して給付を行うことによって本人や家族の生活の安定を図ることを目的としている。

　一定の条件に該当しさえすれば国籍を問わず誰でもこの社会保険に加入できることになっている。

⑴　適用事業所

　健康保険と厚生年金保険は会社や工場など事業所単位に適用される。これらの制度の適用を受ける事業所を適用事業所といい，個人経営の事業所であって 5 人以上の従業員を雇用するものは加入が義務づけられる強制適用事業所となる。

　また，法人の事業所であれば 1 人でも従業員がいれば強制適用事業所となる。

　このような適用事業所（事業主）は，制度加入の手続や保険料納入の義務を負う。

　そして，このような適用事業所に働く従業員はすべて上記制度に加入し被保険者となっている（ただし，強制加入は健康保険では75歳未満，厚生年金では70歳未満である。）。

854   LOCAL TAX etc.

are excluded from the systems).

(2) **Premiums**

Premiums of the Health Insurance and the Employees' Pension Insurance systems are determined by multiplying the "monthly standard remuneration" of the insured person by the prescribed premium rate.

The premium rate for Health Insurance (so-called Kyoukai-Kenpo, managed by National Health Insurance Association) varies with prefectures, from the lowest 96.3/1,000 to the highest 106.1/1,000. The average rate in this year is 100.0/1,000. (99.0 in case of Tokyo Metropolis) of the monthly standard remuneration.

The premium rate for Employees' Pension Insurance is 183.0/1,000 (uniform rate).

Premiums are shared by the employers and employees in equal proportions. The employers are responsible for the payment of premiums due from both the employers and the employees, and are authorized to deduct an amount equal to that of the employees' contribution from the wages to be paid to the employees.

Premiums for both systems are also levied on a bonus, each time it is paid, in the same way as on the standard remuneration.

Note:
Monthly standard remuneration
The Health Insurance and the Employees' Pension Insurance adopt a system of standard remuneration under which the monthly income of insured persons, including wages, salaries, family allowance, over-time allowance, commutation allowance and so on, are classified into bands. The classified monthly income ("standard remuneration") is used to calculate the amount of premiums and benefits.
The monthly standard remuneration is divided into 50 bands ranging from 58,000 yen to 1,390,000 yen under the Health Insurance; and 31 bands ranging from 88,000 yen to 620,000 yen in case of the Employees' Pension Insurance.
The term "remuneration" means wage, salary, allowance and other amounts equivalent thereto paid as consideration for the labor of an employee.
The premium on a bonus is levied in case it is paid more than four times a year.

(3) **Payment of premiums**

The standard remuneration is revised once a year (regularly in July), but a revision is also made whenever there is a significant change in wages and salaries. The amount of the standard remuneration for new insured persons is determined at each time.

¶ 9-860

地　方　税　等　855

⑵　**保険料**

　全国健康保険協会（略称「協会けんぽ」）が運営する健康保険と厚生年金保険の保険料は，被保険者の標準報酬月額に保険料率を乗じて算出される。

　健康保険の保険料率は都道府県毎に異なり，最高は106.1／1,000，最低は96.3／1,000である。全国平均では，当年度100.0／1,000（東京都の場合は99.0）であり，厚生年金保険のそれは183.0／1,000（全国一律）である。

　保険料は事業主・被保険者折半負担である。事業主は事業主負担分と被保険者負担分の両方を合わせて納入する義務を負う。また事業主は従業員に支払う給料の中から被保険者負担分を控除することができることになっている。

　「標準報酬月額」は次頁の表のとおりである。

　健康保険と厚生年金保険では，標準報酬制を採用しており，被保険者の月収（賃金，給与，扶養手当，超過勤務手当，通勤手当などすべて含む。）をいくつかの等級に区分し，これを標準報酬月額と呼んでいる。そしてこれが保険料計算や給付額の決定の基礎になっている。

　標準報酬月額は，健康保険では58,000円から1,390,000円までの50等級に厚生年金保険では88,000円から620,000円までの31等級に分かれている。

　両制度の保険料は，ボーナスに対してもそれが支払われるつど，標準報酬月額と同様の仕組みにより徴収される。

　　(注)：「報酬」には，賃金，給料，手当その他これに準ずるもので労務の対償として支払うもののすべてが含まれる。

　　　　なお，ボーナスは年４回以上支払われる場合に保険料の対象となる。

⑶　**保険料の納入**

　標準報酬は年１回（７月）見直しが行われる。ただし，賃金等に著しい変動があった場合は随時標準報酬の改定が行われる。また，新規加入者についてはそのつど標準報酬の決定が行われる。

　事業主は，被保険者の負担すべき前月分の保険料を被保険者に支払うべき

856 LOCAL TAX etc.

The employers deduct the premiums for the previous month to be shared by the insured from the remuneration paid to the insured. The employers should then pay the total premiums for each month (shared by both employers and employees) to the pension office concerned by the end of the following month.

¶ 9-860

毎月の給与の中から控除し，翌月末日までに所管の年金事務所に納入しなければならない。

Table of standard remuneration and monthly premiums (unit: yen)

Rank (Health Insurance)	Rank (Employees' Pension Insurance)	Standard remuneration Monthly	Actual monthly remuneration		Health Insurance — Employees applicable to the care insurance		Health Insurance — Employees not applicable to the care insurance		Employees' Pension Insurance General	
			more than	less than	114.7/1,000	Employers and employees	99.0/1,000	Employers and employees	183.0/1,000	Employers and employees
1	—	58,000		63,000	6,652.6	3,326.3	5,742.0	2,871.0		
2	—	68,000	63,000	73,000	7,799.6	3,899.8	6,732.0	3,366.0		
3	—	78,000	73,000	83,000	8,946.6	4,473.3	7,722.0	3,861.0		
4	1	88,000	83,000	93,000	10,093.6	5,046.8	8,712.0	4,356.0	16,104.00	8,052.00
5	2	98,000	93,000	101,000	11,240.6	5,620.3	9,702.0	4,851.0	17,934.00	8,967.00
6	3	104,000	101,000	107,000	11,928.8	5,964.4	10,296.0	5,148.0	19,032.00	9,516.00
7	4	110,000	107,000	114,000	12,617.0	6,308.5	10,890.0	5,445.0	20,130.00	10,065.00
8	5	118,000	114,000	122,000	13,534.6	6,767.3	11,682.0	5,841.0	21,594.00	10,797.00
9	6	126,000	122,000	130,000	14,452.2	7,226.1	12,474.0	6,237.0	23,058.00	11,529.00
10	7	134,000	130,000	138,000	15,369.8	7,684.9	13,266.0	6,633.0	24,522.00	12,261.00
11	8	142,000	138,000	146,000	16,287.4	8,143.7	14,058.0	7,029.0	25,986.00	12,993.00
12	9	150,000	146,000	155,000	17,205.0	8,602.5	14,850.0	7,425.0	27,450.00	13,725.00
13	10	160,000	155,000	165,000	18,352.0	9,176.0	15,840.0	7,920.0	29,280.00	14,640.00
14	11	170,000	165,000	175,000	19,499.0	9,749.5	16,830.0	8,415.0	31,110.00	15,555.00
15	12	180,000	175,000	185,000	20,646.0	10,323.0	17,820.0	8,910.0	32,940.00	16,470.00
16	13	190,000	185,000	195,000	21,793.0	10,896.5	18,810.0	9,405.0	34,770.00	17,385.00
17	14	200,000	195,000	210,000	22,940.0	11,470.0	19,800.0	9,900.0	36,600.00	18,300.00
18	15	220,000	210,000	230,000	25,234.0	12,617.0	21,780.0	10,890.0	40,260.00	20,130.00
19	16	240,000	230,000	250,000	27,528.0	13,764.0	23,760.0	11,880.0	43,920.00	21,960.00
20	17	260,000	250,000	270,000	29,822.0	14,911.0	25,740.0	12,870.0	47,580.00	23,790.00
21	18	280,000	270,000	290,000	32,116.0	16,058.0	27,720.0	13,860.0	51,240.00	25,620.00
22	19	300,000	290,000	310,000	34,410.0	17,205.0	29,700.0	14,850.0	54,900.00	27,450.00
23	20	320,000	310,000	330,000	36,704.0	18,352.0	31,680.0	15,840.0	58,560.00	29,280.00
24	21	340,000	330,000	350,000	38,998.0	19,499.0	33,660.0	16,830.0	62,220.00	31,110.00
25	22	360,000	350,000	370,000	41,292.0	20,646.0	35,640.0	17,820.0	65,880.00	32,940.00
26	23	380,000	370,000	395,000	43,586.0	21,793.0	37,620.0	18,810.0	69,540.00	34,770.00
27	24	410,000	395,000	425,000	47,027.0	23,513.5	40,590.0	20,295.0	75,030.00	37,515.00
28	25	440,000	425,000	455,000	50,468.0	25,234.0	43,560.0	21,780.0	80,520.00	40,260.00
29	26	470,000	455,000	485,000	53,909.0	26,954.5	46,530.0	23,265.0	86,010.00	43,005.00
30	27	500,000	485,000	515,000	57,350.0	28,675.0	49,500.0	24,750.0	91,500.00	45,750.00
31	28	530,000	515,000	545,000	60,791.0	30,395.5	52,470.0	26,235.0	96,990.00	48,495.00
32	29	560,000	545,000	575,000	64,232.0	32,116.0	55,440.0	27,720.0	102,480.00	51,240.00
33	30	590,000	575,000	605,000	67,673.0	33,836.5	58,410.0	29,205.0	107,970.00	53,985.00
34	31	620,000	605,000	635,000	71,114.0	35,557.0	61,380.0	30,690.0	113,460.00	56,730.00
35	—	650,000	635,000	665,000	74,555.0	37,277.5	64,350.0	32,175.0		
36	—	680,000	665,000	690,000	77,996.0	38,998.0	67,320.0	33,660.0		
37	—	710,000	695,000	730,000	81,437.0	40,718.5	70,290.0	35,145.0		
38	—	750,000	730,000	770,000	86,025.0	43,012.5	74,250.0	37,125.0		
39	—	790,000	770,000	810,000	90,613.0	45,306.5	78,210.0	39,105.0		
40	—	830,000	810,000	855,000	95,201.0	47,600.5	82,170.0	41,085.0		
41	—	880,000	855,000	905,000	100,936.0	50,468.0	87,120.0	43,560.0		
42	—	930,000	905,000	955,000	106,671.0	53,335.5	92,070.0	46,035.0		
43	—	980,000	955,000	1,005,000	112,406.0	56,203.0	97,020.0	48,510.0		
44	—	1,030,000	1,005,000	1,055,000	118,141.0	59,070.5	101,970.0	50,985.0		
45	—	1,090,000	1,055,000	1,115,000	125,023.0	62,511.5	107,910.0	53,955.0		
46	—	1,150,000	1,115,000	1,175,000	131,905.0	65,952.5	113,850.0	56,925.0		
47	—	1,210,000	1,175,000	1,235,000	138,787.0	69,393.5	119,790.0	59,895.0		
48	—	1,270,000	1,235,000	1,295,000	145,669.0	72,834.5	125,730.0	62,865.0		
49	—	1,330,000	1,295,000	1,355,000	152,551.0	76,275.5	131,670.0	65,835.0		
50	—	1,390,000	1,355,000	more than	159,433.0	79,716.5	137,610.0	68,805.0		

Note: For Health Insurance, the table gives the case of Tokyo Metropolis on Kyoukai-Kenpo. (as of April, 2018)

地　方　税　等　859

健康保険 厚生年金保険 標準報酬月額・保険料額表

（単位・円）

標　準　報　酬			保険料					
等級			健康保険				厚生年金保険	
		月額	介護保険に該当する被保険者		介護保険に該当しない被保険者		一般被保険者	
健保	厚年		報　酬　月　額					
			114.7/1,000	事業主及び被保険者負担	99.0/1,000	事業主及び被保険者負担	183.0/1,000	事業主及び被保険者負担
1	–	58,000	～63,000	6,652.6	3,326.3	5,742.0	2,871.0		
2	–	68,000	63,000～73,000	7,799.6	3,899.8	6,732.0	3,366.0		
3	–	78,000	73,000～83,000	8,946.6	4,473.3	7,722.0	3,861.0		
4	1	88,000	83,000～93,000	10,093.6	5,046.8	8,712.0	4,356.0	16,104.00	8,052.00
5	2	98,000	93,000～101,000	11,240.6	5,620.3	9,702.0	4,851.0	17,934.00	8,967.00
6	3	104,000	101,000～107,000	11,928.8	5,964.4	10,296.0	5,148.0	19,032.00	9,516.00
7	4	110,000	107,000～114,000	12,617.0	6,308.5	10,890.0	5,445.0	20,130.00	10,065.00
8	5	118,000	114,000～122,000	13,534.6	6,767.3	11,682.0	5,841.0	21,594.00	10,797.00
9	6	126,000	122,000～130,000	14,452.2	7,226.1	12,474.0	6,237.0	23,058.00	11,529.00
10	7	134,000	130,000～138,000	15,369.8	7,684.9	13,266.0	6,633.0	24,522.00	12,261.00
11	8	142,000	138,000～146,000	16,287.4	8,143.7	14,058.0	7,029.0	25,986.00	12,993.00
12	9	150,000	146,000～155,000	17,205.0	8,602.5	14,850.0	7,425.0	27,450.00	13,725.00
13	10	160,000	155,000～165,000	18,352.0	9,176.0	15,840.0	7,920.0	29,280.00	14,640.00
14	11	170,000	165,000～175,000	19,499.0	9,749.5	16,830.0	8,415.0	31,110.00	15,555.00
15	12	180,000	175,000～185,000	20,646.0	10,323.0	17,820.0	8,910.0	32,940.00	16,470.00
16	13	190,000	185,000～195,000	21,793.0	10,896.5	18,810.0	9,405.0	34,770.00	17,385.00
17	14	200,000	195,000～210,000	22,940.0	11,470.0	19,800.0	9,900.0	36,600.00	18,300.00
18	15	220,000	210,000～230,000	25,234.0	12,617.0	21,780.0	10,890.0	40,260.00	20,130.00
19	16	240,000	230,000～250,000	27,528.0	13,764.0	23,760.0	11,880.0	43,920.00	21,960.00
20	17	260,000	250,000～270,000	29,822.0	14,911.0	25,740.0	12,870.0	47,580.00	23,790.00
21	18	280,000	270,000～290,000	32,116.0	16,058.0	27,720.0	13,860.0	51,240.00	25,620.00
22	19	300,000	290,000～310,000	34,410.0	17,205.0	29,700.0	14,850.0	54,900.00	27,450.00
23	20	320,000	310,000～330,000	36,704.0	18,352.0	31,680.0	15,840.0	58,560.00	29,280.00
24	21	340,000	330,000～350,000	38,998.0	19,499.0	33,660.0	16,830.0	62,220.00	31,110.00
25	22	360,000	350,000～370,000	41,292.0	20,646.0	35,640.0	17,820.0	65,880.00	32,940.00
26	23	380,000	370,000～395,000	43,586.0	21,793.0	37,620.0	18,810.0	69,540.00	34,770.00
27	24	410,000	395,000～425,000	47,027.0	23,513.5	40,590.0	20,295.0	75,030.00	37,515.00
28	25	440,000	425,000～455,000	50,468.0	25,234.0	43,560.0	21,780.0	80,520.00	40,260.00
29	26	470,000	455,000～485,000	53,909.0	26,954.5	46,530.0	23,265.0	86,010.00	43,005.00
30	27	500,000	485,000～515,000	57,350.0	28,675.0	49,500.0	24,750.0	91,500.00	45,750.00
31	28	530,000	515,000～545,000	60,791.0	30,395.5	52,470.0	26,235.0	96,990.00	48,495.00
32	29	560,000	545,000～575,000	64,232.0	32,116.0	55,440.0	27,720.0	102,480.00	51,240.00
33	30	590,000	575,000～605,000	67,673.0	33,836.5	58,410.0	29,205.0	107,970.00	53,985.00
34	31	620,000	605,000～635,000	71,114.0	35,557.0	61,380.0	30,690.0	113,460.00	56,730.00
35	–	650,000	635,000～665,000	74,555.0	37,277.5	64,350.0	32,175.0		
36	–	680,000	665,000～695,000	77,996.0	38,998.0	67,320.0	33,660.0		
37	–	710,000	695,000～730,000	81,437.0	40,718.5	70,290.0	35,145.0		
38	–	750,000	730,000～770,000	86,025.0	43,012.5	74,250.0	37,125.0		
39	–	790,000	770,000～810,000	90,613.0	45,306.5	78,210.0	39,105.0		
40	–	830,000	810,000～855,000	95,201.0	47,600.5	82,170.0	41,085.0		
41	–	880,000	855,000～905,000	100,936.0	50,468.0	87,120.0	43,560.0		
42	–	930,000	905,000～955,000	106,671.0	53,335.5	92,070.0	46,035.0		
43	–	980,000	955,000～1,005,000	112,406.0	56,203.0	97,020.0	48,510.0		
44	–	1,030,000	1,005,000～1,055,000	118,141.0	59,070.5	101,970.0	50,985.0		
45	–	1,090,000	1,055,000～1,115,000	125,023.0	62,511.5	107,910.0	53,955.0		
46	–	1,150,000	1,115,000～1,175,000	131,905.0	65,952.5	113,850.0	56,925.0		
47	–	1,210,000	1,175,000～1,235,000	138,787.0	69,393.5	119,790.0	59,895.0		
48	–	1,270,000	1,235,000～1,295,000	145,669.0	72,834.5	125,730.0	62,865.0		
49	–	1,330,000	1,295,000～1,355,000	152,551.0	76,275.5	131,670.0	65,835.0		
50	–	1,390,000	1,355,000～	159,433.0	79,716.5	137,610.0	68,805.0		

注：健康保険は東京都における協会けんぽの例　平成30年4月現在

860   LOCAL TAX etc.

Labor Insurance

¶ 9-880 Labor insurance

Labor Insurance is a general term for Workmen's Accident Compensation Insurance and Employment Insurance.

The purposes of Workmen's Accident Compensation Insurance are to give workers prompt and equitable protection against injury, disease, disability or death resulting from employment, or commutation by providing them with the necessary insurance benefits.

Employment Insurance aims to stabilize the livelihood of the unemployed, promote the prevention of unemployment, and to increase employment opportunities by granting necessary benefits in the event that workers lose their jobs.

(1) Applicable undertakings

For the purposes of Workmen's Accident Compensation Insurance and Employment Insurance, all undertakings which employ workers are, in principle, compulsorily "applicable undertakings".

(2) Premiums

Insurance premiums for both systems are levied together in a unified form as "Labor Insurance Premiums".

The premiums which are appropriated for the two systems are calculated by multiplying the total amount of wages paid to all the workers in the undertaking during the insurance year by the total rate of the premiums for both systems.

Of the total amount of the Labor Insurance Premiums, the part which meets the expenses required for the Workmen's Accident Compensation Insurance System is paid in full by the employers.

The premium rates for this system vary by industry, from the lowest 2.5/1000 to the highest 88/1000.

The premiums for the Employment Insurance System are paid by both the employers and the employees. At present, the premium rate in general cases is 9/1000, of which 6/1000 is borne by the employers and 3/1000 by the employees.

(3) Payment of premiums

At the beginning of the insurance year, employers are to pay the premiums as estimations.

¶ 9-880

地 方 税 等 861

労 働 保 険

¶9-880　労働保険
労働保険は，労働者災害補償保険と雇用保険の総称である。

労働者災害補償保険の目的は，労働者の業務上の事由又は通勤による負傷，疾病，障害又は死亡に対して迅速かつ公正な保護を行うため必要な保険給付をすることにある。

また，雇用保険は，労働者が失業した場合に必要な給付を行うことにより，その生活の安定を図るとともに，失業の予防，雇用機会の増大を図ることなどを目的としている。

(1)　適用事業
両制度とも原則として労働者を雇用する事業はすべて適用される。

(2)　保険料
両制度の保険料は「労働保険料」としてまとめて徴収される。

両制度の費用に充てるための保険料は，その保険年度に使用する全労働者の賃金総額に両制度の保険料率を合わせた料率を乗じて算出される。

労働保険料総額のうち，労働者災害補償制度分については事業主が全額負担する。

その保険料率は事業の種類により2.5／1,000から88／1,000までと異なる。

一方雇用保険分については，基本的には労使それぞれが負担することとされており，一般的な事業においては，9／1,000を事業主が6／1,000労働者が3／1,000を負担する。

(3)　保険料の納付
事業主は，保険年度当初に，当該年度の概算保険料を納付しなければならない。

862   LOCAL TAX etc.

At the beginning of the following year, they should report the definite amount of premiums on the basis of the total amount of wages actually paid during the past year, and adjustments are made accordingly.

¶ 9-880

そして，次の年度の当初に，前年度に実際に支払った賃金総額を基にして確定保険料を申告しなければならない。これにより納付済みの概算保険料との調整が行われる。

865

INDEX

Please refer to the chapter and paragraph numbers.

Paragraph number

200% declining balance method 5-160

250% declining balance method 5-160

A

Accident insurance premiums 5-380

Accidental loss
deduction 5-320

Accountants
certified public tax accountant 1-540
foreign taxpayers 1-420
registration tax 2-830
withholding income tax 4-360

Accrual basis of income
calculation 5-140
corporations 6-120

Acquisition of house
tax credit 5-600

Actors
withholding income tax 4-360

Administration system 1-450
chart 1-800

Administrators
liability for inheritance tax 7-020

Adopted children
inheritance tax 7-355

Advocates
registration tax 2-830

Aeroplanes
transfer, consumption tax 8-050

Aggregation of assets
inheritance tax 7-340

Aggregation of income 5-230
capital gains 5-230
forestry income and retirement
income 5-240

Paragraph

Agricultural land 2-345

Aircraft
fixed assets tax 9-580
fuel tax 2-585

Allowances — see also **Deductions**
basic 5-470
comparison of income tax and
income levy 9-090
dependent 5-420
meal 4-230
physically handicapped person 5-430
spouse 5-410
–special allowance 5-412
table 4-230
widow or widower 5-450
working student 5-460

Annuity payments
withholding income tax 4-360
–non-residents and foreign
corporations 4-620

Apartment houses
capital gains from transfer of
suitable land 5-210

Appeal 1-510

Approved contributions,
deduction 5-390

Architects
withholding income tax 4-360

Art work
withholding income tax 4-360

Artists
foreign taxpayers 1-420

Assessable income
foreign corporations 6-875
non-residents 5-880

Assessment income tax 2-080; 3-050
aggregation of income .... 5-230~5-256
basic structure 5-020
blue return 5-030
book-keeping 5-040

Ass

866 INDEX

Paragraph

categories of income 5-120
computation .... 5-010; 5-090~5-200
– examples .... 5-650~5-680
correction or determination
of liability 5-740
deductions and allowances ... 5-310~5-470
exempt corporation 3-410
exempt income 5-070
final payment and refund 5-730
final return 5-720
information return 5-810; 5-820
net loss 5-270; 5-280
non-residents .... 5-850~5-920
prepayment 5-710
rates of tax .... 5-500~5-550
tax credits .... 5-570~5-638

Assets
acquired by bequest or devise 7-275
book value change 6-340
– credits and debits in foreign
currencies 6-345
deferred 6-320; 6-325
definition 8-040
depreciation — see Depreciation
fixed assets tax .... 9-580~9-740
minor 6-265
on lease 6-309
revaluation 6-158
transfers
– acts similar 8-040
– domestic transactions 8-050
– taxable sales ratio 8-580
– time, consumption tax ...... 8-390~8-475;
8-710; 8-720
valuation for inheritance tax 7-550

Athletes
foreign taxpayers 1-420

Automobile acquisition tax 2-870

Automobile tax 2-350

Automobile tonnage tax 2-420

Averaging of income 5-530

Avoidance of tax
thin capital 6-247

B

Bad debts 6-240
computation of business income 5-160
consumption tax 8-640
reserves 6-360

Paragraph

Band players
withholding income tax 4-360

Bank deposits
foreign governments 3-540
withholding income tax exemption. 4-170

Banking business
license fee 2-830

Banking companies 6-090

Barrier-free improvement 5-614; 5-617

Baseball players
withholding income tax 4-360

Basic allowance 5-470

Bathing tax 2-710

Beneficiaries
inheritance tax purposes 7-105
taxation of trust income 3-740

Beneficiary-concealed-
disbursement 6-675

Bill collectors
withholding income tax 4-360

Blue return
corporations 6-056

Bonds
interest, foreign governments 3-540
transfer, consumption tax 8-580

Bonuses
corporations
– deduction 6-215
directors, deemed payment date 4-070
– table 4-270
tax treaties 4-650
withholding income tax 4-130; 4-290

Bookbinding
withholding income tax 4-360

Bookkeeping
consumption tax 8-020; 8-800

Bowlers
withholding income tax 4-360

Boxers
withholding income tax 4-360

Broadcasting
withholding income tax 4-360

Building agents

Ass

INDEX   867

Paragraph

withholding income tax 4-360

Buildings — see also **Capital gains**
enterprise establishment tax 2-430
exchange, replacement, donation 5-210
fixed assets tax 2-360; 9-580
real property acquisition tax 2-850
table of taxes 2-370

Burden adjustment rate 9-680

Burial services 8-155

Business
definition 8-040
enterprise tax .... 9-340~9-440
expenses 6-140
income
– aggregation 5-230
– computation 5-090; 5-120; 5-160;
5-195
– foreign taxpayers 1-420
– offset of losses 5-270
– stocks or shares 5-256

Business consultants
withholding income tax 4-360
business expenses for specific
expenses purpose 5-130

Business year 6-100

C

Capital allowances 5-070

Capital expenditure 6-308

Capital gains 3-040
aggregation 5-230
computation of income 5-130; 5-195;
5-200
– general rule 5-190
– land and buildings 5-200
– land, business income 5-195; 5-200
– long-term, on land, etc. 5-252; 5-555
movable property 5-190
– short-term, on land, etc. ... 5-254; 5-560;
9-120
corporations 6-125
commodity futures trading ... 5-170; 9-120
exempt 5-070
expropriated property 6-505
gross income 6-190
offset of losses 5-270
rates of tax 5-550
special taxation 6-670

Paragraph

stock or shares 5-220; 5-256
– computation of income tax 5-220; 5-256
– per stock capital gain levy 9-111
– tax rate 5-565
– withholding tax 4-400
tax treaties 4-650

Capital transactions
corporations' gross income 6-145

Carry forward of capital loss 5-290;
5-300; 9-100

Carry-over or carry-back
of losses .... 5-280~5-300
corporations 6-570
– accidental loss 6-575

Cash management trusts
withholding income tax exemption . 4-170

Certified nonprofit corporations 5-390;
5-570; 5-638

Certified public accountants
— see **Accountants**

Certified public tax accountants 1-540

**Chamber of Commerce and
Industry** 3-410

Charitable organizations
foreign corporations 3-430

Child allowance 5-070

Children
dependent, allowance 5-420
inheritance tax 7-355

City planning tax 2-390; 9-740

Collective investment trust 6-052

Commutation allowance 8-600

Companies — see **Corporations**

**Conducted for consideration,
definition** 8-040

Conductors, musical
withholding income tax 4-360

Consignment sales 6-178

Consolidated taxation system 6-630

Construction work
consumption tax 8-470

Consumption tax 2-510
aircraft fuel tax 2-585
basic structure 8-020

Con

868 INDEX

Paragraph

bathing tax 2-710
bookkeeping obligations 8-800
  – successors 8-810
business use change 8-660
characteristics 8-010
definitions 8-040
diesel oil delivery 2-680
domestic transactions 8-030
  – determination 8-050
enterprise change from exempt
  to taxable 8-670
exemptions
  – commodities at export
    shops 8-200; 8-210
  – exports 8-170; 8-180
  – Special Taxation Measures
    Law, etc. 8-220
foreign goods 8-060
gasoline tax 2-580
golf course tax 2-650
inheritances 8-280
inquiries and inspection 8-820
interim 8-760; 8-775
liquor tax 2-560
national tax 2-510
non-taxable transactions
  – burial services 8-155
  – disabled persons equipment 8-155
  – domestic transactions 8-070
  – foreign exchange services 8-130
  – foreign goods 8-165
  – international postage service 8-130
  – lease of assets with interest 8-090
  – medical services 8-140
  – midwifery services 8-155
  – postage stamps 8-100
  – purchases by visitors to Japan 2-540
  – rent for houses 8-163
  – school tuition 8-160
  – services rendered by
    governments, etc. 8-120
  – transfer of securities 8-080
  – transfers and leases of land 8-075
  – transfers of exchange checks, etc . 8-110
  – welfare services, etc. 8-150
petroleum gas tax 2-595
petroleum coal tax 2-590
place for tax payment
  – change 8-340
  – corporations 8-320
  – foreign goods removed from
    bonded area 8-350
  – individuals 8-310

Paragraph

  – non-residents 8-355
purchase tax credit 8-530
  – computation .... 8-540~8-570
  – computation, itemized method 8-560
  – computation, proportional
    method 8-570
  – prerequisite, application 8-610
  – refund, etc. of consideration
    for purchase 8-620
  – refund, etc. of consideration
    for sales 8-630
  – simplified tax system 8-680
  – substitutional ratio for taxable
    sales ratio 8-590
  – taxable purchase, defined 8-600
rate of tax 8-510
refunds
  – interim consumption tax 8-775
  – tax on purchase 8-770
returns
  – final 8-750
  – foreign goods removed from
    bonded area 8-780
  – interim 8-760
  – successors 8-810
road tax (local) 2-580
special exceptions, government, etc.
  – business unit 8-700
  – filing date for returns 8-740
  – submission of notification 8-790
tax base
  – domestic transactions 8-490
  – import transaction 8-500
  – special exception 8-380
tax credit
  – bad debt loss 8-640
  – purchase tax credit .... 8-530~8-680
  – simplified tax system 8-680
  – small-scale enterprises 8-680
taxable period
  – individual enterprises 8-360
  – corporations 8-370
taxable sales, calculation 8-270
taxable sales ratio 8-580
  – change, adjustment of tax 8-650
taxation on substance of an act 8-290
taxpayers
  – actual performer 8-290
  – domestic transactions 8-230
  – election 8-260
  – exceptions 8-280
  – joint enterprise, etc. 8-245
  – removing foreign goods from

Con

INDEX   869

Paragraph

bonded area 8-240
– small-scale enterprises,
   exemption 8-250
– trust funds 8-300
time of transfer of assets, etc.
   ....8-390; 8-710
– contract for work 8-410
– installment sales 8-450
– long-term contracts 8-470
– small-scale enterprises 8-475
– transfer of industrial property, etc. 8-425
– transfer of interest and royalties ... 8-440
– transfer of inventories 8-400
– transfer of securities 8-430
– transfer of tangible assets 8-420
tobacco tax 2-640
visitors' tax-free purchases 2-540

Contracts
income, withholding tax 4-155
long-term 6-185; 8-470

Contributions
deduction 5-390
– corporations 6-235; 6-480; 6-485

Cooperatives 6-030
special deductions 6-550

Copyright
registration tax 2-830

Corporate taxation trust 6-052

Corporation levy 9-220

Corporation tax 6-002
accrual basis 6-120
adjustment of net profit 6-110
amendments 1-200
blue return 6-056
business year 6-100
capital gains .... 6-125; 6-470~6-505
– land etc. 6-490; 6-495; 6-505; 6-670
capital transactions 6-145
changes in book value 6-340; 6-345
deferred assets 6-320; 6-325
depreciation ....6-265~6-310
double taxation avoidance 6-010
enterprise tax ....9-460~9-570
exchange, replacement, donation
   of properties ....6-470~6-505
foreign corporations ....6-870~6-920
gross income ....6-150~6-200
– capital gains 6-190
– dividends 6-150; 6-155
– exclusions ....6-150~6-160

Paragraph

– leasehold 6-193
– long-term contracts 6-185
– sales ....6-170~6-180
– technical service fees,
   remuneration 6-188
– transfer pricing 6-200
– undistributed profits, foreign
   subsidiaries 6-195
inhabitant tax ....9-180~9-320
liquidation 6-610
liquidation income 6-070
– tax ....6-820~6-845
mineral prospecting expenditure 6-540
net loss ....6-570~6-590
nondeductible 6-205
ordinary income
– annual basis 6-065
– computation of tax 6-770
– computing ....6-100~6-145
– cooperatives 6-030
– medical care corporations 6-045
– non-juridical organizations 6-050
– public interest corporations 6-040
– rate of tax 6-060
– tax basis 6-060; 6-680
– outline ....6-005~6-090
place for payment 6-055
procedural matters 6-860
return and payment of tax ....6-800~6-810
special deductions etc. 6-550
special taxation
– capital gains from land 6-670
– beneficiary-concealed-
   disbursement 6-675
specific funds 6-090
structure..............................6-005~6-057
tax credits ....6-690~6-755
tax returns
– blue returns 6-056
– white returns 6-057
total costs (business expenses) 6-130;
                  6-140; 6-205~6-247
types 6-005
types of corporations 6-020
– cooperatives 6-030
– public corporations 6-025
undistributed profits ....6-640~6-660
– computation of tax 6-775
valuation of inventory 6-250; 6-255

Corporations
— see also **Domestic corporations**
consumption tax
– place of payment 8-320

Cor

870 INDEX

Paragraph

−tax base period 8-370
corporate division 6-600
domestic 3-340
−definition 3-360
−withholding income tax ..... 4-510~4-570
exempt 3-410
foreign 3-340
−definition 3-360
liquidation 6-610
medical care 6-045
non-juridical organizations 6-050
public interest 6-040
registration tax 2-830
tax liability 3-340
taxes 2-060; 2-090; 3-050

**Credit for contributions to certified
nonprofit corporations** 5-570; 5-638

Curios and fine art
valuation, inheritance tax 7-550

Cycle racers
withholding income tax 4-360

D

Debentures
issued at discount 4-190
−non-residents and foreign
corporations 4-620

Deductions — see also **Allowances**
accidental loss 5-320
assessment income tax 5-090
−computation 5-130
business income 5-160
capital gains on land and buildings . 5-200
categories 5-310
comparison of income tax and
income levy 9-090
contributions 5-390
corporations
−bad debts 6-240
−bonuses 6-215
−contributions 6-235
−entertainment expenses 6-230
−interest 6-247
−reserves .... 6-350~6-435
−retirement allowances 6-225
−salaries, wages 6-210
−social insurance premiums 6-220
earthquake insurance premiums 5-380
enterprise establishment tax 9-820
enterprise tax 9-420
gift tax 7-840

Paragraph

individual inhabitant taxes 9-080
individual annuity premiums 5-370
inheritance tax 7-330; 7-340
land value tax 2-345
life insurance premiums 5-370
long-term care and medical
insurance premiums 5-370
medical expenses 5-330
mutual aid plan contributions 5-350
social insurance premiums 5-340
undistributed profits
.... 6-645; 6-650

Deferred assets
definition and amortization 6-320
special treatment 6-325

Deferred payment
inheritance tax 7-620

Defined contribution pension plan ... 5-070;
5-350

Definitions
approved contributions 5-390
assets 8-040
assessment income 4-540
business 8-040
conducted for consideration 8-040
domestic corporation 3-360
enterprise 8-040
experimental and research
expenses 6-720
family corporation 3-780
foreign corporation 3-360
lease of assets 8-040
long-term contract 8-470
non-permanent resident 3-250
non-resident 3-250
provision of services 8-040
registered owner 2-360
relatives 5-420
resident 3-250
special relationship 6-200
specified payment 5-130
taxable purchase 8-600
transfer of assets 8-040

Dental expenses deduction 5-330

Dependants' allowance 5-420

Depreciation 5-160
accounting 6-305
capital expenditure and
maintenance 6-308
capital sum recoverable 6-300
depreciable assets 6-265

Cor

INDEX 871

Paragraph

increased 6-280
method.. 6-270
minor assets 6-265
purchase during business year 6-285
special 6-310
useful lives 6-290; 6-295

Designated account
– capital gains 5-257; 9-120
– withholding 4-400

Designs
withholding income tax 4-360

Diesel oil delivery tax 2-680

Diplomats
privilege 3-540
staff, exempt income 5-070

Directors
bonuses
– deductibility 6-215
– deemed payment date 4-070
compensation, deductibility 6-210
foreign taxpayers 1-420

Disabled persons, equipment
consumption tax 8-155

Disable spouse 5-410

Discounted debentures 4-190

Discounts 6-175

Distribution of profit
Nin-i Kumiai 4-620
Tokumei Kumiai 4-580; 4-620

Dividends
aggregation of income 5-230
computation of income 5-130
deemed payment date 4-070
distribution from publicly traded
stock investment 4-212
double taxation avoidance 6-010
income, foreign taxpayers 1-420
per dividend levy 9-110
received by corporations 6-150
– constructive dividends 6-155
tax credit 5-580
undistributed profits 6-655
withholding income tax 4-211; 4-212;
4-130
– domestic corporations 4-540
– non-residents and foreign
corporations 4-620
– residents 4-210
– tax treaties 4-650

Paragraph

Domestic corporations 3-340
— see also **Corporations**
definition 3-360
withholding income tax 4-510
– dividends 4-540
– horse owners' prizes 4-570
– income similar to interest 4-550
– interest 4-540; 4-550
– public entertainers 4-570

Domestic transactions
definition 8-040
determination 8-050

Domicile 3-250
inheritance tax 7-110

Donations, property 6-480

Dramatization
withholding income tax 4-360

E

Earthquake restoration surtax 5-020

"Economic substance" 3-710
family corporations 3 760- 3 790
taxation of trusts 3-740

Educational organizations
foreign corporations 3-430

Electric meter men
withholding income tax 4-360

Electric power resources
development tax 2-890

Electric power suppliers
enterprise tax rate 9-480

Employees
exempt income 5-070
foreign taxpayers 1-420
insurance 9-860; 9-880
number, enterprise tax 9-540
salary or wages — see **Salary or wages**

**Employees' Property Formation
Promotion Act** 4-175

Employment income
aggregation 5-230
computation 5-090; 5-120; 5-130
withholding income tax .... 4-230~4-380
– tax treaties 4-650

Energy saving performance 5-617

Emp

872 INDEX

	Paragraph
Enterprise, definition	8-040

Enterprise establishment tax ....2-430; 9-760~9-840
- exemptions and deductions 9-820
- returns and payments......................9-840
- tax authority 9-760
- tax base and tax rate 9-800
- taxpayer...9-780

Enterprise tax 2-240
corporations
- division basis for two or more prefectures 9-540
- gross proceeds taxation.................9-500
- income taxation 9-520
- return and payment 9-560
- tax base and tax rate 9-480
- taxation of corporation by the size of their business 2-270; 9-570
- taxpayer 9-460
individuals
- calculation of income...................9-420
- return and payment 9-440
- taxable income.............................9-410
- taxpayer, categories ....9-340~9-400

Enterprises
consumption tax
- domestic transactions...................8-230
- election to be taxable 8-260
- joint..8-245
- small and medium-sized 8-680
- small-scale 8-250; 8-475; 8-680
- tax-exempt change to taxable 8-670

Entertainment expenses 4-230; 5-160; 6-230

Establishment of corporation 6-600

Exchange checks, transfers
consumption tax 8-110

Exchange non-resident 2-540

Exchange of property 6-470

Excise taxes
deductible 6-205

Executors
liability for inheritance tax 7-020

Exempt corporations 3-410; 3-430

Exempt income 5-070
corporations
- constructive dividends received....6-155
- dividends received 6-150

	Paragraph
- revaluation profits	6-158
- tax refunded	6-160

Exemptions
consumption tax ....8-170~8-220
foreign corporations 6-885; 6-895
gift tax 7-860
- severely handicapped persons......7-870
inheritance tax 7-290
withholding income tax
- interest on employees' savings 4-175
- interest on small deposits etc. 4-170

Expatriates working in Japan 4-410

Expenses, corporations 6-140
— see **Total costs (corporation tax)**

Experimental and research expenses 5-620
corporations....................................6-720

Exports
consumption tax 8-170
- approval etc. of export shop..........8-210
- commodities at export shops 8-200
- exemption 8-170
- exemption, required conditions 8-180
- non-taxable assets 8-580
- scope of exemption 8-190

F

Family corporations
definition 3-780
denial of transactions or entries.......3-760
inheritance or gift tax 7-040
nonpersonal 3-790
undistributed profits ....6-640~6-660

Final payment and refund 5-730

Final return 5-720
corporations....................................6-805
- special treatment 6-810
form...5-950

Finance lease without title transfer ..5-160, 6-309

Fines
nondeductible 6-205

Fire insurance premiums 5-380

Fire or automobile damage appraisers
withholding income tax...................4-360
fixed annuity right 7-550

Fixed assets tax ....2-360; 9-580~9-740

Emp

INDEX   873

Paragraph

tax base as exception 9-660
tax base, general rules 9-640
tax burden adjustment 9-680
tax entity 9-600
tax rate 9-700
taxable fixed asset 9-620
taxpayer 9-580

Fluctuating and extraordinary income 5-530

Foreign corporations
allocation of profits to Japanese sources 6-880
amount of tax 6-895
assessable income 6-875
classification 6-870
definition 3-360
enterprise tax 9-460
inhabitant tax 9-180
place for tax payment 6-055
public corporations 6-025
religious, charitable, etc. 3-430
return and payment 6-910
– operations commenced, ceased 6-905
tax exemptions
 – debentures in foreign currency 6-885
 – interest on deposit from special
  international finance account 6-890
tax treaty concessions 6-900
transfer of withheld tax 4-070
withholding income tax 4-620
 – tax treaties 4-650
 – unilateral concessions 4-680

Foreign currency
credits and debits 6-345
debentures 6-885
deposits, withholding tax 4-155

Foreign embassies and legations
consumption tax 8-220

Foreign exchange services
consumption tax 8-130

Foreign goods
consumption tax 8-060; 8-165; 8-610

Foreign governments, exemption 3-540

Foreign leading shareholders
interest paid to 6-247

Foreign subsidiaries
undistributed profits 6-195

Foreign tax credits 5-630
corporations 1-200; 2-090; 6-740

Paragraph

– credit or deductible expenses 6-755
– indirect 6-750
– ordinary income 6-745
gift tax 7-890
inheritance tax 7-400

Foreign taxpayers 1-420

Forest owners' special deduction 6-550

Forestry income
aggregation 5-240
computation ....5-090~5-130
rate of tax 5-520

Forms
final return 5-950
gift tax return 7-920
inheritance tax ....7-450~7-480
withholding income tax 4-830

G

Gas suppliers
enterprise tax rate 9-480

Gasoline tax 2-580

Gift before death 7 280

Gift tax 2-340; 3-040
basic structure 7-010
computation 7-840
credit, inheritance tax 7-400
deemed gifts 7-850
exempt gifts 7-860
 – severely handicapped persons 7-870
family corporation transactions 7-040
foreign tax credits 7-890
non-juridical organizations or public
 interest corporations 7-030
 – nondeductible 6-205
payment 7-910
returns 7-900
 – form 7-920
tax rates 1-200; 7-880
taxable property 7-780
taxpayer 7-760
US tax treaty 7-050

Golf course tax 2-650

Golfers
withholding income tax 4-360

Goods
purchase by visitors to Japan 2-540
rebate and return 6-175
returned unsold, reserve 6-385

Gol

874 INDEX

Paragraph

Government bonds
assessment income tax interest
exemption 5-070
withholding income tax exemption . 4-170

Government corporations 3-410

Government organizations
special exception .... 8-700~8-740

Gross income, corporations 6-135
capital gains..................................... 6-190
capital transactions.......................... 6-145
consignment sales 6-178
dividends received........................... 6-150
– constructive 6-155
installment sales 6-180
leasehold 6-193
long-term contracts 6-185
ordinary sales 6-170
remuneration and fees, etc., for
technical services........................ 6-188
revaluation profits 6-158
sales reduction, discount, etc. 6-175
tax refunded.................................... 6-160
transactions with foreign related
person 6-200
undistributed profits of foreign
subsidiaries................................. 6-195

H

Handicapped persons
allowance 5-430
dependent 5-420
gift tax exemption 7-870
inheritance tax credit...................... 7-400
mutual aid plan contributions.......... 5-350

Health insurance 9-860

Heirs
inheritance tax purposes.................. 7-105

Horse owners' prizes
withholding income tax................... 4-570

Hostesses
withholding income tax................... 4-360

House
carry forward of capital loss........... 5-290;
5-300; 9-100
rent, consumption tax 8-163
tax credit for acquisition
.... 5-600; 5-611; 5-616; 9-100
tax credit for home improvement
....5-614; 5-617

Paragraph

valuation, inheritance tax 7-550

Hundred (100) percent group 6-590

Hunting tax 2-950

I

Illegitimate children
inheritance tax 7-360

Illustrations
withholding income tax................... 4-360

Imported goods
consumption tax 8-060; 8-500

Income levy
computation of tax amount.............. 9-100
income tax/comparison 9-090

Income tax 2-040; 2-080
assessment — see **Assessment income tax**
corporation — see **Corporation tax**
income levy, comparison................. 9-090
structure.. 3-020
– capital gain, inheritance and gift... 3-040
– withholding — see **Withholding
income tax**

Individuals
consumption tax
– place of payment.......................... 8-310
– taxable period 8-360
enterprise tax .... 9-340~9-440
income tax 2-080
inhabitant taxes .... 9-010~9-160
per capita levy 9-030
per income levy 9-050; 9-080
tax burden............................ 2-040; 2-050
tax liability 3-210

Industrial property
transfer, consumption tax 8-425

Information return 5-810; 5-820

Information service 1-430

Inhabitant taxes 2-110
corporation
– large corporation.......................... 9-320
– per capita levy.............................. 9-200
– per corporation tax levy 9-220; 9-240
– return and payment 9-300
– separate taxation 9-280
– taxpayer 9-180
individual 1-200; 9-010
– assessment and tax disputes.......... 9-160

Goo

INDEX 875

Paragraph	

–income levy, computation of
 tax amount 9-100
–income tax and income levy,
 comparison 9-090
–per capita levy 9-030
–per income levy, income
 computation 9-050
–return and payment 9-140
–separate taxation 9-120
nondeductible 6-205

Inheritance tax 2-310; 3-040
adopted children............................ 7-355
aggregation of net assets 7-340
amendments 1-200
basic structure 7-010
benefits deemed inheritance etc. 7-270
benefits treated as bequest or devise 7-275
computation...........................7-005; 7-250
–example 7-410
–outline 7-260
deductions
–basic estate allowances 7-340; 7-350
–inherited liability 7-330
disputes 7-630
domicile.. 7-110
exempt properties 7-290
family corporation transactions....... 7-040
gift before death 7-280
liability of administrator or
 executor 7-020
non-juridical organizations or public
 interest corporations 7-030
–nondeductible 6-205
payment....................................... 7-620
penalty taxes................................. 7-630
property situated abroad................. 7-320
return 7-420; 7-600
–correction 7-630
–form ....7-450~7-480
scope of liability 7-100
situs of properties 7-120
–Japan-US Inheritance Tax
 Convention 7-130
small-scale land, special treatment.. 7-300
statutory shares of estate 7-360
surtax.. 7-390
tax credits 7-400
tax payable to heirs and legatees 7-380
tax rate.. 7-370
taxpayer.. 7-105
US tax treaty................................. 7-050
valuation of properties................... 7-550

Inheritances
consumption tax 8-280
–filing obligations 8-810

Inquiries and inspections
consumption tax 8-820

Installment sales 6-180; 8-450

Insurance companies 6-090

Insurance payments
inheritance tax 7-270; 7-290

Insurance premiums
fire and other accident 5-380
life insurance 5-370
social insurance 5-340; 6-220

Insurers
enterprise tax rate 9-480

Interest
computation of income................... 5-120
deposit from special international
exempt income 5-070
–foreign governments, bonds
 and deposits 3-540
income.................................5-090; 5-120
income, foreign taxpayers 1-420
nondeductible expenses.................. 6-247
savings, employees property 4-175
transfer, consumption tax 8-440
withholding income tax................... 4-130
–domestic corporations.................. 4-540
–Employees' Property Formation
 Promotion Act............................ 4-175
–non-residents and foreign
 corporations 4-620
–residents.............................4-150; 4-170
–submission of payment slips 4-160
–tax treaties.................................. 4-650

Interim return 8-760
refund of interim tax....................... 8-775

International postal service
consumption tax 8-130

Inventories, valuation ..5-160; 6-250; 6-255

Investment income
foreign taxpayers........................... 1-420

Investment tax credit, specified
equipment 6-730

J

Japan Red Cross 3-410

Inv

876 INDEX

Paragraph

Japan-US Inheritance Tax
Convention 7-130; 7-400

Jockeys
withholding income tax 4-360

Joint enterprise
taxpayer, consumption tax 8-245

Judicial penalty 1-520

Judicial scriveners
withholding income tax 4-360

L

Labor insurance 9-880

Land — see also **Capital gains; Property**
consumption tax 8-075
exchange; replacement, donation 5-210
fixed assets tax 2-360; 9-580
rates of tax 5-550
real property acquisition tax 2-850
sale; succession to book value 6-495
small scale, inheritance tax ...7-300; 7-550
special land holding tax 2-380
table of taxes 2-370
valuation, inheritance tax 1-200; 7-550

Land and house inspectors
withholding income tax 4-360

Land holding tax (municipal) 2-380

Land surveyors
withholding income tax 4-360

Land value tax (national) 2-345

Lawyers
certified public tax accountants 1-540
foreign taxpayers 1-420

Lease of assets
definition 8-040
transfer, consumption tax 8-050

Leases
consumption tax
– land 8-075
– assets with interest 8-090
grant without reasonable initial
payment 6-490
gross income 6-193

Lectures
withholding income tax 4-360

Legatees
inheritance tax purposes 7-105

Paragraph

Life insurance premiums 5-370

Light vehicle tax 2-410

Liquidation 6-610
foreign corporations 6-905
income 6-820
– capital surplus, retained earnings.. 6-080
– final payment 6-835
– merger 6-845
– non-periodic prepayment 6-830
– periodic prepayment 6-825
– tax basis and rates 6-070
– taxation 6-840

Liquor business
license fee 2-830

Liquor tax 2-560

Litigation 1-510

Local government
exempt corporations 3-410

Local special corporate tax 2-100

Local taxes 2-010

Long-term care and medical insurance
premium 5-370

Long-term contract, definition 8-470

Losses
accidental
– corporations, carry-over 6-575
– deduction 5-320
bad debts 6-240
carry-over or carry-back 5-280
– corporations 6-570
changes in book value 6-340
deficit covered by directors,
shareholders 6-580
offset 5-270
reserves
– overseas investment 6-395
– others 6-435

Lump sum gift
educational funds 7-876
marriage and childcare funds 7-877

M

Maintenance
expenses 6-308
reserve for special repairs 6-432

Manuscripts
withholding income tax 4-360

Inv

INDEX 877

Paragraph

Marine agents
withholding income tax 4-360

Meal allowances 4-230

Medical (care) corporations 6-045;
7-317; 7-880

Medical care insurance 9-860

Medical expenses deduction 5-330

Medical services
consumption tax 8-140

Membership fees
consumption tax 8-600

Mentally handicapped persons
inheritance tax exempt property 7-290
mutual aid plan premiums 5-350

Mergers 6-600
consumption tax 8-280
– filing obligations 8-810
liquidation income 6-845

Metals
transactions involving 4-155

Midwifery services
consumption tax 8-155

Mine prospecting reserves 6-435

Mineral product tax 2-950

Mineral prospecting expenditure 6-540

Mining allotment tax 2-950

Mining rights
sale, consumption tax 8-050

Ministry of Finance 1-450

Miscellaneous income 5-090; 5-120

Models
withholding income tax 4-360

Motor vehicles
automobile tax 2-350
automobile tonnage tax 2-420
light vehicle tax 2-410

Motorcar, motorboat racers
withholding income tax 4-360

Movie or stage directors
withholding income tax 4-360

Municipal organizations
special exceptions ....8-700~8-740

Municipal taxes

Paragraph

bathing tax 2-710
inhabitant tax 2-110
– nondeductible 6-205

Music compositions
withholding income tax 4-360

Mutual aid plan contributions 5-350

N

National taxes
basic structure (table) 3-010
domestic and foreign
corporations 3-340; 3-360
exempt corporation 3-410; 3-430
non-juridical organization 3-140
partnerships 3-120
resident and non-resident .....3-210~3-250
structure of income taxation .3-020~3-050
tax treaties 3-510; 3-540
taxation based on "economic
substance" 3-710

Nationality, nondiscrimination 1-400

Navy exchanges
consumption tax 8-220

NISA 5-070

**Non-deductible interest paid to related
corporations** 6-248

Non-juridical organizations 3-140; 6-050
consumption tax 8-730
enterprise tax 9-460
inheritance or gift tax 7-030

Non-permanent residents 3-250; 4-410
definition 3-250

Non-residents
assessable income 5-880
consumption tax
– place for payment 8-355
definition 3-250
exchange 2-540
foreign leading shareholder 6-247
payment of tax 5-920
returns 5-910
tax liability ....5-850~5-920
– computation of amount 5-890
– income from sources in Japan 5-860
– taxable income 5-850
tax treaty concessions 5-900
taxpayers 3-210
transfer of withheld tax 4-070

Non

878　INDEX

Paragraph

visitors' tax-free purchases 2-540
withholding income tax 4-620
– tax treaties 4-650
– unilateral concessions 4-680

O

Occasional income
computation 5-090; 5-120; 5-130

Online tax filing 5-637

Open stock investment funds 5-257;
5-258; 5-566; 9-100; 9-120

Overpaid tax credit 6-700

Overseas investment loss reserve 6-395
specified corporations 6-400

P

Partnerships 3-120

Patent attorneys
withholding income tax 4-360

Patents
registration tax 2-830
tax treaties 4-650
transfer, consumption tax 8-050
payment for obtaining certain
qualifications 5-130

Payment in kind 8-600

Payment of tax
consumption tax ....8-750~8-780
enterprise establishment tax 9-840
enterprise taxes
– corporate 9-560
– individual 9-440
final payment 5-730
– corporations 6-805
– liquidation 6-835
fixed assets tax 9-720
foreign corporations 6-910
gift tax 7-910
inhabitant taxes
– corporations 9-300
– individuals 9-140
inheritance tax 7-620
land value tax 2-345
non-residents 5-920
place, consumption tax 8-310; 8-355
withholding income tax 4-070

Penalties 1-520

Paragraph

Pension insurance 9-860

Pensions
death benefits 7-270
withholding tax 4-390

Per capita levy
corporation inhabitant taxes 9-200
individual inhabitant taxes 9-030

Permanent establishment
foreign corporations 6-900

Personal services
foreign taxpayers 1-420
lump sum payments, withholding
income tax 4-360

Petroleum coal tax 2-590

Petroleum gas tax 2-595

Physically handicapped persons
allowance 5-430
inheritance tax exempt property 7-290
mutual aid plan premiums 5-350

Physicians
registration tax 2-830

Place of tax payment
consumption tax ....8-310~8-355

Postage stamps
consumption tax 8-100

Prefectures
diesel oil delivery tax 2-680
golf course tax 2-650
inhabitant tax 2-110
– corporations ....9-180~9-320
– nondeductible 6-205
– return and payment 9-140; 9-440
local taxes 2-010
real property acquisition tax 2-850

Prepayment of tax
assessment income tax 5-710
corporation tax 6-800
– liquidation 6-825; 6-830
non-residents 5-920

Prizes
withholding income tax 4-360
– horse owners 4-570
– non-residents and foreign
corporations 4-620

Producers
withholding income tax 4-360

Non

INDEX 879

Paragraph	Paragraph

Profits
computation of income 5-130
foreign corporation,
Japanese source 6-880
net, adjustment 6-110

Proofreading
withholding income tax 4-360

Property — see also **Buildings; Capital gains; Land**
acquisition of fixed assets
by subsidy 6-500
donations 6-480
exchange 6-470
excluded for inheritance
tax purposes 7-290
expropriated, exemption 6-505
gift tax 7-780
industrial, transfer 8-425
inheritance tax
– situated abroad 7-320
– situs 7-120
lease granted without reasonable
initial payment 6-490
replacement 6-475
succession to book value 6-495
transfer at low price 6-485
valuation, inheritance tax 7-550

Property taxes
automobile tax 2-350
automobile tonnage tax 2-420
city planning tax 2-390
enterprise establishment tax 2-430
fixed assets tax 2-360
land and buildings 2-370
– land value tax 2-345
light vehicle tax 2-410
special land holding tax 2-380

Provision of services
definition 8-040
domestic transactions 8-050

Public corporations 6-025

Public entertainers
withholding income tax 4-360; 4-570

Public interest corporations 6-040
enterprise tax 9-460
inheritance or gift tax 7-030
– nondeductible 6-205

Public interests corporate juridical person 6-042

Public interest incorporated association
.... 5-638

Public interest incorporated foundation
.... 5-638

Public service corporations
consumption tax 8-720
Purchase tax credit .... 8-530~8-680
special exceptions 8-730

R

Rates of taxes
aircraft fuel tax 2-585
assessment income tax
– fluctuating and extraordinary
income 5-530
– forestry income 5-520
– land and buildings 5-550; 5-555
– progressive rates 5-500
– retirement income 5-522
– tax table 5-505
automobile acquisition tax 2-870
automobile tax 2-350
automobile tonnage tax 2-420
bathing tax 2-710
city planning tax 2-390
comparison of income tax and
income levy 9-090
consumption tax 8-020; 8-510
corporations 2-060
– inhabitant tax 9-240
– liquidation income 6-070; 6-840
– ordinary income 6-060
diesel oil delivery tax 2-680
electric power resources
development tax 2-890
enterprise establishment tax .2-430; 9-800
enterprise tax
– corporations 9-480
fixed assets tax 2-360; 9-700
gasoline tax and local gasoline tax .. 2-580
gift tax 7-880
golf course tax 2-650
individuals 2-050; 9-100
inheritance tax 2-310; 7-370
– surtax 7-390
land and buildings 2-370
land value tax 2-345
light vehicle tax 2-410
liquor tax 2-560
per capital levy
– corporations 9-240
– individuals 9-100

Rat

880 INDEX

Paragraph

petroleum gas tax 2-595
petroleum coal tax 2-590
real property acquisition tax 2-850
registration and license tax 2-830
special land holding tax 2-380
stamp tax 2-820
stock or shares, capital gain 5-565
tobacco consumption tax 2-640
withholding income tax
 – debentures issued at discount 4-190
 – dividends 4-210; 4-540
 – horse owners' prizes 4-570
 – income similar to interest 4-550
 – interest 4-150; 4-540; 4-550
 – payments to non-residents and
   foreign corporations 4-620; 4-650
 – public entertainers 4-570
 – remuneration 4-360

Real estate appraisers
withholding income tax 4-360

Real estate income
aggregation 5-230
computation 5-090; 5-120; 5-130
foreign taxpayers 1-420
offset of losses 5-270

Real estate taxes 1-420; 2-370
registration tax 2-830

Real property acquisition tax 2-850

Receipts and expenses in kind 5-150

Recordings
withholding income tax 4-360

Refund of tax 5-730
consumption tax 8-770
corporations 6-160; 6-805

Regional taxation bureaus 1-450

Registered owner, definition 2-360

Registration and license tax 2-830

Religious organizations
foreign corporations 3-430

Remuneration
technical services 6-188
withholding income tax 4-130; 4-360
 – non-residents and foreign
   corporations 4-620

Rent
consumption tax 8-163; 8-440
non-residents etc, withholding

Paragraph

income tax 4-620

Reorganization 6-600

Replacement of property 6-475

Reserves, tax-free
general outline 6-350
normal reserves
 – bad debts 6-360
 – goods returned unsold 6-385
 – investment loss 6-395
 – special repairs 6-432
 – others 6-435

Residential property, replacement 5-210

Residents
definition 3-250
non-permanent 3-230; 4-410
taxpayers 3-210
withholding income tax .... 4-130~4-410

Retirement allowances
corporations, deduction 6-225
inheritance tax 7-270; 7-290
withholding income tax 4-130; 4-340;
                                          4-350; 4-370
 – non-residents and foreign
   corporations 4-620

Retirement income
aggregation 5-240
computation 5-090; 5-120; 5-130
rate of tax 5-522

Returns
amended 5-740
assessment income tax
 – blue return 5-030
consumption tax 8-020
 – filing 8-750
 – foreign goods removed from
   bonded area 8-780
 – interim returns 8-760
 – refunds 8-770
 – special exceptions 8-740
corporate enterprise tax 9-560
corporate inhabitant taxes 9-300
corporations
 – blue return 6-056
 – interim return 6-800
 – white return 6-057
enterprise establishment tax 9-840
final 5-720; 5-910
 – corporations 6-805; 6-810
 – form 5-950
foreign corporations 6-910

Rat

INDEX 881

Paragraph	

gift tax ....7-900~7-920
individual enterprise tax 9-440
individual inhabitant taxes 9-140
information...........................5-810; 5-820
inheritance tax 7-420; 7-600
– forms..................................7-450~7-480
land value tax 2-345
non-residnets 5-910
pension business etc. 6-855

Revaluation profits 6-158

Royalties
consumption tax 8-440
foreign taxpayers............................ 1-420
withholding income tax........4-360; 4-620
– tax treaties....................................4-650

S

Salary or wages
corporations, deduction 6-210
foreign government or international
    organization staff.........................5-070
withholding income tax.......2-080; 4-130;
                                            4-230; 4-250
– monthly table and daily table........ 4-250
– non-residents and foreign
    corporations 4-620
– tax treaties...................................4-650
– year-end adjustment.....................4-310

Sale of goods — see also **Consumption tax**
succession to book value
    (corporation tax) 6-495

Sales, definition 8-040

Sales reduction 6-175

Salesmen
remuneration, consumption tax 8-600
withholding income tax 4-360

School tuition
consumption tax 8-160

Scientific organizations
foreign corporations 3-430

Securities transactions
consumption tax 8-050; 8-080; 8-430

Services
consumption tax 8-050

Shares
business income 5-256
capital gains........................5-130; 5-565
– computation 5-220

Paragraph	

– tax rate 5-565
– withholding tax 4-210

Ships
consumption tax
– commodities loaded 8-220
– transfer...8-050
fixed assets tax...............................9-580
registration tax................................2-830

Short-term executive 5-130

Simplified tax system 8-680

Small enterprises
mutual aid plan contributions 5-350
corporation tax rate 6-060
deductible entertainment expenses..6-230
special depreciation 6-310
tax credit.................. 6-720; 6-730~6-736

Small scale land
inheritance tax 7-300

Social insurance 9-860

Social insurance premiums,
deductions 5-340
corporations....................................6-220

Social Insurance Treatment
Remuneration Payment Funds
payments to doctors and dentists.....4-360

Social welfare services
consumption tax 8-150

Special land holding tax 2-380

Special measure for taxation on unrealized
capital gains of financial assets at the
time of move from Japan 5-262

Special relationship, definition 6-200

Special Taxation Measures Law
consumption tax exemptions...........8-220

Special tax credit for Additional
construction or home improvement
of a house 5-614

Special tax credit for housing loan for
the acquisition of a qualified
low-carbonic house 5-611

Specified foreign trust 6-197

Specified payment 5-130

Specified stocks issued by specified
small or medium corporation 5-256

Spouse

Spe

882   INDEX

Paragraph

allowance 5-410
– gift tax 7-840
– special 5-410
inheritance tax credit 7-400

Stamp tax 2-820

Standard deduction
from forestry income 5-130

Statement of assets and liabilities 5-721

Stenography
withholding income tax 4-360

Stock
valuation, inheritance tax 7-550

Stock companies 6-090

Stock option 5-070

Stocks or shares — see **Shares**

Students
working students' allowance 5-460

Subsidies
acquisition of fixed assets 6-500

T

Tax Answer 1-430

Tax burden adjustment 2-370

Tax burden level 9-680

Tax credits 5-570
acquisition of house 5-600
consumption tax
– bad debt loss 8-640
– purchase tax credit ....8-530~8-620
– special for small and medium-sized
   enterprises 8-680
corporations 6-690
– experimental and research
   expenses 6-720
– foreign taxes ....6-740~6-755
– income tax 6-710
– investment, specified equipment ... 6-730
– liquidation 6-840
– overpaid tax 6-700
– tax sparing 6-752
– training expenses 6-736
dividends 5-580
experimental and research expenses .. 5-620
foreign taxes 5-630
gift tax 7-890
housing loan ....5-610~5-611
inheritance tax 7-400

Paragraph

special credit for earthquake – proof
improvement of an existing
house 5-636

Tax-free goods 2-540

Tax-free reserves — see **Reserves, tax-free**

Tax havens 6-195

Tax reform 1-200

Tax sparing 6-752

Tax treaties 3-510
concessions
– foreign corporations 6-900
– non-residents 5-900
diplomatic privilege 3-540
foreign governments exemption 3-540
inheritance tax 7-050
tax sparing 6-752
withholding income tax 4-650

Taxable income
— see also **Assessment income tax;
   Corporation tax; Inheritance tax**
consumption tax 8-490; 8-500
enterprise tax 9-410; 9-420; 9-480

Taxable purchase ....8-530~8-620

Taxes
consumption — see **Consumption tax**
corporations — see **Corporations;
   Corporation tax**
enterprise — see **Enterprise tax**
enterprise establishment
   — see **Enterprise establishment tax**
excise — see **Excise taxes**
fixed assets — see **Fixed assets tax**
gift — see **Gift tax**
income 2-040; 2-050; 2-080
inhabitant — see **Inhabitant taxes**
inheritance — see **Inheritance tax**
local 2-010
national ....3-010~3-790
property — see **Property taxes**
table 1-850
transactions — see **Transactions taxes**
withholding — see **Withholding income tax**

Taxpayers
consumption tax
– calculation of taxable sales 8-270
– domestic transaction 8-230
– election 8-260
– inheritances 8-280
– mergers 8-280

Spe

INDEX 883

Paragraph

− removal of foreign cargo from
  bonded area 8-240
− special exceptions 8-280
− taxation on substance of act 8-290
− trusts 8-300
enterprise establishment tax 9-780
enterprise tax .... 9-340~9-400
fixed assets tax 9-580
gift tax 7-760
inhabitant tax 9-010; 9-180
inheritance tax 7-105

Technical services
remuneration 6-188

Technicians, registered
withholding income tax 4-360

Three-part-reform 2-110

Tobacco tax 2-640

Total costs (corporation tax) ...6-130; 6-140;
                                   6-205~6-247
bad debt loss 6-240
bonuses 6-215
contributions paid 6-235
entertainment expenses 4-230; 6-230
− paid to foreign leading
  shareholders 6-247
salaries and wages 6-210
social insurance premiums 6-220
taxes and duties 6-205

Transactions taxes
automobile acquisition tax 2-870
electric power resources
  development tax 2-890
real property acquisition tax 2-850
registration and licence tax 2-830
stamp tax 2-820

Transfer, definition 8-040

Transfer pricing 6-200

Transfer of tax revenue sources 2-110

Translations
withholding income tax 4-360

Travelling allowance 5-070

Travelling expenses 8-600

Trust companies 6-090

Trusts, taxation 3-740
consumption tax 8-300
income tax 5-180
inheritance tax 7-276

Paragraph

gift tax 7-851

U

Undistributed profits
allowance 6-660
basic concept 6-640
computation of tax 6-775
disbursements deductible 6-650
distributions 6-655
foreign subsidiaries 6-195
items added to ordinary income 6-645
tax basis and tax rate 6-060

Union duties 8-600

United States
Armed Forces
− consumption tax 8-220
Inheritance Tax Convention
  with Japan 7-130; 7-400
tax treaty with Japan 7-050

V

Valuation
inventory 6-250; 6-255
properties, inheritance tax 7-550

Visitors' tax-free purchases 2-540

W

Welfare services
consumption tax 8-150

Widows' or widowers' allowance 5-450

Withholding income tax 2-080; 3-050
capital gains from stock
  investment 4-400; 5-220
categories 4-050
exempt corporations 3-410
expatriates working in Japan 4-410
foreign taxpayers 1-420
forms 4-830
general view (table) 4-010
nondeductible 6-205
payments to domestic corporations . 4-510
− dividends 4-540
− horse owners' prizes 4-570
− income similar to interest 4-550
− interest 4-540; 4-550
− public entertainers 4-570
payments to non-residents
  and foreign corporations 4-620
− tax treaties 4-650

Wit

884 INDEX

Paragraph

–unilateral concessions 4-680
payments to residents 4-130
–bonuses 4-270; 4-290
–debentures issued at discount........ 4-190
–dividends 4-210; 4-211
–employment income 4-230
–income similar to interest income . 4-155
–interest 4-150; 4-170; 4-175
–interest, payment slips submission 4-160
–public pensions 4-390
–rates and taxable amounts 4-380
–remuneration fees, etc. 4-360

Paragraph

–retirement allowances 4-340; 4-350;
                                                      4-370
–salary or wages 4-250; 4-260
–year-end adjustment...................... 4-310
withholding and payment................ 4-070

Working students' allowance 5-460

**Workmen's Accident Compensation
  Insurance** 9-880

Wrestlers
  withholding income tax.................. 4-360

Wit

索　引

〈数字はパラグラフ（¶）番号を示しています〉

（あ）

青色申告者の特典　privileges of blue returns	5-030
青色申告書　blue returns	6-056
青色申告特別控除　blue return special deduction	5-160

（い）

異議申立て　request for reinvestigation	1-500, 1-510
遺言　will	7-105
遺言執行人　executor	7-020
遺産管理人　administrator	7-020
遺産に係る基礎控除額　basic estate allowance	7-350
異常危険準備金　unusual accidental loss reserves	6-435
遺贈　devise	7-010, 7-105
一時所得　occasional income	5-120
一時所得の特別控除額　special deduction for occasional income	5-130
一括比例配分方式　proportional method	8-570
一定設備等を取得した場合の法人税額の特別控除　　investment tax credit for specified equipment	6-730
一定の障害者，寡婦に対する少額貯蓄及び国債の利子の非課税　exemption for interest on small deposits and government bonds	4-170
移転価格税制　transfer pricing taxation	6-200
医療等　medical services	8-140
医療費控除　deduction for medical expenses	5-330
医療法人　medical（care）corporations	6-045, 7-317, 7-880
印紙　other stamps	8-165
印紙税　stamp tax	2-820

（う）

受取配当　devidends received	6-150

（え）

益金　gross income	6-135, 6-150〜6-200

886 索　引

役務の提供　provision of services		8-040
延滞税　delinquency tax		5-730

（か）

海外投資等損失準備金　overseas investment loss reserve		6-395
外貨建資産等の換算　credits and debits denominated in foreign currencies		6-345
外形標準課税　taxation of corporation by the size of their business		2-270, 9-570
外交特権　diplomatic privilege		3-540
外国会社の留保金額（タックスヘイブン対策税制）undistributed profits of foreign subsidiaries（tax haven countermeasure）		6-195
外国為替業務　foreign exchange services		8-130
外国組合員　a foreign individual partner of investment fund		5-870
外国子会社から受ける配当等の益金不算入 exemption of dividends received from foreign subsidiary		6-152
外国人職員　foreigners' staff		5-070
外国税額控除（申告所得税）　credit for foreign taxes		5-630
外国税額控除（相続税）　credit for foreign taxes		7-400
外国税額控除（贈与税）　credit for foreign taxes		7-892
外国税額控除（地方税）　credit for foreign taxes		9-100, 9-260
外国税額控除（法人税）　credit for foreign taxes		6-740
外国政府の非課税　exemption for foreign governments		3-540
外国法人　foreign corporations		6-870～6-920
介護保障又は医療保障保険料　long-term care and medical insurance premium		5-370
解散　dissolution		6-820
各事業年度の所得　ordinary income		6-130
各事業年度の所得に対する法人税　tax on ordinary income		6-005
確定拠出型年金　defined contribution pension plan		5-070
確定申告書（消費税）　final return		8-750
確定申告書（申告所得税）　final return		5-720
確定申告書（法人税）　final return		6-805
加算税　penalty taxes		6-860
家事関連費　expenses disbursed for private purposes		5-160
貸倒れ　bad debt loss		8-640
貸倒損失　bad debts loss		6-240

索　引　887

貸倒引当金　allowance for bad debts		5-160, 6-360
加重　heavy penalty		1-520
過少資本対策税制　nondeductible in the case of thin capital		6-247
過少申告加算税　penalty tax for short return		1-520
課税遺産総額　aggregated net assets after allowance		7-260, 7-340
課税売上高　taxable sales		8-270
課税売上割合　taxable sales ratio	8-545, 8-550, 8-580, 8-650	
課税売上割合に準ずる割合		
substitutional ratio for the taxable sales ratio		8-590
課税価格　net taxable assets		7-260
課税期間　taxable period		8-360
課税財産　taxable property		7-780
課税仕入れ　taxable purchase		8-600
課税事業者　taxable enterprise		8-670
課税標準　tax base		8-490
課税標準額　Amount of tax base		8-750
課税文書　taxable documents		2-820
仮装経理に伴う過大申告　tax overpaid due to misrepresentation of		
accounts in financial statements		9-260
仮装経理に基づく過大申告の場合の更正に伴う法人税額の控除		
credit for overpaid tax due to misrepresentation of accounts		
in financial statement		6-700
割賦販売（消費税）　installment sales		8-450
割賦販売（法人税）　installment sales		6-180
合併　merger		6-600
合併による法人消滅届出書　notification of cessation of		
existence of corporation by merger		8-790
寡婦（寡夫）控除　allowance tor a widow or widower		5-450
株式譲渡所得割　per stock capital gain levy		9-111
株式等に係る譲渡所得		
capital gains etc. from stock or shares		5-256, 5-565
簡易課税制度　simplified tax system		8-680
関西国際空港用地整備準備金　reserve for the maintenance of the New		
Kansai International Airport		6-435
間接外国税額控除　indirect foreign tax credit		6-750
完全支配関係　hundred (100) percent group		6-590
還付　refund of tax		8-770

888　索　　引

還付加算金　interest on the refund		5-730
管理支配基準　management and control criterion		6-195
関連者等に係る支払利子等の損金不算入		
non-deductible interest paid to related corporations		6-248

（き）

基準期間　base period		8-250
基礎控除　basic allowance		5-470
既存住宅の耐震改修をした場合の所得税額の特別控除　special credit		
for earthquake-proof improvement of an existing house		5-636
記帳義務　bookkeeping obligation		8-800
揮発油税　gasoline tax		2-580
寄附金　contributions paid		6-235
寄附金控除　deduction for contributions		5-390
寄附金税額控除　credit for contributions		5-570, 5-638
給与所得　employment income		5-120
給与所得控除　standard employment income deduction		5-130
給与所得者　salary income earner		9-140
給与所得に係る源泉徴収　withholding from employment income		4-230
給料，賃金等に係る源泉徴収　withholding from salaries, wages, etc.		4-250
教育資金の一括贈与　Lump sum gift of educational funds		7-876
協同組合等　cooperatives		6-030
居住者　resident		3-250, 5-850
居住者に対する支払に係る源泉徴収		
withholding from payments to residents		4-130
居住用財産の買換え　replacement of residential property		5-210
居住用財産の買換えの場合の譲渡損失の繰越控除		
carry-forward of long-term capital loss on replacement of		
residential property		5-290
居住用財産の譲渡益　capital gains for residential house and land		5-555
金属鉱業等鉱害防止準備金　metal mining pollution control reserve		6-435
均等割額の課税　per capita levy		9-030, 9-200
金融類似商品等に対する源泉徴収　withholding tax on income which is		
similar in nature to interest income		4-155
勤労学生控除　allowance for a working student		5-460

索　引　889

勤労者財産形成住宅貯蓄の利子の非課税
　　　non-taxable interest income from savings for formation of
　　　　　employees' property　4-175
勤務必要経費　business expenses　5-130

（く）

組合　partnership　3-120
繰延資産　deferred assets　6-320, 6-325

（け）

軽自動車税　light vehicle tax　2-410
刑事罰　judicial penalty　1-520
軽油引取税　diesel oil delivery tax　2-680
月額表　monthly table　4-250
欠損金　net loss　6-570, 6-580
欠損金の繰戻還付　carrying back of net losses　9-520
結婚・子育て資金の一括贈与　marriage and childcare funds　7-877
決定　determination　5-740, 6-860
原価基準法　cost plus method　6-200
減価償却　depreciation　6-265〜6-310
減価償却資産　depreciable assets　6-265
原価法　cost method　6-255
現金主義　cash basis　8-475
原子力発電施設解体準備金　nuclear plant dismantling reserves　6-435
源泉所得税　withholding income tax　2-080, 4-010〜4-830
源泉徴収の税率及び課税標準　withholding tax rates and taxable amounts
　　　4-380
源泉徴収のための退職所得控除額の表　withholding tax table for
　　　　　retirement income deduction　4-370
源泉分離課税　withholding income tax only　5-090
現物分配　dividend in kind　6-600

（こ）

公益財団法人　public interest incorporated foundation　5-638, 6-042
公益社団法人　public interests corporate juridical persons　5-638, 6-042
公益法人等　public interest corporations　6-040
恒久的施設　permanent establishment　2-080, 5-870, 6-870

890 索　引

工業所有権　industrial property		8-425
公共法人　public corporations		6-025
航空機燃料税　aircraft fuel tax		2-585
鉱区税　mining allotment tax		2-950
交際費　entertainment expenses		6-230
鉱産税　mineral product tax		2-950
工事完成基準　completed contract rule		6-185
更正　correction		5-740, 6-860
公的年金　public pensions		5-130
公的年金等についての源泉徴収　withholding from public pensions		4-390

公募株式投資信託　open stock investment funds

5-257, 5-258, 5-566, 9-100

公募株式投資信託に係る収益分配金　distribution from publicly traded
stock investment　　　4-212

国外関連者との取引に係る課税の特例（多国籍企業の同一関連グループ内の
移転価格に対する課税）taxation of transactions between corporations and
foreign related persons for transfer pricing　　6-200

| 国外源泉所得　foreign source income | | 6-745, 6-880 |
| 国外財産調書　offshore asset statement | | 5-722 |

国外転出をする場合の譲渡所得の特例
Special measure for taxation on unrealized capital gains of
financial assets at the time of move from Japan　　5-262

国内源泉所得　income from sources in Japan		5-860, 6-875, 6-880
国内取引　domestic transaction		8-040, 8-050
国内の特定の代理人　certain kinds of agents in Japan		5-870
個人事業者の課税期間　taxable period for individual enterprise		8-360

個人事業者の死亡届出書
notification of death of individual enterprise　　8-790

個人事業税　enterprise tax on individuals		2-240, 9-340〜9-440
個人住民税　individual inhabitant taxes		9-010〜9-160
個人年金生命保険料　individual annuity insurance premiums		5-370

国庫補助金による固定資産の取得
acquisition of fixed assets by subsidy　　6-500

固定資産税　fixed assets tax		2-360, 9-580〜9-740
固定資産の譲渡　transfer of fixed tangible assets		8-420
子ども手当　child allowances		5-070
個別対応方式　itemized method		8-560

索　引　891

| 雇用保険　employment insurance | 9-880 |
| ゴルフ場利用税　golf course tax | 2-650 |

（さ）

災害損失の繰越し　carry-over of accidental loss	6-575
財産債務調書　statement of assets and liabilities	5-721
財産に対する租税　taxes on property	2-345〜2-430
財産の所在　situs of properties	7-120
再調査の請求　second review	1-500
再販売価格基準法　resale price method	6-200
債務控除　deduction for inherited liability	7-330
雑所得　miscellaneous income	5-120
雑損控除　deduction for accidental loss	5-320
三位一体改革　three-part-reform	2-110
残余財産の一部分配に係る予納　non-periodic prepayment	6-070
山林所得　forestry income	5-120, 5-130
山林所得の特別控除額　special deduction for forestry income	5-130

（し）

仕入税額控除　purchase tax credit	8-610
仕入れに係る対価の返還等　adjustment of the purchase tax credit in case of refund	8-620
仕入割引　purchase discount	8-620
資格取得費　a payment for obtaining certain qualifications	5-130
事業　business	8-040
事業基準　business criterion	6-195
事業所税　enterprise establishment tax	2-430, 9-760〜9-840
事業所得　business income	5-120
事業税　enterprise tax	2-240
事業専従者　family employees	5-160
事業単位　business units	8-700
事業年度　business year	6-100
事業廃止届出書　notification of discontinuance of business	8-790
事業分量配当金　disbursement according to the degree of utilization	8-620
事業用資産の買換え　replacement of business property	5-210
試験研究費　experimental and research expenses	6-720
試験研究費控除　credit for experimental and research expenses	5-620

892 索　引

資産　assets		8-040
資産の買換え　replacement of property		6-475
資産の貸付け　lease of assets		8-040
資産の交換　exchange of property		6-470, 8-490
資産の譲渡　transfer of assets		8-040
資産の譲渡等の時期　time of transfer of assets, etc.		8-390～8-475
資産の評価益　revaluation profits (exclusion from gross income)		6-158
資産の評価損　loss due to changes in book value		6-340
資産割　assets levy		2-430, 9-800
地震保険料控除　deduction for earthquake insurance premiums		5-380
市町村たばこ税　local tobacco tax		2-640
市町村民税　municipal inhabitant tax		2-040
実質行為者課税の原則		
principle of taxation of the actual performer		8-290
実体基準　substance criterion		6-195
質問検査権　right to make inquiry and inspection		8-820
自動車重量税　automobile tonnage tax		2-420
自動車取得税　automobile acquisition tax		2-870
自動車税　automobile tax		2-350
使途秘匿金　beneficiary-concealed-disbursement		6-675
支払手段の譲渡　transfer of securities and payments		8-080
資本金等の額　capital amounts		6-080, 9-200
資本的支出　capital expenditure		6-308
資本等取引　capital transactions		6-145
資本割　per capital		9-570
社会保険　social insurance		9-860
社会保険料控除　deduction for social insurance premiums		5-340
借地権　leasehold		6-193, 6-490
受遺者　legatee		7-105
収益（益金）　gross income		6-130
収益事業　profit-making business		6-040
重加算税　heavy penalty tax		1-520
従業者数割　number of employees levy		9-800
修繕費　maintenance		6-308
住宅借入金等特別控除　special credit for housing loan		
		5-600～5-614, 9-100
住宅取得等資金の贈与税の非課税		

索　引　893

gift tax exemption of fund used to acquire residential property

7-875

住宅省エネ改修工事等促進特別控除

special credit for promotion of home improvement

for better energy saving performances　　　　　5-614

住宅特定改修特別税額控除

special tax credit for promotion of home improvements for

energy saving performances and barrier-free　　　5-617

住宅バリアフリー改修促進特別控除

special credit for promotion of home barrier-free

improvement　　　　　5-614

住宅の貸付け　rent for houses　　　　　8-163

集団投資信託　collective investment trust　　　　　6-052

収入金額課税　gross proceeds taxation　　　　　9-500

住民税　inhabitant taxes　　　　　2-110

収用資産　expropriated property　　　　　5-210

収用資産に係る譲渡益の特別控除　exemption of capital gains from

expropriated property　　　6-505

酒税　liquor tax　　　　　2-560

狩猟税　hunting tax　　　　　2-950

酒類業の免許　license for liquor business　　　　　2-830

純資産価額方式　value based on the net asset value of the company 7-550

準備金　special reserves　　　　　6-350, 6-395~6-435

省エネ改修工事　energy saving performances　　　　　5-617

障害者控除　allowance for a physically handicapped person　5-430, 7-400

少額資産　minor assets　　　　　6-265

少額貯蓄及び国債の利子の非課税　exemption for interest on small deposits

and government bond　　　4-170

小規模企業共済等掛金控除　deduction for contribution to a small enterprise

mutual aid plan　　　5-350

小規模事業者　small-scale enterprises　　　　　8-475

小規模事業者に係る納税義務の免除　tax exemption for small-scale

enterprises　　　8-250

小規模宅地等　small-scale housing lots　　　　　7-300

償却可能限度額　capital sum recoverable through depreciation　6-300

上場株式　listed stock　　　　　5-565

894　索　　引

上場株式等に係る譲渡所得についての源泉徴収
　　　　　　withholding tax on capital gains derived from transactions
　　　　　　involving stock in listed companies　　　　　　　　4-400
使用済核燃料再処理準備金　used nuclear fuel reprocessing reserves 6-435
譲渡資産の帳簿価額の引継ぎ　succession to book value of old property 6-495
譲渡所得　capital gains　　　　　　　　　　　　　　　　　　5-120
譲渡所得特別控除額　special deduction for capital gains　　　　5-130
消費税　consumption tax　　　　　　　　　　　　2-510, 8-010
消費に対する租税　taxes on consumption　　　　　2-510〜2-710
賞与に対する源泉徴収　withholding from bonuses　　　　　　　4-290
所得及び利潤に対する租税　taxes on income and profits　　2-040〜2-270
所得税　income tax　　　　　　　　　　　　　　　　　　　　2-080
所得税額の控除　income tax credit　　　　　　　　　　　　　6-710
所得の帰属者　to whom income pertains　　　　　　　　　　　3-710
所得割　per income　　　　　　　　　　　　　　　　　　　　9-570
所得割額　per income levy　　　　　　　　　　　　　　　　　9-050
所有権移転外ファイナンス・リース取引
　　　　　　a lease transaction with conditions of non-cancelable
　　　　　　and full payout　　　　　　　　　　　　　5-160, 6-309
資料の提出　information return　　　　　　　　　　5-810, 5-820
人格のない社団等　non-juridical organization　　　　　3-140, 6-050
新鉱床探鉱費等の特別控除　expenditures in prospecting for new
　　　　　　　　　　　　　mineral deposits　　　　　　　　6-645
新鉱床探鉱費又は海外新鉱床探鉱費の特別控除
　　　　　　expenditures in prospecting for mineral deposits or similar
　　　　　　expenditures for foreign mineral deposits　　　　6-540
申告期限　the time limit for filing tax returns　　　　　　　8-740
申告義務等の承継　succession to obligations of filing returns, etc.　8-810
申告所得税　assessment income tax　　　　　　　　　　　　2-080
申告総合課税　comprehensive assessment income tax　　　　　5-090
申告分離課税　separate assessment income tax　　　　　　　5-090
審査請求　reconsideration　　　　　　　　　　　　　　　　1-510
心身障害者扶養共済制度　mentally or physically handicapped persons
　　　　　　　　　　　　mutual aid plan　　　　　　　　　5-350
信託財産　trust fund　　　　　　　　　　　　　　　　　　8-300
信託財産に対する課税　taxation of trusts　　　　　　3-740, 5-180
信託に関する権利の遺贈　bequests and devises of trust interests　7-276

索　引　895

信託に関する権利の贈与　gifts of trust interests　　　7-851

（す）

ストック・オプション　stock option　　　5-070

（せ）

税額控除　tax credit　　　6-060, 6-690, 7-400
税源移譲　transfer of tax revenue sources　　　2-110
清算　liquidation　　　6-610, 6-820
清算確定申告　final return liquidation　　　6-820
清算所得　liquidation income　　　6-820
清算所得に対する法人税　tax on liquidation income　　　6-070
生産高比例法　unit of production method　　　6-270
清算中の予納　periodic prepayment　　　6-070
生前贈与　gift before death　　　7-280
政党等寄附金特別控除　special credit for contributions to
　　　　　　　　　　　　　political parties　　　5-619
税務争訟　tax disputes　　　1-500
生命保険料控除　deduction for life insurance premiums　　　5-370
税理士　certified public tax accountant　　　1-540
税率（消費税）　tax rates　　　8-510
税率（所得税）　tax rates　　　5-500
税率（相続税）　tax rates　　　7-370
税率（贈与税）　tax rates　　　7-890
税率（法人税）　tax rates　　　6-060
石油ガス税　petroleum gas tax　　　2-595
石油石炭税　petroleum coal tax　　　2-590
船舶の早出料　dispatch money　　　8-620

（そ）

増加償却　increased depreciation　　　6-280
相次相続控除　credit for chain successions　　　7-400
相続及び贈与に対する租税　taxes on inheritances and gifts　　　2-310〜2-340
相続時精算課税制度　unified gift/inheritance tax system　　　7-893
相続税　inheritance tax　　　2-310, 7-010
相続税の加算　surtax on inheritance tax　　　7-390
相続税の申告書　inheritance tax return　　　7-450

896 索　引

相続税の税率　inheritance tax rates		7-370
相続税の非課税財産　exempt properties		7-290
相続人　heirs		7-105
贈与税　gift tax	2-340, 7-010,	7-760
贈与税額控除　credit for gift tax paid		7-400
贈与税の申告書　gift tax return		7-920
組織再編成　reorganization		6-600
訴訟　litigation		1-510
租税公課　taxes and duties		6-205
租税条約　tax treaties	3-510, 4-650, 6-900,	7-050
損金　total cost	6-140,	6-205〜6-248
損失の繰越し及び繰戻し　carry-over or carry-back of loss		5-280

（た）

対価　consideration		8-040
代襲相続人　the natural children of a predeceased heir		7-360
退職所得　retirement income		9-120
退職所得控除額　deduction for retirement income	4-370,	5-130
退職手当に対する源泉徴収　withholding from retirement allowances		4-340
退職年金等積立金に対する法人税　tax on specific funds		6-090
代物弁済　payment in substitution		8-490
耐用年数　useful lives		6-290
タックス・アンサー　tax answer		1-430
タックス・スペアリング　tax sparing		6-752
タックスヘイブン　tax haven		6-195
脱税　tax evasion		1-520
たな卸資産　inventory	6-250,	8-400
たばこ税　tobacco tax		2-640
短期在任役員　short-term executive		5-130
短期所有土地等　short-term ownership land		6-670
探鉱準備金　mine prospecting reserve		6-435

（ち）

地価税　land value tax	2-345
地方税　local tax	2-010
地方揮発油税　local gasoline tax	2-580
地方法人特別税　local special corporate tax	2-100

中間申告　interim returns		8-760
中間申告書　interim return form		6-800
中間納付　prepayment		6-800
中高層耐火共同住宅　multi-storey fire-proof apartment houses		5-210
長期工事　long-term construct		8-470
認定長期優良住宅新築等特別控除		
special credit for the acquisition of newly built		
long-term quality houses		5-610, 5-616
調整対象固定資産　fixed assets subject to adjustment		
	8-265, 8-650, 8-660, 8-680	
直接外国税額控除　ordinary foreign tax credit		6-745
著作権，特許権の登録　registration of copyright, patent, etc.		2-830

（つ）

通告処分　notification procedure	1-520
通算課税売上割合　average taxable sales ratio	8-650
積立NISA　installment-type NISA	5-070

（て）

定額法　straight line method	6-270
低価法　cost or market value, whichever is lower	6-255
定期金に関する権利　fixed annuity right	7-550
定率法　reducing balance method	6-270
転換社債　convertible bond	5-220
電源開発促進税　electric power resources development tax	2-890
電子申告　credit for online tax return filing	5-637

（と）

同族会社　family corporation		3-780, 6-640
同族会社の行為計算の否認　denial of transactions or entries of family		
	corporation	3-760, 7-040
同族会社の留保金課税　undistributed profits for a family corporation		
	6-640〜6-660	
道府県たばこ税　prefectural tobacco tax		2-640
道府県民税　prefectural inhabitant tax		2-040
道府県民税利子割　prefecture interest tax levy		9-260
登録免許税　registration and license tax		2-830

898 索 引

特定外国信託　foreign specified trust 6-197
特定口座　designated account 5-257
特定支出控除　specified payment deduction 5-130
特定増改築等住宅借入金等特別控除
　　　　　special tax credit for additional construction or home
　　　　　　improvement of a house 5-614
特定中小会社が発行する株式　specified stocks issued by
　　　　　　specified small or medium corporation 5-256
認定長期優良住宅の新築等を行った場合の住宅借入金等特別控除
　　　　　special tax credit for housing loan for the acquisition of a
　　　　　qualified long-term high quality house 5-610
特別修繕準備金　reserve for special repairs 6-432
特別障害者　a severely handicapped persons 5-430, 7-870
特別償却　special depreciation 6-310
特別土地保有税　special land holding tax 2-380
匿名組合契約に基づく利益の分配　distribution of profit based on the silent
　　　　　partnership (Tokumei Kumiai) agreement 4-580, 4-620
独立価格比準法　comparable uncontrolled price method 6-200
独立企業間価格　arm's length price 6-200
独立企業原則　arm's length principle 6-200
都市計画税　city planning tax 2-390, 9-740
土地譲渡益に対する特別課税　special taxation on capital gains
　　　　　　　　from land 6-670
土地等に係る事業所得等　business income etc. on land etc.
　　　　　　　　　5-195, 5-550, 9-120
土地等に係る事業所得等の金額　business income etc. on land etc. 5-250
土地等に係る短期譲渡所得　short-term taxable capital gains on land etc.
　　　　　　　　9-120
土地等に係る長期譲渡所得　long-term capital gains on land etc. 9-120
土地等の短期譲渡所得　short-term capital gains on land etc. 5-560
土地等の短期譲渡所得金額　short-term capital gains on land etc. 5-254
土地等の長期譲渡所得金額　long-term capital gains on land etc.
　　　　　　　　　5-200, 5-252
土地等の長期譲渡所得に対する税率　tax rates on long-term capital gains
　　　　　　　　on land etc. 5-555
土地の譲渡及び貸付け　transfers and leases of land 8-075

土地の譲渡等に要した販売費・一般管理費
　　　　selling and general administrative expenses in connection
　　　　　with the transaction　　　　　　　　　　　　　　5–195
届出書　notification　　　　　　　　　　　　　　　　　　8–790
取替法　replacement method　　　　　　　　　　　　　　6–270
取引相場のない株式　unlisted stocks　　　　　　　　　　7–550
取引に対する租税　taxes on transactions　　　　　2–820〜2–890

（な）

内国法人に対する支払に係る源泉徴収　withholding from payments to
　　　　　　　　　　　　　　　　　domestic corporations　　4–510

（に）

二重課税　double taxation　　　　　　　　　　　　　　　6–740
日米相続税条約　Japan-U. S. inheritance tax convention　　7–130
200％定率法　200％ declining balance method　　　　　　5–160
250％定率法　250％ declining balance method　　　　　　5–160
日本版ISA（NISA）　　　　　　　　　　　　　　　　　　5–070
入湯税　bathing tax　　　　　　　　　　　　　　　　　　2–710
認定NPO法人　certified nonprofit corporations　5–390, 5–570, 5–638
認定低炭素住宅の新築等を行った場合の住宅借入金等特別控除
　　　　special tax credit for housing loan for the acquisition of
　　　　　a qualified low-carbonic house　　　　　　　　5–611

（ね）

年末調整　year-end adjustment　　　　　　　　　　　　4–310

（の）

納税義務者（消費税）　taxpayer　　　　　　　　8–230〜8–300
納税義務者（相続税）　taxpayer　　　　　　　　　　　7–105
納税地（消費税）　place for tax payment　　　　　8–310〜8–355
納税地（法人税）　place for tax payment　　　　　　　6–055
納税地の指定　designation of place for tax payment　　　8–330
納税地の特例　special exception regarding the place for income
　　　　　tax payment　　　　　　　　　　　　　　　　8–310
ノウ・ハウ　know-how　　　　　　　　　　　　　　　8–425
納付　payment　　　　　　　　　　　　　　　　　　　7–910

900 索　引

延払基準　the deferred payment standard　　　　　　　　　　　8-450

（は）

配偶者控除　allowance for spouse　　　　　　　　　　　5-410, 7-840
配偶者特別控除　special allowance for spouse　　　　　　　　5-410
配偶者に対する相続税額の軽減　credit for a spouse　　　　　　7-400
配当控除　credit for dividends　　　　　　　　　　5-580, 9-100
配当所得　dividend income　　　　　　　　　　　　　　5-120
配当に係る源泉徴収　withholding from dividends　　　　4-210, 4-211
配当割　per dividend levy　　　　　　　　　　　　　　　9-110
販売奨励金等　sales promotion money　　　　　　　　　　　8-620

（ひ）

非永住者　non-permanent resident　　　　　　　　　　　　3-250
非課税　non-taxable transactions　　　　　　　　　　　　8-070
非課税財産　exempt property　　　　　　　　　　　7-290, 7-860
非課税所得　exempt income　　　　　　　　　　　　　　5-070
非課税法人　exempt corporation　　　　　　　　　　　　3-410
非関連者基準　non-related person criterion　　　　　　　　6-195
引当金・準備金　tax-free reserves　　　　　　　　6-350〜6-435
非居住者　non-resident　　　　　　　　　　　　　3-250, 5-850
非居住者及び外国法人に対する支払に係る源泉徴収
　　　　　withholding from payments to non-residents and
　　　　　　　foreign corporations　　　　　　　　4-620〜4-680
非事業用資産　property used for non-business purposes　　　　5-190
非同族の同族会社　nonpersonal family corporation　　　　　3-790
100％グループ内の法人　hundred (100) percent group　　　　6-590
費用（損金）　expenses　　　　　　　　　　　　　　　　6-130
評価通達　evaluation rulings　　　　　　　　　　　　　7-550
標準報酬　standard remuneration　　　　　　　　　　　9-860

（ふ）

賦課及び不服審査　assessment and tax disputes　　　　　　9-160
付加価値割　per value added　　　　　　　　　　　　　9-570
負担水準　tax burden level　　　　　　　　　　　　　　9-680
負担調整措置　tax burden adjustment　　　　　　　　　　9-680
負担調整率　burden adjustment rate　　　　　　　　　　9-680

普通法人　ordinary corporation		6-060
復興特別所得税　earthquake restoration surtax		5-020
物納　payment in kind		7-620
物品切手等の譲渡　Transfers of exchange checks, etc.		8-110
物理的又は経済的減耗に係る償却方法　depreciation according to physical		
	or economic exhaustion	6-270
不動産取得税　real property acquisition tax		2-850
不動産所得　real estate income		5-120
不動産に係る租税　tax burden on real estate		2-370～2-390
不動産の登記　registration of real estate		2-830
不服申立て　tax disputes		1-500, 6-860
扶養控除　allowance for dependent		5-420
分割　corporate division		6-600

（へ）

弁護士の登録　registration of an advocate	2-830
変動所得　fluctuating income	5-530
返品調整引当金　reserve for goods returned unsold	6-385

（ほ）

包括遺贈　inclusive bequest	7-105
報酬, 料金等に係る源泉徴収	
withholding from remuneration, fees, etc.	4-360
法人課税信託　corporate taxation trust	6-052
法人事業税　enterprise tax on corporations	2-240, 9-460～9-570
法人市町村民税　corporate municipal inhabitant tax	2-060, 9-180～9-320
法人税　corporation tax	2-090, 6-005
法人税割額　per corporation tax levy	9-220
法人道府県民税　corporate prefectural inhabitant tax	2-060, 9-180～9-320
法人の課税期間　taxable period for corporations	8-370
法人の合併　merger of corporations	8-280
法人の分割　split-up of a corporation	8-280
法定相続人　heir at law	7-260, 7-350, 7-360
法定相続分　the statutory shares (legal portion of legacy)	7-260, 7-360
保税地域　a bonded area	2-560, 2-580, 2-590, 2-640, 8-060, 8-500, 8-780

902 索　　引

（み）

未成年者控除　credit for a minor	7-400
みなし受取配当　constructive dividends received	6-645
みなし仕入率　deemed purchase ratio	8-680
みなし取得財産　cases treated as inheritances, bequests or devises	7-270
みなし譲渡　deemed transfer	8-040
みなし贈与　benefits treated as gifts	7-850

（む）

無申告　filing no return	1-520
無申告加算税　penalty tax for no return	1-520

（め）

名義株　dummy stock	6-200
免税事業者　tax-exempt enterprise	8-250, 8-450, 8-670

（や）

役員，株主からの私財提供　deficit covered by directors, shareholders	6-580

（ゆ）

有価証券　securities	8-430
有価証券等の譲渡　transfer of securities	8-080
郵便切手類又は印紙の譲渡　transfer of postage stamps and others	8-100
優良住宅地の供給促進　the promotion of the supply of good quality housing or housing land	5-555
優良住宅地の供給促進に係る土地等の譲渡益　capital gains from sales of land etc. which will contribute to promoting the supply of good quality housing	9-120
輸出物品販売場　export shops	8-200, 8-210
輸出免税　export tax exemption	8-170～8-190
輸入取引　import transaction	8-500

（り）

リース期間定額法　straight line（lease period）method	6-270
リース資産　assets on lease	6-309
利益積立金額　retained earnings	6-080

索　引　903

利子　interest	8-090
利子所得　interest income	5-120, 9-120
利子等　interest, etc.	8-440
利子に係る源泉徴収　withholding from interest	4-150
利子に関する支払調書の提出　submission of payment slips for interest payments	4-160
留保金額　undistributed profits	6-640
留保金課税　the tax on undistributed profits	6-640
臨時所得　extraordinary income	5-530

(る)

類似業種比準方式　value based on the value of comparable listed stock	7-550
累進税率　progressive rate	2-080

(れ)

連結納税制度　consolidated taxation system	6-630

(ろ)

労働者災害補償保険　workmen's accident compensation insurance	9-880
路線価　road-tax-rating	7-550

(わ)

割引債　discount bond	4-190

《著者 紹介》

川 田 剛（かわだ ごう）

　昭和42年国税庁に入り，大阪国税局柏原税務署長，在サンフランシスコ日本国総領事館領事，国税庁国際調査管理官，国税庁長官官房国際業務室長，仙台国税局長等を経て明治大学大学院グローバル・ビジネス研究科教授を歴任。

　他に，明治大学商学部大学院講師，学習院大学法学部講師，日本公認会計士協会租税相談員（国際課税）等。

　主な著書として，『基礎から身につく国税通則法（平成30年度版）』，『租税法入門（十四訂版）』，『基礎から学ぶ法人税法（六訂版）』（以上，大蔵財務協会），『国際課税の基礎知識（十訂版）』，『Q&A海外勤務者に係る税務（第3版）』，『節税と租税回避―判例にみる境界線』，『国際租税入門　Q&A租税条約』（以上，税務経理協会），『新版 ケースブック 海外重要租税判例』，『Q&Aタックス・ヘイブン対策税制のポイント』，『早見一覧 移転価格税制のポイント』（以上，財経詳報社）など。他に著作・論稿多数。

平成30年10月29日　発行©

英和対照　税金ガイド　30年版

著　者　川　田　　　剛　《検印省略》

発行者　宮　本　弘　明

発 行 所　株式会社　財　経　詳　報　社

〒 103-0013　東京都中央区日本橋人形町 1-7-10

電　話　03(3661)5266(代)

Ｆ Ａ Ｘ　03(3661)5268

http://www.zaik.jp

Printed in Japan 2018　　振　替　口　座　00170-8-26500番

印刷・製本　創栄図書印刷　ISBN978—4—88177—453—3